ISBN 978-1-330-90019-2
PIBN 10118925

This book is a reproduction of an important historical work. Forgotten Books uses
state-of-the-art technology to digitally reconstruct the work, preserving the original format
whilst repairing imperfections present in the aged copy. In rare cases, an imperfection in
the original, such as a blemish or missing page, may be replicated in our edition. We do,
however, repair the vast majority of imperfections successfully; any imperfections that
remain are intentionally left to preserve the state of such historical works.

1 MONTH OF
FREE
READING

at

www.ForgottenB␣ks.com

By purchasing this book you are
eligible for one month membership to
ForgottenBooks.com, giving you
unlimited access to our entire
collection of over 700,000 titles via
our web site and mobile apps.

To claim your free month visit:

www.forgottenbooks.com/free118925

THE

FOREIGN

QUARTERLY REVIEW.

VOL. VII.

PUBLISHED IN

JANUARY AND APRIL,

M. DCCC. XXXI.

LONDON:

TREUTTEL AND WÜRTZ, TREUTTEL, JUN. AND RICHTER,
30, SOHO SQUARE:

BLACK, YOUNG, AND YOUNG,
TAVISTOCK STREET.

1831.

LONDON:
C. ROWORTH AND SONS, BELL YARD,
TEMPLE BAR.

CONTENTS

OF

N° XIII.

———

THE

FOREIGN

QUARTERLY REVIEW.

ART. I. — *Histoire de Philippe - Auguste,* par M. Capefigue. Ouvrage couronné par l'Institut. 4 vols. 8vo. Paris, 1830.

THE reign of Philip-Augustus belongs to two centuries, the twelfth and thirteenth,—centuries of no little importance in the history of European civilization. At a period like this, when events which have their origin in the progress, decay, and reproduction of past institutions are daily being developed, the study of the different steps by which the citizen has become what he is must be an occupation of the most lively interest. It is a remark of the author of the work before us, that we are apt to consider revolutions in a far too confined point of view; we limit the epoch by its visible signs and its finished results; but these results have been in long preparation. Society does not receive a new form in a day; the ideas cast abroad in one century become the leading principles of the next; in short, in the history of mankind everything is gradual;—a revolution is but the explosion of a train that has been long and curiously laid.

The period in which Philip-Augustus was a great instrument in modelling and arranging the internal forms of society, is marked as the age in which the beginnings of numerous great changes had their commencement,—in which they arose into obvious existence, without, however, then receiving their accomplishment. It was the dawn of the great intellectual reformation, which has since made such rapid progress, and is every day more and more expanding its propitious light.

The two grand elements which operated on society from the establishment of the barbarous invaders in Roman Gaul, and which maintained a continual struggle for predominance over the opinions of men from the seventh to the tenth century, were the material force of the conquerors, and the moral and intelligent force of the clergy. M. Capefigue has traced the fortunes of this singular but most important strife at length; we will do so shortly, as an appropriate introduction to an article on the Spirit of the Twelfth and Thirteenth Centuries, of which the reign of

Philip-Augustus is the great centre, and during which the results of the events of the two or three previous centuries showed themselves in the shape of results.

The annals of the Merovingians and the Carlovingians are filled with the quarrels and mutual encroachments of the warriors and the clerks; the one operated by the seizure of the lands or the treasures of cathedrals and monasteries; the others revenged themselves by interdicts and excommunications. However, at the tenth century the triumph of the Church may be considered complete. Its advantages over its rival are obvious : it was a regular institution, possessed a formal hierarchy, consecrated forms, a written code, invariable maxims : it pursued a given end with order and perseverance. The armed feudality, on the other hand, was but a confused mass of isolated forces—a government without a common object, sometimes prepared to resist, sometimes to succumb. What it gained by its violence it lost by its uncertainty. What ascendancy could the mailed baron preserve, who in the evening was seen plundering a monastery, and the next day, prostrate at the foot of the altar, demanding pardon of holy relics for his offences against God, and loading pious recluses with presents in expiation of his sins? Opposed to him and his physical force were the territorial and monachal clergy, the bishops and their suffragans, the secular priests and the different orders of monks holding their rights from the pope, whose absolute jurisdiction they maintained, all animated with a common spirit, a common object—the triumph of religious ideas and the prerogatives of the Church.

Nearly half of the territory of Roman Gaul belonged to the clergy of the monasteries and the cathedrals; in addition to which they reaped the tenth of the productions of the other half, without the exception of royal domain, baronial castle, or serf's cottage. Besides the influence of riches, the clergy possessed the influence of superior instruction. The little knowledge afloat was confined to them, the scattered elements of some disfigured science, the traditions of sacred and profane literature. They alone could read or write : they were necessary in every castle of France : from the suzerain to the least vassal, all had their chaplain to draw up their deeds, to recite the breviary, or enliven the long nights of winter with some tale or legend of chivalry. They were consulted on all domestic affairs, and they had contrived to connect almost every act of life with religious offices or religious ideas. The Christian faith of the middle ages was a vast polytheism, the deities of which were in continual relation with mankind. The catalogue of the church of Cluny exhibits a list of eleven thousand saints, habitually invoked by the people. The immense power of the Church was preserved in a spirit of unity by the frequent assembly of both general and provincial councils, in which the clerks deliberated upon the means of maintaining the purity of doctrine, or of consolidating the authority of the Church. From the twelfth century to the thirteenth the great collection of the Père Labbe contains four general councils, in which all the bishops of Christendom were assembled to the number of upwards of a thousand, and three hundred and seventeen particular or provincial councils, in which the necessities of the local churches were deliberated upon and provided for by the bishops and prelates of the neighbourhood.

In fact, before we arrive at the end of the eleventh century, we find that the Church had become the unique source of all social existence. From it every thing flowed, the moral and intellectual order of men's ideas were founded on its doctrines, it served as an active and regular authority, the only rational forms of legal jurisdiction were established by it; in short, nothing existed out of its pale but brutal and unorganized force, which could not long oppose any effective resistance, and which was disgraced by every attempt it made against an authority sacred in the eyes of all.

At this period Europe may be considered as a great religious federative republic, governed by a clerical aristocracy, consisting of the Bishop of Rome for its president, and the rest of the bishops of Christendom, their suffragans, their canons, and the monks.

But the Church itself was destined to undergo its revolution: the bishops of Rome set forth their pretensions as true spiritual monarchs placed by God on earth : the famous Hildebrand (Gregory VII.) first established this maxim. The Church then lost its liberal form of government by councils, and assumed an aspect altogether monarchical : this revolution was in progress from the pontificate of Gregory VII. to that of Innocent III. The pope then became the only visible organ of the Church ; and as it had previously become the unique source of power and influence, it naturally followed that the pontiff maintained a sort of universal monarchy over all the princes and people of Christendom; and during the period which forms the subject of the work before us, the proofs of this authority are displayed by the different popes in a manner not to be misunderstood. We find Gregory VII. establishing the doctrine that kings were his temporal bishops. Urban II. made Philip I. of France submit to his will in a point of private morals by relieving his subjects from their oath of allegiance. The emperor Henry IV. submitted to a similar humiliation; and in the long pontificate of Innocent III., contemporary with a great part of the reign of Philip-Augustus, we find this pope excommunicating the king, putting the kingdom under an interdict, proclaiming himself suzerain of England, and, in short, attempting, and successfully, to exercise all the acts of a universal monarch. And his influence was not only exerted over the kings, but it was felt by whole masses of the population, who moved at his beck. In the eleventh century all Europe was put in motion by the voice of Urban II. commanding the delivery of the holy sepulchre. It was he who directed the enthusiasm of the multitude, and regulated its movements. Bulls accorded privileges to the crusaders and relieved them from their debts, and pontifical regulations interfered in the settlement of disputed rights and of the public peace, without consulting any authority but its own. Sometimes it directed its force against the East, now against Spain or England, at another time against the Albigenses; in short, the feudal population of the middle ages appear to have become the devoted subjects of the despotic pontiffs of Rome.

The pontificate of Innocent III. was the epoch of the greatest splendour and energy of the Church, and yet at that very moment its power carried within itself the seeds of decline. The grand principle of the Church was the argument of authority: its science began and ended in the official interpretation of the Scriptures, the regulations of councils and popes. A Christian owed his faith to his Catholic teacher, as the serf his service to his master, as the liege-man to his lord: it was no part of their duty to examine motives, or to look to consequences. But in the period from the eleventh to the twelfth century, the sphere of men's studies became enlarged, manuscripts were multiplied in the libraries of the cathedrals and monasteries; these did not all contain merely the traditions of the Church,—there were found among them the precious remains of Greek and Roman literature. In the twelfth century the classics had become familiar to the lettered clerks; all the pious books of the time display a familiarity with them, and even women had begun to devote themselves to learning the elegant tongues of Greece and Rome. Thus a source of instruction was opened which did not flow from the Church, and by this very fact, and also by the nature of the instruction, its authority received a blow from which it never fairly recovered, and of which the consequences were more strikingly exhibited every day. The philosophical character of many of the authors then beginning to be studied gave birth to heresies, the existence of which had an important influence upon the history of clerical power; and as, moreover, a branch of instruction was discovered which did not emanate from the Church and formed no part of it, it naturally produced a body of teachers devoted to its circulation. Hence arose the continental universities, the great birth-places of heresies; that is to say, of Christian notions combined with the dogmas of ancient philosophy. But this was not the only rival institution to the spirit of the Church that arose out of the studies of antiquity.

Up to this time almost all jurisdiction had been usurped by the clerks, who decided according to certain texts, supposititious or misapplied, of Scripture. The lay jurisdiction was reduced to a few cases of feudal privileges. The discovery of the Roman law produced a great change ; a class of persons arose who acted under a system of notions totally independent of the Church and of religion. The study of the Pandects also enlarged the circle of the ideas of laymen ; and the opinions of the people began, in cases of right and wrong, to refer to entirely different tests and standards from those of the Church. The Pandects becoming objects of especial study, professors arose to teach the codes and institutes. From that moment a limit was set to the influence of the Church. The kings established another mode of procedure than heretofore, by the system of *provost baillis* in the different localities ; the laws were written, and the towns and seigneuries had magistrates, who were placed in a position directly opposed to the ecclesiastical jurisdiction. This rivalry endured up to the complete triumph of the laical jurisdiction.

The progress that had been made in the sciences, although small, tended still somewhat towards the emancipation of the mind, and the weakening of the power of the Church. Every discovery which teaches a man to reflect and compare, gives a blow to all systems of authority. The twelfth and thirteenth centuries are full of the quarrels between bishops and burghers disputing for jurisdiction and power. In former times, the people had been passively obedient : the Pope had but to speak, and all Europe arose or sat down at his wish ; but his wishes no longer found that prompt and enthusiastic accomplishment : the remonstrances of the Church, it is true, continued to produce an effect, but it was faint and temporary. The kings, in their turn, felt the influence of the spirit of the age, and, as soon as they could, threw off the oppressive yoke of Rome : their ability to do so depended on the disposition of the masses ; for it is, in fact, on them, after all, of whatever character they may be, that all power is founded. This is a truth not sufficiently attended to in the history of the middle ages.

With the masses, that is to say, the great bulk of the people, always must rest the supreme force : when they are unanimous, and in motion, there is no other force in a state that can resist it. They have besides a force of inertia : the secret is to know what they will tolerate, and how much they will bear : this is the limit of the authority of a governing power. In the middle ages this force was merely brutal; it was moreover incapable of exercising its real power from want of mutual communication : that is to say, its power was smaller than in a more enlightened state, but still it was supreme. All authority that has ever existed has acted on a kind of instinctive knowledge of the nature of this power. The feudal system tried to cope with it, by multiplying its own force, by means of armour, horses, and implements of war, the building of castles, donjons, and keeps ; and, on the other hand, by reducing the masses into the vilest state possible, and shackling their exertions by every force, physical and moral, that they knew of. The clergy attacked them intellectually : they infused into them certain notions of their own sanctity, and turned the religion of Christianity into a further means of power, by convincing the ignorant man that it was for his *interest* to be guided by them, that his fate in the next world was in their hands. The seigneur bound the body of his thrall, the priest his mind :—the giant was blind. Gradually, with the progress of his intellectual improvement, has the influence of his power been felt; but even in the state of his uttermost darkness, in the middle ages, his power was known, and his temper consulted. They were afraid he would burst his bonds. It may be observed, that reformations, or great changes in the order of things, never take place till the masses are ripe for them. There were many Luthers before the successful one. The history of Italy, and even of Spain, presents numbers, as may be seen in Dr. M'Crie's excellent works on the suppressed reformation in those countries. Why did Luther, from his cell at Wittenberg, pour forth his bulls with more authority than the Pope? Why was he not seized and burnt like so many before him? Simply because his voice found an echo in every bosom ; the *masses* were with him ; and before them, kings, popes, and even armies, are powerless.

In the times of which we are writing, the Church contributed greatly to its own fall from the post of guide and ruler of social existence, by its excessive immorality, by its offences against decency, its open negligence of those rules it prescribed to others, and by prostituting its different sanctions for the sake of extorting money. As the ascetic virtues of the original cenobites had not a little contributed to the establishment of the power of the Church, the vice and luxury of their successors, in a proportional degree, undermined it. The popes and councils were well aware of this consequence. The letters of the popes of this age, both circular and particular, constantly turn on the reformation of the morals of the clergy, for they felt that to be essential to the preservation of the influence of the Church, no doubt perceived to be declining. The spirit of the age also required such a reform-

ation. The authority of the Church demanded for its maintenance the extinction of heresy; hence the establishment of the
Inquisition. The violence of this atrocious institution may be
considered as the last effort of a tottering authority.

When the people were emancipated from the slavery of the
Church,—that is to say, when the Church ceased to hold despotic
sway over the minds of men—for it has never entirely lost its
power as a political body—the feudal institutions remained,
though greatly changed and mutilated. The suzerain had erected
himself into a king, and greatly extended his feudal powers; to
the extension of this power the barons were still opposing a continual resistance. In the mean time another form of government
had arisen; the people collected in towns began to be conscious
of their force, and vindicated to themselves certain privileges.
Scattered abroad in the fields, or collected in small hamlets, the
serfs were the slaves of their masters' will; but when once they
had gathered together in communes, had learned to sympathize
with each other, and to act in concert, they disdained the seigneur's
authority. In some countries they succeeded in establishing the
independence of the commune; in all they accomplished a certain
degree of liberty. We have before traced the emancipation of
the people from the Church. The history of the communes is
the history of the emancipation of the people from the feudal
system, and in fact the foundation of society as it exists at this
moment. Attention has been more peculiarly called to them of
late by the very admirable letters of M. Thierry[*] on the History
of France.

An observation of M. Capefigue on these communes is full of
practical wisdom. He observes that the desire of liberty broke out
in these communes pretty nearly about the same time; and during
the twelfth and thirteenth centuries, the collections are full of
charters giving the name of *right* to that liberty that was enjoyed
in *fact*. Thus a popular revolution was afterwards sanctioned
by the royal and feudal power. A grand lesson, says our author,
for societies. The best way to obtain freedom is, to take it first
of all, and get it written down afterwards.

The spirit of association, arising out of the necessity of mutual
protection, was the characteristic of the middle ages. Every
society fell into the form of a corporation,—a sure indication of

---

[*] The author of the *History of the Norman Conquest of England*, reviewed in our last
number: the same, we believe, whose lectures were suspended by the ministry some
short time previous to the glorious Revolution of July. Lady Morgan, in her "France
in 1830," speaks with praise of a *History of France* by M. Thierry. There is no such
work. She probably, speaking on the recommendation of some friend, alludes to these
excellent letters in her chapter on History.

the absence of a central authority. Although the establishment of municipal institutions was widely spread, yet there were shades of difference between those adopted in the towns of Italy, France, Flanders, and England. In Italy the municipal system was converted into a regular republican government. The cities of Lombardy elected their own magistrates, and treated of war and peace, as independent sovereignties. They differed in no respect from the republics of antiquity, resembling more especially the Achæan league of the latter ages of Greece.

The municipalities of Languedoc were constituted after the same model. If there were any hope of securing absolute sovereignty, the citizens never hesitated to proclaim it. Marseilles, Montpellier, Toulouse, and Arles, several times declared themselves republics in the middle ages, and maintained their independence against the counts and bishops who claimed authority over them. Wherever in the cities a power was retained by some feudal lord, it was the occasion of perpetual revolt on the part of the burghers. In the space of fifty years the inhabitants of Avignon put to death one of their viscounts and two of their prelates.

In the communes of France the municipal privileges were not so extensive. The communal charters guaranteed to them the elections of their magistrates: the meetings in which their elections were held took place at the sound of the church bells, in the public square, and neither king nor seigneur had any right to interfere with them. The magistrates regulated the police, the management of the contributions, superintended the walls, fosses, and roads. The cities had their own military establishments, a jurisdiction independent of that of the king, which was administered by their mayors and echevins. The municipia of Languedoc differed from the republics of Italy in this, that very few of them had been able to shake off their dependence upon some superior power, whether of the king, the counts, or the bishop.

The towns of Flanders were ruled by a sort of federative system, founded on their commercial relations. They were strictly devoted to their counts, but still so jealous of their municipal privileges, that they would admit no feudal banner to approach their walls without permission. The sole right possessed by the seigneurs was to man the citadel and appoint the governor of the castle. The citizens undertook to support the troops, in return for the protection and privileges they enjoyed from the feudal lord. Their exertions were chiefly of a mercantile cast; their commerce embraced all the known world.

The municipal rights in England were mixed up, as in France, with the feudal system, though to a greater extent. The Conquest was recent, and the military vassals had preserved a good deal of their authority over the citizens. The municipal privileges partook largely of the character of fiefs, and in fact existed by and under the swords of the barons. A great principle was however proclaimed in Magna Charta. The immunities of the towns were recognised by the King, and the representatives of the communes were called to parliament to vote in matters of aid and subsidy.

In the heart of the cities interior municipal bodies were formed : all was corporation and exaggeration. Every trade and branch of industry had its peculiar laws, privileges, and magistracy. The glovers, the butchers, the fishermen, as well as the rest, boasted of their banners, their guard, and their provost, as well as the towns and the barons.

The cities became in no long time the depositories of all the wealth of the country, and the kings soon discovered that they were the readiest sources of supply. The baron, possessor of the soil, lord of a rude and empty castle, was a poor contributor to the wants of the state in any other metal than steel, which he was more ready to draw in his own quarrel than that of the country at large. The citizen, on the other hand, constantly exchanging his merchandize against coin, always had the means of relieving the wants of the king in the way most agreeable to rulers in general. But he who has the power to grant supplies, or withhold them at will, is sure sooner or later to be consulted in the disposition of them : this leads to the great step in the history of modern government, the representation of the commons in parliament by their deputies.

If we may apply the term " opposition" to the government of the middle ages, we may distinguish three bodies in which it was severally centred. First, the Church made its weight felt by its discourses, its interdicts and excommunications, by its promises as well as by its wealth : then came the barons with their opposition of pure physical force : at last it centred in the citizens, and had its foundation in their power to refuse or grant supplies. Of these three oppositions, the burghers were the one which gave the least trouble ; and as it was the only one which turned upon the only sole true principle of government, viz. the interests of the governed, it is the one which has remained, has been greatly expanded and extended, and must continue to be so in proportion as the people learn the nature of their rights, and the art of self-government. We must not suppose that the commons were ever cited to council, because their advice was wanted. It is the remark of an old French writer, " he must sadly want eyes who does not see that the *roturier* was never added to the States General, contrary to the old order of France, for any other reason

than that he was sometimes wanted to bear all the principal burdens and charges."—*Pasquier, Recherches sur la France,* liv. ii,
c. 5.

After the junction of the commons with the other two elements
of feudal government, the barons and the king, a sort of fusion
was established between all three, out of which the composite
form of modern states has arisen.   The extinction of some feudal
privileges, the aggrandizement of the power of the suzerain, and
the existence of the commons as a separate power, enabled the
government to assume a general character.   Previously, the king
treated with his vassals, the barons were sovereigns of their own
domains, and the people only had privileges when they were collected in sufficiently large masses to take them.   Since the period
of junction, the race of power has been between the kings and
the people, in which the former have had greatly the superiority.
The kings took advantage of the generalization which their authority had acquired, and published edicts and ordinances, which,
though they respected particular privileges, still gradually gained
an authority, controlled certainly by the states, which the kings
took care to call as seldom as possible.

The generalization of the royal authority was also greatly aided
by the action of the Roman law, and the works of the jurisconsults, who, taking for guides the maxims of the Pandects, and for
models the absolute monarchy of the emperors, warmly and industriously maintained the plenitude of the royal legislation and
administration.   The number of works written by the ancient
jurisconsults is immense.   The theory that it was the courts of
justice which greatly contributed to generalize and render absolute the authority of the kings, is admirably developed by Mon-
tesquieu.

Such may be considered a general picture of the political
movement of the 12th and 13th centuries: but civilization embraces the progress of mankind in other points besides those
which relate to the character of the governing body.   We will
again follow M. Capefigue in collecting the facts which mark the
developement of the human mind during the period which we
have described as the age when so much was begun for the future, and so little finished for the present: this is as applicable to
the *literary, scientific,* and *intellectual* history of the time as to its
moral and political institutions.   We will proceed in our endeavour to convey the character of these centuries, by noting down
the facts which will of themselves mark the progress of the world
in the various departments of mental culture.

The exact sciences in the 12th and 13th centuries had made
but small progress : nevertheless the period which produced

Roger Bacon and Albertus Magnus cannot be considered sterile. The fault of the times was, that the sciences were made the subject of dissertation rather than of observation. The corrupt translations of Aristotle, derived through the medium of the Arabs, were the source of the philosophy of the age; even *Aristotelism* had not made any great progress; but so far as it was known, no changes were permitted in the doctrines of the ancients, but such as were drawn from the prevalent system of Christian Theology. Three celebrated men have written descriptions of the physical world, Saint Thomas, Saint Bonaventure, and Albertus Magnus, and each falls into the same train of ideas. The following short summary of them is taken from Brucker:—"The different aspects of the celestial bodies are the causes of generation and corruption. All the properties and faculties of terrestrial bodies are nothing more than the forms and conditions impressed upon them by the stars, and above the stars by superior intelligences: their motion is produced by a mutual but secret action: it is thus that the attractive virtue resides in an occult form, which the celestial spheres confer on the magnet. An element is the simple principle of composed or composable bodies: the quintessence is an existence which is distinguished from all bodies, and which contains in itself no principle of contrariety, and consequently of corruption."

Such verbiage necessarily rendered no assistance in the acquirement of a knowledge of nature. The absurdest discoveries and pretended facts are recorded in the writings of this age. In the *Speculum Naturale* of Vincent de Beauvais, the unicorn is placed in the list of the animal kingdom: to catch it, a young virgin must be employed, because she is the emblem of purity. The ostrich is said to hatch her eggs by the heat of her looks.* Rigord relates, that, after the taking of Jerusalem by Saladin, children ceased to have more than twenty-two teeth, and the Chronicle of St. Denys carefully informs us, that the death of Philip Augustus was announced by a comet.

The compass, one of the properties of the magnet, gunpowder, and the properties of convex glasses, are discoveries that belong to these centuries.

The most complete description of the compass is in the book of Guyot de Provins, known under the name of the *Guyot Bible*, published in the reign of Philip Augustus. Its utility to mariners is also spoken of by other poets and writers of the same age.

The discovery of gunpowder is attributed to a German monk: the much more ancient description of it by Roger Bacon would

---

* Vincentii Bellovacensis Opera: Specul. Natural. § 68.

seem to give the credit of the invention to England. He says in his work *De nullitate magiæ,* "in order to imitate thunder and lightning, take some sulphur, nitre, and charcoal, which when separate produce no effect, but when mixed together discharge themselves the instant a light comes in contact with them, from any hollow machine in which they may have been shut up, with an explosion which equals the report and flash of thunder." As early as the year 1200, the Arabs used this mixture in order to shoot stones and balls from tubes. Nevertheless the first mention made of the employment of this powder in France, is in an account of the year 1338, of Barthelemy de Drake, treasurer at war, in which is registered a payment to Henry de Faumechon for powder and other things necessary for the cannon employed at the siege of Puy-Guillaume.

To Roger Bacon are also attributed the principal discoveries in optics; such as the first idea of the *camera obscura,* spectacles, telescopes, &c. In a manuscript of 1299, the author complains that he is no longer able to read without spectacles; and in a sermon preached in 1305, it is said that they were invented about twenty years before.—(*Tiraboschi,* t. iv. p. 196—199.)

The progress of the mathematical sciences was not so considerable as the physical ones. However, calculation by ciphers was already applied to geometry, astronomy, and even to music and architecture. The principal object of these studies was to get at the mysterious connection between numbers and the occurrences of human life. The introduction of the Arabian numerals contributed greatly to the extension of the arithmetical calculus. The first use made of them in France was by an Englishman of the name of Holywood, (Joannes de Sacrobosco,) a professor in the University of Paris, in a treatise on the sphere. They are there used for multiplication, and even for the extraction of cubic roots.

There still exists a commentary on Euclid by Campanus de Navarre, which belongs to these times. But geometry was confounded with architecture, and certainly, whether by theory or practice, seems to have been carried to a considerable degree of perfection. In the middle of the 13th century Alain de Lisle defined right lines, curved and circumflex, the triangle and tetragon. Euclid's Elements began to be taught. Two MSS. remain of treatises of geometry in these times, written in French, in which all the figures are drawn in gold.

Mechanism made considerable strides. Albertus Magnus made a speaking head, and an automaton human figure, which arose and opened a door when it was knocked at. Roger Bacon made a mechanical flying pigeon.

The first Latin Book on astronomy is by the before-mentioned Campanus de Navarre. It is a complete treatise of the sphere, and contains a planetary theory. He adopts the system of the ancients, with the corrections of the Arabs, who were our masters in this science. The most remarkable monument of the epoch is the undertaking of Alphonso X. in Spain, who employed some Jews and Arabs to compile the astronomical tables which still retain his name, and which served for a long time as the basis of all astronomical calculations.

Astrology, of course, occupies a large place in the state of the sciences of these ages. Talleyrand-Perigord, bishop of Auxerre, an adept in the art of divination, wrote a special treatise on astrology: it served as the basis of the vast labours of Albertus Magnus, whose works contain an immense quantity of cabalistic theories, and of those systems of numbers and signs which are supposed to indicate the course of mundane affairs. Albertus also teaches us the art of preparing the simples, the alchymical mixtures of blood and mud, for the purpose of fabricating living beings: he gives us a description of these imperfect and horrible creatures, into which he tried to infuse the breath of life. The works of Albertus Magnus form twenty-one volumes in folio, (Lyons, 1631); they are composed of separate treatises on all the occult sciences.

Astronomy made also some progress under the more exact and rational observations of Roger Bacon. His labours on the magnitude and refraction of the heavenly bodies, on the equinoxes and the solstices, prove that his mind had taken the only right direction in philosophical inquiry, the procedure by experiment. He rectified numerous errors in the calendar then in use, and proposed to Clement IV. that it should be remodelled; but the time had not then arrived for that change. The ordinary writings of the times betray the prevalence of the most absurd ideas on this subject. Alberic, the monk of Trois Fontaines, speaks of leaps which he has seen the sun take. (Chronic. ad ann. 1212.) The chroniclers tell us, with perfect simplicity, that the sun passes the night in lighting up Purgatory: that the earth is sustained by water, water by stones, the stones by the four Evangelists, and they by the fire of the Spirit. The universe was compared to an egg, the earth is the yolk, the water the white, and the air the shell.

The little geography that was known in these centuries was derived from the Arabs. The Chronicles abound in the most absurd geographical mistakes. The blunder of Shakspeare, who speaks of the sea shore of Bohemia, probably after some old chronicle, may be taken as a specimen of the notions of a prior age. Paradise is found in their writings in the centre of Asia, whence flow the four great rivers, the Nile, the Ganges, the Tigris, and the Euphrates. Gautier de Metz occupies a whole book with the description of the island of Méroès, where there is six months of day and six months of night. "As for us," says Gervase of Tilbury, "we declare the world to be a square placed in the middle of the seas." The *Speculum Naturale* of Vincent de Beauvais, which has been already mentioned, must be distinguished from the ignorant descriptions of his contemporaries. His work contains a tolerably exact picture of the state of geography in the middle ages. He gives a methodical list of the different countries of Asia, Africa, and Europe. Concerning Palestine, as his information was founded on the observation of pilgrims, his report is pretty accurate. When he comes to the north, then but very little known, numerous errors occur. He supposes that Europe is terminated by the ocean at the 60th degree of latitude: beyond which islands only occur. Albertus Magnus has rectified many of his imperfect notions on this point.

The spirit of travelling, whether under a religious or mercantile form, which took possession of the Christian world during the middle ages, with all the ardour of a passion, necessarily extended the geographical knowledge of the time. The second part of the Annals of Roger Hoveden contains a detailed description of Syria and the countries visited by the crusaders. The hope of converting infidels led several missionaries into distant regions at this period, and some have left interesting memorials of their observation. Such are the travels of Pietro Carpini, who made known the great rivers of Russia under the names of the Dnieper, Don, Jaik, and Volga; of the monk Rubruquis, who was sent to Tartary on a rumour of the conversion of the great Khan. He gives a living picture of the manners and usages of the nations he traversed in his journey to Caracorum. The most important of the writings of these travellers is however undoubtedly the work of Marco Paolo. He may be considered as the creator of Asiatic geography.

The habit of composing chronicles, as shown in the stupendous quantity of these monuments of monastic patience, might, it may be supposed, have had a salutary influence on chronology. For it was in a chronological form that they preferred to record the events of history; they put down the transactions they describe day by day. The confusion of their geography is, however, not more decided than that of their chronology. They are only to be depended upon for the events which occurred immediately under their eyes, and in recording these they differed greatly in their calendar. In most of the provinces of France, in Burgundy, in Narbonne, at Foix, as in Italy, the year began at Easter; at Rhodez, Cahors, Tulle, and in Spain, on the 25th March. The first of January rarely occurs as the commencement of the calendar year.

M. Capefigue attributes the slow progress of science during the dark ages to the method of instruction. " Adopt," he observes, " a philosophical course, and the result obtained will show, by the liberality and elevation of the studies pursued, the admirable effects which flow from such a source. Shut up," he adds, " the intelligence in narrow bounds, and you will have an education without end, aim, or result." This may be very true,—*truistical* even as far as it is intelligible, for unluckily M. Capefigue is sometimes misled by sound,—but it seems to us that the defect of the middle ages was rather in the matter than the method of instruction. Observation had as yet done so little for them, that there was scarcely any actual knowledge to teach, and as, when their bodies are idle, men's minds must be actively employed, they occupied themselves in the boundless regions of the imagination. The intellectual occupation of the scholastic ages was the comparison of ideas: as that of the eighteenth and nineteenth centuries has been that of facts. The one, it is true, is a barren study, and leads to no result; the other is the gate of all happiness and improvement. In composing their logical treatises of the times, the most thorny and disputable points were selected from the works of Aristotle and St. Augustin, on the groundwork of which the art of reasoning was taught. M. Capefigue says that this was not the art of reasoning, but the art of abusing reason. But the fault was not in the art, but in the subject; a constant comparison of ideas, without guide or standard, can lead to no stable conclusion. For instance, they discussed the interior structure of Paradise: whether Jesus Christ ascended into Heaven in his clothes, and whether his body, as administered in the sacrament, is naked or clothed? In discussing such absurd questions, it is possible to reason very correctly and ingeniously, but where is the result to be obtained? and if obtained, of what utility is it? This appears to have been the fault of the middle ages, that the intellect was employed *per se*, and with no other end than its occupation. Its influence on the happiness of mankind when employed in the collection and classification of facts was not dreamed of.

There was certainly one important error in the method of instruction, which was the laying down *in limine* of certain *formulæ* which it was necessary to receive as articles of faith. Science was divided by the doctors into four grand classes: theology, jurisprudence, philosophy, medicine: all four were subject to the common method of authoritative instruction, which was termed scholastic.

Theology was one of the essential studies of these two centuries; and such parts of the Scriptures were selected for commentary and interpretation as fell in with the tendency of the age towards mystical discussion. The prophecies of the Apocalypse were a favourite subject. Albertus Magnus, Saint Thomas, Saint Bonaventure, commented on the most mystical parts of the Old and New Testament, the Epistles of Paul, the Psalms, and the sufferings of Job. We owe to this age the first concordances, and the division of the Bible into chapters, as it exists to this day. The study of the sacred languages was not entirely neglected. Two doctors of the University of Paris were able to translate the Talmud. The theological works of the time, used as text books for the purposes of education, are derived from two sources: the one class are commentaries upon the great book of *Sententiæ*, by Peter Lombard; the other are *Summæ*, or abridgements of religious science, and answer to the *Syllabus*, or rather the *Elements*, of the modern professor. The *Summa* of Saint Thomas, which has been handed down as an elementary book of theology, embraces three parts: the first treats of the nature of things, of the Creator and his creatures; the second of morality; the third of the sacraments and the incarnation. In this work Aristotle is referred to in every page, along with the Fathers of the Church and the texts of the Old and New Testament. One of the first books printed was the *Summa* of William Durand, bishop of Mende, under the title of *Durandi Rationale*, Mentz, 1459.

The study of the canon law was one of the principal branches of scholastic instruction. It was drawn exclusively from the collection of pontifical decisions, published by Gratian, in the middle of the 12th century. This code attributed absolute power to the Popes, as the sole ecclesiastical authority. Raymond de Pennafort, a Spanish Dominican, added five books to those which Gratian had published; they contain the Decretals from Innocent III. to Gregory IX. These two collections are the basis of the canon law, and were exclusively consulted by theologians, in preference to the councils and all the other acts of the church. Italy was peculiarly the theatre of this melancholy study. When the rising schools of the civil law gained a footing, a noisy rivalship was commenced between the two chairs, and the University is said, by a contemporary, to have resounded with the thunder of their disputes. Civil jurisprudence began to be studied in the 13th century, at Paris, Toulouse, Orleans, Montpellier, Angers, where flourished the celebrated professor Thomas

Desfontaines. In Italy, where the Roman jurisprudence naturally regenerated with vigour and brilliancy, flourished several of its most distinguished professors. Alzon published at Bologna two juridical *Summæ* and an *Apparatus* of codes. Accursius, his most illustrious disciple, wrote a collection of glosses on all the texts of the Roman law at that time known, which displays a singular example of patience and industry: this work is still used in the schools of law; though it was only in the subsequent century that the study of the Roman law took its present enlarged and liberal character, under the guidance of the celebrated Barthole.

Philosophy produced nothing in the middle ages except commentaries, more or less obscure, on Aristotle, which were by turns upheld and condemned by the Church. It was about the 11th century that Aristotelism began to appear in the schools, and it reigned till the condemnation of Amaury de Chartres, who had applied it too boldly or too subtilely to the doctrines of Christianity. Amaury thus proved that God and matter were indivisible—" A simple being," said he, " is one that has neither quantity nor quality. Such is God—such is also primal matter; but can there be two simple beings? No—for they could only be distinct by qualities, or by parts which one had, or the other had not. But this is incompatible with the nature of a simple being : consequently it follows that God and matter are one and indivisible." Amaury de Chartres was compelled to retract, and his disciples were burnt outside the walls of Paris. Aristotle was proscribed in the schools, with the exception of his logic; at the request of Philip - Augustus, Cardinal Robert de Courçon forbade the teaching of the Greek philosopher in the University.

Medicine was the fourth faculty of the University. This science, which had made so considerable a progress in ancient Greece, appears to have been totally lost in the dark ages; except some feeble traditions of the art of healing, that appear to have been preserved in the monasteries. Medicine returned into Europe through the medium of the Arabs. The works of Mesué, Geber, Rhasès, Avicenna, Avenzoar and Averroes, were the sources of instruction for the Western physicians. Unfortunately anatomy and physiology were neglected, and surgery was left in the hands of the barbers. It was in the thirteenth century that anatomy, the true foundation of all medical knowledge, was commenced, and that in the West. The Emperor Frederick ordered that no person should be admitted to his degree who had not studied anatomy and the dissection of the human body. There remain some remarkable works on medicine written at this period, among which is the *Tresor des Pauvres*, or Manual of the Art of

Curing, composed by John Peter of Spain, who afterwards became pope under the name of John XXI.   The most complete works on medicine of the age are those which were published by Gilles de Corbeil, canon of Paris, in Latin verse.   They consist of two treatises, one *De Pulsibus* and the other *De Urinis,* besides a poem in four cantos on the *Virtues of Medicaments.*

Neither the object nor result of all the intellectual activity of these centuries can be said to have much advanced the true interests of mankind. Nevertheless, some of the indirect effects have had great influence upon subsequent ages.   One of these undoubtedly is the multiplication of manuscripts and the formation of numerous libraries, where were to be found not only contemporary works, but also all the remaining productions of antiquity. Libraries then began to multiply.   Philip de Dreux, Bishop of Dreux, had more than 300 MSS., which he bequeathed to his cathedral.   "There is at St. Medard a beautiful library," says Gauthier de Coinsi, in speaking of the Abbey of St. Medard of Soissons.   Vincent de Beauvais is in raptures when he speaks of that of St. Martin of Tours.

In these centuries commenced the great struggle for preeminence between the Latin and the vulgar tongue, the parent of the French language.   Latin reigned in the schools, the sciences, the church, and the formal documents of public and civil life. It was taught in the grammar of Priscian, of Albertus Magnus, and the grammatical "Elements" of Alexander de Villedieu, and the *Dictionarum Locupletissimum,* the only lexicon which dates from this age.   The vulgar tongue was the language of conversation among the laymen, and even among the clergy.   In spite of the efforts of the universities and the monastic orders to arrest its progress, it began to make its way into the business of instruction.   In the thirteenth century especially some books were translated into French for the use of the people.   The *Gospels* and the Bible passed from the oriental to the vulgar tongue, greatly to' the scandal of the Church.   A curious fusion was made of the two idioms: they were mixed together in the rhymes and verse of the times, as in this example—

> " Je maine bonne vie *semper quantum possum.*
> Si tavernier m'appelle, je dis *ecce adsum.*
> A despendre le mien *semper paratus sum.*"*

The chronicles were among the first productions of the national tongue.   The Latin chronicles are in general written with tolerable correctness, but they are bare and meagre enumerations of facts.   Most of the chroniclers were witnesses or contemporaries

---

* Dos Fames, des Dez et de la Taverne, p. 74.   Fabliaux, tom. iv. pp. 485—488.

of the events they record; so that they either speak from actual observation, from the communications of eye-witnesses, or the rumour of the day. But it is chiefly in the chronicles written in French, such as those of Joinville and Villehardouin, that we find those traits of manners, that pleasing simplicity, or that liveliness and picturesque narrative which gives them their chief value. They are also less clerical, and written rather with feudal than ecclesiastical prejudices: they recount all they have seen in the course of their pilgrimages or their adventures in court and castle.

The number of chroniclers of the two centuries is very great. We have mentioned the names of the two principal ones, who wrote " *soit en naif français, soit en ramage de leur pays.*" The history of Rigord, though in Latin, was translated in " *biau parlier en les grandes et incomparables chroniques de Saint Denis.*" Guillaume-le-Breton, the author of the *Philippiad,* has also written a history in prose, which is only valuable where it continues that of Rigord. Matthew Paris is certainly the most remarkable of the narrators of this period. His chronicle is a bulky folio, comprising the national history of England. It is characterized by a spirit of opposition to, and independent criticism on, the Church of Rome, not a little remarkable in a monkish author of the middle ages. Jacques de Vitri, who writes chiefly of affairs connected with the Holy Land, presents us with a most interesting report of all that was known in the West of the history, manners and customs of the Saracens, as well as a very animated picture of the corruptions of the clergy. The work of Alberic, the monk of Trois Fontaines, is a compilation of chronicles anterior or contemporary. The same may be said of the *Miroir Historial* of Vincent de Beauvais. The number of chronicles of this period which relate to particular provinces or special events, such as the crusades against the Albigenses, is almost infinite, and they partake pretty generally the character of the history of the period.

Philippe Monski, Bishop of Tournay, wrote the history of France in Latin verse, " *en rimes dilectables.*" He begins with the Trojan origin of the Franks. Guillaume-le-Breton's poem on Philip-Augustus contains twelve thousand verses. It is a metrical chronicle, with metaphors and figures borrowed from the classics. Lisyer, in his Literary History of the Poets of the Middle Ages, counts upwards of 180 in these two centuries. The middle ages are equally abundant in sermons, epistles, tracts, essays, in short in all those kinds of works favoured by the religious spirit of the time. Sermons by Saint Bernard, Peter of Blois, and John of Salisbury remain, on reading which it is difficult to conceive wherein lies the spirit which shook the whole world, and ruled the society of Christendom with such absolute power.

It was during the thirteenth century, from the year 1201 up to 1280, that the songs of the troubadours were chiefly in vogue. During this period occurred the crowd of *gai chanteurs*, such as Cadenet, Blacas, Giraud, De Borneuil, Boniface de Castillane, Pierre Cardinal, Isarn, the Monk of Montaudon, Giraud Riquier, &c., whose poems were so celebrated in castle hall and lady's bower. These men impressed a literary character on their age by their productions: they are the only ones of the time in which the spirit showed itself in freedom and truth, and are the best monuments of the history of the period.

The productions of the *Gai Savoir* are of several kinds. The *sirventes* are satires, general or personal, in which no one is spared, lord or priest, king or people. The *sirventes* of the Monk of Montaudon and Peter Cardinal are full of interest; the one paints the dissipation of the castle, the other of the clergy. The troubadour of Montaudon is especially severe upon the ladies; their infidelity, their ornaments, their gallantry, are each in their turn the subject of his caustic raillery. The *tenson* is a dialogue in verse between two persons on any question in the code of love, of poetry or chivalry: they are generally of a tame description, but sometimes exhibit a satirical turn. In one of them Rambaud de Vaqueiras reproaches the Marquis of Malespina with robbing on the high road. The marquis does not deny the truth of the allegation, but excuses himself by saying that it was for the purpose of giving away, and not of hoarding. Avarice was a crime, but robbery a violence in harmony with the feelings of the times. *Epistles* in verse sometimes occur, in which the poet addresses advice to his correspondents respecting their conduct in life. Amadieu des Escas teaches his mistress how she ought to arrange her toilette, to put rouge on her cheeks in such a manner as to eclipse the brilliancy of the painted glass, how she should soften and whiten the skin of her whole person, receive her lover secretly at night at the foot of the little tower, and take him to her heart. The *pastorals* are more monotonous than the *tensons*, and invariably turn upon the hacknied ideas of the rural eclogue. It is always a shepherd wandering in the fields, who meets his shepherdess gathering flowers; or a lord who in vain attempts to seduce the fidelity of the shepherdess, who prefers her swain. There are also some *tales* which have been used by the Italian poets of the fourteenth and fifteenth centuries; and another species of poems, termed *plaintes*, which are elegies on the death of a friend or mistress. Sometimes political misfortunes are deplored in them, such as the taking of Jerusalem, or the unhappy state of Languedoc during the crusade against the Albigenses. The *aubades*, the song of the dawn (*l'aube*), and the *serenade*, the song of the evening (*ser*), were dedicated to feelings of gallantry and pleasure. In the aubade every strophe necessarily ended with *alba*, in the serenade with *ser;* in the *ballade* the first verse was uniformly repeated.

The poetry of the *trouvères*, or songsters of the north of France, had a different character from that of the *troubadours*, or minstrels of the south. The latter are more gay, and more satirical: the former have less variety, are more monotonous in their tone, and also more elaborate in their execution. To the *trouvères* may be attributed those vast and complete productions, the Romances of Chivalry, the descriptions of a new world and an imaginary state of manners, a stock of heroes and adventures of a most marvellous character, but uniform, consistent and striking. Such are the romances comprised under the three great classes, 1. of the Round Table; 2. of Charlemagne; 3. of Amadis, which belong to a later date. To them and to this age belong the *Roman de la Rose*, and the *Bible Guyot*, one of the most faithful memorials of manners. The author of the last named work announces his design in these verses:

> " D'un siècle puant et horrible,
> M'estuet (me convient) commencer une bible,
> Pour poindre, et pour aiguilloner,
> Et pour grant example donner."

Every class of society passes in review before the author—kings, counts, barons, clerks, bishops, lawyers; and the vices of each profession are unsparingly depicted. " The clergy," he says, " had married three virgins, Charity, Virtue and Justice, but after having deflowered and repudiated them, they put in their places Treason, Hypocrisy and Simony." The *Bible* of the Seigneur de Bèze is written in the same spirit. In the *Chemin d'Enfer* of Raoul de Houdon, he puts many of his contemporaries, princes and prelates, among the *dampnés*.

The *batailles* of the *trouvères* are dialogues, like the *tensons* of the troubadours, in which there are frequently discussed scholastic questions of great nicety. The *chastiements* are didactic poems, in which the *trouvères* embrace complete bodies of instruction for the use of particular individuals. The *bestiaires* are fables; frequently translated from Æsop: at other times they contain bitter satires in the form of an apologue, the most famous of which is undoubtedly the romance of " The Fox." These poems of different kinds have still their admirers, and many find in them, not only talent and power, but also consider them as the source of the modern school of poetry. Be this as it may, and it is not a little doubtful, there is one thing certain, that the historian who would attempt to seize the spirit of this age without consulting them, would commit an irreparable error.

Amidst a state of society so rude and so unsettled, the fine arts cannot be expected to have made much progress; nevertheless a style of architecture arose and was carried to perfection in these times, which is not surpassed for beauty and harmony, and aptitude to its purposes, by that of any other country or age. The cathedrals of the twelfth and thirteenth centuries, with their elegant arches, their clusters of light and lofty columns, their elaborate portals and gorgeously painted windows, are monuments of skill, science, industry, and religious enthusiasm. The details exhibited in the ornamental parts show the utmost facility in the art of sculpture, and by their grotesque character and varied nature, add greatly to our means of understanding the history of the times. It is true that the figures want animation; and the same remark applies to the exquisitely beautiful illuminations of the MSS. of the time. The art of invention, the art of colouring, the art of grouping—all are there, excepting that appearance of motion and life which makes the difference between representing an animate and an inanimate object. This step in the progress of the arts of sculpture and design was reserved for a subsequent period. In music, however, a discovery was made, which effected a complete revolution in that science. Hitherto that which is called *accompaniment* was utterly unknown even to the ancients: it was tried in the cathedrals under the name of *dechant* or double chant, and was, like so many other good things, forbidden and condemned by the pope. The *dechant*, however, continued, and ended in completely discarding the old method of singing in unison, and accompanying the voice with the same part on the instrument. For this discovery we are indebted to that noble instrument the organ, itself a creation of the middle ages, in admirable harmony, both in sound and appearance, with the vaulted roofs and carved chapels it adorns.

We have thus, with the aid of M. Capefigue, run through the principal facts which mark the character and tendency of this age, with the exception of those which relate to commerce. Commerce is itself an element in civilization, the activity of which is rarely taken into sufficient account.

We have seen how much the liberties of Europe were indebted to the spirit of association which prevailed among the middle classes of persons during these two centuries. The origin of this spirit is doubtless partly attributable to motives of self protection against the force and discipline of powerful chiefs; but it also arose in part out of the necessities of trade and commerce. Persons practising the same arts of life must necessarily come to some understanding respecting the general conduct of their business, and consequently they must associate. Also in carrying on commerce with distant countries, in venturing property far from home, and in order to facilitate communication, it was again necessary to associate. These wants induced the people of the middle ages, after the birth of trade and commerce, to unite themselves into corporations and guilds, from which union they derived great part of their force. The influence of their wealth has already been alluded to, besides which a moral strength doubtless arose from the commercial intercourse with other nations; for it is one of the blessings of commerce, amongst the many it carries with it, that, by constant communication with other countries, it greatly contributes to the acquisition of knowledge, and the consequent enlargement of the mind.

The merchants of the middle ages, feeling the necessity of protection from power, and being already considered a useful and valuable body as administering to the increasing wants of a luxurious nobility, demanded and procured various grants of privileges *pour le faite des marchandises,* such as safe conducts through the territories of plundering barons, and freedom from tolls and exactions of various kinds, which every *seigneur* of the time imposed upon the unhappy persons obliged to pass through his demesne. These privileges naturally gave rise to others, and as they were likely to be as beneficial in similar cases, they were granted. At length the citizens grew strong enough to take such as they wanted.

When communication between different parts of a country is difficult, the utility of *fairs* is obvious. They are characteristic of this period. Every city and village, even monasteries, solicited the privilege, as a royal or seignioral concession, of holding a fair on a given day in each year. Some of these fairs were celebrated over the world: at that of the Landit, at St. Denys, even Armenians were present; and the chroniclers describe with wonder and astonishment the quantity of merchandize exposed for sale, and the number of purchases completed within the short space of time allowed for traffic.

These centuries were rich in events, and no reign is more striking in the character of its transactions, or of the persons that figured on the stage of Europe during its continuance, than that of Philip-Augustus. The *personal* history, if we may use the term, of the time, is equally curious with the philosophical view of the elements of civilization then in operation, which we have endeavoured to take. The heroes of the age are innumerable. Our own Richard, the model of the warriors of his time, brave, passionate, ignorant,

.coarse, unsurpassed in feats of arms, and gifted with a taste for song; Philip, himself a perfect knight in the field, violent in his wrath, wily in his plans, unscrupulous in his means, unfeeling and unrelenting.   Innocent III., the ruling spirit of the times, the indefatigable, the indomitable, mild and persuasive as long as gentle measures were likely to effect his purpose, fierce, uncompromising, and inexorable when strong measures alone could serve his ends.   His power was felt everywhere, his influence settled even questions of private life: disputes were submitted to his arbitration from all quarters of the world, and when they did not interfere with the domination of the Church, of which he was the great upholder, his decisions were prompt and just: his activity, and almost omnipresence in Europe, is one of the marvels of the age.   The immense collection of his letters remains a monument of his authority.   Our John possesses a large place in this history, but it is one of distinguished baseness.   He possessed not a single virtue of his age, and there is scarcely a vice of any other for which he was not notorious.   The sovereigns partook of the character of the chivalry of which they were the head; civilization and refinement had not as yet set them apart from their fellow men.   In some relations they were suzerains, and in others vassals, doing homage to their own liege men; and the vassal and the suzerain were not unfrequently at war; in some great fief, as in Guienne and Poitou, the vassals had a feudal right to carry on independent wars. Under such circumstances a degree of equality and parity, both in character and bearing, existed between kings and seigneurs, inconsistent with the modern notions of sovereignty.   Philip-Augustus was indeed the first who, in establishing a general authority, and concentrating a vast mass of power and property, first raised the throne of France high above the seats of the nobles.   It was his system to undermine the feudal power of his *grand-tenanciers,* and his long and active reign enabled him to make great advances towards the completion of his project.   When he commenced his reign, the King of England was the actual sovereign of a territory in what is now France, fully equal to all the rest of the French king's dominions. The fiefs of Normandy, Britanny, Poictiers, Anjou, and Guienne, compose the richest and most valuable half of France; while the counts of Flanders, whose authority extended over Artois, the counts of Champagne, and the dukes of Burgundy, owed but a formal homage to him as their suzerain, and as often carried their gonfanons against him in the field as on his side.   At his death, the whole of the fiefs of England had passed into his hands, and besides greatly humbling the independent authorities of the great feudatories on the other side, he had consolidated and generalized his authority over the whole of his own kingdom, in which previously there had been as many kings as there were castles.

With the view of illustrating what we have called the *personal* history of these centuries, we will select some details of a few of the events and characters which stand out most prominently on the historical canvass. They who are slow at gathering the spirit of the times from general remarks may perhaps get more instruction from the living pictures which abound in the work before us. We shall not dwell upon the great movements of the period, such as the crusade of Philip and Richard, which ended in the captivity of the latter; nor the expedition of the Franks to the East, when they took Constantinople, and made a count of Flanders emperor of Byzantium, and a count of Champagne lord of the Morea; nor yet the great league of the barons against Philip, which was dissolved by the decisive battle of Bovines, (which Mr. Capefigue compares to the battle of Waterloo); nor yet the wars of Richard or John in France, nor those of Louis of France in England, which have been so imperfectly narrated by English historians; to do justice to all these, a space would be required far beyond the allowed limits of an article. But by some insulated facts which will not take up much room, we can gage the spirit of the age. By the description of the establishment of a single *commune*, we will give a specimen of the manner in which these bulwarks of our modern liberties were built up, and it is not improbable that, abridged as it is from the contemporary chronicles, it will better conduce to a due impression of the nature of this struggle for privileges, than any thing we have hitherto stated.

The history of the commune of Laon presents as complete a picture of the progress and developement of these municipal guarantees as that of perhaps any other. The town of Laon was subject to the temporal authority of its bishop. It had no police, and was constantly the scene of the greatest disorders. The nobles and their followers exercised every kind of cruelty and injustice upon the burghers; the burghers, in their turn, oppressed the peasants and serfs; taxes were levied by the strongest, and property was not respected. In the year 1106, the bishopric had been got possession of by dint of money by one Gaudri, a Norman, who frequented the altar but little, and was mightily given to horses, dogs, and falcons. To these unseemly pursuits he joined the greatest cruelty of character. Among his followers was one of those black slaves brought by the barons on their return from a crusade. This slave had been one of the instruments of the bishop's cruelties exercised on the burghers: in the bishop's palace he had torn out the eyes of one inhabitant of the town, and by his orders had assassinated another in the metropolitan church. The burghers were naturally exasperated by this treatment, and conspired to establish a *commune.* Gaudri was at that time in England with the Norman king. The burghers addressed propositions to the nobles and the chapter of the church, offering to purchase their municipal liberties. The deeds were drawn up, and considerable sums of money paid. On his return from England, Gaudri himself confirmed them, " because he had himself a great want of money." But the bishop had soon squandered, in horses, dogs, and gambling, the money of the burghers, and he found that the duties payable by the town, and fixed by the municipal charter, were not enough to satisfy his wants. He resolved, therefore, to abolish the commune, and he persuaded the nobles, and even the king Louis VI., to second his designs. The king came to Laon on Holy Thursday, A. D. 1112; the next day it was published by sound of trumpet that the commune was dissolved, and that the burghers should no longer retain their banner, their town-house, and their belfry. This news created great confusion : all the shops and hostelries were immediately shut, and the burghers took arms. Forty of them took a mutual oath to kill the bishop and all the nobles who had threatened the existence of the rising commune. This conspiracy got wind, and Gaudri was informed of it. His friends beseeched him not to go out on the day of the Easter procession. " For shame?" said he, " *I* die by the hands of such folks as them! If John, my black, was to amuse himself by pulling the nose of the stoutest among them, he durst not even grumble." However, he caused himself to be surrounded in the procession by his knights and servants, who wore arms under their robes. Whilst the procession was winding down one of the streets, the mob began to cry " *Commune! Commune!*" but owing to some want of understanding among themselves, this time the project of the conspirators fell to the ground. On Easter Thursday, while the bishop, in complete security, was conversing with an archdeacon named Gauhier, the cry of " *Commune! Commune!*" was again heard. At this signal, numbers of banded burghers, armed with lances and bows, clubs and axes, surrounded the episcopal palace. The nobles, who ran from all parts to its succour, were massacred, and the citizens by main force entered the palace, crying, " Where is the traitor of a bishop, the scoundrel?" Gaudri had hid himself in a vat, where he would not have been found but for the treachery of a servant. One Thergand, a serf of the church of St. Vincent, who was the ringleader of the insurrection, having taken off the cover of the tun, struck it with his club, crying out " Is there any body within here?" The trembling bishop answered, " Ah! it is an unhappy prisoner." " Oh, it is you, then, master fox," said the serf of St. Vincent's, " that have hidden yourself in this tun?" Saying these words, he dragged the bishop by the hair out of his hiding place : the poor Gaudri prayed and supplicated, promising on the Gospel to abdicate the bishopric, and leave the country for ever. But his prayers were not listened to ; and the serf gave him a blow on the head with his two-edged axe. The second blow finished him. The burghers cut off his little finger, in order to take his rich pastoral ring; his body was dragged into the street, and every one that passed threw mud and stones upon it.

When the exasperation of the burghers had subsided, they saw the danger to which they were exposed. Feeling that they could not resist the vengeance that was sure to fall upon the town, they resolved to put themselves under the protection of Thomas de Marle, seigneur de Coucy, whose name figures in all the popular tales which describe the violence of the barons of the middle ages. The Sire de Coucy promised them his protection, but only in his castle, for the town of Laon was incapable of defence. The burghers abandoned their town in tears, and it was sacked by the troops of Louis VI.; the lands of de Coucy were overrun by the forces of the barons; the victory was followed by vengeance : more than three hundred burghers were hung. But such was the perseverance of the population in the pursuit of their privileges, that sixteen years after the murder of Bishop Gaudri, the burghers of Laon succeeded in obtaining a new charter under the title of *Institutio Paci;* it was only, however, confirmed in the reign of Philip-Augustus.

The story of Philip's marriage with Ingeburg, the Danish princess, his disgust, his divorce, and his subsequent passion for Agnes de Meranie, his forced separation from her, her death, and again his forced resumption of Ingeburg by the authority of the pope, who laid the country under an interdict, and, in effect, deprived Philip for the moment of his kingdom and his subjects, is one which, in all its parts, is not only of great interest, but an admirable practical illustration of the manners and modes of thinking of the times.

The king seems to have married Ingeburg on the credit of the praises of the Bishop of Hamburg, who, in a letter to Philip, enlarged with rapture on her great beauty, and—as the clergy were always special in these matters—on the brilliancy of her fair hair, and the dazzling whiteness of her hands. Philip went to meet her on his charger, with his casque on his head and his hauberk of silver mail on his shoulders : she met him riding on her white hackney *(hacquenée).* He looked, misliked, but yet married her.

But it was with great difficulty that he could be prevailed upon by the priests to consummate the marriage, and he immediately resolved on a divorce.   The obedient clergy then set to work, and arranged some genealogical trees, by which they proved that the parties were within the prohibited degree of consanguinity : they were related within eight degrees by the marriage of some great grandfather.   The queen was ignorant of French, but when she was called into the Council, and an interpreter explained to her the decree that had gone forth, all she could say was " *Mauvaise France! Mauvaise France!*" then, after a pause, she added " *Rome! Rome!*"   She meant by this that she intended to appeal against the injustice committed against her to the Pope, and in good time he interfered effectually in her behalf.   In the meanwhile, however, she was sent by her capricious husband into the confinement of remote castles and convents, where her wants were so little attended to, that she was indebted to the charity of some churchmen for subsistence.   Stephen, Bishop of Tournay, wrote a most pathetic letter in her behalf to the Cardinal of Champagne, which, however, does not seem to have produced its proper effect ; it remains an honourable testimony of his humanity, and the sufferings and virtues of the unhappy Ingeburg.
    Stephen says,

" There is a precious stone in these realms which men tread under foot, but which the angels honour, and which is worthy of the royal treasury.   I speak of the queen, shut up in Cisoin as in a prison, overwhelmed with grief and misery.   We bewail her destiny, and leave to God alone to pronounce on the cause and end of her disgrace ; but who has such a heart of stone as not to be touched by the misfortunes of a princess, the descendant of so many kings !—to see her in such a state of poverty, so young, so beautiful, so venerable in her manners, so modest in her words ; with a face more lovely than that of the Ambrosian Virgin.   I would say she is better made than Sarah, more virtuous than Rebecca, more pleasant than Rachel, more devout than Anne, more chaste than Susanna.   They who are judges of the beauty of women assure us that the queen is not less lovely than Helen.   Her daily occupation is to read, to pray, or to work ; she plays at no game of chance, nor even at chess : she prays to God with sighs and tears from morning till the sixth hour, not only for herself, but for the king our sovereign : she is never seated in her oratory, she is always either standing, on her knees, or prostrate on the earth.   This princess, so beautiful and so noble, is forced to sell and pawn her clothes and furniture for the means of subsistence : she asks for the means of life, she solicits alms, she stretches forth her hands to receive them.   She weeps, and often do I weep with her : my heart is melted within me.   I exhort her to put her trust in the Lord : she answers, ' My friends, my near relations are as much estranged from me as if they did not belong to me ; my only refuge is the Lord Archbishop of Rheims, who has protected me, kept and fed me so liberally since the commencement of my misfortunes.' "—*Baluze, Miscellan.* t. i. p. 420.

While the divorced wife was in this pitiable condition, Philip married Agnes, sister of Otho, Duke of Moravia. Agnes was a lady of ravishing beauty; and the monks tell us of her fair hair, which descended to the ground, and of her little foot and her white hand. She was, moreover, a huntress, indomitable in the chase, and on her fiery horse in the depth of the forest, like another Diana or Camilla, gave the death-blow to a stag or boar, with a grace which enchanted the whole chivalry of the court. At tilt or tourney, she distributed the prizes with a dignity and sweetness that won all hearts; many were the young chevaliers that wore her colours. The King became desperately in love with her, and she appears to have duly returned the passion.

The news of Agnes's beauty and accomplishments reached even the remote tower where the pious Ingeburg was confined: she confided her griefs to the bosom of the Pope. In her letter, among other touching things, she says, " By some diabolical counsel of the great, he has just espoused Agnes; more beautiful, perhaps, she may be than me, but not one who loves him more; while I, a sad plaything of fortune, am shut up in the depths of a castle, where I cannot even see the heaven to which I hourly lift my supplicating hands."

These letters produced but little effect as long as Celestin occupied the pontifical throne: but the scene changed as soon as Innocent assumed the tiara. The divorce had been granted by a council without reference to the papal authority; and he determined not to let so flagrant an encroachment of his prerogatives pass with impunity. What might have been overlooked in the injustice to Ingeburg was unpardonable in its offence against the Pope. On the other hand, opposition only strengthened the passion of the royal lovers. " Agnes is my wife," said the king; " no person shall separate me from her?" Gentle measures were at first tried and failed, and at last the fatal tremendous interdict was laid on the country.

The legate convened a sort of council at Dijon. The archbishops of Lyons, Rheims, Besançon, Vienne, eighteen bishops, and a great number of abbots were present. Two abbots were charged to summon the king, who had them put out of the palace. On the 6th of December, the bishops and priests assembled, each with a torch in his hand. In the dead of the night the clerks chanted in a funeral tone the *miserere*, and prayers were addressed in the names of the culpable to the God of mercy: the echoes of the church repeated the melancholy sound, and immediately the bells, heard for the last time, rang the dead peal. The Christ on the altars was veiled, the last consecrated wafers were burnt, and the bodies of the saints and images of the patrons were carried down into the crypts. In presence of the assembled people, the legate, attired in his violet-coloured stole, used on Passion Day as in the service of the dead, elevated his voice, and announced to the multitude on their knees, in the name of Jesus Christ, that all the domains of the king of France were laid under an interdict, until he ceased his adulterous intercourse with Agnes de Meranie his concubine. A deep groaning was heard in the church; the old men, the women and children wept: it seemed as if the hour of judgment was come, and that all were going to appear before the avenging God without the succour of the church.

The influence of this proceeding can only be calculated by those who know the depth of superstition in which the masses were at this period plunged. From the moment of the fulmination of the bull, all religious offices were suspended, the images of our Saviour outside the church were covered up, as also those of the Apostles and the Virgin, the guardian angel, before whom the baron and his vassals were accustomed to kneel every sabbath and feast day. The cross on the steeple was also covered with black cloth: the gates were closed, and the noisy bells, which announced the close of labour for the day and the hour of prayer, were alike muffled: service ceased from one end of the kingdom to the other, the choir was silent and the monasteries still: marriages and baptisms were celebrated in the churchyard, and they who died during the interdict did not receive Christian burial. People left the kingdom to attend the ceremonies of the church in neighbouring countries; they flocked to Normandy, into Britanny and the fiefs of England. At many points of the kingdom violent commotions took place: the multitude attempted to force the bishops and priests to reopen the chapels, and to celebrate the holy mysteries.

Philip tried in vain every means of resistance, and at length was obliged to send two clerks to ask that the interdict should be taken off, protesting that he was ready to put the question of divorce to a trial of its validity. The Pope answered, " I am willing: but first of all let him send away his concubine and take back Ingeburg: then, and then only, will I proceed to examine the case of divorce, and take off the interdict!"—" My God! my God!" cried Agnes, " where now shall I take my grief?" Philip in a moment of fury exclaimed: " Well then, I will turn my back on the Church—Saladin was happy to have no pope." Philip assembled his parliament and summoned the principal barons and prelates of his realm: Agnes appeared before them, in a suit of mourning, in grief, but beautiful in her tears; a mortal paleness marked her face, and her far-advanced pregnancy did not diminish the interest her appearance excited. The barons and the prelates, however, could find no means of relieving their sovereign : they decided that the king must obey the wish of the pope, that Agnes de Meranie should be dismissed, and Ingeburg brought back from her prison.

Agnes wrote an affecting letter to the pope, who only answered by sending a legate to inquire into the affair of the divorce. She retired to a castle in Normandy, where she died at the end of two months in child-bed. In the mean time the council sat at Soissons to deliberate on the validity of the divorce, and it was joined by envoys from the king of Denmark. The affair was every day assuming a more serious character, when one morning the assembly was informed that the king had all of a sudden arrived on horseback, and had rode away with Ingeburg on the croup behind him. Here was an end of their grave deliberation on the divorce, and the council was dissolved. Philip, however, had no further intention than that of confounding a council debating on a point that no longer concerned him: he again shut up Ingeburg in an old palace, and in spite of the repeated entreaties of the Pope that he would take carnal knowledge of his lawful wife, his capricious disgust remained in all its force, and it was only on his death bed that he ever again consented to see her.

The extraordinary power of the Church under Innocent is also strikingly displayed in the treatment of the Comte de Toulouse, when Provence, which was a fief of the king of Arragon, was invaded by the crusading barons, bent upon destroying the Albigenses by fire and sword. When this powerful prince—for such was the Comte de Toulouse—saw that it was impossible for him with his vassals and allies to make head against the Frank seigneurs under Louis of France, he determined on making his peace with the Church, which charged him with heresy or the protection of heresy. After promising to give up into their hands seven of his strongest castles, and taken an oath to confirm it, the Comte was admitted to make his abjuration. Advancing towards the sanctuary, an altar covered with relics, naked to the waist, a rope was drawn tight about his neck, and two bishops held the ends of it, as if they were holding a beast of burden; the Comte then pronounced an oath, beginning thus : " In the 12th year of my lord, the Pope Innocent III,. I Raymond, in presence of the holy relics, the host and the wood of the true cross, swear, that I will obey all the orders of the pope and yours, Master Melon (the legate) touching the articles for which I am excommunicated, &c." When the ceremony of reconciliation commenced, the legate put a stole on the neck of the count instead of the cord, and taking the two ends, he took him into the sanctuary, whipping him with a rod. The lord count cried out, and was red with shame: at last the legate gave him absolution. The crowd in the church was so great, that they were obliged to send him out of the church all covered with blood, by the subterranean passage leading into the fields.

We shall now pass to another aspect, in which the church, or at least a churchman, was exhibited to an admiring multitude. In one of the engagements between Richard and Philip, the Bishop of Beauvais was taken prisoner: he was found by the side of Philip, with his helmet on his head and lance in his hand : and in the course of the battle had made great carnage among the English. Richard treated him harshly, and locked him up in a fortified tower. He wrote a bitter complaint to the pope that a churchman should be so treated: the pope answered rationally enough : " You quitted the peaceful rule of the shepherd for the turbulence of war, the mitre for the casque, the pastoral crook for the lance, the cup for the cuirass, the ring for the sword, and you write me word that evil has befallen you. I am not astonished: you sought—well! you have found : you struck, and lo! you are stricken in your turn: however, I shall write to Richard to ask your deliverance." At the great battle of Bovines, the same bishop was again in arms, and distinguished himself greatly by his marvellous prowess. The venerable prelate fought with a massive iron club, for he had a scruple of conscience about taking life away by an effusion of blood. The chance of the fight brought him in contact with the Earl of Salisbury, upon whom he fell with his club, and quickly brought him to the earth. The bishop had by him a *chatelain*, the Sire de Nivelle. " John de Nivelle," said he, " drag this Salisbury along for me : say it was thou that struck him, for I am doing unlawful work. I should not change my staff for this club." Saying these words, he went forward gaily upon the English, knocking them down with his club, right and left.

Among other signs of the times recorded in the history of this remarkable reign, is the crusade of the children. The spirit of an age may be indicated by the turn of the infantine mind : in a country engaged in a popular war, the children will always be found playing at soldiers. But the religious duty of the Crusades had taken such universal hold of men's minds, that it produced a movement, even among the children of Europe, of a kind unparalleled in the history of the world.

In the year 1212, many thousands of boys and girls abandoned their homes, not only in France, but in Germany and Italy, giving out that they were bent upon delivering the Holy Land. The eldest were not more than eighteen years of age. It was in vain that their parents attempted to restrain them. They watched opportunities of escape, and got away by making holes in the walls; and sallied forth from the paternal mansion with as much joy as if they had been going to a festival. The fate of these unhappy children, as may be supposed, was most unfortunate; they were entrapped in numbers by merchants of Venice, Genoa and Marseilles, who were at that time engaged in the infamous traffic of supplying the seraglios of the East with children. A great many were shipped in the Mediterranean ports, and many died of hunger and fatigue in the long journies to which they had voluntarily devoted themselves, but for which their strength was utterly inadequate.

It would be very ungrateful, after having made such copious use of a book as we have done in this article, to speak ill of the author, and therefore we feel easy in strongly recommending M. Capefigue's history to general attention. It is written after a plan as yet unpractised in England, and which can scarcely be called history. It consists almost wholly of a reproduction of morsels of the old contemporary writers, monks, chroniclers, poets and letter writers, frequently in their own words, and almost always partaking of their simplicity, at the same time occasionally varied by a remark which belongs to the present century. In itself this style of weaving history produces a kind of party-coloured performance, which is far from being agreeable at first sight: a little attentive contemplation, however, shows that the natural result is that of deeply imbuing the reader in the colours of the time.

ART. II.—1. *Prolegomena zu einer wissenschaftlichen Mythologie.* Von Karl Otfried Müller. (An Introduction to a Scientific System of Mythology. By C. O. Müller.) Göttingen. 1825. 8vo.

2. *Aglaophamus, sive de Theologiæ Mysticæ Græcorum causis libri tres.* Scripsit Chr. Augustus Lobeck, idemque poetarum Orphicorum dispersas reliquias collegit. Königsberg. 1829. 2 vols. 8vo.

THE subject of mythology may be considered in two points of view, either in regard to the *religion* or the *history* of ancient nations. The first branch of this subject comprises investigations into the origin and nature of the different modes of worship, the rites, ceremonies, festivals, and sacred symbols prevailing among the nations whose mythology we possess; and it is this which has attracted the chief notice of the writers of France and England. These authors, actuated by different motives, either like Volney, Dupuis and others, by a hatred, or like Bryant, by a love of the Christian religion, have by the most absurd etymogies, the most fanciful hypotheses, and the most illogical reasoning, attempted to set up a fabric which the faintest breath of criticism at once demolishes. Though the efforts of these writers have probably been more barren of good results than those of any other labourers in the field of literature, yet the utter worthlessness of their books is to be attributed, not to the nature of the subject, (for the history of religion is the history of the human mind,) but to their eagerness to explain upon one theory, or to refer to one origin, a mass of phenomena wholly unconnected, and springing from numberless causes. Dupuis and Volney with their astronomy, and Bryant with Noah and the ark, resemble the advertising quack, whose infallible and instantaneous cure for *all* diseases would probably turn out not to be of use in *one*. But in explaining the sacred symbols so prevalent in the ancient religions of India, Egypt and Greece, a new path has been struck out by several modern writers, avoiding the absurdities of the authors just mentioned. Whatever errors may have been committed by the symbolical mythologists, and to howsoever well-grounded objections parts of their systems may be liable, it cannot be denied that the labours of Creuzer and others on the continent, and in this country of Mr. Payne Knight,[*] have thrown much light on the modes of expression adopted by the early priests and religionists for the objects and powers of nature which they worshipped. The general use of these holy symbols is proved by their constant occurrence on the temples of Hindostan and Egypt, and the coins of the Greek states, which last were exclusively reserved for sacred devices; nor were ever, till late times, polluted by portraits of human princes. The *historical* school of mythology has had no followers in this country, nor indeed in any country but Germany. The attempts of some of the French and English historians, such as Mitford, Raoul-Rochette, and many others, to elicit history from fable, are ludicrous in the extreme. Instead of perceiving that the legends of mythology bear only an *analogy* to the truth, that they are false when understood literally, but frequently true when interpreted metaphorically, they have

---

[*] See his *Inquiry into the Symbolical Language of Ancient Art and Mythology.* London. 1818. Printed for private distribution, and afterwards published in the Classical Journal. It was intended to be prefixed to the second volume of " Select Specimens of Ancient Sculpture," published by the Society of Dilettanti, which is, we understand, in course of preparation.

taken them as the narratives of real facts, embellished by credulity or a poetical imagination; and having struck out the wonders, they took the *caput mortuum* which remaiued for real history.   It was left to the inquiring genius of the Germans to detect the fallaci- ousness of this process, to discover the real nature of the legendary accounts of early nations, and the possibility of extracting truth from fiction.   Among those who have clearly perceived the true difference between traditional and contemporary history, and have assisted by their researches to unriddle the secrets of mythology, Otfried Müller, the celebrated author of *Orchomenus, the Dorians, the Etruscans,* and other works, stands in the first rank.   His sketch of a system of mythology was in some measure intended to set forth the principles on which the mythological investi- gations in his former works had been founded; he has, however, gone through the subject in a regular order, and illustrated his positions with numerous and well-chosen examples.   At the end of the volume is added a statement of the mythological systems of Heyne, Creuzer, Voss, Hermann, Buttmann and Welcker, the chief writers on this branch of learning, together with an exami- nation of their respective merits.   On this and several other sub- jects treated in this work with great learning and ability our limits prevent us from entering; but we shall proceed to lay before our readers an abstract of that part of Mr. Müller's work which re- lates to the nature, origin and treatment of mythological fables : while in the discussions respecting the religion, and particularly the mystical worship and ceremonies of the Greeks, we shall be assisted by the late admirable work of Lobeck, of which more will be said hereafter.

The fables of mythology (μῦθοι), and the mythological collec- tions, such as the work of Apollodorus, the κύκλος μυθικὸς of Dionysius, &c. consisted of narrations of the acts and adventures of certain individuals belonging to a time divided with tolerable precision from the regular history of Greece.   These stories are not true in their plain and literal sense, but must be interpreted and explained before their proper meaning can be understood. To assist us in this solution we have the Greek language, which shows that many mythological names have a meaning correspond- ing to the acts of the persons designated by them, and a know- ledge of the local circumstances of the Greek territory, of the history, religion and civil institutions of the Greeks.   By these means it may be observed that all mythological fables are either statements, clothed indeed in a peculiar language, of real facts ; or are merely fanciful, and represent nothing derived from out- ward observation.   Of the first class are the historical fables, such as the national genealogies, the legends respecting the foun-

dation of the Greek cities and colonies: of the second, the fictions concerning the attributes and actions of the gods. Frequently these two kinds of fable are mixed in the same legend,
religious tales being often invented to account for some actually
existing worship or sacred solemnities. Thus it was said that
Ceres in her wanderings came to Eleusis, and taught the Eleusi-
nians her mysteries. The existence of the mysteries of Ceres at
Eleusis was a real fact, but the story that Ceres had taught them
to her votaries there, neither was true, nor bore any analogy to
the truth.

Our knowledge of the Grecian mythology is derived from the
poets and prose writers. From almost every kind of both classes
some information may be derived—from the epic, lyric, tragic and
elegiac poets, the writers of hymns and idyls—from the early and
late compilers of mythology, historians, geographers, orators,
sophists, grammarians and ecclesiastical writers. There is, perhaps, scarcely an ancient author in whom some mythological notice is not to be found. Hence the great difficulty of treating the
subject; as a knowledge is required far more extensive than is necessary for purely historical inquiry, and the characters and peculiarities of the different writers must be estimated before their
style of narrative and application of the allegorical and fanciful
legends of antiquity can be rightly seized.

From an examination of the different poets and prose writers
of Greece as regards their mode of handling mythological fables,
it follows that we are not in possession of the original source
of these fables or μῦθοι, but that the Greek writers borrowed
them from some more remote origin. These fables were never
the work of pure invention; nor did the Greeks ever receive
the story of the Choice of Hercules by Prodicus, of Eros and
Anteros, &c. into their works of mythology: a μῦθος, meaning
originally a story or narration, came to signify an *ancient* story or
legend, referring to a time separated both by distance and character from the historical age—a time in which prodigies were still
common, in which the heroes and gods still lived together, which
conferred nobility on all who could trace up to it their pedigree,
and which long furnished the only subjects for poetry, painting
and sculpture. The common source from which all these writers
borrowed, who did not borrow from each other, was *popular tradition.* That many of these fables could not have been invented by
the poets is proved by the accurate knowledge which they show
of the districts to which they refer, and the temples, worships and
fates of the native tribes. For it cannot be supposed either that
there was a poet to every small region of Greece, or that there
were wandering bards who travelled over Greece in order to col-

lect materials for mythological fables. These popular legends were not invented by the priests or *cicerones* of a particular sanctuary, or by a caste of men elevated by their knowledge above the mass of the people, but were the forms which the popular narratives and fictions naturally took at an early era of the Greek nation. This distinction between the original source of mythological fables and of our knowledge of them, between the writers who have recorded and embellished and the people who invented them, is of great importance; but though perfectly evident when stated, it has been often implicitly denied. Thus it has been argued that a certain fable could not have existed in the time of Homer, *because* it does not occur in the Iliad or Odyssey; as if Homer must have mentioned every legend, profane or religious, which he had ever heard; as if many traditions might not have lived in the mouths of the Delphians, Thessalians, and other tribes of Greece, without having reached the ears of the Ionic poet. The fable must itself furnish its own history: an analysis of its component parts will frequently, though not always, show, approximately, the date and object of its invention, and the race of its inventors. At the same time a chronological arrangement of the authorities to a fabulous legend is not only useful, but necessary. Of the various versions of the same fable given by different writers, that recorded by the most ancient writer is probably the most ancient. A comparison of these varieties frequently throws much light on the objects and interests of those who successively changed the legend. In determining the time when legendary fables arose, the greatest assistance is derived from the dates of colonies; for instance, Byzantium was founded in the 30th Olympiad (about 660 B. C.) by Megarians, with whom were a party of Argives. The fables of Io connected with the worship of Juno (who had a temple on the citadels both of Argos and Byzantium) were local at Argos, and the place was there shown where she had fed in the shape of a cow. Now Io was also said to have fed as a cow on the promontory of Κέρας ("the Horn"), near Byzantium, and to have borne a daughter, named Κερόεσσα ("the Horned") who was the mother of Byzas, the national hero. The name *Bosporus* appears to have had the same origin. It is evident that these fables were invented in their new form *after* the thirtieth olympiad, and probably not long after, as there was not in later times such a connection between Argos and Byzantium as to cause a transmission of worship and sacred legends. In like manner it may be shown that the fables of the Alpheus and Arethusa, and of Medea and Jason, were not earlier than the fifth olympiad; and many other examples might be given of legends which thus arose in the historical age.

But the difficulty of this process is much increased when we come to events lying beyond the historical period. Indeed it is evidently impossible to determine the exact date of any event in an age anterior to authentic chronology. We must therefore be satisfied with ascertaining the succession, or the relative antiquity, of mythological fables which were invented before the time of memory. Many examples might be given of such investigations; but without entering on a subject which would be unintelligible unless treated in detail, it is sufficiently plain that the largest number of mythological legends arose in the fabulous age, and that they preceded the existence of a regular school of poetry. The invention of such fables did not, however, altogether expire till the time when philosophy and history began to flourish in Greece. Such records put an end to a mode of narration fitted only for oral tradition. A like cessation of these fictions would also have been caused by the revolution in the religious opinions of Greece. In the earliest time the various religious ideas and feelings of this nation produced an endless variety of mythological fables, which the next age handed down with implicit faith as the history of a miraculous antiquity; then followed the age of Pindar, when religious feelings were influenced by philosophical speculations opposed to many of the ancient fables; and lastly, the age of sophistical explanation, when Euripides, and other philosophical poets and poetical philosophers, treated the ancient fables, not as primitive modes of expression, but as the vehicles of their own perverse notions and subtle refinements. These changes, however, only took place in the cultivated part of the Greek nation; and primitive tribes, such as the Arcadians, which still retained their ancient simplicity and barbarism, might still retain also their ancient mode of expression. But it is this very circumstance which forms the difference between the genuine mythological fable and the idle tale of fiction. Such stories arise in the lowest classes of society, and do not harmonize with the spirit of the age, bearing about the same relation to the legends of mythology as a belief in ghosts to true religion.

The great difficulty in all mythological researches is to separate the embellishment of the poet, the *rationalizing* of the historian, and the explanation of the philosopher, from the true body of the ancient legend; to discriminate between the original and the altered form. The chief business of the poets was to assign motives and reasons for the acts of their heroes—to *account for* the circumstances related by tradition. Thus Æschylus found in Hesiod that Prometheus stole fire from heaven, that he was chained to a rock, &c.; but the motives for these acts, the rebellious and proud thoughts of the enemy of the gods and the friend of man, he drew from his own fancy. (We may compare this with the first part of the Paradise Lost, the outlines of which alone are derived from the sacred tradition; but the councils and characters of the infernal princes, their " considerate pride waiting revenge," their fierceness made fiercer by despair, their sullen and inactive discontent, came from the mind of Milton.) On the whole, where the original legend often embodied the feelings and acts of large masses of men into one hero, the poets individualized these characters, and gave them personal wishes and dispositions. Thus it has happened, that where the original tradition contained in it a germ of historical instruction, the poets have changed the representative of a nation into a single man, and described as the casual and unimportant acts of an individual, feelings and measures in which large numbers coincided. The poetry of Greece likewise had great influence in assimilating the different local worships and deities, and in this respect its powers were far greater than that either of intercourse between different races, or the authority of distinguished sanctuaries. Thus, in the ancient mythology of Athens, Athene or Minerva, attended by the three Agraulian nymphs, was a goddess presiding over agriculture. In Homer, however, she is represented as the goddess of practical wisdom, and this character is extended by later poets to the ancient Attic legends, where her attributes were originally quite different.

" Hence," says Mr. Müller, " the Greek nation in general, at least wherever the influence of poets reached, had scarcely any other notion of a deity than that which they had derived from Homer; and the earlier and discordant ideas left only in some ancient names, ceremonies and obscure local legends, dubious traces of their former existence. It was this astonishing influence of poetry which caused Herodotus to make the assertion (which, however, must be received with great limitations) that ' Homer and Hesiod taught the Greeks their theogony, gave the gods their names, allotted to each his office and art, and established their forms.' "—p. 213.

In cases where the local tradition represents the deity under a different character from that in which it appears in the received poetical mythology, there is no doubt that the former is the more ancient, as it could scarcely have arisen after the other notions had become generally prevalent.

As to the treatment which the fabulous legends received from the ancient historians, it is very necessary to observe, that when a definite statement respecting some ancient race occurs in Herodotus or Thucydides, it is not to be set down as an indubitable truth; and a mythological account in Pausanias relating to the same subject to be thought unworthy of serious notice. But in general the historical statement is the *result;* the fabulous legend is the source from which the historian drew his information, as neither Herodotus nor his successors had on the matters of early. history any other authority than popular tradition.   The object, therefore, in examining such accounts derived from tradition, is to single out the statements from which the narrative of the historian appears to be derived, to examine how far these accounts bear out the relation founded upon them, and to discover what parts of the supposed history were gained by inference, and how far these inferences are correct.

But, in order to restore a mythological tale to its original state, a different process is required; the whole must be resolved into its component parts, and each be separately examined.   A process, the very reverse of that which these fables had undergone in the hands of the ancient compilers and revisers, who sought to form them into uniform bodies, having an apparent harmony and connexion.   At every step the mythologist will discover what discordant elements, both in meaning, place, and time, have been moulded by a truly levelling spirit into one consecutive fable. The web of mythology, which had been woven in the full day of Grecian learning and criticism, must be laboriously unravelled in the comparative darkness of modern times.

It is, however, necessary to guard against an abuse of this process of separation by dissolving parts which were originally connected.   For this purpose, before examining a mythological narrative, the inquirer should ask himself three questions—Where was it invented ?   By what persons ?   And on what occasion ?

As to the first question, it is evident that every fable must have arisen in *some one* place, and that, if this can be ascertained, much assistance will be given towards separating the earlier and later parts of the legend.   In most cases, this is not a difficult problem; as we have only to ask, whom the story most concerns? The inhabitants of a country naturally speak of their native heroes; the founders of a town are celebrated as such in the traditions of its citizens; the hills, and streams, and fountains, are changed into mythological personages by those who dwell about them, and have experienced the peculiar feelings which they awaken.   The chief exceptions are the fables relating to imaginary nations, such as the Æthiopians and Hyperboreans, (who were not till late times respectively identified with the negroes and inhabitants of the north,) and the extension of an originally Grecian legend to a foreign country, as the expedition of the Argo to Colchis, the residence of the Gorgons in Libya; and sometimes a foreign fable has been received into the Greek mythology, on account of some supposed resemblance or affinity.   Thus the army of Alexander found in India a god worshipped with the same frantic rites as Dionysius or Bacchus in their own country: whence arose the fable of the expedition of Bacchus to the East.

To decide *by whom* a mythological story has been invented, we must keep in mind that it is not always to be referred to the inhabitants of the country known to history. Many parts of a national mythology owe their origin to races subdued or expelled; and have survived, in fragments and ruins, the dominion, or even existence of the tribes which gave them birth. Thus many of the Bœotian legends belong to the ancient Thracians, Cadmeans, and Minyans; of the Athenian to the Pelasgians, and most of the Peloponnesian traditions were earlier than the Doric invasion. (In like manner the fabulous exploits of the British hero Arthur became the favourite theme of the Norman minstrels, whose only right to the fame of this prince was derived from the conquest of the Anglo-Saxons, who had themselves conquered the Britons.*)

Thirdly, in many, though not in all cases, the fable relates to some real fact or event. One legend refers to an ancient rite, another to the festival of some god and the exhibitions accompanying it; a third to some institution or custom of early times. In these cases the object is to account for these facts by stories which are indeed false, but which would explain them *if they were true.*† It is singular that in numerous instances the occasion for such legends was furnished by *false etymologies.* Proper names were explained by an incorrect derivation, and then a story was invented to agree with the false meaning thus obtained. So, for example, the Athenian and Ionian festival of Apaturia doubtless signified an assemblage of the members of the patræ or clans;‡ but the ancients derived the word from ἀπάτη, or deceit, connecting with it the story of a border-war between the Athenians and Bœotians.

From the circumstance of the fables of mythology so frequently referring to real facts, it is necessary to know those which gave occasion to the tradition. Among these there is no class of facts which so often come into question as the rites and observances of the different worships of Greece, the sacred places, priests, festivals, &c. Hence in a system of mythology it is proper to take a general survey of the religion of the Greeks; though only in a subsidiary point of view, as the correctness of the mode of

---

* See Sir J. Mackintosh's History of England, vol. i. p. 26.

† " In commune opinio valebat, *quæ ab hominibus maximeque in re sacra fierent, suas debere causas habere.* Arnob. vii. 25." Lobeck, vol. i. p. 171.

‡ Ἀπατούρια, from a and πατόρες, " the members of a πάτρα." See Müller's Dorians, vol. i. p. 95. Eng. translation. See also Lobeck, vol. i. p. 168.

mythological interpretation above detailed is independent of the correctness of any views on the ancient *religions*, which it assumes as existing, whatever may have been their origin.

The religions of Greece appear to have been originally very numerous, and to have varied greatly in character. The frantic and tumultuous orgies of Bacchus differed as much from the solemnity and gloominess of the worship of Ceres, as both differed from the cheerful, serene, and energetic feelings inspired by the worship of Apollo. These various deities and modes of worship did not arise at successive stages of civilization, as appears to have been the case in the Indian religion ; but their variety is to be attributed to the dissimilar characters of the numerous races which peopled the Greek territory. All inquiries go to prove the originally limited sphere of the several religions of Greece. Each god has his favourite abode, his favourite territory, generally likewise the place of his birth ; and, however obscure and scanty the vestiges which guide us, the worship of Apollo may be traced to northern Thessaly, the orgies of Bacchus to Bœotian Thrace, and the worship of Neptune to the shores of the Saronic and Corinthian bays, while all the temples of Juno were derived from Argos. Although this original diversity of worship was much softened by the influence of the poets, the peaceful intercourse of different tribes, or their mixture by conquest and by political incorporation, (such as the union of several boroughs into one city or state, the conversion of gentile into national rites, &c.) yet it was never wholly obliterated, and the idea of a national and tutelar deity, having local attachments, and demanding them in return, always remained a predominating article in the religious opinions of the Greeks. In early times the worship of the national deity was common to the whole nation ; whence the performance of its rites, as being a national concern, belonged to the princes or kings (βασιλεῖς). The celebration of this public worship was one of the most important offices of these petty rulers, particularly in the less warlike tribes ; and it may nearly as well be said that the priests were kings, as that the kings were priests. The royal families frequently retained these sacerdotal functions after their political power had expired. The same inheritance of priestly offices sometimes also took place in other noble families : in the historical age such heritable priesthoods were however less numerous than those which were given by the state to the persons of its choice. There are moreover the strongest reasons for believing that there never was a sacerdotal caste in Greece, or a division of the community into priests and laymen. Had this been the case, the distinction would have been shewn in the performance of some acts by one which were inter-

dicted to the other order.   Now the duties of the Greek priests
were sometimes to deliver a short, simple form of prayer ; to perform sacrifices, in which great stress was laid on the manual dexterity and skill of the sacrificer ; and various ceremonies, such, for
instance, as the rite of atonement for blood, the consecration of
sacred objects, places, &c. ; the singing of hymns, and sometimes
divination.*   All these functions might however be performed by
persons who were not priests : thus the Ephetæ, a court of judges
at Athens, purified from the guilt of homicide ; hymns were
generally sung by public choruses ; and any one was free to exercise the art of soothsaying.   It sometimes happened that certain
religious rites were attended with peculiar sanctity, and were
looked on with great superstitious awe ; but there is no trace of
their affording the priests any opportunity or encouragement for
gaining important political privileges.   No ascetic discipline was
perpetuated from father to son, or from generation to generation ;
no alliance or concert, expressed or understood, existed between
the priests of different states.

If the priests of Greece would ever have formed themselves
into a powerful body, linked together by their participation in the
same rights, their precise division from the rest of the people,
and their knowledge of a secret theology, it might have been expected that the hereditary ministers of the sacred *Eleusinian mysteries,* would, above all others, have enjoyed these privileges.   Nevertheless, the members of the family of the Eumolpidæ, which
had the privilege of shewing to the initiated the sacred symbols
(ἱερὰ φαίνειν, δεικνύναι); of the family of Callias and Hipponicus, and
afterwards of the Lycomedæ, which had the office of torch-bearer
at Eleusis ; and of the *Hieroceryces,* or sacred heralds, who performed various duties at the celebration of the Eleusinian mysteries, were by no means exclusively priests, or restricted from
following any other employments or professions.   The statesman,
the ambassador, the orator, the general, or the merchant, would
at the appointed time put on his sacred dress, and perform his
honourable duties in the temple of Eleusis, and then return to
his usual course of life.   The privileges which belonged to these

* It was the priests' duty, according to Apuleius, " Callere leges cerimoniarum, fas
religionum, jus sacrorum." *Apol.* p. 446.   " Deorum cultus (says Lactantius) non habet sapientiam, quia nihil ibi discitur quod proficiat ad mores excolendos vitamque for-
mandam ; nec habet inquisitionem aliquam veritatis, sed tantummodo ritum colendi,
qui ministerio corporis constat." *Instit.* iv. 3.—Varro, in his first book on *Divine Antiquities,* made three kinds of theology :—1. The fabulous or mythological, used by the
poets : 2. That relating to natural philosophy, used by men of science : 3. The popular theology ; which last kind (and not the philosophical theology) " maxime sacerdotes
nosse atque administrare debent, in quo est, quos deos colere, quæ sacra et sacrificia
facere quenquam par sit." p. 224. ed. Bipont.—The above and other passages of like
import are collected in Loheck, vol. i. p. 11.

families may be compared with the rights, honorary rather than valuable, which are hereditary in some families in England ; such as the office of king's champion, falconer, &c.; only the duties entailed on the three noble families of Athens were more frequently exercised, and were (not accessory but) essential to a more solemn and awful ceremony than the English coronation.

It is, however, on the supposed rites of the Eleusinian mysteries that many modern writers have founded their notions of a system of secret and sublime doctrines inculcated by the priests of Greece, handed down from the earliest times, the remnants of a primitive civilization. Admitted into the inmost shrines of the temple at Eleusis, listening to the oracular lessons of Hierophants, and gradually trained for a participation in such holy secrets, the trembling neophyte learned to despise the silly tissue of fables which the vulgar called religion, and imbibed the doctrines of a pure theology, the immortality of the soul, and the prospect of a recompense for virtue in another life. The following summary of the celebrated Creuzer's opinions on this subject is given by M. Silvestre de Sacy :—

" When there had been placed under the eyes of the initiated symbolical representations of the creation of the universe, and the origin of things, the migrations and purifications of the soul, the origin and progress of agriculture and civilization in Greece, there was drawn from these symbols and these scenes in the great mysteries an instruction destined only for the more perfect ; and to the epopts were communicated the doctrines of the existence of a single and eternal God, and the destination of the universe, and of man in particular."—tom. i. p. 448.

For the detailed refutation of these and other exaggerated opinions, we are indebted to the admirable work of Lobeck, named at the head of this article, of whose arguments we will now attempt to give our readers a short abridgment.

It appears that instead of a few persons being admitted with care, and after long preparation, to a knowledge of the hidden doctrines of the Eleusinian priests, these mysteries were open to all men and women,* except Greeks defiled by the commission of some atrocious crime, and barbarians. The Eumolpidæ and Ceryces called upon all to approach " whose hands were clean, and who spoke the Greek tongue." The citizens of other states besides Athens were (in later times at least) admitted, and perhaps also the Athenian slaves. It is clear that the Hierophants could not have proceeded to attack the popular religion of their country, and teach a purer doctrine, before this promiscuous crowd of different nations, ages, and sexes. But had they not two sets of

---

* Lobeck, vol. i. p. 202.

doctrines, one esoteric, one exoteric; the one destined for the vulgar and illiterate, the other reserved for the learned and refined? It has been imagined that some sign or watchword was used by those who entered the temple. This notion is however contradicted by a story in Livy, that " two Acarnanian youths, who had not been initiated, accidentally entered the temple of Ceres during the days of the mysteries. They were soon detected by their absurd questions, and being carried to the managers of the temple, though it was plain that they had come there by mistake, were put to death for so horrible a crime." (xxxi. 14.) The temple at Eleusis was therefore protected rather by the opinion of its sanctity, than by any contrivance of tickets or watchwords. All the introduction requisite was the company of a friend previously initiated; and it seems not to have been an uncommon duty of an Athenian host to take his guest to the Eleusinian festival. There were some stages of initiation, or at least a succession of different ceremonies, which came at certain intervals of time ;* no one could be admitted to the great, who had not been initiated at the lesser mysteries :† but there is no proof of a gradation of *doctrines*, religious or moral. When Alcibiades and his associates were indicted for insulting the public religion of Attica, the writing of accusation set forth that " *Alcibiades had committed sacrilege towards Ceres and Proserpine, by imitating the mysteries, and shewing them to his companions in the same dress in which the hierophant shewed the sacred things; and by calling himself the hierophant, Polytion the torch-bearer, and Theodorus the herald.*" (*Plutarch. Alcib.* 22.) And Lysias accuses Andocides of " *putting on the sacred dress, and showing in mimicry the sacred things to the uninitiated, and uttering the secret words.*" (p. 107.) What were the sacred things shown in the original of this mimic representation? Probably the Hierophants displayed some images and statues of the gods, sacred vessels and caskets containing holy symbols‡ and relics, such as are exhibited in Roman Catholic churches. It appears also that a veil or curtain was at some part of the solemnity withdrawn, which discovered statues of the gods set off with lighted torches and much splendour of ornament. The whole ceremony was doubtless contrived so as to produce a grand and imposing spectacle:§ and when the severe and simple beauty of the sacred architecture and sculpture of the Athenians was contrasted with the brilliant decorations of the temple, the procession, and the priests, when the gold and

---

* τὴν τελετὴν ἅπασαν ἀπὸ τῶν μικρῶν ἄχρι τῶν ἐποπτικῶν παραλαβεῖν. Plutarch, vit. Demosth. 26.

† Lobeck, p. 140. 188, note.   ‡ See Lobeck, vol. i. p. 703.

§ Muller, p. 255.

silver vessels were displayed, when the sacred hymns were chaunted, and the sublime impression was strengthened by a deep superstitious awe, we may imagine that the celebration of the Eleusinian mysteries awakened feelings very different from those produced on common occasions. The rites, however, were not performed in silence; the Hierophant (as we learn from Lysias,) " spoke the secret words." These words were doubtless nothing more than short litanies or invocations to the deities of the temple,—short ritual *formulæ ;* or at the most, brief narrations of some mythological fables relating to the Eleusinian deities, illustrative of allegorical paintings or sculptures. Sometimes an adventurous priest or hierophant might volunteer a mystical discourse on some simple natural facts, on the benefits or origin of agriculture, and on the plainest moral duties ; and it cannot be doubted that the mythological character of Proserpine, as a deity of Hades, the receptacle of departed spirits, gave occasion for allusions to a future life. The choice of these subjects seems to have been in great measure arbitrary, and to have varied in the same place at different times.* But (whatever might be the subject) these effusions were probably mere mystical rhapsodies, devoid of rational information, and by no means contained religious tenets or articles of faith. Of the three parts of which the priest's duty at the mysteries is made by ancient writers to consist, the things which he *shewed*, which he *did*, and which he *spoke*, (τὰ δεικνύμενα, τὰ δρώμενα, τὰ λεγόμενα,) the last was by far the least important, and is sometimes omitted as implied in the others. Thus Aristotle stated that " persons initiated in the mysteries were not to learn any thing, but to experience certain feelings, and be put into a certain frame of mind, having previously been prepared for such sentiments."† Nevertheless, what the initiated did see and hear, they were bound not to reveal; and the Greeks, even of the latest times, always approach a mystical subject with reluctance, and shrink from divulging any explanation or fable related to them at the mysteries.‡ This secrecy was considered by the Greeks as a solemn religious duty; to infringe which was to render a man impious and accursed. A

---

* Lobeck, vol. i. p. 136.

† Ἀριστοτέλης ἀξιοῖ τοὺς τετελεσμένους οὐ μαθεῖν τι δεῖν ἀλλὰ παθεῖν καὶ διατεθῆναι γενο-μένους δηλονότι ἐπιτηδείους Synesius Dion. p. 48. A. This passage seems to us quite decisive. " Quæ Hierophantæ Cerycesque (says Mr. Lobeck,) sacris aut præfabantur aut accinebant, plurimum fortasse ad commovendos audientium animos valebant, ad erudiendos nihil, multoque magis veteres errores confirmabant quam tollebant, quippe cum deorum dearumque invocatione conjuncta." vol. i. p. 147.

‡ Lobeck, vol. i. p. 131. 151, vol. ii. p. 1287., has collected some examples, the number of which might be much increased.

belief not confined to Attica, or even to Greece, but taken up by neighbouring nations.

> " Vetabo (says Horace) qui Cereris sacrum
> Vulgarit arcanæ sub isdem
> Sit trabibus, fragilemque mecum
> Solvat phaselon."

The splendour of the name and arts, the renown of the writers of Athens, the well-known superstitious turn of the Athenians, and the expense and magnificence with which they celebrated all religious solemnities, were the chief causes of the fame of the Eleusinian mysteries, and gave them a sanctity founded rather on fancy and enthusiasm than cool reason. Hence the poets and panegyrical orators speak of these holy rites with raptures which we find it difficult to account for, who contemplate with a cold and critical scrutiny those ceremonies, which to the Athenians were hallowed by the warmth of devotion and the memory of sublime and religious aspirations. " Happy the man (says Pindar) who descends beneath the hollow earth, having beheld those mysteries. He knows the end, he knows the divine origin of life." In a like strain are the verses of Sophocles: " Thrice happy they who descend to the shades below after having beheld these rites ;* for they alone have life in Hades, while all others suffer there every kind of evil."—" Those (says Isocrates) who have been initiated in the mysteries of Ceres, entertain better hopes both as to the end of life and the whole of futurity."† That such hopes were raised in the breasts of the initiated by the Eleusinian mysteries, hopes (as Cicero says) not of a better life only, but also of a better death, is easy to believe ; only it must be remembered that they were not founded on any solid conviction, but resembled rather the expectations of reward which the Mahomedan founds on his visit to the Prophet's shrine, or the Roman Catholic on his pilgrimage to Rome or Loretto, than the reasonable, fixed, and calm persuasion of a life to come, and a return for good and evil deeds, which the enlightened Christian draws from the book of revelation.

It is impossible for the student of antiquity to impress too strongly on his mind two characteristics of the Greek polytheism ; *viz.* the local nature of the different worships, and the absence of all doctrines or articles of faith. To us, a religion without doc-

---

* It is worthy of remark, that both Pindar and Sophocles speak of *seeing* the mysteries: (ἰδὼν ἐκεῖνα, ταῦτα δερχθέντες τέλη,) as if that which struck the eye was more important than that which struck the ear. In like manner Hercules says, in Euripides, " I rejoiced at *seeing* the orgies of the Mystæ," τὰ μυστῶν ὄργι᾽ εὐτύχησ᾽ ἰδών. Herc. Fur. 613.

† περί τε τῆς βίου τελευτῆς καὶ τοῦ σύμπαντος αἰῶνος ἡδίους τὰς ἐλπίδας ἔχουσι. Paneg. p. 59. See the other passages in Lobeck, p. 69.

trines seems like a wood without trees, or a town without houses, a plain contradiction in terms. Nevertheless, it is certain that the Greeks never looked to their priests for instruction or exhortation, whether moral or religious. They considered them as the manual operators in a set of outward ceremonies intended to gain the good-will or appease the wrath of some deity, whose protection was supposed to be confined exclusively or chiefly to the inhabitants of a particular family, town, or district. Hence the expression of Livy, which to our ears sounds so strange, that " the Etruscans were the more devoted to religious observances because they excelled in the art of performing them ;"* the sacerdotal duties being considered as a sort of sleight-of-hand and curious mystery; like the feats of a juggler, or the occult science of a magician. The chief excellence of a priest consisted in knowing what deities were on such and such an occasion to be appeased ; in what manner this was to be done, in what order the rites followed each other ; and in performing these operations in an adroit and skilful manner. The priests were as much the performers in the religious ceremonies of the Greeks as the actors are in a play-house : the spectators of a sacrifice, a purification, or a mystery, might gain the favour of a god, be cleansed from the stain of homicide, or be elevated by the communication of holy secrets, as the audience are affected by the mimicry of the actors; but in neither case was the effect produced by the agency of the lookers-on. That the education of the youth should, as in England, Spain, Italy, and other countries, be entrusted to the clergy, or order of priests, would to a Greek have been as incomprehensible as that any one doctrine, such as that of the immortality of the soul, should have been inculcated as an article of faith by all the different priests of all the different religions of his country. Where there was a regular hierarchy, possessed of large political privileges, and trained to their duties by a long and laborious education, as in India, Egypt, Etruria, and Gaul, the inculcation of religious doctrines was possible; and thus the Druids taught the eternity and transmigration of the soul as a fundamental dogma of the Gaulish religion,† which probably was the same in the island of

---

* " Gens ante omnes alias eo magis dedita religionibus, quod excelleret arte colendi eas." Livy, v. i. An idea of some state of the mind is so inseparably connected with our notion of religion, that it is impossible to render these words faithfully into English.

† The passages of the ancients on this point are collected by Amédée Thierry, *Histoire des Gaulois*, tom. ii. p. 81. According to Strabo, " the Druids teach that the human soul and the world are imperishable ; but that fire and water will one day gain the mastery." It does not clearly appear whether he means that the souls of men will as well as the world be destroyed by fire and water; if he does, Dr. Whately is excusable for omitting all notice of these testimonies in his argument to show that the doctrine of the immortality of the soul was unknown to, or at least disbelieved by the ancients. See his *Essays on the Peculiarities of Christianity*, Essay 1.

Mona as in Armorica, and was maintained so by the communication of the priests.   But in Greece, Asia Minor, Sicily and Italy, there was (especially in early times) no one universal religion or worship ; here the territory was (as it were) parcelled out among numerous deities, each of whom was the tutelar, national, hereditary, or paternal god of some race, state, city, clan, or family. The gods, though generally recognised out of their own domains as having a divine power, and celebrated with almost equal honours by the various poets of Greece and Rome, yet had a peculiar local influence, and a decided predilection for certain places and persons.   Thus when Veji was razed and incorporated with Rome, the Romans, wishing to naturalize in their city the Veientine worship of Juno, before they proceeded to move her statue first asked the goddess " whether she was willing to go to Rome."*
Hence it was that the worshippers of any particular deity, so far from wishing to force their own religion upon others, or even to make proselytes by gentle means, considered themselves rather as having a preference over their neighbours, which would be lost by such a communication.   They enjoyed the favour of some powerful, placable, and beneficent god, who would assist them in the hour of need ;† they were the repositories of a most precious secret in knowing the best means, by proper rites and ceremonies, of obtaining his assistance.   In this spirit is conceived the advice of Ajax in Homer, that the Greeks should pray apart and in silence,‡ lest the Trojans might overhear them, and, by imitating them, be able to pray with equal effect.   Originally the Eleusinian mysteries were closed to all but Athenians ;§ the liberality of later times and the eagerness of strangers to gain admission abolished the monopoly of the benefits supposed to flow from these holy initiations.‖   The Greeks were rather happy to be allowed a free trade in religion, and to import sacred rites from foreign countries,¶ than desirous to make converts by the sword or the stake. The worshippers of any particular god conceived themselves in the possession of a valuable religious monopoly and pre-eminence, as knowing a short and easy road to divine protection ; and they were no more anxious to make others participate in these advantages than the members of the Bank of England or the East India Company would wish to extend to others the privileges of their respective monopolies.   Religious persecution, except for

---

* *Visne Romum ire Juno.*—Livy, v. 22.
† See particularly Lobeck, vol. ii. p. 1218, on the Samothracian deities, who were celebrated for the prompt assistance which they gave in time of danger to those who ad been initiated in their mysteries.
‡ Iliad, vii. 195.   § Lobeck, vol. i. p. 273.   Muller, p. 241.
‖ See the inscription in Boeckh's Corp. Inscript. No. 71.
¶ Lobeck, vol. i. p. 271.

religious innovations by individuals, as in the case of Socrates, or for impiety, as in those of Æschylus,* Diagoras, Aristotle, &c. was therefore unknown to the Greeks. The national deities appeared to possess by prescription such pre-eminent privileges, that they were not to be disturbed by the unauthorised introduction of fresh gods, which was rather a national concern;† nor were an insult of the mysteries, a revelation of mystical fables,‡ a deification of men,§ or a total denial of all divine power, tolerated by the Greeks; though blasphemies against the popular deities, whether of bitter invective, as in the Prometheus of Æschylus, or of ludicrous burlesque, as in the Frogs of Aristophanes, did not offend the ears of an Athenian audience.

It would be easy, if our space allowed, to extend our views on the peculiarities of the polytheism of the most civilized nations of antiquity, and to contrast them with the character of the true religion. We will, however, only remark, that no change worked by the spreading of Christianity, not even the substitution of the worship of one for many gods, is so great as the complete abolition, we might say extinction, of the idea of local worships, of privileges, and preferences in religion, and divine predilections for places and nations. For these petty territorial worships Christianity has substituted one religion for all men; has made them *one* fold, under *one* shepherd; and, by removing all temptation for a jealous appropriation of peculiar rites, has no less benefited mankind politically, in destroying local prejudices and forwarding national union, than morally, by teaching the duty of imparting religious instruction to brethren, to foreigners, and even to enemies.‖

It is much to be desired that many writers, who undertake to institute comparisons between the Christian and the ancient religions, would first take the trouble of gaining a more perfect knowledge of both sides of the parallel. Ancient mythology seems to be considered as a licensed field for the wildest conjectures and the most farfetched combinations and etymologies; and there are few books on this subject which can be safely consulted by the general reader. So far as the mystical worships of Greece,

---

* Lobeck, vol. i. p. 76—84.   † See Herodotus, vi. 105.
‡ See Lobeck, vol. ii. p. 1285.
§ See Athenæus, XV. p. 696 A.   Compare Bentley's *Remarks upon a late Discourse of Freethinking*, S. 47, p. 192, ed. 8.
‖ " Sprung from the same extraction, preparing together for the period of all worldly distinctions, reminded of their mutual infirmities and common dependency, imploring and receiving support and supplies from the same great source of power and bounty, having all one interest to secure, one Lord to serve, one judgment, the supreme object of all their hopes and fears, to look towards; it is hardly possible, in this position, to behold mankind as strangers, competitors, or enemies."—Paley's *Moral Philosophy*, book v. ch. 6.   See also Dr. Arnold's notes on Thucydides, book ii. 16 72, and p. 639; and Dr. Whately's *Sermons on Scripture Revelations concerning a Future State*, 178, ed. 2.

the Eleusinian, Orphic, and Samothracian mysteries, are concerned, the work of Lobeck has exhausted, and to a certain point decided the question. To learning and industry perhaps never surpassed, he joins a cool discriminating judgment, a power of original investigation, a disregard for the authority of great names, and a perfect controul over his imagination, which lead him to doctrines the furthest removed from the fanciful and enthusiastic mysticism of many German, French, and English writers. In short, he is the *rationalist* of the ancient religions; and as such his reasonings are to be watched with care; nor can it be denied that he has sometimes strained them some points beyond their proper limits; but the scrupulous accuracy and the fulness of his citations (for all the chief passages are given at length) enable the reader to judge as he proceeds of the correctness of the argument. Mr. Lobeck is by no means a laudatory or assenting writer; his pen is against every man, and it will be well for him if every man's pen is not against him. At the same time we have not observed any rancour or vituperation in his censures. Sainte Croix and Creuzer fall chiefly under his critical lash, and the opinions of the chief antiquarians of Germany, Boeckh, Müller, Welcker, Boettiger, &c. are frequently attacked. We are sorry, however, that a writer of this country, Mr. Thomas Taylor, shares the worst fate; who is convicted not only of ignorance almost incredible, but is charged with the heavier imputation of literary dishonesty,* which, if not disproved, must in future deprive his assertions of all claim to belief. A blunder, more innocent but more ludicrous than the errors of the modern Platonic Theologian, is pointed out by Lobeck in the writings of another mystic mythologist, Captain Wilford, of Indian celebrity.

" At the conclusion of the mysteries of Eleusis (we learn from this judicious writer) the congregation was dismissed in these words : Κόγξ, Ὄμ, Πάξ. These mysterious words have been considered hitherto as inexplicable; but they are pure Sanscrit, and used to this day by Brahmins at the conclusion of religious rites. They are written in the language of the gods, as the Hindoos call the language of their sacred books, *Candscha, Om, Pacsha. Candscha* signifies the object of our most ardent wishes. *Om* is the famous monosyllable used both at the beginning and conclusion of a prayer or any religious rite, like *Amen. Pacsha* exactly answers to the obsolete Latin word *vix;* it signifies change, course, stead, place, turn of work, duty, fortune, &c."— *Asiatic Researches*, vol. v. p. 300.

This interpretation has been approved by Creuzer and Schelling, by Münter, who is " thrown into amazement by reading that these words are pure Sanscrit," and by Uwarow, who calls it " the

---

* See Lobeck, vol. i. pp. 93—96. 219—221.

E 2

most important of modern discoveries." This great discovery is founded on the following article in the Lexicon of Hesychius. Κόγξ, ὅμπαξ· ἐπιφώνημα τετελεσμένοις. Καὶ τῆς δικαστικῆς ψήφου ἦχος, ὡς ὁ τῆς κλεψύδρας· παρὰ δὲ ᾿Αττικοῖς βλόψ. In the first place it should be observed that, allowing the Sanscrit doctrine to be true, there is no trace of these holy words being used in the *Eleusinian* mysteries. It appears, however, from the explanation of Lobeck, that we should read Κόγξ, οἶον, or ὁμοίως πάξ ; and that these portentous words mean no more than that " κόγξ and πάξ were exclamations used when anything was finished (like the Italian *basta ;*) also the sound of the ballot-box of the judges, and of the Clepsydra. The Athenians likewise used the sound βλόψ."* Such are the ridiculous mistakes into which half-learned men fall when hurried away by a love of fanciful etymologies and mystical erudition; nor is there much hope that there ever will be a want of such dreaming mythologists, of whom it is true beyond any other class of writers, that " they are the slaves of the folly of the day, and the despisers of all received and sober learning."†

ART. III.—*Clinique Médicale, ou Choix d'Observations recueillies à l'Hôpital de la Charité (Clinique de M. Lerminier).* Par G. Andral, Professeur à la Faculté de Médécine de Paris, &c. (Clinical Medicine, or a Selection of Cases from the Clinical Waids of M. Lerminier, at the Hospital of *La Charité.* By G. Andral, Professor in the Faculty of Medicine of Paris.) Deuxième Edition. Paris. 1829. 2 vols. 8vo.

NOTHING has so much exposed the public to the designs of those who profess to cure diseases by methods unknown to the regular faculty, as the extreme ignorance of the public in general concerning the structure and functions of the human frame, and the nature of the diseases to which it is liable. The studies of anatomy and physiology are so extremely interesting, that their addition to what is commonly called a general education would afford a most agreeable occupation for many hours now much less profitably employed, and do more to abolish quacks and quackery than half-a-dozen acts of parliament, or the verdicts of

---

* See Lobeck, vol. i. p. 775—781. Mr. Lobeck compares the very undignified sounds εναξ, ταξ, παξ, κνάξ, πύπαξ, πάπαξ, βομβάξ, παπαιαξ, ἰαττατΗαξ. The word *pax* is often used by the Roman comic poets in the familiar sense indicated in the text. See Forcellini in *v. pax ad fin.* M. Eusèbe Salverte, in his work on Occult Sciences, reviewed in our last Number, may be added to the number of those who have been deluded by Captain Wilford's supposed discovery, (tom. i. p. 258). This writer has implicitly adopted, and pushed to a ludicrous length, the current erroneous notions respecting the mysteriousness of the Grecian religion and philosophy.

† Δοῦλοι ὄντες τῶν ἀεὶ ἀτόπων, ὑπερδρῶται δὲ τῶν εἰωθότων.—Thucydides.

a hundred juries. It would be seen that the human body is a very intricate and a very delicate machine, and that in order to rectify its movements it is necessary to understand them.

Of all the subjects of quackery, the most profitable are those diseases which are in their nature either extremely lingering or avowedly incurable. Nobody flies to a quack doctor for relief in a violent attack of sore throat, or sends for him when afflicted with inflammation of the bowels. He is never thought of when all the children have the measles, and would be justly looked upon as a dangerous intruder when the father of a numerous family is lying ill of a typhus fever. These are acute disorders, and may not be trifled with. There is no sophistry in them; neglect to repel them and they become dangerous. The mummeries of *Mesmerism,* and the manipulations of the skilful in the employment of the metallic tractors, would be quite out of place ; and to rub the patient with a liniment would be deemed nearly of as little use before death as after. But the territory of quackery is chronic disease—disease that calls for patience, which is a rare quality, and for perseverance, with which few patients are endowed. Some chronic diseases are curable; and those who exhibit under the direction of the quack that patience and perseverance in which they were defective under the regular practitioner, furnish to the former his purest triumphs. Other chronic diseases, which are incurable, are yet capable of alleviation, and sometimes of remarkable and protracted mitigation. Here the quack achieves his greatest apparent victories over the regular doctor, for he seems to cure what regular art gives up in despair. Even when the unfortunate patient, transferred in the latter stage of his malady to the irregular practitioner, and living for one week on his promises, dies in the next of his medicine, the quack is not a loser in reputation; all the blame of the murder is thrown upon the more regular physician who had the previous care of the case. Now and then, however, the survivors are not content with the proceedings : the work has been done too hastily even for their credulity; and then, not with very great justice, they try to overwhelm the pretender, in whom they were silly enough to confide, simply on the ground of his own recommendation, with all the vengeance of the law.

Of those diseases in which quackery is productive of the most unfortunate effects, and yet of which the character most exposes the friends of the patient to the delusions of unprincipled interlopers in medicine, is consumption. It is often lingering in its course, and it is almost invariably fatal in its termination. It exhibits fluctuations which encourage hope, and it is sometimes simulated by such general disorder of the health as is curable by

great attention to diet and regimen, the chief remedial agents of
those who profess to use secret remedies.   It may be that regular
members of the faculty sometimes overlook this distinction, and
deservedly incur some loss of reputation; but it is no less true,
that many consumptive patients, by being consigned to the care
of the quack, are subjected to modes of treatment which hasten
the termination of the malady, and fill the latter days of their lives
with unnecessary discomfort.   It may, therefore, not be an unac-
ceptable service to our readers, if we avail ourselves of the opportunity afforded by the appearance of the second edition of M. Andral's valuable practical work, to lay before them, in a simple and
popular form, such information with respect to this too common
disorder, which occupies a considerable portion of the work, as
may be readily understood.

The chest, or that part of the body which is enclosed by the
ribs, may be said to be entirely occupied by the heart and the
lungs.   The heart is one of the simplest organs in the body, composed of muscular fibres, and divided into four cavities, namely, a
right auricle and ventricle, and a left auricle and ventricle.   Red
blood is sent from the left side of the heart into the aorta or large
pipe leading from it, which soon forms an arch in the chest, and
descends to carry blood to the abdomen and lower limbs; other
vessels being given off from the arch itself, which supply the
upper limbs and the head.   Losing its florid colour in its course,
the blood is brought back of a dark hue to the right side of the
heart, by the veins; and before it again passes to the left side of
the heart, it is driven through the lungs, in them to be recon-
verted, by the action of the inspired air, into its florid or arterial
state; after which it is again propelled into the aorta, to travel
through the arteries as before.   Just before the blood in the veins
of the head and neck is transmitted to the heart, it receives, from
a peculiar duct, a supply of chyle, which has been brought upwards along that duct from the organs of digestion, in a state to
be mixed with the blood; and in the lungs the mixture becomes
complete.

The lungs, in which this doubly important office of converting
the chyle into blood, and the venous blood into arterial, is performed, cannot consequently but be regarded as organs of extreme importance; and it is found that their well-being is quite
essential to health, and even to ordinary comfort.   They are of
great size, filling up all the chest not occupied by the heart.
Their texture is light and spongy, and they are divided into innumerable cells, communicating with the countless ramifications
from the two great divisions of the wind-pipe: these two main
divisions, uniting at the upper part of the chest, form a cartilagi-

nous tube, passing upwards along the front of the neck, and terminating superiorly in the larynx, of which the cartilages are distinctly felt at the upper part of the throat. At each inspiration, air is received between these cartilages, and through this tube, and passes down the wind-pipe into its two great bifurcations, and from them into every corner of the elastic and expanding lungs. Each little cell, or at least each minute ramification, to its very extremity, becomes dilated with air, and the admitted blood, travelling in small vessels along the walls of these cells, undergoes the changes already mentioned. The air is then expired, altered in its qualities, and the renovated blood passes to its destination in the left cavities of the heart; the next inspiration bringing fresh air into the cells, and more blood into the lungs to receive the benefit of it. This wonderful process, on which life hangs, is performed by day and by night, whether we are sleeping or waking, from birth until the last moment of life.

Now the term pulmonary consumption has been applied to two distinct affections of the lungs. One of these, being nothing more than a chronic inflammation of the lining membrane of the wind-pipe and its many ramifications, is perhaps generally a curable disease. The membrane becomes very irritable, and even thickened or ulcerated, and sometimes the patient sinks under the malady. But this form is so often relieved, as not unfrequently to create an opinion of the probable cure of a true pulmonary consumption much more favourable than medical experience sanctions.

The nature of a true pulmonary consumption is this :—numerous small, hard, greyish bodies are deposited in the soft, elastic, spongy tissue of the lungs themselves. These are, commonly at least, very numerous. They are sometimes in clusters, and sometimes scattered all through the lungs; sometimes confined to one lung, often extended to both. These small bodies are what, in medical language, are called *tubercles.* It is their nature to enlarge, and, beginning to soften in the centre, to break down into a fluid mass. The lung immediately surrounding a tubercle which is undergoing this change becomes inflamed; a communication is established between the softened tubercle and one of the many ramifications of the air-passages, and thus the tubercle is expectorated in the form of a yellow or purulent fluid. When the tubercles are in a cluster, many commonly break down together, and, being expectorated, leave a considerable cavity in the lungs. If the tubercles are not numerous, all of them may be thus got rid of, the cavity may be obliterated, or cicatrised, and a person who has been affected with true pulmonary consumption may in this way actually recover. But this is a rare occurrence. The tubercles generally exist in great number. When some are softening, others are forming; and when the first are got rid of, the second have yet to be got rid of. This long process irritates the constitution; and the irritation, being protracted, destroys life. The action of the heart becomes quickened, the stomach and intestines become highly disordered, the patient is tormented with hectic fever, and wasted to a skeleton; although often, notwithstanding these obvious sources of suffering and symptoms of decay, cheerful and full of hope to the last. i

The progress of the tubercles through their changes of character is not always uniform; peculiarities of constitution and various accidents retard or accelerate those changes, and sometimes the progress is long suspended; all the symptoms of constitutional irritation for a time subside, and the friends of the patient delude themselves with the hope of a perfect recovery. Not unfrequently the symptoms suddenly reappear, and the disease becomes speedily fatal, even before the tubercles have undergone the ultimate changes which have been described.

Human skill, we fear, has yet achieved little, either for the prevention or the cure of this terrible malady, to which, it has been calculated, that no less than sixty thousand persons fall a sacrifice in every year in Great Britain alone. Whilst it is most common in temperate climates, no degree of heat or of cold seems an absolute protection from it. It is no less fatal, and it is hardly less prevalent, in France than in England, and it is very common all along the shores of the Mediterranean. It is found in all parts of our own island, and is almost equally common in all; though perhaps most common in the maritime counties.

The presence of tubercles in the lungs is generally first indicated by some slight oppression of the function of respiration. The chest seems not to be sufficiently expanded in the act of breathing, and the inspirations are short and frequent. Next in order comes a hard and peculiar cough, first heard, perhaps, in the winter or spring; but not disappearing in summer or in autumn. Sometimes there is a slight spitting of blood thus early, although that circumstance, taken by itself, is by no means decisive of the nature of the malady. Conjoined with habitual frequency of pulse, or in a female with a defect or suspension of functions peculiar to the female constitution, it is a symptom well calculated to excite alarm. There is often little or no expectoration; but the cough is distressing when the patient lies down at night, or begins to dress in the morning. The face and figure soon put on the peculiar external characters of consumption. The hair becomes thin, and the circumscribed scarlet heu of the cheeks is strongly contrasted with the paleness of the face and of the white part of the eyes. The shoulders seem pointed, and the chest narrowed. The hands become pale and slender: emaciation and debility keep pace together.

From the very commencement of the disease the action of the heart and pulse is frequent, above a hundred, pulsations being generally counted in a minute. Morning chilliness is succeeded by evening heat and thirst; and to evening hectic, for such the exacerbation soon becomes, succeed wasting night perspirations. The appetite for food is often little affected, although irritability of the stomach and vomiting are common. The bowels are generally irritable as the disease advances, and diarrhœa alternates with the night perspirations. The lining membrane of the air passages becomes irritated, inflamed, ulcerated, or even studded with tubercles. Worn and harassed by these complicated sufferings, the patient still, very commonly, indulges in sanguine hope of recovery: there is, in fact, a mental excitement, which passes on, in the latest stage, to a mild delirium. The consumptive constitution is characterised by great susceptibility to impressions, and the delicate nervous system is readily excited, even before the disorder itself commences. With the commencement of the disorder, or soon afterwards, the signs of an irritable brain are generally very perceptible; the sensations of the patient become unfaithful, and the materials for a correct opinion of their actual condition being thus withheld, the patients entertain confident hope when all around them despair.

The cure of this disorder being so rare, the practitioners of medicine have anxiously sought for the means of prevention, by investigating, with much diligence, those circumstances in the constitution of the patient, and the local disordered actions, which predispose to the deposition of tubercles in the lungs. As is usual in investigations of such a nature, many of the investigators have been content to generalise on the foundation of a very small number of facts, and the causes of consumption assigned by various authorities are contradictory, often frivolous, and sometimes absurd. Foreign pathologists in particular have ascribed phthisis to almost every ordinary article of diet and regimen; to animal food, to vegetables, and even to the use of butter. It would be very unprofitable to repeat all the fanciful opinions which have thus in succession been advanced with the solemnity of discoveries.

The majority of pathologists, we believe, will assent without difficulty to the proposition of M. Andral, that " pulmonary tubercles are the product of a morbid secretion." p. 25. The supposed necessity for a previous state of active sanguineous congestion in the lungs, or in portions of them, which was maintained in

the first edition of the " Clinique Médicale," is, we observe,
abandoned, and, we think, justly abandoned, in the second.
Such a state may occasionally precede the deposition of tubercles,
and hasten their formation: every circumstance favouring such
a state in the lungs may favour the formations of tuberculous
matter; but the invariable precedence of it has not been proved,
and several circumstances throw great doubt upon it.   Disordered secretion may often be attended with vascular disturbance,
or be induced by it; but secretion is a compound process, the
work of the nerves and blood-vessels in associated office; it may
be disturbed or depraved by nervous commotion; and even when
disturbed or depraved by disorder primarily affecting the blood-
vessels, this disorder may not necessarily consist of or produce
active sanguineous congestion.   It is of more than theoretical
consequence to make this admission, for the opinions entertained
on this point must inevitably influence the practice of the physician.

What constitution of body most predisposes to the creation of
tubercles in the lungs can only be expressed by saying, that it is
one of which the predominant feature is debility.   This debility
is often connected with a scrofulous character, but not invariably
or necessarily.   The progress of the ravages effected in the frame
by the irritation which supervenes on the formation of tubercles
seems, however, to be more rapid and more marked when the
patient is already affected with any form of scrofula.   But consumption may unquestionably appear, and does unquestionably,
we believe, appear in a majority of instances, in those who are
not of a scrofulous constitution.   An altered complexion, an
unhealthy state of the skin, a disordered digestion, and many signs
of imperfect health, and commonly of defective nutrition, precede
the declaration of a decided phthisical affection; or the complaint
arises in those who have been from their birth delicate, if not
absolutely sickly.   Circumstances of a nature to reduce the
strength, and perhaps at the same time to affect the nervous system, may bring a healthy individual into that state in which tubercles may become formed in the lungs.   Thus nothing is more
common than for symptoms of consumption to appear not long
after a patient has struggled through a fever; or for the complaint
to be induced by a course of reckless dissipation; and we have
seen it plainly brought on by deep and long-continued mental
affliction.   Frequent exposure to wet and cold, with its common
consequences, frequent attacks of catarrh, undoubtedly dispose
the lungs to disease and to the creation of tubercles; and that poor
diet may be a powerful predisposing cause will readily be credited
by those who know how invariably some of the inferior animals

may be brought into a state of disease, and that tubercles are formed in their lungs at will, by confining them to particular kinds of food.   Habitual confinement in a deteriorated air, in close apartments, in crowded manufactories, or in schools where a number of scholars are kept together for several consecutive hours, seems to be not an uncommon cause of that state of body which favours the development of tubercles.   In these cases, the nervous and vascular systems are probably first debilitated, and the process of digestion is commonly also much impaired, before the phthisical disorder appears.   To the predisposing causes M. Andral adds, want of sufficient exposure to the influence of the sun. Early life, too, he observes, must be enumerated among the predisposing causes.   Some of the diseases of early life—as the measles and hooping-cough—are presumed to dispose to the formation of tubercles, by producing a considerable accumulation of blood in the pulmonary tissue.   The same circumstances occurring in females, on the cessation of the periodical functions, renders, it is also supposed, the occurrence of phthisis at that period of life, in female subjects, not a rare occurrence.

It is to be observed, that the age at which symptoms of consumption may appear is not so constant, or even so limited as has frequently been asserted, and as many medical authors still assert. The age of puberty is attended in both sexes with constitutional changes, not effected without a degree of tumult which becomes a source of both sanguineous and nervous disorder to the feeble constitution; and at this period consumption does, without question, very often show itself.   More rarely, it is seen at an earlier age.   But its supervention at a later period is still more common than at the age of puberty.   We are ourselves disposed, after some attention to this particular fact, to believe, that of all ages at which phthisis shows itself, the most common is that between thirty and forty.   Instances have not been wanting in which the malady has become fatal at a much later time of life, or in which it has even made its first appearance in advanced age.   M. Andral mentions the case of a patient of sixty-eight, who had enjoyed previous good health, and in whom symptoms of phthisis then first showed themselves; the complaint proved fatal after a few months, and numerous tubercles were found in both lungs; which, judging from the patient's health having previously been uninterrupted, would seem to have been recently developed.

The duration of the malady after it has been incontestably declared is also very variable, or rather, to speak more correctly, the malady is capable of suspension for considerable intervals, with occasional returns, which at length prove fatal.   In such cases the patient is generally more or less a valetudinarian; can-

not endure much exertion; his respiration is soon oppressed, and
his heart is irritable: he suffers much on every attack of common
catarrh, and seems at last, from this cause, to fall into consumption.   M. Andral says he has known individuals remain in this
intermediate state, between illness and health, from early life to
thirty or forty years of age.

Far more commonly, consumption destroys the patient in a
much shorter time.   The average duration of life, after the disorder is actually established, cannot be stated as greater than two
years.   Many patients are worn out by the disease much within
that period; some sink in less than a year, and some are hurried
to the grave in a few months, or, though more rarely, even in a
few weeks.   The latter description of cases are so striking, even
to common observers, as to be designated, in popular language,
galloping consumptions.   Of these M. Andral gives some examples.   In one, death took place four weeks after the first appearance of cough; in another, five weeks after the first symptom of
ill health; in a third, the symptoms of phthisis had been observed
in a slight degree for many years, without affecting the patient's
health or strength; and then the softening and expectoration of
tuberculous matter, occurring apparently for the first time, were
followed by death in the short space of eleven days.   It cannot
be a matter of surprise that the patients are in these cases generally unconscious of their danger, and unprepared for death.   We
have known them chiefly complaining of symptoms which had
little connection with the pulmonary disorder, and loath to acknowledge any cough or other affection of the respiratory organs,
only a few days before they died of pulmonary consumption in
the last degree.

Such being the hopeless character of consumption when once
established, the fact of its establishment becomes of the greatest
importance, and the means of determining either its absence or
its presence cannot be too carefully studied.   By these means,
supposing them to exist, a protection may be given against the
deceptions of the quack, who pretends to cure what does not
exist; and in other cases, where the disorder is but too well established, a protection of another kind may be afforded to the
unfortunate patients themselves, who may be spared the infliction
of remedies which are powerless to heal, and may yet obtain much
relief by palliative measures, adopted in consequence of sound
views being entertained of the actual state of the lungs.

Two methods of investigating all diseases of the lungs and of
the heart have, for some years past, occupied the attention of medical practitioners, in addition to an observation of what are commonly called symptoms.   These are, percussion of the chest, and

auscultation. The first is a revived invention, the second a very recent discovery; or, at least, recent and novel in the extent and accuracy of its application. As these are methods by which the presence of tubercles in the lungs may sometimes be positively ascertained, and as the principle of their employment is very simple, it may be worth while shortly to explain both of them to readers to whom it is probable that the terms percussion and auscultation may convey no very clear signification.

The light texture of the lungs, the manner in which their innumerable cells are filled with air, and the extent to which they fill the chest, have already been described. What is called the chest, therefore, may in some sort be compared to a box or barrel filled with air; and when the chest is struck with the fingers it returns, in most parts of it, exactly the sound we should expect to be given. Percussion of the chest is but the eliciting of this sound, by the steady and consecutive striking of the ends of two or three of the fingers on all parts of the chest. It requires to be done with some care; the points of the fingers should be held evenly, and the chest be struck smartly; the examination of each part of one side of the chest should be compared with that of the corresponding part of the other side of the chest; and the same parts on both sides should be struck as nearly as possible at the same angles. When the front part of the chest is subjected to this kind of examination, it is most convenient that the person examined should cross his arms behind him; and when the back of the chest is examined, the arms may be folded before the patient. Thus examined, the whole of the chest returns a hollow sound, except on the lower part of the left side, where the heart intervenes between the lung and the hand; and on the lower part of the right side, where the liver is situated, and seems to encroach on what is commonly called the chest. Where there is the least soft and unsonorous substance interposed between the lungs and the hand, the sound is clearest; as at the sides and along parts of the front of the chest: where there is the most soft matter, muscle, fat, or other substance, there the sound is duller; as at the top of the chest behind, above the shoulder blades, and in fat persons and females on the front of the chest. But the sound of the corresponding parts of each side of the chest will still, in health, be equal, and the natural differences of sound are consequently soon appreciated.

The application of these simple facts to the investigation of diseases of the lungs is very direct. Whatever becomes interposed —*within* the chest as well as without—between the hand and the air-expanded lung, lessens or modifies the sound returned when the chest is struck with the fingers in that part in which the interposed matter exists. The interposed matter may be a fluid, and

then the sound on the side of the chest where the fluid is, or to a
certain height from the lower part of the chest, will be dull;
whilst on the other side of the chest, or above the level of the
fluid, it will be clear and natural. The difference in these cases
may be appreciated by any ear. The same effect, or dulness of
sound, may be produced by any part of the soft lung having become less pervious to air. This is the case in inflammation of
the lungs: the substance of the lung, when the inflammation is
severe, destroys for a time the elasticity of the lung, and its capacity of receiving air in the portion inflamed; and here also the
dull sound will be returned when the chest is struck over the inflamed part, unless in the single case of the inflamed portion of
lungs being in the centre, and healthy lung being interposed between it and the hand.

The description of tubercles which has already been given, will
make it readily intelligible to all, that if they are numerous, or if
many of them are collected together, they must constitute a mass
of such a degree of density as to produce modifications of sound
when percussion is employed. If they are not numerous, and
not grouped together, little or no modification of sound can be
expected; and the same want of distinct modification exists even
when they are numerous, if they happen to be scattered over all
parts of the lungs. When, however, in a patient who has some
of the symptoms of consumption, a dull sound is returned on one
side of the chest, particularly at the upper part, and the corresponding part of the other side of the chest returns the usual
sound, there is the strongest reason to believe that many tubercles
are collected in the part of the lung where the dull sound is
given, and the opinion given in such a case is generally very unfavourable. We have several times found this sign distinct at
an early stage of the ordinary symptoms, and have seldom been
deceived by it.

The principle of what is called auscultation is no less simple
than that of percussion. The manner in which blood and air
are received into the lungs, and transmitted from them, has been
already explained. When the ear is applied to the chest, these
actions are found to be productive of a low but distinct sound,
or murmur, which murmur is heard all over the chest, with the
exceptions just alluded to when speaking of percussion. Whatever diminishes the elasticity and light texture of the lungs—
whatever intervenes between the lungs and the ear,—and whatever obstructs, in any degree, the passages through which the air
passes into the pulmonary substance, diminishes or modifies the
respiratory murmur, and thus becomes an indication of disease,
and of the nature of the disease. *Mediate* auscultation signifies
the employment of a perforated cylinder of wood, called the

stethoscope, one end of which, scooped out like a funnel, is placed steadily and evenly on the chest, whilst the ear is accurately applied to the other.

It will be seen at once, that the use of the stethoscope, or of auscultation, must be limited in the case of consumption by the same circumstances which circumscribe the utility of percussion in the same disorder. If the tubercles are numerous, if clustered together, if near the surface of the lungs, they will render the respiratory murmur less distinct. If few in number, if small, if scattered over the lungs, they so slightly modify the respiratory sounds that, even if we admit that the practised ear can appreciate the modification, such modification cannot be understood as being available to the general course of practice; and we may almost say, therefore, that in such circumstances the stethoscope is of no use in phthisical cases. The strong and decisive evidence, however, which is afforded by its employment in those cases in which percussion has indicated a dull sound on one side or in one part of the chest, and the certainty acquired in such cases by the employment of both methods in conjunction, are sufficient to show that even in consumption the stethoscope is an instrument not to be neglected. Its use, too, is by no means thus limited in this disorder, in the progress of which it affords other and perhaps infallible diagnostics. In a number of cases, observes M. Andral, auscultation renders the recognition of phthisis more precise and more exact; and it marks, much better than any other method of investigation, the extent, the seat, and the degree of the alteration which the lungs have undergone. By its means, the existence of cavities in the lungs, the product of softened tubercles, has been ascertained in cases in which the patients were previously supposed to be suffering from a simple bronchial affection, or perhaps only suspected of being in the very first stage of consumption.—(p. 68.)

One of the most striking of the phenomena which may be discovered by the use of the stethoscope in consumption is what is called pectoriloquism, or the sensation, if the patient speaks during the time when the stethoscope is applied to the chest and the ear to the stethoscope, of the voice of the patient passing *directly through the instrument.* This sign is found when a cavity is already produced in the lungs by the softening of numerous tubercles; and it is of course not often heard in cases affording the least hope of recovery. The exceptions with which the indications of the stethoscope and of percussion are to be received in consumption, are very clearly and ably stated by M. Andral; and even the sign last-mentioned, so important when it is heard, is sometimes, it seems, not heard, even when a cavity

really exists. The reader, who is desirous of being master of all
that relates to this sign, should carefully peruse the explanations,
cautions, and valuable directions of the great inventor of the stethoscope, M. Laennec, contained in the chapter on Phthisis
Pulmonalis, in his masterly Treatise on diseases of the Chest and
on Mediate Auscultation, and also in the notes of his distinguished
translator, Dr. Forbes.

Such are some of the principal facts relating to the nature and
progress of this malady, and to the means of detecting its existence. Its treatment does not obtain much consideration in the
work before us, of which the chief objects are to illustrate the
symptoms and the morbid anatomy of diseases. But we cannot thus
dismiss the subject at a time when the public attention has been
challenged with more than common effrontery, and in the face of
facts of an appalling kind, to the efficacy of a mode of cure professed by a man apparently unacquainted with the rudiments of
medical science. The declared destruction of a few patients,
and the suspected murder of many more, are probably less calculated to shake a confidence which rests on no reasonable ground,
than a mere consideration of the prospect of cure afforded by the
actual nature of the malady itself.

If we suppose the disease to be established, or tubercles to be
actually formed in the lungs, there would seem to be two especial
indications of treatment; namely, to prevent the progress of these
foreign bodies, and to check the symptoms of irritation produced
by them, not only in the lungs but in other organs. The presence of the tubercles is often declared more strongly by the
supervention of these secondary irritations than by any primary
embarrassment in the functions of the lungs themselves. It is,
consequently, against these secondary states that the efforts of the
practitioner are very frequently directed; and some of them—inflammation of portions of the pulmonary tissue for example—demand the promptest attention, inasmuch as they tend to hasten the
progress of the tubercles, before existing in a passive condition,
into that stage in which they work the most serious effects on the
general constitution. The means of preventing at once the in-
conveniencies of the different supervening irritations, and the ac-
celeration of the process of tubercular change, are, generally, all
such as are calculated to prevent excitement of the vascular system.
The presence of actual inflammation may make it necessary to
prescribe moderate bleeding, and this may become again occasionally necessary, although the wasting character of consumption
is sufficiently declarative of the impropriety of the repeated, and
as it were periodical, bleedings, to which practitioners have sometimes resorted. Blistering the chest, as near as possible to the

inflamed part of the lung, the exact situation, of which may be ascertained by the stethoscope, is a powerful auxiliary to the venesection; and, in many cases, if resorted to after the application of leeches, may render it unnecessary to incur the inconvenience of a general bleeding. Irritations of the larynx and trachea (windpipe), and also of the bronchial ramifications, may generally be alleviated by these means, and by other methods of producing external irritation; as well as that distressing disturbance of the stomach which is exceedingly troublesome to the greater number of phthisical patients. With the same intentions, various soothing medicines, chiefly mucilaginous and anodyne, are found to be serviceable; and the adoption of a system of diet which is moderately nutritious, but from which every thing that could cause excitement is carefully excluded. Every part of the regimen of the patient should be so ordered as to conform to this system; violent bodily and mental exertions, late hours, exposure to vicissitudes of weather, insufficient clothing and every kind of irregularity are to be diligently avoided.

By the early and rigid adoption of measures of this kind, many individuals in whose lungs tubercles actually exist, are enabled to maintain a condition of health very little interrupted, and the duration of life may, in some cases, be greatly prolonged. Both of the indications already mentioned are indeed thus simultaneously accomplished.

In variable climates like our own there is always an additional difficulty to be contended against, arising out of the perpetual irritation of the air-passages, by the actual contact and unavoidable reception of the air itself. If, desirous altogether to avoid this inconvenience, the patient is restricted to the air of rooms of which the temperature is carefully regulated, the want of invigorating freshness is too often productive of general effects which induce some other disadvantages, both as regards the general health and the pulmonary disease; and if attempts are made to secure the benefit of that freshness which the external air alone can impart, hardly any care or watching can long prevent some accidental exposure which brings on an aggravation of symptoms which it is most desirable to repel. The hope of securing the advantage, without incurring the counterbalancing disadvantages, produces the numerous annual migrations of the consumptive to various parts of foreign countries and of our own; and these again impart a high degree of interest to the character of particular countries of the continent, or of particular islands to which so many sail in quest of health, or of particular parts of our own island, to which those who are unwilling or unable to leave their native country commonly resort. The desired climate for a consumptive patient is one which is dry, warm or temperate, and subject to few vicissitudes. There is, unfortunately, much difficulty is finding such a climate in our own country. We may obtain warmth in Devonshire, and generally along the southern coast of England; but not warmth with dryness, or warmth free from vicissitudes. Dryness is to be found on the heights of Clifton or Malvern, but dryness without sufficient warmth, or sufficient protection from severe winds. The sheltered vallies in the neighbourhood of Clifton, or the coast of Devonshire, or the southern parts of the Isle of Wight, seem to afford the best winter residence. During that season the temperature of Devonshire is 5° above that of London. Hastings, and the beautiful part of the Isle of Wight called Undercliff, are perhaps the most sheltered from the piercing winds of spring. In the heat of summer, the heights of Clifton or of Malvern offer some advantages; and during the autumnal heats, probably no situation is better than Brighton.

That which gives to any one place or district a decided superiority over another, is the equal distribution of heat throughout its year. A climate, like that of Paris, where the heat of summer is very great, and the coldness of the winter excessive, is worse for the consumptive patient than any part of our own island. Yet patients are sometimes contented to " go abroad for their health," leaving their residence to be determined by accident; and seeming to imagine that some peculiar virtue is attached to every acre of a foreign soil. But the same country, or certainly a country so extensive as France, may contain climates of the most opposite character. That of the south-east of France, for instance, differs exceedingly from that of the south-west of that country, which, like the south-west parts of England, is warm and relaxing, but subject to violent winds; whilst that of the south-east, although 3° above the south-west in mere temperature, is subject to sharper winds, which try the consumptive invalid much more severely. No where in Europe is there perfect shelter from the winds of the spring. Even at Nice, where the winter is so mild, the months of March and April are particularly unsuitable to pulmonary invalids; and the same may be said of Montpellier and Marseilles. There are spots in Italy which are less exposed to these disadvantages. Yet even in Rome, distinguished for its soft and delightful air, and for its general dryness, it is very common in spring to have cold winds prevailing until sunset; and the malária renders it an undesirable residence in the summer. The winter of Naples is well adapted to an invalid; but at Naples also they complain of the coldness of the spring. Summer, too, brings its disadvantages in a warm climate; although there are situations in the neighbourhood of that city which are considered agreeable even in that season; but excepting such situations, and the baths of Lucca, the warmth of an Italian summer is much too great for invalids to bear with impunity. For this reason the suffering patient is often compelled to undertake a fatiguing journey, either to England or into Switzerland, or to what seems better than either, for a summer residence, to Ems on the Rhine. By a sufficiently prolonged residence at any one of the places which we have mentioned, particularly if care is taken to guard the invalid, from the particular vicissitudes which are found most to distress him, we feel confident that the progress of consumption may be delayed, and all the inevitable irritations attending its progress much alleviated.

More sanguine hopes arise at the mention of the island of Madeira; which boasts of a climate far superior to that of France, or of any part of Italy; and one which combines the requisites both for a summer and a winter place of residence. Almost wholly exempt from the keen winds which prevail so generally over the European continent, and enjoying a high winter temperature, the equability of its climate is quite remarkable; and the summer is not so hot as to drive away those who seek its shelter from the severe winter of their own land. Thus it is stated by Dr. Clark, in his very valuable work on the Influence of Climate in the Cure of Diseases, that whilst the Madeira winter is 20° warmer than that of London, the summer-heat of Madeira only exceeds that of London by 7°; and whilst the winter at Madeira is 12° warmer than the winter in Italy, the Madeira summer is 5° *cooler* than the Italian summer. Nor are the variations of temperature from day to day sudden or considerable; and the rain which falls is commonly confined to the autumnal season. So that, altogether, there does not seem to be on the face of the globe a place more likely to preserve the life of those threatened or affected with consumption than Madeira. Still, it is to be remembered, that such is the state of the lungs in confirmed consumption, that much relief, or much prolongation of life, are not to be expected in any climate whatever; and that the cases benefited even by the salubrious air of Madeira are incipient cases. Of these, a large majority undergo such improvement as to maintain a very high character for the island as a place of refuge for consumptive invalids.

On the whole, a consideration of the nature of tubercles, and of the inevitable changes which they undergo, and the testimony of all experience, do but too strongly confirm the opinion, that human resources against the fatal progress of consumption are few and limited in power; that the retardation of the malady, and some mitigation of its attendant inconveniences, are nearly all that can be hoped for; and that perfect recovery, where the tuber-

F 2

cles are numerous and far advanced, is not, under any circumstances, to be · expected.   In the retardation of the malady, however; and, we would add, in its prevention in persons predisposed
to it by biith or natural constitution, so much' may yet be done
by careful diet and regimen, by attention to clothing, and exercise
more' especially, as well to 'reward the pains required to order
these particulars properly and effectually.

·   That tubercles already deposited in the lungs may be removed
by absorption, or that the constitution can be supported through
the processes by which even a large collection of them might possibly be eliminated from the ₁ungs, are things which yet exist only
in the dreams of the sanguine, or in the bold promises of those
whom ignorance endows with confidence.   That the public should
readily believe in the curative power of inhalation, or in the efficacy of barbarous methods of destroying large portions of the
integuments of the body by corrosive substances, unknown in
medicine, and presumptuously borrowed from the coarser arts,
can only, 'we fear, be regarded as a proof of the limited diffusion,
even in these times, of really useful knowledge.

ART. IV.—1. *Hinterlassene Schriften* von Carl Maria von Weber, *herausgegeben* von Theodore Hell.   (Posthumous works
  of Carl Maria von Weber, published by Theodore Hell.) Dresden, und Leipzig, 1828.   3 vols. 18mo.

2. *Lebensbeschreibung* von Carl Maria von Weber.   (Life of ditto.)
  Gotha.   1829.   4to.

MR. THEODORE HELL, " a name *unmusical* to Volscian ears,"
announces himself as the executor of Weber and guardian of his
sons; and in this capacity of executor he has laid before the
public the posthumous works of his deceased friend, accompanied with various dissertations of his own, critical and biographical.   We are sorry we cannot congratulate him either on the
care or judgment with which he has performed his task; his materials follow each other in most admired disorder;—now a portion of a romance by Weber himself; now, a thin layer of biography from Mr. Hell: then a set of musical critiques and occasional notices of matters musical by Weber; then, another portion of his biography by the executor " in linked sweetness long
drawn out:"—then Weber and his criticisms again.   But want of
order is not all we have to complain of.   Musicians, who cannot
afford time, like Gretry, to exhibit a portrait of their own mind,
should at least confide their musical MS. to a musical executor.
Their life is not safe in any other hands.   What the public expect
from the biographer of Weber is a sketch at least of the peculiar

features of his mind as an artist, of the gradual culture by which it was formed, the circumstances which furthered and the obstacles that repressed its progress;—his habits of study and composition, and some attempt to trace those influences which, operating upon his peculiar temperament, gave rise to that wild spirit of romance which breathes through his compositions. What Mr. Hell on the contrary gives us, is a long prosing discussion on his literary abilities as a poet and a novelist, in which field the executor seems to look upon him as another Salvator; vague and general tirades about his wit, humour and conversational powers, and the cordial fellowship in which he lived with Kind the editor, and some other of the better spirits of Dresden; while with regard to the immortal part of him, his habits and efforts as a musician— every thing which gives importance or value to the other trifles, his book preserves a decorous silence; Hamlet, in short, is entirely omitted in his own play.

Probably the same reasons which led the country manager to the suppression of the part of the Prince of Denmark have weighed with Mr. Hell. He feels he has no one to take the part. In stage language, Mr. Hell cannot *double* the musical critic with the literary; and so consoling himself with the reflection that Weber's fame as a musician will probably stand high enough without his aid, he devotes himself, with much executorial piety, to the task of elevating his *nugæ literariæ* to a corresponding altitude.

We fear, therefore, that any information we may have it in our power to communicate through the medium of this work, must be meagre and scanty; but with the aid of one or two other sources we shall endeavour to lay before our readers some authentic particulars relative to this great, we may truly add this good, man. Some features of his mind, we think, will be clear enough from this sketch, others will be indicated more or less plainly; where we can avail ourselves of his own correspondence or remarks we shall allow him to speak for himself; where we are destitute of information, we shall leave the blank to be filled up by some future biographer.

Weber was born at Eutin, in Holstein, on the 18th Dec. 1786. Like almost every other great composer, his father was a musician. He was an accomplished violinist, and at an early period anxiously devoted himself to the education of his son. The retired habits of his family, his early intercourse with persons older than himself, and his seclusion from the society of rude and boisterous playmates, soon excited in his mind a disposition to thought, and taught him to live in a world of his own imagination. " I heated my fancy," says Weber in a letter to a friend, written long afterwards, " with the reading of romances, and pictured to myself models of ideal excellence." These sedentary pursuits and early ·wanderings of imagination, while they matured his intellectual faculties, not improbably laid the foundation of that physical weakness which ·too soon terminated in disease. His occupations were incessant. Music at first only shared his attention' with painting and drawing. He wrought in crayons, in oil, in water-colours; he etched very tolerably; every thing, in short, indicated that restless activity of mind, which, whether it be spread over the whole field of art, or poured into a single ·channel, seems to be· the inseparable concomitant of genius. Gradually the master-feeling of his soul assumed the preponderance, and banished' its rivals from the scene; painting and etching· dropt silently into abeyance, and music engrossed the whole energies of his youthful mind.

His studies in this art were not a little· retarded by his father's' frequent change of residence, and the consequent alteration which took place in the 'systems and 'modes of tuition' to which' he' was' subjected; On the other hand, these changes, by leading him to reflect, and compare,- and analyse, probably developed and assisted the constitution of an enlarged musical taste. To Hauschkel of Hildburghausen, in particular, Weber, in a little fragment of autobiography which he began at Dresden, expresses his high obligations for the acquisition of whatever skill he professed as a pianoforte player; particularly in rendering him equally adroit in' the use of both hands. His father, who witnessed his progress with pleasure, took him when' about eleven·years old to Saltzburg, and placed him under the care of Michael Haydn. " But there was too awful a distance," says Weber, " between the old man and the child. I learnt little with him and with great difficulty." To encourage him, however, his father printed, in 1798, six fugues which he had composed, and in the end of that year took him' to Munich, where he received instructions in singing from Valesi, and in harmony from the court-organist Kalcher, to whose clear, progressive and unwearied instructions, particularly in regard to the grand elements of composition, the treatment of subjects in four parts, he expresses himself as greatly indebted. Weber's inclination towards dramatic music soon began to display itself. Under the eye of his master he now wrote an opera entitled " The Power of Love and Wine," besides a mass, numerous sonatas for the piano-forte, violin trios, &c., all of which, however, he afterwards committed to the flames. Even the field of music, it seemed, was not wide enough for him. Senefelder's discovery of lithographic printing all at once inspired him with the resolution of turning lithographer. He thought he had discovered an improved process in lithography, and forthwith set about reducing his invention to practice, by removing to Freyberg and actually commencing the practice of the art. But the mechanical, "spirit-killing" drudgery, as he calls it, of this employment soon became repulsive, and throwing away his alkalies and his dabbers, he returned with a warmer and now unalterable attachment to his former studies.

In 1800, he composed the music of the Chevalier Steinberg's opera, "The Maid of the Woods," (Das Waldmädchen,) which though he himself characterizes it "as a very immature production, only not entirely destitute of occasional invention," appears to have been received with approbation even in Berlin and Petersburgh, no trifling distinction for the work of a boy of fourteen. An article in the Musical Gazette about this time, (1801,) suggested to him the idea of composing a piece in a different style, in which old and forgotten instruments should be introduced. To this archæological opera he gave the name of "Peter Schmoll and his Neighbours," (Peter Schmoll und seine Nachbärn.) It was played in Augsburg, as he himself drily and significantly observes, "without any remarkable consequences;" the most agreeable circumstance attending this antiquarian capriccio being, that it procured him the following kind notice from his old master, Michael Haydn:—"As far as I may pretend to judge, (says he,) I most truly and candidly say, that this opera not only possesses great power and effect, but is composed according to the strict rules of counterpoint. To spirit and liveliness, the composer has added a high degree of delicacy, and the music is moreover perfectly suited to the words." Another of his masters, in alluding to the same opera, with respect to its author, made use of the remarkable and prophetic expression "erit mature ut Mozart;" and even Weber himself seems to have thought some portions of it deserving of preservation, for he afterwards retouched the overture, and had it printed by Gambard.

In 1802 he accompanied his father on a musical tour through Leipzig, Hamburg and Holstein, in the course of which he collected and studied various theoretical works on music, with the greatest assiduity, but, as would appear from his own confession, with no other result than that of filling his mind with conflicting and undigested theories. While in this bewildered state, he seems to have been grievously annoyed by an unlucky physician, who with the perplexing question "Why?" used to assail and generally overturn the principles, such as they were, which he had gathered in the course of his reading. "A confounded Doctor of Medicine," says he, "to whom I was giving instructions in thorough bass, pestered me so with his queries, had so little

respect for the authority of names, and was so determined to get
to the bottom of every thing, that with all my omniscience, I felt
myself now and then fairly nonplused.   I resolved at last to treat
music as other studies are treated, to be able to assign a reason
for every progressive step." By these means, proceeding in his
investigations with the most undaunted perseverance, and, as
nearly as possible, upon the same method to which modern research has been indebted for its success in the physical sciences,
after a time Weber not only emerged from the limbo of doubt,
into which the faulty and hypothetical systems of his predecessors had cast him, but brought with him a more philosophical
system of his own, based upon experience and the observation
of nature.   Having thoroughly grounded himself in the principles
of his art, he now sought a proper field for its display.

Vienna is, in Germany, the Holy Land to which all musical
devotees make their pilgrimage, and Weber also turned his face
to the east.   His reception was kind and cordial.   Musicians, iu
general, are not conspicuous for the harmony of their intercourse
with each other; but Weber was received with generous sympathy by those in whose minds his rising genius and boundless application might have excited envy.   The Abbé Vogler, the most
distinguished of his new acquaintances, advised him at once to lay
aside all premature attempts to acquire distinction, and to devote
himself silently and steadily for two years more to the critical
study of the works of the great masters, a course which he rigidly
followed out under the Abbé's personal superintendence, though
he admits that the effort which it cost him, was at first, a painful
one.

Anxious to perfect his education by a more complete acquaintance with dramatic and musical effect, he about this time
accepted of the situation of music director in Breslau.   Here he
formed a new orchestra and chorus, remodelled several of his
earlier works, and composed the greater part of Rode's opera of
Rubezahl.   His numerous duties left him little time for original
composition, but the contrasted nature of those works which, in
his official situation, he had to bring out and superintend, served
to exercise his mind, as he says, in discriminating musical
effects, and in exhibiting the practical application of those views
which his theories had suggested, while it prevented him from
falling into the beaten track of any one composer.

For a short time, in 1806, he took the direction of the theatre
at Carlsruhe, at the request of Prince Eugene of Wirtemberg,
but his employment, and the neat little theatre itself, were soon
put an end to by the ravages of war.   Music he found for a time
to be an unprofitable servant: a *march* was the only movement

which was popular, and the only instruments which were heard were the drum and the trumpet. During these evil times, Weber found an asylum in the house of the Duke Louis of Wirtemberg, at Stuttgard, where he rewrote his opera of the *Wood Girl*, and composed various smaller pieces, including *Der erste Ton* (The First Sound), till the political atmosphere began to clear in 1810, and restored him again to his profession. " From this time," says he, (writing afterwards in 1817,) " I may consider my opinions as pretty much made up on the subject of music, and all that time has since done, or can do, is merely the rounding-off of sharp angles, and the imparting additional clearness and comprehensibility to principles which were already firmly established in my mind." He now travelled through Germany in various directions, and his operas were played with success in Frankfort, Munich, Berlin, and Vienna. In conjunction with Meyerbeer and Gänsbacher, he enjoyed (and with more beneficial results than before) all the advantages which the fine taste, profound knowledge, and great experience of Vogler could impart. The Abbé was on the verge of the tomb, and Weber seems to have received his last instructions as a sacred legacy. " Once more only," says he, " I saw him in Vienna, fully sympathising with my success. Peace be to his ashes !" The opera of Abon Hassan was the composition of this period.

In January, 1813, he undertook (with some reluctance, for he foresaw the Augean nature of the task which awaited him,) the direction of the opera at Prague. Every thing had to be re-organized, and his efforts at reform were retarded by intrigues and obstacles of every kind. He wrote to Liebich, the stage-manager at Prague, on the subject of these annoyances, with feeling, but with that calm and dignified sense of his own uprightness and superiority which was blended in his mind with a singular modesty. He mentions that he had at last come to the resolution of giving up his obnoxious situation at Prague. " Think not, however," he observes in conclusion, " that this resolution is founded on any feelings of irritation or pride, but in the firm conviction that I can no longer remain here for good. While I continue to hold the helm, my management will always afford me the same pleasure and be distinguished by the same exertions." Accordingly with unpretending patience, he laboured for months before laying down the direction to complete and simplify all the arrangements of the opera for his successor, to fill up catalogues, inventories, and so forth, so as to reduce the operatic chaos into order and regularity. Having done so as well as he could, almost at the sacrifice of any attempt at composition of his own, (for his residence at Prague is hardly distinguished by any work of conse-

quence, save his cantata of " Kampf und Sieg," and his music to
Körner's " Leyer und Schwert,") he resigned his office.

" I now," says he, (March 26, 1818,) " set out on my pilgrimage
through the world, calmly waiting for that sphere of operation which
fate might assign to me., Numerous and tempting offers reached me from
all sides; but an invitation to assist in the formation of a German opera
in Dresden was the only one sufficiently attractive to decide me. And
here I am labouring with might and main at the duties assigned to me ;
and when they shall lay a stone upon my grave, I trust they will be able
to write on it—HERE LIES ONE WHO MEANT HONESTLY TOWARDS MUSIC,
AND TOWARDS MEN."

Well might Weber describe himself as working with might
and main during his residence at Dresden. He had come thither
in January, 1817, and though his residence was on the whole a
happy one, it was the contentment derived from successful, but
unceasing and laborious exertion—varied only by the occasional
society of a few congenial minds, and the constant and well-
merited tribute of " respect from the respected." Even if Weber
could have eaten the bread of idleness, it was not in his nature to
sit down in indolence. The same activity of mind, which in early
youth engaged him in painting, etching, and even the more mechanical labour of lithography, made him devote the *horæ inter-
cesivæ* which he could spare from his professional avocations (and
these intervals were not many) to the cultivation of poetry and
general literature. He published from time to time short criticisms on professional subjects, new operas, concerts, or elementary works on music generally, anonymously or under the signature of Melos, Simon Knaster, or some such pseudonym, most
of them distinguished by acuteness and depth, often by force and
happiness of expression, and uniformly by a noble candour and
sensibility to the merit of others. Many little poems and copies
of verses, epigrams, and translations from the Italian, also dropped
from his pen at these times, though in general they were communicated only to some of his friends, or left to repose in his
desk. They indicate, as might be anticipated, a fine ear for versification, and a considerable turn for humour. This quality appears a little overstrained in the longest of his productions, which
he did not live to complete, entitled "Tonkünstlers Leben, (" the
Life of a Musical Artist,") a humorous arabesque, in which
scenes from Weber's own musical life, or that of others, criticisms upon existing notions in the art, or in dramatic literature,
are worked up into a Shandean kind of romance, of which some
specimens appeared in various German periodicals, and are reprinted in the present work. His humour, there is reason to
believe, appeared to more advantage in his conversation in

society, where his good-natured playful satire and variety of conception are spoken of by his friends in high terms. Often in those quiet evening circles where Weber used to unbend after the fatigues of a laborious day, and where each of the company was called on alternately to contribute some poem or tale, or perhaps to take up and carry on a story begun by another, his readiness of invention and command of language rendered him a delightful visitor.

These *symposia*, however, exhibit the bright side of the composer's life; " the weariness, the fever, and the fret," of incessant occupation and wavering health, to which he was exposed during this his residence at Dresden, as he describes it' himself in a letter written in 1818, must be taken into view, to complete the picture. Weber had been rash enough, in an unguarded moment, to promise to review some musical production of a brother artist, and had been prevented by his multifarious avocations from fulfilling his promise. He had in the meantime received a most impertinent and vexatious letter from the brother of the musician, to which he thus replied:

" I was indebted, when I left Prague, to my publisher, in a variety of works already begun and paid for. I went to Berlin. I gave no concerts that I might lose no time. I worked day and night, and had almost completed my task, when I was invited to Dresden to assist in the formation of a German opera there. I came and found prejudices to contend with, obstacles of every kind to overcome, engagements to form, correspondence to carry on with all quarters of Germany, a corps to organise from the foundation, for an opera, which, with all its limited means, has since obtained the approbation of the court and the public. It was a hard time of restlessness and care, and my health was broken by it. The pressure of employment on all sides was so great, that I had no time to think of composition. I had been deprived of all social intercourse with my friends, some of whom had scarcely received a token of my existence for a twelvemonth. I had hoped to carry through my arrangements for my marriage in the end of August, when the task was suddenly imposed upon me of composing an Italian cantata for the nuptial ceremony of our Princess Maria Anne, to be completed at the very moment when I was in the midst of my arrangements for my new residence. The ceremony was put off from day to day, and this period of uncertainty, night and day, I shall never forget. At last, on the 30th of October, I was allowed to set out. I completed my marriage at Prague on the 4th of November, and paid a visit on family matters to Manheim. I had taken your brother's work with me in the carriage, that I might avail myself of any moment I could find, but it was impossible. In the end of December I returned, when a fearful heap of arrears awaited me. I had pledged myself to the king to prepare a mass for his birth-day, which was to be my greatest work. It was completed on the 8th of March, 1818, being the fruit of nocturnal labour, at a time when I was on the point of taking leave of this world altogether. My colleague Morlacchi had been travelling in Italy on leave ever since the end of August, 1817, and thus every thing lay on my shoulders * * * * Can a man, who has been conducting the opera for the last three years and a half, without playing a single piece of his own, though he had every facility for so doing—who is still indebted to his publisher in the completion of works begun a year before,—who has been for the same time, in a manner, dead to his friends, who has been unable to complete the opera which was expected at Berlin, be accused of thinking only of himself, or of wishing to suppress the talents of others? Both here and in Prague I have purposely represented nothing of my own, in order to convince the world that there may be such beings in it as directors who can foster the talents of others, and can be contented without listening eternally to their own music. I have not succeeded, it would seem, and it grieves me to the heart."

His marriage, to which he alludes in the above letter, was a happy one. His wife was the celebrated actress, Caroline Brand, with whom he had formed an acquaintance when at Prague. Wéber had, in his extreme love of simplicity, and fear of display, forbidden all music on the occasion; but, to his surprise and emotion, no sooner had the priest concluded the ceremony, than a burst of music from the organ, and the voices of his scholars, who had been anxious thus to express their sympathy, greeted the newly-married pair.

These proofs of sympathy from his scholars were not undeserved. The task of instruction, even amidst his numerous and distracting avocations, had always been discharged by Weber with that zeal and conscientiousness which pervaded his conduct in all the relations of life. Young as he was, his distinguished talent and enthusiasm for the art had early attracted towards him many pupils, and he seems to have mingled with his musical tuition an almost parental regard and anxiety for their success in life, and the general formation of their character. He censured their moral errors with the same readiness as their musical, he harmonized their whole mental constitution, and endeavoured to impress upon it that piety, charity, and unshaken but unpretending rectitude of purpose, which distinguished his own. Some passages, in a farewell letter addressed by him to a pupil who was about to leave him to commence his career in the world, indicate a remarkable union of tenderness and good sense.

" I feel myself called on, dear Emilius, before our parting, to repeat to you in writing what I have so often verbally endeavoured to impress upon your heart. When you became my scholar, I felt myself charged with the care of your whole being, for I cannot separate the artist from the man. You know how thoroughly I despise that miscalled ' geniality,' which considers the life of an artist as a license to all excesses, and a permission to violate all the restraints of modesty and decorum. True, an indulgence in the dreams of fancy is but too apt to infect our intercourse with real life; it is pleasant to feel ourselves so carried away. But here it is that a man must preserve his strength of mind, and make his choice, whether by governing his feelings he shall move at once freely and steadily along the path which is pointed out for him; or whether, not possessing, but possessed by his feelings, he shall be whirled giddily about like an insane Fakir in the worship of a wretched idol.

" Persevering diligence is the true spell by which these mischievous influences on the heart are to be counteracted. How absurd to suppose that the mind is cramped by the serious study of means? Free creative power is the result of habits of self-control alone; the mind must be content to move along beaten paths, if it would finally reach the region of novelty. * * * * Dear Emilius, with your acuteness, ambition, and talent, you sin against heaven, your parents, your art, and your instructor, if you abandon yourself any longer to idle dreams and extravagant excesses; if you do not study with firm perseverance, and with that order and method which alone can teach a man how to live in and for the world. Your unsteadiness, your disregard of promises and appointments have become a bye-word among your friends. It is the proud distinction of a man to be the slave of his word. Do not flatter yourself with the illusion that you may be careless in such matters, and not in things of greater importance. It is little matters that make up the mass of life, and the fearful power of custom will soon prevent the best intentions from being reduced to action. I trust, however, in HIM who directs all things for good. In the life of all of us there are turning points which are decisive of our future existence for good or evil. Let it be your care to enter on the right path; keep before your eyes the duties of your art; learn to be true to yourself, and your own feelings will richly reward you for any sacrifices which the effort may cost."

It is gratifying to learn, that the individual to whom this paternal remonstrance was addressed, justified by his after conduct the hopes of his instructor. He died early, but not without manifesting in the subsequent part of his conduct the impression which Weber's advice had left upon his mind.

In these laborious duties, Weber's time had passed down to 1818. The absence of Morlacchi, to which he alludes in the letter already quoted, had thrown upon him the whole duties of the opera. In May, 1818, after finishing the Grand Mass for the birth-day of the King, the state of his health was such, that he received permission to return to the country. Until about the close of 1819, he had been in the habit of furnishing a series of regular criticisms on dramatic music. These he now abandoned, partly from the state of his health, partly from an invidious attack upon him in a Dresden newspaper, where he was accused of labouring to suppress all talent but his own and that of his

flatterers and protegés. These observations were on occasion
of the announcement of Meyerbeer's " Emma di Rodrigo," and
" Alimelec," which had been played at the Royal Theatre that
spring, and their object was to produce the impression that
Weber had been unjust to the merit of his old friend. This consideration alone induced the former to notice the attack, which he
did in a most conclusive reply. But perceiving by experience
the thousand vexations to which the most honest reviewer is exposed, he in a great measure abandoned his musical criticisms.
During his tranquillity in the country, however, he composed
part of his *Preciosa*, the story of which is taken from one of Cervantes's " Novelas Exemplares;" and commenced another opera
which had been long before commissioned for the Berlin Theatre,
the well-known " Freyschütz," founded on a romance of Apel's.
His friend Kind, by whom the text of the opera was to be framed,
had at first given it the name of the " Jager's Bride," which was
afterwards changed for the more striking title (to a German ear)
of " The Enchanted Bullets." These labours were for a time
interrupted by the sickness of his wife ; but in spring, 1820, the
Preciosa was, for the first time, played at Berlin; and in 1821, the
newly-erected royal opera there was opened with " Der Freyschütz."

The effect produced by the first representation of this romantic
opera, which we shall never cease to regard as one of the proudest
achievements of genius, was almost unprecedented. It was received with general acclamations, and raised his name at once
to the first eminence in operatic composition. In January it
was played in Dresden, in February at Vienna, and every where
with the same success. Weber alone seemed calm and undisturbed amid the general enthusiasm. He pursued his studies
quietly, and was already deeply engaged in the composition of a
comic opera, " The Three Pintos," never completed, and had
accepted a commission for another of a romantic cast for the
Vienna stage. The text was at first to have been furnished by
Rellstab, but was ultimately written by Madame de Chezy, and
written in so imperfect and impracticable a style, that, with all
Rellstab's alterations, never had a musician more to contend with
than poor Weber had to do with this old French story. As it is,
however, he has caught the spirit of the tale.

" Dance and Provençal song, and vintage mirth,"

breathe in his melodies ; and although a perplexed plot and want
of interest in the scene greatly impaired its theatrical effect, the
approbation with which it was notwithstanding received by all
judges of music on its first representation in Vienna (10th Oct.

1823) sufficiently attested the triumph of the composer over his difficulties. He was repeatedly called for and received with the loudest acclamations. From Vienna, where he was conducting his Euryanthe, he was summoned to Prague, to superintend the fiftieth representation of his " Freyschutz." His tour resembled a triumphal procession ; for, on his return to Dresden, he was greeted with a formal public reception in the theatre.

But while increasing in celebrity, and rising still higher, if that were possible, in the estimation of the public, his health was rapidly waning, amidst his anxious and multiplied duties. "Would to God," says he in a letter written shortly afterwards,—" Would to God that I were a tailor, for then I should have a Sunday's holiday !" Meantime a cough, the herald of consumption, tormented him, and " the slow minings of the hectic fire" within began to manifest themselves more visibly in days and nights of feverish excitement. It was in the midst of this that he accepted the task of composing an opera for Covent Garden Theatre. His fame, which had gradually made its way through the North of Germany, (where his Freyschutz was played in 1823,) to England, induced the managers to offer him liberal terms for an opera on the subject of Oberon, the well-known fairy tale on which Wieland has reared his fantastic but beautiful and touching comic Epos. He received the first act of Planché's manuscript in December, 1824, and forthwith began his labours, though he seems to have thought that the worthy managers, in the short time they were disposed to allow him, were expecting impossibilities, particularly as the first step towards its composition, on Weber's part, was the study of the English language itself, the right understanding of which, Weber justly considered as preliminary to any attempt to marry Mr. Planché's ephemeral verses to his own immortal music. These exertions increased his weakness so much, that he found it necessary to resort to a watering-place in the summer of 1825. In December he returned to Berlin, to bring out his Euryanthe there in person. It was received, as might have been anticipated, with great applause, though less enthusiastically than the Freyschutz, the wild and characteristic music of which came home with more intensity to the national mind. After being present at two representations, he returned to his labours at Oberon.

The work, finally, having been completed, Weber determined, himself to be present at the representation of this his last production. He hoped, by his visit to London, to realize something for his wife and family ; for hitherto, on the whole, poverty had been his companion. Want had indeed, by unceasing exertion, been kept aloof, but still hovering near him, and threatening with the decline of his health, and his consequent inability to discharge his duties, a nearer and a nearer approach. Already he felt the conviction that his death was not far off, and that his wife and children would soon be deprived of that support which his efforts had hitherto afforded them. His intention was to return from London by Paris, where he expected to form a definitive arrangement relative to an opera which the Parisians had long requested from him. He left Dresden early in 1826, accompanied by his friend Furstenau, a celebrated performer on the flute, travelling in a comfortable carriage, which his health rendered indispensable. His cough was less troublesome on the journey than it had latterly been. He reached Paris on the 25th of February, where he was received in the most flattering manner by all the musicians and composers of eminence, among others by Rossini, who was so anxious to see him, that he had called before his arrival, that he might ascertain the exact moment of his coming. On the 27th he was present at the first representation of Spontini's " Olympia;" and though no great admirer of the composer, the way in which the opera was performed elicited his warmest approbation. " How splendid a spectacle;" says he, " is the opera here ! The noble building, the masses upon the stage, and in the orchestra, are imposing, almost awful. The orchestra in particular has a strength and a fire such as I never before witnessed." The longer he remained in Paris, the more the number of his visitors increased. " I cannot venture to describe to you," he writes to his wife, " how I am received here. It would be the excess of vanity. The very paper would blush for me, were I to write down half of what the greatest living artists here tell me. If I don't die of pride now, I am ensured against that fate for ever." Though thus breathing an atmosphere of flattery, and feeling his health and spirits improving amidst the novelty of the scene, his letters betray his longing to revisit his domestic circle, and his resolution never again to undertake so long a journey without the comfort of their society.

On the 2d of March he left Paris for England, which he reached on the 4th amidst a heavy shower of rain,—a gloomy opening to his visit. The first incident, however, that happened after his arrival, showed how highly his character and talents were appreciated. Instead of requiring to present himself as an alien at the Passport Office, he was immediately waited upon by the officer with the necessary papers, and requested to think of nothing but his own health, as every thing would be managed for him. On the 6th he writes to his wife from London.

" God be thanked! here I sit, well and hearty, already quite at home, and perfectly happy in the receipt of your dear letter, which assures me that you and the children are well; what more or what better could I wish for? After sleeping well and paying well at Dover, we set out yesterday morning in the Express coach, a noble carriage drawn by four English horses, such as no prince need be ashamed of. With four persons within, four in front, and four behind, we dashed on with the rapidity of lightning through this inexpressibly beautiful country; meadows of the loveliest green, gardens blooming with flowers, and every building displaying a neatness and elegance which form a striking contrast to the dirt of France. The majestic river, covered with ships of all sizes, (among others the largest ship of the line, of 148 guns,) the graceful country houses, altogether made the journey perfectly unique."

He took up his residence with Sir George Smart, where every thing that could add to his comfort or soothe his illness had been provided by anticipation. He found his table covered with cards from visitors who had called before his arrival, and a splendid pianoforte in his room from one of the first makers, with a request that he would make use of it during his stay.

" The whole day," he writes to his wife, " is mine till five, then dinner, the theatre, or society. My solitude in England is not painful to me. The English way of living suits mine exactly, and my little stock of English, in which I make tolerable progress, is of incalculable use to me.

" Give yourself no uneasiness about the opera (Oberon), I shall have leisure and repose here, for they respect my time. Besides, the Oberon is not fixed for Easter Monday, but some time later; I shall tell you afterwards when. The people are really too kind to me. No king ever had more done for him out of love; I may almost say they carry me in their arms. I take great care of myself, and you may be quite at ease on my account. My cough is really a very odd one. For eight days it disappeared entirely; then, upon the third (of March), a vile spasmodic attack returned before I reached Calais. Since that time it is quiet again. I cannot, with all the consideration I have given it, understand it at all. I sometimes deny myself every indulgence, and yet it comes. I eat and drink every thing, and it does not come. But be it as God will.

" At seven o'clock in the evening we went to Covent Garden, where Rob Roy, an opera after Sir Walter Scott's novel, was played. The house is handsomely decorated, and not too large. When I came forward to the front of the stage-box, that I might have a better look of it, some one called out, Weber! Weber is here! and although I drew back immediately, there followed a clamour of applause which I thought would never have ended. Then the overture to the Freyschutz was called for, and every time I showed myself the storm broke loose again. Fortunately, soon after the overture, Rob Roy began, and gradually things became quiet. Could a man wish for more enthusiasm, or more love? I must confess that I was completely overpowered by it, though I am of a calm nature, and somewhat accustomed to such scenes. I know not what I would have given to have had you by my side, that you might have seen me in my foreign garb of honour. And now, my dear love, I can assure you that you may be quite at ease, both as to the singers and the orchestra. Miss Paton is a singer of the first rank, and will play Reiza divinely. Braham not less so, though in a totally different style. There are also several good tenors, and I really cannot see why the English singing should be so much abused. The singers have a perfectly good Italian education, fine voices, and expression. The orchestra is not remarkable, but still very good, and the choruses particularly so. In short, I feel quite at ease as to the fate of Oberon."

The final production of the drama, however, was attended with more difficulty than he had anticipated. He had the usual prejudices to overcome, particular singers to conciliate, alterations to make, and repeated rehearsals to superintend, before he could inspire the performers with the proper spirit of the piece.

" Braham," says he, " in another of his confidential letters to his wife, (29th March, 1826) " begs for a grand scena instead of his first air, which, in fact, was not written for him, and is rather high. The thought of it was at first quite horrible; I could not hear of it. At last I promised, when the opera was completed, if I had time enough, it should be done; and now this grand scena, a confounded battle piece and what not, is lying before me, and I am about to set to work, yet with the greatest reluctance. What can I do? Braham knows his public, and is idolized by them. But for Germany I shall keep the opera as it is. I hate the air I am going to compose (to-day I hope) by anticipation. Adieu, and now for the battle. * * * * * * * * * * So, the battle is over, that is to say, half the scene. To-morrow shall the Turks roar, the French shout for joy, the warriors cry out victory!"

The battle was indeed nearly over with Weber. The tired forces of life, though they bore up gallantly against the enemy, had long been wavering at their post, and now in fact only one brilliant movement remained to be executed before they finally retreated from the field of existence. This was the representation of Oberon, which for a time rewarded him for all his toils and vexations. He records his triumph with a mixture of humility, gratitude, affection, and piety.

" *12th April,* 1826. ·

" My best beloved Caroline! Through God's grace and assistance I have this evening met with the most complete success. The brilliancy and affecting nature of the triumph is indescribable. God alone be thanked for it! When I entered the orchestra, the whole of the house, which was filled to overflowing, rose up, and I was saluted by huzzas, waving of hats and handkerchiefs, which I thought would never have done. They insisted on encoring the overture. Every air was interrupted twice or thrice by bursts of applause. * * * * * So much for this night, dear life: from your heartily tired husband, who, however, could not sleep in peace until he had communicated to you this new blessing of heaven. Good night."

But his joy was interrupted by the gradual decline of his health. The climate of London brought back all those symptoms which his travelling had for a time alleviated or dissipated. After directing twelve performances of his Oberon in crowded houses, he felt himself completely exhausted and dispirited. His melancholy was not abated by the ill success of his concert, which, from causes we cannot pretend to explain, was no benefit to the poor invalid. His next letters are in a desponding tone.

" 17th April, 1826.
" To-DAY is enough to be the death of any one. A thick, dark, yellow fog overhangs the sky, so that one can hardly see in the house without candles. The sun stands powerless, like a ruddy point, in the clouds. No : there is no living in this climate. The longing I feel for Hosterwitz, and the clear air, is indescribable. But patience,—patience—one day rolls on after another ; two months are already over. I have formed an acquaintance with Dr. Kind, a nephew of our own Kind. He is determined to make me well. God help me, that will never happen to me in this life. I have lost all hope in physicians and their art. Repose is my best doctor, and henceforth it shall be my sole object to obtain it. * * * *
" To-morrow is the first representation of my (so called) rival's opera, ' Aladdin.' I am very curious to see it. Bishop is a man of talent, though of no peculiar invention. I wish him every success. There is room enough for all of us in the world."

" 30th May.
" DEAREST Lina, excuse the shortness and hurry of this. I have so many things on hand, writing is painful to me—my hands tremble so. Already too impatience begins to awaken in me. You will not receive many more letters from me. Address your answer not to London, but to Frankfort—*poste restante*. You are surprised ? Yes, I don't go by Paris. What should I do there—I cannot move—I cannot speak—all business I must give up for years. Then better, better, the straight way to my home—by Calais, Brussels, Cologne, and Coblentz, up the Rhine to Frankfort—a delightful journey. Though I must travel slowly, rest sometimes half a day, I think in a fortnight, by the end of June, I shall be in your arms.
" If God will, we shall leave this on 12th June, if heaven will only vouchsafe me a little strength. Well, all will go better if we are once on the way—once out of this wretched climate. I embrace you from my heart, my dear ones—ever your loving father Charles."

This letter, the last but one he ever wrote, shows the rapid decline of his strength, though he endeavours to keep up the spirits of his family by a gleam of cheerfulness. His longing for home now began to increase till it became a pang. On the 6th June he was to be present at the Freyschutz, which was to be performed for his benefit, and then to leave London for ever. His last letter, the thirty-third he had written from England, was dated the second of June. Even here, though he could scarcely guide the pen, anxious to keep up the drooping spirits of his wife, he endeavours to speak cheerfully, and to inspire a hope of his return.

" As this letter will need no answer, it will be short enough. Need no answer! Think of that! Furstenau has given up the idea of his concert, so perhaps we shall be with you in two days sooner— huzza! God bless you all, and keep you well! O were I only among you. I kiss you in thought, dear mother. Love me also, and think always of your Charles, who loves you above all."

On Friday, the 3d of June, he felt so ill that the idea of his attending at the representation of " Der Freyschutz" was abandoned, and he was obliged to keep his room. On Sunday evening, the 5th, he was left at 11 o'clock in good spirits, and at 7 next morning was found dead upon his pillow, his head resting upon his hand, as though he had passed from life without a struggle. The peaceful slumber of the preceding evening seemed to have gradually deepened into the sleep of death.

He was interred on the 21st, with the accustomed solemnities of the Catholic Church, in the chapel at Moorfields, the Requiem of Mozart being introduced into the service. In person, Weber is described as having been of the middle height, extremely thin, and of dark complexion. His countenance was strikingly intelligent, his face long and pale, his forehead remarkably high, his features prominent, his eyes dark and full. His usual look was one of calm placid thought; an expression which was increased in some degree by spectacles, which he wore on account of his shortness of sight. The force and acuteness of his mind were indicated in the occasional brilliancy of the expression of his countenance; the habitual patience and mildness of his disposition, in its permanent look of placidity and repose.

To characterise such a man as Weber is not an easy task, though we may now approach it with more chance of impartiality than amidst the excitement and regret which followed his early death. When " Science' self destroys her favourite son," and a great and good man drops suddenly into the grave from the very earnestness of his pursuit after immortality; dies too—far from his home and friends—in a land " where other voices speak, and other sights surround," our feelings are so mixed up and blended with our judgment, that we are at first inclined to overrate his services, or to exaggerate the range and compass of his ability. Something perhaps analogous took place in the case of Weber. Much vague and unmeaning compliment, much idle declamation, and many false views, would require to be cleared away before the man himself could be seen and appreciated in his simplicity. But Weber is, fortunately, one who, even when deprived of these trappings, retains the dignity and the honours of a great artist; nay, perhaps, like the Sybilline books, he loses little or nothing of his value by their abridgement.

As a composer, amidst the flood of excellence which his works display, we have some difficulty in singling out the quality for which he stood most pre-eminent. We think, however, that he was in no respect more distinguished than for the perfect originality of his style. He imitates no particular master, he is the slave of no particular school, and can scarcely be said to take the cue from any of his predecessors or cotemporaries. He walks in a path decidedly and peculiarly his own; and yet with all this originality, with a style so strongly, so indelibly marked, that it can never be mistaken, he is perhaps less of a mannerist than any composer of his day. The character of his music always varies with the subject. Unlike that of some, it is no Procrustes'-bed, to which all themes whatever are forcibly subjected and fitted in so as to correspond with its precise form and dimensions. On the contrary, his compositions, as they invariably spring from the contemplation of the subject, possess all the beauty and variety incident to it; and when we turn to his laughing chorus, the striking and singular effect of which is produced by the adaptation of the very phenomenon which usually takes place on the vocal organs when the risible faculties are agitated—to the cries of terror and dismay which break from Max when struggling to escape from the demon, and to many other passages of his works, we are impressed with the idea that the object which he had constantly in view was simply to modulate the voice of nature so as to bring it within the laws of musical expression. So completely, indeed, has he followed the course which nature points out, that we may apply to him with the most perfect justice the high eulogium which Pope pronounces on Shakspeare, when he describes him as being " less an imitator than an instrument of nature," and adds " that it is not so just to say of him that he speaks from her as that *she* speaks through *him*."

The consequence of this is, that his works are remarkable for the individuality of their character; and, in this respect, they admit of being favourably contrasted with those of his great rival Rossini. His Freyschutz, his Preciosa, his Oberon, his Euryanthe, are so distinct from each other, we may venture to say that, with a person ignorant of their author, they might pass for the productions of a different artist; but let any one for the first time hear a series of Rossini's operas, and if he did not, without

being informed, very soon find out that the author of Tancredi
wrote the Barber of Seville, we should have no very high opinion
of his musical discrimination.   There are, indeed, many points in
which it would be desirable to institute a comparison between
these two great masters, and there is one in particular which we·
cannot resist alluding to, but which at the same time we do not
feel ourselves at liberty to dilate upon.   We should be sorry to
praise the dead, at the expense of the living; and while we are
quite ready to hold up the pure, spotless, amiable, and *unpre-*
tending character of the one, as a perfect model for the imitation of his professional brethren and of his fellow-men, we
feel that we have no right, and we have certainly no wish, to
assume the ungracious office of censors upon the conduct of the
other.   To contrast his *morale,* or that of almost any man, with
the career of the former, would be putting it to a severe test;
and with regard to Rossini, when we reflect upon the loose and
profligate society in which he passed his earlier years, the vagrant
life which he led, the temptations by which he was surrounded,
and his own ardent temperament, we should be uncharitable
indeed, if we did not regard, with every feeling of indulgence,
errors and irregularities which the matured man has outlived,
and, we trust, atoned for.   If, therefore, we recall to mind
the following little circumstance, we do so simply because we
consider it highly characteristic of the slovenly way in which
operas are got up in Italy, and the sort of judgment which is
there exercised on the part of the composer and the audience.
What we allude to is the well-known incident which happened at
Venice some years ago, upon the production of Rossini's opera
of " Odoardo e Cristina," which went off with prodigious *eclat;*
because, as his biographer tells us, no one in Italy ever thinks
of reading or attending to the "*words*" of an opera; for had
they done so they would have discovered, that what they admired
so excessively consisted of a mere jumble, a piece of patchwork,
which, in point of conception and character, could have had no
earthly relation to the piece, as it had all been most carefully
selected by the *maestro* himself out of two of his own operas
which had shortly before been performed at Naples with great
success.   The fact was, that when the libretto arrived, unhappily for the unfortunate *impressario,* who was nearly ruined in
consequence, the composer was too deeply engaged in the affairs
of the heart to trouble his head with the business of composition.

We need hardly say that a German audience would have been
more critical, and a German composer more scrupulous.   In
regard to Weber, he never wrote without having studied his subject in all its bearings, and deeply imbued his mind with its

spirit and sentiment. In the execution, every thing manifests the utmost care and refinement, the most consummate judgment and propriety; the most admirable congruity pervades the *tout ensemble*, and the result always is, what can scarcely ever be said in regard to any of Rossini's works, one perfect and uniform whole. This unity extends even to the overture, which it most certainly ought to do (although his illustrious rival seems to be so little of that opinion, that he makes use of the self-same overture to preface no fewer than three of his operas); and in this particular we know no composer who has been more felicitous. Whatsoever he has written in this shape is the perfect *beau ideal* of this class of composition. His overtures, particularly his greatest, that of the Freyschutz, contain a sort of miniature representation of the plot and design of the opera: they are like a mirror, in which all its rays are collected into one focus; and thus, they fix the tone and character of the piece in the mind, and form an excellent preparative for what follows.

We see in Rossini a perpetual recurrence to the same series of modulation, and as in *Di piacere* and *Una voce*, he is constantly reproducing the same ideas in different shapes; he is always, in short, revolving and re-revolving within a limited sphere. Doubtless, within that sphere, his pretensions to originality, to a felicity, a light, a brilliancy unequalled, to a genius, which, at the age of twenty-four, had subjected all Europe to its power, are incontestable. But genius, that clear fountain from which all original ideas flow, will sometimes run dry when the soil from which it springs is not occasionally moistened by the dews of study and contemplation. We are convinced that it is only in this way that the faults to which we have alluded—mannerism and an exclusive partiality for a particular style—are to be avoided. "How absurd," says Weber, in one of the letters we have quoted, "to suppose that the mind is cramped by the serious study of means." As well might it be said that a knowledge of mankind contracted our notions, and strengthened our prejudices, as that an intimate familiarity with the works of the great masters, their principles, and their practice, had a tendency to repress the natural expansion of the faculties! It may have occasionally happened that individuals by no means destitute of talent, by losing sight of the ends to which the acquisitions they were engaged in amassing were truly subservient, or from too great a veneration for a particular model, have been led to become followers in a path, where nature, had they obeyed her dictates, had qualified them to take the lead; but in all vigorous and well organised minds, application judiciously directed has always, and will ever, produce an opposite effect, and impart fresh impulse to the creative powers.

ɛ. Such certainly. was the case with Weber. We may consider the production of the Freyschütz as the great land-mark of his fame—the brightest spot in his existence; and when we take a retrospect of his previous career of patient, laborious industry, it would appear. as if till then he. had been proceeding, step by step, to the lofty eminence to which it raised him. He had never previously undertaken a work of equal magnitude. His antecedent operatic productions had been of a much lighter and less elaborate fabric; but, besides these, his detached pieces, consisting, as they chiefly did, of Masses, Symphonies, Cantatas, Concertos and Sonatas for stringed and wind instruments, were of a nature to render him well versed in every species of style, and intimately acquainted with the uses and capabilities of the different instruments. By. these means, in conjunction with the experience he had acquired in dramatic as well as musical effect, he was enabled, when the occasion at last presented itself, to develop his great talents in the fullness. of their maturity, by producing an opera equally remarkable for the beautiful, expressive, and novel character of its melody, and the ingenious and scientific nature of its instrumentation. If we were to assign a reason why we think this opera should place its author only a little lower than Mozart, it would be the inimitable manner in which the charms and expression of the vocal department are heightened and enforced by the happiest and most skilful choice and distribution of all the means and resources which the powers of harmony could call into operation. These are the *chiaro oscuro*, the colouring, the filling up of the picture; and unless they are effected by the hand of a finished aitist, the production is by so much the less perfect; nothing, therefore, can be more clear than that wherever any imperfection exists in the sinfonial parts, it must proportionally detract from the excellence of the whole. The operatic scores of Paisiello and Cimarosa, exquisite as are their melodies, are but meagre and unsatisfactory in comparison with those of Mozart, of Beethoven in his Fidelio, of Weber, nay, even of Mayer, Paer, Weigl, and Winter.

We are now treading upon debateable ground; we have passed the confines of the question which has so long divided the Italian and the German school. But we cannot regard as a matter of doubt, or as any thing short of a violent national prejudice, the opinion of those dogmatists who, for upwards of twenty years after his death, would deny a hearing to the *chef d'œuvres* of Mozart, and who even yet turn a deaf ear to many of his happiest effusions. If the most appropriate, the most varied, and the most effective accompaniments are not to be called in to the aid of the song, and if these are not to be adjusted with that degree of skill, delicacy and judgment which a great symphonist alone possesses, —or if, when thus accomplished, we are to be told that the effect produced is an interruption to the *cantilena*—an unwarrantable encroachment upon its prerogative,—let our orchestra be at once dismissed—a few chords struck upon one of Broadwood's grand-pianofortes, or at most a *septett* of performers, will produce all the body of sound which admits of being tolerated. Accompaniment is the art of enforcing and setting off to the greatest advantage the effect of the principal part, and as such, both in the composition and in the performance, it has always been regarded as perhaps the most arduous and delicate branch of the art. Now, if the objectors to the German school could show, that its most illustrious masters had failed in the execution of this part of their task—that their accompaniments, instead of being subservient, had actually predominated, to the injury of the vocal effect, we should not for a moment hesitate to concur with them. But we have never observed this to be the case, except when they happened to be ill performed, a circumstance of which the Italians had frequent experience on the first introduction of Mozart's music into Italy, and which, we have no doubt, had its influence in rivetting this prejudice. Upon this occasion we are told, that it was remarked, by one of their *cognoscenti*, that the German accompaniments were not "mere guards of honour to the song, but actually *gens d'armes*," a simile which conveys a lively idea of the miserable style in which the orchestra had performed its functions, while it affords a fair enough exemplification of what these judges consider that the art of accompaniment should consist of. "Guards of honour!" by which we are of course to understand, a sort of military *cortege*, whose duty it is to stand sentry for the protection of the song, holding no farther communication with it than by firing an occasional salute—a mere piece of etiquette in short, of about as much importance as the sentry who used nocturnally to mount guard at one side of the proscenium of the opera house, to let us know that we were sitting in the King's theatre.

That the human voice is the most delicious of all instruments none will be hardy enough to deny, nor will any one be surprised to find that where it exists in perfection, it will be cultivated in preference to instruments of an artificial kind. We need not, therefore, wonder that the Italians, gifted by nature with the richest vocal organization, should luxuriate in the delights of melody, in preference to all other species of musical gratification—that they should prefer to listen to their Pacchierottis, their Marchesis, and their Davids, to all the instrumentalists in the world—and that their composers, giving way to the public *penchant*, should, like so many jackalls, exert all their efforts to supply them with the necessary wherewithal to enable them to display their powers, and that, so far from rendering permanent, they would do all in their power to sink a branch of the art which might rival, or occasionally hold a *divisum imperium* along with them. Thus it is, that in this country melody has expanded itself into a rank and excessive luxuriance. The Germans again seem to have steered a middle course. As nature has not been quite so bountiful to them with respect to voice, they have not been seduced to cultivate one branch of the art to the exclusion of the other. With them, accordingly, melody and harmony have grown up like twin sisters, reciprocally to sympathize with and support each other. It is in this relation, we think, they appear most graceful. Melody, as the elder of the two, may be entitled to a certain degree of deference; but we are always sorry when we observe any coldness or reserve existing between them; and herein, we apprehend, the great error of the partizans of the opposite opinion lies—they consider them as strangers to each other, and discourage that mutual affection which is constantly prompting the one to cling to the other.

The point at issue here seems to us to be so very clearly in favour of the German school, that it is quite unnecessary to extend the argument farther. Our only reason for entering on it at all, is, that Weber's proudest distinction seems in great measure to hinge upon it. In this particular, however, we are happy to think that he has one powerful and more than sufficient guarantee—his fate is linked with that of Mozart; and those who are of opinion (and there are few who are not), that Don Giovanni and the Zauberflote are the best models of operatic composition, will not be slow to admit that Der Freyschutz and Oberon follow closely after them. The reputation of that artist is built upon a rock who to the inspiration of the purest melody has superadded all the means and resources of the most accomplished symphonist. If, however, these qualities are, as we suspect, the veritable stamina to ensure length of fame, what are we to say to the earlier works of the greatest of living composers? Are we to conclude that all his delicious arias are doomed to premature oblivion? The magic of genius, we trust, will avert that fate; but that the superstructure would have promised a longer term of endurance if it had been built of less flimsy materials, the author of the *Siege of Corinth* and of *William Tell*, we dare say, would be the first to avow. Except that his accompaniments are more massive, that there is more reduplication of parts, and the work is less minute and *travaillé*, Rossini seems now to have fairly gone over to the German faction, and never regards his operas as complete until he has given the last finishing touch to the orchestral arrangements; and the result has been that his latter works have raised him in the estimation of connoisseurs. But they are not received with half the enthusiasm and delight which ushered in his earlier operas. The days are gone, when, in all the fire and buoyancy of youth, he was wont to transport his hearers into extacy with such strains as " Di tanti palpiti" and " Amor possente nome." Some may think that such scintillations of genius are only to be struck out in the morning of life; but of this we are by no means certain. If we advert, for instance, to the compositions of Haydn, we shall find that the flowing and graceful melody of his latter works is as instinct with beauty and life as any which he produced in the early part of his career. Rossini is yet in the vigour of life, and if his works do not sparkle now as they once did, it can only be because the vein which he has so long excavated, and the ore of which he has expanded until it is reduced to the highest possible state of tenuity, is at last exhausted. Had he adopted the same course which Weber followed—had he, instead of squandering, in the very wantonness of extravagance, the rich patrimony which nature had given him, replenished his stores and refreshed his invention by study and thought, his success might not have been so electrifying, but it would have been more lasting, and at the present moment, instead of finding his resources abated, they would, perhaps, have been inexhaustible; instead of being the *facile princeps* of his own style, leaving so many tracks uncultivated, he might have been the successful rival of almost every great master in his own department; finally, instead of being merely great in his generation, which we fear he is, with posterity, we venture to say, he would be still greater.

If Weber struck out a new path any where, it was in modulation, and in this respect he is eminently distinguished above the imitators of Mozart and Rossini, who are content to pursue the even tenor of their way, availing themselves of the identical route which they had travelled with so much greater advantage, and who have consequently done nothing to extend the boundaries of their art. The melody of Weber is characterized by a total freedom from all restraint. It is bold, striking, and diversified ; so much so, indeed, that he has sometimes been accused of having wandered too far from the beaten track. For ourselves, we think that this is the very quality which throws around his music the inspiring freshness which constitutes its greatest charm. Weber no doubt felt, that, in this age of imitation, we were wearied to death with the monotony of the many, and that it was absolutely necessary that our jaded appetites should be regaled with something a little more piquant and *recherché*. If we look back a few years in the annals of music, we behold the art of melody regulated entirely by the dictates of theorists, who laid down its laws *ex cathedra*, and appointed the course in which it was to run. But the genius of Haydn arose, and taught musicians the great truth, that melody knew no bounds but those which nature had set up, and that the true criterion of accuracy was to be found not in its correspondence with certain factitious systems, but in its effects upon the ear; that music, in short, instead of being, as of old, a prisoner of the schools along with arithmetic and geometry, belonged entirely to the regions of sound, where it merely consisted, as he quaintly expressed it, of the study and apprehension of " what was good, what was better, what was bad." The old moulds of the contra-puntists were now broken, and their system gradually wore out. Composers henceforth wrote in utter defiance of antiquated fashions and prejudices, and the improvements which took place in the art were like those which ensued on the introduction of the modern style of gardening. The parallel and rectangular walks, the interminable avenues, and the formal rows of clipped hedges, vanished; and in lieu of them the face of nature was decked in her most artless and picturesque array. With regard to the melody of Weber, it may be said to be laid out in the most captivating and beautiful variety, at one time resembling a rich and luxuriant garden, at another a tangled wilderness,—now opening to us, in Oberon, glimpses of fairy land, or surrounding us with the associations of the east,—now suddenly recalling us to the darker sources of northern superstition, and

> " Wonders wild of Arabesque combin'd
> With Gothic imagery of darker shade."

Like Salvator, he gloried in delineating the wild and savage aspects of nature, and in wandering, like Beethoven, in her sullen and more gloomy recesses. The romantic turn of his mind, inspired by his early studies, rendered the wild legend of the Freyschutz, perhaps, the most suitable subject on which he could have employed his talents. In depicting, or rather in aggravating the horrors of the wolf's glen, with its fearful omens, and all its unearthly sights and sounds, in painting the grief and despair of his hero and the gloomy demoniacal spirit of the lost and abandoned Casper, he found full scope for his peculiar talent. Were we to compare him with any of our romance writers we would say that he possessed, though mingled with and controlled by a finer taste and far greater discretion, a congeniality of soul with Monk Lewis, or Mrs. Radcliffe; and rich as the dramatic literature of his country is in tales of superstition and diablerie, we think it is to be regretted that he did not, at least, furnish us with another romantic opera from that prolific source. His forte certainly lay in the treatment of this description of subjects.

To have formed a full and complete estimate of Weber's talent as a composer, it would have been necessary to have entered into a minute analysis of his works, but our readers must be aware that to have done so would of itself have exhausted all the space which we have devoted to this article. We have accordingly been obliged to confine ourselves to a brief and general survey of some of those more prominent traits which appear to us in an especial manner to have contributed to his exalted reputation. We rise from the task as much impressed with the sterling worth of his musical compositions as with the excellence of his private character. Both were masculine and nervous, disdaining trick and hating all vulgar appeals to popularity; as an artist and a man, Weber reposed in the consciousness of his own strength and a confidence that in due time his merits would be appreciated by those whose approbation alone he was anxious to obtain. Although a national composer, in so far as he followed up the course in which his compatriots have so nobly set the example, the great success of his productions in other countries, particularly in our own, sufficiently attests their universal character, and leads us to hope, that, like the works of all truly great and inspired genius, they will form the delight of future ages as they have done of this, and obtain a hearing when the more ephemeral productions of the day are forgotten.

ART. V.—*Histoire de l'Art par les Monumens, depuis sa déca- dence au IVe siècle jusqu'à son renouvellement au XVIe*; par J. B. L. Seroux d'Agincourt. Ouvrage enrichi de 325 planches. 6 tomes. folio. Paris. 1823.

IT has sometimes been said, that he who would see self-conceit in its utmost perfection ought to visit the abode of savages; for the savage admires nothing but himself, and atones by the excess for the very limited range which he suffers his admiration to take. Few, however, have the opportunities, the inclination and the qualifications that are necessary for verifying this remark. It is more easy, indeed, to be convinced by actual observation, that the clown esteems only the inhabitants of his own village; that the countryman, who is somewhat less rude, extends his good opinion over the whole of his county; and that the people of towns and cities, being still further advanced in toleration, will applaud any deserving citizen of the state to which they belong. A larger improvement softens national prejudices, and teaches the natives of a country that foreigners may possibly have a just claim to their esteem, as well as their own countrymen; that another people have their peculiar merits; and that in civilized nations the balance, as to good qualities and defects, is nearly equal.   A person who has reached this point has already made considerable progress in liberality; nevertheless much still remains to be learnt; for those who are acquainted with no other age than that in which they live, although they may estimate fairly the pretensions of men remote only in place, will be very apt to undervalue, through the prejudice of ignorance, the merits of other days—to over-rate prodigiously the worth of their own age—and to suppose that whatever it affords of good, great or beautiful, has then appeared for the first time.   They will fondly imagine that they are basking in the fulness of genial light and meridian warmth, and that all who preceded them groped about miserably in an universal and most pitiable darkness.   Men who have enjoyed the greatest blessing which Providence can bestow, the unspeakable advantage of a liberal education, uniformly except two bright spots in the long night of moral and intellectual helplessness from the sweeping sentence of condemnation under which even they include the entire history of their species, the age of Pericles and that of Augustus; or rather they allow, if they have derived a reasonable benefit from the precious instruction they have received, that for several centuries, in Greece and in Rome, the inhabitants of those favoured countries were in a state in some measure resembling the refinement of modern times; and in proportion as their studies have been profound, and as they are familiar with the classical productions of those ages and of their own, are they inclined to set a higher value on the former.   A long period intervenes between the last of the classics and the first of those writers who may properly be termed modern.   With the character and productions of this period of at least a thousand years, few are acquainted; the most liberal and best instructed, the most accomplished and philosophical of scholars, alone can estimate them correctly.

" We often think of, and represent to ourselves," these are the words of a distinguished philosopher, " the middle ages as a blank in the history of the human mind—an empty space between the refinement of antiquity and the illumination of modern times.   We are willing to believe that art and science had entirely perished, that their resurrection, after a thousand years sleep, may appear something more wonderful and sublime.   Here, as in many other of our customary opinions, we are at once false, narrow-sighted and unjust; we give up substance for gaudiness, and sacrifice truth to effect.   The fact is, that the substantial part of the knowledge and civilization of antiquity never was forgotten, and that for many of the best and noblest productions of modern genius, we are entirely obliged to the inventive spirit of the middle ages.   It is upon the whole extremely doubtful whether these periods, which are the most rich in literature, possess the greatest share of moral excellence, or of political happiness. We are well aware that the true and happy age of Roman greatness long preceded that of Roman refinement and Roman authors, and I fear that there is but too much reason to suppose, that in the history of modern nations we may find many examples of the same kind. But even if we should not at all take into our consideration these high and more universal standards of the worth and excellence of ages and nations, and although we should entirely confine our attention to literature and intellectual cultivation alone, we ought still, I imagine, to be very far from viewing the period of the middle ages with the fashionable self-satisfaction and contempt."

" Even in the Christian age," he adds, " the national distinctions of Greeks and Romans were still kept alive; and if the former were remarkable for skill and subtilty, the latter were no less so for practical intellect and soundness of understanding. These qualities of the Roman mind, embodied as they were in that admirable system of laws, which was preserved all over the Roman west among the learned and the clergy, are entitled more than any others to our gratitude. It is to the influence of the Roman jurisprudence, united with the spirit of freedom and natural feeling introduced by those German tribes that conquered and restored the Roman empire, that we must ascribe the successful developement and dignified attitude of modern intellect."

We must postpone for the present the consideration of the literature of the middle ages, and of the assiduous and salutary culture of the civil law, which continually opened new springs of freshness and vigour, and not only maintained in perfection and purity the Latin tongue, and encouraged a diligent study of the choicest and chastest of the Roman classics, but tended powerfully in due time to the revival and encouragement of Greek letters; for he who, being acquainted, however perfectly, with Latin only, would discourse of the civil law, feels and seems, in comparison of one who is armed from head to foot in the panoply of Greek, like a child amongst men. It is of the history of art only during the middle ages that we now undertake to speak, an interesting subject, to the elucidation of which the author of the work before us devoted his whole life. We learn from the short biographical notice prefixed to it, that the ingenious author was born precisely a century ago, in the year 1730, at Beauvais, of an ancient and noble family. The details of his earlier years are not interesting, except perhaps that he had botanized in company with Rousseau, and that he had been entertained at Ferney by Voltaire, who honoured him moreover by addressing an obliging letter to him, which has been published. In his forty-seventh year he visited England, Holland, Belgium and a part of Germany, and returned to Paris, which city he quitted in the following year, 1778, intentionally for a long period, and in fact for ever. He proceeded to Italy, and passed the remainder of his life in that country, residing chiefly at Rome, where he died in the year 1814. During thirty-six years he enjoyed and most diligently availed himself of every opportunity of investigating the remains of antiquity that are found in Italy, and laboured with singular zeal and industry in the composition of his *History of Art.* He had published some numbers, when the Revolution deprived him of the greater part of his property; and the long and cruel wars that were caused by anarchy and despotism, threatened to bury learning for ever under the ruins of the social fabric, and checked still more rudely the cultivation of the fine arts. The publication of the remainder was retarded by various causes, which it is unnecessary to state, and it has but lately been completed. Although the laborious and anxious duties of editors have been well performed by MM. Dufourny, Emeric David, L. Feüillet, Gence and de la Salle, in their respective departments, it would be an ill compliment to the author not to regret that he did not live to superintend the impression of his work; the ingenious editors must have felt that certain further elucidations are sometimes wanting, which no one but the venerable historian himself could supply.

After a preface and a preliminary discourse, according to the practice of the writers of all countries, the author adopts the custom of France, and sets forth at some length a historical sketch of the political and civil state of Greece and Italy, from the first epoch of the decline of art to that of its complete restoration. The twenty-eight chapters, consisting of the history of the world from Constantine to Leo X., would form, as M. d'Agincourt well observes, a separate work; and we confess we wish that he had made the separation in fact which he could in idea. We are well aware, however, that every composition that sees the light at Paris would be born in vain, whatever might be its subject, if it were not preceded by a *Tableau Historique;* and we will not blame the historian of Art for being a Frenchman, and faithfully obeying the law of his country. He has done what we verily believe he thought was quite indispensable, and we must acknowledge, that although most of his readers could repeat the historical facts, " *suivant l'ordre des temps et des lieux,*" he has interspersed so much matter that concerns the proper subject of his valuable work, especially in the notes, that a great deal of curious information may be gleaned by rapidly skimming over the rapid sketch. The body of the work demands a more attentive perusal; the *History of Art* deserves, and will repay, a careful and deliberate examination.

The author treats of a period of twelve centuries, from the fourth to the sixteenth, and, that we may understand his method, it is necessary to consider·the precise meaning of the title he has chosen, " *Histoire de l'Art* PAR *les Monumens;*" he endeavours to give a *History of Art* BY MEANS OF *Works of Art.*   His object is not to compose a history from the testimony of others, but to make his reader an eye-witness of the events, and thereby enable him to form his own conclusions, not from the descriptions of others, but from actual inspection. · It is,' therefore, a demonstration, not in a' mathematical sense exactly, (although in geometry the diagram ·is placed before the student,) but, as it were, a demonstration in anatomy; the organ is laid upon the table, and the lecturer explains its structure and points out the different parts in their order. This method has a two-fold advantage; the demonstrator explains more accurately and plainly when the object is in sight, and the pupil not only understands more clearly, and remembers more tenaciously what he sees, but in doubtful cases he can judge for himself whether he actually sees all that his tutor says may be seen.   So is it with the present work.   Every word was written deliberately when the object of which he wrote was before his eyes.   There is no opening for ignorance or mistake, and it may be read as it was written; the representation is present to us; we have the same means of knowledge as the author had; we may compare him with himself.   It follows, therefore, that reflections composed under such circumstances, by a person of vast experience,·are entitled to great respect; and although we may not always accept his conclusions, it is impossible to slight or neglect his opinions.   The entire number of the plates on which the history is founded amounts to 325: they are divided into three classes, and the history into three parts; 73 belong to Architecture, 48 to Sculpture, and the remaining 204 to Painting.   An entire plate is sometimes occupied by a single subject, but more commonly it comprehends several.   The extent of the work will be understood when it is stated that more than 1400 monuments are represented, and its value, when it is known that more than 700 of these were never engraved before.

, Many of the figures are sufficiently large to be perfectly intelligible; others are so small that it is difficult to comprehend them. It was a natural desire to include as many illustrations as possible, and had they all been of a full size, the price and magnitude of the publication would necessarily have been enormously increased. If we wish sometimes that the style of engraving had always been such as would have done ample justice to the works of the great masters, we must moderate our wishes by remembering that in an extensive collection this is for many reasons impossible.   The numerous plans, sections and elevations of remarkable buildings, although they are often on a small scale, are very interesting.   It is more easy to judge of the general effect of an edifice from these miniatures than of a painting. ; Many curious architectural specimens are brought together within the compass of one plate, which facilitates comparison; but as the size of the plate augments the cost, similar representations might be given in a more economical manner in a work of much smaller dimensions. A collection of ample materials for forming the taste and exercising the judgment would be a valuable manual to a person who sought to enter into an enlarged study of architecture. , The elementary writers on that art generally imagine that they discharge their duty by giving specimens of the five orders from those buildings which are supposed to furnish the most approved models, together with a few details and two or three ancient temples, and with the latter their illustrations terminate. The task of collecting views of so many buildings must have been troublesome and expensive, and would demand a long time and great activity. Of his great care to obtain accurate drawings, M. d'Agincourt thus speaks. After returning thanks by name to many architects from his own country, with whom he had been acquainted whilst they were studying in Italy, he continues :—

" As a recompense for the interest which they had always found me take in their studies during my long residence in Italy, they have always had the kindness, when they discovered in their travels any monuments which they thought would be of use in my undertaking, to make drawings of them for me, or to verify the accuracy of those which I already possessed and had communicated to them. These careful verifications have been the more useful, because the monuments of the period of the decline of the arts, that had been published before my time by other authors, are often very negligently drawn, and it is not with these buildings as with those of a better age, where one part is always like its corresponding part; the irregularity and extravagances of those of which I treat impose upon the artist the necessity of seizing all the details, and upon the historian that of mentioning all their peculiarities."

The History, as we before observed, is divided into three parts. The first part, or Historical Discourse, as it is termed, treats of Architecture, and the subject is again sub-divided into three distinct heads; in the first of which the author, having pourtrayed the condition of the art at the beginning of the period of which he writes, in a short introduction, describes its gradual decline and decay; under the second head he relates the story of its revival, of the second infancy of the art; the third head comprehends the narrative of its complete restoration. The next part is given to Sculpture, which is handled in a manner precisely similar, under the same three-fold division. Painting occupies the last part, and it is divided and explained exactly like the two former arts.

In each part, and in every sub-division of each part, he steadily pursues his favourite method. He narrates the history of art *by means of* works of art. If the principles he lays down are not always derived from a careful induction of particular instances, they are at least always illustrated by examples. He has of course selected such specimens as favour his own views. In order that we may finally be led to just conclusions, we must hope that others of equal zeal and ability will be excited by this illustrious example to publish other selections, that by sedulous and patient comparison we may arrive at the truth, or rather, speaking with that humility which befits mortals, may approximate towards it. If we are hardly permitted to attain to certainty in any department of knowledge, such a consummation is least to be expected in matters of taste, which are proverbially uncertain and indefinite. The third volume consists entirely of an explanation of the plates, in which however much interesting and instructive matter is brought before us.

We think it our duty to point out such defects as have occurred to us, and we feel ourselves bound, in the honest exercise of our critical office, to do so the rather because on many accounts we take considerable interest in the present work; and we are afraid therefore to suffer ourselves, or our readers, to be deceived by our gratitude and respect towards the memory of a most meritorious benefactor of the Fine Arts, of a liberal contributor to one of the most fertile sources of human enjoyment. These defects are of small import, but it is fit nevertheless that they should be pointed out. We have already mentioned that the figures are sometimes too minute; an opposite fault might be found in the inconvenient magnitude of the volumes; and although we will readily concede that a large expanse of paper is often required for the plates, we think the letter-press would have been more accessible in a smaller form. The luxury of typography is doubtless striking, but it interferes with the quiet privacy of attentive study. A new novel, perhaps, would lose its interest, if it were printed with the largest and most beautiful types of M. Didot, upon the scale of an Atlas.

A distinguished anatomist of Germany begins a chapter of a work, in which he describes very scientifically the structure of the human body, with these words:—

' " This important organ"—he speaks of the nose—" occupies a conspicuous position on the human face, of which it is a prominent feature, being situated in most subjects immediately below the forehead, between the eyes and above the mouth."

It is evident that this kind of writing would be very instructive to a person who does not know where his nose is, and who cannot devise a more ready manner of finding it; but others may, per-haps, conveniently postpone it to books treating of matters that are equally true, but less obvious. M. d'Agincourt, in like manner, forgetting that it is necessary to assume that his reader is acquainted with something besides his letters, favours us occasionally with such passages as the following:—

"The productions of the arts of design, architecture, sculpture and painting, consist of objects sensible to the sight, under forms peculiar to each of them, and the effect of which only reaches the understanding through that organ."

This fault is that of the times, and more particularly that of his nation; his countrymen conceive that they are logical, philosophical, and so forth, when they gravely put forth flat, stale, meagre, jejune, stupid truisms; it is the same error as if a host sought to show his extraordinary hospitality by placing before his guests a first course of vacant dishes and empty bottles. Our author, however, rarely offends thus; his table is usually loaded with a profusion of choice viands, and his liquors are excellent and abundant. Nor does he often annoy us by another national vice, which is far more offensive, by a display of frigid sentimentality clothed in the tawdry trappings of false eloquence. We have selected one sample, which, through a filial reverence for our mother-tongue, we forbear to translate.

"Voilà ce que Rome inspire! Eh! que n'inspire-t-elle pas, cette ville toujours éloquente? Quel est celui qui, à l'aspect de ses monumens, ne se sente l'âme profondément émue, ou le génie vivement enflammé? Je les y ai vus, je les y ai entendus, au milieu des ombres de leurs antiques prédécesseurs, ces modernes maitres du monde, ce Joseph II. qui aurait voulu le remplir de son nom, ce Gustave III. digne d'un meilleur sort; ces savans meditatifs, ces poëtes à l'ame brûlante, Herder interrogeant la divinité dans ses temples superbes, Dolomieu expliquant les crises de la nature sur le théâtre même de ses convulsions, Goethe nourrissant sa verve originale des grands souvenirs de l'antiquitè. Recemment encore j'y fus témoin des rêveries touchantes d'un génie ouvert à toutes les grandes impressions philosophiques et religieuses, de Châteaubriand, cherchant un aliment à sa vive imagination au milieu des décombres du palais des Césars, et dans la poussière sacrée des anciennes basiliques."

These bursts of eloquence, however, are of rare occurrence, and the history is usually written with plainness, sobriety, and good sense. We find in it the peculiar defects of a Frenchman, but we find also that ability, which has given a great preponderance throughout Europe to his nation and language.

The instruction and information that are conveyed in an elementary work, must necessarily be somewhat superficial, but they are on that account more valuable to a student; and the writer,

who would embrace a subject of vast extent, must content himself with treating parts of it imperfectly. The notices of works
of art, notwithstanding the quantity of matter comprised in the
huge volumes of M. d'Agincourt, frequently err through brevity.
His observations concerning the arts of Greece would have been
more valuable, had his knowledge of Greek been more profound
than certain inaccuracies we have occasionally observed will allow
us to believe it to have been.

Having spoken according to our promise, with freedom and
candour, of the defects of the work, we proceed to give some
account of each of the three great divisions of the entire subject.
The narrow limits to which we are confined must be our excuse
for the omission of many important topics, and for the scanty and
inadequate consideration that is given to those which we mention.

I. The first part is devoted to ARCHITECTURE, to which all that
remains of the first volume after the prefatory and historical
matter, and seventy-three plates, are assigned.

· We think that M. d'Agincourt has done the most in this department, for although he has effected a great deal for a single
individual in the other two branches, yet so many researches
must still be made, and so much remains to be discovered,
that, without detracting in any degree from the credit that is
justly due to him, we may say that we look forward with confidence, and even with some impatience, for the additions, which
the prosecution of similar investigations by others, will undoubtedly supply. The various structure of edifices of different ages
and countries is explained with remarkable perspicuity and felicity; the view of the subject under consideration is never unnecessarily impeded by a pedantic accumulation of technical terms.
" The terminology of Kant," says one of his countrymen, " is a
barbarism; it is writing philosophy in cypher;" and the censure
might be applied to some amongst ourselves, who have the
barbarism of the German philosopher without his learning.
The Historian of Art, however, is not only exempt from this vice,
but he rarely uses even the recognized terms of art, unless a more
familiar expression, will not fully convey his meaning. Having
exhibited a few specimens of the ancient Architecture in its
utmost perfection, and shown that in that art, as in others, the
more attentively we study the remains of a wise antiquity, the
more shall we be astonished at the good taste and skill that are
displayed; and that to attain to the full comprehension of their
merit the mind must be invigorated by a wholesome discipline;
" *robustæ mentis esse solidam sapientiam sustinere;*" he proceeds
to unfold, by a series of well chosen examples, the architectural
history of the twelve centuries his work embraces. It is not to

be dissembled that the task is arduous: Dr. Moller observes, " As far as it is possible to judge from these plates, which are on a very small scale, and admitting, what however still requires proof, that the delineated buildings are really the original churches erected by the Lombards, &c." the history certainly has this grand difficulty to contend with, (and it is beset by many others,) that amongst the successive reparations, additions, and alterations, it is not easy to assign accurately the date of the existing building, or of any part of it; nevertheless, absolute certainty being unattainable, we ought gratefully to receive such conjectures as a learned experience shall deem probable. As it is impossible to decide the age of a MS., within a few centuries, from the form of the letters, and the other criteria which diplomatists have established, so is it from the style to fix with precision the epoch at which an edifice was erected.

In the history of the Architecture of the middle ages, an honourable place must necessarily be assigned to the Gothic, the most enthusiastic admirers of which have not hesitated to affirm, that the Greeks and Romans were only the precursors who prepared the way for this more glorious style; that the columns of the former and the arches of the latter were the elements out of which, with a large admixture of other and peculiar artifices, this sumptuous manner of building was compounded. They declare that this system has adopted and made a part of itself whatever merits the ancient edifices possessed, and has superadded a prodigious richness, a native grace, and an inexhaustible variety. They assert in praise of a favourite style, perhaps somewhat imprudently, much that we cannot accept and will not repeat; nevertheless, we are by no means inclined to deny its intrinsic excellence, or to undervalue the aids that M. d'Agincourt has contributed towards the investigation of an obscure and difficult subject. It seems that we are not permitted to discover the origin of things, but the vain pursuit is eminently engaging. He remarks that the architectural decorations painted on the walls in Herculaneum and Pompeii, in respect of lightness and in the variety and abundance of fantastic ornaments, have some slight resemblance to the Gothic style: we cannot admit however, that they exhibit any traces of declining art. He might have added, that by an attentive observation of the remains of antiquity we may discover other points of likeness. We find the form of the buttresses and some other resources of this style, to name one instance only, in the ground plan of the baths of Diocletian, as delineated by Desgodetz. He illustrates carefully the gradual substitution of the arch for the entablature, which admitted wider intercolumniation, and, in consequence of the superior strength, of greater lightness, but at the expense of simplicity.

' The pointed arch, which may be termed the specific difference of the Gothic species, of course receives much attention; the earliest specimens he has been able to collect are brought from churches that are either entirely, or in part, underground, being built on the sides of hills. It is possible, but the observation does not occur to this acute critic, that the form was chosen, because it throws off the weight of superincumbent earth or rock, from the centre, and the water also, which perhaps is of more importance; on this account it might deserve to be adopted in our cellars and other subterranean structures, instead of the semicircular arches that are at present used. There is some difference of opinion as to the relative strength of the semicircular and pointed arches, but the weight of authority is decidedly in favour of the latter. The erection of the beautiful Church of St. Sophia, at Constantinople, by Justinian, first proved that a cupola may be raised upon a square base, and furnished many hints of which architects afterwards availed themselves in the construction of Gothic temples. The miracles of Grecian architecture were effected by means of a few very large stones; when the Romans imitated the Greeks they used similar materials, but in their most national, peculiar, and characteristic works, they employed small stones, or more commonly bricks. The Romans possessed an entire and most masterly command over bricks, as many stupendous remains testify. The artists, who adopted or invented the Gothic style, used small stones also, and have left us many specimens of wonderfully solid building. The stones were selected with the utmost care for the more important parts, hard, solid, and free from flaws; they were fitted together with extreme accuracy, and much attention was paid to the composition of the mortar. In consequence of the goodness of the materials and the workmanship, and of the enormous pressure, the pillars and arches frequently ring like a bell when they are struck. On account of the sound, and a certain remarkable elasticity, it is difficult to believe that the vibrating body is not a surface of metal, but merely an assemblage of small and often not very hard stones laid in mortar, like the walls of our houses. This perfection of construction alone proves that we might learn much from ages which we are apt hastily to condemn in the mass as entirely barbarous.

We sometimes try to picture to ourselves the wonder and delight with which the less prejudiced architects of Greece and Rome would inspect the most perfect specimens of the Gothic style that our cathedrals supply: their penetrating minds would doubtless discover the principles of construction, which escape the observation and exceed the comprehension of modern visitors.   The hardness of marble is so great, that we are not surprised to find Gothic buildings executed in that material firm and lasting, but the softer substance, free stone, which is more commonly used, does not seem to promise sufficient strength and consistence to bear the enormous strain and immense pressure, to which it is frequently subjected.   The contrivances for locking the different parts together, and the various resources for giving firmness, unity, and solidity, are curious and almost infinite; and more resemble the endless artifices of nature displayed in the structure of animals, than the limited and monotonous routine of human art.   In all respects, indeed, the Gothic architecture reminds us rather of the unceasing variety and unwearied luxuriance of nature, than of works of art; consequently it is very difficult to classify and arrange the specimens, such is their complexity and delicacy, and so minute the gradation through which the one species melts almost insensibly into the other: it is not impossible however, for, except some trifling imperfections, the nice observation and spirit of order of Linnæus have reduced vegetables to a satisfactory and intelligible system, and a similar classification has been effected in every province of the three great kingdoms of nature.   We may borrow an illustration, and a very commodious system of arrangement, from the science of comparative anatomy : we usually find the same parts in all the animals of the higher ranks; in some a given organ is fully developed, in others it is exaggerated, in others it is barely indicated, being useless and unimportant, whilst in a few it disappears and is altogether wanting.   The beautiful, lofty and most transparent cathedral of *Notre Dame*, at Paris, for example, wants that remarkable member, the central tower, but we see the four massive buttresses, on which it might have been erected; and the transept, although in many respects it seems to assert its dignity, falls very far short of its ordinary and characteristic importance.   Some cathedral, of which the organization is complete in all its parts, ought to be assumed as the standard; as the comparative anatomist takes man as the most perfect animal, and points out in what respects the various tribes deviate in structure,—the form, functions and position of the different organs in the human prototype having been first fully described.   M. d'Agincourt has furnished the means of instituting the comparison, and of commencing this delightful and instructive study.

The propriety of the term *Gothic,* which has long been applied to this style, and is almost universally received, has given occasion to many unimportant discussions.   Some writers have taught, that the Goths and other Germanic tribes were savages, like those who subsist by the chase in North America;, Frederick Schlegel and others maintain, with patriotic zeal, that they have never been in that wild state during any period since we have had accounts of them. M. d'Agincourt is not by any means satisfied with the name Gothic, but he maintains the civility of the Goths, at the time they invaded Italy, with much ability and success; and strives to make gentlemen of the Germans of old so strenuously, that he ought to satisfy even those of their descendants, who are the most punctilious concerning the character and good behaviour of their ancestors. Nor is he less patriotic; for he affirms, that the Norman Architecture is the appellation by which this style is generally known in England, where the introduction of it is attributed to the conquerors : in this respect he is entirely mistaken, for it is universally termed Gothic here, except by a very few persons, who seek to distinguish themselves by the affectation of unusual words, and who would therefore adopt the name Gothic, if it should be ordinarily called Norman. He rejects at once, as utterly unfounded, the title Saracenic, which has sometimes been proposed. It is evident that he is inclined to forge a new designation: when we find such a name as *anti-Greek* or *anti-Roman* offered as a substitute for Gothic, we are disposed piously to return thanks that Adam was not a Frenchman. This ingenious people are singularly unlucky in the difficult and delicate task of naming, and unhappily they imagine that they possess the very rare faculty, and they exercise it licentiously and unsparingly. The name Gothic has been adopted almost universally; in all ages, we fear, a few unhappy persons will be afflicted by that incurable and very disfiguring disease, a mania for innovation; and these passages, " miro opere Gothica manu ;—miro opere per manum Gothicam ;—miro opere constructa ab artificibus Gothicis," which are cited by Gori from ancient chronicles, prove that the style received its present name very early. By selecting specimens well, a *primâ facie* case may be made out in favour of almost any theory that is designed to account for its origin; and by choosing others judiciously it may be successfully answered, and another, wearing equal plausibility, may be substituted. The Germans have not been idle in enriching with paradox and mystery a subject in itself very obscure, especially as they lay claim to the invention of the style. We have been so often captivated by the ingenuity which they have displayed in creating theories, and in the novelty of them, that we have felt ourselves bound in gratitude to make them the only compensation in our power, by supposing that they do not themselves believe one word of what they so confidently assert, and apparently demonstrate with so much solidity.

Whatever doubts may exist as to the origin of the Gothic style, it is impossible to question its prodigious merits. Although we have had the advantage of viewing the remains of other schools, we are deeply penetrated by the merit of that which had the power of raising structures that are able to affect with a sentiment of religious awe, not only the apathy of boorish ignorance, but even that apathy which is the result of long accumulated erudite experience, and of exquisite and recondite learning.

We will cite the words of an imaginative writer respecting this view of the present subject.

" As to that style of Christian architecture which is characterized by its lofty vaults and arches, its pillars, that have the appearance of being formed out of bundles of reeds, its profusion of ornament, its flowers and leaves; and which is in all these respects essentially distinguished from that older Christian architecture, the first and best model of which is to be found in the church of St. Sophia at Constantinople; I am rather of their opinion who conceive that this system of architecture was perfected and diffused over all Europe by a small society of artists, who were very closely connected with each other.

" But whoever might be the builders, this much is certain, that they were not mere heapers together of stones, but they all had thoughts, which they meant to embody in their labours. Let a building be ever so beautiful, if it be destitute of meaning, it cannot belong to the fine arts. The proper display of purpose, the immediate expression of feeling, are indeed denied to this eldest and most sublime of all the arts. It must excite the feelings through the medium of thought; but perhaps the feelings which it does excite are on that account only so much the more powerful. All architecture is symbolical, but none so much so as the Christian architecture of the middle ages. The first and greatest of its objects is to express the elevation of holy thoughts, the loftiness of meditation set free from earth, and proceeding unfettered to the heavens. It is this which stamps itself at once on the spirit of the beholder, however little he may himself be capable of analysing his feelings when he gazes on those far-stretching columns and airy domes. But this is not all; every part of the structure is as symbolical as the whole, and of this we can perceive many traces in all the writings of the times. The altar is directed towards the rising of the sun, and the three great entrances are meant to express the conflux of worshippers from all the regions of the earth. Three towers express the Christian mystery of the triune god-head; the choir rises, like a temple within a temple, with redoubled loftiness; the shape of the cross is in common with the Christian churches even of the earlier times. The round arch was adopted in the earlier Christian architecture, but laid aside on account of the superior gracefulness supposed to result from the crossing of arches. The rose is the essential part of all the ornaments of this architecture; even the shape of the windows, doors, and towers, may be traced to it, as well as the accompanying decorations of flowers and leaves. When we view the whole structure, from the crypt to the choir, it is impossible to resist the idea of earthly death leading only to the fulness, the freedom, and the solemn glories of eternity."

If this passage be somewhat fanciful, it is at least eloquent and ingenious, and it is certainly in the German taste. It is impossible to doubt that the higher works of art, in all countries and in all times, were essentially religious. It is necessary, therefore, in order fully to comprehend them, to seize the spirit of the age in which they were produced. It is not easy at the present day to acquire the feelings that animated the painters of Italy in the time of Leo X., still less to enter into the state of mind of the artists who constructed the marvellous cathedrals of the middle ages; it is impossible to feel as the architect felt who designed the Pantheon at Rome; and perhaps even more so to call back precisely the same sentiments of devotion that inspired him who built the Parthenon, or the author of the Temple of Neptune at Pæstum. To invent like Phidias, the soul must be filled with the same impressions as those out of which he selected and composed his unrivalled works, hence is the attempt hopeless: Time will not stand still, much less can we persuade him to retrace his steps and to return to that point of his journey which we desire to revisit.

The mixture of jest with earnestness is perhaps the most characteristic feature of the literature of the middle ages, and of the manners of the Teutonic races; it is certainly a striking distinction of the Gothic architecture. We commonly find in the details various samples of the ludicrous, the general effect of the whole edifice being serious, and eminently solemn and impressive. Whenever we examine the ornaments closely, we shall find ridiculous scenes and characters, and a number of grotesque representations, reminding us of the tragedies of Shakspeare, which, if they resemble the productions of nature in many other respects, are not less similar to them in this also, that in the great drama of human life we always find joy and sorrow near together, and often almost in contact. The character and expression of these ludicrous representations are very peculiar, and some of them have been copied with great fidelity, (as for instance, those in the cathedral of York by Halfpenny,) but no one has afforded a satisfactory explanation of the object of the comedy. It has been conjectured, with apparent probability, that the figures allude to stories that were well known at the time when they were executed, and that by bringing them together and comparing them with whatever information the writings of the day will afford, the whole subject might be made intelligible. They frequently contain satires on the clergy, especially the monks and nuns; but as the architects were often ecclesiastics, as the building was carried on under their superintendence, and as they were always the paymasters, we cannot suppose the sculptors would incur the hazard of offending their employers and patrons by irritating strokes of ill-judged satire. We may believe, therefore, that these visible railleries were executed with the knowledge and approbation of the clergy, that they had the good humour and liberality to expose and to deride their own infirmities, and that they were convinced their authority was so firmly established that no danger was to be apprehended from the exposure. The most frequent subjects of these ludicrous representations, however, are demons. It was natural enough that the churchmen should hold up to scorn and derision their grand adversaries, the spiritual enemies of the human race; that these beings should be gibbeted on the roof, exposed to the wind, the rain, and the frost, impaled in conspicuous situations, bound captive at convenient posts, distorted into painful attitudes, and jammed and miserably crushed by the enormous pressure of arches and columns; that they should be represented in pain, ugly, and therefore odious, and rendered ridiculous, that they might be despised: all this is in accordance with the dictates of hostility and revenge. There is a certain generosity, however, and a magnanimity not unworthy of the age, (it was an age of chivalry,) in representing their vanquished foes in the only state that could conciliate a kind of sympathy; in the midst of their monstrous ugliness there is a laughing indifference, an air of high, disdainful, unconquerable scorn, that seems to make light of their misfortunes, and was essential to the notion then entertained of the character of demons, that commands respect; for a being that endures calamity bravely awakens a fellow feeling in man, who knows that it is his lot to suffer. The whole of the sacred edifice often swarms with life; besides the jocular designs, serious representations abound everywhere; innumerable niches line the walls both within and without, and each is the shrine of a Christian hero: it seems probable that some fixed plan was observed in the arrangement, that every part was the effect of design, that every image had its story. The veneration bestowed on martyrs was a new and an impressive sentiment; in these ages there was a deep feeling of reverence for the most venerable of all objects before which the human mind can bow down, a man, who has suffered persecution and punishment, even death itself, rather than renounce the faith which he conscientiously holds. He who can contemplate, without interest and emotion, these figures of the victims of human violence and injustice, and of their own noble constancy and courage, which were once the objects of universal homage, is an object truly to be pitied.

The art of designing and executing Gothic edifices has been totally lost; modern structures, although they are the productions of the first architects of the age, who have been sometimes successful in other manners, and have been built with prodigious care and cost, are not only ugly, but they want the distinctive character of the style at which they aim, and are a deformed and mongrel breed, equally removed from that order and every other. Ancient buildings have no doubt been restored very successfully; but these operations have, it must be confessed, commonly penetrated only skin-deep, and have been confined to the renovation of battlements, pinnacles, and ornaments, of which the types also were usually to be found in the same building; the frames and stone work of windows, and other similar matters, which it would be tedious to enumerate; the inspection of the restorations at Westminster and in other churches will explain them more intelligibly than any verbal description. The churches lately erected on the Gothic model have been eminently infelicitous; and if the defects in the halls and castles are less glaring, we have never seen any building of modern date that would entirely satisfy the least fastidious critic, whose taste had been formed by studying the pure and faultless models which the middle ages plentifully supply. The wretched ill-fated objects that testify the total absence of all sense of the Gothic in our builders, have no profile, no projection; they are as unlike the buildings of which they are imitations, the workmanship of better times, as the dry, colourless, shapeless specimen, pressed flat in a *hortus siccus,* is to the living plant.

Many works might be named, in which the principles of Grecian architecture are well explained; but it is not so with the Gothic; it should seem that the present age is ill supplied with men capable of discovering and unfolding principles. We cannot suppose that such wonderful erections as our cathedrals were executed without much reflection and much writing; it is possible, that in the unexplored recesses of the chapter-libraries in some of our cities, not only plans and working drawings of the neighbouring edifice might be found, but treatises mouldering in MS., in which the true principles of construction are distinctly and intelligibly laid down and expounded.

It is probable also, if the best monuments in this style were examined with as much care and accuracy as have lately been bestowed on the Grecian and Roman remains, and by men of ability and education, that the system might be learned, which is doubtless somewhat complex and abstruse; but the effects that are produced, and the difficulties' that are, overcome, prove that it is extremely scientific. Many competent judges have decided, that the Gothic architects must have been better skilled in the rules of construction than any of their predecessors.

.The Gothic architecture of every century has its peculiarities; in like manner that of every country has its points of difference, but the style has much in common in all ages and in all places, and the comparison of the agreement and disagreement is agreeable and instructive. The style of many of the ancient churches of Germany, that are represented by Dr. Moller, is peculiarly tame, ugly, and feeble ; but on the other hand, that country contains many examples of the utmost perfection of the art, several of which are delineated in the work before us. It is a piece of national vanity in M. d'Agincourt, which is pardonable—and moreover a most innocent deceit, for it cannot impose upon any one—to include the stupendous cathedral at Strasburg amongst the French specimens: it is as little the production of Frenchmen as St. Peter's at Rome, St. Peter's at Westminster, or that St. Peter's, which is commonly called the Minster, at York. France comprehends, however, many fine Gothic churches, especially in the north, to which the ingenious author is undeniably entitled, and which he of course represents. He has assembled with exemplary diligence whatever Italy affords that is in any degree connected with this style. He does not give us much information relative to Spain, where the Arabian architects, together with much grace, beauty, and peculiar cheerfulness, have not hesitated to adopt considerable extravagance. For illustrations of the oriental style, and of the Gothic edifices in that country, we must apply therefore to the works of M. de Laborde and Mr. Murphy.* The plans, elevations, sections, and views, which the latter gentleman has published, have already made us acquainted with the chaste and pure composition of the majestic Abbey of Batalha, in the province of Estremadura in Portugal. The present work is most deficient in a department which the English reader can readily supply; he treats scantily and imperfectly of our English cathedrals: it is a proof of the vast extent of the subject, that although so much has been done, so much also has been omitted.

Mr. Cottingham, by a series of rough engravings on stone, has enabled us, as far as the eye can judge for itself, to discover the principles of the florid Gothic, by inspecting the plans, elevations, sections, and details, of King Henry VII's Chapel; but he has not unfolded the doctrines of the artists who executed this

* Laborde, Voyage Pittoresque de l'Espagne, 4 vols. folio, Paris. Murphy's Arabian Antiquities of Spain, 1 vol. folio, London.

remarkable work. The exterior of this highly elaborated building is perhaps less successful in effect, and a less satisfactory result has been produced, than the cost and art of the construction ought to have created; the interior, however, if he were permitted to examine it at his ease, would satisfy the most fastidious critic. Why is it shut up? Why are not the public allowed to enter, and to admire an edifice, on the restoration and reparation of which they have lately, and at a time when they were oppressed by so many and such heavy burthens, expended enormous sums? The guardians have an undoubted right to furnish, at their own cost, as they are well able to do, a careful person to attend constantly and to prevent damage; but so long as the sun is above the horizon they have no right whatever to exclude their fellow-citizens. If the two cathedrals of our metropolis were open to the public, as in reason and justice, and we may add by law also, they ought to be, they would be excellent schools for forming the taste in Roman and Gothic architecture. If the walls of the interior of St. Paul's were painted with lightsome and somewhat gay colours, to overcome, as far as is possible, the darkness, smoke, and fogs; and if something of its ancient ornament were restored to Westminster Abbey, (ample funds are attached to these sacred edifices, a part of which might be thus applied without injury to individuals, and with important benefits to the arts,) immense gratification would be afforded to a very meritorious nation, which, although well provided with the necessaries of life, is certainly not so well supplied with refined enjoyments as it ought to be.

The sense of the beautiful, which is one of the grand distinctions of the human species, may be classed amongst our most valuable possessions; our countrymen have not had fair play; but we are strongly inclined to think, that so far from being deficient in this sense, nature has abundantly gifted them with it, and that culture alone is wanting to lead them to distinction in the arts. Our cathedrals prove that it abounded formerly; and the taste of the English in laying out gardens, and indeed in the whole department of landscape, is peculiarly excellent; that the sentiment of beauty has not been entirely eradicated by the discouragement which it has met with, is of itself a satisfactory proof that it is deeply rooted. Our cathedrals have frequently been restored with judgment and intelligence; but in some instances a venerable pile has been botched in a sordid, illiberal, and ignorant manner. The touching prayer or adjuration of Cardinal Baronius ought to be inscribed in a conspicuous place in every antique edifice. In an ancient church in Rome, dedicated to two martyrs, which the father of ecclesiastical history had repaired, with a profound and dutiful reverence for the original construction, he caused these remarkable words to be engraved, that they might breathe a like respectful spirit into succeeding incumbents :

> Presbiter, Card., successor quisquis fueris,
> Rogo te per gloriam Dei et
> · Per merita horum martyrum,
> Nihil demito, nihil minuito, nec mutato ;
> Restitutam antiquitatem piè servato :
> Sic te Deus Martyrum suorum precibus
> Semper adjuvet.

· We have discoursed somewhat largely of Gothic architecture, because it occupies a considerable portion of M. d'Agincourt's work ; and the illustrations of it, which his industry has furnished, are perhaps the most valuable part of that work : to our countrymen, moreover, this style is eminently interesting, since the only native monuments of art that we can boast, are many most admirable specimens of every kind of Gothic structure. Many plates are devoted to the noble productions which the restorers of architecture placed in that country, where the spirit of art almost forms the character of the nation ; the 56th plate in the department of architecture proves with how much zeal and industry they studied the precious remains of antiquity ; and plates 47, 48, and 49, are alone sufficient to demonstrate their genius, taste, and invention. · The edifices of Michael Angelo claim a considerable portion of the whole work : in contemplating the originals themselves, or the engravings of them, we equally feel, that his greatness of style, when exercised on the interior, caused a large building to appear small ; we will not presume to decide whether that be a merit or a defect : in the inside of a building the eye rather requires beauty than sublimity. St. Peter's, the grand cathedral of the diocese of Rome, receives its due share of attention. Would it not have been better if the close porticos, (or corridors,) which lead to St. Peter's on both sides, had been parallel and at right angles to the front ; at present the ends that are farthest from the building approach;—is not this a deformity? would it not be better, if it were possible, to pull them open, till they were as distant as the two ends that join the church, and to remove therefore the open and round portico so far to the right and left as would be required to admit of this arrangement? what was the motive of the architect for placing them obliquely? was it that the visitor might catch occasional glimpses of the church through the open windows, and does this advantage compensate for the defect, if such in truth it be? This objection occurred to us on the spot, and plate 61 brought it to our recollection; we would gladly see the proposed alteration represented in a large drawing, all other changes being made that symmetry might demand, in order to estimate the effect of it.

Baptism is performed in this country on very young children, and is considered as a matter of course even by the most scrupulously pious ; we are apt to forget therefore the importance of the institution, that it distinguished the Christian from the Pagan, was often preceded by a difficult conversion, and exposed the person who underwent it to many hazards. Having accustomed ourselves to forget the dignity of the initiatory rite, we consequently possess no buildings analogous to those magnificent edifices which, under the name of Baptisteries, are frequent in Italy, —churches dedicated to St. John the Baptist, usually of a circular form ; they will perhaps appear to be disproportionate to the purpose for which they are used, unless we permit our imaginations to go back to the times of the first establishment of Christianity. In most of the principal cities of Italy there is a beautiful baptistery, on which all the decorations of architecture have been profusely lavished ; there only is that sacrament administered, and all the infants who receive it must be brought thither, as a practical admonition, it is said, of the value of the benefit that is conferred. Of these sacred structures M. d'Agincourt has presented some elegant examples.

He has supplied several instances also of that agreeable and useful building, the cloisters,—they abound in Italy ; we have some specimens in England, but not so many as we could desire, and the far greater part of those we have are shut up.

The *History of Architecture* includes several structures of great singularity, two or three of the most remarkable of which we shall mention. Plate 55 exhibits the remains of a theatre, forming part of a monastery at Velletri, near Rome ; it was erected in the fifteenth century. The front of the scene reminds us of the ancient theatres, which it also resembles in being in the open air; it was used for the representation of the sacred dramas, which, under the name of Mysteries and Moralities, were a favourite recreation in the middle ages. Plate 18 shows us a church near Ravenna, now called from its form *S. Maria della Rotonda*, which is commonly supposed to have been the tomb of Theodoric ; the roof consists of one enormous round stone hollowed into a bowl, which being turned down forms a cupola ; the stone is 36 feet in diameter, and about 10 in height ; this monument surpasses the marvels of Egypt, and deserves to be enumerated among the wonders of the world. Plate 23 is very interesting ; it also represents a church at Ravenna, which is remarkable on account of its roof, although on a very different account. The cupola of the beautiful church of St. Vitalis, of which the span appears to be between 50 and

60 feet, is composed entirely of jars of earthenware arranged in
a spiral with much ingenuity; it is not easy to describe in words
the peculiar construction, which combines lightness with strength;
the building is as entire in the present day as it was when the architect had just done his last office to it in the time of Justinian.
Plate 71 supplies many examples of the use of similar vessels in
important erections by the ancients; the advantages to be derived from this application of pottery seem to be obvious, and the
practice deserves attention; indeed, M. d'Agincourt informs us
that several French architects had lately employed it with success.
The tax levied on bricks in England, and the numerous and
inconvenient regulations by which it is secured, are formidable,
perhaps insuperable, impediments to the attainment of excellence
in the manufacture and application of these materials, and would
probably be obstacles to the revival of this usage of antiquity.

At the conclusion of the portion devoted to architecture we
find a curious table, which the author has composed, indicating
the number of churches that were built at Rome from the commencement of the Christian era to his own time; the total comprehends 303; the sixteenth century is the richest, for it boasts
93; the tenth century has 1 only, and is the poorest, except the
first century, which presents a dreary blank; to the second, 2
are assigned; to the eighteenth, 7; it is a curious speculation
how many the nineteenth will add to the list. A work containing
engravings of all of them, and a short account of the authorities for
ascribing to each its date, would be in itself a most interesting
history of architecture from its monuments. We lament that M.
d'Agincourt has not given us even the names of the several churches,
and that we are often compelled thereby to guess at his meaning;
we presume that he assigns an earlier date than the vulgar era to
the finest of them all, the Pantheon, as he has not ascribed a single church to the first century.

II. We quit with reluctance the department of Architecture,
which has detained us longer than we had intended, and proceed to
the second part of the History, which treats of SCULPTURE, under
the usual threefold division. The treatise on Sculpture is the shortest and the least valuable portion of the work, and seems to be
that department of art with which the author was least familiar;
he meekly bows his head before the great Winckelmann, and acknowledges that he is unable to add any thing to that distinguished critic's illustrations of the majesty of antiquity. The
investigations of M. d'Agincourt as to its condition in the middle ages have been less extensive or less successful than with respect to architecture and painting, and the graphic illustrations of
them are confined to forty-eight plates. Eight of these present

an accurate and faithful representation of the great bronze doors of the church of St. Paul without the walls of Rome, which were cast at Constantinople in the time of William the Conqueror; they are covered with sacred subjects and inscriptions, inlaid with silver; a laborious and costly operation, but there is nothing of Byzantine superiority in the workmanship. It is probable, that they would have been executed nearly as well in London in those days. The figures are hardly, if at all, superior to those of the famous piece of needlework, in which Matilda, the Conqueror's queen, embroidered the fortunes of her husband. We cannot doubt, however, that the best artists of the East must have been superior to those of the West at that period; it is the good critic, however, who insures the excellence of the artist, and we may suppose, that as Hildebrand was no great judge of art, the Byzantines contrived to cheat the Pope. The least honourable trait of the religion of the venerable Greek church was its frequent addiction to the extravagances of the Iconoclasts, which has no doubt thinned the monuments of sculpture: the Byzantines, however, are not responsible for the sweeping destruction of statues that was perpetrated in their city, A.D. 1204; the avarice of their barbarous Latin conquerors, and not domestic superstition, anticipated the brutal ravages of the Turks.

M. D'Agincourt has deduced some information and many examples of the sculpture of the middle ages, from the *diptychs*, of which several are preserved in various museums; the posthumous work of the learned Gori, entitled " *Thesaurus Veterum Diptychorum,*" however, had already exhausted the subject. A diptych, (that we may not enter into a vast mass of erudition, by which the matter has been illustrated, or obscured,) is a little book, or small tablets of box or other wood, or of ivory, which at first consuls, on being elected, used to present to men of rank and to their private friends, afterwards other civil magistrates, and in process of time ecclesiastical also, containing the names of the magistrates for the year and similar memoranda, embellished with carving, painting, and gilding, according to the magnificence of the giver, or the rank of the receiver. This custom has perhaps been retained and is still continued by sending at the close of the year a pocket-book as a present, which often contains an almanack for the following year. This couplet is the poesy inscribed in one that was presented by a consul to the senate :—

τουτὶ τὸ δῶρον τῇ σοφῇ γερουσίᾳ
ὕπατος ὑπάρχων προσφέρω Φιλόξενος.

The diptych represents the consul on horseback, or clothed in his robes of state, and seated in his curule chair—or it shows the different games of the circus, or types, symbols, and allegorical figures; sometimes it is anonymous, and contains nothing but carving; no letters, not even the name of the consul : occasionally it is not only ornamented within and without, but enclosed in a splendid case. When Christianity became the prevailing religion, bishops took the place of consuls, and we see Christian symbols and heroes, prophets, apostles, saints, and martyrs, but chiefly and especially our Lady; or scenes taken from the Scriptures, or the Lives of the Saints : a pious aspiration was sometimes added, as, " *Sancte Laurenti, propitius esto mihi miserrimo peccatori!*" which is inscribed under a figure of St. Laurence. The death, or the falling asleep, as it is respectfully termed, ἡ κοίμησις τῆς Θεοτόκου, is a favourite subject, those words being written above. In later times, and in a few instances, hunting, hawking, masques, tilting, and other sports were introduced. When it was composed of three pieces, or tablets, it was called a *triptych.* The diptych, or triptych, was often placed upon the altar, and it is the origin of the altarpiece, as well as of the pocket-book, two very different inventions being derived from the same source. An altarpiece, with its two wings, two smaller paintings, turning upon hinges and shut to defend the picture from dust, from the sun and from other injuries, but not locked or fastened, (as the hand that has opened many in silent and solitary churches, and with grateful piety, when the painting was examined, has closed them again, thankfully testifies,) so that a liberal curiosity may be gratified at all times, often boasts the work of a great master, and on a larger scale retains the precise form of the ancient triptych.

· M. D'Agincourt has drawn some specimens of sculpture from sepulchral monuments, but his field of observation, it should seem, was not very extensive; they are, for the most part, taken from Rome, where, as he remarks, ancient bas-reliefs were often pressed into the service, and after some slight alterations, compelled to form part of a more modern tomb. In the sepulchral effigies of the middle ages we often observe a great inequality; extreme stiffness, a want of symmetry, figures disproportionately tall, especially those in drapery; yet notwithstanding these and other defects, the same work will sometimes exhibit much merit, pathos, and truth of expression. The faces commonly seem to be taken from casts made after death; in a statue that was to be placed in any other situation than a church or a cemetery, this melancholy condition of the countenance would be intolerable; there perhaps, a literal copy of the deceased, as he appeared when last seen by his friends, when he was dearest and most observed, may be touching and appropriate, and being seen seldom, and for a short time, the spectacle is not too distressing. Monumental statues often show that the artist had no model of the whole figure, but only of the face and some other parts; they resemble therefore the trunk of a tree carved into the human shape, but still retaining traces of what it originally was. The dresses are often much laboured; it would be easy to obtain the forms of the apparel of the times from monuments, and to learn the entire costume: the fashion of the hair and beard of Edward the Third, in the chapel of St. Edward, in Westminster Abbey, is not unworthy of a Greek patriarch. The monumental sculpture of France is usually superior to that of England, but the latter is sometimes not without merit; the oldest are not unfrequently the best, (although these are comparatively modern,) as the effigy in Gloucester cathedral, which is said to represent Robert Duke of Normandy.

Engraved gems, however beautiful the execution, are less interesting than larger works, for being designed, not for the gratification of the public, but for the use of individuals, there is something private, exclusive, solitary, and selfish in this application of the art of the sculptor; few examples of the display of exquisite talent, within a narrow circle, have been given in the present work.

III. The third and last portion of the *History of Art* is dedicated to PAINTING. To this subject the largest number of plates has been dedicated; they amount to 204, and are illustrated with many valuable and curious descriptions: we lament that we are unable to enter more fully into the examination of the very various matters to which the ingenious author directs our attention. Many of the observations at the commencement of his discourse would serve as a valuable and favourable commentary upon such parts of the Natural History of Pliny as relate to the painters of Greece. He opens his practical illustrations by producing some specimens of the ancient paintings that have been recovered at Herculaneum and Pompeii, the inspection of which will suggest many reflections. Figure 9, in plate 1, is an instance of the modern and most approved practice of grouping the figures in a pyramid; the painters of antiquity commonly arranged them in a row, as in bas-reliefs. We have not seen any thing in the pictures of the ancients, that have hitherto been discovered, to prove that they were acquainted with the famous *di sotto in su*, (as from that favourite kind of it, where the figure is seen from below, the marvellous foreshortening of the Italian school is called); great as their merits are, they may be even superior, in other respects. We will not speak at present of the prodigious spirit and infinite skill in drawing that appear in these ancient designs, on which qualities, and not on the materials that are employed, excellence depends; nor will we refer to the paintings in the tomb of the family of Naso, or to the other works of antiquity from which examples have been selected. The remarks of M. D'Agincourt, as to the importance of correct drawing, a part of the art of the painter, which unfortunately is often neglected, and especially by his countrymen, are well worthy of the attention of artists and of critics; we will therefore transcribe them.

" O you young artists, to whom Nature has assigned what you call talent; and you, still more fortunate, whom her beneficence has endowed with a poetic imagination, and a feeling heart, allow me to repeat to you this advice—study daily, study incessantly, that fundamental part of your labours, drawing; give yourselves up to this study even to the end of your days. I find at Rome a hundred proofs, in tradition and in monuments, that attest that my immortal countryman, Nicolas Poussin, made drawings, both after nature and the antique, to his very last moments—a painful labour, which is rarely that of a head radiant with glory and covered with hoary locks."

The singular comic or satirical scene delineated in plate 3 deserves notice, because it has never been published before. The fragments were found in the year 1787, in an antique subterranean chamber, situate beneath the beautiful gardens of the Villa Pamphili, that was accidentally discovered in consequence of the falling in of the earth.

We hasten to a topic, which has taken strong hold of the imagination of M. D'Agincourt, and to which he attributes a vast importance: it has drawn forth much learned illustration in other countries, but has hitherto received little attention in England. Protestants have been excluded, perhaps with too much jealousy, from the consideration of certain Christian antiquities, because they have been eagerly pursued at Rome; but as the political impediments to our advancement in the fine arts have happily been removed of late, we may with the less hesitation advert to a source, whence the illustrious author would derive large and valuable assistance. We mean the Catacombs at Rome. It is well known that these are numerous, being situated in different parts of the city, and are of vast and unknown extent. In these catacombs, sepulchral chambers and chapels have been excavated, the roof and walls of which are frequently adorned with paintings; from these works M. D'Agincourt proposes to deduce the history of the art for several centuries. With an ardent zeal, with indefatigable industry, and at considerable expense, he explored these mysterious recesses during several years and at various periods, nor was the enterprize always free from danger, as the following passage proves:—

" A great number of inscriptions enrich the staircase of the church of

St. Agnes without the walls: they have been brought from the cata-combs, which extend a great way in the valley around this basilica, and they join others that are very famous, and of which the branches reach as far as the river on the Salarian way. These catacombs had long been closed; I had them opened some years ago in the hopes of finding monuments. My undertaking was unsuccessful, and it exposed me to considerable peril. My guides, who did not know all the turnings in these caverns, were lost, as well as myself, for more than an hour. We had some difficulty in keeping our feeble light and were all very near ending our lives there. The same accident happened before to an artist, my old friend, M. Robert; and my draughtsman, Macchiavelli, when he was alone, was once exposed to the like danger. Montfaucon in his *Diarium Italicum* relates, that a similar accident happened to another Frenchman *and himself.* We got out of this catacomb at last, through one of the openings which served for the purpose of letting down the dead bodies in the first ages of Christianity. This opening is in the mid-dle of the ruins of a monastery, which, if it be not of the same epoch as the churches of St. Agnes and St. Constantia, is not of a much later date."

We have extracted the passage to which our author refers, which relates to the catacombs near the Church of St. Sebastian. Montfaucon (ὁ πάνυ,) says,

"Narrant enim quempiam nobilem, qui cum familia incautè in hæc sese loca conjecerat, nunquam postea comparuisse. Incidi haud ita pridem in schedas cujusdam peregrini Galli, *qui emunctæ naris homo videbatur,* narrabatque se sociosque paucos cum in hos sese obscuros tramites immi-sissent, horis plus quinque ultro citroque oberrâsse, nec sine discrimine nunquam evadendi, nisi in operas incidissent quæ corpora eruebant."— p. 154.

It appears that Dom Bernard was not a partner in the danger, as M. d'Agincourt has erroneously stated, and as in truth it seemed to be altogether incredible to us; nor did he share in the perilous expedition of his countryman, whose sagacity he praises; the learned Benedictines took too much care of themselves to place unnecessarily a member of the congregation of St. Maur in such jeopardy. If our space would permit us, we would gladly extract all that M. d'Agincourt says on this subject, that, on a matter in which he is so deeply interested, he might have the ad-vantage of speaking for himself; but his observations are long, and are moreover scattered throughout different parts of his work. The following account of one of his researches gives an interest-ing picture of the last faint traces of humanity which a long and slow decay had left.

"The receptacles were hollowed out for one or more bodies. In that which I opened on the 12th of May, 1780, I found two, the head of one body touched the feet of the other. This position, as well as a slight difference, which I thought I observed in the structure, induced me to believe that these two persons had been a man and a woman.

I could only distinguish, as to the form, some vestiges of the principal bones. The extremities were nothing more than an almost insensible dust; what was left of the bones turned, when touched, into a moist yellow paste of a reddish hue. It would be difficult to form an exact idea of the remains of a human body, reduced to a condition so near to absolute annihilation. A little whitish dust marked the place where the head had been, and showed the bones of the shoulder, of the thigh, the knees, and the ankles; vestiges of this dust still traced, with broken lines, the direction of some of the bones; but it was not a body, it was not a skeleton that we saw, they were vestiges hardly to be distinguished, and at the lightest breath the whole disappeared. The two bodies that I saw in this state had been buried for fourteen or fifteen centuries. That of the woman, or at least that which I took for such, was the least destroyed."

The next passage will prove that the ingenious author was considerably excited by these unusual and mysterious investigations.

"After these testimonies of veneration from men who have themselves merited divine honours, after the affecting descriptions which they have given of the Catacombs, ought I to risk the expression of the sentiments which I have so often felt, whilst wandering through these celebrated places in search of the *monuments* my work required, and sometimes remaining alone, far from my guides, under these dark vaults, where no plant, no bird, no animal, presents the image of life, I found myself seated amongst so many tombs constructed above my head, or hollowed out beneath my feet, or when I traced by the light of a torch those winding passages which presented themselves on all sides to my astonished eye. A vague anxiety at first seized me; my fancy was overwhelmed by the multitude of ideas which religion, history, philosophy offered to me at once; the deep silence that surrounded me gradually restored the calm of my spirits; an agreeable reverie took possession of me, and I enjoyed a repose almost like that of the millions of dead who have slept in these cemeteries for fifteen hundred years. And I also, I said, will sleep here one day with you; but before my dust is laid here, I desire to honour your manes by the brilliant recollections that are attached to the history of the arts, of the arts that have often been indebted for their cultivation and their success to the homage which the faithful have paid to your holy victories."

It is evident that he attaches the reputation of his great work in a peculiar manner to this part of the subject. M. d'Agincourt has given us a portrait of a Roman sexton, or rather to speak the truth, of an anti-sexton, plate 12, fig. 2, and the remark he makes upon the countenance of this old resurrection-man proves how much his visits to the catacombs had exalted his fancy.

"This man, Pietro Luzi, was for more than forty years the guide of the excavators of the Catacombs, and consented to be mine for four or five years in the labyrinth of these astonishing subterraneous caverns.

The peace of his soul imprinted on his countenance, appeared to me to be the sign of the recompense awarded to his long labours in the mansion of eternal happiness."

It is not to be denied that the aspect of Peter Luzi is cheerful and contented, but there are temporal causes that are perhaps sufficient in themselves to account for " *la paix de son âme empreinte dans ses traits:*" there is a society consisting of twenty-four persons, who are entitled " *Cavatori delle Catacombe,*" whose only business is to explore the catacombs when required, and to search for the remains of martyrs. Their duty is very light, and by a whimsical appropriation of a part of the revenue of the Holy See, the fees that are received for dispensations to marry within the prohibited degrees, and for other matrimonial indulgences, are set apart for their maintenance; out of this fund they receive a competent salary, together with their sacristan and the keeper of the catacombs, " *Custode delle Catacombe,*" and a prelate, who is of course well paid for yielding auspices. Peter is a distinguished member of this fraternity, and during a long life has known no other care than the trouble of receiving his stipend and of being in attendance as a spiritual butler, to produce from the proper bin in his vast cellars whatever relics His Holiness may think proper to order.

After patiently inspecting not only the plates which M. d'Agincourt has given us, but those which are well and faithfully engraved in the enormous and most erudite folio of Bosio, and in several other ponderous works, which it is unnecessary to name, and after carefully examining some of the originals at Rome, we must confess that we think the importance of these works in the History of Art has been greatly over-rated: the subjects are few in number, and they are treated vulgarly and unskilfully. The raising of Lazarus is often repeated, he is always represented as a babe in swaddling clothes. We see Moses striking the rock and two children drinking the water that issues; Noah standing in a small tub to denote the ark, whilst the dove flies towards him with the olive branch in her mouth: Jonah swallowed by the whale, and afterwards thrown up again, is a favourite incident, and the throat of the monster is remarkably narrow, as it were to make the miracle greater. We ought not to judge of the state of painting in England at the commencement of the 19th century, of the portraits of Sir Thomas Lawrence and the landscapes of our best artists, from the cuts that adorn the farthing, or even the half-penny editions of the *Death of Cock Robin,* or to estimate the merits of Chantry and the present condition of sculpture from the cherubs' heads garnished with gilded marrow-bones that enliven our country church-yards. Besides, the early Christians were poor and obscure persons; if we were satisfied as to the authenticity of the works of art that are connected with them, it would still be unfair to measure the ornaments of the wealthy and powerful Pagans by that scale.

It is impossible for any one, who is even moderately sceptical, to be satisfied of the genuineness of works of art that are described in the writings of men of great learning, like Marangoni, but unhappily of great credulity also.   When we meet with such a relic as that of which he tells in the 39th chapter of his *" Istoria dell' Antichissimo Oratorio o Capella di S. Lorenzo commune-mente appellato Sancta Sanctorum,"* 4to. *Roma,* 1747, we must acknowledge that the odour of sanctity is too powerful for us; to borrow his own words—"nell' atto di aprire la cassettina, tosto ne uscì da essa un odore così veemente, che quantunque soave, non potea, per la sua veemenza, soffrìrsi:" there is no chapter in the entire history of the phenomena of the human mind which we ever read with a stronger and more indescribable feeling than this.   The Catacombs at Rome were originally quarries, from which various minerals were extracted; there is no doubt that they are very extensive and of great antiquity.   Little labour or art was required to give them the forms of tombs or chapels; the paintings are not very numerous, and, as we before observed, they are rude and inartificial; a few subjects, perhaps twenty or thirty in all, are constantly repeated, and are treated in nearly the same way, but never with moderate ability.   These caverns were commonly connected with churches and monasteries, and were used as cemeteries, for which purpose they are well adapted, and as they usually had other entrances, and the galleries often led to a great distance, we may imagine that they were useful to the monks, as they could go in and out of their convents without being observed. Persons who are acquainted with the passages would be able to find their way even in the dark, whilst strangers would be afraid to venture into the unknown labyrinth, the dangers of which the religious, for obvious reasons, would be disposed to magnify, and superstitious terrors would be added to the real hazards.   They would be safe retreats in troublesome times, and convenient hiding places for property that was liable to be seized by lawless plunderers.   Since there were so many motives to induce the monks to retain possession of them, in addition to the reputation for sanctity which the habit of frequenting such gloomy places would give them with the common people, it is probable that they bestowed upon their walls and roofs many of the barbarous decorations that are still seen there.   We must remember, that a thousand years are a long time, and that during that period swarms of monks had abundance of leisure; consequently it is quite impossible not to regard these compositions with considerable distrust. It is a hasty inference, that the tenant of every tomb in which an empty bottle or other vessel was found was a martyr, and that it was once filled with the blood of the victim, for we know that vessels were placed in tombs in more ancient times, and long before the great cause in which they were supposed to have been suffering witnesses was ripe for trial. Legends of martyrdoms and the exhibition of relics may be of sovereign potency in kindling anew the zeal of the people when it begins to wax cool, but it is not necessary on that account to impose upon the learned in matters that respect only the history of the fine arts. We must also be permitted to doubt, whether the forms of churches were ever derived from the chapels in the Catacombs, or whether the latter are as ancient as they are commonly supposed to be; it is not certain that they were made in times when the Christians, on account of the predominance of the Pagans, were afraid to build churches above ground, for in a superstitious age the supposed advantages of being near the dead, amongst skulls and mouldering bones, in dark and gloomy recesses, would induce men to make subterranean oratories. We find, indeed, crypts and calvaries that were constructed in times and countries when the Pagans were extinguished, and when the true faith was universal. It was usual formerly, and the custom still prevails, to offer prayers and to perform services for the dead, which rites could be performed more efficiently in the opinion of many in the immediate vicinity of their resting-places, and the dismal scenes would well accord with the sentiments and impressions that would be deemed suitable to such offices. Many epitaphs have been transcribed from the Catacombs; like the numerous specimens of this species of composition, which have descended from early times by other channels, they are chiefly remarkable for an extreme simplicity, as " Victoria dormit"—" Porcella hic dormit in pace;" sometimes this simplicity is touching, as Χᾶιρε Τύχη, ψυχή καλὴ, Τύχη θυγάτηρ. In the following the epitaph *fortissima* seems strange, unless we suppose it to be adequate to our familiar phrase, " a brave girl;" " Faustinæ, virgini fortissimæ, que vixit annos XXI.;" this most resolute virgin died early, the resolution of many lasts much longer.

A sane criticism will teach us to view with suspicion specimens of the arts extracted from the Catacombs at Rome; the specimens, however, are not uninteresting in themselves, and we refer our readers to them, in order that every one may judge for himself. It may sometimes be perilous to estimate the age of Christian antiquities by the style, for it is easy to confound the stiffness of affected sanctity with the stiffness that arises from the imperfection of art. M. d'Agincourt, however, investigated the Catacombs so completely and with so much diligence and activity, whilst we were able to explore them ourselves in so very limited and unsatisfactory a manner, that it is with extreme diffidence we have ventured to express our opinions on this part of the subject, especially whenever we have been compelled to dissent from his views, and we freely offer them to be corrected by those men of learning who have enjoyed opportunities of forming a larger experience.

It has been conjectured with some probability, that during certain periods in the middle ages an orthodoxy was established, not merely in doctrines, but in art; that it was esteemed heretical and criminal to represent any subjects, except those that were constantly repeated, or to treat them in a new manner, or in positions or arrangements different from those in which they were usually shown; that "*une liturgie pittoresque*" had been sanctioned by custom, and that the pious *virtuosi* of the day commended a painter, not because he was a skilful master, but because he was orthodox : this theory would account for the insipid sameness of the ecclesiastical sculptures and paintings. The same pernicious conformity, however, was not strictly enforced in architecture; so that the necessary and indispensable parts were duly placed in cathedrals, the artist was permitted to indulge his genius; we accordingly find great variety in these edifices, perhaps we may add that fanciful invention seems to luxuriate, and to take holiday as it were, in compensation for the grievous restraints that were imposed on the other branches of art. For several centuries the eldest sister appropriated to herself the portions of the other two, and profusely squandered the property of the family in fantastic and ostentatious, but tasteful, magnificence.

After the decline of painting in the west, the art still maintained a considerable superiority at Constantinople, and was preserved by Greeks, who resided in places that communicated with the capital. We read that a school of Greek painters always subsisted in the city of Otranto, which a channel about forty miles across separates from Greece. M. d'Agincourt has furnished many examples of the productions of Greeks, and of their Italian disciples. The adoption of the monstrous errors of the Iconoclasts is the greatest stain upon the character of a reverend church, to which the learned and pious willingly acknowledge many important obligations. The Greek worship was on the whole favourable to painting. We have seen some Greek pictures of the Panagia full of sentiment; the Virgin is hard-featured, ugly and somewhat old, but as the artist often sought to compose a *Ma-*

donna di San Luca, a portrait of our Lady painted by St. Luke, or at least such a one as he would have painted, and according to the tradition the Virgin was fifty years old, when her likeness was taken by the Evangelist, who was a painter by profession, as well as a physician, it was necessary to represent a female of that age and not a young mother, as in pictures that do not affect extraordinary sanctity and authenticity. The original portrait is commonly plain, but there is a remarkably touching expression in the countenance; the copy aggravates the plainness into ugliness, and the expression is altogether omitted, especially if it be taken by a French artist, upon whom all sentiment is inevitably lost, save the airs of a coquet and the affected simpering of a shepherdess of the opera house. It is not to be denied, however, that many of the old Greek pictures are black, ugly and unmeaning. Nothing can be more frightful, for example, than the engraving of the Virgin and Child in plate 87: it may be a faithful imitation, or the original may possibly have some merits that have escaped the observation of the engraver. We have observed and admired in the works of the oldest masters—"nos in antiquis tabulis illo ipso horrido obsoletoque teneamur"—a stronger and a more affecting expression of sentiment than in the compositions of their successors, in the productions of Pietro Perugino than in those of his disciple Raphael, and when we have examined the originals of the elder painters, and especially of the Greeks of the middle ages, we have been sometimes penetrated by this mute eloquence. But, unfortunately, it is precisely this quality which is the most fugitive and the most difficult to be transferred: through want of skill in the engraver or in the person who made the drawing from the original, it will entirely evaporate, and to render it with fidelity consummate ability is required. When an artist of superior merit copies one of the most ancient pictures of the middle ages, the defects, the stiffness and the other peculiarities forcibly strike his eye, and by rendering them faithfully, or rather by augmenting them a little, a coarse imitation is produced that satisfies the vulgar by its obvious resemblance, whilst through a want of faith in their existence, he is rendered insensible to the refined excellencies which can only be perceived by an intelligent and unprejudiced spectator. We are perhaps less dissatisfied with the old traditional mode of representing religious subjects than with certain modern variations. The attempts of Raphael and other artists in an age of refinement to adapt oriental scenes to the critical and fastidious taste of the west were unsuccessful; if it be necessary to innovate, the extravagancies of Michael Angelo, which at once boldly bid defiance to reason and probability, are more tolerable.

The same observations will apply to the numerous plates which have been deduced from another and a very copious source, for the purpose of illustrating the History of the art of Painting by monuments of art. We refer to the miniatures, the illuminations, Dante would probably call them *alluminations;*

—————— Arte
Ch' alluminare è chiamata in Parisi,

which M. d'Agincourt has extracted with indefatigable industry from Greek and Latin MSS. of the middle ages. His specimens have been principally derived from the unknown treasures of the Vatican Library; with his accustomed courtesy and piety he apologizes for the want of a catalogue of that collection; we will extract his lame and impotent excuse in his own words.

" Still less would I venture to celebrate the riches of the Vatican Library in the department of ecclesiastical manuscripts. It is in that respect, for Christianity, what the Greeks called *panoplia*, a *sacred arsenal*. The key of this depository, an object of reverence, may be ranked among those which the Vicar of Jesus Christ, the guardian of the true faith, holds in his hand. It is doubtless to the respect to which it is entitled, and not to any timid jealousy, that we must attribute the want of a catalogue of this prodigious collection."

The Protestants have affirmed less charitably that the real motive is the unwillingness of the guardian of the true faith to set any limits to the unbounded exercise of forgery and falsification. It is certain that no sovereigns have done so much for the fine arts and for literature as the Popes; gratitude forbids us, therefore, to inquire too narrowly whether new arms may not have been occasionally forged in the sacred arsenal upon an emergency, but we may lament that pious laziness denies to the anxious desires of the learned a complete catalogue of the library of the Vatican.

So many curious topics are connected with these illuminations, many of which were never before published, that many observations suggest themselves to us, but we must produce those only which can be most shortly expressed, not those which appear to be the most important. They are as numerous as the stars, and in the language of the unpublished verse which he has produced the author has made his book as various as another sky;

ὡς ἄλλον ὄντως οὐρανὸν τεύξας βίβλον.

Some works have been too much neglected, others, on the contrary, disproportionately admired; as for example the Vatican Virgil, in which every thing is represented meanly: Dido, for instance, burns herself in plate 24, fig. 2, not on a lofty pile, but like a good housewife, in the most economical manner, by placing about sixpennyworth of wood under her bed. Yet it is not altogether to be despised; we see the dresses, implements, utensils, &c. that were used in Italy in the fourth and fifth centuries: the simple loom with which Circe is weaving in the back-ground, pl. 25, fig. 1, is curious. In a more modern MS. of the same poem, the soldier, who is sitting and keeping off the rain by placing his shield above his head, whilst Dido and Æneas are snugly sheltered in the cave, plate 64, may perhaps claim the invention of the umbrella. The art of botanical drawing has been much improved, since the specimens given in plate 26 were executed. A biblical scene, inscribed βουνὸς τῶν ἀκροβυστιῶν, is represented with more truth than delicacy in plate 29, fig. 3, and a similar subject is rather whimsical than refined, as shown in a mosaic, plate 18, fig. 5. By reversing the painting, the marriage of the Virgin, plate 137, has been made literally a left-handed marriage. Nothing could have helped the transfiguration of St. Francis, for a saint traversing the air in a flying wheelbarrow, with the wheel on fire, cannot but be ridiculous. Plate 119 was taken from a good fresco, which was soon afterwards destroyed by white-washing, as many others have doubtless been. We would gladly learn something more concerning the contents of a Greek MS. of the eleventh century on surgical operations, of which plate 48 contains some curious specimens; and we should above all things desire to know whether it has been ascertained that none of the ancient MSS. which M. d'Agincourt examined were palimpsests, whether they do not contain the lost decads of Livy? M. d'Agincourt deserves at least the thanks of the diplomatist for having added to the science of palæography many alphabets extracted from ancient writings, in some of which the letters luxuriate until they nearly lose all shape and distinguishable form.

In the department of painting, Mosaic is included, an art by which, at the expense of infinite patience, eternal duration is given to a picture: the Romans have been eminently successful in all ages in this difficult and elaborate kind of representation; at first the effect of even the best specimens is unpleasant, but by degrees the eye accustoms itself to it, and learns to regard only the beauties and to forget the grand defect, that the piece has the same appearance, as if it were seen through a sieve.

Engraving has been called " a marvellous invention, to which the productions of the art were indebted for immortality;" M. d'Agincourt adopts the eulogium in its utmost extent, and has devoted some attention to this part of the graphic art. The history of engraving cannot be brought within a narrow compass: the invention of paper made of linen or cotton necessarily preceded the discovery of printing, and was still more indispensable to engraving. The use of rituals was favourable to the invention of printing; there was perhaps no volume in the ancient world which it was deemed necessary that every person should possess, like a prayer book or missal; the art of engraving received during its infancy similar assistance. We acknowledge the manifold benefits that have been derived from this elegant art; we feel, nevertheless, that much money, time and skill are employed upon engravings, which afford a gratification that is somewhat selfish; prints are hidden in the portfolios of the rich, and when they are framed and exhibited, the exhibition is confined within the walls of a private house, but we must except our printshops, which are spectacles for the public at large.

M. d'Agincourt speaks of some unusual modes of painting, to which we have not leisure to refer at present, and he discourses very fully of the revival of the art by the great masters of Italy, and accompanies his remarks by specimens of their works; as that part of the subject is more generally understood than some others upon which we have enlarged, we pass it over altogether, merely referring those who may desire information to the judicious observations of the author, to the valuable work of Lanzi, whose extraordinary merits are often recognised with due respect by the Historian of Art, and to other popular volumes.

The following passage, in which an old Italian historian of painting endeavours to account for the eminence of the painters of the Florentine school, is not less just than it is interesting for its quaint simplicity.

" In Florence more than elsewhere," says Vasari, " men become perfect in all the arts, especially in that of painting, because in that city men are spurred on by three things. The one is the blame, which many men bestow, oftentimes indeed in order to keep up the fashion of minds that are somewhat negligent by nature, and not to rest contented with works that are only moderate, but always to consider them more for the credit of the good and the beautiful than with respect to the maker. Another is, that in order to live it is necessary to be industrious, that is to say, to exercise continually the genius and the judgment, to be dexterous and ready in business, and to know how to make money, Florence not having an extensive and abundant country that could easily support the expenses of its inhabitants, as where good land is abundant. And the third cause, which perhaps would not be sufficient without the other two, is the desire of glory and honour which this air generates to a great degree in men of every profession, and which in all persons who have spirit, will not permit them to remain equal to, much less behind others, whom they see to be but men like themselves, although they acknowledge them to be masters; it forces them therefore so greatly to desire their own greatness, that unless they are naturally kind or sensible, they are apt to become censorious, ungrateful, and forgetful of kindnesses. And it is very true that when a man has learned enough, if he desires to do otherwise than live, like the beasts, from day to day, and wishes to become rich, he must depart from thence and sell elsewhere the goodness of his work and the reputation of this city, as the doctors do that of their studies. For Florence does with her artists the same as Time with all things, she makes them and then unmakes them, and consumes them by degrees."

The last plate is occupied by a representation of the bust, which in his enthusiasm for the glory of the French school, M. d'Agincourt erected in honour of his countryman, Nicholas Poussin, in the Pantheon at Rome, with the following inscription:

Nic. Poussin,

Pictori Gallo

Joa. Bap. Lud. Gior. Seroux d'Agincourt.

1782.

His biographer is delighted with the homage that is paid to the artist by the amateur, and finds a noble simplicity in the inscription. Austere critics have asserted that the desire of engraving his own name in that famous and much visited temple, under the pretext of honouring another, was the true motive of the dedication, and that the inscription, simple as it is said to be, is a correct example of a rhetorical climax, in which the sense artfully rises in three steps, and the importance of the subject with it: first, we have the glory of Poussin, which is tolerably great; secondly, that of France, which is far greater; and thirdly, that of M. d'Agincourt himself, which is incomparably the greatest: and they add that more than twice as many words, without reckoning the date, are employed upon the last topic, as on both the former. This censure, however, is too severe; the vanity, if such it be, is harmless, perhaps laudable; and precedents are not wanting to justify it; the Chevalier d'Azara, the Spanish Ambassador at the court of Rome, had lately erected a similar monument in honour of Mengs, and the like offerings had been previously made by other worshippers at the shrine of art.

We have spoken with the utmost freedom of a work, which is possessed of so much merit, that it would have been easier to have bestowed upon it unqualified praise, and we have done so from a persuasion that it is incumbent on those, who differ from the received opinions on such attractive topics to state their own sentiments with entire frankness and an honest boldness, because the great cause of *virtù* must necessarily be forwarded by liberal inquiry, and can only be retarded by a servile submission to the imposing authority of great names.

Art. VI.—G. F. Sartorius Freyherrn von Waltershausen *Urkundliche Geschichte des Ursprunges der Deutschen Hanse.* Herausgegeben von J. M. Lappenberg. (G. F. Sartorius, Baron of Waltershausen's Documentary History of the Origin of the German Hanse. Published by J. M. Lappenberg.) 2 vols. 4to. (Vol. I. pp. xxxiv. and 314. Vol. II. pp. 762.) Hamburg. 1830.

DURING the anarchy which followed the subversion of the Empire of Charlemagne, commerce of every sort was almost entirely proscribed. The seas were covered with pirates; while the nobles, unacquainted with any other profession than that of arms, and despising the laborious and servile occupations of the husbandman and artizan, were engaged in perpetual contests with each other; and scrupled not to commit every sort of outrage on the property and persons of those who were unable to defend themselves. But notwithstanding these multiplied disorders, the seeds of improvement were not wholly destroyed. In Germany, as in Italy and elsewhere, the foundations of a new and better order of things were laid in the towns. Being associated together in considerable numbers the citizens became conscious of their strength; and began, at a very early period, to resist the tyrannical proceedings of the lay and ecclesiastical lords who had obtained an authority over them. Unluckily the citizens were themselves divided into the classes of nobles, freemen or burgesses, and serfs or slaves. According, however, as commerce and industry gained ground, the class of burgesses acquired a marked ascendancy over the nobles, while the lowest and most numerous class was, partly through its own efforts, partly through the influence of the Christian religion, and partly through the policy of the emperors, gradually raised to an equality with the burgesses. Henry V., who began his reign in 1106, abolished every legal distinction between the burgesses and *cives opifices,* or serfs of Spires, Worms, and some other towns: and it was about the same time enacted that a serf belonging to a stranger who should take refuge in any free city, and continue there for a determinate period, without being claimed by his master, should be declared free. In truth, however, this privilege was carried much farther; and few instances occurred in which a fugitive serf was given up, whatever might have been the length of his residence.

In order to strengthen themselves still further, the German towns like those of Italy, entered into associations for the purpose of mutual defence, or in order to advance their common interests. In 1255 more than seventy cities, at the head of which were Worms and Mentz, joined with the Archbishops of Mentz and Cologne, in a league the object of which was to repress the exactions of the nobles, to procure the abolition of the tolls by which they had entirely obstructed the navigation of the rivers and even the intercourse by land, and the establishment of some sort of law and police. William the King, for so he was termed, of Germany, having approved of the objects of the confederacy, the efforts of its leaders were crowned with success. Several objectionable practices were abolished. And to use the words of the learned M. Pfeffel, " Les nobles, resserrés dans leurs châteaux, surveillés des toutes parts, et menacés de toute la rigueur des loix, *cessèrent pour quelque tems de voler sur les grands chemins.*"* Similar leagues were·formed at subsequent periods; the efforts of the princes to deprive the cities of the power of entering into such associations, having proved entirely ineffectual.

In consequence of the liberty and security enjoyed by the inhabitants of the free towns, while the rest of the country was a prey to all the evils of feudal anarchy and oppression, they made a comparatively rapid progress in wealth and population. Nuremberg, Augsburg, Worms, Spires, Frankfort, and other cities became at an early period, celebrated alike for the extent of their commerce, the magnificence of their buildings, and the opulence of their citizens. The famous·Eneas Sylvius, afterwards Pope Pius II., the envoy of the Court of Rome at the councils of Constance and Bale, and who had travelled over the greater part of Europe, says that the kings of Scotland would wish to be as well lodged as the meaner burgesses of Nuremberg. *" Quot ibi civium ædes invenias Regibus dignas? Cuperent tam egregiè Scotorum Reges, quam mediocres Norimbergæ cives habitare."*†

·The commercial spirit awakened in the north, about the same time as in the ·south of Germany. Hamburgh was founded by Charlemagne in the beginning of the ninth century, in the intention of serving as a fort to bridle the Saxons, who had been ʼsubjugated by the emperor. Its favourable situation on the Elbe necessarily rendered it a commercial emporium. Towards the close of the twelfth century, the inhabitants, who had already been extensively· engaged in naval enterprizes, began to form the design of emancipating themselves from the authority of their counts, and of becoming a sovereign and independent state; and in 1189 they obtained an Imperial charter which gave them various privileges, including among others, the power of electing councillors, or aldermen, to whom in conjunction with the deputy of the count, the government of the town was to be entrusted. Not long after Hamburgh became entirely free. In 1224 the

---

. * Histoire d'Allemagne, Anno 1255.   † De Mor. Germ. p. m. 1055.

citizens purchased from Count Albert the renunciation of all his rights, whether real or pretended, to any property in or sovereignty over the town, and its immediate vicinity. And the government was thus early placed on that liberal footing on which it has ever since remained.

Lubeck, situated on the Trave, was founded about the middle of the twelfth century. It rapidly grew to be a place of great trade. It became the principal emporium for the commerce of the Baltic; and its merchants extended their dealings to Italy and the Levant. At a period when navigation was still imperfect, and when the seas were infested with pirates, it was of great importance to be able to maintain a safe intercourse by land between Lubeck and Hamburgh, as by that means the difficult and dangerous navigation of the Sound was avoided.* And it is said by some, that the first political union between these cities had the protection of merchandize carried between them by land for its sole object. But this is contradicted by Lambec in his *Origines Hamburgenses* (lib. xi. pa. 26.) And it is, indeed, quite obvious that they must have been anxious to acquire protection against pirates at sea, as well as robbers by land, and to place themselves in a situation to make head against the princes who had begun to envy their wealth and prosperity. But whatever may have been the motives which led to the alliance between these two cities, it was the origin of the famous *Hanseatic League,* so called from the German word *hansa,* signifying a corporation. There is no very distinct evidence as to the time when the alliance in question was established; but the more general opinion seems to be that it dates from the year 1241.

Adam of Bremen, who flourished in the eleventh century, is the earliest writer who has given any information with respect to the commerce of the countries lying round the Baltic. And from the errors into which he has fallen in describing the northern and eastern shores of that sea, it is evident they had been very little frequented and not at all known in his time. But from the beginning of the twelfth century, the progress of commerce and navigation in the north was exceedingly rapid. The countries which stretch along the bottom of the Baltic from Holstein to Russia, and which had been occupied by barbarous tribes of Sclavonic origin, were then subjugated by the Kings of Denmark, the Dukes of Saxony, and other princes. The greater part of

* Among the interesting documents in the appendix to the work before us, is a proclamation (No. CXIV.) of the magistrates of Lubeck, dated in 1304, announcing that they used the same mint and the same coins that were used by the citizens of Hamburgh; and that they maintained at their own expense *thirty-two* horsemen, and the magistrates of Hamburgh *eight* horsemen, for the protection of merchants and merchandize going by land between the two cities, and stating the sums charged for their escort.

the inhabitants being exterminated, their place was filled by German colonists, who founded the towns of Stralsund, Rostock, Wismar, &c. Prussia and Poland were afterwards subjugated by the Christian princes, and the Knights of the Teutonic order. So that in a comparatively short period, the foundations of civilization and the arts were laid in countries whose barbarism had ever remained impervious to the Roman power.

The cities that were established along the coasts of the Baltic, and even in the interior of the countries bordering upon it, eagerly joined the Hanseatic confederation. They were indebted to the merchants of Lubeck for supplies of the commodities produced in more civilized countries, and they looked up to them for protection against the barbarians by whom they were surrounded. The progress of the league was in consequence singularly rapid. Previously to the end of the thirteenth century it embraced every considerable city in all those vast countries extending from Livonia to Holland; and was a match for the most powerful monarchs.

The Hanseatic confederacy was at its highest degree of power and splendour during the fourteenth and fifteenth centuries. It then comprised from sixty to eighty cities, which were distributed into four classes or circles. Lubeck was at the head of the first circle, and had under it Hamburgh, Bremen, Rostock, Wismar, &c. Cologne was at the head of the second circle, with twenty-nine towns under it. Brunswick was at the head of the third circle, consisting of thirteen towns. Dantzic was at the head of the fourth circle, having under it eight towns in its vicinity, besides several that were more remote. The supreme authority of the League was vested in the deputies of the different towns assembled in Congress. In it they discussed all their measures; decided upon the sum that each city should contribute to the common fund; and upon the questions that arose between the confederacy and other powers, as well as those that frequently arose between the different members of the confederacy. The place for the meeting of Congress was not fixed, but it was most frequently held at Lubeck, which was considered as the capital of the League, and there its archives were kept. Sometimes, however, congresses were held at Hamburgh, Cologne and other towns. They met once every three years, or oftener if occasion required. The letters of convocation specified the principal subjects which would most probably be brought under discussion. Any one might be chosen for a deputy; and the Congress consisted not of merchants only, but also of clergymen, lawyers, artists, &c. When the deliberations were concluded, the decrees were formally communicated to the magistrates of the cities at the head of each circle, by whom they were subsequently communicated to those below them; and the most vigorous measures were adopted for carrying them into effect.   One of the burgomasters of Lubeck presided at the meetings of Congress; and during the recess the magistrates of that city had the sole, or at all events the principal direction of the affairs of the League.

Besides the towns already mentioned, there were others that were denominated confederated cities, or allies.   The latter neither contributed to the common fund of the League, nor sent deputies to Congress; even the members were not all on the same footing in respect of privileges: and the internal commotions by which it was frequently agitated, partly originating in this cause, and partly in the discordant interests and conflicting pretensions of the different cities, materially impaired the power of the confederacy.   But in despite of these disadvantages, the League succeeded for a lengthened period, not only in controuling its own refractory members, but in making itself respected and dreaded by others.   It produced able generals and admirals, skilful politicians, and some of the most enterprizing, successful and wealthy merchants of modern times.

The *Golden Bull* proscribed all sorts of leagues and associations, as contrary to the fundamental laws of the empire, and to the subordination due to the emperor and the different princes. But Charles IV., the author of this famous edict, judged it expedient to conciliate the Hanseatic League; and his successors seem generally to have followed his example.

As the power of the confederated cities was increased and consolidated, they became more ambitious.   Instead of limiting their efforts to the mere advancement of commerce and their own protection, they endeavoured to acquire the monopoly of the trade of the North, and to exercise the same sort of dominion over the Baltic that the Venetians exercised over the Adriatic.   For this purpose they succeeded in obtaining, partly in return for loans of money, and partly by force, various privileges and immunities from the Northern sovereigns, which secured to them almost the whole foreign commerce of Scandinavia, Denmark, Prussia, Poland, Russia, &c.   They exclusively carried on the herring-fishery of the Sound, at the same time that they endeavoured to obstruct and hinder the navigation of foreign vessels in the Baltic. It should, however, be observed that the immunities they enjoyed were mostly indispensable to the security of their commerce, in consequence of the barbarism that then prevailed; and notwithstanding their attempts at monopoly, there cannot be the shadow of a doubt that the progress of civilization in the North was prodigiously accelerated by the influence and ascendancy of the

Hanseatic cities. They repressed piracy by sea and robbery by land, which must have broken out again had their power been overthrown before civilization was fully established; they accustomed the inhabitants to the principles, and set before them the example of good government and subordination; they introduced amongst them conveniences and enjoyments unknown by their ancestors, or despised by them, and inspired them with a taste for literature and science; they did for the people round the Baltic what the Phœnicians had done in remoter ages for those round the Mediterranean, and deserve, equally with them, to be placed in the first rank amongst the benefactors of mankind.

" In order," as it has been justly observed, " to accomplish their purpose of rendering the Baltic a large field for the prosecution of commercial and industrious pursuits, it was necessary to instruct men, still barbarous, in the rudiments of industry, and to familiarize them in the principles of civilization. These great principles were laid by the confederation, and at the close of the fifteenth century the Baltic and the neighbouring seas had, by its means, become frequented routes of communication between the North and the South. The people of the former were enabled to follow the progress of the latter in knowledge and industry. The forests of Sweden, Poland, &c. gave place to corn, hemp and flax; the mines were wrought, and in return the produce and manufactures of the South were imported. Towns and villages were erected in Scandinavia, where huts only were before seen: the skins of the bear and the wolf were exchanged for woollens, linens and silks: learning was introduced; and printing was hardly invented before it was practised in Denmark, Sweden, &c."

The kings of Denmark, Sweden and Norway were frequently engaged in hostilities with the Hanse towns. They regarded, and it must be admitted not without pretty good reason, the privileges acquired by the League in their kingdoms, as so many usurpations. But their efforts to abolish these privileges served, for more than two centuries, only to augment and extend them.

" On the part of the League there was union, subordination and money; whereas the half-savage Scandinavian monarchies were full of divisions, factions and troubles; revolution was immediately followed by revolution, and feudal anarchy was at its height. There was another circumstance, not less important, in favour of the Hanseatic cities. The popular governments established amongst them possessed the respect and confidence of the inhabitants, and were able to direct the public energies for the good of the state. The astonishing prosperity of the confederated cities was not wholly the effect of commerce. To the undisciplined armies of the princes of the North—armies composed of vassals without attachment to their lords—the cities opposed, besides the inferior nobles whose services they liberally rewarded, citizens accustomed to danger, and resolved to defend their liberties and property. Their military operations were combined and directed by a council, composed of men of tried talents and experience, devoted to their country, responsible to their fellow-citizens, and enjoying their confidence. It was chiefly, however, on their marine forces that the cities depended. They employed their ships indifferently in war or commerce, so that their naval armaments were fitted out at comparatively small expense. Exclusive too of these favourable circumstances, the fortifications of the principal cities were looked upon as impregnable; and as their commerce supplied them abundantly with all sorts of provisions, it need not excite our astonishment that Lubeck alone was able to carry on wars with the surrounding monarchs, and to terminate them with honour and advantage; and still less that the League should long have enjoyed a decided preponderance in the North."*

Waldemar III., who ascended the Danish throne in 1340, engaged in a furious contest with the League. Success seemed at first rather to incline to his arms. Ultimately, however, he was completely defeated by the forces of the League and its allies, and was even obliged to fly from his kingdom. In his exile he prevailed on the Emperor and the Pope to interpose in his favour. But neither the imperial rescripts nor the thunders of the Vatican were able to divert the confederated cities from their purposes. At length, in 1370, the regents, to whom the government of Denmark had been intrusted during the absence of the monarch, concluded a peace with the League on the conditions dictated by the latter; one of which was that most of the strong places in the kingdom should be given up to the League for fifteen years, in security for the faithful performance of the treaty. Waldemar having assented to these humiliating terms, returned soon after to Denmark. In the early part of the fifteenth century the Hanse towns having espoused the side of the Count of Holstein, who was at war with Eric X., King of Denmark, sent an armament of upwards of 200 ships, having more than 12,000 troops on board, to the assistance of their ally. This powerful aid decided the contest in his favour.

Nearly at the same time the League raised their ally, Albert of Mecklenburgh, to the throne of Norway, who confirmed to them several important commercial privileges. In their contests with Sweden, during the fourteenth and fifteenth centuries, the League were equally successful. Such, indeed, was their ascendancy in that kingdom, that they were authorized to nominate some of the principal magistrates in most of the Swedish maritime towns of any importance!

The extirpation of piracy was one of the objects which had originally led to the formation of the League, and which it never ceased to prosecute. Owing, however, to the barbarism then so

* L'Art de Verifier les Dates. Troisième Partie, tome viii. p. 204.

universally prevalent, and the countenance openly given by many princes and nobles to those engaged in this infamous profession, it was not possible wholly to root it out. But the vigorous efforts of the League to abate the nuisance, though not entirely successful, served to render the navigation of the North sea and the Baltic, comparatively secure, and were of signal advantage to commerce. Nor was this the only mode in which the power of the confederacy was directly employed to promote the common interests of mankind. Their exertions to protect shipwrecked mariners from the atrocities to which they had been subject, and to procure the restitution of shipwrecked property to its legitimate owners,* though, most probably, like their exertions to repress piracy, a consequence of selfish considerations, were in no ordinary degree meritorious; and contributed not less to the advancement of civilization than to the security of navigation.

The town of Wisby, situated on the west coast of the island of Gothland, became, during the ascendancy of the League, one of its principal depôts, and also one of the best frequented emporiums of the North.† But Wisby is chiefly famous from its name having become identified with the code of maritime laws that was long of paramount authority in the Baltic. Grotius has spoken of these laws in terms of high and deserved commendation. " Quæ de maritimis negotiis," says he, " insulæ Gothlandiæ habitatoribus placuerunt, tantum in re habent, tum æquitatis, tum prudentiæ, ut omnes oceani accolæ eo, non tanquam proprio, sed velut *gentium jure,* ûtantur." The principal Northern jurists and historians, regard the Wisby code, or compilation, as anterior to the code, or compilation, denominated the Rules or Judgments of Oleron, and as being in fact the most ancient monument of the maritime laws of the middle ages. But no learning or ingenuity can give plausibility to so improbable a theory. Navigation had made a considerable progress in Italy and the more southern countries of Europe, which had preserved some knowledge of the maritime laws of Rome, while the countries round the Baltic were sunk in the depths of barbarism. It is, therefore, far more reasonable to suppose that the magistrates of Wisby, or the individuals who framed the rules or regulations issued in that city,

---

* In the Appendix (No. LXVII.) to the work before us, is a series of resolutions, purporting to have been unanimously agreed to by the merchants frequenting the port of Wisby in 1287, providing for the restoration of shipwrecked property to its original owners, and threatening to eject from the " *consodalitate mercatorum*" any city that did not act conformably to the regulations laid down.

† Olaüs Magnus, speaking of Wisby, says, " Confluxere illuc Gothi, Suedi, Russi seu Reutheni, Dani, Prussi ; Angli, Scoti, Flandri, Galli, Finni, Vandali, Saxones, Hispani, singulæque gentes, suos proprios vicos et plateas incolentes, *nulli preclusum municipium.*"—Lib. ii. cap. 24.

compiled them from the codes or customs of the foreigners
frequenting their port, than that the latter should have derived their maritime laws from the former.   There are many
things, indeed, mentioned in the laws of Wisby, that are quite
inexplicable on any other hypothesis.   Had the code been an
original compilation, that is, had it been drawn up from observations made by native merchants or jurists on the conduct and
proceedings of those engaged in the commerce of the Baltic, and
not copied from foreign codes or customs, the illustrations given
in it would undoubtedly have been, for the most part at least, derived from the laws and practices of the principal trading towns
on that sea.   But the very reverse of this is the fact.   Almost all
the places mentioned in the laws of Wisby are situated without
the Baltic.   Repeated references are made to the Scheldt, to
Hamburgh, Amsterdam, Rochelle, Bordeaux, &c.; and regulations are laid down as to what should be done in the event of
certain occurrences taking place in them.   But from one end
of the code to the other there is not a single allusion to Stockholm, though in the immediate vicinity of Wisby, to Dantzic or
Riga, or indeed to any port in the Baltic, with the exception
of Lubeck and Copenhagen!   The 25th article gives particular
directions as to the stowage of wine, and the circumstances under
which the owners should be obliged to indemnify the merchants
for any injury that had happened to it; but we look in vain for
a single word respecting timber, iron, corn, or any one of the
peculiar productions of the countries contiguous to the Baltic.
It is not conceivable that such should have been the case had the
laws of Wisby been an original compilation; and, in point of fact,
the article now alluded to is a literal translation of the 11th article
of the Judgments of Oleron, in which, being intended for the regulation of the maritime affairs of France, it was most properly
placed: but for a detailed statement of the various matters connected with the history of this celebrated code, we beg to refer
our readers to the chapter upon it in the first volume of the very
learned and excellent work of M. Pardessus, " *Collection des Loix
Maritimes anterieures au dixhuitieme Siècle.*"   It is there shown,
in the most conclusive manner, that the laws of Wisby have been
copied with very little variation from the ancient maritime laws of
Lubeck, the Rules of Oleron, and the ancient maritime laws of
Holland.

The northern jurists have not been less erroneous in their
statements as to the antiquity of the Wisby code.   It is abundantly certain, from allusions in the code itself and other circumstances, that it was not compiled previously to the end of the
fourteenth, or the beginning of the fifteenth century.   A more

ancient and extended body of maritime law, compiled under Magnus, King of Sweden, was promulgated with his sanction and authority between the years 1320 and 1360. But this code seems to have attracted no attention, and was entirely forgotten when it was published, for the first time, by Hadorph in 1681. The code referred to by Grotius, Leibnitz, Loccenius, &c., under the name of the " Supreme Maritime Law of Wisby," to which the preceding remarks exclusively apply, consists, in M. Pardessus's edition, of sixty-six articles, and was first printed at Copenhagen in 1505.

But whatever may have been the origin or the date of the laws of Wisby, the regulations embodied in them are for the most part consistent with the soundest principles, and are, and ever will be, of great authority in all questions of maritime jurisprudence. Their promulgation must have been of great use to navigation. As the historian observes, maritime suits were much more expeditiously decided by them, than other causes by the courts upon the main land. " Ab hâc etiam Insulâ (Gothlandiâ) in omni navigantium controversia, præsertim a Consulatu Visbycensi petitur et datur jus, et sententia definitiva, quid unicuique permittendum vel auferendum erit. *Certe, jus hoc mercatorum, ac nautarum, valde prudenter digestum, citius lites admit in fluidis aquis, quam aliorum decisio in terra firma.*"

In order to facilitate and extend their commercial transactions, the League established various factories in foreign countries, the principal of which were at Novogorod in Russia, London in England, Bruges in the Netherlands, and Bergen in Norway.

Novogorod, situated at the confluence of the Volkof with the Imler Lake, was, for a lengthened period, the most renowned emporium in the north-eastern parts of Europe. In the beginning of the eleventh century, the inhabitants obtained considerable privileges that laid the foundation of their liberty and prosperity. Their sovereigns were at first subordinate to the Grand Dukes or Czars of Russia; but as the city and the contiguous territory increased in population and wealth, they gradually usurped an almost absolute independency. The power of these sovereigns over their subjects, seems, at the same time, to have been exceedingly limited; and in effect, Novogorod ought rather to be considered as a republic under the jurisdiction of an elective magistrate, than as a state subject to a regular line of hereditary monarchs, possessed of extensive prerogatives. During the twelfth, thirteenth, and fourteenth centuries, Novogorod formed the grand entrepôt between the countries to the east of Poland and the Hanseatic cities. Its fairs were frequented by an immense concourse of people from all the surrounding countries, as well as by numbers of merchants from the Hanse towns, who engrossed the greater part of its foreign commerce, and who furnished its markets with the manufactures and products of distant countries. Novogorod is said to have contained, during its most flourishing period, towards the middle of the fifteenth century, upwards of 400,000 souls. This, however, is most probably an exaggeration. But its dominions were then very extensive; and its wealth and power seemed so great and well established, and the city itself so impregnable, as to give rise to a proverb, Who can resist the Gods and great Novogorod? *Quis contra Deos et magnam Novogordiam?* *

But its power and prosperity were far from being so firmly established as its eulogists, and those who had only visited its fairs, appear to have supposed. In the latter part of the fifteenth century, Ivan Vassilievitch, Czar of Russia, having secured his dominions against the inroads of the Tartars, and extended his empire by the conquest of some of the neighbouring principalities, asserted his right to the principality of Novogorod, and supported his pretensions by a formidable army. Had the inhabitants been animated by the spirit of unanimity and patriotism, they might have defied his efforts; but their dissensions facilitated their conquest, and rendered them an easy prey. Having entered the city at the head of his troops, Ivan received from the citizens the charter of their liberties, which they either wanted courage or inclination to defend, and carried off an enormous bell to Moscow, that had been long regarded with a sort of superstitious veneration as the palladium of the city. But notwithstanding the despotism to which Novogorod was subject, during the reigns of Ivan and his successors, it continued for a considerable period to be the largest as well as most commercial city in the Russian empire. The famous Richard Chancellour, who passed through Novogorod in 1554, in his way from the court of the Czar, says, that " next unto Moscow, the city of Novogorod is reputed the chiefest of Russia; for although it be in majestie inferior to it, yet in greatness it goeth beyond it. It is the chiefest and greatest mart town of all Muscovy; and albeit the emperor's seat is not there, but at Moscow, yet the commodiousness of the river falling into the gulph of Finland, whereby it is well-frequented by merchants, makes it more famous than Moscow itself."

But the scourge of the destroyer soon after fell on this celebrated city. Ivan IV. having discovered in 1570, a correspondence between some of the principal citizens, and the King of Poland, relative to a surrender of the city into his hands,

---

* See *Foreign Quarterly Review*, vol. iii. p. 155.

punished them in the most inhuman manner.* The slaughter by which the blood-thirsty barbarian sought to satisfy his revenge was alike extensive and undiscriminating. The crime of a few citizens was made the pretext for the massacre of twenty-five or thirty thousand. Novogorod never recovered from this dreadful blow. It still, however, continued to be a place of considerable trade until the foundation of Petersburgh, which immediately became the seat of that commerce that had formerly centered at Novogorod. The degradation of this ill-fated city is now complete. It is at present an inconsiderable place, with a population of about 7,000 or 8,000; and is remarkable only for its history and antiquities.

The merchants of the Hanse towns, or Hansards, as they were then commonly termed, were established in London at a very early period, and their factory here was of considerable magnitude and importance. They enjoyed various privileges and immunities; they were permitted to govern themselves by their own laws and regulations; the custody of one of the gates of the city (Bishopsgate) was committed to their care; and the duties on various sorts of imported commodities were considerably reduced in their favour. These privileges necessarily excited the ill-will and animosity of the English merchants. The Hansards were every now and then accused of acting with bad faith; of introducing commodities as their own that were really the produce of others, in order to enable them to evade the duties with which they ought to have been charged; of capriciously extending the list of towns belonging to the association; and obstructing the commerce of the English in the Baltic. Efforts were continually making to bring these disputes to a termination, but as they really grew out of the privileges granted to and claimed by the Hansards, this was found to be impossible. The latter were exposed to many indignities; and their factory, which was situated in Thames Street, was not unfrequently attacked. The League exerted themselves vigorously in defence of their privileges; and having declared war against England, they succeeded in excluding our vessels from the Baltic, and acted with such energy, that Edward IV. was glad to come to an accommodation with them, on terms which were anything but honourable to the English. In the treaty for this purpose, negotiated in 1474, the privileges of the merchants of the Hanse towns were renewed, and the king assigned to them, in absolute property, a large space of ground, with the buildings upon it, in Thames Street, denominated the Steel Yard, whence the Hanse merchants have been commonly

---

* See Foreign Quarterly Review, vol. iii. p. 173, and following.

denominated the Association of the Steel Yard; the property of
their establishments at Boston and Lynn was also secured to
them; the king engaged to allow no stranger to participate in
their privileges; one of the articles bore that the Hanse merchants
should be no longer subject to the judges of the English Admiralty Court, but that a particular tribunal should be formed for
the easy and speedy settlement of all disputes that might arise between them and the English; and it was further agreed that the
particular privileges awarded to the Hanse merchants should be
published as often as the latter judged proper, in all the sea-port
towns of England, and such Englishmen as infringed upon them
should be punished.   In return for these concessions the English
acquired the liberty of freely trading in the Baltic, and especially
in the port of Dantzic and in Prussia.   In 1498, all direct commerce with the Netherlands being suspended, the trade fell into
the hands of the Hanse merchants, whose commerce was in consequence very greatly extended.   But, according as the spirit of
commercial enterprise awakened in the nation, and as the benefits
resulting from the prosecution of foreign trade came to be better
known, the privileges of the Hanse merchants became more and
more obnoxious.   They were in consequence considerably modified in the reigns of Henry VII. and Henry VIII., and were at
length wholly abolished in 1597.

The different individuals belonging to the factory in London,
as well as those belonging to the other factories of the League,
lived together at a common table, and were enjoined to observe
the strictest celibacy.   The direction of the factory in London
was entrusted to an alderman, two assessors, and nine councillors.
The latter were sent by the cities forming the different classes into
which the League was divided.   The business of these functionaries
was to devise means for extending and securing the privileges and
commerce of the association; to watch over the operations of the
merchants; and to adjust any disputes that might arise amongst
the members of the confederacy, or between them and the English.
The League endeavoured at all times to promote, as much as
possible, the employment of their own ships.   In pursuance of
this object they went so far, in 1447, as to forbid the importation
of English merchandize into the confederated cities, except by
their own vessels.   But a regulation of this sort could not be
carried into full effect; and was enforced or modified according
as circumstances were favourable or adverse to the pretensions of
the League.   Its very existence was, however, an insult to the
English nation; and the irritation produced by the occasional
attempts to act upon it, contributed materially to the subversion
of the privileges the Hanseatic merchants had acquired amongst us.

By means of their factory at Bergen, and of the privileges which had been either granted to or usurped by them, the League enjoyed for a lengthened period the monopoly of the commerce of Norway.

But the principal factory of the League was at Bruges in the Netherlands. Bruges became, at a very early period, one of the first commercial cities of Europe, and the centre of the most extensive trade carried on to the north of Italy. The art of navigation in the thirteenth and fourteenth centuries was so imperfect, that a voyage from Italy to the Baltic and back again could not be performed in a single season; and hence, for the sake of their mutual convenience, the Italian and Hanseatic merchants determined on establishing a magazine or store-house of their respective products in some intermediate situation. Bruges was fixed upon for this purpose, a distinction which it seems to have owed as much to the freedom enjoyed by the inhabitants, and the liberality of the government of the Low Countries, as to the conveniency of its situation. In consequence of this preference, Bruges speedily rose to the very highest rank among commercial cities, and became a place of vast wealth. It was at once a staple for English wool, for the woollen and linen manufactures of the Netherlands, for the timber, hemp and flax, pitch and tar, tallow, corn, fish, ashes, &c. of the North; and for the spices and Indian commodities, as well as their domestic manufactures imported by the Italian merchants. The fairs of Bruges were the best frequented of any in Europe. Ludovico Guicciardini mentions, in his description of the Low Countries, that in the year 1318 no fewer than five Venetian galleasses, vessels of very considerable burden, arrived in Bruges in order to dispose of their cargoes at the fair. The Hanseatic merchants were the principal purchasers of Indian commodities; they disposed of them in the ports of the Baltic, or carried them up the great rivers into the heart of Germany. The vivifying effects of this commerce were every where felt; the regular intercourse opened between the nations in the north and south of Europe made them sensible of their mutual wants, and gave a wonderful stimulus to the spirit of industry. This was particularly the case with regard to the Netherlands. Manufactures of wool and flax had been established in that country as early as the age of Charlemagne, and the resort of foreigners to their markets, and the great additional vent that was thus opened for their manufactures, made them be carried on with a vigour and success that had been hitherto unknown. These circumstances, combined with the free spirit of their institutions, and the moderation of the government, so greatly promoted every elegant and useful art, that the Netherlands early became the most civilized, best cultivated, richest, and most populous country of Europe.

" Flanders," says Mr. Macpherson under the year 1301, " being the seat of the best manufactures to the northward of the Alps and the Pyrenæan mountains ; and, consequently, crowded with people, the greatest exertions were made to render the fields as productive as possible; and the encouragement afforded by so numerous a population was a most powerful stimulus to the industry and ingenuity of the agriculturists. It is generally allowed that the other countries in the west of Europe have been instructed in agriculture and horticulture by the Flemings; and have been earlier or later in their improvements in those arts in proportion to the earliness and frequency of their intercourse with their masters. Literature and the fine arts were also more flourishing in Flanders than in the neighbouring countries during the prosperous ages of· their manufactures and commerce. So true is it that plenty and politeness are produced and nourished by the genial influence of well-directed industry."

·The commerce of Bruges continued to flourish without interruption till about 1490, when the Emperor Frederick III., in revenge of the imprisonment of his son Maximilian, treated the city with great severity. In consequence, the commerce that had been previously carried on at Bruges was gradually transferred to Antwerp, which speedily rose to the ·highest rank among commercial cities.

From the middle of the· fifteenth century the power of the confederacy, though still very formidable, began ·to decline. This was not owing to any misconduct on the part of· its leaders, but to the ·progress· of that improvement it had done so much to promote. The superiority enjoyed by the League resulted as much from the anarchy, confusion, and barbarism that prevailed throughout the kingdoms of the north, as from the good government and order that distinguished the towns. But a distinction of this sort could not be permanent. The civilization which had been at first confined to the cities, gradually spread from them, as from 'so many centres, over the contiguous country. Feudal anarchy was every where superseded by a system of subordination; arts and industry were diffused and cultivated ; and the authority of government was at length firmly established. This change not only rendered the princes, over whom the League had so frequently triumphed, superior to it in power, but the inhabitants of the countries amongst which the confederated cities were scattered, having learned to entertain a ¡just sense of the advantages derivable from commerce and navigation, could not brook the superiority of the association, or bear to see its members in possession of· immunities of which they were deprived: and in addition to these circumstances, which must speedily have occasioned the dissolution of the League, the interests of the different cities of which it consisted became daily more and more opposed to each other. Lubeck, Hamburgh, Bremen, and the towns in their vicinity, were latterly the only ones that had any interest in its maintenance. The cities in Zealand and Holland joined it, chiefly because they would otherwise have been excluded from the commerce of the Baltic; and those of Prussia, Poland, and Russia did the same, because, had they not belonged to it, they would have been shut out from all intercourse with strangers. When, however, the Zealanders and Hollanders became sufficiently powerful at sea to be able to vindicate their right to the free navigation of the Baltic by force of arms, they immediately seceded from the League; and no sooner had the ships of the Dutch, the English, &c. begun to trade directly with the Polish and Prussian Hanse Towns, than these nations also embraced the first opportunity of withdrawing from it. The fall of this great confederacy was really, therefore, a consequence of the improved state of society, and of the development of the commercial spirit in the different nations of Europe. It was most serviceable so long as those for whom its merchants acted as factors and carriers were too barbarous, too much occupied with other matters, or destitute of the necessary capital and skill, to act in these capacities for themselves. When they were in a situation to do this, the functions of the Hanseatic merchants ceased as a matter of course; their confederacy fell to pieces; and at the middle of the seventeenth century the cities of Lubeck, Hamburgh, and Bremen were all that continued to acknowledge the authority of the League.

ART. VII.—1. *Geschichte des Teutschen Volkes.* Von Heinrich Luden. (History of the German Nation. By Henry Luden.) 5 bänden. Gotha. 1825—1830.

2. *Geschichte der Alten Deutschen, besonders der Franken.* Von Konrad Mannert, Hofrath und ordentlicher Professor an der Universität zu München. (History of the Old Germans, especially the Franks. By Conrad Mannert, Aulic Counsellor and regular Professor at the University of Munich.) Stuttgart und Tübingen. 1829. 8vo.

THE early history of Germany is, perhaps, less generally known than that of any other country, amongst those usually prominent in our thoughts when we speak of the European commonwealth. Various causes may have contributed to this. One not uninfluential is the frequent disappearance of the parent stock from the busy scene of general action, even whilst the swarms successively thrown off were either locust-like temporarily over-running and desolating the world, or permanently hiving themselves in its happier districts—a disappearance renewed in later times after the fall of the Hohenstauffen or Swabian emperors. Another cause may be the want of a good German history, either in the languages more familiar to the reading public, or even in the vernacular tongue, the Germans themselves usually proving, it must be confessed, heavy historians. But the principal cause we conceive to be, that one of the last of those conquering swarms already mentioned, the Franks, bestowed their own name upon a part of the land they conquered and occupied; whilst they so amalgamated themselves with the more civilized vanquished inhabitants, whose language they adopted, that they lost even those personal characteristics described as almost universal amongst the Teutonic races, and soon came to be considered, if not actually as Gauls, yet as French, in contradistinction to Germans. Hence, as also from the general adoption of the Frenchified version of his Latin title Carolus Magnus, that most brilliant meteor illuminating the dark ages, Charlemagne,* is to this day esteemed a French prince, although he was not only a German Frank, but one of those Franks who, having settled in the provinces upon the Rhine, had remained pure unadulterated Germans; although he habitually held his court at Aachen, or Aix, (which even to a late period continued to be a sort of metropolis of the German empire, where the emperors were, or ought to be, elected,) and spoke German as his mother tongue; nay not only spoke, but endeavoured to raise it to the dignity of a written and cultivated language, by collecting all the national poems then extant, including perhaps those metrical records of ancestral fame mentioned by Tacitus as common amongst the early Germans. These songs, so invaluable to the historian, the philosopher and the philologist, to say nothing of the antiquary and the poet, were rejected, if not destroyed, by the piety of his son Louis *le Debonnaire*, on account of their heathenism.

But however naturally it may have arisen, such ignorance concerning the only nation that, with permanent success, resisted the gigantic power of Rome, partially at least foiling her vaticinated destiny, *regere imperio populos*, and which, in the end, actually subjected the larger portion of the western Roman empire, is not to be therefore approved or justified. Assuredly there is no other modern nation whose early history can possess equal claims to

* More brilliant, perhaps, than our Alfred, though less wise, less great, and less good.

general interest with the German, to whom we may, with but little alteration, apply what Sismondi, in the Introduction to his *Histoïre des Français,* says of France.

" The central situation of France, her power, the long duration of her monarchy, the supremacy which at two or three different intervals she has acquired over the whole of the West, have so linked her destiny with all the others, that the revolutions of European nations proceed almost always from those of France, so that next to the national history, the history of France is that which each of them ought to study. Germany, Italy, Northern Spain, Savoy, Belgium, Holland, and Switzerland, all formed part of the monarchy of the Merovingian or Carlovingian Franks. With their subjection to that monarchy commences, for these countries, the history of all the nations which now inhabit them."

Of course we cannot here pretend to supply the historical *desideratum* to which we have alluded, but we may briefly indicate the points of striking and general European interest that mark the early annals of the Germans.

The Germans first present themselves to our notice as warriors alarming, nay terrifying, the arrogant Romans, and that not in the infancy of their power, when the Samnites or the Volscians were formidable antagonists, but in the very fullness of their strength, in the first vigour of youthful manhood, when Italy, Spain, part of Gaul, the northern coast of Africa, Greece, Syria and Asia Minor were subdued to the republican yoke. Then was it that the Cimbri and Teutones, issuing from the North of Germany, (which, with the northern coast of Gaul, is the situation where we first find the Teutonic races, the southern division of both countries being occupied by Celtic or Keltic tribes,) invaded and harassed Italy, chilling the mistress of the world with fear. Nor was the fear groundless. They were only to be kept from thundering at the gates of the Capitol by the talents and energies of that mighty plebeian Caius Marius, who, upon this occasion, was allowed by the haughty patricians to hold the consulate year after year, unopposed, and we apprehend unenvied. Marius repulsed and utterly defeated these dreaded barbarians, and the Eternal City recovered her disdainful confidence.

The Germans next meet us in Cæsar's Commentaries. The principal resistance which the future usurper experienced in subduing Gaul, appears to have been offered either by German tribes settled in that country, or German armies from the right bank of the Rhine. Of such an army was Ariovist the leader. He entered Gaul as the ally of one small Gallic state against another; made himself, after the fashion of such allies, master of both parties; and was acknowledged by the Romans as King of the Germans in Gaul. When Cæsar's victory over the Helvetians had filled the Gauls, conscious of their hopes and schemes, with terror, they hastened to lay their submission and homage at the feet of the conqueror, and endeavoured to propitiate him by bitter complaints against the oppression and tyranny of Ariovist. Cæsar promptly undertook to relieve them from all despotism but his own. The superiority of the Romans in military science, joined to his own extraordinary abilities, enabled him to defeat Ariovist, and drive him back across the Rhine, with the remainder of his forces. The German tribes occupying Belgium and some provinces in the north of Gaul, were next compelled to submit, if that state may fairly be called one of submission, in which the reluctant native watches for every opportunity of insurrection, and seizing it, often inflicts great and serious evil upon the detested master. Twice Julius Cæsar crossed the Rhine; but if we judge from the shortness and inactivity of his stay upon the right bank of the river, rather for the purpose of dazzling the imagination of the Romans by the name of the thing, than with any hope of really extending in that direction the dominions of the haughty Republic, of which he was even then meditating the subversion.

From this period the Germans inhabiting Germany beyond the Rhine seem for some centuries to have contended merely for their own independence, leaving their brethren in Gaul (who formed four Roman provinces, *i. e.* 1st and 2d Germania, 1st and 2d Belgium) to themselves. The struggle was attended with fluctuating success, according to the individual character of the several emperors who successively occupied the throne of the world. During the reign of the all-powerful Augustus, repeated and successful incursions into Germany were made by Drusus and Tiberius; but they effected no permanent establishment, and their temporary success was amply avenged by the defeat, the actual annihilation, of Varus and his army of occupation. The son of Drusus was sent to avenge the disgrace of the Roman eagles, and is stated to have been still more fortunate in his enterprizes than his father or his uncle. But he was recalled from the theatre of his triumphs by the suspicious jealousy of Tiberius, and his own surname of Germanicus was the most durable monument of his achievements. Perhaps the success which he and his predecessors did obtain, might in no small measure be ascribed to the perpetual divisions of the different German states amongst themselves.

As the power of Rome dwindled in the hands of insane or profligate tyrants, and of a people corrupt enough to submit to an authority only redeemed from contempt by its atrocity, the complexion of the contest betwixt the empire and the Germans changed. The latter, instead of merely struggling to preserve their own freedom, became in their turn the aggressors. Rome was still not altogether fallen, and the fortunes of either party alternated as before, but with a constant tendency in favour of the purer and nobler, if more barbarous Germans. Whilst German adventurers now occasionally wore the imperial crown, different tribes gradually extended their conquests in different directions, until, towards the close of the fifth century,—the Ostrogoths occupying Italy—the Visigoths, Suevi and Burgundians Spain, Portugal, Southern Gaul and Switzerland—the Franks Northern Gaul, and the Saxons England, the western Roman empire was at an end. In the course of this contest, the Germans, by repulsing Attila and his Huns, saved Europe, perhaps, from being assimilated to the barbarism of Central Asia, (the Franks and Visigoths under their respective kings, in conjunction with Ætius and a Roman army, consisting almost entirely of Germans, defeated Attila near Chalons); and within the next 300 years the Franks under Charles Martel merited similar gratitude from Christian Europe, by defeating the Saracens near Tours.

But it is not in their martial character alone, it is not merely as the conquerors of ancient Europe, or even as the founders of the states of modern Europe, that the early Germans command our attention, or our interest. Their simple institutions, either such as we first find them, or as they necessarily developed themselves in the course of their conquering career, are the true source of all the systems of polity that have since prevailed. From these are derived alike the feudalism of the most enthralled of continental nations, and the free constitution of England, her parliaments, and her trial by jury. Further, to the pure chastity of their manners, and the consequent respect entertained for the weaker sex, may be ascribed much of the lofty spirit of chivalry, much of the just rank now held by woman, and consequently much of the immeasurable superiority of the modern structure of society, even in its lowest state, over the boasted civilization of Greece and Rome; and we think we discover the origin of much of the spirit of Protestantism, certainly of the mysticism that characterizes modern German piety, in the deep religious feelings with which our common ancestors, disdaining idols and temples, worshipped an invisible divine influence in the solemn gloom of their forests.

Nor to the philosopher, to the classical scholar, and to the historical student, is it the least of the claims of the Germans that our knowledge of those institutions and manners is chiefly derived from Tacitus. His countrymen, if they could not actually contemn the bold warriors, whose prowess they dreaded, still regarded them as mere savages, whose courage was the only quality they possessed deserving notice. But the high-minded moralist, who shrank in disgust from the vices that surrounded him—the philosophical politician, who beheld in those vices the source of the slavery and degeneracy of the once sovereign Republic, felt his best sympathies kindle into admiration whilst he contemplated the rude, perhaps, but genuine virtues, the uncompromising spirit of liberty that dwelt in the primeval forests of Germany. He *may* have coloured these excellencies too highly (he is taxed with having so done) to enhance the contrast with Roman license and baseness, but he has painted them with a graphic truth, which, through all the changes of times and seasons, of government and religion, of refinement and corruption, we can still recognise.

We must now turn to the two distinguished authors whom it is our present business to review. Both are known and esteemed for various historical, biographical and geographical works, and will assuredly not lessen their established reputation by the productions before us, which the historical student will find invaluable magazines of information, although we would by no means recommend either for translation, German history being in truth untranslatable. Both Luden and Mannert profess to write their several Histories for the purpose of instilling into their readers a veneration like their own for their early ancestors. In other respects they not only treat their subject very dissimilarly, but take very opposite views of some main points; the differences being, perhaps, of the kind that might be anticipated from the comparative bulk of their Histories. Konrad Mannert, who gives us the history of the Franks to the death of Charlemagne in one moderate octavo volume,* takes facts, for the most part, as he finds them recorded in ancient authors. He is somewhat dry and cold, from his brevity, (an uncommon fault, by the way, in a German,) but his statements are clear. He presents the received opinions of historians and legal antiquaries in a distinct and compact form, paints broadly the good and bad qualities of all parties, and if he neither interests nor delights, instructs his reader. We should add, that he occasionally illustrates his positions with incidents of the times he is describing, which are well told, and afford a pleasing relief to the mind.

Heinrich Luden, on the other hand, is a true German. His History is of the German nation, and to be completed in ten thick octavo volumes; or should it extend to a few more, he thinks no reasonable man can object. He begins with the very first mention of the Germans in Roman history, and intimates that he may possibly end with the fifteenth century. He does not impart his reasons, and we confess ourselves unable to discover, why the

---

* We observe that a *second* volume has just appeared.

·history of the German nation should cease when the German empire was about to resume an active part in European politics.
But of this when the time comes; that is to say, when our author
shall have brought down his work to the period in question. For
the present we have only to do with the first four volumes, which
end with the coronation of Charlemagne as Roman emperor; and
we take them without awaiting the forthcoming of more, because
they comprise the whole of the interesting period concerning
which we have just given our own views, and moreover nearly
coincide with that selected by Mannert.

Unlike Mannert, Luden takes no fact as he finds it in ancient
authors. Of him might indeed be said what Sismondi says of
German jurists. " their prodigious research, their ingenious
criticism, their skill in detaching resemblances and connections,
drawing new truths out of the well of old facts, have in more
recent times, thrown a blaze of light on the antiquities common
to both Franks and Germans," (a part and the whole.) Luden
reasons upon the prejudices and interests that must have coloured
the statements of former historians, upon what they say and what
they suppress. He puts together hints casually dropped by different writers; shows where the subsequent course of events convicts them of misrepresentation, or at least of omission; and supplies a conjectural narrative from all these sources. This he does
by the Greek and Latin authors in behalf of the Germans collectively; and by the Frank chroniclers, on behalf of the Saxons,
Bavarians, Thuringians, and in short of all the tribes who resisted
the supremacy assumed by their conquering Frank brethren. We
hardly need subjoin, that the facts thus elicited or surmised are all
favourable to his and our common ancestors, or that it is requisite
to read so speculative an historian with caution, lest the unlearned
should take these fanciful relations for established and admitted
history, at least for what, according to the French wit, *on est con-
venu de croire.*

Many of these argumentative disquisitions have, we must say,
afforded us considerable pleasure. Before reaching the end of
the fourth volume, however, such unceasing, laborious, subtle and
conjectural investigations of what must or may have been the con-
catenation of events, becomes wearisome; and Luden's illustrative
incidents want the contrast which gives effect to Mannert's. In
short, although this *plaidoyer* on behalf of the old Germans has to
us proved on the whole gratifying in the perusal, we would nevertheless fain hope, that the author may not deem it necessary to pursue the same course through all his remaining volumes, whatever be
their number. But we doubt such hope were idle, since he tells
us in an apologetical introduction prefixed to his fourth volume—

" Had I had nothing new to offer, I should assuredly never have undertaken to write the History of the German nation;" and we grievously fear that such novelty must still be evolved out of the same kind of sifting of old records.

Some of the new opinions advanced in the present volume are sufficiently bold and original. Of course we cannot pretend, within our limits, to discuss, or even to enumerate them all; nor, if we could, would the subject prove entertaining to the general reader; whilst to the lover of historical investigation we decidedly recommend the original work. A few of these historical heresies, however, we shall briefly mention, selecting such as possess most general interest for a degree of detail that may give a fair idea of Luden's talents and manner. Amongst these are his denial of any wandering propensity in the early Germans as nations, and consequent assertion that almost all their conquests were made by bands of youthful adventurers without property at home, led forth by some distinguished prince or leader similarly circumstanced; his defence of Brunhildis and Fredegundis, more commonly known and reprobated as Brunehault and Fredegonde; his averment that the last Merovingian kings, the *Rois fainéans* of French history, were treated with all external decorum by the aspiring Carlovingian *Maires du Palais*, whom he denominates *Haus Æltester*, or House-Elder, and conceives to have originally been the fiscal chief of the *Geleit*, or body of adventurers constituting the king's household, or family; from the very nature of which *Geleit* he ingeniously deduces the necessary rise and development of the feudal system. This subject is, we think, skilfully handled; so is his inquiry into the name of Germans, given by the Gauls to their warlike neighbours, as our author conceives, because the frontier guards, with whom they came most into contact, called themselves the *Wehr Münner,* men of war or defence; further deriving many names of tribes or states from similar sources, as Marcomanni, Marchmen; Bavarians, *Wehren* against the Baji or Boji; Franks, not from *frank,* meaning free, nor from Φρακτοι, meaning armed, nor from their favourite weapon the *francisca,* which he thinks more likely to have been so named from them, but from the word *Wrangen,* still used in Lower Saxony for to fight or to brawl; whence the name might mean quarrelsome, or, perhaps, bold warriors. But Luden's speculations concerning Tacitus's treatise *De Moribus Germanorum* must, we think, whether approved or rejected, interest every classical scholar, every admirer of the great Latin historian. This treatise Luden considers as merely notes or materials, prepared beforehand by Tacitus for that portion of his History which was to treat of his countrymen's wars with the Germans. The German author says,

" This work, single in its kind, has often been over-valued, as well on account of its author, as of the great importance which the nation to whom it is dedicated, has since acquired; yet, never can it be sufficiently valued. Wrongfully has it been esteemed a masterpiece; but it contains the essence of all that the Romans knew concerning Germany and Germans. Every statement is written with the genius that never deserted Tacitus, because it was peculiarly his, and the whole of his notices present themselves in that pure light of lofty morality through which his works so powerfully affect well ordered minds. But the detached statements seem loosely strung together, as the facts became known to the author; they are not wrought into a whole, into a lucid representation. Hence, it is not probable that Tacitus designed to make these remarks upon Germany known in this form. There is scarcely any thing in the writing that should induce such an opinion. It would rather seem that Tacitus had collected these notices for the sake of the other works which he had written, or might intend to write. They were materials for historical representations, — separate sketches, such as every historian makes or needs. To give his history the truth, life, and intrinsic truth, capable of compensating for want of fullness, he felt it indispensable to know the world which had produced that Prince Armin,[*] before whose might the Roman eagles had fled. As he might judge it impossible to obtain a complete knowledge of this world, he sought from the detached pieces of information he met with to elicit general principles, the individuality distinguishing the German from other nations, the peculiar nature of the land upon which their life developed itself. He sought to attain to a perception of the original constitution of their civil society, of which the constitution of so many states, which separately he could neither understand nor describe, were only branches, similar in character, with particular deviations, produced by situation and circumstances. In like manner he sought to investigate the essence of their morals and religion, because the customs of single nations could rarely be known to him. And what information he gained he put together inartificially, in order to stand upon a spiritual ground-work, in his representation of great events. Circumstances unknown to us led him perhaps, afterwards, to publish the crude remarks which he could not work up, or they may have been made known accidentally, and then may a necessary connexion have been given to the detached parts, which originally they neither had nor wanted. Thus, it should seem, arose this admired and incomprehensible *booklet*."

To this statement of opinion is appended a note, explaining the grounds upon which it rests, far too long to translate, but which we will try to condense and extract so as to do it justice.

" Hardly any one can have read and meditated this treatise through, without feeling himself staggered, and compelled to acknowledge that he does not well know what to make of the tiny *booklet*, and that it wants the pure historical character.

" As for myself, I confess a doubt has often crossed my mind whether it really were written by Tacitus. From this doubt I was scared by the

---

* The Arminius of Latin, the Hermann of most German writers.

genius that in various detached parts spoke to me irrefragably, and which I could only agnize as the genius of Tacitus ; this doubt was likewise opposed by a feeling of bitter pain that I could not subdue."

This terrible doubt rested chiefly upon the circumstance of the *MS. de Mor. Germ.* not being found with any of the oldest MSS. of Tacitus's other works, and of its not being mentioned by any ancient writer upon Germany except Cassiodorus, who quotes it thus, *quodam Cornelio scribente,* and who could say ' one Cornelius,' of Tacitus? This *quodam,* however, Luden argues from the context to be the blunder of a copyist for *quondam,* and thence that Cassiodorus knew the Germany as the work of Tacitus. A stone fell from our author's heart ; still it was not a book meant for publication, but *notamina,* studies for his own use, an opinion grounded upon nine reasons.

1st. The title is borrowed from Livy, with the mere addition of the word *populis,—de situ, moribus, populisque Germaniæ.*

2dly. It has no introduction. The first sentences of the Annals, History, and Life of Agricola, respectively state the purport of the several works.

" It may therefore be confidently averred that it was the style of Tacitus, in the works he designed for publication, to establish a friendly understanding with his readers, to greet them, and give them notice what they would and what they would not find. But the *Germania* begins without address, without definition, without the appearance of the author, or mention of the reader, in a word, without introduction : *Germania omnis— separatur,* &c. No one will deny that this beginning is a deviation from the usage of Tacitus, no one will deny further that this deviation is the more unaccountable from its striking resemblance to Cæsar's *Gallia est omnis divisa,* &c. So bald an imitation would certainly have been avoided by such a writer as Tacitus, though it is natural enough if he thought of no reader but himself."

3dly. The same absence of all communication between author and reader prevails throughout the book, except when some habitual turn indicates it, or where single sentences may have been subsequently inserted.

" 4thly. The whole character of the book presents a want of solidity, of completeness, as belongs to general remarks and portraitures. What it contains are sketches, often singularly happy sketches ; but nothing is wrought out. The outline only is given ; the frames only are prepared. Observe, for instance, the few notices relative to Germany's geographical position, rivers, mountains, nature, and character, the doubtful notices of the sites of different nations. Impossible that Tacitus should have thus written, had he purposed a picture of Germany for the world, a *rationarium Germaniæ.* Other parts again are so circumstantial and so positive as not to accord with a whole, containing parts so loose and uncertain.

" 5thly. The whole work is in a manner taken out of time. In vain do we ask ourselves—when did the state of things described in the *Germania* exist in Germany ? We find no fixed epoch. Sometimes we incline to think of an earlier, sometimes we are forcibly referred to a later age. It is no condition evolved by the changes of life, and extant at any definite period; it is rather a generalization of life, the ground-work, the permanent throughout all change."

The 6th, 7th, and 8th reasons are the apparent want of plan, or order in the book, instanced by the frequent introduction of reflexions, of irrelevant, or rather misplaced matter, suggested by a mere expression employed. The abruptness of some sentences, unlike any thing but memoranda ; and finally, sentences, or portions of sentences in prose or verse, taken, without alteration or acknowledgement, from other authors.

" 9thly. The notices constituting the *Germania* are used in the Annals and History. Their impression is indisputably manifest in the account of the wars of Armin and Civilis. Parts are literally repeated, as, for instance, in the Annals, compare cap. 29, with Ann. iv. 12; cap. 31, with Ann. iv. 61; cap. 28, with Ann. xii. 27. Yet more occurs in the Histories. Other passages are improved, so as wholly to deviate from the *Germania*. And had we the rest of the Histories, it would perhaps appear that the whole of the *Germania* had been used. When, therefore, any contradiction appears between the *Germania* and the Annals or History, these last indubitably merit the preference upon single points, since they relate actions ; but the general truth is in the *Germania*, which contains the permanent, the essence of German life, wherein those actions originated.

" But enough of indications ! It would require a large treatise thoroughly to establish a view, which, for the present, can only solicit toleration and pardon."

We have already said that we do not propose entering into controversy for or against Luden's opinions, and we shall adhere to our determination now, notwithstanding the vivid interest attaching to every thing connected with the name of Tacitus. We cannot, however, quite forbear observing, that we have ourselves been struck with the unconnectedness of which Luden speaks, with the verbal repetitions and the occasional discrepancies, although without considering their hearings quite as profoundly, as critically, or as alarmingly, as our German historian. We shall next select, as our specimen of Luden's historical style, his History of Arminius, a favourite hero, whose adventures, since the rise of a more national patriotic spirit in Germany have again become a chosen subject for the national muse. We shall proceed as before, alternately abstracting and extracting.

Our diligent author first devotes a page and a half to an investigation of the character of Quinctilius Varus, from the accounts of different historians, from known facts, and from probabilities, deciding that he was a man very much as men go, and that his idiosyncrasy had nothing to do with the catastrophe, which, entirely through the force of circumstances, occurred during his command of the German provinces. Germany, after the successes of Drusus and Tiberius, appeared to be tranquillized; peace and amicable intercourse between Germans and Romans prevailed, the former discovering an incipient taste for the higher cultivation and fine arts of the latter. It would thence be inferred at Rome, that the country was ripe for the establishment of the customary forms of provincial administration; and Varus was accordingly instructed to introduce them. This the *routinier* Varus, incapable of appreciating the difference between the worn-out Syrians and the youthfully vigorous Germans, set about as a common-place business. He observed the usual military, but no moral precautions. He left two legions under his nephew to guard the passage of the Rhine and secure his communication with Gaul, and advanced with three of Rome's best legions, six cohorts, three squadrons of cavalry, and a number of Gallic auxiliaries, in all 50,000 men, from the Rhine to the Lippe. In the country of the Cheruscans, upon the left bank of the Weser, he fixed a stationary camp, where he sat in prætorian dignity, issuing edicts of civil administration, imposing tributes, ordering contributions, investigating and judging the disputes of Germans with Romans or amongst themselves, according to foreign laws, pronouncing sentence in a foreign tongue, and inflicting corporal punishments undreamt of by the free natives, whom he was thus bending to the yoke. All this was enough to exasperate a gallant race, independently of the probable individual vexations and outrages practised by an insolent soldiery.

"Amongst the men who most deeply felt the whole weight of misfortune pressing upon their country, a youth named Armin stood by far the highest. He was the son of Segimer, a Cheruscan prince * * * When Armin placed himself at the head of his nation, he was twenty-five years of age. The beauty of his person, the strength of his arm, the keenness of his faculties, the promptitude of his judgment, have been extolled by his enemies; they have acknowledged that the fire of genius flashed from his eyes and animated his features. But no details of his earlier life have been transmitted to us. He had long been in the service of Rome, perhaps during the expedition of Tiberius. He now sojourned in the Roman camp, as the leader of one of the auxiliary bands which the Cheruscans were bound to supply. Rome had honoured him with the rights of citizenship, and with equestrian rank. Varus preferred him above all his fellow countrymen, and with him, for his sake, his father Segimer. It was the esteem which genius, energy, and activity must always meet with. In this youth the barbarian disappeared to the Roman eye, and only the distinguished man was seen."

Segestes, another Cheruscan prince, was one of those whom idleness, vanity, or blindness, had reconciled to the Roman yoke. He also had been honoured with the rights of citizenship, but was jealous of Armin's superiority of every description, and sought by calumnious accusations of falsehood and treachery, to ruin him in the opinion of Varus. Varus might possibly see through the motives of Segestes; or in his proud sense of Roman greatness he might disdain such insinuations; or he might be naturally unsuspicious. He rejected the information of Segestes, and continued to confide in Armin. The insurrection of a distant German nation, neither the name nor the seat of which are known, first disturbed the security of Varus. He broke up his camp, and summoning the German princes to accompany him, marched against the insurgents. But considering himself still in a friendly, or rather a subject land, he marched without the order or discipline requisite in the neighbourhood of an enemy. The legions moved at a distance from each other, separated and encumbered by their baggage, by women, children, and a crowd of other unwarlike and unarmed persons, who had gathered around the stationary camp, and would not be left behind.

"But when the adjacent German states beheld the advance of the Roman army, when the distant heard of it, the long-suppressed rage burst forth. A strong light flashed through the midnight darkness, enkindling the hearts of men. The cry of freedom rang from community to community, the cry of vengeance from district to district. Every man saw his own danger in the danger threatening his brother. One feeling impelled all to one resolve. The whole German people, as far as the tidings spread, rose like one man * * * Every where the Roman soldiers were surprised, every where the Roman citizens slain, and from all sides the *Landsturm** came roaring on to surround the Roman army, to check its march, to assault, to annihilate the foe, and deliver the common country. So universal was the inspiring indignation, that Sigismund, the son of Segestes, who had been sent by his father to serve at the altar of the Roman deities beyond the Rhine, tore off his sacerdotal fillet at the voice of his country, and hurried back across the Rhine to join his struggling brethren. Not Segestes himself remained unmoved—the torrent hurried him onwards with his people despite his previous blindness, despite his envy and hatred of Armin.

"Meanwhile the Romans leisurely pursued their march down the Weser, sensible only to the difficulties of the way, unconscious of the circle of woe that was rapidly closing around them. Varus, upon the first report of disorder and opposition amongst his German auxiliaries, issued a juridical summons to the ringleaders, either because his delusion was still undissolved, or, what is more likely, because he judged it needful to maintain a show of unalterable constancy. But the distress

---

* The rising of the population *en masse* at the call of government.

grew, the danger came nearer. The paths were already obstructed with large trees: the compatriot gods, favouring the pious enterprise, sent tempests and deluges of rain; the discomfort and shivering of the chilled body rapidly increased the anxiety rising upon the mind; and the shaken spirits were further harassed by ghastly apparitions in heaven and upon earth. Bloody passages already occurred between the Romans and the German auxiliaries accompanying the army."

Varus was now aware of his danger, but still affected unconsciousness, treating all as mere ordinary squabbles, and issuing useless orders for their suppression. The various evils continued to augment, and thus the army reached the defiles and quagmires of the Teutoberg forest. Then did Armin stand forward with his Cheruscans. His known character, or evident abilities and energies, procured him the chief command; and he felt that the embarrassment of the situation of the Romans rendered this the moment to effect their destruction.

" The Romans hindered, pressed, and weakened, by repeated attacks under his guidance, wearied by the forest, the wind, and the rain, and perhaps not less exhausted by hunger than by their growing anxiety, saw the day draw to a close, without bringing them nearer the end of their troubles. They once more attempted to fortify the camp they had pitched upon a clear space, but their strength and courage proved unequal even to this work of habitual discipline. The wonted fortifications, however deep the sense of their necessity, remained unfinished. But Armin did not assault the open camp during the night. His Germans likewise required rest, the enemy could not escape ; and a nocturnal engagement might be hazardous from the mode of warfare of his countrymen, and from the total want of order amongst their hastily assembled masses.

" But when on the following morning the Roman army, discouraged or hopeless, broke up from its encampment, the projected attack began on all sides. Armin, stationing himself upon an eminence whence he could overlook the field, directed the efforts of his men by word and gesture, by shout and exhortation, and directed the shock of the wedge * to the point where he foresaw that it would fall most destructively. A fearful battle ! The Romans in gloomy despair, fought for the last of earthly possessions, life ; the Germans in joyous expectation for the first of blessings, liberty ; both with the utmost exertion of which human nature is capable. On the one side the moan of suffering, the yell of agony ; on the other, the battle song, the shout of triumph ; both mingling in the splash of pouring rain,† and the howling of tempestuous winds ! Varus was wounded. Overpowered by the pain of his wound, unmanned by the sense of calamity, discovering no chance of preservation, but perceiving in himself hereditary courage sufficient to brave death, he with

---

* The usual German form of battle array, or attack.

† In a note Luden expresses his doubts concerning this incessant bad weather, judging that the vanquished might deem it less mortifying to have been defeated by the elements than by men.

his own hand plunged his sword into his breast, thus at once escaping from the sight of inevitable misery, and from the just revenge of an enemy intoxicated with success. Many followed this example of despair; many lost all recollection in the terror of impending death; few were energetic enough for the resolve to seek for death in battle. Cejonius, one of the camp-prefects, would have purchased life by surrender, but his colleague Eggius prevented such a disgrace. Both fell honourably. Vala Numonius, Varus's legate, attempted to fly with the cavalry, but destruction overtook the fugitives. A very few accidentally escaped the common lot. At last, the multitude, deprived of their commanders, and rendered indifferent to life or death by long exertion and suffering, allowed themselves to be cut down without resistance. And now, when a hostile weapon was no longer seen, the slaughter ceased, the defenceless were made prisoners. Then did the inspired warriors send up from the ensanguined field an infinite shout of victory, a thanksgiving to the patron gods of their native land, a signal of recovered liberty to their wives and fathers.

Such is Luden's view of the great battle in the Teutoberg forest. Now follow the contrary statements of the Roman historians, who attribute the whole series of events from Varus's passing the Rhine, to a deep-laid conspiracy of the Germans, organized by Armin, and carried on and kept secret for three years, by which the Roman general was lured away from his resources. Against this our patriotic author argues upon the general principles of human nature, the ordinary course of human affairs, and the national character of the Germans. He observes moreover, that Tacitus, although he tells the same tale of treachery, refers it wholly to the authority of the renegade Segestes, concluding, " Varus fell a victim to fate and to the might of Arminius." Luden adds :

" The Roman authors undertook a tortuous work in a tortuous spirit. They endeavoured by inculpating the German nation, and Armin, its saviour and founder, to maintain the honour of the Roman arms, misused in unsuccessful attempts against God and nature. The duty of a German historian of the German nation is to defend and assert the holiest possession of that nation,—its honour, and to clear the founder of that nation from the stains which have now, for 1800 years, hung upon his name. This is so much the more his duty as he is able fully to refute such imputations, and need not meet them by counter charges.* * * The German nation avenged its wrongs and asserted its liberties, hurried on by the force of its own spirit, impelled to resolve and to act by the holiest feelings of the human heart. Armin served the Romans faithfully so long as his engagement lasted. He joined his countrymen with his whole soul when they burst the chain upon which that engagement hung; and he took the high station befitting him; when the force of circumstances, the pressure of the hour, brought on the decision of the great question, whether a German nation—whether liberty,—should thenceforward exist, or whether a universal slavery should enthral the world, stifling genius, virtue, and all that is great, noble, and beautiful? This was the conspiracy of the Germans, this the treachery of Armin."

Luden next endeavours to disprove the cruelties alleged by Roman survivors, to have been practised by the conquerors upon their prisoners. He allows that some few deeply outraged individuals might thus revenge themselves, but that the main body must have preserved their captives to till the soil; a business always devolved upon those whom Latin authors designate slaves, but modern Germans *leibeigene* or *hörigen*, the German terms for the worst degree of feudal villenage.

" When the first burst of passion, of rage, and revenge, of joy and rapture, uncontrollable in the intoxication of victory had subsided, Armin raised his voice amidst the sons of freedom. As in the hour of pressure he was the leader, so in the hour of victory he was the orator of his nation. What had been gained was now to be preserved. Cheruscans and Bructeri, Marsi and Chatti had fought the great fight in common. But it was a mere impulse of patriotism, irresistible in anxiety and danger, that, like blind Chance, had drawn them together. Nothing was accomplished, if every state, every warrior should now go their several ways to enjoy the booty, to employ the thrales obtained in the fight. What had originated in accident was to be maintained by reason. In this sense, over the corses of slaughtered foes, in the fair and proud moment of victory, spoke Armin of the German nation, of a German country. He found open ears and minds, and thus became the founder of a great confederation for common defence against a common enemy, now doubly to be dreaded after such disgrace. Armin himself became the head of the confederation, because, in the battle he had earned the highest meed of glory, because he governed men and things with the most potent genius.*** Armin sent the head of Varus to Marobod.* It was a token by which Marobod might learn that if his formidable position had enabled him with inactive might to preserve the German name untainted in the South, every spot had now been washed away in the North by battle and victory; that fame and power were great here as there; and that henceforward it would be proper to act in one sense, in one alliance. We know not what Armin said to Marobod; we know not what Marobod answered to Armin. But the token was understood. Marobod transmitted the head to Tiberius. The Romans might perceive that there existed one great German confederation, extending from the Danube to the Ocean."

The Germans now cleared the right bank of the Rhine of all Roman stations, but seem not to have thought of passing the river. And as Tiberius, whom Augustus hastily despatched to the left bank, in alarm as to their possible intentions, contented himself with re-establishing the strictest discipline amongst the

* Marobod had led a body of Marcomanni into the South of Germany, where, by conquest, he founded a considerable kingdom.

legions, and making one short excursion across the river after the earlier fashion, in which he does not appear to have seen an enemy, we learn little of the proceedings of the Germans. Luden, however, judges that the confederation produced by danger must have become relaxed in tranquillity, and that Armin's power and influence must have declined.

" Betwixt Armin, the deliverer of Germany, and Segestes, the blinded creature of Rome, arose a bitter enmity, which led to war and treachery. This enmity doubtless sprang from the irritation felt by Segestes, when he saw the man whom he had laboured to ruin by calumniating, crowned with glory, and idolized by the whole nation. He hated Armin because he was conscious of having fruitlessly as craftily plotted against him, and he persecuted him the more acrimoniously the higher he saw him raised above himself and his artifices. We know not the cause of the explosion. Armin was married to a daughter of Segestes, whose name, Thusnelda, we learn from Strabo only. The time of his marriage is unknown, its manner is enigmatical: according to Tacitus, he carried her off forcibly."

The improbability of Armin's having committed so lawless an act is discussed at great length, but no important fact is brought forward, save that Thusnelda's first and only child was unborn in the fifth year after the great battle, whence it seems probable that the marriage took place subsequently to that event. What is known is, that Segestes, a little before the death of Augustus, surprised Armin, seized him and Thusnelda, and for a while held them both in captivity. At this period the Roman legions upon the left bank of the Rhine were in a state of mutiny, provoked by their desire to raise Germanicus to the imperial throne instead of Tiberius; and the Cæsar, Germanicus, after having in a manner reduced them to obedience, sought to give a vent to their ill-humours by leading them across the boundary river to surprise the unprepared Marsi in their sleep, of whom they made a great slaughter, without incurring any loss. But the news of this incursion aroused the slumbering confederation, and, as Luden conjectures,

" awoke a longing for Armin, so that the hero of his country's liberty probably owed his own to the companions of his fame. He appeared once more at their head. But his wife was parted from him, remaining in her father's custody."

When the Romans had recrossed the Rhine, Armin attempted to recover Thusnelda out of her father's hands; but Segestes, through his son Sigismund, applied to Germanicus for assistance. The Cæsar detained Sigismund as a prisoner or a hostage, but hastened to the relief of his father, then besieged by Armin or his friends. He attacked and defeated the be-

siegers, delivered Segestes, recovered much of the booty taken
upon the day of Varus's disaster, and captured Armin's wife and
unborn heir.   Segestes made a long speech to his deliverers, but
was too insignificant, too much despised by his countrymen, to
be valuable as an ally.   He was sent across the Rhine by Germanicus, and Thusnelda bore her son in a Roman prison, to
languish with herself in thraldom.

Armin, maddened by grief and rage at this complete loss of
his wife and expected child, flew from state to state of the Confederation, imprecating curses upon the false Segestes, calling
upon every German to arm in vengeance for the wrongs inflicted
upon their chief, their brother.   The Cheruscans and other allied
nations obeyed his call, and his uncle, Inguiomer, for the first
time gave them the sanction of his concurrence.   Inguiomer was,
like Armin and Segestes, a Cheruscan prince, (for every district
had its own prince,) but his dominions lay remote from the
Roman borders, and his consequence was enhanced in the eyes
of friends and foes by distance.   The Cæsar, fearing an attack,
endeavoured to prevent it by again carrying the war into Germany.   He sent one division of his army under Cæcina, by land
to the banks of the Ems; embarked in person with the remainder; sailed, or rather rowed, for the mouth of the same
river, which he entered, and landing, re-united his forces.   The
Chauci submitted to the terror of his arms.   The Bructeri,
according to a common German practice, removed or destroyed
their property, leaving the enemy a desart to traverse.   Germanicus advanced unchecked, and reached the Teutoberg forest,
where he collected and interred the bones of the Roman legions
that had lain five years unburied.   The army raised a tumulus, or
barrow, to their honour.

When this pious duty was discharged, the Cæsar proceeded to
the Lippe, where he found Armin.   The German leader fell
back to the edge of a forest, and the Roman sent forward his
cavalry to occupy the open ground; but Armin now turned
suddenly upon the foe, and some ambushed troops, rushing forth
at this signal, assailed them in flank and rear.   The Roman
cavalry were broken and fled, hurrying along with them the
auxiliary cohorts sent by Germanicus to their support.   The
legions remained in battle array, and were not attacked.   Nevertheless the Cæsar's plans seem to have been foiled, his high-
raised hopes disappointed, and he began his retreat.

He himself re-embarked with his division, and returned as he
had come, except that he suffered some loss through Roman inexperience of the ocean tides, landing his men upon ground left
dry by the ebb, where they were surprised by the returning flood.

Cæcina had to retrace his steps by land, and experienced many of the evils that had attended the march of Varus. Armin and the Germans attacked his troops in every difficult pass. The Romans were cut down in numbers, they lost their baggage, and, upon one occasion, they were indebted for the power of pressing forwards, solely to the Germans' eagerness for plunder. The next day the same scenes were repeated, the progress of the Romans being still less, and thus it would probably have continued, to the consummation of a second Teutoberg forest catastrophe, had Armin's authority been equal to the emergency; but Inguiomer was impatient of his nephew's prudent dilatoriness: he urged the immediate storming of the Roman camp, at once to complete the annihilation of the enemy, and to secure a larger booty in better condition. This advice suited the temper of the impetuous warriors: Armin was overruled, and the camp attacked. This operation created a good deal of confusion amongst the disorderly Germans, of which Roman tactics and discipline enabled Cæcina to avail himself. He broke through with the remnant of his division, and made his way to the Rhine; but tidings of their disasters had preceded them, and the bridge by which they were to cross would have been broken down, and their destruction thus rendered inevitable, had it not been preserved by the firmness of Agrippina, the wife of Germanicus, and grand-daughter of Augustus. The Germans did not pursue their advantage, hindered probably by dissensions betwixt Armin and Inguiomer.

Germanicus now determined to transport his whole army by water, thus avoiding the evils seemingly inseparable from a march by land, and prepared a considerable fleet. Again he directed his course to the mouth of the Ems, landed and proceeded towards the Weser. Upon the left bank of this river the Romans halted; upon the right was drawn up the German army, with Armin at its head. Armin accosted the Romans across the river, to request that the Cæsar would allow him an interview with his brother, who had remained in the Roman service, and to whom Latin authors give the name of Flavius. Germanicus complied, and the brothers met, with the Weser flowing between them.

" Armin first accosted his brother, inquiring, in accents of horror and sympathy, how he had lost his eye? Flavius named the place and the battle. Armin, in hopes of recalling his brother from his delusion, inquired further, what had been the reward of so great a sacrifice? Flavius replied, that his pay had been increased; that he had received a chain, a crown, and other military decorations. Armin, not without bitter mockery, depreciated all these things, as the paltry wages of labour,

M 2

as the common pay of servitude. Flavius, compelled to defend the whole produce of his life, strove to convince Armin of the madness of offering resistance to Rome. He spoke of Rome's greatness, of the Cæsar's power; of the hard lot of conquered nations; and the mildness displayed towards such as submitted. Even Armin's wife, and the son she had borne him, were not, he said, hostilely treated. Armin rejoined more urgently; 'More than once has Rome's greatness bowed before the strength of German nations; even thy Cæsar's might has repeatedly yielded to German arms; and now will victory again be with us and our cause. Come over! our country has the first right to her sons; only her miserable or criminal offspring will endure the overthrow of her hereditary liberty. The Gods of Germany recal thee! The mother whose womb bore us both implores thee conjointly with me. So long as thou abidest with the Romans must thou be a deserter, a traitor, in the eyes of friends, of kindred, and of the world. Come over, and be one of thy nation's leaders to victory and glory.' Flavius burst into a rage at the energy of this fraternal exhortation, and the more so for its being shouted to him in the face of the Roman army, within ear-shot of spies and eaves-droppers. Furiously he called for his horse and arms, and would have crossed the river to fulfil his unhappy destiny by trying his sword in single combat against his brother. Stertinius hardly withheld the wrath-inflamed man; and Armin, postponing all personal considerations to the interests of his country, referred the decision to the impending battle."

The following day the Germans again appeared upon the right bank of the Weser. Germanicus prepared to cross the river, and sent over his cavalry, together with his Batavian allies, who were practised swimmers, to drive back the Germans and protect the construction of the bridges. The Germans, always ready to facilitate an engagement, did not, it should seem, dispute their passage; but a conflict ensued upon the right bank, in which most of the Batavians, with their leader Cariobald, fell. The Germans then retired into a forest, and suffered the Romans to cross uninterruptedly. The noise of men and horses thronging in the forest, and intelligence imparted by a deserter, led the Cæsar to apprehend a nocturnal attack from a formidable gathering of the confederated nations. He made his preparations accordingly, sought to encourage his troops by depreciating the Germans, and listening unseen to the conversation of the soldiers, satisfied himself of their alacrity for the engagement, an alacrity professedly inspired by gratitude for his kindness, affability, and generosity. The expected night-attack was not made. What prevented it, and how the Germans spent the night, are points, unknown to history. But Luden images to himself and his readers the probable anxieties of Armin, and his exhortation to his army in the morning, when both generals gave the signal to engage.

٬. This battle is described by Tacitus; but Luden, notwithstanding his professed admiration for the Prince of٬Historians, as he calls him, cavils at the whole account, which, as he avers, rests less upon the authority of Tacitus than upon that of the Cæsar Germanicus, from whose statements the former must have derived his information, and who, having undertaken his German expeditions against the inclination—if not the express injunctions—of his imperial uncle Tiberius, and being upon the whole unsuccessful, would inevitably be the more desirous of redeeming his reputation by partial victories. We must confess that the account given by Tacitus of the two divisions of the German army flying, the one backwards, the other, as it should seem, forwards, is somewhat perplexing to ordinary apprehensions; but we doubt whether our readers would thank us for detailing all our enthusiastic historian's reasons for believing that Germanicus, who by the bye is no favourite of his, saw his eight eagles in a. waking vision; that the battle, so far from being unbloody, was hard-fought; that the division which fled forwards really gained the advantage; and that the failure of Armin's plans, with his consequent discomfiture, arose from the unbridled impetuosity with which this forward-flying Cheruscan division attacked prematurely. The certain facts are, that Armin was wounded, and that the Romans remained masters of the field, where they erected a trophy in honour of their victory.

What is equally certain is, that the Germans were not so thoroughly routed but that they were ready to renew the. conflict, even before Armin was sufficiently recovered from his wound to resume the command, which in consequence of his incapacity devolved upon his uncle. This second battle gives birth to a second disquisition like the last. Tacitus allows this one to have been hardly contested, since he states that Germanicus, in the hour of pressure, taking off his helmet in order to be the better known by his men, hurried from post to post exhorting them to perseverance; and that Armin, notwithstanding his wound, did the same. Tacitus further asserts that night put an end to the engagement; that the Romans, in the camp which one legion had fortified during the continuance of the battle, erected a trophy of captured arms, dedicated to Mars, Jupiter, and Augustus, and recording their subjugation of the nations between the Rhine and the Elbe; immediately afterwards, though but little past Midsummer, beginning their retreat. Upon reaching the banks of the Ems the army re-embarked. The fleet was surprized, we are told, by a violent tempest, in which many vessels, a large part of the troops, and almost all the horses and baggage perished. We need hardly add Luden's conclusion that upon this occasion his countrymen gained the victory, at least remained in possession o the field, and that the tempest was merely an excuse of the Roman leader to account for his losses.

In the autumn, Germanicus, to revive the spirit of his army, undertook two simultaneous devastating expeditions across the Rhine, leading the one in person, and committing the other to Caius Silius. Both committed great ravages without encountering an enemy. The Cæsar, who had set his heart upon the conquest of Germany, meditated greater exertions for the next campaign; but his ambitious projects were finally checked. Tiberius, either jealous of the reputation—or fearful of the power—his nephew was acquiring, or perhaps impatient of his thus lavishing Roman blood in fruitless if not disastrous wars, recalled him to Rome, and after allowing him the honour of a triumph over the German nations between the Elbe and the Rhine, sent him to Asia, where he died, as was supposed, by poison. The principal ornaments of Germanicus's triumph were the wife and son of Armin, of whose subsequent fate nothing is known, except that Tacitus says, the son, Thumelicus, grew up at Ravenna, where *ludibriis conflictatus est,* which Luden translates, was exposed to insult and outrage.

After the recal of Germanicus, the Roman commanders, by the orders of Tiberius, confined themselves to precautionary measures against German aggression. But the Germans meditated not as yet such aggression. Content to enjoy their own freedom, or perhaps engrossed by intestine discord, they sought not to emancipate the trans-Rhenane German and Belgian provinces from the yoke of Rome. Of their history for some centuries from this period we know little, the Romans deeming the squabbles of insignificant barbarians unworthy of notice; and their domestic records were probably lost with the songs collected by Charlemagne. Some few hints touching Armin, however, Tacitus has preserved, and with the use Luden makes of them we shall conclude our extracts from his History of the German Nation.

The first of the remaining events of Armin's life known to us is his quarrel with Marobod. Marobod, as we have said, was king of the Marcomanni, and by conquest sovereign of an extensive realm, or rather perhaps confederation, in Southern Germany. Whilst the free northern confederation headed by Armin was struggling against the power of Rome, the authority exercised by a German monarch, however arbitrary, could be no object of jealousy or dissatisfaction; and Armin, after the victory in the Teutoberg forest, had evidently courted an alliance with Marobod. The recal of Germanicus, and the subsequent forbearance of the Romans, changed the relative position of the German leaders.

" Armin was, according to the nature of man, the author of the contest. Marobod, as an absolute prince, although by no means indifferent to the gradual enlargement of his dominions, might easily rest satisfied with his situation. Armin, on the contrary, as the free chief of a free confederation, must necessarily desire and strive to effect the union of all Germans in one and the same association. But with regard to Marobod such an attempt involved a contradiction. He could not place himself under Armin ; Armin could not be willing to own him as his superior, and side by side there was no room for them."

This difficulty, combined with the incompatibility of Marobod's monarchy with the free Cheruscan Confederation, and, as Luden imagines, the discord-promoting arts of Rome, produced dissensions, only to be decided by the sword ; and in the year of our Lord 19, the North-west of Germany marched against the Southeast. But neither army was unanimous. The people subject to Marobod inclined to Armin, attracted by his splendid fame, and by the liberty of the Cheruscan Confederation ; whilst some of the princes who followed Armin were at once, perhaps, envious of that very fame, and dazzled by the brilliancy of Marobod's station. Amongst these last was Inguiomer, who had long been jealous of his nephew's pre-eminence, and now with his whole force deserted the Cheruscans to unite with the Marcomans. The place where the kindred foes encountered has not been ascertained. Each leader sought to animate his army by a harangue ; Marobod endeavouring to transfer the reputation of Armin to Inguiomer, who was now his own ally ; and Armin recapitulating the achievements of the Cheruscans and their allies against the dreaded Romans, whilst he reviled Marobod for basely striving through a servile submission to Rome to revel undisturbed in his regal pomp. In the hard-fought battle that followed, the right wing of either army was defeated, and night interrupted the mutual slaughter, leaving both parties in their original positions. With the dawn of morning the Cheruscans prepared to renew the engagement ; but Marobod had shunned it by retiring to a new position upon a hill in his rear. This retrograde movement appeared to many of his followers tantamount to a defeat ; and such numbers consequently deserted, that he was constrained to retreat into Bohemia, the chief seat of his power ; and the war seems to have been for a while suspended. Marobod, eager for its prosecution, sought for assistance in an alliance with Rome. But Tiberius met his advances coldly, reproached him with his own neutrality during the recent wars between the Romans and the Cheruscan Confederation, and sent his son Drusus into the adjacent Illyrian provinces, manifestly to watch, direct, and profit by the course of events. Drusus, whose mission was of course to act against either party, as should seem best, appears to have craftily induced Marohod to cross the Danube, and trust himself, nearly unarmed and unattended, in the power of the Romans. He did not recross it, but was sent into Italy, where he passed the remainder of his life in a sort of rather honourable captivity.

The fate of Armin was not subjected to the caprices, even if it were hastened by the arts of his natural enemies, although it was decided much about the same time as Marobod's. From Tacitus alone do we learn the catastrophe, and Luden, as usual, distrusts the accuracy of his narration. Tacitus mentions a proposal made by a Prince of the Chatti to Tiberius to poison Armin, and rejected by the Emperor with a noble indignation similar to that with which such a proposal for poisoning Pyrrhus was rejected by the Roman Senate in its prouder days. A comparison by which our patriotic historian conceives that his great predecessor meant to intimate his disbelief of the rejection. For his own part at least, Luden believes only so much of the tale as goes to prove that the idea of murdering Armin had been entertained at Rome. Tacitus adds, that Armin, aiming at sovereignty, was opposed by the free spirit of his countrymen, attacked in arms, and whilst struggling with fluctuating success, was slain by the artifices of his kindred.

" Except these few words we have not the slightest hint. With these does Armin, the man of such mighty deeds, disappear from history. But upon these no conjecture can be founded, from them no conclusion can be deduced. *   *   * It was his happy fortune to meet death in the flower of his age, in the vigour of his powers, in the plenitude of his fame, in the full consciousness of his deeds, without spot, disgrace, or error, pure and free beyond all historical prototype, a great example for every generous spirit in days of oppression and anguish, a brilliant star in the night of time. His task was fulfilled. His country was saved, her liberty was assured. But a sorrowful and inexorable destiny lay upon his beloved wife and upon the son whom he had never seen, whom he must never hope to see. He had no further ties to life. *   *   * So far as the history of the human race goes, no nation can boast of such an early age as the Germans, of such a man, and of such deeds. And yet how different might all appear, how much greater, more beautiful and more sublime, if in addition to the reports transmitted from the enemy's camp, we possessed the German traditions of Armin and his faithful followers. *   *
*   * It is from the annals of the hostile power that Armin and his times have passed into the annals of the German people. Rome hated the living man, and when dead gave him not due fame. Rome had cause for her hatred; she trod her own path, and fulfilled her own

destiny. Amongst us Armin wants not for admirers and eulogists; but we should honour him more if a Tacitus arose amongst our enemies who bore witness to the world and to posterity that we are worthy of him. Then will the last hour of Germany strike, when none is found amongst her children who wishes to live and to die like Armin."

Enough, and we trust our readers will not say more than enough, of Arminius and Luden. We have given more pages to them than we had intended, seduced by feelings in which we would fain hope for some little sympathy; *i. e.* a real love for the genuine enthusiasm of the historian, a thrilling sense of the romantic and patriotic interest glowing around the earliest Hero of Germany, through the dim haze with which time has veiled him, and a warm delight in the fervid admiration that has impelled the national German poets of our own day to sing his exploits. Our bosoms do not equally yearn towards the heroes of the subsequent struggles between the Empire and Germany, and without bestowing a thought upon the barbarian Emperors who successively arose, or upon the conquests of Ostrogoths, Visigoths, Burgundians, Longobards or Lombards, and Saxons, we shall at once proceed to the Franks and their long-haired Sicambrian kings of the Merovingian dynasty, who according to their own early Chronicles derived their origin from Troy; Faramund being a grandson of old Priam, notwithstanding the little chronological difficulty of his being likewise a contemporary of Attila, the king of the Huns. And with the Franks we shall take up Professor Mannert.

The Franks first appeared upon the stage in the last quarter of the second century. From this time the names of nations with which we have previously been familiar, as Cheruscans, Chatti, &c., are gradually superseded by those of Franks, Saxons, Allemans, and Goths, which, with the exception of the last, the name of a distinct tribe from the north-east, seem to be the appellations assumed by different confederations. As the Franks are first mentioned during the reign of the philosophic and pacific Antonines, Mannert concludes that their confederation was not the result of hostile aggression from Rome, but of internal wars; and these wars he conceives to have been chiefly of self-defence against the Saxon confederation, which, occupying the north of Germany, sought to extend itself westward to the Rhine. The nations lying between the Saxons and that river, found it necessary to unite in order to resist their northern invaders, and did so successfully, under their new name of Franks. The Saxons then turned their energies to the sea, and became formidable pirates, whilst the Franks in the consciousness of power invaded Gaul, and incorporated the first and second *Germania* and *Belgium* of the Romans with themselves.

About the year 500, Clovis, or Chlodwig, his proper Teutonic name, by reducing the several Frank principalities under his own sceptre, and conquering the last remnant of the Western Roman Empire in Gaul, is held to have founded the French monarchy. His Frank kingdom was, nevertheless, by no means commensurate with modern France, consisting of the northern German provinces on probably both banks of the Rhine, of the present kingdom of the Netherlands, and of so much of France as lies north of the Loire, with the exception of Britanny, where large bodies of Britons, expelled from their insular home by the Saxons, had established themselves, and long maintained their independence. Of the southern half of France, the larger part situated to the west of the Rhone was included in the Visigothic kingdom of Spain; whilst the provinces to the east of that river were held, together with Savoy and Switzerland, by the Burgundians. Chlodwig attacked both. Against the Burgundians he effected little or nothing; but he was more successful against their western neighbours. Assisted by the hatred which the Catholic natives entertained towards their Arian masters, (the Franks were the only orthodox barbarians,) he before his death reduced the Visigothic dominions in Gaul to the single province of Languedoc, incorporating all the rest in his Frank realm. His sons and grandsons in time not only subdued Burgundy, but brought many German states, as the Thuringians, Allemans, and Bavarians, into complete feudal subjection.

The sovereignty of the Merovingian dynasty is, almost uninterruptedly, a scene of reckless, one might really fancy of unconscious cruelty, of moral and political profligacy, from which the mind recoils in disgust. Wherefore, as we are not bound to narrate its loathsome annals, we shall dismiss this period with the single remark, that the incessant division of the realm amongst the sons of every deceased king, constantly severing the eastern provinces, under the name of Austrasia, from the western, or Neustria, tended much to prepare the way for the subsequent separation of France and Germany, by promoting two distinct nationalities: since Austrasia being inhabited entirely by Germans, (a few towns upon the left of the Rhine, that had been Roman colonies, excepted,) remained German pure and unadulterated, whilst in Neustria and the western portion of Burgundy, Franks, Goths, and Burgundians being thinly intermingled with colonized Romans, and Romanized Gauls, amalgamated with their more numerous subjects, conformed insensibly to their manners, becoming more polished and more corrupt, learned to speak their language, (a barbarous Latin, which slowly formed itself, through the intermediate state of the *langue Romane* of the

Troubadours, into modern French,) and in process of time lost in the French character almost every trace of their German origin.

We come now to the vigorous and genuinely German Carlovingians; and from the history of their rise, which may, we conceive, be less familiarly known to the general reader than their more brilliant era, the reign of Charlemagne, we shall take our specimen of Mannert's mode of treating his subject, alternately abstracting and translating as before.

The Carlovingians, or Pippins, were a wealthy and noble Netherland family, whose landed domains comprised nearly the whole tract of country between Liege and Holland. The first mention of them occurs during the final contest of Brunhildis, (called Brunechild by Mannert,) in behalf of her great grandson, Sigibert the Second, of Austrasia, against Chlotar the Second, of Neustria, which was decided in favour of the latter by Arnulf, Bishop of Metz, the most influential man in Austrasia, who, from enmity to the old Queen, induced a large body of the nobles, with PIPPIN at their head, to join the Neustrians. The consequence of their defection was the defeat of Brunhildis's army, the death of the royal family of Austrasia, (the old Queen's being attended with circumstances of the most atrocious cruelty,) and the re-union of the whole Frank monarchy under Chlotar the Second.

But the union of the monarchy under one king did not now imply its union under one administration. Austrasia retained her separate *Major domus*, an officer who had now become rather the actual sovereign than the prime minister of the kingdom he ruled. The first Major domus of Austrasia appointed by Chlotar was one Rado; but he quickly disappears from the annals of the times, and is succeeded by Pippin, strengthened by a family connexion with Bishop Arnulf, whose son Adalgisil married Pippin's daughter Begga: a marriage no wise disreputable to the Carlovingians, inasmuch as married nobles, fathers of large families, frequently entered the church late in life for the sake of wealthy bishoprics. But indeed the celibacy of the clergy was a law which in those early days it was found so difficult to enforce amongst the German nations, that the chroniclers have not thought it worth while to inform us whether Adalgisil was born before or after his father's taking orders. These two allies, thus wielding the temporal and spiritual power, now governed Austrasia in fact independently, though nominally under a Merovingian king; and after a few years, choosing (it is hard to conjecture why) that this king should be a separate one of their own, they compelled Chlotar to appoint his infant son, Dagobert, king of Austrasia.

Chlotar retained a nominal sovereignty over his son, which might have been bought derogatory to the dignity of Austrasia.

But what was only nominal was not considered so deeply, we' imagine, in the seventh as it is in the nineteenth century, and, that Chlotar enjoyed no power over his son's kingdom which could in any manner controul the free-agency of the Major domus and his episcopal colleague, may be judged from the following anecdote :—

" The young monarch had been taught by the influence of the reve-. rend Bishop Arnulf, of the Major Domus Pippin, and of the great men of their faction, to detest Chrodoald, an Austrasian noble and a member of the illustrious family of the Agilolfingas, whom they had represented to him as having amassed immoderate wealth, as rapacious and over-bearing. Chrodoald's death was decreed; but he fled to King Chlotar, to negotiate a reconciliation through his means. The old king" (a curious epithet for a monarch who did not live to be forty-five,) " obtained a promise that his petitioner's life should be spared on condition of his improvement. But for this no time was allowed him, his head being struck off upon his reaching Treves. Chlotar's intervention in Austrasia was no longer of any avail. This private quarrel with a great man of the opposition is the more deserving of historical notice, from its being the first time that the family of the Agilolfingas* appears by name. We have often before seen Dukes of the Allemans personally interfering in Austrasian affairs, but never any of the royal or rather ducal family of the Bavarians, who must long have been part of the Frank monarchy, ere a branch of the Agilolfingas could appear amongst the most exten-sive Austrasian landowners; and we learn from subsequent history that a large part of the present Wetterau was the property of Chrodoald, inasmuch as we find his son possessing it as his patrimony."

Under the tutelage of Bishop Arnulf and Pippin, Dagobert's separate reign in Austrasia was energetic and prosperous; and upon the death of his father Chlotar, he was acknowledged King of Neustria and Burgundy, the duchy of Aquitaine, consisting of the provinces that had formerly belonged to the Visigoths, being given to his younger brother Charibert. But now the aspect of affairs changed, Bishop Arnulf died, and Pippin lost his influence, to which the Neustrian Major domus Æga succeeded. Æga is described as a wise and good man, and the chief transactions of his government were the wars carried on with the Sclavonian nations for the protection of Austrasia; nevertheless his original subjects presently conceived an aversion to Dagobert, which could only be appeased by his appointing his infant son Sigibert, King of Austrasia, sending him to Metz, the usual residence of the Merovingian sovereigns of that kingdom, and committing him to the superintendance of Chunibert, Bishop of Cologne, and of Pippin's son-in-law Adalgisil. These regents were pre-sently joined by Pippin himself, and for a short time the govern-

---

* The Dukes of Bavaria were always chosen from the Agilolfinga family.

ment prospered as previously to the disfavour of the able Major domus.

The death of Pippin produced general confusion. His son Grimoald and Adalgisil co-operated strenuously for the preservation of their joint authority, but a strong party was formed against them by Radulf, Duke of Thuringia. Such contests for power were decided in those days, not by the votes of Lords or Commons, nor even by court intrigue, but by the swords of partizans. The political antagonists met at the head of their respective armies, Grimoald and Adalgisil carrying the young king with them. The treachery of some of their adherents turned the fortune of the day against them; but they still retained possession of Sigibert's person, and the benefit derived by Radulf from his victory was not ascendancy in Austrasia, but a degree of independence as Duke of Thuringia.

At court the influence of the Pippin family increased daily. Of Adalgisil we hear no more; but Grimoald gradually got rid of his various opponents, and in the year 640 obtained the post of Major domus.

" Meanwhile Sigibert had ripened to manhood, and was already the father of a son; it was time he should die,* being in the twenty-first year of his age, and the eighteenth of his nominal reign. Grimoald now deemed himself so secure that he ventured, through the instrumentality of the Bishop of Poictiers, to send away the baby-prince, Dagobert, to Scotland or Ireland, spread a report of his death, and proclaimed his own son Childebert king, under pretence of the deceased Sigibert's having adopted him. By this violent measure many of the crooked paths to the throne would have been shortened; but it failed. Men's minds were too much accustomed to the glory of the Merovingians to bear the transition to a short-haired† race without more preparation. Streams of blood were yet to flow, ere gradually such an idea could gain admittance; and even Grimoald's partizans do not appear to have concurred with him on this occasion. He was fraudulently overpowered without any one's moving to his assistance; was carried a prisoner to King Chlodwig of Neustria, and thrown into a dungeon, where he found the end of his life. The fate of his son Childebert is unknown to me."

The Pippin family was now thrown for a while into the back ground. Chlodwig the Second was acknowledged king of the whole realm, a separate Major domus of a different race being chosen to govern the German half. Upon Chlodwig's death

---

* This was the regular lot of the latter Merovingian Kings; and considering that their history is transmitted to us by Carlovingian Chronicles, certainly offers ground of suspicion against those who profited by their deaths.

† Was there in those days no substitute for Macassar oil that could promote the growth of Childebert's short hair? Bear's grease was surely not wanting, but perhaps no one knew its use.

Austrasia and Neustria were again divided between two of his sons; and afterwards, upon the death of their King Childerick, the Austrasians applied to Wilfrid, Bishop of York, to negotiate the return of the royal exile Dagobert. Dagobert came, and was at first well received, but ere long murdered, at the instigation, it is said, of his bishops and nobles. And now the Pippins recovered their power, not again to lose it, until they in their turn should degenerate as the Merovingians had done before them. Pippin of Heristall, (so called in history from his family estate near Liege,) the son of Adalgisil and Begga, and consequently the grandson of Bishop Arnulf and of the elder Pippin, together with Martin, another grandson of Arnulf's, now took the lead in Austrasia, supported by all the malcontent nobles. Ebruin, Major domus of Neustria, with his King Theuderich, marched against and defeated them; Martin fled to Laon.

" Thither repaired Agilbert, Bishop of Paris, and Riol, Bishop of Rheims, for the purpose of luring him to court, by pledging their oaths for his security. A Frank was not to be duped by an ordinary oath; even when sworn upon the Bible, he knew that it was broken and laughed at. But when a shrine containing the relics of any celebrated saint was brought forward, an oath taken thereon was deemed binding, because a firm conviction was entertained that the martyr himself would instantly avenge a perjury which thus became a personal offence. So did the bishops swear, and Martin, feeling himself perfectly secure, went to court, where Ebruin immediately put him to death. When complaint was made of the perjury, the bishops proved that they had indeed sworn upon the shrine, but had first carefully taken out the relics."

The pious fraud was of little use, as Pippin could not be ensnared like his cousin, and remained alone at the head of the Austrasian government. After some vicissitudes he gained, A.D. 687, a decided victory over the Neustrian King Theuderich, and his new Major domus, Berchar, at Tistri, near St. Quentin: Pippin entered Paris as a conqueror, but offered no injury to the king beyond seizing his treasures, and did not even take upon himself the office of Major domus, when Berchar was murdered by treacherous friends. Contenting himself with appointing a Neustrian partizan of his own to the vacant post, he returned to Austrasia, and governed that state untroubled by any separate king, although acknowledging the sovereignty of Theuderich. In process of time he made his second son, Grimoald, Major domus of Neustria, and the eldest, Drogo, Duke of either Champagne or Burgundy,* and was thus really master of the whole Frank realm.

---

* Which of the two it was, is matter of great dispute, because Burgundy had never been a duchy. But Champagne would have been nothing for Pippin's eldest son; and as a Major domus was an unaccustomed officer in Burgundy, we do not see why Drogo should not have had the third distinct kingdom with a new title.

But Pippin had the misfortune of losing both his sons, nor did they even leave him the consolation of lawful heirs to their greatness—an illegitimate infant child of Grimoald's, Theudoald, was all that remained of these late mighty rulers. To this boy the dying Pippin endeavoured to assure the inheritance of his power; and his able and energetic widow Plechtrud or Bilichtrud, a Bavarian Princess, assuming the regency for her grandson, maintained herself in full authority. Theudoald, however, did not prove long-lived; and upon his death came forward the celebrated Charles Martel, from whom his family derive the patronymic Carlovingian. Charles was the son of Pippin by a second wife; for Christianity had not hitherto abrogated the old German privilege allowed to princes of marrying more than one consort, as matter of state or policy, not of appetite; and Pippin, anxious for more sons, had thus espoused the high-born Alpheida, whom the ecclesiastical chroniclers, however, treat as merely a concubine, and whom the influence of the clergy, or of Plechtrud, prevailed upon him to repudiate after she had borne him two sons. The eldest of these, Charles, Plechtrud held in custody during her grandson's life. Upon Theudoald's death she had no further motive for confining, and probably released him, although the chroniclers attribute his liberation to the immediate intervention of angels. However it was effected, the Austrasians gladly welcomed the youthfully blooming son of their old ruler.

They wanted such a leader; and his hereditary talents were forthwith put to the proof; Austrasia was invaded by the combined arms of the Neustrians, the Saxons, and the Frieslanders. Charles was defeated and put to flight. But Plechtrud appears to have purchased the retreat of the enemy, who had besieged her in Cologne, with a part of Pippin's treasures; and the following year Charles found himself strong enough to retaliate by the invasion of Neustria. King Chilperic led an army to oppose him, and the enemies encountered near Cambray, where, after some fruitless negotiation, a battle was fought. Charles defeated and routed the Neustrians, pursuing them as far as Paris, but made no further use of his victory. He returned to Cologne, where Plechtrud delivered up to him the remainder of his father's treasures, and retired with her daughter, his half-sister, to Bavaria.

Charles now set up a separate King of Austrasia, Chlotar the Fourth, respecting whose birth we are uninformed, (of course it was Merovingian,) and under his auspices again invaded Neustria. Chilperic had recourse to Eudo, Duke of Aquitaine, who is conceived to have been a grandson of Charibert, the brother of Dagobert the First. Chilperic confirmed Eudo in the possession of his ·duchy, loaded him with presents, and besought his assistance.· ·Eudo led an army to his support; but A. D. 7l9,

" Charles routed the allied forces near Soissons, who all fled in the utmost disorder into Aquitaine, carrying with them however the royal treasure. ¦ The whole conduct of Charles, though clearly known to us only in detached and prominent points recorded by the continuator of Fredegar, displays so well combined and well digested a plan, as could hardly have been anticipated from his youth and inexperience. With reasonable expectation of a happy result, might he have pursued the beaten and scattered enemy into Aquitaine; but he did not pursue them. He remained upon the Loire, procured his own election as Major domus of Neustria and Burgundy, entered into negotiation with all his adversaries collectively, and concluded a treaty affording security and advantage to all parties. Charles acknowledged Chilperic the Second as King of the Franks, whereupon his Chlotar died;* Duke Eudo obtained peace, and the recognition of his sovereignty, in return for which he delivered Chilperic into Charles's hands; the former Major domus, Raginfried, was made Count of Anjou, and retained uninterrupted possession of his county, although his conduct occasionally compelled Charles to make war upon him. A universal peace suddenly prevails; and Charles, the ruler of the re-united Frank monarchy, entitles himself Major domus of the Franks, Duke, and sometimes Prince, of the Austrasians. Austrasia would have no Neustrian king, consequently no separate Major domus. Charles was, under whatever title, the freely elected ruler of the Austrasians."

The condition of the Merovingian kings was now changed. They no longer took the field at the head of their armies; but with the least possible show of royalty, were kept in a species of confinement in a country house, which they were only permitted to quit at stated times, to receive foreign embassadors, and to preside over the assemblies of the nation, or rather of the nobles and warriors, in the fields of March or of May, which it should seem had previously fallen into disuse, and been revived by Charles or his father. Upon these occasions the captive king was brought, it is said, in a carriage (a waggon probably, for we hardly conceive there were any other,) drawn by oxen, and driven by a servant clad in the garb of a peasant. On his arrival, he was placed upon a throne, with the Major domus by his side, performed the external functions of royalty, delivering the speeches dictated by the Major domus, and was then re-conducted to his villa in the same form in which he had come from it. This mode of conveyance, Mannert, in common with most other historians, considers as intended to degrade the Merovingian kings in the eyes of their subjects, and thus prepare the way for a change of dynasty. Luden, more subtly, argues that the actual rulers

---

* Was he one of the parties to whom this treaty afforded security and advantage?

would have disgraced themselves in the opinion of foreign powers, and insulted the national warriors, by producing the nominal sovereign under circumstances of contumely; that if the Merovingians did still possess influence or interest with the nation, they could not safely have been insulted; that if they possessed neither, they would not have been permitted to wear the crown during another half century; and he concludes that the team of oxen, &c. is either an idle story invented in after times, or was the remnant of some old national custom, not mentioned by earlier writers, only because it was universally and familiarly known when they wrote.*

Charles was now the acknowledged master of the Frank monarchy; he was addressed by the Pope as Prince of the Franks; and he further secured to himself the oddly hereditary rights of his family to an independent and uncontrolled prime ministership by marrying his niece, the daughter of Pippin's daughter by Plechtrud, his first, and in fact only lawful wife. But Charles did not enjoy his sovereignty in peace. Upon his eastern frontier the Sclavonian nations harassed the southern provinces, as the heathen Saxons and Frieslanders did the northern. At home, several Burgundian nobles, though too weak to rebel openly against the potent Major domus, took advantage of his being occupied with foreign wars to elude his authority, and Eudo of Aquitaine endeavoured to establish his own absolute independence by means of an alliance with the Saracens; who, having conquered the Visigoths, were at this time the sovereigns of Spain. Against these external and internal foes Charles was invariably successful; although to be so he was obliged to take the field incessantly against one or another. But the great, the splendid feature of his government, was his war against the Saracens of Spain, and the ever-memorable victory by which he finally repulsed their repeated invasions of France, and thus, perhaps, saved Europe from Mahometanism.

Charles was first called upon to oppose these dreaded—and as it was believed irresistible—children of the desert, in defence of his rebellious vassal, the Duke of Aquitaine.

" Eudo was soon taught to feel that an alliance with the sworn foe of the Christian name was an impossibility.† To the former Moslem

---

* We shall not deviate from our resolution of waiving the discussion of these novel views of Luden, but we cannot refrain from observing, that in the present case his opinion is also that of the learned and philosophical Dr. Jacob Grimm, in his *Deutsche Rechts Alterthümer* (German Legal Antiquities).

† Such alliances were afterwards frequent, and it must be remembered that Eudo made a mistake. He gave his daughter in marriage to Munuza, Governor of Saragossa, and like himself a subject aspiring to sovereignty. When the Emir of Spain had subdued the rebellious Munuza, Eudo's connection with him was necessarily a cause of Moslem enmity, not friendship.

generals succeeds the enterprising Abderrahman; irresistibly he presses forward over the Pyrenees of the Basques, defeats the opposing Duke Eudo at the confluence of the Dordogne and Garonne, and devastating and plundering every thing, but especially the churches, rapidly possesses himself of the whole open country, even beyond Poitiers. His desires now fix themselves upon the richly endowed Church of St. Martin at Tours, without the slightest consideration of the circumstance that this city belonged not to Aquitaine, but to the dominions of the West Franks. The whole Christian world was his enemy.

" But now the ever-ready Charles appeared as his antagonist, with his well ordered Frank troops: Charles's aid had been implored by Duke Eudo, and he required not solicitation to march against the common foe. The two armies met between Tours and Poitiers, and for seven days did they remain in position observing each other. To the Franks the rapid evolutions of the Saracens were novel phenomena, whilst the latter beheld with equal wonder the steady regularity of the Frank order of battle. At length the general onset begins (732). Vain are the ever renewed assaults of the Mahometans; the Franks stand immoveable as walls, and pressing forwards with steady aspect, cut down all that oppose them. Abderrahman fell in the action; yet was nothing decided, and night put an end to the mutual slaughter. The next morning found the Christians ready to renew the engagement; before their eyes stood the tents of the hostile camp, behind which they conceived the army to be arrayed for the encounter. When after long waiting no foe appeared, the out-posts were ordered to reconnoitre, and all was found vacant; the Arabs had employed the night in rapid flight. He who knows the Franks need not be told that their first thought was not the pursuit of the enemy, but the plunder of a camp teeming with wealth. Even Charles, who earned in this hard-contested battle the name he bears in history of the Hammerer (*Martellus*), thought not of pursuit. For the moment he was satisfied with having established the superiority of steady tactics and endurance over the impetuous onslaught of Arabian fanaticism, which esteemed death in battle the surest pledge of future happiness. * * * * It is true that the Franks derived no other immediate advantage from their victory. The Saracens long retained possession of Southern Gaul, where Charles Martel repeatedly fought with them in after years; and it was only his son Pippin, who, by immense exertions, succeeded in expelling them. But it is likewise true that the Saracens thenceforward lost all inclination to be the aggressors with regard to the Franks; that upon this battle rested the question whether Europe should remain Christian or become Mahometan; (or Mohammedan, as Mannert more etymologically denominates the followers of Mohammed;) for had Charles been defeated and slain, like the Moslem general, the strong band which held the Franks together would have vanished, and internally divided, they must have remained exposed to the rapid and violent inundations, which had recently brought destruction upon the Empire of the Visigoths in Spain."

These extracts will, we think, be sufficient specimen of the

Munich professor's historical manner; but as his dryness may have been found wearisome, we will, ere concluding this article, at once display his best style, and endeavour to refresh our readers by translating the most amusing of the incidents he relates in illustration of the state of Frank society under the Merovingians.

" At Tours dwelt two noble Franks who possessed extensive domains in the vicinity. One of these, named Austregil, slew and plundered some of the *Pueri*, or armed attendants of Sichar, the other. As the slain were not free-born Franks, but *hörigen*, or thralls, although appertaining to that armed portion of the household without whose escort no man of any consequence undertook a journey, the affair was referred to the burgher tribunal, which decided that Austregil had incurred punishment. But Sichar learning that the stolen goods were in his antagonist's house, troubled himself no further about the verdict, collected a body of armed followers, attacked the mansion by night, slew Austregil, and plundered his property. The town was alarmed for the consequences, and the bishop in conjunction with the judge, (probably the Frank *Gravio*,) invited the parties to appear before them. They came, the assembled citizens being likewise present. ' Prosecute this quarrel no farther,' said Bishop Gregory, ' be placable, and let him who has done the wrong make compensation; should his wealth prove insufficient, the church shall buy him off with her gold.' But Chramnisind, the nearest kinsman of the murdered man, refused to accept any composition, and the assembly broke up. It was soon afterwards reported that Sichar had been murdered upon a journey by his own attendants; (he was merely wounded). Immediately Chramnisind and his party fall upon Sichar's country residence, kill some of his servants, burn his houses, and drive away his cattle. Both parties were again summoned before the *Gravio*, and the judges decreed that he who, rejecting a just composition, had burnt the houses, should forfeit one half of the composition previously adjudged to him, but that Sichar must still pay the other half. This was a proceeding contrary to law, devised as a means of restoring peace. The church paid the money; both parties respectively swore that neither would speak a word against the other, and so the dispute seemed to be ended.

" Not an idea appears of royal intervention, or of the 200 *solidi* fixed by Salic law as the price of the blood of a free-born Frank. It was to be a voluntary bargain in which neither party could be compelled to concur; and the sum offered must have been large, since it was presupposed beyond the pecuniary ability of the wrong-doer.

" But what has been related is only half of this strange incident, which so clearly marks the lawless habits of the Franks. The foes were so thoroughly reconciled that they frequently feasted together and slept in the same bed (an old German custom). As they sat one day at Chramnisind's table, drinking together in mirthful mood, Sichar said, ' Thou shouldst thank me, good brother, for having killed thy kinsman, since the composition has made thee a rich man.' Then thought Chramnisind in his heart, ' If I leave my kinsman's blood unavenged, I am

N 2

not worthy to be called a man.' ·He put out the lights, clove· Sicbàr's head in twain, and hastening to the king, told how the thing had happened, and prayed for assurance of his life. ·He believed, therefore, that he had acted with perfect propriety;·but he had Brunechild against him, because Sichar was a follower of bers, and Chramnisind was constrained to seek for safety in exile."*

ART. VIII.—*Briefwechsel zwischen Schiller und Goethe, (Correspondence between Schiller and Goethe.)* 6 Bde. sm. 8vo. Leipzig. 1830.

THESE " *Epistolæ Clarorum Virorum,*" we are afraid, will somewhat disappoint expectation; not because they do not contain many letters eminently characteristic of the writers, and important towards forming a right estimate of their respective minds and literary habits, but because these letters are not separated with sufficient. care from others which are neither characteristic nor important.   Men in real life, who write with the view of communicating their respective wants and wishes to each other, must touch on many topics which a judicious collector would omit as in no way interesting to any but the parties themselves.   " What the deuce is it to me," said the elder Scaliger, " whether Montagne loved white wine or red;" and this querulous observation is somewhat apt to occur to one's mind in perusing these letters, particularly those in the first volume, which were principally written, shortly after Schiller had begun to publish the periodical work called " Die Horen," and relate chiefly to matters of bookselling and bookbinding; questions of fine or coarse paper copies ; engravings, contributions to writers, and so on.   Not but that these little details are occasionally amusing enough ; but they suit better with such persons as Madame de Genlis, than with the two greatest names in German literature, Schiller and Goethe.   Hence, we must say; it would have been better for the purses and patience of the reader, if nearly a third part of these letters had been retrenched.

One extremely interesting point about them, however, is the perfect confidence which they prove to have subsisted between the writers, each, in his respective style, at the head of literature in Germany ; Goethe, the more Catholic in his genius, the more

* This article was entirely written, and in types, previously to the appearance of Luden's fifth volume, copies of which have only recently arrived in this country.   That Volume carries on the History to the final division of the Frank empire into its French and German portions, during the dissentions of the sons of Louis *the Pious,* an appellation which the French authors have translated, strangely enough, *le Debonnaire.* · We shall probably return to the work, when some more volumes have appeared, and enable us to exhibit a period of similar character, although of shorter duration, than that embraced in the present article.

comprehensive in his views, the calmer in his opinions, the more, classically graceful in his compositions; Schiller, with more of that irregular strength still clinging to him with which he had at first entered the field of literature, hardly yet settled in his notions, either of philosophy, life, or art itself, and, therefore, constantly changing his principles of composition; yet, from his industry and fervour, making a deeper, if not a wider, impression on the public of Germany, and certainly far more generally read and understood in Europe. These men, so closely united in some points, and so very different in others, had not altogether harmonized on their first meeting; Goethe even thought that some of the doctrines in Schiller's " Essay on Dignity and Grace" were aimed at himself; and as the one resided in his civil capacity at Weimar, while the other was attached to the university of Jena, considerable time had elapsed without materially altering the terms of mere acquaintance on which they stood. The circumstance which brought them into that union which gave rise to these letters, and to which both acknowledge their obligations for many important reciprocal benefits, was Schiller's undertaking the literary and philosophical periodical already mentioned, (" The Hours,") with the view of counteracting, in some measure, the false principles in philosophy, taste, and morals, which about that time, (1794,) disgraced the literature of Germany, in common, indeed, with that of the greater part of Europe. The co-operation of Fichte and Jacobi in the philosophical department, of the Schlegels in the critical, and of Meyer in matters relating to art, had been secured; Schiller, who had already shown that he could pass from poetry to philosophy, and from philosophy to history, was himself a host. But Schiller felt the want of some one who would teach the public more by example than by precept, and who with his lighter productions would counteract the too didactic tendencies of his other coadjutors. This assistant he sought and readily found in Goethe.

From the commencement of their acquaintance to the death of Schiller, in 1805, these two great men continued in almost daily correspondence; communicating to each other the projects in which they were engaged, soliciting or giving advice on the conduct of their respective works, and exchanging opinions also on general questions of taste and literature. Each felt that the criticism or encouragement of the other was the strongest incitement to renewed exertion; though the feeling with which Schiller contemplated some of the productions of his rival was occasionally blended with a distrust of his own powers, and dissatisfaction with his own performances. Speaking of Goethe's Wilhelm Meister, he writes, " I cannot express to you the painful sensation I feel on turning from a production of this nature to look into my own being. With you, all is so cheerful, so loving, so harmoniously blended, so true to humanity; with me, every thing so harsh, so rigid and abstract, and so unnatural; for all nature is hypothesis, and all philosophy antithesis." In another letter, after alluding to what he conceives to be the peculiar characteristic of Goethe's mind, its intuitiveness, he observes; " My understanding works rather by symbols, and thus I waver between idea and perception, between rule and sentiment, between technicality and genius; I was surprised into poetry where I ought to have been philosophical, and into philosophy where I should have poetised. And even now, imagination too often destroys my philosophy, and cold understanding my verse." Both his estimate of Goethe's genius and his own were to a certain extent incorrect, though both were also substantially true. Goethe had undoubtedly succeeded in effecting a rare blending of all the different elements of feeling, fancy, wit, and pathos in his works, but he had often carried this principle of repose, and this balance of contrary qualities, too far for the actual practical effect of his compositions, and thereby given to them an Utopian and unreal aspect of tranquillity. Schiller, on the other hand, though doubtless the intellect and the imagination had never co-operated in his mind with that complete fusion which they had done in that of Goethe, had, on the whole, addressed himself with more effect to the mind of his countrymen, and if his intellectual armoury was less numerously furnished than that of his rival, he made up for it by the skill and strength with which he launched his weapons. It is certain, however, that his intercourse with Goethe was of essential benefit to him in that particular in which he felt his deficiency;—the effecting a harmonious union of his imagination with that abstract spirit of research which too often destroyed the creations of his fancy, even in the moment of their formation.

On the other hand, the restless activity, the intensity and fervour of Schiller, exerted amidst all the depressing influences of almost continual sickness, together with his lofty principles of morals and criticism, seem to have imparted a no less striking and beneficial influence to the mind of Goethe. " I rejoice," says he, " to tell you what pleasure I have derived from your conversation, that I reckon those days to have been an epoch in my life, and how glad I am to have proceeded on my way without much encouragement, since it seems now, that after so unexpected a meeting, we are destined to proceed together. I have always valued the honest and uncommon earnestness which shows itself in all you have written and done." He speaks still more decidedly on the subject in the late notices of his literary life, (vol. xxxi. p. 42.) " Amidst this pressure of annoyances, what surpassed all my expectations was my increasing connection with Schiller; from the first it was an irrepressible progress in philosophical culture and literary activity; the burst of a new spring, in which every twig and seed shot forth with renewed activity." Of this the newly collected and arranged letters on both sides are the best evidence.

They certainly do afford evidence of extraordinary and most varied literary activity on both sides. While Goethe is performing his duties as minister, and losing of course much valuable time in the ceremonial of a court, he is at the same time finishing William Meister, composing Faust and Hermann and Dorothea, each a master-piece in its way, throwing off innumerable little poems, many of them gems of art, writing philosophical essays, translating plays and novels from the French, Memoirs of Benvenuto Cellini from the Italian; criticising, and that carefully too, and with many suggestions and alterations of his own, the ballads and poems of his friend; and blending with all this the study of galvanism, of a new theory of colours, and of butterflies. Nothing, in short, is too exalted for him, nothing too insignificant, in his desire of knowledge and enlargement of mind. Schiller, on the other hand, confines himself a little more to matters more strictly literary; but he supplies, by the most careful study for each particular subject, his want of general preparation; if he writes a poem, he studies the habits and customs of the country, or the features of the scene which he describes, in order to reflect them at once with force and with fidelity. Many of the most interesting letters in these volumes relate to the composition of his Wallenstein, in which the magnitude and conflicting nature of the materials with which he had to deal, occasioned the most important and repeated alterations. Of Goethe's works, that which is most frequently alluded to is Wilhelm Meister, which was submitted to Schiller in its progress, and appears to have been viewed by him with the greatest admiration as a whole; though in reference to particular parts he suggested many valuable corrections and improvements, of which several were adopted by Goethe. Many other interesting particulars may be gleaned from these letters relative to Faust, The Maid of Orleans, William Tell, Schiller's smaller Poems and Ballads, and other works on which the writers were engaged during the period to which the correspondence relates. And to the future biographer of either, they will undoubtedly, when divested of the many trifling and unimportant matters with which they are at present clogged, afford most valuable materials. We would recommend, however, the addition of an index of subjects, without which, particularly in their present form, reference to them is exceedingly troublesome.

ART. IX.—*Der Aufstand der Braunschweiger am 6ten und 7ten September, seine Veranlassung und seine nächsten Folgen.* (The Insurrection of the Brunswickers on the 6th and 7th of September, its Causes, and its immediate Consequences.) Brunswick. 1830. 8vo.

THE pamphlet of which the title-page is prefixed to this article, has been lately published at Brunswick without a name. The author of it, however, seems to have had access to the best information, and it contains a detailed and apparently impartial account of the events which led to the late expulsion of the reigning Duke of Brunswick. We will avail ourselves of it to lay before our readers a brief narrative of that remarkable revolution.

Few princes ever ascended a throne with greater advantages than Charles, Duke of Brunswick. Under the enlightened and paternal sway of his grandfather and father, Charles William Ferdinand and Frederick William, the Brunswickers had learnt, not only to honour and revere their rulers, but to esteem and love them, as mixing in private with their subjects, and identifying their own interest with that of their people. Equally well satisfied were the citizens of Brunswick with the public administration under the Regency of George IV., which followed the death of Frederick William at Quatre Bras. From experience, therefore, they had reason to think well of their rulers. Nothing, accordingly, could exceed the loyal hopes and enthusiasm of the people of Brunswick at the accession of the young Duke Charles. In the tumult of popular joy, the suspicions of those were drowned who thought that they could trace in the deportment of the duke marks of coldness and want of sympathy with his subjects. The first year of his reign passed in apparent tranquillity, but not a day went by which did not damp the hopes and increase the melancholy forebodings of the people. The taxes were either increased or retained unaltered; while the expenditure for the public benefit was diminished. Faithful counsellors were dismissed. The assembly of the estates, re-established during the Regency, was not convened. The people in vain looked for one act of the sovereign directed to the public welfare; nor had they even the poor consolation to think that the misgovernment was owing to the irregular passions of a youthful prince, when they saw his deliberate distrust and the phlegmatic indifference of his disposition. Soon afterwards, the chief ministers of state, who had earned the gratitude and esteem of the people, were dismissed, and, with one exception, forced to seek an asylum in foreign countries from the insults and oppression to which they were exposed at home. It was after the duke had thus got rid of the disagreeable restraint of honest advisers, that he openly quarrelléd with his former guardian, the late King of England. This indecent proceeding was accompanied with a rescission of the laws passed during the last year of the Regency, and a plain avowal never to recognise the representative constitution, re-established during that administration. A set of servile flatterers now rose into the favour of the duke. Foreign parasites, prostitute writers, lawyers and professors of low reputation, obtained the highest posts of the state. With these willing tools of despotism the duke soon broke out into acts of lawless violence. A young man who had passed some censure on the theatre, was, at the command of the duke, thrown into prison, and detained there for several weeks. The citizens began to tremble for their personal safety, and to communicate their fears to confidential friends. To prevent such expressions of alarm, police agents were sent about in secret—letters were opened and read in the private cabinet of the duke. To be favoured or countenanced by the prince, once the highest favour, was now the greatest misfortune, as it was surely followed by universal distrust and aversion. But no measures of the government were more unpopular than its financial regulations. Although many offices, even in the courts of justice, were left unfilled, and a parsimony very different from a wise economy introduced into the public expenditure, the public burdens were not only not diminished, but increased; and taxes seemed only destined either to increase the duke's treasure, or to buy up newspapers. By these acts of rapacious extortion and short-sighted avarice many opulent families were driven from the capital; the poor were thrown out of employment; the rent of houses fell a third, their value one half; and the sums expended upon public works and improvements were still further reduced. Not satisfied with this unjust appropriation of the taxes, the duke next raised large sums by a sale of public lands, which was expressly prohibited by an edict of Duke William Ferdinand. Bitter, a man who had risen into high office from being a common clerk, and was employed by the duke in opening private letters, had full powers for effecting these sales; and was paid by a percentage on the purchase monies, and a permission to receive gifts from the purchasers. It would be needless to enumerate the other illegal and outrageous measures of the duke. Men of rank and station were wantonly insulted and driven into banishment; members of the Assembly of the Estates were annoyed with petty persecutions; just punishments were improperly remitted; the sentences of the regular courts of justice were attacked, and the Estates were not convened. When at last this assembly, in accordance with its constitutional right, met without summons from the sovereign, in May, 1829, the duke applied without success to the German Diet for an abrogation of the law for the assembling of the Estates, which produced an open breach with the Diet, and destroyed all hope in his subjects of his ever exercising a legal and constitutional rule.

In this state of things, with the decrees of the Diet hanging over his head, the duke left Brunswick in the early part of 1830. The country was suffering from the various evils of the most deplorable misgovernment; anxiety, mistrust, despondency, alarm, distress, every where prevailed. As was expected, the absence of the duke tempted him to measures which might have endangered his personal safety if he had been within the reach of those who were to suffer by them. The *Cammer-Collegium,* a high board of administration, was remodelled, contrary to the law which required the consent of the Estates, and was filled with men of the desired subserviency. Even new tribunals were erected, so as to make the administration of justice dependent on the duke's will. At the same time an edict was issued, prohibiting all public servants from being absent from their place of residence a single night without permission. In some matters the ministers had no discretion without receiving instructions from Paris, to the great hindrance and embarrassment of public business: in others, Bitter, who was the organ of communication with the duke, had full powers, and chiefly in the sale of the public lands. The grants which had always to that time been annually made for agricultural works were for the first time withheld, and immense sums of public money sent to be squandered at Paris.

Such was the state and such were the feelings of the Brunswick people, when they received the news of the French revolution. All were naturally eager to learn how this event would influence the conduct of their sovereign. They soon heard that the duke had fled from Paris, on foot, attended by a single officer, and that after a walk of several hours, he had hurried to Brussels in a miserable carriage. All his money and treasures had been left in the custody of another officer, who was forced to give up most of the arms to the people of Paris, but saved the other effects without any loss. On the 13th of August, the citizens of Brunswick, who had expected that the duke would cross to England, heard that he had arrived that morning in his own city, attended only by a Frenchman named Alloard, having travelled on horseback, and had reached his castle, unobserved, by a back-way. Bitter, the duke's favourite, in vain attempted to persuade the people to illuminate their houses at the return of their sovereign; and a procession of torch-bearers, composed of the lowest public servants and other dependant persons, alone, amidst the silence of the crowd, saluted the duke with a few faint shouts when he appeared on the balcony of his palace.

The duke immediately after his return appeared to anticipate a repetition of the events which he had witnessed at Paris.   He went to the theatre by a circuitous way; he rode out armed with pistols; and one day when a wheel came off his carriage, and some foot-passengers called out to warn him of his danger, mistaking their exclamations for seditious cries, he took refuge in a neighbouring house.   It was generally understood that he was prepared to resort to extreme measures.   The Baron von Sierstorpff, who had been illegally banished from the territory of Brunswick, and was expected to return under a decision of the German Diet, was to be received with some public rejoicings by his neighbours. Orders were accordingly issued by the duke, that in this case the military were to fire grape-shot into the crowd—orders which the consequent absence of Sierstorpff alone prevented from being carried into effect.

The unpopularity of the duke was further increased by his breaking up a stud kept for the general improvement of the breed of horses, which was sold to trading Jews at low prices.   The intimacy of an unknown foreigner at the palace likewise heightened the suspicions of the people: and placards were posted in remote quarters of the city, complaining of want of bread, and calling on the duke to remain at home, and dismiss his foreign favourite.

At this time an event happened which nearly brought matters to an issue between the prince and the people, and affords a striking example of the truth of the remark of Aristotle, that revolutions, though made for great objects, often arise immediately from unimportant circumstances.   The vice-master of the horse, von Oeynhausen, an officer of old standing, who had distinguished himself at Waterloo, and generally esteemed and respected by his fellow citizens, was, even at the duke's table, assailed with the most humiliating reproaches.   The old soldier, overcome with mortification and anguish at such a cowardly insult, was suddenly seized with an illness which seemed to threaten his life.   When he had partially recovered, the duke was pleased to bestow on him a long visit, in which the subject of the former conversation was renewed in the same style, and with such effect, that the unhappy man died the next day.   As soon as the duke was apprized of this event, he hastened to the room where the corpse lay almost warm; began reviling the wretched man who had just expired, ordered his remains to be forthwith removed from the castle, and exclaimed, that " he must accustom himself to the sight of dead bodies." The diffusion of these words through the city naturally created an instantaneous alarm.   Every one appropriated to himself this fearful prophecy: and when such was the avowed determination of the duke, all hopes of a peaceable arrangement between him and his subjects were plainly at end.

Only one peaceable act followed this sad tragedy. On the 1st of September a deputation of citizens waited upon the duke to represent to him the deplorable state of public affairs, and the necessity of convening the Estates in order to consult with them on the best means of relieving the general distress, as the ministers possessed neither the confidence of the duke himself nor that of the people. The only reply vouchsafed to this application was, that " Circumstances would give a clearer answer."

Orders were immediately given to increase the watch, to recall all soldiers on leave of absence, and to serve out cartridges to the men. On Monday, Sept. 6th, sixteen cannons with ammunition were drawn out in front of the barracks. Up to this time there had been no disturbance or riot on the part of the people : no breach of the public peace had been committed. But after the signal had been thus given by the duke, the contest could not long be deferred. In the evening of that day the duke's carriage was attacked while returning from the theatre. Alloard, the favourite, was mistaken for his master, and pulled back by the crowd, as he was mounting the steps. Several stones struck the carriage, and one passed through the window ; but the duke succeeded in regaining the castle amidst the shouts of the populace. The crowd dispersed over the town in separate bodies, and broke some lamps and the windows of different public buildings. The infantry were soon seen marching from their barracks into the castle-yard : and the duke appeared on horseback with his sword drawn. The people, unarmed, stood in crowds outside the castle : but nothing further took place than that Lieutenant-General von Herzberg was 'sent to parley with them, and that the duke was with difficulty persuaded not to order the cannon to fire on the multitude. At last the space near the castle was cleared by a regiment of hussars, and at half-past two in the morning of the 7th all was quiet.

Early in the same day 5500lbs. of gunpowder were, by the duke's order, brought from their usual place of deposit to a church within the city ; but, in compliance with the immediate remonstrance of a tradesman, the order was recalled, and the gunpowder restored to its former magazine.

At 11 o'clock in the morning, the chief magistrate of the town, with six deputies, appeared at the castle, and requested an audience of the duke. They were twice repulsed by Bitter with the answer, that the duke was not yet dressed : but, at last, at 12 o'clock, they were informed that in an hour's time the duke would grant them an interview. At the appointed hour, therefore, the deputation, having been admitted, represented to the duke the strong excitement of all classes of his subjects, and the necessity of some immediate measures to avert the impending storm. They recurred to their former petition for the assembling of the Estates, and requested, as the first step towards an adjustment, that the cannons should be removed to the arsenal. In answer to these proposals, the duke promised, in general, relief to the poor, and labour to the unemployed; authorized the chief magistrate to withdraw the cannon into the arsenal, and gave into his hands a paper in which 5000 dollars were promised for the indigent, and employment in some public works. On the assembling of the Estates, the duke was silent: but he desired that no citizen should be allowed to carry fire-arms, or come near the castle, adding, that he knew how to defend his own castle, and they had only to defend the rest of the city. " The King of France," added the duke, " had taken imprudent measures, had not kept his word, and had thus offended his subjects: but that *he* would not adopt any half measures, and suffer things to come to such a pass as at Paris." The deputation returned dissatisfied: and a proclamation, announcing the results of the negotiation, was received with distrust. All the cannons, with the exception of those in the castle-yard, were carried back to the arsenal, and the crowd dispersed.

On the same morning the duke sent a notice to the inhabitants of the street opposite the castle to remove their effects from the front of their houses, as it was intended to fire upon the people with grape-shot on the first symptom of a tumult, and no damage would be made good except that done to the buildings. The effect produced by the diffusion of this announcement may be easily conceived.

After the departure of the deputation, the duke, in the presence of several of his household and his ministers, communicated to General von Herzberg his intention to repress any future commotion of the people by military force. The general represented to the duke the danger of such violent measures, and the expediency of listening to the demands of the citizens: the difficulty of maintaining any of the public buildings besides the castle, and the inutility of holding that post when the rest of the town was either occupied or destroyed. He also reminded his master, from a late example, of the difficulty of resisting a people when all are animated by the same spirit. The duke inquired if he could depend on the fidelity of the army. He was answered, that the officers knew only the duty of obedience, but, on account of the ill-treatment which they had of late years received, the scantiness of their pay, and the privations to which they had been exposed, they could not be well affected to their sovereign, and that the privates could not be expected to act with zeal and determination against a multitude formed of their kinsmen and friends. To this statement the duke rejoined, " that it might be true that he had not been sufficiently liberal to the officers : it was not, however, too late to remedy the omission : that the public monies were at his disposal: but that the officers must first fight for him against the rebels, and show that they deserved their reward." The general declined to be the bearer of such a proposal; and the conversation here terminated.

About noon the duke was anxious and uneasy, moving from place to place, and giving instructions to his officers. The commander of the artillery twice received orders to fire among the people at the first disturbance. At 7 o'clock in the evening the military again assembled in the castle-yard: they were distributed by the duke himself, so as best to defend the castle: the body-guard was posted in the castle-garden, and all the outer doors and wickets were closed. By this time a large crowd had assembled without the gates, and after committing some smaller outrages, proceeded, with loud shouts and imprecations, to attack the Chancery, or Archive-Office (the Canzlei), a building connected with the main body of the castle, and two other door-ways, one leading into the castle, the other into the garden. At this critical moment, the duke, by the representations of his attendants, was convinced, that even if he ordered the military to fire, his life would be exposed to the utmost danger, on account of the great number of the assailants. While, therefore, the people were as yet kept back by the military, he determined on instant flight. This resolution was immediately executed. Taking with him two aides-de-camp, a regiment of hussars, and the body guards, as an escort, he sallied from the garden just as the people were breaking into it. He was escorted for some miles on his flight by these regiments; and about midnight, neither disturbed by the loss of his crown, nor the anxious conversation of his followers, nor the sight of the flame of his palace which lighted him from his dominions, he unconcernedly took leave of those who returned, threw himself into his carriage, and drove away.

In the mean time the efforts of the attacking party had not been relaxed. The duke at his departure had left General von Herzberg with full powers to act as he might think best. Herzberg attempted to gain the assistance of the chief municipal magistrate and the civil force, but his efforts were fruitless, and he nearly lost his life in returning to the castle. The decision was now to be taken, whether the castle should be defended or not. With the advice, and in accordance to the general feelings of the officers, he gave the command to the troops *not to fire*, but to retreat when the crowd could not be resisted without firing. At the moment of the duke's departure the Chancery had been forced, and the entrances into the castle and garden broken open. The troops accordingly withdrew by degrees to the back of the castle-yard, and thence into the gardens. The fire now burst forth from the windows of the Chancery; in vain had the chief magistrate attempted to check the fury of the multitude; nothing could be heard but the yells and imprecations of the victorious besiegers. The right wing of the castle, in which were the rooms occupied by the duke, was next on fire: every thing, of whatever kind, found in them, was thrown out of window, and eagerly destroyed. The chief magistrate wished to use the fire-engines, which had been brought up by the burgher-guards, but a thousand voices exclaimed that the engines would be broken if the attempt was made; that the castle must be levelled with the ground. By midnight the fire had seized the whole right wing of the castle. The roof had not yet fallen in, but blazed on high, throwing a red glare on the castle-yard and all the neighbouring buildings. The fire-engines were now used for securing the houses of the citizens, which were endangered by the intense heat of so vast a conflagration. In this work both soldiers and citizens joined. In the midst of the stunning noise caused by the crackling of the flames, the crash of the falling walls, and the shouts of the infuriated crowd, and impeded by the concourse of men, some plundering, some saving from destruction, Herzberg contrived to preserve many of the most precious effects contained in the castle, and particularly the contents of the treasury. Numerous valuable articles and papers were the next day restored to the proper authorities. It was not till break of day that fire-engines could be brought into the castle-yard, and even then the offer of four days' wages would not persuade any of the crowd to join in working them. At last, when it became evident that the flames would spread from the left wing of the castle to the adjoining houses, some few hands gave assistance. But it was not till near noon that, with the help of the military, the fire was completely extinguished; after the right wing, the centre, and part of the left wing of the ducal castle had been destroyed.

The chief magistrate now perceived the necessity of organizing a Burgher-guard, before the lower classes could proceed to other acts of violence, unconnected with the expulsion of the reigning duke, and not prompted by the desire of wreaking vengeance on an oppressor. In the course of the day a body of 1800 men was organized, and at seven o'clock in the evening the most profound tranquillity prevailed throughout the whole city.

On the same day a committee of the Estates met and debated; and in a declaration of the 9th of September, the assembling of the whole body was promised within a short time. It was now necessary to provide for the vacant throne. All eyes were turned towards William, the younger brother of the late duke. An address, inviting him to appear in the midst of the Brunswickers, and by his presence to strengthen the bond of the laws and of the social union, was prepared for signature, and numerously signed. On the 10th of September, Duke William made his public entry into the town, amidst the cheers and congratulations of the people. He soon addressed his new subjects in a proclamation; new ministers were appointed; and in the space of a week the general tranquillity was so far restored, that all persons had returned to their usual occupations and amusements.*

The revolution of Brunswick, no less than those of Saxony and Belgium, was the child of the French revolution of July last. Although in all three cases, and particularly the first, the government had been most oppressive both from the interest and ignorance of the rulers, the oppression would doubtless have been endured, if the people had not been roused to resistance by a sympathy with the French, and the example of their successful conflict with the military.† It was said, we believe, by Madame de Staël, that the Russian constitution was a " despotisme limité par l'assassinat." The four revolutions of the last six months must constantly and forcibly remind all monarchs, whether constitutional or absolute, that if all laws are trampled upon, their power is at least limited by insurrection. The memory of these revolutions, following each other in such quick succession, will be a warning to all future princes, however bent on arbitrary rule, that it is their interest no less than their duty, to respect the written laws, the established constitution of the state, and the unanimous wishes of their subjects—

> " Ne populus frequens
> Ad arma cessantes, ad arma
> Concitet, imperiumque frangat."

---

* A general persuasion has prevailed in this country, founded on the conduct of the Duke of Brunswick to our late king, that the mind of the duke was, partially at least, deranged. There is no intimation of such a suspicion in the pamphlet which we have reviewed; whether because the belief does not exist among his former subjects, or out of respect to his brother, the reigning duke, we know not. There is certainly no part of the duke's conduct, as there represented, which might not have been the act of a weak, selfish, obstinate and unprincipled man. An account of his quarrel with his guardian, the late King of England, may be seen in the Foreign Review, No. VI. and the Annual Register, Vol. LXIX. p. 288.

† We use this expression with reference only to the *issue* of the contest. In fact, the military were not beaten by the populace either at Paris or Brunswick. In the one place they retired for want of ammunition and provisions; in the other they refused to act.

All revolutions, however good and desirable the object for which they are effected, are evils in themselves. It is a dangerous thing for the friends of order and the laws to set the example of destroying that order and breaking those laws, and to call in the assistance of the lowest ranks for that purpose. If the disease is deadly, the remedy is also perilous. A double guilt, therefore, is incurred by rulers such as the Duke of Brunswick and Charles X. that by their misgovernment they not only inflict great sufferings on their subjects, but drive the people to relieve their sufferings by a desperate remedy; when recourse is had to that *summum jus* to which all laws must indeed bend, but which is never resorted to without destruction of property and life—the disturbance of credit—the suspension of commerce—and confiscations, banishments and executions for political opinions and crimes.

When a nation has past safely through such a crisis, and has recovered from the effects both of the disease and the cure, it is the part of all honest men, who wish well to their country, to attempt to perpetuate the constitution in its new form, and to withstand a *counter-revolution.* These considerations should weigh not only with native statesmen, but also with foreign courts : nor can any thing but the necessity of self-preservation justify an interference to restore a fallen dynasty or a deposed monarch. In the case of Brunswick there seem to be the strongest reasons why the German Diet and the chief nations of Europe should abide by the decision of the people. The reigning duke is of the ancient dynasty, and now rules by the free choice of his subjects; the deposed sovereign has proved himself to be a cruel, heartless and incorrigible tyrant; and the territory of Brunswick is of so small an extent that the changes in its internal government cannot be of much importance to foreign nations. We have therefore seen with sincere pleasure the recent communication of the King of England to the Estates of Brunswick, that " they may look to him for protection and aid in their endeavours to obtain redress of their just grievances, and that he will proceed to take such measures as are best calculated to secure to his beloved nephew, Duke William, the rights of sovereignty." This declaration of a powerful and beneficent monarch cannot fail (whatever may be the secret wishes of the German courts) to secure the reigning Duke of Brunswick on his throne, and to save the Brunswickers from a second infliction of their former oppressor.

ART. X.— 1. *Lafayette en Amerique en* 1824 *et* 1825, *ou Journal d'un Voyage aux Etats Unis.* Par M. Levasseur, Secretaire du General Lafayette. Paris, 1829. 2 vols. 8vo.

2. *Lafayette in America in* 1824 *and* 1825, *or Journal of a Voyage to the United States.* By M. Levasseur, Secretary to General Lafayette during his Journey. *Translated* by J. D. Godman, M. D. Philadelphia, 1829. 8vo.

3. *Lettres sur les Etats Unis.* Par le Prince Achille Murat. Paris, 1830. 12mo.

WE have been singularly unfortunate in the class of travellers, who have professed to give the English public information on the subject of America. While our Clarkes, our Burckhardts, and our Denhams, men on whose candour and powers of observation we could implicitly rely, have explored every other part of the globe with the minutest attention, we are not aware that any traveller of unimpeached character for impartiality and accuracy has yet published a volume on the United States, which has the slightest pretensions to be called philosophical. Perhaps, however, it is less necessary that we should have any direct or minute accounts of the state of affairs in that country. An acute observer of human affairs would arrive at a knowledge of the state of the people without them. He has only to consider (a difficult task we allow) what would be the condition of man in a highly civilized state, untouched by the corruptions of fashion, unbiassed by a veneration for antiquity, his faculties allowed to expand free from those checks which the mannerism of long established governments and the despotism of opinion impose among ourselves, excepting such as are absolutely necessary to the security of his person and property. This possibility of duly appreciating the American character and condition, by means of a simple knowledge of the fundamental principles on which their government is founded, seems to have struck Talleyrand in a letter to Madame de Staël from the United States.

" J'avois envie," he observes, " d'écrire quelque chose sur l'Amerique et de vous l'envoyer; mais je me suis aperçu que c'etoit un projet insensé. Je renvoie le peu d'observations que j'ai faites aux conversations que j'espere avoir quelque jour dans les longues soireés avec vous. L'Amerique est comme tous les autres pays : il y a quelques grands faits que tout le monde connaît, et avec lesquels on peut d'un cabinet de Copenhague deviner l'Amerique toute entière. Vous savez quelle est la forme du gouvernment; vous savez qu'il y a de grands et immenses terrains inhabités, où chacun peut acquérir une propriété à un prix qui n'a aucun rapport avec les terres d'Europe : vous connaissez la nouveauté du pays, point de capitaux, et beaucoup d'ardeur pour faire fortune, point de manufactures, parceque la main-d'œuvre y est et y sera encore long-temps trop chére. Combinez tout cela, et vous savez l'Amerique mieux que la majorité des voyageurs."

We would not have it supposed that it is our intention or recommendation to discard or under-rate the accounts of travellers, in estimating the social and political condition of the United States, but we think that this principle may be safely opposed to the assertions of the Americans themselves, that they are the most difficult people in the world to understand. On the contrary we consider them the most easy. They have none of the artificial distinctions of rank, none of the multifarious restrictions which, in the Old World, warp and oppose the developments of the human mind, and which form the chief obstacles to all *a priori* reasonings on political subjects. The Americans are left by their government in a state of nature, or nearly so: we do not use the phrase in an offensive sense, but on the contrary as implying the highest praise to their rulers: our definition of a good government being, that it is one that leaves its subjects in a state of natural and uncontrolled freedom, so far as is consistent with the preservation of peace and the maintenance of justice. Such *is*, or we ought rather perhaps to say, such *was*, with some exceptions, the condition of the American people, for they have lately begun to swerve from that wise course which had hitherto marked their conduct.

Captain Basil Hall is the latest of our own travellers in the United States, who has favoured us with his observations. Captain Hall is an able and accomplished man, who, we have no doubt, wrote in perfect sincerity, and believed himself to be as free from prejudice as he says he was; but an impartial reader can hardly rise from a perusal of his work, without concurring in the opinion of one of his American reviewers, that " he was under the influence of a feeling, which utterly incapacitated him from seeing the country as it is." He has consequently been led into innumerable errors, which have been exposed in detail, though in a spirit far removed from that of fairness or impartiality, in a pamphlet lately published in this country.* We trust that the observations which we shall have occasion to make in the course of this article will be such as not to lay us open to similar imputations. We do not mean to limit ourselves to the topics suggested by the two works whose titles we have prefixed, but shall draw freely from other sources, and also endeavour to turn to account the opportunities derived from some personal acquaintance with the subject. But we must first say a word or two on the books before us.

* A Review of Capt. Basil Hall's Travels in North America. By an American. London, 1830.

M. Levasseur accompanied General Lafayette in the capacity of secretary, in the visit which the General.paid to the United States, in the years 1824 and 1825, at the invitation of the Congress. . On his return he wrote an account of this interesting expedition, of which the original, and a.translation, published at Philadelphia, are ·now before us. We cannot conceive a more heart-stirring sight·than the spectacle of the friend of Washington and Franklin visiting, in his old age, the scenes of his early renown, and,' as one risen·from the dead, beholding the splendid maturity of a nation, in establishing whose liberties he had played so conspicuous a part. It is seldom given to man to witness such a magnificent realisation of' his hopes. Lafayette had fought for the' United. States .when they contained but three millions. of inhabitants, when they were engaged in a war, the success of which.appeared. almost hope-less,. and which, when their independence was secured, had .left them in a state of poverty and impotence, with ,no other' re-sources but in the genius of the people. Now, when he returned to visit them after the lapse of nearly half a century, the,three millions had increased to twelve,.they possessed a territory equal in extent to two thirds of Europe, their poverty was a revenue of five millions sterling without internal taxes, and their flag was known and respected in every quarter of the globe. ,

Of course the General was received with the most unbounded· enthusiasm ; his ,journey was a triumphal progress from one' end of the Union to the other, and his whole time was taken up in receiving addresses, and attending meetings, balls .and dinners, given in honour of his visit. Amidst .such. continued scenes of festivity, it was of course impossible for M. Levasseur to take an impartial view of the condition of the country, and his book is consequently tinged with the agreeable feelings, which he must have experienced at so hospitable a reception. His account must therefore be received with caution, except in those points .where he criticises what he saw; for precisely the same rea-sons we put confidence in these statements, as we do in the few laudatory paragraphs with which Captain Hall has inter-spersed his travels: in both cases they are the evidence of an unwilling witness. The Emperor Alexander, when he visited England, surprised at the number of well-dressed persons that crowded his steps wherever he went, asked where were the *canaille?* M. Levasseur, less shrewd than the autocrat, .seems to have almost persuaded himself that there really were none in America. The quantity of unappropriated land must doubtless cause their number to be infinitely fewer than in old countries, but the fact that in the city of New York alone, which reckons under 200,000 inhabitants, 31,000*l.* is sometimes expended in a single year for the support of the poor, ought to make us hesitate in believing in the non-existence of pauperism among our Transatlantic brethren.*

The unpretending letters of M. Achille Murat, son of the celebrated King of Naples, are written in an amusing style, with all the vivacity of a Frenchman, and with a fair mixture of candour and impartiality. Having lost all hopes of succeeding to his father's crown, he collected the scattered remains of his fortune, naturalized himself in America, and is now a slave-holding proprietor in the state of Florida.

———

There is not a little to excite the *amour-propre* of England in the contemplation of the United States, particularly when we compare their condition with that of the ill-starred colonies of Spain. In the former case, we see the seeds of liberty, which ourselves have sown, flourishing with unrivalled luxuriance, and the tide of civilization, to which we have given the first impulse, rolling on with continually increasing force, carrying our name and language over the almost boundless regions of the New World. In the Spanish part of America, since the inhabitants have thrown off the yoke of the mother country, revolution has succeeded revolution with awful rapidity; the state of ignorance and debasement in which they were kept is now visited on the unhappy colonists themselves as well as on Spain, who, by obstinately refusing to recognise their independence, deprives herself of those advantages which she might derive from their commerce, small as those advantages are to what they might have been, had she acted from the beginning in the liberal spirit of England. We are far, however, from joining in those anticipations which the prognosticators of evil and abettors of despotism are for ever ringing in our ears. It is difficult to collect authentic accounts of the state of Spanish America before the revolutions, but from the slight grounds we have for forming an opinion, we should doubt whether the disturbances that ensue from their present anarchical liberty are greater than the miseries which were inflicted by the murders, robberies, legal confiscations and executions, which resulted from the *protection* of Spain.

The state of the *laws and judicial polity* of the United States is, or ought to be, to Englishmen a subject of the deepest interest. Burke, in his speech on American conciliation, said of his American contemporaries, " in no country perhaps in the world is the law so general a study." This is still substantially true;

their descendants have translated Bynkershoek, Martens, Pothier, and, in fact, we believe the greatest part of the continental jurists, and added to them valuable notes, while several periodical publications are specially devoted to the discussion of legal questions. Deriving their laws from the same sources as our own, the traces of the feudal times, so indelibly marked on the whole system of English jurisprudence, were, at the period of their revolution, equally prominent in the American. It becomes consequently a subject of no slight importance, particularly when we are endeavouring to remove those blemishes which the lapse of time and change of manners have caused in our laws, to investigate by what means those which were equally felt on the other side of the Atlantic, have been got rid of. We are confident that a richer harvest than is commonly imagined may be gathered by the legal inquirer, from a consideration of the several judicial systems in the twenty-four states of the Union. The constitution of the Union guarantees to each individual state a republican form of government, without which it would cease to form a member of the confederacy. Consequently the main features of each of the state governments, that is, the governor, the senate, and the house of representatives, as well as the general mode of elections, being the same, the effect of the difference in the criminal and civil laws may be more accurately judged than in the case of Europe, where the dissimilarity in the forms of government, to say nothing of the difference of language and manners, oppose far greater obstacles to our endeavours to discover the real excellencies of the several systems.

· In conformity with that apathetic spirit, with which Englishmen, we know not why, have usually regarded every thing relating to the United States, little is known among us of the numerous ameliorations of our law, which have been carried into effect by the Americans. Perhaps it may be little flattering to our pride to see our ancient colonists so much in advance of ourselves in the application of the principles of jurisprudence to practice. Some there are doubtless among us who imagine that little is to be gained in any point of view by an acquaintance with the legal system of America; but whether pride or ignorance is the cause of this indifference, we submit that, considering the source from whence it has sprung, a system cannot be undeserving of our attention, to which M. Comte, one of the most celebrated French political writers of the day, and who at least will be taken as an impartial witness, has applied the following brilliant eulogy:—

" Nos théories les plus brillantes sont, sous le rapport des institutions, de beaucoup en arrière des pratiques Américaines; les legislateurs de l'Amerique ont exécuté, sans violence et presque sans efforts, ce que les philosophes anciens ou modernes n'auraient pas osé concevoir."

A useful introduction to a knowledge of American law has lately been published in this country by Mr. Parkes, of Birmingham, in a single octavo volume. It contains the statutes and orders of the Court of Chancery and the statute law of real property in the State of New York: the author has prefixed to this a short but clear account of the equity jurisdictions and law of real property, as it exists throughout the whole of the United States, and we shall make considerable use of this introduction in the following observations on American jurisprudence.

It is now more than four years since Mr. Humphreys, in his able work on real property, pointed out the defects of, and suggested remedies in the English system. These defects, which existed equally in the American laws, have long since been removed, while interminable delay seems to characterise every endeavour at a similar reformation of our own. It is remarked by Mr. Parkes, as a singular fact, and we may add not a little humiliating, that the parliamentary reports and discussions on the English Court of Chancery have actually been of more use to the Americans than to ourselves.

Though in the charters which were granted to the original colonists, the feudal rights of the sovereign in the soil were formally recognized, yet even then, for all purposes of enjoyment and alienation, the lands were really allodial; by a statute passed by the legislatures of New York and Massachusetts, since the establishment of their independence, this allodial title of the proprietor in his lands has been placed beyond all doubt, and thus those numerous sources of litigation, which proceed from our absurd adherence to the forms required by the obligations of military fealty, are among our ancient colonists entirely removed; for though laws distinctly recognizing this principle have not (as far as we are aware) been passed in all the other states, yet for all practical purposes the allodial right of the landed proprietor is formally established. The grievances resulting from our system of copyholds and manorial services, from uses and trusts, from the incapacity of married women to convey, from the necessity which exists with us of naming the heirs of the alienee in all alienations in perpetuity, and from the cumbrous machinery of fines and recoveries, are in America either considerably ameliorated or entirely removed. The state of the law respecting estates tail may be seen from the following extract from Mr. Duponceau's " Dissertation on the Jurisdiction of the Courts of the United States," quoted by Mr. Parkes.

" Of estates tail in the several States of the Union., In four states these estates were never known to have been in existence, viz. Vermont, Illinois, Indiana, and Louisiana. In one, viz. South Carolina, the statute *de donis* never was in force, but fees conditional at common law prevail. In twelve they have been abolished, or converted by statutes into fee simple absolute, viz. New York, Ohio, Virginia, North Carolina, Georgia, Missouri, Tenessee, Kentucky, Connecticut, Alabama, Mississipi, and New Jersey; but in the last four a species of estate tail still exists, being for the life of one donee, or a succession of donees then living. In six they may be barred by deed, acknowledged before a court or some magistrate, viz. Rhode Island, Maine, Pennsylvania, Massachusetts, Maryland, and Delaware; but in the last four they may also be barred by fine and common recovery. And in one only do they exist as in England, with all their peculiar incidents, viz. New Hampshire."

All the improvements that Mr. Brougham desired respecting the conveyances of estates held by married women in their own right, or in which they would be dowable, have been effected.* The absurd doctrine of *tacking*, by which a second mortgagee, if he was ignorant of the prior charge when he advanced his money, may, with us, by getting an assignment of any legal interest anterior to the first mortgage, take precedence of the first mortgagee, has been utterly exploded, and the simple rule of " qui prior est tempore, potior est jure," is every where observed.

The absurd rule in our law, by which, if an estate is given to a plurality of persons, without adding any explanatory words, they become joint tenants of the lands, has been remedied in the United States by the obvious plan of reversing the rule, as in nearly every case the interest of the parties requires that they should have a tenancy in common and not a joint tenancy.

" In New York and Delaware, estates conveyed to executors and trustees are excepted from the rule of construction introduced by statute. The propriety of this exception is obvious. The actual law of New York and Delaware, both with regard to the general principle and the exceptions, coincides exactly with the provision proposed by Mr. Humphreys, who says, ' where land is aliened to two or more jointly, whether with or without distinction of shares or interests, or in whatever terms, the share of each of them, upon his death, shall pass to his real representatives, and not to any surviving proprietor, unless an express right of. survivorship be given, or in the case of active trustees.' "†

The custom of primogeniture, so firmly rooted in the English system, would of course cause the American law of descent to be in great measure inapplicable in England; still, however, the Americans have introduced several improvements in the law of descent not touching on this point, which might be advantageously

---

* Purkes's Introduction, p. 77.　　　　　† Ibid. p. 72.

transplanted to this side of the Atlantic. The English law, by which a parent cannot succeed to the son's estate, and which requires a collateral heir to be of the whole blood of the ancestor dying seised, a law, which Mr. Humphreys justly stigmatizes as " repugnant to every principle of property, and to the moral feelings of kindred," has been abrogated in all the states. Blackstone's seventh canon of descent, by which kindred derived from the blood of the male ancestors, however remote, are admitted before those from the blood of the female, however near, which Mr. Parkes properly characterises as violating the feelings of nature, is observed in very few districts of the Union. There is no uniformity, however, in the several states in the laws relating to this subject: in Georgia a preference is given to the brothers and sisters of the half-blood in the paternal line, while in Pennsylvania the inheritance is divided among the next of kin of equal degree to the intestate.

The very obvious improvement on the English law, recommended by Mr. Humphreys, which should render the real as well as personal estate of the deceased liable for his simple contract debts, has been carried into effect in most of the states. Also during the life of the debtor, his real estate is liable for the payment of his debts, except in the State of Virginia, which all travellers concur in describing as the most aristocratic part of the Union, and of which, it appears, the large landed proprietors have felt that reluctance, which Mr. Humphreys anticipates would be felt by ours, at a proposal of subjecting their real estates to the payment of their debts of every description.

M. Levasseur was much struck, and well he might be, at the absurd law in the State of New York, which incapacitates a person from sitting on the bench after he has attained the age of sixty years; an absurdity, which could not be more glaringly exposed, than by the fact of the appointment of Mr. Kent as a commissioner to revise the laws of the State, after he was superannuated as a judge. This gentleman, whose learning and abilities justly entitle him to the appellation of the Blackstone of America, is the author of " Commentaries on American Law," which, like the Commentaries of our celebrated English judge, were originally delivered in the form of lectures at Colombia College. They contain a full and luminous account of the legal institutions of the republic, and though not quite completed, are considered, we believe, throughout the States, as the standard work on American jurisprudence.

It is an anomalous circumstance, that in a land which we are accustomed to consider as a model of simplicity and uprightness, the practice of gambling in lotteries, and places devoted to this purpose, which has been some time forbidden in England, and now appears on the point of meeting with a similar fate in France, should be sanctioned by legislative authority in the United States. In New York, several lottery offices exist with the connivance of government; the legislature, it is true, has forbidden the establishment of new ones, but with what we cannot but consider as a culpable weakness, it has refused to withdraw its protection from the old ones, on the plea that they exist in virtue of privileges anterior to the constitution; the city is consequently exposed, in the words of M. Levasseur, " to a scourge more terrible than drunkenness or prostitution, which extends its ravages through the city of New York, and daily taints the public morals."* New Orleans also contains numerous gambling establishments, to which licenses are granted by the government in the same way as at Paris.

Slavery and the laws relating to the free persons of colour form a foul spot in the picture of the American Union. On this subject we are persuaded there is little accurate knowledge in England. The travellers of our nation who have visited the slave-holding states, have, as far as our observation goes, been either persons whose morbid horror of slavery has prevented them from taking a sufficiently close view of its state, or whose unfounded prejudices against the whole American nation have utterly disqualified them from judging impartially on any subject relating to that great republic. For this reason we shall abstain in the following observations from quoting the work of any Englishman, and should have done so even though we had not been warned of its danger by the sweeping denunciation of M. Murat, who declares that on the subject of slavery, there is not a single page, in any English traveller, that has been dictated by common sense.† M. Murat himself, however, is chargeable with entertaining prejudices against the English government, on the subject of slavery, not less unfounded than those which he ascribes to our countrymen, when he accuses it of employing writers to exaggerate the evils of American slavery, with the view of discouraging emigration to the United States. This is a mistake into which, to say nothing of its intrinsic improbability, he could hardly have fallen, had he been aware of the evils which excess of population is now inflicting on England.

In thirteen out of the twenty-four States slavery has been abolished by law; in the eleven others it exists in full vigour, though variously modified according to the genius and character of the several governments. Much more inquietude is felt with respect to the free blacks than the slaves, for there, as every

---

* Lafayette in America, vol. i. p. 124.　　† Lettres sur les Etats Unis, p. 114.

where else, the whites have an unconquerable aversion to any connection or intercourse with persons of colour; and ·this puts a complete check to an amalgamation of the two races. Discontent is not unfrequently excited amongst the slaves by the sight of their black free brethren, who usually live in a state of complete idleness. By a law lately passed in the State of South Carolina, every traveller who enters that province with a black servant is deprived of him on the frontiers, where he is imprisoned, and only returned to his master when he is about to leave the State. The reason given for the enactment of this law is the fear that tumults may be excited among the slaves by free black strangers, who never fail to talk to them of liberty.* A negro, whether free or enslaved, cannot travel without a passport, and every white has a right to stop and detain him in prison† if he is not able to prove his freedom. The desire of some States to rid themselves of the free blacks has induced them to impose a heavy capitation tax on these unfortunate persons, and even to authorise their sale if they are unable to pay it.‡ This appears to be a most impolitic measure, as without diminishing their numbers in the Union, it can only serve to increase the dislike between the two races; and in case of an insurrection the contest between them would be maintained with a more determined hate and ferocity. In most of the States, they may be sold to pay the debts of their masters contracted before their emancipation, and even the expenses of their imprisonment, if they should be detained while travelling for not having certificates of their liberty.§ In thirteen of the States, the constitution expressly forbids them to vote, and in all the others, except Pensylvania and New York, they are deprived of this privilege by special laws. Some of the southern States have forbidden free negroes to enter their domains under severe penalties—a law which, equally with some of those above-mentioned, has given rise to long discussions as to its constitutional character. The constitution of the United States declares that " the citizens of each State shall be entitled to all privileges and immunities of citizens in the several States." But a free negro of New York is a citizen of that State: now we have just seen that so far from enjoying the privilege of a citizen in some of the southern States, he is even forbidden to enter them— a plain violation of the constitution. In some parts, slaves are only allowed to be emancipated, on the understanding that they shall quit the State immediately on obtaining their freedom.

" On the admission of Missouri into the Union, in 1821, an article of

---

* Lafayette in America, vol. i. p. 206.   † Lettres sur les Etats Unis, p. 143.
‡ Lettres sur les Etats Unis, p. 147.   § Ibid. p. 144.

its constitution which forbids the entry of free persons of colour into the legislature, gave rise to long and violent discussions. The article was, however, at length admitted, on the understanding that it should not apply to any citizen of another State,—a result which only serves to perplex the question in a greater degree than before. The debate on the admission of this State, commonly called the ' Missouri question,'* violently agitated the Union, and gives reason to fear that at some future period it may be the cause of its dissolution."*

The question of slavery in all its aspects is evidently surrounded with difficulties which appear almost insurmountable. It is impossible to get rid of so vast a number by exportation; besides, degraded as they are, the country in which they are born is still looked upon by the negroes with the same feelings with which we regard our native land: to the generality, Africa is as great an object of abhorrence as to a white. If they are freed, the question is as far removed from settlement as ever, as we have seen that the free blacks are as great sources of disquietude as the enslaved, and in most States subjected to laws of Draconian severity. Jefferson says, in his Memoirs,†

" Nothing is more certainly written in the book of fate than that these people are to be free; nor is it less certain that the two races, equally free, cannot live in the same government. Nature, habit, opinion, have drawn indelible lines of distinction between them. It is still in our power to direct the process of emancipation and deportation peaceably and in such slow degree, as that the evil will wear off insensibly, and their place be, *pari passu,* filled up by free white labourers.. If, on the contrary, it is left to force itself on, human nature must shudder at the prospect held up."

The increase of the slaves renders the application of this remedy absolutely impossible. In Jefferson's own State, Vir-

---

* Lettres sur les Etats Unis, p. 147.

† Jefferson's Memoirs and Correspondence form one of the most important and authentic works on American affairs ever presented to the public; they are especially valuable for the insight which they give us into the character and views of the American government. Whoever expects to meet in them eloquent passages, finely turned sentences, or deep erudition, will be woefully disappointed. Nearly all his letters bear marks of being written *currente calamo,* and have never since received any polish or correction from his hand. The writer was above all subterfuge or chicanery, he always went directly to the point he had in view,—he was one of that rare class of statesmen, who speak as they think, and act as they speak. Some prejudices, it is true, totally unworthy of his liberal mind, defile many pages of these memoirs. His detestation of federalism was only equalled by his hatred of England. Federal, he declares, is synonimous with lie. " Nothing like honour or morality," he says, " can ever be counted on in transactions with England," and he accuses us of playing the hypocrite to Spain, on the occasion of its invasion by Louis XVIII.; a charge which, it is almost needless to say, is wholly false. These, however, are blemishes of a trivial cast, compared with the valuable information which his volumes afford; wherever he relates a fact from his own knowledge, we can place implicit confidence in his testimony, and his work may be safely referred to as a record of facts of the most unquestionable authority.

ginia, nearly half the population are blacks. It reckons 1,065,366 inhabitants, among which 462,281 are coloured people, and of these only 37,113 are free. Georgia also, in a population of 340,000 inhabitants, reckons 150,000 slaves.

It is unjust, however, not to mention that the Americans are fully sensible of these enormous evils, and are doing all in their power to mitigate them. In 1821 the American Colonization Society entered into an agreement with some African chiefs for the purchase of some land at Cape Mesurado.* There they have founded a colony under the name of Liberia, and it is their intention to people it with free blacks, to be transported thither from the United States: we trust that they will have better success in their philanthropic attempt than has been experienced in our kindred colony of Sierra Leone. There are numerous other societies dispersed throughout the United States having a similar object in view, to describe which would require, says M. Murat," cent bouches, chacun avec cent langues, et des poumons d'airain." Not possessing these requisites, we shall content ourselves with referring to the fact of their existence, as a proof of the groundlessness of the taunts that are sometimes thrown out against the Americans on their indifference to the continuance of those evils, and to the inconsistency which they display with the free tone of their institutions. Notwithstanding all these drawbacks to the prosperity of the southern section of the Union, M. Murat contends that there arise from this very system many advantages, which in some measure counterbalance the numerous evils. According to him, the custom of being perpetually in the habit of commanding, gives the slave-owner a more noble bearing in his intercourse with his equals, and an independence of views in politics and religion, which form a perfect contrast with the reserve and hypocrisy which often characterise the inhabitants of the North. He declares that the southern inhabitants display an infinite superiority of talent over the rest of the Union, and that the elections, instead of being those scenes of tumult and confusion which the lower classes, who reign supreme in the North, cause them to be there, are conducted " tranquillement et raisonnablement" by the agency of the upper classes.

All this must of course be received with many grains of allowance, especially as M. Murat is a slave-holder himself, and desirous of inducing his friend, to whom these letters are addressed, to emigrate to his part of the country. When we hear of the public business being conducted in a way that is characterised by

---

* Holmes's Annals of America, vol. ii. p. 497.

the above oily epithets, and in the same breath compared with the
" turbulent" scenes which are charged on a freer state of things,
we are instinctively recalled to the established language among
despots and tyrants, and are led to suspect that M. Murat has
not yet forgotten some of the ideas that were instilled into him,
while he was yet heir to the throne of Naples. M. Murat, however, seems to be rather prejudiced against the northern section,
and particularly against the six States which go by the name of
New England: these, he insists, consider religion to consist in
eating nothing else on Saturday but cod-fish and apple-pies, and
relates a story of a New England brewer who was publicly censured in the church for having brewed on Saturday, by which the
beer was made to *work* on Sunday.

By way of counterpoise to the ex-prince's notions on this subject, we shall translate a passage from M. Comte's late work, entitled *Traité de Législation*, quoted in an article in the *Revue
Française*, and we do so because the able reviewer declares that
the author, to whom he is by no means favourably inclined, has
put forth all his talent on the discussion of the slavery question,
and has left nothing to desire; that he has investigated it among
both the ancients and moderns, and considered its effects in every
possible variety of aspect. M. Comte is speaking of Louisiana.

" It is expressly forbidden to every slave-holder to cultivate the intellectual powers of his slaves. A master who should be convicted of
teaching one of his slaves to write, is subjected to a punishment seven
times greater than what he would incur if he was to cut off his hands
and his tongue. Any slave-holder who chances to meet on the public
road more than seven slaves collected together, is empowered to flog
them. A slave, unless he be blind or maimed, is forbidden to appear in
public with a cane or stick, under the penalty of receiving twenty-five
lashes; if attacked, he is interdicted from defending himself. If he is
found sleeping, without a written permission, in a place belonging neither to his possessor nor to the person by whom he happens to be employed, he is punished by the infliction of twenty-five lashes. Even
these precautions are insufficient to remove all fear from the minds of the
masters; they believe themselves perpetually menaced with an insurrection, and always go armed with daggers. The custom of indulging in
arbitrary rule and violence towards the slaves, renders the masters uncontrolled in their passions, vindictive and cruel towards each other.
Quarrels, which ordinarily terminate in a duel, are frequent among them,
and the general result is the death of one of the combatants. When disputes take place among the inferior classes, they are conducted with a
degree of violence almost unknown in countries where domestic slavery
does not exist. The combatants in their fury endeavour to maim each
other, to cut off the nose, to tear away the eyes and ears. The wives of
the slave-holders go themselves to the markets to buy whatever slaves

they want, *et font elles-mêmes, pour n'être pas trompées,*[*] *toutes les vérifications usitées en pareille circonstance; elles ne paraissent pas même se douter des lois de la pudeur.* A white condemned for his crimes would disdain to eat at the same table with a man of colour, and it is necessary in the prisons to have separate tables for each race. In those parts where there exist a great number of slaves, esteem attaching almost exclusively to the aristocracy of colour, a white woman loses nothing of her reputation or self-respect by the most debauched course of conduct; while a woman who carries in her veins the slightest tinge of African blood, cannot rise into public esteem by the most virtuous behaviour. The wives of the Louisiana slave-holders are so proud of the whiteness of their skins, that it is difficult to conceive the extent to which this feeling is pushed. One of them, famous for her incontinencies, entering one evening into a ball-room, exclaimed in an imperious tone, ' there is black blood in the room.' This was instantly spread about, and it was discovered that two ladies, one quarter of whose blood was African, and who were well known for the excellent education they had received and the propriety of their conduct, were in the room. They were immediately advertised of the disgust their presence occasioned, and were obliged to decamp in haste from the presence of a woman whose company should rather have been considered as a stain in their society."[†]

The *constitution* of the United States presents a novel and imposing spectacle in political history. It was an experiment, according to Washington, to try with how much power the subject may be safely entrusted, and it is impossible to say that it has been as yet unattended with success. There are, however, germs of discord in its bosom, which, it would be presumptuous to deny, may at some future time, when the population begins to approach more nearly to the condition of a European State, cause a civil war, or dissolution of the Union. The Missouri question, which we have adverted to before, is of this nature. While it was under discussion it produced the most violent agitation from one end of the Union to the other. Jefferson declared that it filled him with alarm. Ten years ago he wrote, with reference to this question,

" I have been among the most sanguine in believing that our Union would be of long duration. I now doubt it much, and see the event at no great distance, and the direct consequence of this question; not by the line which has been so confidently counted on—the laws of nature controul this; but by the Potomac, Ohio and Missouri, or more probably, the Mississippi, upwards to our northern boundary."[‡]

---

[*] Surely, with respect to this fact as well as the preceding one, M. Comte must either have exaggerated or been grossly imposed upon. Had we met with it in the pages of an English traveller in America of the common class, we should at once have set it down as a misrepresentation.

[†] The testimony of Duke Bernard, of Saxe Weimar, as to the state of society at New Orleans, (see our Third Volume, page 634,) confirms the fidelity of this picture in all its essential points.

[‡] Jefferson's Memoirs, vol. iv. p. 331.

M. Murat also declares, that in the present state of the Union, the annexation of Canada to it would probably cause its dissolution, owing to the great preponderance of power which this addition would give to the Northern States, and which would enable them to pass measures dictated simply by a regard to their own interests, in hostility to the wishes and welfare of the South. What effect these causes may have in bringing about this much to be deprecated result, it would be idle to conjecture, on this side of the Atlantic. But this much we may say, that the causes which we hear commonly given as likely to bring about this event, are utterly inefficient to that end. The old feud between the Federalists and Republicans, which is not unfrequently referred to as tending to a dissolution, has been extinguished by the annihilation of the former party; nor indeed did it ever threaten more serious results than the contemporaneous contentions of Whigs and Tories in this country. We have as little confidence in the assertion which we have sometimes heard, that the election for the Presidency will endanger the permanent tranquillity of the country. We are aware that Kent, in his Commentaries, maintains, that if ever a civil war arises, it will take its origin in this cause; but we cannot help thinking that the experience already obtained, particularly in the celebrated contest between Jefferson and Burr, warrants a contrary opinion. The nation, it is true, is violently agitated while the choice is making, and the vilest calumnies and reproaches which the bitterest spirit of party can suggest, are scattered with the most unsparing hand. But the day after the election, quiet is restored, and the threats which have been used by either party are in a moment forgotten. " How soon do you lay siege to the Capitol?" was the natural question of M. Levasseur to some violent supporters of General Jackson, the day after his opponent, Adams, had been elected. Such also, we are confident, would have been the inquiry of most foreigners. It is curious, indeed, to see the perpetual mistakes which are made by nations in judging of the dangers to which their neighbours are exposed by popular commotions. England has been predicted by the French a hundred times to be on the eve of a revolution. A public meeting in this country is invariably supposed to menace the existence of the monarchy. We are now making almost daily the same mistakes with respect to France. Not a petition can be presented to the king, but the alarmists are instantly on the alert with their prophesyings of secret plots and conspiracies against the nation. Even Jefferson is perpetually falling into the same error with respect to England, which he imagines is visited with an insurrection every six years on an average; and his countrymen seem all to be labouring under similar delusions. Englishmen are in general equally incorrect in their notions of tumults in America, which they usually set down as being in a state of civil war once every four years, on the election for the president.

At present, no State has the power to withdraw from the Union, as the act would be illegal, unless its constitution contained an express provision empowering it to declare its independence.* No State has an article to this effect in its constitution, and it would doubtless be impolitic to insert one, though we do not imagine that this will oppose any obstacle to a separation, should their real or supposed interests ever seem to require it.

In 1798 Jefferson writes, " Our general government has in the course of nine or ten years become more arbitrary, and has swallowed more of the public liberty, than even that of England !" In the eight years of his government, from 1801 to 1809, the impulse was in the contrary direction, that is, the state governments appear rather to have encroached on the powers of the general, and we are confident Jefferson judged rightly, in encouraging this tendency, a conclusion, to which we have arrived, from looking at what has been done of late years, when there seems a wish to invest the Congress with a power of regulating the internal concerns of the States. That the government can ever become really arbitrary we cannot for a moment believe with Jefferson, nor do we put any faith in another of his assertions, that if a common law was in force in the United States, it would become the most corrupt government on earth. Where such an eagle eye is kept on every movement of men in place, that the erection of a billiard table in the President's house could give occasion to a serious charge of immorality, we cannot hesitate to reject the opinion that the taint of corruption can there at least ever creep in.

In her *intercourse with foreign countries,* North America has always conducted herself in a way that commands our most unqualified praise. The Memoirs of Jefferson afford innumerable proofs of the open and candid spirit by which her government has ever been actuated. Her policy appears to have been invariably straightforward and undisguised, and all attempts at cunning and subterfuge utterly banished from her diplomatic intercourse: that this mode of transacting business has been as successful as what is called *refined* policy could have made it, the terms on which she has obtained the cession of Louisiana and the Floridas are a sufficient proof. In the first treaty of alliance contracted with France in 1778, she incautiously imposed on herself the obligation of protecting the French West India Islands against all aggressions. When war had broken out between England and France, in 1793,

---

* Rawle, on the Constitution of the United States, p. 295.

the performance of the stipulations in this article would instantly have involved the United States in hostilities with this country. Upon this, Washington issued a proclamation enforcing the strictest neutrality on the part of America, and this was the commencement of that system of non-interference in the affairs of foreign nations, to which the government has ever since inflexibly adhered. Happily, the circumstances of the case, and the wording of the article, enabled America to remain neuter with perfect good faith; there being at that time no firmly established government in France, America might refuse the fulfilment of the guarantee on this plea, and though it was not expressly mentioned in the Treaty, she certainly could not be justly required to stand to the strict terms of the obligation, unless the war in which her ally was engaged was defensive. This is the implied principle on which mutual guarantees of territory are always made; it was expressly stated by Mr. Canning on the occasion of our sending troops to Portugal, a measure to which we should not have resorted, had the hostilities been justly provoked by our ally.

Ever since that time America has cautiously avoided entangling herself with any similar obligation. The spirit of her government is essentially pacific; her army counts under 6000 men, and war, unless with a nation far inferior to herself in power, must seriously diminish the only sources of her revenue, importation duties. The most conciliatory demeanour has always been displayed by her government in negotiations with foreign states, never showing any want of dignity or spirit in urging just claims, on the one hand, or of readiness to enter into any reasonable arrangement that might be proposed, on the other. When Napoleon's Berlin and Milan Decrees and the English Orders in Council rendered it impossible for American ships to cross the ocean in safety, she resorted to the strong and, we believe, unexampled measure of detaining all her vessels in port. Afterwards all intercourse between France and Great Britain was prohibited; and on the expiration of this law, a proposition was made to both powers, that if either would revoke its hostile edicts, that law should be revived against the other. Surely no government could go farther in its efforts to maintain peace; and it was not till after England had tried her patience to the utmost, having stationed ships of war before all her principal harbours, and boarded and searched every American vessel that appeared, having captured more than 900 of her ships, and impressed some thousands of her seamen, among whom were two nephews of Washington, that she was reluctantly compelled to engage in hostilities with this country.

Nothing indeed can be more honourable to the American government than the temper and forbearance which it displayed throughout the trying times that succeeded the French revolution. For some time it had even to struggle with the opposition of the people. When Washington issued his celebrated neutrality decree, the feelings and prejudices of the majority of the American people were in open hostility to the measure, and even the venerable character and well known patriotism of the president did not preserve him from those attacks, which were now, for the first time, openly directed against him. The talents of that administration, to which America has never since seen one equal, carried the vessel of state safely through the dangers that menaced it; Washington and Adams filled the offices of president and vice-president, Hamilton, one of the authors of the Federalist, and Jefferson, were also in the cabinet. Had the European governments constantly shown the same spirit of moderation, the same disinclination causelessly to plunge their countries into the miseries of war, it is not too much to say, that half the evils which this pestilence has inflicted on Europe might have been avoided.

We must now, however, turn with regret to a point, in which, it appears to us, that the Americans have sadly fallen off from the wise course pointed out by their forefathers, namely, their *commercial policy.* It is singular indeed to remark the deep root which antiquated notions, that are beginning to be scouted by every enlightened nation in Europe, have already taken in the United States. England has for some time proclaimed her recognition of the principle of commercial freedom, and though a long course of contrary policy offers innumerable obstacles to its immediate and universal application, she is assiduously endeavouring to introduce it into every part of her system. Sweden also has been throwing off the shackles that bound her trade, and prevented the importation of foreign goods. Prussia again, to whom belongs the merit of having forced us to relax our navigation laws, has been for some time pursuing the same policy. Under it her manufactures are daily increasing, and her commerce proportionally advancing; her iron manufactures have so prodigiously improved since she has enjoyed her free trade, that we have some fear lest in that quarter our pre-eminence in this art may be endangered. France, we doubt not, will shortly follow in the same course. This journal has in some former articles given pretty strong proofs of the misery she has inflicted on herself by the prohibitive system. Three fourths of the wars that have desolated Europe for the last two centuries have taken their rise in the irritation caused by commercial prohibitions. Napoleon's adherence to this policy was one of the main causes of his downfal, and by it he inflicted perhaps as great miseries on the nations under his control, as by the direct oppression of his conquests. If there ever was an invention by which the halcyon state of universal and perpetual peace can be secured, in free trade the secret lies, the application of which binds men together by the strongest and most indissoluble ties that human nature can feel—those of mutual interest and common advantage. Well has it been observed of the prohibition system by Sir Henry Parnell, in his excellent work on Financial Reform, " that those statesmen who invented this system, who have supported it, and who still support it, deserve to be classed among the greatest enemies of mankind."

Can it then, ought it to do otherwise than raise our warmest indignation, to see the Americans, whom we have been accustomed to consider as among the great promoters of civilization, as the steadiest friends to the improvement and refinement of the human race, thus casting off their philanthropy, and wilfully taking their station " among the greatest enemies of mankind?" Their adoption of the prohibitive system is of very recent origin ; down to about six years ago, the policy of unrestricted trade with all the world, a policy under which their wealth and prosperity advanced in a degree unparalleled in the annals of nations, had been constantly adhered to; " the system of the United States," writes Jefferson, " is to use neither prohibitions nor premiums. Commerce then regulates itself freely, and asks nothing better." We shall presently see how their progress has been checked since they have departed from this wise course.

While reproaching the Americans with the folly of their tariff, we do not wish to conceal that the example of England has, more than any thing else, induced them to maintain it. For centuries the " mercantile theory of wealth" was firmly fixed in the minds of our statesmen; the history of our commercial legislation presents a continued series of laws (made only to be broken, for it was impossible to enforce them) having for their object the prevention of the importation of foreign goods. And of late years, when wiser counsels have ruled the empire, it cannot be denied that the good effects which might have resulted from the change, in the way of example to foreign nations, have in a great measure been neutralised, by the reasons which our ministers have adduced for abandoning the prohibitive system, reasons which were never the strongest, and sometimes even not the true ones. They have acted right, but reasoned wrong. No greater advantage can be given to the enemies of truth, than by maintaining right principles on erroneous grounds. This is what has unfortunately been done in England. Mr. Huskisson, with free trade in his heart, had prohibition perpetually on his lips. He declared he took off the importation duty of 75 per cent. on cotton goods, because their superior cheapness in England was an effectual prohibition to their introduction without the aid of this high duty. One of his principal reasons again for reducing the duty on woollen goods from 50 to 15 per cent., and on silk goods from prohibition to 30 per cent., was, that these low imposts were still high enough to prevent the foreigner coming into competition with the English manufacture, or, in other words, these measures were to be utterly inefficient, and to leave us in the same state of prohibition as before. In the words of Mr. Senior, "these measures are defended as useless, and opposed as beneficial;" it being the constant practice of those who oppose them to declaim on the quantity of foreign goods which they will introduce, that is, on their beneficial tendency. Far too much use is also made of the argument deduced from smuggling. Mr. Huskisson constantly urged, and with perfect truth, "if you wont allow the fair trader to introduce foreign goods, the smuggler will do it:" but he did not add, which he ought to have done, with equal earnestness, "if you can shut out the smuggler, the result will be still more disastrous than it is with him." Pressing as he did with undue force on this argument, powerful as it no doubt is, he led his hearers to believe, that if we could suppress the smuggler, prohibitive laws would be highly beneficial; whereas, in truth, we should be infinitely worse off without than with him; for this great evader of our taxes applies a salutary correction to the evils of our faulty commercial legislation, and as such deserves to be looked upon with peculiar veneration and esteem.

Unhappily for the Americans, by this faulty reasoning of Mr. Huskisson their attention has been principally caught; and they have been wofully deceived by it, as the result has proved. If Mr. Huskisson made such a point of not lowering the duties to that level, which should readily admit foreign goods, why, asked the Americans, inconsiderately enough we allow, but with some degree of plausibility, should not we raise our duties to that height, which should produce the same effect as is intended in England? The speeches of our free-trade minister supplied no answer, and their tariff is the result.

While we object to the species of argument that prevailed in Mr. Huskisson's speeches, we must not forget that he was in a great measure forced into it by the prejudices and interests he had to deal with. Firmly convinced of the sound policy of his measures, the unceasing clamour of his opponents was perpetually compelling him so to arrange them that nearly the minimum of effect might be produced. He consequently struck a balance between the free-traders and the prohibitionists. To the latter, he declared that the effect of his measures would be to admit few, very few, foreign goods; to the former, who naturally inquired in what then consisted their utility? he answered, they would admit some, and that too large an importation would cause great immediate distress. He had a difficult part to perform, and the improvements he had at heart could only be carried into effect by throwing dust in the eyes of those whose opposition would otherwise have overwhelmed him. His error lay in *saying* too much, from necessity we admit, to please the prohibitionists; for his *acts* were all against them, and in fact, as far as they went, were in complete accordance with the doctrines of Adam Smith; this the Americans will discover if they will condescend to examine " the Wealth of Nations" a little more closely. They are perpetually accusing us of being inconsistent supporters of the free-trade theory, while we impose duties as high as 20 or 30 per cent. on foreign manufactures. We answer in the words of Adam Smith, " the second case, in which it will generally be advantageous to lay some burden upon foreign for the encouragement of domestic industry, is, when some tax is imposed at home upon the produce of the latter."* Now this is exactly the case with England. Several of our manufactures are directly taxed, but it will be said not to the extent of 20 or 30 per cent., consequently, only part of the duty is accounted for. Again, with the same illustrious authority, we say, " the case in which it may sometimes be a matter of deliberation, how far or in what manner it is proper to restore the free importation of foreign goods, after it has been for some time interrupted, is, when particular manufactures, by means of high duties or prohibitions upon all foreign goods which can come into competition with them, have been so far extended as to employ a great multitude of hands. Humanity may in this case require that the freedom of trade should be restored only by slow gradations, and with a good deal of reserve and circumspection." This again is the case of England, and forms a sufficient reason why our duties should not in the first instance be lowered to a less rate than 20 or 30 per cent., considering that the old duties were 75 per cent., or prohibition. Now neither of these cases applies to America; they have not our burden of internal taxation, and they *had* not their tariff, consequently, in vain can they assert the example of England in raising their duties even to this height; and we are surprised that Mr. Cambreleng, in his excellent Report to Congress on Commerce and Navigation, should say that 30 per cent. duty

---

* Wealth of Nations, book 4, ch. 2.

"has been ascertained and settled in Great Britain, as the safest for the revenue, the best for manufactures, and the most equitable rate for all classes and interests."* The only reasons why there should be any duty at all, are contained in the above two quotations from Adam Smith, both of which are inapplicable to America. It is true that importation duties may be made a source of revenue, but in that case there can be no doubt that the amount levied would be much greater if the duty is lowered considerably beneath 30 per cent. After what we have said, it is almost needless to state that we are as much opposed to our corn laws as the Americans are. They should learn, however, that their reproaches for our inconsistency on this score fall utterly pointless, as those who advocate freedom in other matters (with one or two exceptions) advocate it in this also, and *vice versa*; consequently, the imputed inconsistency does not exist.

It is curious to read the reasons given by the American prohibitionists for imposing some of the additional duties contained in their last tariff. By their previous tariff, they had imposed duties sufficiently high, it was supposed, to prevent the importation of our woollen goods, when their nice calculations were completely upset by that politic measure of Mr. Huskisson, which reduced the duty on foreign wool imported into England from 6*d*. to 1*d*. or ½*d*. per pound, which of course gave our manufacturers an unlooked-for advantage. This was not to be borne; an indignity, it was declared, was put on the republic; could it be endured, exclaimed the Transatlantic wiseacres, that our revenue laws should be repealed by an act of the British legislature? A simple and obvious course was suggested by some, that they should also repeal their duties on foreign wool, and thus place the home manufacturer on the same footing with the British; but here another difficulty occurred. The wool-grower must have his *protection* as well as the manufacturer, and would it not be a disgrace to the country to allow this protection to be taken away by the act of a foreign nation? Only one other course remained, which was to increase the duties on woollen goods, and they were accordingly raised to from 45 to 108 per cent. As might naturally be expected, the effect of these impolitic probibitions has been sensibly felt in the extended distress and smuggling which they have occasioned. Mr. M'Vickar, the intelligent lecturer on political economy in Columbia College, says, in his introductory lecture,

" Our population is not only checked, it is actually diminished. Last year there was a falling off of 1,413,000 dollars in the amount of duties

---

* Report on Commerce and Navigation, p. 38.

collected in this port, equal to a diminished importation of 4,000,000; dollars. Our ship-yards are abandoned, our ships rotting at the wharves, and our tonnage less than it was twenty years ago."

The prohibitive system, once admitted as true, can stop no where till every trade is subjected to it. The American hemp-growers asked why they should not be protected as well as the wool-growers, the iron manufacturers, &c.; the duty on hemp was consequently raised to 12*l.* 5*s.* a ton, and after 1831 it is to be 13*l.* 8*s.* The consequence is, that the manufacture is fast disappearing under the competition of the Russians, who imported into the United States, in 1819, only 251,356 pounds of cordage, and in 1829, 1,848,254 pounds, while in four years, ending 1829, the consumption of the Boston cordage mills decreased from 430 tons to 147.* But there are other results behind even worse than this; the ship-owners, naturally preferring the untaxed cordage of Russia to the taxed American, send their ships out on the Russian voyage half-rigged, to the hazard of the seamen's lives, for the sake of completing their equipments at St. Petersburgh, and bringing back a double supply, thus depriving the revenue of the duty on its consumption; for large as is the use of Russian cordage, as stated in the figures given above, it is in fact more than one third greater than this, as appears from the Russian accounts of exportation to the United States; the mode in which the vessels are rigged explains why the addition does not appear in the American revenue accounts. By these various duties on sail-cloth, on hemp, on iron, and in fact on every thing that is employed in ship-building, Mr. Cambreleng states, that a premium of nearly four hundred pounds sterling is enjoyed by an English as compared with an American ship-builder in fitting out a ship of 500 tons. Need we then wonder that the ratio of foreign to American tonnage, entering American ports, has been rapidly increasing? that of England in particular has advanced from 15½ per cent. in 1820, to 38½ per cent. in 1828, while, under the system of free-trade granted them by England, our North American colonies, in spite of their small population, have a greater quantity of tonnage engaged in foreign trade than the whole United States.

But even articles which are solely produced in the country have not escaped this duty fever, and the freedom from internal excise, so long the boast of America and the envy of England, is no more. Salt and brown sugar are subject to taxation, not wholly, however, excise, from 80 to 275 per cent., though the internal duty alone is in some of the States as high as 100 per cent.

---

* Report on Commerce and Navigation.

Under this mistaken system, smuggling has of course increased to an enormous extent, principally across the Canada frontier. If every man in the American army, which reckons under 6000 men, was employed in guarding the frontier, there would be too few to prevent the ingress of the smuggler. If that army was increased twentyfold, it would be still insufficient to watch the immense boundaries. How can the Americans suppose that, with such small means, they can effect what France and England have been utterly unable to do with their small comparative extent of frontier, and immense array of preventive service? The answer, which the American prohibitionists make, when pressed with this argument, is inconceivably absurd. A pamphlet, published at Baltimore, with the appropriate signature of Mephistopheles, as an answer to Mr. Cambreleng, declares that American manufactures have been so improved in quality and lowered in price, since the passing of the tariff, that they are now beating the English in foreign markets. " Even now the British cottons in South America owe their currency to fraud. They are flimsy imitations of substantial American wares, bearing counterfeit marks." The *North American Review,* which seems to be the Coryphæus of American illiberalism, in its 66th Number, has a long and laboured article in defence of the tariff. It endeavours to repel the assertion, that encouraging their manufactures by these protective duties will produce a spirit of insubordination and ferocity in their border inhabitants, from the smuggling pursuits in which they will be constantly engaged. An article in the *Edinburgh Review* is alluded to; the American writer begins with the following flourish :—

" Lest the reader should be tempted to question the testimony of our eyes, which we have found some difficulty in believing ourselves, we quote the passage as it stands in the article before us. 'The Americans, instead of having the population on their frontier engaged in the clearing of land, and extending the empire of civilization, will imbue them with predatory and ferocious habits, and teach them to defy the laws, and place their hopes of rising in the world, not in the laborious operations of agriculture, but in schemes to defraud the public revenue.' The Latin poet tells us that it is the cultivation of the arts that prevents men from being ferocious ;

> Ingenuas didicisse fideliter artes
> Emollit mores, nec sinit esse feros.

Our critic, on the contrary, has discovered that it makes them so, and that the interior of the republic, which has now, it seems, become all at once a paradise of innocence and refinement, is to be demoralised by the invasion of the demon of domestic industry !"

We pass over the ignorance of the sense in the above hack-

neyed Latin quotation (we should be sorry to take it as a
specimen of American classical knowledge) displayed by the
critic, with a recommendation to inquire of some schoolboy the
meaning of " ingenuas artes" before he again applies it to manufacturing or " domestic industry." What we wish to remark is, the species of reasoning and misrepresentation, by which
the Americans are deluded into a support of their tariff. No one
that we ever heard of, certainly not the Edinburgh Review in
the passage quoted by the American critic, ever maintained that
the practice of domestic industry imbued the people with predatory and ferocious habits, as the writer intimates. The Scotch
critic expressly says, " population on the frontier," the American
transforms this into " the interior of the republic," as gross a misrepresentation as could well be made. The introduction of manufactures by these means must infallibly cause these ferocious
habits to become general among the border peasantry. Does
the example of England and France go for nothing, or are not
our coast peasantry in Sussex and Hampshire in the state here
described from the effects of our clinging to a small part of the
prohibitive system? Nations, it seems, are always unwilling
to be taught from the experience of each other, and the Americans must learn in the school of adversity, by the actual infliction of these evils, the truth of this unhappy effect of prohibitions.

Another injurious effect of these measures, of the most vital
importance to America, is the diminution they have caused in
her shipping. Mr. Cambreleng gives ample proof in support
of this. Notwithstanding the vast increase of her population
since 1807, and the addition of the commerce of the fertile countries of Florida and Louisiana, it appears that the tonnage belonging to the United States, entering from abroad, in 1828, was
actually 265,095 tons less than entered in 1807. Some of these
statements of Mr. Cambreleng the tariff arguers have endeavoured to controvert. But it is quite clear, without reference to
facts, that some diminution must have taken place. This is one
of those questions on which the unassisted aid of theory throws a
clear and certain light, and in which, the data being laid down,
we may arrive at a conclusion without the hazard of being wrong.
How is it possible, that when the Americans have imposed prohibitive duties on almost every article of foreign growth and manufacture, when they have done all in their power to exclude
from their country every thing that foreigners had to give in exchange, the result can be otherwise than Mr. Cambreleng asserts
it to be? When there are fewer things to be carried, must there
not be fewer carriers? But, besides the accounts of the American shipping, we can give other proofs of the truth of the con-

clusion to which Mr. Cambreleng has arrived. As Cuba lies close upon the borders of the United States, and possesses a soil abounding with the richest products, and a capital city, which is one of the greatest centres of commerce in the American archipelago, the trade between it and the United States is consequently immense. A late number of the "Revue Encyclopédique" contains extracts from some Spanish official documents, from which we have formed the following table of the number of ships belonging to the United States and England, which entered and departed from its ports in 1827 and 1828. The amount of tonnage is not given; but it is to be observed, that the proportion, which the English bears to the United States shipping, is really much larger than is indicated by the number of the vessels, a circumstance which arises from the greater size of the English ships, owing to the length of the voyage they have to make.

Number of vessels belonging to the United States and England respectively, which entered and departed from the ports of Cuba in 1827 and 1828.

	ENTERED.		DEPARTED.	
	United States Vessels.	English Vessels.	United States Vessels.	English Vessels.
1827	1242	166	1107	151
1828	1175	206	990	175
Difference	—67	+40	—117	+24

Thus it appears, under the different systems of the two countries, the United States shipping entering Cuba decreased 67 vessels in a year, while ours increased 40. We also add, from the same source, a table of the value of the imports into Cuba from the two countries, which shows more unequivocally the decaying condition of the trade of the United States and the increase, *pari passu*, of that of England.

Value of imports into Cuba from the United States and England respectively, in the years 1827 and 1828.

	1827.	1828.	
United States.	£1,432,535	£1,319,819	*Decrease.* £112,716
England. . .	323,674	354,017	*Increase.* £30,343

It appears, therefore, that while our exports to Cuba with our unshackled trade increased upwards of thirty thousand pounds sterling in a year, the exports of the United States fell off in the same time more than a hundred and twelve thousand pounds. And yet the Americans talk of their having supplanted British goods in foreign markets. Is Jonathan so utterly blind as not to see, that if this statement be true, if they do undersell British goods in foreign markets, if their manufactures are really cheaper than ours, the tariff is entirely useless, and the only ground for maintaining it cut away? Were this the case, is it not as clear as any axiom in Euclid, that if the admission of British goods into New York were as unrestricted as that of the wind, not a bale could possibly be sold? And yet the Mephistopheles answer* to Mr. Cambréleng's report, which we have alluded to before, speaks of this supplanting of our manufactures as a fact, and the Harrisburg delegates gravely state, that " large quantities of American manufactured cotton goods are exported from New York to Canada, and the people are supplied with cottons cheaper than they can import them from England, the import duty of 15 per cent. being honestly paid!" and still more extraordinary, that they smuggle cottons into England, finding it now convenient not to pay the duty, that duty, be it observed, being 10 per cent.! We have either formed far too high an estimate of American intellect, or the Harrisburg delegates must have grossly libelled it.

The declamation and reasoning with which the American tariff advocates pretend to controvert the free-trade doctrines of British writers are almost incredible, and would lead one to believe that they had their origin in the latitudes of Spain and Sicily, rather than in a country professing to contain the most intelligent and sagacious population on the face of the earth. The Harrisburg delegates, an assembly chosen by the manufacturers to represent their wishes, and therefore, we should suppose, not the least sagacious of their body, state that our free-trade doctrines are manufactured, like our cloths, for exportation to America; as if there were no French, Russian, or Italian writers who maintained the same opinions, or as if the " Wealth of Nations," which was published some years before the American independence, had just been written to deceive the Yankees. The same enlightened assembly, in answer to the assertion that

---

* In passing, we cannot help remarking, that the American tariff advocates seem to have a *cacoethes* of misquoting Latin. This writer, alluding to the clamour of some citizens for free trade, mangles the well-known line of Horace into *ardor prava civium jubentium.* Perhaps it would be too much to expect a knowledge of the Horatian metres in such a writer, but the unfortunate collocation of the words unhappily betrays his mode of construing them.

their prohibitions will injure the cotton grower and agriculturist, by diminishing the exportation of raw goods, or rendering it less profitable, state that this cannot be the case, because we lie under an absolute necessity of taking their cotton, and that when we can do without it, we shall in spite of them ; as if they were to give us their cotton, good people, for nothing, or as if the time when we shall be able to do without it will not be greatly hastened by the premium which these prohibitions give to the Brazilian, East Indian, and Egyptian cotton growers.*

We fortify these opinions with a quotation from an author, who must be allowed, even by the Americans, to be free from the imputation of manufacturing doctrines for exportation to America to the profit of England. M. Say, speaking of the injurious results which would accrue to the South American States if they endeavoured to raise manufactures by impeding the production of English, says, " Il est à craindre que les Etats-Unis de l'Amérique du Nord aient fait une faute pareille, pour *protéger*, selon leur expression, leurs manufactures. Ce qui mériterait d'être protégé chez eux, ou plutôt ce qui n'a pas besoin de protection, ce sont leurs produits agricoles, qui peuvent se multiplier indéfiniment, et dont ils contrarient le développement, en refusant de recevoir des marchandises manufacturées dont les étrangers seraient obligés de faire, venir les retours en produits de l'agriculture."†

* As another instance of American tariff reasoning, we give the following from a work of high character and circulation :—

" As all commerce is an exchange of equivalent values, and as the value of all objects is determined by the quantities of labour respectively bestowed upon their production, it is certain, that if we send to Europe in exchange for manufactures the produce of the labour of three million of persons, or whatever other number we choose to assume, the manufactures we receive in return must also be the produce of the labour of the same number, and if made at home would give employment to an equal number of our own citizens, and create a new demand of proportional extent for the agricultural produce necessary to their support. In other words, the domestic manufactures, competent to supply us with the articles we now receive from Europe, would give us, on the above supposition as to the number of persons employed in producing our exports, which will probably not be thought too high, a manufacturing population of three millions, and an *additional agricultural one of three more*, making a total addition to the population of six millions, and of the products of the labour of six million persons to the annual revenue of the community .... another effect of the same cause would be, as we have already shown (?), to occasion a greatly increased consumption of manufactures ; and in the same proportion in which this increase should take place, would the *addition to the population and wealth of the country be greater than we have stated it above.*"—*North American Review, No. 66.* The millions mount like Falstaff's men in buckram ; with the last addition, the writer calculates that between seven and eight millions are to be added to the American population by the enactment of their tariff! He also says that the only effect of the tariff will be to make England send gold instead of manufactures to the United States, that he is not a partizan of the balance of trade, and he recommends his antagonist to read Adam Smith ! *Risum teneatis.*

† Cours d'Economie Politique. Quatrieme Partie, ch. 19.

Another point in which the Americans have also lately gone astray is what they call " the system of internal improvement." Indeed, they seem to be fully aware of the advantage that may be gained by the advocates of a cause by giving it a good name. There is no better way of concealing a fallacy or preparing for an attack on an opponent. The prohibitive system, which we have described above, they have christened the " American system," and every one opposed to it they have accused of being un-American, in the interests of England, &c. In like manner, whoever is not favourable to the " system of internal improvement," they charge with being adverse to internal improvements, forgetting, that besides the goodness of the end there is something else to be considered, viz. the fitness of the means.

This system consists in investing the general government with a power to spend the public money in making roads and canals over the whole country. The Americans, it seems, have conceived the most extravagant ideas of what may be effected by these means. Lines of communication by land and by water are to branch out from Washington to every part of their immense territories; from a town which, though the capital, does not contain above 13,000 inhabitants, which is not situated in any of the great lines of traffic, and yet is to be made the centre of works equalling, in American imaginations, any thing that old Rome or Napoleon ever produced. We believe the first attempt to introduce this innovation was made in 1817, when a bill giving the government this power, after passing both houses, was lost by the veto of the President. Jefferson opposed it to the utmost of his power; in 1825, when the system appears to have taken firm root, he writes, that he had for some time considered the question as desperate, and that those who thought with him were " in a state of perfect dismay, not knowing what to do or what to propose."* He declared that the assumption by government of these powers was an open infraction of the constitution, and prepared an energetic protest from the State of Virginia to the general Congress, in which he plainly intimates, that if Congress proceeded in this course, his State, though long-enduring, would at length raise the banner of disaffection. A short time before his death he wrote, with reference to this question :

" We must have patience and longer endurance, then, with our brethren, while under delusion ; give them time for reflection and experience of consequences ; keep ourselves in a situation to profit by the chapter of accidents ; and separate from our companions only when the sole alternatives left are the dissolution of our union with them, or submission to a government without limitation of powers."

* Jefferson's Memoirs, vol. iv. p. 424.

' But this advice was utterly thrown away on the American statesmen: Jefferson declares, that one might as well reason with marble columns. The present President, General Jackson, has, however, had the firmness to oppose the general current, by putting his veto on a road bill, which passed the Houses last session: and in his recent message to Congress, he has entered at great length into the policy of the system, and expressed himself opposed to it: he has, however, lost popularity by this conduct, and most of the newspapers, which we have seen, declare this veto to have been not only highly injurious to the general welfare, but absolutely unconstitutional. At the ceremony of commencing the Mohawk and Hudson rail roads in New York, last July, being the first rail road ever attempted in that State, Mr. Cambreleng made some judicious observations on this subject.

" No general government," he says, " ever did, or ever will, manage roads and canals, or distribute the funds for their construction with the justice, economy, or discretion, that private corporations, local authorities, or state governments, are compelled to exercise. But this question does not rest merely on the maxims of philosophy. We have evidence more unquestionable—the examples of France and England. The former acts on the national system, and the consequence is a few good roads radiating from the capital, and the rest, by far the most numerous, almost impassable; in the latter, they have been suffered to grow up under the local authorities, and the whole country is covered with good roads."

This reasoning is perfectly correct, and the examples are appositely chosen, except that Mr. Cambreleng might have gone still farther in depreciating the results of the French intermeddling system. The roads branching from Paris are even for the most part infamously made; the lines of communication to Lyons and Rouen, the first towns of France after the capital, are during the winter almost impassable, while in many parts the crackbone *pavé* system still exists, to attest the inherent slowness of governments in adopting improvements which have been long effected by individuals. We would not only prohibit the General Congress, we should even doubt the propriety of allowing the State Governments to engage in making roads and canals. The ridiculous mode in which even those works, the execution of which would seem to fall more peculiarly within the province of government, are sometimes carried on, affords ample reason for permitting it to do as little in this way as possible. Our mast-pond at Portsmouth is a memorable instance of this, it having been ordered to be discontinued after being six years in progress, on its being proved to the Finance Committee that it would require 176 years for its completion, and cost the public £132,000,000! an instance of official folly, which we can only parallel by what occurred in France with respect to the national map, an undertaking which, when it had been laboured at for ten years, was declared by M. de Tracy, in the Chamber of Deputies, impossible to be completed under a hundred years, or at a less expense than four millions sterling.

· Unlimited *toleration of religious opinions* is so generally the rule in the United States, that it would be perhaps invidious to remark the few exceptions that exist, were it not for noting the anomalous fact, that our Parliament was, last session, on the point of passing a bill, which would have granted to a religious sect political privileges, of which that sect is still deprived on account of their opinions in some sections of the Union. In Maryland, the Jews, as well as all persons who deny the truth of the Christian religion, are prohibited from holding all offices of trust or profit; while in North Carolina the exclusion is extended to all who do not hold the Protestant faith. In no other States are there any political disabilities on account of religious belief; the last named State may still take example from us on the subject of toleration.

The publication of *newspapers* is carried in the United States to an extent unparalleled in any other quarter of the globe. A settlement is no sooner made in any of the back woods than a newspaper is instantly established; indeed a vehicle for the communication of ideas, by which the inhabitants may, as it were, hold converse with the remotest parts of the Union, is deemed almost as indispensable to a village as houses; and, we imagine, this fact may serve to account for the universality with which education is extended throughout the Union. In many, we believe we may say in most, parts, it is impossible to meet with a person in any rank of life who is unable to read and write; such being the case, it is evident, that so powerful an instrument of civilization, unless perverted to a bad end, must bring into play a mass of intelligence which we might expect would produce the happiest effects.

But is it perverted to a bad end? We regret we cannot answer this question so satisfactorily as we could wish. Jefferson, whom we love to quote whenever his testimony can be made available, gives a harsh opinion on this point.

" It is a melancholy truth," he says, " that a suppression of the press could not more completely deprive the nation of its benefits than is done by its abandoned prostitution to falsehood. Nothing can now be believed which is seen in a newspaper. Truth itself becomes suspicious by being put into that polluted vehicle."*

---

* Jefferson's Memoirs, vol. iv., p. 83.

Again, writing to Doctor Jones :—

" I deplore with you the putrid state into which our newspapers have passed, and the malignity, vulgarity, and mendacious spirit of those who write for them; and I enclose you a recent example, the production of a New England judge, as a proof of the abyss of degradation into which we have fallen. These ordures are rapidly depraving the public taste, and lessening the relish for sound food. As vehicles for information and a curb on our functionaries, they have rendered themselves useless, by forfeiting all title to belief."

This is a lamentable picture, which happily could not be drawn in the first thirty years of their independence; for it is fearful to think what would have been the result if Washington had been driven from his post, which Jefferson states he certainly would have been, had he been assailed with the degree of abandoned licentiousness afterwards practised, " which," he writes in 1805, " is confounding all vice and virtue, all truth and falsehood, in the United States."

Let it not, however, be concluded that the freedom of the press is the cause of its licentiousness. The French press, which is much freer, is, at the same time, infinitely less open to the imputation of slander than our own, which seems to hold a middle station between the American and the French, being as much superior to the former as it is inferior to the latter. The abusive tone of the American press is to be sought for in other causes. Mr. de Witt Clinton, the late Governor of New York, attributes it, in a great measure, to the injudicious provisions relative to the office of the President. The election to this office engenders party spirit to so violent a degree, that, says the Governor, " it has violated the sanctity of female character, invaded the tranquillity of private life, and visited with severe inflictions the peace of families." This cause, doubtless, has some share in the result complained of; but we imagine that a more fertile source of the evil is to be found in the unintellectual character of the population, arising from the non-existence of any means of advancement in knowledge beyond the merest elements. In support of this fact, the unimpeachable testimony of Dr. Channing may be adduced. He says—

· " That there are gross deficiencies in our common schools, and that the amount of knowledge which they communicate, when compared with the time spent in its acquisition, is lamentably small, the community begin to feel. There is a crying need for a higher and more quickening kind of instruction than the labouring part of society have yet received; and we rejoice that the cry begins to be heard. We do and must lament, that however we surpass other nations in providing for and spreading elementary instruction, we fall behind many in provision for the liberal training of the intellect, for forming great scholars, for communicating that profound knowledge, and that thirst for higher truths, which can alone originate a commanding literature. The truth ought to be known. There is among us much superficial knowledge, but little severe persevering research; little of that consuming passion for new truth, which makes outward things worthless; little resolute devotion to a high intellectual culture. There is nowhere a literary atmosphere, or such an accumulation of literary influence, as determines the whole strength of the mind to its own enlargement and to the manifestation of itself in enduring forms."*

This is confirmed, if, indeed, the statement of such a writer requires confirmation, by the accounts of most travellers. In fact, it is the natural effect of the situation of the country. When such a quantity of land remains unappropriated, it is not to be supposed that the college student will prefer the intellectual toils and uncertain gains of a literary life to the easy independence that is offered in the back woods; and, accordingly, he leaves the university or school long before he has acquired that degree of knowledge which is considered indispensable in European society. It would be as impossible to find readers as editors for publications which should discuss subjects with any degree of learning or profundity; consequently, light reading, which is too apt to degenerate into slander, is the prevailing taste, and we have been assured that novels alone return any considerable profit to the publishers.

This evil is, however, doubtless, only transient, and as America becomes more peopled, and intercourse more easy and rapid, must progressively diminish. Though while we ascribe this effect, in great measure, to natural causes, we cannot but think that the growth of literature might be considerably hastened, if government would co-operate in removing some obstacles which prevent its expansion. One of these is the utter want of good public libraries, than which there cannot be a greater drawback to literary exertion. Philadelphia, one of the largest and most literary cities in the Union, is said to contain 65,000 volumes in its public institutions. This, at first sight, looks considerable; but when we learn that sixteen public libraries make up this number, giving much under 5,000 volumes to each, it is evident that there must be many duplicates, and its literary treasures very small. The absurdity of imposing a duty of 15d. per pound on imported books must be a great impediment to the formation of libraries; what reason there can be for keeping up this duty we cannot conceive; it seems to be the determi-

---

* The Importance and Means of a National Literature, by W. E. Channing, D.D. London. 1830.

nation of the Americans to cause the blasting effects of their tariff policy to be felt by every interest. But that spirit of pride, which leads us to contemn what we do not possess, has unhappily had its effect on the Americans, and induced them to undervalue the advantage of public libraries, as well as of many other European institutions, which might have been usefully introduced among them. Mr. Dwight, a traveller from the United States, who published a tour in Germany, makes some laudatory observations on the splendid libraries in that country, and laments their want in his own, as placing a great impediment to the advancement of its literature. For this he is taken to task by his American reviewer, who assures him that discoveries will not be made, or the taste of foreign literature promoted, by "the facility of accumulating quotations by means of huge libraries,"* and that the taste of the Republic will not be dictated to, a strain of remark, which also forms the burden of some of Mr. Cooper's observations, in that mass of conceit and self-complacency, *Notions of the Americans, picked up by a Travelling Bachelor.* Dr. Channing, who possesses a mind superior to these vulgar prejudices, boldly acknowledges that they "want universities worthy of the name, where a man of genius and literary zeal may possess himself of all that is yet known," and that "intellectual labour, devoted to a thorough investigation and a full developement of great subjects, is almost unknown among us."† Jefferson also makes continual complaint, in his Memoirs, of the parsimonious spirit and utter disregard of the interests of literature evinced by the Virginian legislature, in refusing all aid to the university he was struggling to found.

The removal of the *seat of government* from Philadelphia, in 1800, and its establishment in a city which even now does not contain more than thirteen thousand inhabitants, we cannot but consider as having been, in many respects, highly injurious to the country. The small increase of their capital in thirty years must have convinced the Americans of the error they have committed; had it been situated in any of the great lines of commercial intercourse, as it ought to have been, it would long since have attained a respectable rank among cities. The various good effects that result from establishing the government in a populous city are almost too obvious to require mentioning. There, men of science, of business, and of pleasure, naturally resort; there, all that the wealth, the talent, the industry of the country can produce, is, in a great measure, condensed; far greater facilities are

---

* North American Review, No. 65.
† Importance and Means of a National Literature, p. 36.

given to the executive for obtaining intelligence and sounding the wishes and feelings of the people; while the presence of the representatives, and the excitement of constant political discussion diffuses juster notions of the wants and situation of the country, which diverge from this point as from a focus to every corner of the empire. The establishment of the government in a comparatively uninhabited spot must also deprive it in a great degree of that weight and influence which it ought to possess and would exercise, if situated in a populous neighbourhood. An incidental effect of this is also seen in the non-existence of leading newspapers in the United States; for there is no city which possesses all the requisites combined for furnishing a daily journal with information on those important topics which are constantly agitating the public mind. A stranger, wishing to know the state of France or England, refers to a newspaper published in their respective capitals, and would never think of consulting any other. If the United States are the object of his inquiries, is he to read a journal published at Washington, the seat of government, at Philadelphia or Boston, the seats of literature, or at New York, the most populous and mercantile town in the Union? In Paris and London these requisites are all combined; the Americans have it in their power to cause at least two of them to be found in the same place; besides, we should think, convenience would require that the seat of government should be fixed, not in the centre of the territory, but in the centre of the population; the disadvantage under which a few of the deputies would lie, by having a greater distance to travel, being more than counterbalanced by the much smaller space which the great majority would have to traverse. The establishment of some leading newspapers might also have the effect of banishing the piebald English and the general want of talent which characterize their journals, and of introducing a better tone of discussion among them. At present, the most ably conducted American newspaper does not sell more than 2,000 copies, a number to which very few attain, while half that quantity is considered to constitute a very respectable circulation. With the small profits which so limited a sale can produce, it is evidently impossible to induce a person of high intellectual attainments to devote his time and talents to the drudgery of daily composition; in fact, the greatest part of their journals are merely vehicles for advertisements, like many of the English provincial ones, whose small sale is the cause of similar results.

We cannot close this article without making some observations *on the mutual dispositions of England and America.* With respect to the latter country, were we to take the tone of the newspapers as the test of public opinion, the conclusion, as far as our observation goes, would be any thing but flattering to England. But, for the reasons above given, we are unwilling to take these as authorities on the subject; though as periodical literature, from its very nature, must always afford some index to the state of public feeling, and as the Americans have several Reviews, which, in point of general talent, will stand a comparison with the best of our own, we may refer to these as indicating, in some slight measure, the disposition of well-informed Americans towards this country. An examination of them, we regret to say, leaves a very disagreeable impression on our minds, such, at least, as convinces us that the Americans cannot with any degree of propriety complain of that illiberality of sentiment, which, they maintain, always pervades one or two of our Reviews when treating of the affairs of their country. As an instance of this, we give the following quotation from the last number of the *American Quarterly Review*, edited by Dr. Walsh,* a work which bears the highest character in the United States. In it, England is thus described:—

" A haughty and interested nation, long since arrived at that state which makes it indispensable for her to sacrifice all the obligations of national reciprocity to that great monopoly of commerce, without which she must become bankrupt. In such a contest, whether of enactments of congress and orders in council, or by a resort to arms, it ought never to be forgotten that we can expect nothing but what is conceded to our strength and resources, to our means of offence and defence, to our courage and skill. The present calm with England is, we think, destined to be of short duration; nor will she ever sincerely seek our friendship, until admonished, perhaps at no distant period, by her waning influence in the Old, she shall feel herself obliged to link her sinking fortune to the rising strength and glories of the New World. It is far from our will or intention to revive or strengthen the recollection of ancient grievances or recent struggles, with a view to perpetuate or aggravate them. But, at the same time, we feel it our duty to indicate to this young nation, apt as it is to forget the lessons of experience and adversity, the danger and the folly of being cajoled by Mr. Canning's lullaby of ' Mother and Daughter,' or the time-serving praises lavished on the Message of our present distinguished Chief Magistrate. Every thing indicates that the popular feeling is hourly acquiring force and influence in England, and, in proportion as it operates upon the government, will be the impracticability of establishing any thing like a reciprocity in their commercial relations with the United States. The great mass of the people of England dislike the Americans, and certainly the Americans are no way backward in this species of reciprocity. No ad-

* This gentleman resided some years in Europe during the earlier part of his life, and it is understood, (though we are bound to disbelieve all reports of articles in Reviews being written by *single* individuals,) that he contributed *one* remarkable article at least, (if not more,) to the *Edinburgh Review;* we allude to that on the *French Conscription*, which appeared in the 26th Number of that Journal.

ministration in England will gain popularity by concessions to the United States, nor will the government of the United States ever probably much strengthen itself with the people, by toying with England. Even the people of England have been taught by a system of exaggerated falsehoods, unquestionably countenanced and encouraged as a matter of policy by the government, to look upon us with feelings of mingled contempt, hatred, and jealousy."

We would fain hope that the writer of this passage has made as false an estimate of the feelings of Americans as he certainly has of those of Englishmen. The ignorance which seems to prevail in America with respect to this point is perfectly astonishing, and we have a strong belief, which we most ardently hope is well founded, that their misapprehensions on this subject have contributed in no slight degree to cherish those feelings of dislike, which are described above as existing in America. In two parties, the existence, or supposed existence, of hate on one side quickly engenders a similar disposition in the other: may we not then hope that some advantage will be gained to the cause of peace and mutual goodwill, by denying in the most unqualified manner the truth of the assertion in the above paragraph, that " the great mass of the people of England dislike the Americans?" That the preceding extract rightly describes the sentiments of the Americans towards this country cannot, we are afraid, though we should be happy to find ourselves in error, be so easily denied. We have seen similar assertions repeated, and their correctness assumed, in numerous Transatlantic publications. The *North American Review*, a periodical which enjoys, with the one above named, the highest credit in the United States, writes in an exactly similar strain. In one of its latest numbers we read : " In England, generally speaking, the government party, inheriting the feelings of the year 1775, has not only retained the soreness and irritation of that period, but through the literary organs under its influence has libelled America, its institutions, its manners, and its citizens atrociously and systematically, and still does it." Captain Hall also states that in a debate, which he attended in the Congress, every speaker seemed determined in some way or other to drag in England for the sake of abusing it. We have diligently searched the American reviews of his Travels, in the hope of finding a refutation of this assertion, and should not have quoted it, had it not received a negative confirmation in the silence of his critics, who have ransacked the Captain's Travels for the purpose of exposing his misstatements with the minutest attention. To the complaint, which the Americans are perpetually making, that our government has instigated and sanctioned the attacks that have been made upon them, we can give no other answer than by expressing our utter disbelief of the fact. We cannot credit that any set of ministers has ever incurred the disgrace of thus endeavouring to excite animosities between the two nations; at any rate the present ones cannot be liable to this imputation, and we trust the calumny will never be repeated. We do not deny that there is a party, or rather the remnant of a party in this country, to whom abuse of America as well as of every other nation where a free and liberal government is established, is always palatable. There are also some persons among us, (as there are in America—Mr. Cooper is a signal instance,) who are affected with that feeling of ultra-nationality, which can see no merit in that which is foreign, no fault in that which is at home. But the publications which lay themselves out for catering to the appetites of these two classes, are few in number, and we may safely assert, that their feelings are in no degree general or even common in England. By far the greatest part of our newspapers, magazines, and other periodical literature, not only are wholly free from the reproach which the Americans cast on them, but are generally disposed to treat with more than ordinary favour and goodwill America and her institutions. Let the people of the United States look at our parliamentary debates which relate to them, particularly on the sore subject of their tariff, or the still sorer one of the duty they imposed on rolled iron, in direct contravention of the spirit of a treaty, being in fact a discriminating duty in favour of a Russian and Prussian manufacture against an English one. Throughout the numerous speeches, not a sentence, not a word will they find in the least degree indicative of that deeply-rooted spirit of hostility or dislike, that malignant feeling, which they charge us with entertaining towards them.

But the real truth is, there is very little known or thought of in England concerning America. We do not profess to account for this utter indifference—we simply assert the undoubted fact, that Englishmen seldom bestow a moment's attention on Transatlantic institutions, manners, literature, or government; whatever the Americans do, or think, or propose, seems to be looked upon by us with the most listless disregard. Hence they are continually committing errors from ignorance of this fact. The 68th number of the *North American Review* contains a petulant article in reply to a British critic, who had asserted that not more than three or four American authors enjoy any reputation among us. Now we are confident that nineteen-twentieths of our readers would be puzzled to mention half-a-dozen American writers, whose works they were acquainted with. The Transatlantic reviewer, endeavouring to make out a list of writers, exclaims in a tone of indignant reproach, "Did our critic never hear of Fisher Ames?"

We ask, have a dozen of our readers read his works? Another American genius is thus described by the reviewer.

" The beloved, admired, the lamented Buckminster, a miracle of genius, cut off indeed in the early morning of his brilliant promise, but not till he had produced works, which may well be compared with the mature efforts of the highest talents in the same departments of learning. His discourses are among the most elegant, finished and really valuable production of their class to be found in the English language . . . . considered simply as written sermons, they are undoubtedly superior to any that have appeared in England since the beginning of the present century."

Critics are supposed to know every thing, and we shall doubtless astonish our brethren by our boldness, when we confess that this is the first time the name of Buckminster has reached our ears. Have any of our readers heard of this writer, whose sermons are " superior to any that have appeared in England since the beginning of the present century ?" On inquiry we find his works have been reprinted at Liverpool, and this is literally all the additional information we have been able to obtain concerning him. A book is advertised to be published in London, entitled " Specimens of American Poetry," which of course contains extracts from American writers of the greatest reputation. From the published list of the authors, whose works have contributed to form the selection, we take the following in the order in which they are given, " Sigourney, Pierpoint, Pickering, Ware, Bryan, Haven, Doane, Hillhouse." Have any of our readers ever even heard before of a single name among these? For aught we know, there may be Miltons, and Popes, and Byrons in the list, but unread they have been and will remain in England until some unexpected revolution takes place in the public mind. We trust it will not be supposed by the Americans that this indifference towards them arises from a feeling in any degree approaching to contempt; we do not profess to account for it, but we certainly share it in common with the inhabitants of the European continent. The " Biographie Universelle," which is by far the completest biographical dictionary that has yet appeared, and the standard work on the subject, is almost bare of American names. Neither " Fisher Ames," nor " Patrick Henry," who is considered the first of American orators, and who, according to Jefferson, spoke as Homer wrote, have a place in it, though they both died long before the volumes in which they should have appeared were published.

Perhaps the greater proximity of the civilized nations of the Old World to each other causes them to fill so large a space in the public eye, that there is no room to take in what is worth observing on the other side of the Atlantic. Perhaps it is supposed that so lately formed a nation can present nothing worthy of remark. We give no opinion on this question, because, in truth, we have none to give. Certain it is, that we are infinitely more engaged in watching what is going forward in France and Germany, and the literature of those countries is infinitely better known to us than that of America. We are far from wishing to excuse this ignorance and apathy : we allow that both reason and interest should induce us to become better acquainted with the Americans, and utterly reject Captain Hall's theory, that it would be a " foolish wisdom" to extend our knowledge of their writings. At the same time we cannot but remark that they would do well to improve their acquaintance with England, superior as it no doubt is to ours of America. An American review just published uses as an argument against the dissolution of the Union, (a question to which the impolitic enactment of their tariff has given rise,) that the separated parts would soon fall into the power of England. Little do they know the opinions prevalent here, if they imagine we think we have not colonies enough, or that we would not infinitely sooner have them as allies than as subjects. This is a branch of the same system of error, which leads them to suppose that the remembrance of their successful rebellion still rankles in our breasts, and that we view their growing prosperity with malignant dissatisfaction. It can never be too often repeated, that such is not the feeling or the spirit of Englishmen. If we have spoken harshly of the Americans in this article, the commendations which we have unsparingly intermingled will show that our minds are unbiassed by prejudice, and capable of duly appreciating whatever may seem worthy of praise ; and in our strictures, we have been particularly careful to take as authorities only such writers as every American could not but allow are wholly free from what they call British hatred or preposessions against America. We look upon the course they have run—and in this we are sure we speak the sentiments of every thinking Englishman— with wonder, admiration, and pleasure; and we can assure them, that it is no less our wish than our interest, a wish which we hope to see re-echoed from beyond the Atlantic, that the ties of the sincerest friendship, and the mutual benefits of a continually increasing intercourse, may bind together England and the United States in the bonds of a never-ending alliance.

Art. XI.—1. *Minerva.*—2. *Orphea.*—3. *Taschenbuch zum geselligen Vergnügen.*— 4. *Frauentaschenbuch.*— 5. *Urania.*—6. *Musen Almanach.*—7. *Taschenbuch der Liebe und Freundschaft gewidmet.*—8. *Penelope.*—9. *Vergissmeinnicht.*—10. *Wintersgrün.*—11. *Cornelia.*

It has often appeared to us not a little singular that our annuals, considered as literary performances, should, on the whole, be so remarkably poor, tedious, and commonplace. Their outward presence is most imposing: they " walk in silk attire," fringed with gold ; their embellishments are triumphs of the pencil and the graver ; great names adorn the lists of their contributors, while the high pressure of exorbitant remuneration is lavished on the getting-up of articles. And yet when the glossy binding has been admired, the plates examined and canvassed, what is an annual? A collection in general of trifling tales, without interest either of plot or execution, poems generally below mediocrity, tragical attempts at mirth, or feeble washy sketches " in the soft line," —all many degrees inferior to similar productions in any respectable magazine. And what at first adds to our surprise, the compositions which bear the greatest names are, in nine cases out of ten, the worst. If by any chance we light upon something less commonplace than the rest, the probability is, that it bears the superscription of some one unknown to fame. Now we think there are two reasons, among others, which make our annuals flat and unprofitable. Booksellers will have great names to dignify their list of contents ; and in this country, where the annuals, succeeding the pocket-books or memorandums of last century, have always been looked upon as a kind of *parvenus* in literature, —very gaudy, assuming, and empty-headed : the best productions of great names (we say it to the credit of our literary men) are not so to be purchased. A scrap from some unfinished tale which the author has found himself unable to wind up, some copy of verses for a lady's album, a stray sonnet, or some juvenile indiscretion in the shape of a tragedy, may no doubt, by the proper application of the golden key, be extracted from the recesses of an author's writing-desk, and ushered with much pomp and a strong flourish of the editorial trumpet before the public. But invariably their better works are reserved for other purposes, and with the exception of a few pieces, bestowed " for love, not money," we hardly know an article in any of our annuals to which, in a separate shape, any of our distinguished authors would have cared to set his name.

Another cause of this defect is the shortness of the articles in such periodicals. The British public, it seems, must have variety, and thus, in order to bring together some twenty or thirty imposing names, the space allowed to each must be proportionally narrowed. Hence there is no room for developement, no means of exciting interest by a complicated well-evolved plot, still less for any novel of manners, where the characters develope themselves in dialogue instead of being described by the narrator: and thus little else is ever exhibited with us but insulated scenes, or meagre outlines without detail or colouring.

There is much less of both these faults in Germany. Their annuals have long been admitted within the literary pale, and the greatest names have voluntarily chosen this vehicle of communication with the public. Goethe still continues in this manner to present his new year's greeting to his countrymen. Schiller's 'Thirty Years' War was written for a lady's almanack. The philosophic Kant and Jacobi, the majestic Klopstock, the wild and original Hoffman, have in this insinuating form instructed the public with their wisdom, or delighted and agitated it with their striking and grotesque combinations. Here the graceful Undine of Fouqué first awakened our sympathy for her fate ; Apel, with the invisible world at his command, bewitched us with his dark and terrible fantasies ; Laun, with his alternate tales of broad humour or romance ; Lafontaine, with his calm domestic pictures of German life ; Blumenhagen and Van de Velde, with their sketches of chivalry and the life of the middle ages ; Richter, with his quips and cranks, his " Selections from the Devil's Papers," and " Dog-post Days," at once the laughing and crying philosopher—have in this shape passed before us in every aspect of the terrible, the tragical, the tranquil, or the humorous. There are but few years in which one delightful volume at least of elegant extracts from the Taschenbücher might not be made up. An author in Germany is not hampered as he is here; four or five tales in general fill the volume, so that he really has space enough, if he possesses the other requisites, to make the tales interesting and effective, not as fragments but as a whole. And accordingly many of the cleverest and most interesting romances and novels which have for years past formed the Christmas supply of our German neighbours, have been contained in these little volumes.

In one particular only, it must be admitted, the German progenitors of the annuals are sadly thrown into the shade by their descendants—we mean in the graphic and pictorial embellishments with which they abound. Now and then Retzsch condescends to employ his graceful hand on a design or two, or Naecke, as in his clever illustrations of Van de Velde's novels in the present number of the *Frauentaschenbuch;* but generally speaking, the " *hard* line," or drawing and engraving department, is in the hands of such persons as Ramberg, Wagner, and Fleischman, and most extraordinary devices they do exhibit. There are illustrations by Ramberg to the *Minerva* of this winter, from the Sorrows of Werter, which we consider as (unintentionally) superior to any thing in the *Comic Annual;* and the situations and costume in which really would appear to be taken from that clever burlesque upon Goethe's youthful extravaganza, with which Matthews some years ago amused the public at the English Opera. There is the same wild disorder in the cravat, the same convulsive energy in the pantaloons, the same desperation in the cock of the hat. His attitude in the scene where he meets the crazed notary, and that where he is sprawling on the ground with Charlotte's children, are inexpressibly ludicrous. After all (we merely throw out a doubt), may not Mr. Ramberg be a wag, who thus with a grave face plays off his comic plates upon the public?—a German George Cruikshank, fighting in ambush under cover of sober and sentimental descriptions? Really, when we look at another set of illustrations by him to Marschner's Vampyr (a romantic opera of the Freyschütz school, of which the plot is taken from our own melodrama of the Vampyre,) which grace the *Orphea* of this year, we feel these doubts materially increased, for there is one plate representing Lord Ruthven tumbling over a precipice, while a boy seems to be firing a squib or other combustible behind him, which we regard as a deliberate and scarcely disguised joke. But the truth is, plates are after all a very secondary matter, and provided the text has that which passeth show, the suits and trappings of gilding and copperplate embellishment may almost be dispensed with.

Our readers need not fear that we intend to inflict upon them a complete *catalogue raisonnée* of the articles in these same periodicals. We propose to ourselves nothing more than a few rambling remarks on some of them, for the list contained in this article does not comprehend half of those " autumnal leaves" which strew the drawing-room tables of our fair German friends about this season. Even as it is, among this chaos which lies before us of

" Blue covers and white,
Green covers and grey,"

we hardly know where to begin ; and so, waving all questions of precedency, either on the ground of age or merit, we put our hands into the wheel of this literary lottery, and the first ticket that comes up is

Minerva—a decided prize, were it only that it contains a drama by Oehlenschlager, founded on a portion of the life of Charlemagne. Of the living dramatists of Germany, this distinguished

Dane is now the first. His Aladdin, Axel and Walburg, and Hakon Jarl abound with striking scenes. His classical play of Correggio, with much of the severe purity of taste and high poetry of Goethe's Tasso, and exhibiting the struggle of genius against the pressure of adverse circumstances, as Goethe's play paints the contest between poetical enthusiasm and the prosaic spirit of the world, is more touching and more natural than its predecessor. There is much fine poetry too in Charlemagne, but it wants dramatic interest, and the character of Pepin, his son, is destitute of any thing either morally attractive or theatrically effective. Oehlenschlager has not in this case been fortunate in a subject. There is nothing particularly striking in the other contents of this volume. The " Tournament at Worms," by Caroline Pichler, is a tolerable tale, but scarcely worthy of the authoress of Agathocles. Then follows a very amusing travelling sketch by that authoress of all work, Johanna Schopenhauer, descriptive of a journey to Vienna and Austria; sundry poems, all pretty bad; and another tale by Storch, " Mineta's Ruin," a story of paganism, a great deal too Ossianic and antiquarian to be interesting. Minerva is further adorned by the melancholy scenes from Werter above alluded to.

" Proximus ardet Ucalegon"—*Orphea* is the next that presents itself, with more plates from that insidious wag, Ramberg, illustrative of the Vampyre. The two most interesting pieces in this volume are, one of Blumenhagen's chivalrous pageants, " Castle Leuenrode," and a tale of mystery, by Kruse. There is great life and bustle in Blumenhagen's sketch, particularly in that scene where the Duke of Hanover receives the deputation from the city, who come to intimate to him the rejection of his proposals, which reminds us, by its energy and truth, of Crevecœur's magnificent defiance to Louis, or the stirring scenes with the insurgent Liegeois. Blumenhagen has great intensity and power of conception in such scenes, and more ingenuity in the construction of his plots than his predecessor in the same line, Veit Weber. " The Black Heart," by Kruse, is a story in a different vein. Kruse is a man of very peculiar, and at the present day, *rare* powers of invention ; for at present, though there is no deficiency in clever romance writers in as far as regards the painting of manners or character, or the natural construction of dramatic dialogue, there is a woeful deficiency in good plots. Indeed, with the exception of some of those stories in real life which sometimes adorn our Newgate Calendar, or the still more extraordinary occurrences which now and then are disclosed by the criminal records of France, we hardly know now-a-days where a good plot is to be met with. Now these are exactly the sources from which Kruse has chiefly derived his materials. Tales of murder or secret crime, discovered by a chain of gradually emerging evidence, are his favourites, with which he is fond of blending the superstitious interest arising from the use of the ·supernatural. These may seem vulgar instruments for a novelist who addresses himself to the public mind, and so in truth they are in themselves. But they are applied in a manner so new and so artful—the chain of complexities winds itself about us so gradually, so naturally, and apparently so inextricably—and then unrolls itself again with such consummate art and vraisemblance, that in this respect we consider some of the tales in his *Criminal-Geschichten* as unrivalled. The story called the " Dance of Death," published by him in a separate volume, and a romance in three volumes, *Deodati's Birth*, are also most successful specimens of the circumstantial-evidence school of writing ; though some parts of the latter would perhaps render it a perilous task for a translator. The present tale, though not equal to his best, is yet very good. The *nodus* of the tale turns on the principle of *resemblance*, an idea which, though as old as Plautus, seems still capable in the hands of a dextrous artist, who knows how to steer clear of a double Dromio and a double Antipholis, of producing a strikingly perplexing effect; while such tales of real life as that of Martin Guerre satisfy the reason of the possibility of such caprices of nature. Here, it is artfully managed, and combined most ingeniously with the supernatural. If an abridged outline could have given any idea of this tale, we should have been tempted to the task, but every thing lies in the art of the filling up. The other materials of this volume are trifling.

Taschenbuch zum geselligen Vergnügen, edited by Kind; a very venerable annual, now nearly forty years old, an age by no means common among this short-lived class. The illustrations are by Ramberg again; but to do him justice, they are far better than either of the other two productions we have noticed ; they are from poor Heinrich Kleist's strange play of Catharine von Heilbronn—after all, the best, and unquestionably the most dramatic of his productions, and one or two of them are really good. The literary contents are decidedly so. The first tale, " Clemenza l'Hopital," by a very industrious and occasionally successful novelist, Frederika Lohmann, is varied and interesting. There are good things too in the editor's own contribution, "The Angel Seer," though it is too long drawn out. Kruse's novel, " Magnetic Love," which follows, is not one of his happiest efforts, though still the power of exciting curiosity never forsakes him. The tale, which is a story of animal magnetism, opens well, but it diverges into other channels very slenderly

connected with the first, and the winding-up is extremely unsatisfactory. Wolffe's " Humoreske," the " auto-biography of the
Village Schoolmaster, Cyrillus Spangenbeck," is one of those
pieces of heavy wit in which our neighbours now and then indulge,
as they are said by Grimm to do, in leaping over chairs, in their
anxiety to be lively. Some copies of verses which diversify the
prose tales are pretty.

Frauentaschenbuch, by George Döring. There is a story of a
Scotch author, who, after having tried Garrick with a tragedy
and a comedy, both of which were rejected; and being told by
the manager that his genius did not lie in either, begged him to
tell him where it *did* lie. We feel something in the same way as
to M. Döring. After reading his plays, we were instantly satisfied his genius did not lie in that direction; and on perusing a
few of his novels we felt equally convinced that it did not lie in
romance: and yet we had a kind of impression that he had some
available talent about him, if he could only find a field for it.
And when some years ago he took the editorship of the *Frauentaschenbuch,* once in the hands of a man of different calibre,
La Motte Fouqué, we thought he had exactly found his sphere.
But the unlucky Doctor, we suspect, is determined to disappoint
us once more. His volume has not this year even the merit of a
good selection. His own contribution is mawkish, and the
others, by Schefer, Nidda, and Wilebald Alexis, are all indifferent. The best story in the volume is anonymous, viz. " the Mil-
ler's Daughter." This is told with a good deal of naïveté and
grace. To balance the dullness of the literary part, the plates,
which are illustrative of Van de Velde's novels, are better than
those in many of its rivals.

Urania. We generally open the Urania with good hopes, and
this year they will not be disappointed, for here the first and
longest tale in the volume is by our old friend Tieck—the acute,
learned, and tasteful Ludwig Tieck—an Italian head with a German heart—a deep-feeling, deep-thinking writer, but scattering
over all his works a sunny glow of cheerfulness, and airy lightness,
though not levity. This is he to whom Shakspeare and the
writers of the days of Elizabeth are familiar as household words;
who in his own country has touched upon every department of
literature, and adorned them all, and moved the minds of his
countrymen to laughter or tears, as he laid down or took up the
comic mask or the tragic pall; the dramatist of Blue Beard and
Puss in Boots, and the World turned Upside Down, of Fortunatus
and Genoveva; and here he carries us back to the days of Baldwin,
" the Emperor of Greece," and with that lightness and felicity of
touch, which, next to Goethe, he peculiarly possesses, exhibits to

us in transitory glimpses the tumultuous scenes in Ghent under
the nominal regency of his daughter.

Compared with some of the better tales in the Phantasus, "the
Emperor of Greece" may appear deficient in force, but none can
be insensible to the beauty of the verses which are liberally interspersed through the story.   One ballad sung by Ferdinand,
(p. 75,) "Will alles mich verlassen," is among the sweetest of
the many little canzonets to which his prolific muse has given
birth.   Victor Hugo's "Orientals" have found a translator in
Gustavus Schwab.   He might have made a more ¡judicious
choice from the works of that clever but most unequal poet.
"Schaifenstein," by Frederick von Heyden, which follows, is
poor; and "Duvecke," which concludes the volume, a tragical
tale from the History of Denmark, by Leopold Schefer, rather
too broken, and too much in Veit Weber's elliptical manner for
our taste.   The plates to this volume are from French designs.
The editor prefaces his volume with the announcement of a *prize*
of ten louis d'or a sheet for the best Tale or Novel for next
year's Urania (not to exceed five sheets); will not this magnificent prize tempt some of our readers to qualify themselves for
the "concurrenz" by studying German on purpose? We recommend the project to all rejected contributors to our own annuals.

"Flectere si nequeant superos, Acheronta movebunt."

The *Musen Almanach* is entirely poetical, and consists of short
pieces, lyrics, elegies, and so forth.   It boasts great *names* amongst
its contributors, but little more.   This year it seems to us any
thing but interesting.   A few trifles from Goethe's pen no doubt
it contains, but they are the merest trifles, and valuable only
from recollection and association.   Tieck's portrait adorns the
volume,—a calm countenance, marked with strong traces of refinement and taste, "*con occhi tardi e gravi*," and with that good-
humoured expression which we should naturally ascribe to him.

Taschenbuch der Liebe und Freundschaft gewidmet. We never
particularly admired this pocket book, though it is rather a
favourite in Germany, and we do not think it appears this year
to advantage.   Its comic plates by Ramberg, (who on this occasion *really* wishes to be comic,) are trifling and absurd. Its
literary contents are "The Last Love," by Blumenhagen, a
pathetic and well-told story; the "Swallows," by Frederika
Lohmann, a clever tragical picture from the days of "Faustrecht;"
and the "Birdnester," by Baron von Miltiz, a writer whom we
never greatly liked, though he seems to be a persevering, if not a
powerful, contributor; poems, by Döring, Schutz, (the editor,)
Langbein, Chamisso, and others, complete the volume.

Penelope this year is good. Two drawings by Retzsch, one from Deinhardstein's play of Hans Sachs, the other from Auber's opera of Masaniello, are interesting, particularly the first. These are intended as the commencement of a Series of Theatrical Designs, to be continued through future volumes. " A day in the Vintage," by (thank heaven we have merely to write, not pronounce, the name,) the Ritter von Tschabuschnigg, is a pretty sentimental love story; the description of a poor student's Romance of a day, which is suddenly dissolved by discovering that he might as well have fallen in love with some particular star, as the exalted fair one who, in an " unguarded moment," has been betrayed into an apparent reciprocity of feeling. The story, however, is well told, and we have good hopes of the Great Unmentionable. " The Cataline of Hanover," by Blumenhagen, is also good, and so is the " Battle of Hochkirchen," by Frederika Lohmann; " Elizabeth, Countess of Holstein Schauenberg, a romantic historical picture," is rather deficient in interest; but Waiblenger's " Sketches from Italy," which follow, are piquant and interesting. " The Quartett," by Lehring, which concludes the volume, is cleverly told, and the poetical contributions, which are from Tiedge, Castelli, Hell, &c. more varied than usual.

The *Vergissmeinnicht* is this year edited by Spindler, who is favourably known here by his novel of the Jew, and, as usual, contains no poetry, but an interesting selection of tales. There are " The three Sundays, from the papers of an Artist;" " The Court at Castellaun;" " Dressing Gown and Cloak ;" " The Romance of an Evening;" and " Forget me not." All these are from the pen of the able and industrious editor himself, and really the reader feels no want of variety in the volume. " The Court at Castellaun," and the " Forget me not," will, we think, be considered as the most generally interesting.

Wintersgrün. " Wintergreen," a very plain and unassuming annual published at Hamburg, contains nothing but a translation of Paul de Koch's novel " La Maison Blanche."

Cornelia is this year embellished with a set of engravings illustrative of German traditions, but none of any great merit. Nor are the literary contents at all striking, though the first story, which turns on the loves of Suffolk and Margaret, the sister of Henry VIII. is from the pen of Tromlitz. Tromlitz is, in general, a writer of great fertility of invention, and considerable skill in the conduct of a plot; he is, besides, a most industrious novelist, being generally a contributor to at least two or three of the annuals, but this year we seldom meet with him, and this, which is the only tale of his we have perused, has disappointed us. The opening promises a great deal, but it is not adequately followed up. We anticipate a great deal from certain characters, who, after all, have no prominent influence on the story.

But we really feel the necessity of drawing to a close; and though we have not exhausted more than a third of the pocket books of the year, we can only assure the much-respected editors and contributors to the remaining twenty, that if we could have noticed their labours it should have been done. Next year the wheel of fortune may be more favourable to them, and the neglected Aglaias and Fortunas of this season take precedence of their rivals; for this purpose we recommend them to send us early copies, addressed to the care of our publishers. We wish well to them all, for to their varied contents—their tales of love and chivalry, of terror, and mystery,—their humoresques and capricci, we have been indebted for many a pleasant winter evening, and the reviving of many a pleasant association connected with the country of their birth.

CRITICAL SKETCHES.

Art.XII.—*Pensées sur l'Homme, ses rapports, et ses intérêts,* par Frédéric Ancillon. 2 vols. 12mo. Berlin. 1829.

This is a beautiful book, full of profound thinking and good feeling, and calculated to be especially useful to the small wits of the nineteenth century. It is the production of a man whose fertile pen has already given to Europe a numerous collection of valuable essays on philosophical and political subjects, and who, in all his works, is remarkable for the noble purity of sentiment which pervades them, and for the force, clearness, and precision, with which his views are expressed. It would, perhaps, have been scarcely excusable for any writer, whose opinion had not already obtained great weight in the world, to put forth his ideas in detached fragments, as Ancillon has here done, but he had previously acquired a reputation which fairly entitled him to comply, as he says, with the solicitations of his wife, to collect and arrange the fragments in his portfolio, and publish them in their present form. They are well suited for a relief and diversion to the scholar, wearied with long arguments and disquisitions—to the man of business, who wants often to seek other materials for reflection than are afforded by the busy hum of the world—and to the victim of *ennui,* who would be glad of some aid to the process of thinking, which should enable him, without fatigue, to take that wholesome exercise. Experience has shown that fragments of this kind, when really good, are much relished by the public, as the Thoughts of Labruyère and Pascal have especially testified, as well as the Maxims of La Rochefoucault, the Table Talk of Selden, and more recently, Mr. Colton's *Lacon.*

It is scarcely fair towards the author to judge, from one or two isolated extracts, of the general tone of his opinions. On Religion, particularly, *the whole* of his Thoughts deserve much attention, but we select the following as applicable to the connection between Church and State, the expediency of which is a point of so much difference of opinion in this country.

" Religion and law, the church and the state, exercise upon each other a reciprocal action and re-action. They are inseparable. Their respective wants ally and unite them. The laws protect religion, and religion supplies the wants of the laws, vivifies them, makes them loved and respected. From thence it in no way results that religion should be in the state, or the state in religion, or that either of them ought to be subservient to the other. They are two powers, or means, which concur to the same end, each in its manner, and after its nature. That end is the reign of justice, and of true liberty. Religion tends thereto by inward means; the laws by outward means. The one takes human actions in their source, judges them by their principles, and desires to perfect them in purifying their motives. The laws take them in their effects.

They are two distinct forces, which have many points of contact, but which can and ought never to be confounded. If you place the government of the state in religion, you will have a theocracy, and those who manage it, will cultivate religion and morals systematically for their own profit. If you make religion subordinate to the government, and place it in the state, you will see religion descend from its elevation to become a mere engine of police, and that the government will denaturalize it, by removing it from its proper sphere, to make it enter that of the government."—p. 39.

The degradation of Religion, by converting it into a political engine, is undeniable. There is also much truth in the following contrast between Catholicism and Protestantism.

" In the Catholic Church there is the more fixity; in the Protestant Church there is the more agitation of men's minds. In the former the authority of the Pope and of Councils weakens the authority of the Gospel. In the latter the total absence of external authority may weaken that of the Gospel. In the one liberty may expire in anarchy, in the other in despotism. In the one there is no church firmly established, for want of unity; in the other, the church is so stereotyped, that there is no real life in it, nor principle of sentiment and action."—p. 44.

Under the head of Science this passage is remarkable.

" The contradictions of men arise from each of them having different sensations, and from all of them associating the same terms, whilst some judge by sentiment, others by understanding, and others again by reason. But these three ways of judging cannot lead to the same results. The sentiment judges of objects by relation to itself; the understanding judges by relation to notions which are often arbitrary; the reason alone seizes truths by a peculiar and intuitive evidence "—p. 85.

Ancillon's views of Social Order and Governments are those of a man wholly beyond the reach of those petty political squabbles, and those party-coloured opinions, with which the peace of society is in all countries disturbed. As a proof how well he appreciates the difference of feeling between an aristocracy and a people, we may refer, among other sentences, to this very brief one.

" The nobles look back on the past, and in looking back on it they often remain motionless. The other classes look to the future, and march on."—p. 268.

The division, entitled " Jugemens Historiques," has convinced us how much historical matter may be read to no purpose, unless the reader possesses some of that philosophical discernment of which our author has so ample a share. His love for the ancients is thus beautifully expressed by Ancillon, himself an ancient, in respect of almost all the qualities he refers to.

" One loves the ancients as one loves freshness, calmness, simplicity, and nobleness. They transport us into a younger world, less agitated by the petty passions of society; they have less desire to produce effect than the moderns; they appear at a much greater height above things and events. Have they in fact, or do they only appear to have, these qualities? Have they them because their genius was in fact more original and their character more elevated? Do they seem to have them because the world in which they place us, so different from our own, makes us forget the latter? We may differ in opinion on the causes of the fact; the fact itself is incontestable."—p. 358.

" To read the ancients is to take a journey; journeys in time refresh and vivify perhaps more than journeys in space."—p. 358.

Although these volumes are written in French, their style strikes us as wholly different from that of a Frenchman, and we have, indeed, observed in other instances that German French has about it a solemnity, a simplicity, and a force of eloquence, in perfect accordance with the German character. We love the Germans, for the same reason that Ancillon loves the ancients, for the freshness, the simplicity, and the noble purity of their minds. In them we are never disgusted with attempts to catch at ephemeral applause, with impertinent *badinage*, or with materialism assuming exclusively the name of philosophy. To the following passage (the last we have space to quote) we cordially agree.

" The Liberals of a good sort in Germany love liberty as the first condition of intellectual life, and as the appendage of the liberty of man. In France the Liberals of a good sort love liberty as the principle and guarantee of all the advantages and pleasures of social life. The fact is, that every thing in Germany has a secret tendency towards the invisible world. In France it is just the reverse."—p. 357.

In Germany the principle of the *finite*, the mechanical, calculating, materialist principle, does not, and is not likely to, predominate over men's minds. Can such an assertion be made of Great Britain, any more than France, with any degree of truth? We think not.

ART. XIII.—*Poetæ Scenici Græci. Accedunt perditarum fabularum fragmenta.* Recensuit Guil. Dindorfius. Leipsic & London. 1830. 8vo. pp. 960.

MR. WILLIAM DINDORF, the Professor in the University of Leipsic, whose name is too well known in this country to require any comment, has published, in one thick octavo volume, all the extant plays of Æschylus, Sophocles, Euripides, and Aristophanes, together with the extant fragments of their lost tragedies and comedies respectively. The plays of the different poets are arranged in a chronological order, and we observe that Mr. Dindorf is one of those critics who believe the Rhesus to be genuine, and the most ancient of the remaining plays of Euripides; and that he does not agree with Mr. Hermann, in supposing that it was the work of some Alexandrine scholar. As Mr. Dindorf had already published text editions of Æschylus, Sophocles, and Aristophanes, and as his brother, Mr. Lewis Dindorf, has edited Euripides, no very remarkable novelties in the recension of the text could be expected in this edition. The editor, however, with his accustomed diligence and acuteness, has in his preface suggested many improvements in the text of the four Greek dramatic poets, in addition to his former labours. We will select a few of these critical remarks.

In the *Prometheus* of Æschylus, v. 354, Τυφῶνα θοῦρον, πᾶσιν ὃς ἀντέστη θεοῖς, where Porson corrected Τυφῶνα θοῦρον, ὅστις ἀντέστη θεοῖς, supporting his emendation with numerous instances of the intrusion of πᾶς, Mr. Dindorf (after Wunderlich) reads—Τυφῶνα θοῦρον, πᾶσιν ὃς ἀνέστη θεοῖς, citing *Iliad*, Ψ. 634:

πὺξ μὲν ἐνίκησα Κλυτομήδεα, Ἤνοπος υἱὸν,
Ἀγκαῖον δὲ πάλῃ Πλευρώνιον, ὅς μοι ἀνέστη.

In *Prom.* 1056, the Medicean MS. has τί γὰρ ἐλλείπει μὴ παραπαίειν εἰ τοῦδ' ἐντυχῇ. Mr. Dindorf restores, ἢ τοῦδε τύχῃ.

On *Sept. ad Theb.* 562, Mr. Dindorf attempts to show that the particle ἂν is sometimes lengthened by the Scenic poets. We confess that the small number, and the uncertainty of the instances which he adduces, are not, in our estimation, sufficient to weigh against the numberless examples of the contrary usage. It should be remembered, moreover, that the natural progress of all languages is to contract and shorten; and that some instances of this particle being lengthened would probably occur in Homer or the early epic poets, if its quantity had in later times been doubtful.

Soph. Electr. 882, ἀλλ' οὐχ ὕβρει λέγω τάδ', ἀλλ' ἐκεῖνον ὡς παρόντα νῷν. Mr. Dindorf, following the traces of the manuscripts, reads— ἐκεῖνον ὡς παρόντα νῶ, for νόει; and in like manner in *Æsch. Pers.* 1054, καὶ στέρν' ἄρασσε κἀπιβόα τὸ Μύσιον, he would get rid of the anapest by reading κἀπιβῶ. He likewise removes the anapest in *Soph. Œd. C.* 1466, by writing ὀρανία γὰρ ἀστραπή.

Eurip. Electr. 497, παλαιόν τε θησαύρισμα Διονύσου τόδε. Mr. Dindorf defends the shortening of the diphthong in παλαιὸς by two examples, one from Sophocles, the other from Aristophanes. It is very difficult to form any safe judgment on short fragments, but we are doubtful whether in the verse of Sophocles we ought not to read Φοίβου παλαιὸν κῆπον without the conjunction.

The fragments of Æschylus and Sophocles appear in this volume in a much more correct and complete form than in any former edition. Mr. Dindorf states that he had not originally intended to add the fragments of Euripides and Aristophanes, as they had been so recently published by Mr. Matthiæ* and himself; but that, in compliance with the wishes of his bookseller, he afterwards consented to introduce them. We rejoice that he was induced so to do, as the work is not only thereby rendered complete, but considerable improvements have been made upon Mr. Matthiæ's revision of the numerous and beautiful fragments of Euripides.

Æsch. fragm. 302. "*Eustathius*, p. 641, 59, Οὔτε δῆμος οὔτ' ἔτης ἀνήρ." The same words are cited by the scholiast to Homer, whose words are given by Mr. Dindorf in *Eurip. fragm. incert.* 158. Compare in the Elean inscription (Boeckh, *Corp. Inscript.* No. 14.) αἴτε Fέτας αἴτε τελέστα αἴτε δᾶμος.

Soph. fragm. 209:—

γλῶσσ' ἐν οἷσιν ἀνδράσιν τιμὴν ἔχεις,
ὅπου λόγοι σθένουσι τῶν ἔργων πλέον.

"V. i. Ἡ supplet Brunckius et ἔχει scribit. Fort. ὦ γλῶσσ'." *Dindorf.* Besides these suggestions there is the emendation of Jacobs, in his *Lec-*

---

tiones Stobenses—γλῶσσ' ἐν κενοῖσιν ἀνδράσιν τιμὴν ἔχει. But the article
is necessary. Whether the emendation of Brunck or Mr. Dindorf is
admitted, it seems that the sense requires ἐκεῖ for ὅπου.

In *Soph. fragm.* 464, the following line occurs :—

ἐνῆν δὲ συμμιγὴς ὀλαῖς παγκαρπία.

Perhaps : ἐνῆν δ' ὀλαῖσι συμμιγὴς παγκαρπία.

Soph. fragm. 584, from the *Tyro* :—

τίκτουσι γάρ τοι καὶ νόσους δυσθυμίαι.

In fragm. 588, Mr. Dindorf has, "*Antiatticista*, p. 89, 19, Δυσθυ-
μία: Σοφοκλῆς Τυροῖ." The gloss of the grammarian probably refers
to the above line preserved in Stobæus.

Eurip. Æol. fragm. 2 :—

ἃ μὴ γάρ ἐστι τῷ πένηθ', ὁ πλούσιος
δίδωσ', ὃ δ' οἱ πλουτοῦντες οὐ κεκτήμεθα,
τοῖσιν πένησι χρώμενοι θηρώμεθα.

This elision of ι in the dative case is not noticed by Dr. Elmsley in his
note to the *Heraclidæ*, v. 693; and it appears to offer more difficulty
than any of the passages there corrected.

Cress. fragm. 9 :—

πλούτου δ' ἀπορρυέντος ἀσθενεῖς γάμοι·
τὴν μὲν γὰρ εὐγένειαν αἰνοῦσιν βροτοί,
μᾶλλον δὲ κηδεύουσι τοῖς εὐδαίμοσιν.

The two last lines are thus cited in a fragment of the work of Aristotle
περὶ εὐγενείας preserved in Stobæus, 86, 25, and Plutarch, περὶ εὐγενείας, c. xiv.—καίτοι... οὐκ ὀρθῶς ἐπιτιμῶσιν ὁ Θέογνις οὐδ' ὁ ποιητὴς ὁ
ποιήσας

ὡς τὴν μὲν εὐγένειαν αἰνοῦσιν βροτοί,
μᾶλλον δὲ κηδεύουσι τοῖσι πλουσίοις.

In Stobæus the MS. A. and ed. Trinc. have ποιήσας ὡς ὅτι τὴν μὲν,
whence Mr. Gaisford, transposing the words, has edited ποιήσας ὅτι,
ὡς τὴν μὲν, &c. In Plutarch the word ὅτι is omitted. We think it
more probable that one word arose from the other, and would read—

οὐδ' ὁ ποιητὴς ὁ ποιήσας ὡς
τὴν μὲν εὐγένειαν, &c.

Peleus, fragm. 3 :—

οὐκ ἔστιν ἀνθρώποισι τοιοῦτο σκότος,
οὐ δῶμα γαίας κλειστόν, ἔνθα τὴν φύσιν
ὁ δυσγενὴς κρύψας ἂν εἴη σοφός.

Mr. Dindorf does not mention the unfortunate conjectures of Mr. Gaisford and Mr. Matthiæ, κρύψας νομισθείη σοφός, and κρύψει' ἂν εἰ κείη
σοφός. We propose, as a more probable conjecture than any yet advanced, κρύψας ἂν οὐκ εἴη κακός. See *Welcker ad Theognin.* p. 29.
Few mistakes are more frequent in manuscripts (and even in printed
books) than the improper addition or omission of the negative. In this
case the negative had probably fallen out, and a later transcriber restored the sense by changing κακὸς into σοφὸς, but in so doing spoiled
the metre.

Philoct. fragm. 12 :—

πατρὶς καλῶς πράσσουσα τὸν εὐτυχοῦντ᾿ ἀεὶ
μείζω τίθησι, δυστυχοῦντα δ᾿ ἀσθενῆ.

These senseless and unmetrical lines are preserved in *Stobæus* xxxviii. p. 230 ; where one MS. has δυστυχοῦσα for δυστυχοῦντα. Mr. Matthiæ conjectures τὸν τυχόντ᾿ ἀεὶ for τὸν εὐτυχοῦντ᾿ ἀεὶ. Hence read :

πατρὶς καλῶς πράσσουσα τὸν τυχόντ᾿ ἀεὶ
μείζω τίθησι, δυστυχοῦσα δ᾿ ἀσθενῆ.

" *Every man, whoever he may be, is raised by the prosperity, and depressed by the sufferings of his country.*"

Eurip. Trag. incert. fragm. 55 :—

μητέρα κατέκτα τὴν ἐμήν· βραχὺς λόγος·
ἑκὼν ἑκοῦσαν, ἢ θέλουσαν οὐκ ἑκών.

We would read βραχὺς ὁ λόγος. Compare *Archel. fragm.* 29 :—

ἁπλοῦς ὁ μῦθος, μὴ λέγ᾿ εὖ· τὸ γὰρ λέγειν
εὖ δεινόν ἐστιν, εἰ φέροι τινὰ βλάβην.

Ibid. fragm. 57 :—χαλεποὶ πόλεμοι γὰρ ἀδελφῶν· From Plutarch. The same verse is also cited by Aristotle, *Polit.* vii. p. 433, E.

The fragments of Aristophanes are repeated, in an abridged form, from the late excellent edition of Mr. Dindorf, which has left little for either the diligence or ingenuity of succeeding critics. Of the fragments of Æschylus an edition is expected from Mr. Hermann, which, if we may judge from the dissertations on some of the lost plays published in his *Opuscula*, will be of the highest merit. In the mean time, the volume before us contains the best collection of the fragments of Æschylus and Sophocles now in existence ; and the fragments of Euripides, though not given with such copious detail as in the work of Matthiæ, appear in a much purer form than in that edition. The paper is good, and the type, though small, very distinct. On the whole, we consider this volume as a most useful and laudable publication, and for the purposes of reference and occasional consultation, very convenient to all admirers of the ancient Greek drama.

ART. XIV.—*Memoires d'une Femme de Qualité sur Louis XVIII., sa Cour, et son Regne.* 4 vols. 8vo. Paris, 1829.

THE mass of *soi-disant Memoires secrets et inedits,** published in France within the last few years, has, in this country at least, actually glutted even to nausea the natural propensity of mankind for that agreeable and erst favourite style of composition, which combines, or combined, the easy pleasures of light reading with the dignity of historical study. For our own part, we have looked upon all these innumerable *pseudo-*biographies merely as so many historical novels, deprived, for the memoir-title's sake, of the story and the interest which fascinate our atten-

---

* The descriptive title sins rather by incompleteness than positive falsehood, since what was unwritten was certainly unpublished, and what was unknown, even to its supposed authors, may well be called secret.

tion, in the delightful productions we have latterly been accustomed to receive under the humbler name. As such, we have esteemed them undeserving our notice. The work now before us, however, (though in so far belonging to the same class that it is not written, we understand, by its presumed anonymous author,) distinguishes itself from its fellows in one very important point; as we are assured that the best-informed foreigners believe the *Femme de Qualité* in question to have really supplied the—what shall we say?—not facts; for the word would involve an assertion which we are by no means prepared to maintain; but the raw material, afterwards wrought into its present form by three or four gentlemen constituting a very respectable firm in the book-manufacturing line. Now since, in compositions of this description, the substance is assuredly of far more consequence than the workmanship, or the auctorial claims and abilities of any memoir-scribbler of either sex, we deem the volumes in question worthy of some attention, as showing the view which *Madame Olimpe*, Comtesse Du Cayla, (so her editors *initially* entitle her) took, or wishes to give, of her royal friend.

Respecting Madame Olimpe, Comtesse Du Cayla, herself, we hardly need remind the reader, that she was the reputed mistress of Louis XVIII. She herself, indeed, declares that the attachment was altogether Platonic, save as far as her ears were concerned,* and insinuates, with French delicacy, proofs of, or reasons for, its being so, which our English delicacy forbids us even to allude to more distinctly. The lady further declares herself to have passed unscathed through ordeals where no such reasons are alleged to have guarded her virtue, preserving her maiden purity through sundry nocturnal interviews with that fanatic and unfortunate Bonapartist, Charles Labedoyere, and her nuptial fidelity through various suspicious intimacies with the Duke of Rovigo and others, the gallant duke himself not appearing to entertain any very high respect for the propriety of the lady's conduct. In fact, she confesses to only one failure of her virtue, and that was in favour of a noble Venetian *Carbonaro*, her love for whom, nevertheless, if stronger than her virtue, was weaker than her loyalty, for she betrayed to the king the secrets she wrung from Morosini's passion, and was thus remotely the cause of his suicide, which she wept for a whole week. Let us not, however, be understood to blame the lady's reserve. We fully agree with Madame de Genlis, that a memoir writer is not bound to tell the whole truth, provided he or she tell nothing but the truth; and we think a woman of incorrect conduct would doubly offend against public morality by proclaiming her frailties. What we quarrel with is the unnecessary mention of supposed intrigues for the purpose of asserting their purity. We know nothing, and had no' desire to hear any thing, of her girlish amours, and we think it would have been in better taste to have left the reader to form his own opinion of her connexion with the gouty old king, unless indeed she could have boldly pronounced his affection for her to have been wholly paternal.

---

* She for ever represents the king's words and anecdotes to be such as she cannot repeat.

,. This connexion, however, be its character what it might, manifestly afforded Madame Du Cayla such opportunities of knowing Louis the XVIIIth's opinions and feelings upon most subjects, as stamps her statements, her records of conversations, her court-gossip in short, with a considerable degree of authenticity, and makes the book worth running through. Moreover, although parts of it would certainly never have been written by any Englishwoman above the condition of the Harriette Wilsons, it contains nothing so objectionable in points of delicacy, as need exclude it from the drawing-room. We have, accordingly, no hesitation in recommending, even to our female readers, *Les Mémoires d'une Femme de Qualité* as amusing and not uninstructive ; and, expecting our recommendation to be acted upon, we shall in consequence abstain from offering either an abstract of their contents— which, indeed, is pretty nearly an impossibility—or many long extracts. We shall further take leave to decline the labour of refuting the absurd notions which the fair memorialist (as allowable a denomination, we think, as Mr. C. Butler's Reminiscent) ascribes to His Most Christian Majesty touching the perfidy and selfishness of British politics upon all and every occasion, and the excessive feudal oppression and total want of liberty we poor English groan under, and the correctness of General Pillet's accounts of English women and English manners.* Neither do we intend to trouble ourselves with such a work of supererogation as the vindication of the Duke of Wellington from the extraordinary faults detected in *Sa Grace* by the keen eyes of the king and his *belle amie*, such as coxcombry, vanity, silliness, theatrical trickery, cowardice, and what not. We shall content ourselves with mentioning a few of the leading traits of the king's character, as drawn by himself in his biographer's statements, and conclude with extracting a short conversation, illustrative of his opinion of the ultra-royalists, amongst whom ranked Madame Du Cayla herself ; and, as she silently gives us to understand, the royal brother, nephews, and nieces.

Louis XVIII. appears, from this account, to have been rationally convinced of the actual impossibility of restoring the *ancien regime*, and of the absolute necessity of conforming, partially at least, to the spirit of the age ; and therefore bent upon upholding his *Charte*, to which he was besides attached with the blind fondness of a parent and an author ;† but being withal deeply imbued with the feelings, opinions, recollections, and habits of the days of absolutism, he enacted the constitutional king in a somewhat despotic vein, more diverting than is consonant with English ideas of limited monarchy. Jealous of his power,

---

* For the benefit of such readers as may know neither the disgusting work itself, nor the extracts given, at the time of its publication, by one of our brother periodicals, we will just mention, as a sample, that according to General Pillet, every Englishwoman who has attained to the matronly age of forty, gets more than tipsy every evening during the temporary after-dinner separation of the two sexes, and that every Englishman kills his wife with impunity when tired of her ; most men thus disposing of three women a-piece, in punishment, we conceive, for their inebriety.

† Their preference of other constitutional forms to his *Charte* was, it should seem, in Louis's eyes, the original sin of the Spanish, Portuguese, Neapolitan, and Sardinian revolutionists ; and we are not sure but we are of his majesty's opinion.

jealous of his ministers, and of their reputation, he yet appears to have been led by every favourite who, to use an expressive vulgarism, could get the length of his foot, (Decazes gained his favour, it seems, by receiving Latin lessons from his majesty,) and whom he forgot the moment he was teazed into dismissing them. His laudable ambition to be beloved by his subjects, his desire to be supposed indebted for both his restorations to their loyalty, led him naturally enough, but less laudably, to hate the allies who placed, and, while needful, supported him upon his throne, more especially George IV. and the Duke of Wellington, the last, as the commander of the army of occupation, the former, for making pu l c a letter in which Louis had professed to owe his crown, under God to the Prince Regent of England, which letter was meant solely for the private gratification of the British sovereign's own vanity, not of his people's. But the most original part of the picture is the king's literary vanity. Louis appears to have occupied himself in concocting articles for newspapers, to have claimed a sort of partnership concern in divers comedies and operas, to have written, corrected, polished, copied and recopied his parliamentary speeches, with a diligence worthy of Pope or Gray, and altogether without the participation of his *responsible* ministers, and to have bored every creature within his reach with these and all his other compositions, swallowing the grossest, baldest flattery, like mother's milk. The surest recipe for putting him into good humour was to request the gratification of hearing him read the *Voyage de Paris à Bruxelles.* But the most important point in Madame Du Cayla's representation is the manner in which the whole *clique* of ultra-royalists tormented the poor old king, if not to death, out of all the comforts of his life, in order to goad him, whom they treated as little better than a jacobin, into counter-revolutionary measures. Upon one occasion they exploded a barrel of gunpowder upon a back staircase, and accused the liberals of having designed thereby to blow up the Tuileries and its royal inmate. After public congratulations upon his escape, the *belle amie* presented herself, and was thus accosted —:

" Do you know that your friends, whom you call my faithful subjects, give me proofs of their attachment that are any thing but agreeable to me?

" How so, sire?

" Did you not hear the explosion?

" Can you suspect the royalists, whilst the jacobins—

" For this once are very innocent. It is a machination of your right-thinking men; a little plot to frighten me.

" Impossible!

" For the sake of your friends' honour, would to God I may be mistaken! But ere long we shall have an irrefragable proof of their guilt.

" What proof, sire?

" That nothing will be found out concerning this plot.

" Truly an extraordinary proof!

" My dear Countess, (returned the king,) if the Jacobins, the Bonapartists, or the Liberals, are the authors of this explosion, before two days are over our heads, we shall have thirty people arrested, and a regular prosecution set on foot by M. Jacquinot and his underlings: if, on the contrary, all this is, as I I suspect, a pretty little trick of my good friends, no one will be arrested;

neither M. Jacquinot, nor his underlings, will institute any legal proceedings. If I seem angry, the Keeper of the Seals and the Minister of Police will come with downcast looks and implore me not to follow up inquiries which may disturb the public tranquillity, rekindle animosities, bring hostile parties face to face, and expose honourable names to unjust imputations. I shall be obliged to give way, the conspirators will continue to call themselves my best friends, and I—I shall not even be at liberty to tell them that I would gladly dispense with their friendship!"

Need we add, that Louis's anticipations were, upon this occasion, fully verified. We must not conclude without mentioning, that in literature Louis XVIII. was a rigorous *classiciste,* and that he would not have objected to M. de Chateaubriand as a politician or a minister, had he not reprobated and envied him as an author.

Art. XV.— 1. *Le Gueux de Mer.*   2 vols. 12mo.   Paris. 1830.
2. *Le Gueux des Bois, ou les Patriotes Belges de* 1556 ; *suivi de la Bataille de Navarin.*   4 vols. 12mo. Paris. 1830.
3. *Phillippine de Flandre, ou les Prisonniers du Louvre. Roman Historique Belge.*   Par M. H. G. Moke.   4 vols. 12mo. Paris. 1830.

The innumerable works of fiction, good, bad, and indifferent, hourly littered by the Parisian press, is not the portion of our brilliant neighbours' literature to which we usually direct the attention of the British public ; those only can pretend to be mentioned in our pages, that are peculiarly distinguished by genius, character, or circumstances. Upon a late occasion we reviewed at some length the productions of one of the most popular French novelists* of the present day, for the double purpose of making his style and talent known to our readers, and of guarding such of them as do not wish to sully their minds with gross images, against being tempted by his indigenous celebrity, to open any of his multifarious volumes. Our present object is the very reverse, and may be more shortly attained, being to recommend to general perusal the writings of M. H. G. Moke, whom we must however confess to be an author much inferior in brilliancy to Paul de Koch.

Moke's principal merit, in our eyes, is the having opened what we may call a new field of romance, since the very few splendid scenes that Sir Walter Scott has sketched of Netherland transactions, can scarcely be deemed sufficient to render the term incorrect.† Moke has painted, and we really think to the life, the free, bold, wealthy, virtuous, and turbulent burghers and yeomen of the Low Countries, in their struggles for their civil and religious rights: and we should, at any time that we had happened to meet with them, have recommended his *Romans Belges* for the mere novelty and vivacity of their Flemish pictures. But we are more especially impelled to do so now, when the revolutions, bursting out around us on every side, give additional and important interest to these clever delineations of popular commotions; of

---

* Paul de Koch, No. 10.
† Whilst we are writing, the publication of Mr. Grattan's Heiress of Bruges seems to tax us with incorrectness ; M. Moke, however, was first in the Belgian field.

the humane and patriotic forbearance with which William of Nassau, Prince of Orange, and his confederates, sought redress by every legal and pacific means ere they would be provoked to insurrection; of the horrors and atrocities nearly inseparable from civil war; and of the almost inevitable involvement, upon such occasions, of the best, of the most determined to refrain from violence, in bloodshed, if not in guilt. The happy choice of his subject-matter is not, however, M. Moke's sole merit. He has managed it reasonably well, and he has drawn many of his characters with vivid energy. We could, indeed, have wished that in his *Gueux des Bois* he had coloured less heavily the vices of the Spanish governors, commissioned by Philip the Second to establish the inquisition; but we acknowledge with pleasure that the little he has given us of the Prince of Orange and his party is good and striking. In the same work the bold and benevolent Capuchin is well opposed, not only to the intolerant and persecuting Roman Catholic priests, but to the equally worthy and conscientious Protestant zealot, himself further contrasted with the *pseudo*-fanatical demagogue, after whom the novel is named, who, by the criminal excesses to which he instigates his followers, gives a show of justice to the most flagitious proceedings of the inquisition. In *Philippine de Flandre*, the rude and half brutal soldier of fortune, the loftily chivalrous noble, are as happily painted amongst the French characters, as are the Bear of the Butchers, and the Deacon* of the Drapers amongst the Flemings. Expecting that these novels will be generally read, we shall say nothing of the story of any of them, (the *Gueux de Mer* we as yet know only by name,) but shall try to select a short, detached scene from the last, *Philippine de Flandre*, such as may give an idea of our author's graphic and dramatic powers, observing however that it would require a longer and more continuous extract to do him justice.

Count William of Juliers, a warlike ecclesiastic, is escorting a damsel, wrapped in a peasant's cloak, into Bruges, which city is in a state of insurrection against Philip the Fair, King of France.

"Scarcely had he entered the city, when a barricade stopped him. 'What means this?' exclaimed Count William, 'do the people leave their ramparts unguarded and entrench themselves in the street?'

"'It is the smiths, who fortify their quarter,' said a peasant, with a flail in his hand, and a quiver on his shoulder; 'and by the blood of our Lord, well they may, having hostile trades to right and left! But you will find the street to your right clear, Sir Knight.'

"The young Count followed his advice, and reached the market place without impediment. Here bands of drapers and boatmen were in garrison * * * In front of their respective stations they had erected posts, to which they had affixed barrels filled with combustibles; and the flames that rose eddying from those immense brasiers lighted the whole place. By this sinister light were seen small parties of armed men hurrying to and fro, and ranging themselves under the banners of their several guilds. The lugubrious sound of the bells, the shouts occasionally uttered by the furious multitude, the distant aspect of

---

* We translate the French *Doyen*, by the Scotch name of the elder of a guild or corporation, for want of an English word.

the close columns forming in the adjacent streets, all announced an approaching and inevitable commotion.

" There was something so frightful in the whole picture that William of Juliers felt his hair bristle on his head. ' Let us retrace our steps,' said he to his companion, ' It fits not you should brave such dangers. Perish rather the name of Flanders and the lion of our ancestors !'

" The young maiden cast upon him a severe look. ' Already have I sacrificed more than life,' she replied in melancholy accents, ' and nothing shall now make me turn back. And wherefore should I ? Better die here than in exile.'   *   *   *   ..   *   *   *   *

" A troop of pikemen, whom their blue frocks showed to be weavers, surrounded a mean-looking house. At sight of the horseman they lowered their pikes, opposing an iron rampart to his progress, whilst different voices clamoured.

" Who are you?—What do you want?—Nobody may approach Master Peter's house. Priest or devil, you pass not!

" ' Where is the deacon?' asked he, impatiently.

" ' If we did but know l' they returned, brandishing their long pikes.

" ' But his sons?' resumed William of Juliers.

" ' At the old castle,' replied the Flemings.

" ' Well then, I must speak with his wife.'

" ' Yes, Yes!—No, no!—Call the deaconess!—Cross your pikes!—Let him pass !—Drive him back!'—shouted a thousand voices.

" The house door now unclosed, and a woman appeared, whose still handsome and proud face bore the traces of deep affliction. She glanced at the equestrians, and apparently recognizing them, exclaimed; ' Open your ranks! It is the hope, the last hope, of Flanders !' "

The deaconess now introduces the strangers into her best apartment, and displays the warmest loyalty towards the lady, the daughter of the unfortunate Count of Flanders, who, deserted by his rebellious subjects, had been perfidiously invited by King Philip to the French court, and upon his appearing there, treacherously seized and imprisoned. The deaconess eagerly divests Philippine of her rustic disguise, and the latter anxiously inquires for the Deacon de Koning, who, in expiation of his rebellion, has devoted himself to her father's cause, and upon whose aid she relies, for gaining over the good city of Bruges, already in open revolt against French oppression.

" They were interrupted by a masculine voice that called out from the lower story, ' Be of good cheer, Deaconess. Master Peter is in the Count's palace, and we are going to fetch him out.'

" ' What mean those words?' asked the young Countess, starting up. ' Has the fatality that pursues our family reached to de Koning ?'

" The deaconess in tears led her to an open window, and showing her a crowd of pikemen jostling each other, she said, ' Those are the weavers returning to town; the trades, inimical to ours, had taken advantage of their absence to throw the deacon into prison. Now they will pay dearly for it. Do you see how the arms glitter on the *Place du Bourg?* They are lighting the torches; they are unfolding the banners. The hour of vengeance is come!'

" From the window William and Philippine saw part of the great market place, and of the neighbouring strongly fortified castle. The night was dark, the sky clouded; but the blazing casks and torches cast a ruddy and flickering light over the discoverable space. The stately edifices of the old castle and the market place presented a vague and imperfect outline, appearing to tremble as the wind agitated the eddying fire and smoke, or to move with the motion of the torches.

"The weavers were mustering at the old castle. They were compressed between a church of antique and gigantic architecture, and ramparts, recently half destroyed by fire. They set forward, and such were their numbers that they seemed rather turning upon themselves than proceeding, when the head of their column appeared entering the market place by a dark and narrow street. Presently they stopped, without any perceptible cause. Loud cries arose. * *

"Philippine clasped her hands, and for a moment seemed engaged in prayer; then raising her beautiful head, she murmured, ' I will stay them.'

"She sprang upon her horse with the grace and lightness of a daughter of air. Her white robe floated in large folds over her courser's back; her tresses fell in curls upon her shoulders. Pale, but not timid, she urged her steed amidst the throng, forbidding all attendance.

* * * * * *

"When Philippine reached the spot, the column was again in motion. The weavers had driven back a body of enemies who had opposed their progress, and the conflict was raging round the palace of the Counts of Flanders. She saw the butchers and fishmongers, who guarded the palace, hurling large stones at their assailants. She heard battle cries and groans of pain. But it was impossible to make way through the infuriate mass of the draper's faction, and for a moment the young Countess forgot her purpose, whilst gazing on the spectacle that now fixed her attention. A party of carpenters, smiths, and tilers, had undertaken to penetrate into the palace, by throwing a sort of bridge across from the roof of a neighbouring house to one of the turrets. Thrice they succeeded in placing beams across, upon which the boldest immediately sprung; but every time their enemies overthrew their bridge, and with it were seen to fall those who had trusted to its support. But the assailants were not discouraged. A fourth attempt was made. A longer beam was more securely placed, and a throng of brave spirits rushed on to the tottering bridge. Again some fell, but many reached the turret; and immediately large planks afforded a passage to their comrades. A shout of triumph resounded through the adjacent streets. The body of the column pressed on. The palace of the Counts was won!

"Philippine could now urge her horse forward, and she arrived in the palace court just as de Koning, released from his dungeon, was lifted up in triumph on a shield.

"Insignificant in person, old, and blind of one eye, there was nothing in the appearance of the deacon of the drapers that could awe, flatter, or dazzle. He was a low-born man, with ordinary features, an ignoble carriage, a hard and sharp eye; but the indomitable resolution stamped on his bald and bony forehead recalled to the imagination those antique bronze statues. unchanged by time or tempest. His fetters had been broken, but some links still hung upon his arms, which, with looks of the fiercest resentment, he was displaying to his avengers. Those who bore him in triumph, almost all wounded and covered with blood, presented such contrasts as only popular commotions can offer. Here was a plaisterer white with lime, there a smith with blackened hands and face; weavers, dyers, fullers, all differently dressed and armed, but all alike robust, bold, and eager. Some prisoners of the hostile trades, who had been brought to the deacon's feet, seemed condemned to certain death. Most of them were on their knees ejaculating their dying prayers; but a few, more intent on braving their enemies than on the salvation of their own souls, stood upright, with threatening looks and insulting words, defying the revenge of their conquerors.

"' What shall we do with them, de Koning?' inquired some of the leaders.

" ' To death with them! ᛁ To death with them !' shouted the impatient crowd.

" And the deacon, his heart still ulcerated, seemed to smile at the idea of their execution. He bowed his head in token of assent; his lips moved to pronounce the fatal word. But a voice, to which every nerve in his frame vibrated, murmured, ' de Koning!' He shuddered, raised his eyes, and met the severe gaze of the young Countess.

· " The cheeks of the proud draper were crimsoned with shame. , ' Of what mud is man's soul formed," exclaimed he bitterly, ' that for petty quarrels I should every minute betray the cause to which I have dedicated my existence !' And springing down from the buckler, he resumed in a loud voice.

" ' No more honours, no more authority for me ! Behold her whom we must all obey !'

" All eyes were already fixed upon Philippine, who appeared amidst the ferocious multitude as a being of a higher nature. At first, the superstitious notions of the populace mingling with the illusive charm spread over that pure, white, and aerial form, they shrank from her in mute alarm. But when the name of Philippine of Flanders had been pronounced, all pressed around her whose misfortunes had excited so much interest and compassion. The offences imputed to her father were forgotten, together with the municipal enmities of the different trades, and innumerable voices enthusiastically raised the battle cry of her house, *Flanderen den Leeuw*—The Lion of Flanders !" .

Having thus awarded to M. Moke his due meed of praise, and given a fair specimen of his talents, we shall further prove our opinion of his merit, by pointing out some of the faults which we should wish him to avoid whilst pursuing the career so happily begun, uninterrupted, as we trust it may in future be, by such *hors d'œuvre* as his Battle of Navarino. His characters are exaggerated, and that sometimes to a degree of coarseness; and he unscrupulously deviates from the species of historical truth, which we expect in a historical novel, *i. e.* truth of characters and manners. In fact we think *that* the best style of historical novel, in which the historical personages are well interwoven with the story, the hero and heroine being fictitious, as in Ivanhoe, and indeed as in M. Moke's own *Gueux des Bois*. This is our taste. Nevertheless we would not quarrel with our author for rescuing Philippa, or as he pleases to call her, Philippine of Flanders, the affianced bride of Edward II. of England, from the premature death to which the remorseless Philip the Fair is said to have doomed her in his own palace as the surest way of preventing her marriage; nor yet for sinking this resuscitated princess into the *inamorata* of a French knight. But why, to take our example from the same novel, has he loaded with obloquy the memory of a queen, Jeanne de Navarre, of whom the last and ablest French historian, after ransacking, as in duty bound, all sources of information, expressly says, " History has preserved nothing respecting her that can enable us to judge of her character or of her influence with her husband;"—?* And yet more, why has he done this, falsifying the date of her death to effect it, for the sake of diminishing the odium that rests upon her husband, Philip the Fair, one of the most contemptibly detestable of modern tyrants; the ruffianly virtual

* Sismondi, *Histoire des Français,* vol. ix. p. 170. ..

assassin of an aged pontiff, whose chief faults sprang from partiality to that very Philip; the legal plunderer and murderer of the whole order of Knights Templars; in a word, for we have no leisure to enumerate his crimes, the cowardly robber, who effected by gross frauds, by the tricks of a pettyfogging attorney, those spoliations of his neighbours and vassals, which he had neither courage nor skill to achieve as a conqueror? Further, descending to minutiæ, and still confining our remarks to his last production, why has M. Moke given the Heiress of Navarre a brother, (who must have unheiressed her,) in her cousin, Robert of Artois? Or why has he made the name of the deacon of the weavers unplebeian by the addition of the French preposition, *de?*

Art. XVI.—1. *Verhandelingen over de Vraag: Welke Verdiensten hebben zich de Nederlanders vooral in de 14e, 15e, en 16e eeuw in het vak der Toonkunst verworven ; en in hoe verre kunnen de Nederlandsche Kunstenaars van dien tijd, die zich naar Italien begeven hebben, invloed gehad hebben op de muzijkscholen, die zich kort daarna in Italien hebben gevormd: Door* R. G. *Kiesewetter en* F. J. *Fétis.* [Discussion of the question: What services have the Netherlanders, especially in the 14th, 15th, and 16th centuries, rendered to the art of music, and how far could the Netherlandish artists of that period, who went into Italy, have influenced the schools of music, which shortly afterwards arose there? By R. G. Kiesewetter and F. J. Fétis.] 4to. Brussels, 1830.

2. *Curiosités Historiques de la Musique, complément nécessaire de la Musique mise à la portée de tout le monde.* Par M. Fétis, Directeur de la Revue Musicale. 8vo. Paris, 1830.

In 1824, the foregoing question, was proposed by the fourth Class of the Royal Institute of Literature and the Fine Arts of the Netherlands, as the subject of a prize essay. It produced, among other answers, one in German, by M. Kiesewetter, of Vienna, and one in French, by M. Fétis, of Paris, which that learned body justly esteemed worthy of the gold and silver medal. Both candidates hold, we believe, appointments in royal or national libraries, and they therefore came to their task with those advantages of access to ancient MSS. which were indispensable to its successful execution. The result of this investigation, which has been upon both hands sufficiently diligent, is highly honourable to the genius of Flanders, and proves satisfactorily that the composers of that nation, if not the discoverers of counterpoint, were the first who turned its resources to their legitimate ends—expression and refinement. With the honour of producing the first practical application of the principle of florid counterpoint, they may be well content; and a view of contemporary compositions of various nations during the era of their most celebrated masters, renders their title to it unquestionable. To us, the examples and illustrations which have been industriously collected by M. Kiesewetter furnish the most valuable part of the volume. They prove that from the time of Ockeghem and Josquin des Pres (whose country, by-the-bye, is not satisfactorily determined,) to Orlando di Lasso, the Flemings were supreme in the musical art ; and the Italians, whom we are accustomed to look upon as the regenerators of music in Europe, have with native frankness and candour been the first to acknowledge their obligations. The school of Italy was, in fact, much the younger one, commencing only with Palestrina, in the latter half of the 16th century, during the career of Orlandus Lassus, one of the last of the eminent musicians of Flanders. Such was the reputation of the latter school from the time of Ockeghem, to that of Lassus, that its masters or their pupils stocked all the foreign courts, and certainly with the happiest influence upon the taste for composition. Josquin appears to have been a prodigious man ; his writings are the earliest extant, in which are found an instinct of the poetical, as regards conception and design ; and he is remarkable, too, for expression at a time when his contemporaries were too much occupied with rules, and calculations, to believe imagination, or feeling, necessary to music. He was the admiration, of the Italians, for the constant variety of plan in his compositions ; every one of which seemed to extend the domain of art. Nothing need be said beyond this in proof of his great genius. Roland Lassus, better known by his Italian cognomination, Orlando di Lasso, flourished about a hundred years later than Josquin, under the happiest circumstances that could befall a musician ; and a life of ease and competence enabled him to leave a name as imperishable as the art itself. Many of his compositions are sought with delight at the present day, from the grace and elegance of their style. Palestrina, the founder of the Roman school, the first great name in the church music of Italy, and the contemporary and rival of Orlando di Lasso, was the disciple of Claudius Goudimel, a Fleming. M. Kiesewetter divides the history of Flemish art into three epochs—the age of Josquin, from 1450 to 1500 ; that of Hadrian Willaert from 1500 to 1540, and that of Orlando di Lasso from 1540 to 1590 : from this period the genius of the Flemish masters declined. It is convincingly clear, that, for a century and a half, the composers of the Netherlands took precedence of those of civilized Europe, and that their contemporaries, generally, could not pretend to equal their skill in the higher order of counterpoint.

We wish M. Kiesewetter had been satisfied with showing this, without attempting to prove that music was in a manner *born* in Flanders. In our opinion, he would not have deserved the gold medal the more, for labouring to show, that Melpomene came down from Heaven, *via* Holland, and landed in Flanders from a *treckschuyt*. Truth is the grand object in historical inquiry,—not the flattery of national vanity. Who the first discoverer of counterpoint, or rather of the combination of musical tones, was, cannot be known, nor is it important. Tinctoris, one of the earliest and most reputable authorities upon music, ascribes the origin of this art to England ; but M. Kiesewetter, who will hear of no partition of honours with that classical territory, the history of whose performances he is examining, quotes the authority of **Dr.** Burney in opposition. It is a matter of the most perfect indifference, since counterpoint has been discovered and brought to perfection, what country has the majority of conjectures in its favour. The love of displaying knowledge, particularly where nothing can be known, is a foible in historians, which has provoked the good-humoured laugh of satirists from the time of Cervantes to the present. To our mind, the reeds and rural pipes of Ovid and Lucretius are worth a hundred pages of dry disquisition upon the origin of music. The essay of M. Fétis does not manifest any important variation from that of his fellow-labourer. He ascribes, however, to the Flemish, the honour of forming the organ school, for which Germany has become celebrated.

The volume entitled *Curiosités Historiques de la Musique* is a piece of genuine book-making. It has no more connection with *La Musique mise à la portée de tout le Monde* than if it were an essay on the steam engine. One volume having sold off quickly, M. Fétis thought it expedient to try his fortune with another. He has accordingly reprinted several essays from the *Revue Musicale,* his letters on the state of music in England (not omitting the falsehoods contained therein), and joined to these certain extracts from a general biographical dictionary of musicians, which he is about to publish. This the *complément necessaire* to *La Musique mise à la portée de tout le Monde!* The author means that the profits are a *complément necessaire* to his pocket.

ART. XVII.—John Pettersson's *fullständig Hebreisk Grammatika efter egna forskningar och ny åsigt af ordlens grundformer.* (John Peterson's Complete Hebrew Grammar, &c.) Lund. 1829. 8vo.

GRAMMATICAL treatises are showered down upon the world as thick as hail-stones. Every man who sets up for a teacher seems to think he must establish his title by the publication of a School-book or a Grammar. This is particularly the case in Germany, where it is difficult to say whether the class of writers or of readers is the most numerous. Amidst the shoals of books upon languages, there are few worth resening from obscurity; they are generally dull repetitions of one another—amidst a century of which, not one ray of novelty throws out even a momentary brightness. We could mention a man who has written four Grammars of the same language, all unlike one another, yet each of course pretending to be *the* desideratum. Nay, in an Italian Grammar just published, the illustrious and candid author confesses that if he had understood the subject as well when he began his work as he did when he had completed it, he should have made a much better book. As soon as he had ended his task his notions changed, both of the fundamental character and the component parts and affinities of the language; and he should therefore have felt it his duty, had he been thoroughly acquainted with the topic, to give his production *eine ganz-andere Gestalt*—quite another shape. It would seem that the literary rule was not to write because you understand—not to write because you have knowledge; but to write because you do not understand—to write because you have not knowledge.

The oriental languages, requiring more attention for their competent understanding, have been tolerably safe from the intrusions of ignorant and presumptuous men; they are in their very form and appearance repulsive to vain and shallow scribblers; and the book before us is an admirable specimen of what elaborate study and thorough acquaintance with the subject can produce. It is the fruit of long labour, and of an exhaustive examination of the whole field of which it treats. No portion of it is written without due care; there is no haste, no presumption any where; its different parts are all complete in themselves and harmonious in their union. It is the work of a teacher in the University of Lund, in Sweden. His system of derivations is, we believe, original: he defends it with great erudition and ingenuity; and it is much to be regretted that the small extent over which the Swedish language is spread, must give to his theories a share of attention very far less than that to which they are entitled. We wish this Grammar were published in Latin, so as to give orientalists in general an opportunity of estimating it; and in this case we would respectfully suggest to the author, that his arrangement of the different parts of speech might be improved, and that he would do well to take the derivate forms of the verb in the order employed by Arabic grammarians, (viz. *gatal, gittel, gôtel, higtíl, hithgattel, hithg'otel, nigtal*); and these forms should also be distinguished from the variations of *gal* (gatal, gatel), which in fact, in Hebrew as well as in Arabic, alone deserve the title of conjugations. The conjugations should be distinctly and fully explained before any the slightest reference is made to their derivatives. It was, perhaps, the high authority of Gesenius, Ewald, and other German orientalists, that led our author to introduce pronouns before nouns—a precedence wholly unsanctioned by true philosophy; for the distinctions of sex went long before their abbreviated representation in the pronominal form. The difference between *hú* and *hí* (he and she) would neither have been invented nor understood until man and woman, father and mother, brother and sister, son and daughter, and the thousand other gender-distinguishing words, had obtained currency. The substitute should on every account follow the principal. And it is curious to observe, by a reference to the venerable authority of the Bible, what was the progress of language, and how the noun substantive was made the ground-work of the whole. " And the Lord God formed every beast of the field, and every fowl of the air, and brought them unto Adam to see what he would call them; and whatsoever Adam called every living creature, that is the name thereof." (*Gen.* ii. 19, 20.) Here, before even the creation of Eve—here we find the elements of the infant language of the world: verbs followed nouns; and afterwards came those conventional abbreviations which give so much flexibility and variety to' language, and those modifications which represent the different shades of thought.

We think the author's verbal system susceptible of much simplification. He has adopted eight conjugations, which in truth might be reduced to one, with seven derivative forms; nay, he has gone further, and introduced active, passive and reciprocal, which it will be obvious to the Arabic scholar, are only new derivatives. He employs two constructive forms, which are truly only two separate classes of verbs, and by thus encumbering his pages with needless refinements and distinctions, destroys the lucidity of his general views. For example, he thus gives the first conjugation in the present tense.

active	intransitive	passive	reciprocal
gatal	gatel gatol	(gatúl)	nigtal

We do not think this a happy arrangement—we doubt even its correctness.

We regret that we cannot praise our author's orthography. Taking the Swedish alphabet as his instrument of pronunciation, we think his pupils must be led astray. He gives, for example, to the letter *zajin* the character of *ds*. It is simply and purely the French and English *z*. He writes *waw*, *vav*, and describes the sound to be *v*. It is in reality *w*. And this misconception is curiously illustrated by a note, page 9, where he says the aspirate *b* has not, as is commonly supposed, the sound of *v*, *because* it is but rarely interchanged with *waw;* which is just as if he said *v* is not *v* in English, because it is rarely replaced by *w*. He represents Q*of* by *k* instead of *q*, which is in fact the identical letter. These misconceptions will be understood when we observe that the sounds of *z*, *w* and *q* are unknown to the Swedes, unless as represented by *s*, *v* and *k*.

In the vowels too, we think he is mistaken in representing the long *Khôlem* by *å*, which has the sound of *oa* in our word *broad ;* while the true sound is that of *oa* in the word *load*, and might, according to the system of Sir William Jones, have been very appropriately written *ó*. The writing of Jôd and Qôf Jåd and Kåf cannot be maintained, for the Greek ιωτα and the Latin *qu* evidently predicate the long and close *ó* in the original Phœnician names. The letter *å* might, however, be used as a fit representative for those cases where, as in Swedish, the fulcrum for the Khôlem (o) is an Aleph (a), as, for instance, *lå* (not), where the Arabic sound also closely approaches to the *a*, as in *lá* (not).

These remarks have been elicited by our high estimate of this Grammar, and our desire to contribute a hint or two towards its perfection. It is rather too elaborate for beginners, as it extends to 500 pages.

ART. XVIII.—*Die Römische Kampagne : in topographischer und antiquarischer Hinsicht, dargestellt von* J. H. Westphal ; *nebst einer Karte der römischen Kampagne, und einer Wegekarte des alten Lazium.* (The Campagna di Roma; exhibited in Topographical and Antiquarian Delineations, by J. H. Westphal ; with Maps of the Campagna and Ancient Latium.) 4to. With Maps in Folio. Berlin. 1829.

THOUGH a great variety of works are constantly appearing on Italy in general, and on Rome especially, still an accurate description of the " Roman Campagna" in its greatest extent—the classic soil of the origin of Roman greatness—was much wanted. Most travellers visit

but few spots outside the gates of Rome; more remote points are less
frequented, partly on account of their distance from the high road,
partly because they are, without any reason decried for being unsafe.
It was therefore of no small importance to find a properly-qualified
traveller to examine carefully the whole country from Civita-vecchia to
Terracina, from Narni to Sora, in order to give an accurate account
of the present condition of the country, with an exact description of
the antiquities, and to fix the points, where it may be desirable to
make further researches. In the work now before us this difficult task
is not only satisfactorily performed, but it contains moreover an entirely
new investigation of the old Roman causeways or military roads, the
old itineraries and *Tabula Peutingeriana* are frequently revised and corrected, and the positions of a great number of ancient towns and military stations is now fixed with the utmost precision. By the exactness of his measurements the author was enabled to delineate two
maps, grounded upon entirely new data. Proceeding from the different
gates of Rome, as points of departure, the text of the work is divided
into eleven sections, each of which comprises one particular branch of
roads, together with the adjacent relics of antiquity. The first map,
inscribed " Contorni di Roma Moderna," not only gives a distinct
image of the present shape of the soil, but indicates also all those spots
where ancient remains are still to be seen. Every place, down to the
smallest " casale," is marked, and the roads leading to them pointed
out, so that this map will be even more useful to the stranger than the
best-road book. The other map, bearing the title " Agri Romani Tabula," specially recommends itself by the delineation of the old Roman
high-roads. A small plan of Rome, with its Seven Hills, its gates,
and bridges, affords a distinct view of that ancient classical soil. The
index of the ancient and modern names annexed is a most useful addition to a work which, for completeness and accuracy, surpasses any
previous work on the subject.

Note to the Article on Codification in **No. XII.**

WE have heard, with much regret, that Mr. Cooper, the learned and enlightened author of the *Lettres sur la Cour de la Chancellerie*, reviewed by us in a former Number, has conceived that the omission of any reference to his work in the article *on Codification*, in our last Number, was intentional. Nothing could be further from our intention, than to be guilty even of the appearance of a slight towards so distinguished a writer. We were as well aware that Meyer's work had been occasioned by Mr. Cooper's Letters, as that Savigny's tract had been occasioned by that of Thibaut. Neither of these facts was stated formally to our readers, as we did not profess to give a literary *history* of the controversies respecting codification. The chief object of our article was to examine the arguments of Mr. Bentham, as a representative of those, who, by codification, understand a total repeal of the existing law, and a substitution of new law in its place. In exposing (what appeared to us) the errors and inconsistencies of that doctrine, and the inconclusiveness of those arguments which oppose codification as necessarily implying an enactment of new law, we took occasion to refer incidentally to some passages in the works of Savigny and Meyer, and some other publications; but we neither professed to exhaust the subject, and to weigh all the arguments of different writers on each side of the question, nor even to enumerate the principal English authors on the subject. Had such been our intention, we should not have despaired of being able to show that the grounds on which we rested our argument are not to be overthrown even by the temperate and erudite discussion of Mr. Cooper.

***

*** We willingly give insertion to the following correction of a mistatement relative to the late Mr. Marryat, in our last Number, the origin of which we cannot at this moment exactly trace.

To the Editor of the Foreign Quarterly Review.

SIR,

In the article in the last Number of your Review, entitled " The French Prohibitive System," I see with surprise, at page 403, the following paragraph:

" Amongst other acts of conciliation, the late Mr. Marryat persuaded us to deprive them (the French captured colonies) of the power of selling in our markets the few hogsheads of sugar which they produced; and they ceased to grow it."

So far from this being the case, my father was, I believe, the only member connected with the West Indies, who opposed the Bill brought forward in 1809, by his Majesty's ministers, for the purpose of excluding the produce of the island of Martinique from the home consumption of Great Britain, for which he received a vote of thanks from the inhabitants of that colony.

Referring you to the reports of the debate on that question, for the confirmation of what I state, I remain, Sir,

Your obedient humble servant,

CHARLES MARRYAT.

12, CLARENCE TERRACE, REGENT'S PARK,
13th December, 1830.

MISCELLANEOUS LITERARY NOTICES.

No. XIII.

FRANCE.

Necrology.—COUNT Louis Philip de Segur died on the 27th of August last, in the 77th year of his age. He was one of the most elegant and popular writers of the present day, as his works, which are very voluminous, bear evidence. One of the latest of these, the *Memoirs of his Life*, in 3 vols. 8vo., which only come down to the period of the French Revolution, have been extremely well received both in France and England, and it is to be hoped that the sequel of them is yet destined to see the light. M. de Segur served in the American war of independence, under Lafayette, was afterwards sent ambassador to Russia, and subsequently to Prussia, at the beginning of the revolution, by which event his fortune was entirely ruined. During the first years of the revolution he contrived to escape the guillotine, although he was proscribed, and retired into complete seclusion, from which he was drawn by Bonaparte, when he assumed the helm of affairs. He enjoyed the favour and confidence of the Emperor to the last. After the restoration he again went into retirement, but in 1818 was called to the Chamber of Peers by M. De Cazes. He has left a son, General Philip de Segur, the heir of his talents and his liberal opinions, and whose literary merits have already obtained him a seat in the French Academy.

The French Society for Universal Statistics, whose formation we noticed in our last, has commenced a monthly journal of its labours. It is divided into two portions, the first, or *Bulletin*, giving an account of the meetings, reports and decrees of the Society and its council, and miscellaneous articles; the second portion consisting of documents, tables and statistical statements, and memorials, &c., of which the publication has been directed by the Society and its council.

The first number contains the following documents:—1. A comparative statement of the gross revenues of France, with the expenses of their collection. 2. A view of the progress of the gross revenue from 1816 to 1829. 3. Four statements relative to the vine-cultivation. 4. The number and classification of the 5 per cent. rentes.

Besides the 600 French members of whom the Society consists, as we mentioned in our last, it includes nearly 200 foreign members selected from the best informed of all nations, exclusive of Austria and including Egypt. Several princes and sovereigns have not thought it beneath them to associate with private individuals for the purpose of disseminating a species of knowledge on which the art of government is in a great degree founded.*

A volume has recently appeared at Paris, containing some hitherto unpublished documents relative to the massacre of St. Bartholomew, which throw considerable light on the leading points in the controversy which was revived about four years since between Dr. Lingard and the Edinburgh Reviewers. The theory of Dr. Lingard, it will be recollected, was founded on the story told by the Duke of Anjou (afterwards Henry III. of France), when he was in Poland, of the circumstances of the massacre. According to this the St. Bartholo-

---

* Among our own countrymen, we understand, the distinguished name of Mr. Malthus appears as a foreign member.

mew arose out of an unsuccessful attempt to assassinate the Admiral Coligny, undertaken by direction of the Queen-mother and her son the Duke of Anjou, without the concurrence or knowledge of the King; on the failure of which the Queen and her Catholic councillors, partly by insinuation and partly by threats, obtained an order from the King to put the admiral and his principal adherents to death. By this tale the odium of a preconcerted plot, concealed for many months, and disguised with infinite art and dissimulation, is avoided; and the guilt of the original authors of the massacre is reduced to the intended commission of a single murder, which by accident was extended to a greater number, and by the fury of an exasperated and fanatical populace was converted into a general massacre of all the Hugonots in Paris. The publication we allude to, entitled " Monumens Inedits de l'Histoire de France: 1. Correspondance de Charles IX. et de Mandelot, Gouverneur de Lyon, pendant l'année 1572.; 2. Lettre des Seize au Roi d'Espagne Philippe II." shows the entire fallacy of this theory. The letters of Charles IX. and of Catherine de Medicis, here published, with the answer of Mandelot, prove that on the 13th of August, several days prior to the attempt to assassinate the admiral, and eleven days before the massacre, Catherine and her son had ordered the Governor of Lyons to intercept all communication between France and Italy, thus preparing beforehand for the night of the 24th of August, and arranging the means of preventing the flight of their victims and the arrival of any letters from Italy (where the plan had been no doubt submitted to the approbation of some superior power) which might serve to put the Protestants on their guard. Other letters of the King and Mandelot throw additional light on a matter which has been too long controverted. The other documents which the book contains are curious.

The year 1830, which may well be designated *the year of revolutions,* has been an unfortunate one in the annals of French literature. However beneficial the results of the memorable week of July may *ultimately* prove to the liberties and permanent interests of the nation, it is a melancholy truth that its immediate effects have been most especially disastrous to the cause of literature. This has been proved by the extraordinary number of failures which have taken place among the booksellers in Paris since that time ; it falls little short of two hundred. Some relief has been afforded by the loan which was advanced by the government to the commerce of the metropolis. But the results will be more readily seen by a comparison of the books published in 1829 and 1830. The total number of books registered in the weekly list, entitled *Journal de la Librairie,* for the year 1829, was 7823—the same for the year 1830, was 6739. If we take the numbers for the corresponding periods of the two years, the difference will be still more striking.

From January 3 to July 25, 1829, the number was . . .	4651
From January 2 to July 24, 1830	4176
Difference . . .	475
From August 1 to December 26, 1829, there were . . .	3172
While from July 31, (the week of the Revolution,) to December 25, 1830, there were only	2563
Difference . . .	609

Histoire Littéraire de la France. The twelfth volume of this important work, originally published by the Benedictines in 1763, and which has been long out of print, has been recently reprinted by Firmin Didot. There are no alterations, excepting that in this new edition there are twenty-three pages added, containing sixty-five critical remarks, corrective of omissions and inaccuracies to be found in certain articles in the volume, and which are almost inevitable in these biographical notices. The first volume of this work was published in 1723 by Dom Rivet, who is the author of that and the subsequent volumes, to the ninth inclusive, which last was published in 1750, five years after his death, by Taillander; the tenth is by Clemencet; the eleventh by Clemencet and Clement; the twelfth by Clement; the thirteenth to the sixteenth inclusive, (which have appeared since 1814,) and the seventeenth, not yet published, but in a state of forwardness, were edited by Messrs. Brial, Ginguené, Pastoret, Daunou, Amaury Duval, Petit Radel, and Emeric David.

Mr. Beltrami, the traveller in Mexico, has recently made a tour to the Pyrenees, accompanied by Professor Boubé, (quere Boué,) and has announced the intention of shortly publishing a description of these celebrated mountains.

The *Memoirs, Correspondence, and Unpublished Works of Diderot* are about to appear in four or five volumes 8vo. These will include the memoirs of his life by his daughter, Madame Vandeul, from which we have already given an extract. One of the most interesting portions of this collection is his correspondence addressed to his mistress, Mademoiselle Volland, in which he was in the habit of noting down a kind of diary of his actions, his labours, and all his ideas. This correspondence embraces twenty-five years of Diderot's life. Several amusing extracts from it have appeared in the *Gazette Litteraire.*

The second livraison of the Chevalier Bronsted's Travels in Greece, the appearance of which, from the long delay that has taken place, was almost despaired of, has at last been published. It contains among other things a description, with plates, of the metopes of the Parthenon at Athens.

The French Academy, in its sitting of the 18th of November last, elected Messrs. Victor Cousin and Viennet to the seats vacant by the decease of the Comte de Segur and M. Fourier.

A new and handsomely printed collection in 8vo. at an extremely cheap price, of the best French Classics, is just announced by Messrs. Treuttel and Würtz, at Paris. The following are some of the advantages of this collection, which will commence with the *chefs-d'œuvre* of the French Theatre :
1. The best works *only* will be given of each author, and for this purpose the Editors have been compelled to reject several productions of various authors, that are either erroneously attributed to them, or are unworthy of their otherwise deserved reputation.
2. The text will be accurately printed, from the best editions.
3. Biographical Notices, for the most part original, will be given of the life and character of each author, together with a systematic table of contents.
4. The type and paper will be in a corresponding style of neatness and beauty.
5. A beautiful and well-engraved portrait will be given of each author.
6. And, above all, the chief recommendation of this edition will be its *cheapness.*
The object of this Collection is to place it within the reach of every description of readers ; and at the present period, when the cultivation of the mental faculties of all classes of the community has received so mighty an impulse, the publishers, we trust, are not mistaken in anticipating a rapid and extensive sale,

both in France and in foreign countries. The dramatic portion will consist of 23 volumes, 8vo., the price of each volume, containing on the average 400 pages, being only 4s.! From the 1st of March, 1831, two volumes will be published regularly every month. For the sake of those who may wish to have an edition printed on still finer paper, an edition is prepared at 4s. 6d. per volume.

The following is the arrangement of the dramatic portion :—

Œuvres de Molière, 7 vols. 8vo. with portrait.
Œuvres Choisis de P. Corneille, 4 vols. 8vo. with portrait.
Œuvres de J. Racine, 5 vols. 8vo. with portrait.
Théâtre Choisi de Voltaire, 7 vol. 8vo. with portrait.
The whole Collection, it is supposed, will not exceed eighty volumes.

GERMANY.

The second volume of the second edition of Mr. Niebuhr's Roman History has lately been published. Contrary to the intention which the author had expressed in the preface to the first volume, it has been greatly enlarged and remodelled throughout, so us to be almost as much a new work as the previous part. The internal history is brought down to 374, A.U.C.; the military history to 384, A.U.C. The account of the Licinian rogations, with which the first edition of the second volume closed, and which form a great epoch in Roman history, is not, therefore, included in the new edition.

The author states, in his preface, that as this volume has appeared three years later than he had intended, some explanation is due to the well-wishers to his work, who might lament so long a delay. This has arisen from the conviction which he acquired in attentively revising the second volume for publication, that " a substantial and credible history might be established from the beginning of the period which it embraces ;" and that consequently it would reward the labour of the historian to examine minutely into every detail of the historical narrative. For this new labour, however, he had become in some measure unfitted, by the uninterrupted exertions of sixteen months devoted to the first volume; and he felt the necessity of a change of subject, which he found in the new edition of the Byzantine Historians. Some time afterwards, when his power of useful application had returned, and the manuscript for the first sheets of the second volume were ready for the press, a fire which broke out in his house at midnight consumed these papers. The notes were, however, preserved, and the loss restored by the labour of seven weeks. " At other times (says Mr. Niebuhr,) this delay would not have had any effect on the progress of my work ; but I had only completed two-thirds of this task, when the madness of the French Court broke the talisman with which the demon of revolution lay spell-bound : the rest was written in order to perform a duty in finishing that which had been begun ; and with a constant effort to keep off the anxious cares with which I was haunted, for the destruction which threatened all property, and the dearest and happiest relations of social life. The first volume was written in a season of perfect tranquillity, and in the grateful and perfect enjoyment of it, in the most complete security for the future : now, if God does not providentially interfere, we see before us an impending ruin, such as befell the Roman world about the middle of the third century of our era ; an annihilation of prosperity, of freedom, of civilization, and of science."

Such were the gloomy forebodings which occupied the mind of this great historian at the publication of the last work which he has been permitted to complete. The hopes which he there expresses of continuing his labours on Roman history can now no longer be realized:

> " A greater Power than we can contradict
> Has thwarted his intents."

It seldom happens that a man of a comprehensive and vigorous mind, of great acquirements, of unwearied industry, and of honest and upright character, is cut off in the midst of his useful and honourable career, without such a loss suggesting a painful regret that the hand of death should fall there, while it spares the ignorant, the indolent, and the mischievous. But it is no less unwise than it is impious to cherish such an involuntary feeling, and to cavil at one out of the numerous forms of evil which surround us : we must in this, as in other like cases, bow, without repining or inquiry, to the inscrutable decrees of Providence.

Mr. Niebuhr states, in his preface, that the manuscript of his history is nearly completed up to the first Punic war. We trust that this remaining part of his labours will be given to the public as a posthumous work. But we despair of this history being continued in a style worthy of its beginner; there is no one left who can bend the bow of Ulysses.

The Annual assemblage of the Society of German Naturalists and Physicians took place in September last at Hamburgh. The first meeting was held on the 18th, in the Great Hall of the Exchange, the galleries of which were filled with spectators, and was attended by more than 490 members, of which number above 250 were foreigners. Among these were Professors Berzelius, of Stockholm, and Agardh, of Lund, Count Sternberg, of Prague; besides several men of science from London, Edinburgh, Copenhagen, Vienna, and even from Baltimore, in the United States. Among the representatives of the German Universities there were Professors Oken, Jacquin, Lichtenstein, Pfaff, Harless, Osiander, Mertens, Tiedemann, Brandes, &c. Several of the Russian professors attended, such as Fischer, of Moscow, Fischer of St. Petersburgh, Struve, of Dorpat, and Bornstorf, of Helsingfort; also Professors Sazochy, Emile, and Isubert from Warsaw. The burgomaster, Bartels, one of the most influential and well-informed citizens of Hamburgh, acted as president of the assembly. Four public sittings were held, at each of which some discourses of a nature generally interesting were delivered. At the last sitting, on the 26th, it was settled that the next year's meeting should take place at Vienna, the Emperor having signified through Count Sternberg his desire to that effect, and that the Austrian government would be gratified by the opportunity of showing every attention to the members of the assembly.

The most perfect harmony reigned among the members who attended on this occasion, and it is to be hoped that the exchange of ideas, of observations and discoveries which took place between them, will be attended with great benefit to science; the ties which should unite them must have been cemented, and it is not saying too much that some petty jealousies and scientific rivalries have been banished by this personal intercourse. The Senate of Hamburgh, and especially the president of the Society, deserve the highest praise for the kind reception which they gave to the members, and the attentions of every sort with which they loaded them during their stay.

A very beautiful lithographic map of the Course of the Rhine, from Huningen to Lauterburg, in nineteen sheets, has recently been completed by Herder, of Friburg.

Dr. Brand, Professor at Bonn, has just published, in 2 vols. 8vo., a General Repertory of the whole science of Heraldry, with critical and other remarks, and directions relative to the books and literary history connected with it. The work contains 3331 articles arranged according to countries, with appendixes, indexes, &c. It seems to be a most laborious production, and entitles the compiler to the thanks of every heraldic student.

The first volume of a Collection of celebrated Criminal Trials, by the Chevalier de Feuerbach, has recently appeared at Giessen.

HOLLAND.

Katherine Wilhelmina Bilderdijk, the wife of the celebrated veteran poet of Holland, died at Haarlem, on the 16th of last April. Mivrouw Bilderdijk was herself a woman of considerable literary abilities, and distinguished by her talent for poetry. Her productions, however, have generally been printed along with those of her husband. In 1816, she obtained the prize offered by the Letterkundige Genootschap at Ghent, for the best poem on the Battle of Waterloo. Her longest performance is her translation of Southey's ' Roderick, the Last of the Goths,' which is also generally considered her masterpiece.

Few works of more general interest have lately issued from the Dutch press than Olivier's *Land en Zeetogten in Nederlands Indie.* These volumes give the result of the author's travels in Java and the Molucca islands, in the years from 1817 to 1826 inclusive, and contain a variety of important details relative to the geography and political state of that portion of the eastern world. His descriptions are frequently very animated and graphic. He depicts Amboyna as quite an earthly paradise, combining the advantages of extreme healthiness of climate, the most luxuriant vegetation, and scenery rivalling that of Switzerland.* Of a very different description is his account of an eruption of Mount Tomboro, on the island of Sumbawa, which seems to have exceeded in horrors all that the imagination can conceive. The shock was felt within a circumference of more than twelve geographical miles, and produced in its vicinity the most terrible convulsions. The relation the author gives us of the Alfocrezes, one of the native tribes inhabiting the island of Banda, is exceedingly curious. From a most inhuman law, requiring a human head to be delivered to their priests, before any one may marry, it might be concluded that this race were the most barbarous savages; whereas they are remarkable for chastity, honesty, temperance, gratitude, and fidelity, and the revolting, sanguinary custom just mentioned, only shows how far a degrading superstition can triumph over nature and humanity, even in a virtuous people. A work so full of information as the present will hardly be confined to its original language.

Holland is not greatly behind either Germany or England in the number of her literary annuals, and although they cannot compete with those of the former country in the talent they display, and are infinitely inferior to our own in the article of embellishments, several of them possess considerable merit. The *Belgische Muzen-Almanak,* which first appeared in 1826, is one of the most popular, and generally contains some pieces by Tollens, Bilderdijk, and other admired poets. Of a similar character is the *Nederlandsche Musen-Almanak,* and some of the contributors to the preceding work have also pieces in this.

---

* One half of the population are now Protestant Christians ; a proof that the Dutch government have not been indifferent to the spiritual concerns of the natives.

The volume for 1830 contains many productions of merit, particularly Box-man's *Onafhankelijheid des Dichters,* and one or two poems by Madame Bilderdijk, Tollens, Immergeel, and Van der Hoope, while the short biographical notices of Pruimers, Cleve, Rielberg, Nierstrasz, and other poets who have died within the last two years, impart to it an additional value. The *Groningen Studenten Almanak* is also a poetical authology. That entitled *Voor het Schoone en Goede,* which has now been published for a number of years, is conducted more upon the plan of our own annuals, but the prose department is generally inferior to the other. The last volume, however, is, in this respect, far superior to its predecessors, and contains a very clever tale, by Louwense, *De Minnezangster,* or Minstrel, which gives an animated and faithful picture of the province of Gelderland, in the fourteenth century. Neither are the engravings without merit. The *Almanak tot Nut en Verpoozing* has, likewise, a variety of prose articles. Besides the above, there are several others adapted to the tastes of different classes of readers; one of the best is Hazelhoff's *Tijdkorter,* which is now nearly past its teens, the volume for the present year being the nineteenth.

The poets of Holland are far more prolific than any other class of its literary men. Tollens has lately published another collection of poetical pieces by him, in two volumes, many of which will add to his former reputation; none detract from it. Several of them, indeed, are fraught both with true poetical inspiration and deep religious feeling. Nearly the same remark will apply to Warnsnick's *Gedichten.* In general, the subjects are rather too much what are designated " occasional poems," to please an English taste; yet there are many noble pieces among them, particularly that entitled the " Constellations." Although of a different turn of genius from the two preceding writers, Van Hell is a poet of indisputable merit and refined taste. His intimate acquaintance with classical literature manifests itself in his poems, particularly in his lyric compositions, many of which are imitations, or rather revivals of his favourite, Horace, whose spirit seems frequently to animate him, and to have dictated some of his most felicitous passages. Nor is M. Van Hell less admirable as a prose writer, in which character his reputation is established by his two original and exceedingly interesting works, *Plinius Secundus* and *Messala Corvinus;* the former of which, if not the other, has been translated into French.

==========

ITALY.

WE have, under the date of Rome, the following publication, in one volume, octavo:—*Memorie Storiche del Ministero, de' due viaggi in Francia, e dell, prigionia nel Forte di S. Carlo in Fenestrelle, del Cardinale Bartolommeo Pacca scritte da lui medesimo. Edizione seconda, riveduta dall' autore e corredata de nuovi documenti.* Cardinal Pacca was Secretary of State to Pius VII., in 1808, when Napoleon, after having occupied Rome by force, began a long course of annoyances and petty warfare against the Pope, who kept himself confined to his palace on the Quirinal, and which ended with the latter being carried away in the middle of the night by the gens-d'armes, and taken to Savona. Pacca had the difficult and dangerous task of defending strenuously, by arguments and protestations, the rights and independence of his sovereign. His zeal and abilities drew upon him the wrath of the conqueror, who had him confined for more than two years in the dismal fortress of Fenestrelles, among the Alps of Piedmont; when at last, in 1813, the reverses of Napoleon indaced him to come to terms with the Pope, and liberate the Cardinals, it was not without difficulty that he consented to Pacca's release. It was during his captivity that Pacca began to write the memoirs of his ministry, and of the events that followed it. He wished the other Cardinals, who had been concerned in those transactions, to follow his example, in order to form a body of authentic materials for a general history of the times. It appears from some fragments written by the illustrious Gonsalvi, which Pacca has inserted, that that distinguished prelate and statesman had adopted his suggestion. As documents by a witness and a party concerned, the facts related by Cardinal Pacca are valuable to the historian, however partial his judgments may appear to be. The work has produced a sensation in Italy, and is now passing through a third edition.

Lucien Buonaparte, Prince of Canino, having effected some excavations on his estate near Montalto, which district formed a part of ancient Etruria, has been successful in finding a vast quantity of fine vases bearing paintings and inscriptions, and which appear to be of a similar kind to those found at Nola, in Campania. He has now published an account of this collection, in a 4to. volume, *Muséum Etrusque de Lucien Buonaparte, fouilles de* 1828-9, with forty-two plates of the inscriptions; and has also begun a splendid work in folio, which will contain a hundred coloured plates representing the paintings. The latter comes out in monthly numbers of five plates each, and is sold by Piatti, of Florence. This discovery has revived the question about the so called Etruscan vases, which the archæologist Zannoni contends are Greek, or at least of Greek invention, and not specimens of original Etruscan art anterior to Greek civilization, as the Prince of Canino seems inclined to think them.

C. Troya, of Naples, announces the speedy publication of an important work to which he has devoted years of researches, during which he has visited all the principal libraries of Italy. The subject is *a Political History of Italy, and of the social condition of the people under the dominion of the Longobards.* This has been, till now, the most obscure part of the history of that country.

The learned Tuscans, with Professor Rosellini at their head, who accompanied M. Champollion in his Egyptian scientific expedition, in 1828-9, are about publishing the account of *their* researches and discoveries, under the title of *Relazione del viaggio fatto in Egitto e in Nubia dalla spedizione scientifico-litteraria Toscana negli anni* 1828-9. It will consist of two volumes.

The long-announced continuation of Guicciardini's History of Italy, by Carlo Botta, may soon be expected to appear, as the eighth part of the MS., which comes down to the year 1748, has been delivered by the author to the society which has undertaken the publication. The ninth, or concluding part remains, which will come to the epoch of the French revolution, and thus join Botta's already published history of Italy from that time to the peace of 1814.

The Marchese Vacuni announces, at Rome, a new and splendid edition of *Vitruvius*, in five volumes, folio, printed at his own press, established for the purpose, and illustrated with 140 plates. The first volume will contain an apparatus of dissertations relative to the author's life, character and style, the various MSS. editions and translations, and the more difficult passages of his work. The second and third will contain the ten books of the treatise *De Archi-tectura,* the text carefully revised by a critical collation. The fourth will con-tain a collection of various readings from forty-five MSS. and printed editions, an ancient compendium of the architecture of Vitruvius, ancient inscriptions relative to architecture, and various indexes. The fifth will contain the 140 plates from entirely new designs, and partly taken from monuments for the express purpose.

Another handsome edition of this classic has been recently completed at Udino, in four large 4to volumes, each consisting of two parts. The editor is Signor Simeon Stratico, and the Italian Journals speak very highly of the execution of it.

SPAIN.

NECROLOGY.

CEAN-BERMUDEZ.—So little is known of the past and present state of the fine arts beyond the Pyrenees, even to those who are conversant with their history in the rest of Europe, that many will perhaps now learn, for the first time, that Spain has recently lost, in the person of Cean-Bermudez, one of the most ingenious critics and industrious historians of art, whose labours have opened to the inquirer highly interesting and valuable stores of hitherto inaccessible information. Juan Agustin Cean-Bermudez was born at Gijon, a sea-port of Asturia, in the year 1749, and was educated in the Jesuits' College at Oviedo, where he remained till the age of sixteen. It was his good fortune to become the early and intimate friend of one whose name reflects glory on his country, and whose virtues were an honour to humanity—his townsman, Jovellanos. The latter lived to experience the base ingratitude of that country ; Cean-Bermudez to have the melancholy task of recording how ill requited were the services of the enlightened and zealous patriot. After having spent two years with Jovellanos, at Alcala, and one at Seville, Cean-Bermudez accompanied him to Madrid, where, in 1778, Jovellanos was appointed chief judge of the king's court. Whether he continued with him in any official capacity, is not known ; but he afterwards proceeded with him to Seville, and it was among the treasures of art with which that city abounds, that Cean-Bermudez first turned his attention to those studies in which he afterwards distinguished himself. During his residence there he applied himself to architecture, anatomy, and drawing ; and, in conjunction with some other individuals, succeeded in founding an academy for the arts of design, which was afterwards further established by royal confirmation from Charles III. He was now advised by Jovellanos to visit Madrid for the purpose of availing himself of Mengs's instructions in painting, which he accordingly did ; but he did not long enjoy that advantage, as, within a few months, Mengs repaired to Rome. About this period he obtained, through the influence of his friend and patron, who had returned to the capital, some situation in the Bank of San Carlos, in which, uncongenial as it must have been to one of his turn of mind, he continued till the end of the year 1790, when he was sent to arrange the papers in the archives of the Office of India Affairs at Seville, a labour that occupied him during the following seven years. The intelligence and assiduity, however, which he displayed in this protracted task, secured for him the appointment to the secretaryship for India Affairs at Madrid, to which he had been recommended by Jovellanos. The subsequent disgrace and exile of the latter, caused also the removal of Cean-Bermudez, who was obliged to quit Madrid, and to resume his labours at Seville. He continued to discharge his official employments with punctuality during the stormy period that ensued, and until he finally retired on a pension. From that time he devoted himself exclusively to those studies, the fruits of which have so materially enriched that department of literature. . These were the solace and occupation of his declining years, until they were interrupted by a stroke of apoplexy, in September 1827, which, however, he survived two years; his death not taking place till December 3d, 1829. When we consider for how long a period Cean-Bermudez was engaged in occupations so remote from the course of his favourite studies, we cannot but wonder at the industry which enabled him to complete so many works, several of them not only voluminous, but demanding great application and research. His first undertaking was a Biographical Dictionary of Spanish Artists, (*Dicionario Historico de los mas ilustres Professores,* &c.) which appeared at Madrid, in six volumes 8vo.; 1800; and in executing it he could derive but little assistance from the meagre work by Palomino, the only previous one of the same kind. In 1804, he published his *' Descripcion Artistica de la Catedral de Sevilla,'* which is exceedingly interesting and valuable for the sketch it contains of the history of the different styles of architecture; and in the same year he also published a description of another very remarkable building at Seville, the Hospitel del Sangre. To this succeeded, in 1806, an essay on the Seville School of Painting. His next literary production was one to which we have already alluded—the biography of his patron Jovellanos, entitled ' *Memorias para la Vida,*' &c. 1814. But his last and most important work is a history of the architects and architecture of Spain, in four volumes 4to., 1829. This was originally commenced by Llaguno, who terminated his history with the year 1734; but Cean-Bermudez not only brought it down to 1825, but made so many additions, and inserted so many notes, that at least three-fourths of it are entirely his own. Besides the above and a few other publications, which we have not named, he left in manuscript a history of the Roman Antiquities of Spain, which will shortly appear; a General History of Painting, a Catalogue Raisonné of his own collection of engravings, and an architectural work.

RUSSIA.

The Russian Government has offered a prize of 25,000 rubles, (about 1000*l.* sterling) for the best " Treatise on the Cholera Morbus," a disease which has lately made dreadful ravages throughout the empire, and threatens, it is said, to overspread all Europe. The following is a translation of the announcement of the prize :—

" The Imperial Government of Russia proposes, on behalf of suffering humanity, to the physicians of Russia, Germany, Hungary, Italy, France, England, Sweden, and Denmark, that they shall write a treatise on the *Cholera Morbus,* embracing—1. a clear and minute description of the *nature* of the disease. 2. The causes which produced it. 3. *Description* of the manner of its propagation. 4. Whether it is contagious or not. 5. The means of *preservation* from its attack. 6. The method of cure.

" The treatises may be written in Russian, Latin, German, French, English, or Italian, and must be forwarded to the address of the ' The Medical Council at St. Petersburg,' before the 1st (13th) September, 1831. The name of the author to be sent in a separate note, carefully sealed up. The author of the treatise, which shall be considered to have best answered the terms of this invitation, shall receive the above reward of 25,000 rubles in bank assignations."

A complete edition of Von Visin's works, in 4 vols. 8vo., with a portrait and a facsimile of his hand-writing, has just appeared, and contains, besides many productions of which only extracts had previously been given to the public, or which were scattered in various periodicals, several that have never been before printed. All admirers of Russian literature must feel grateful to M. Beketov, the editor; for this collection of the writings of one of the most original and talented authors of the age of Catherine. This edition is further enriched by a biographical notice of Von Visin's life, and some account of his literary works.

Professor Dvigubsky has commenced a work that has long been a desideratum, and which cannot fail to add many important contributions to the study of zoology, namely a "Description of all the Animals of the Russian Empire." It is computed that the whole will extend to about eight fasciculi, two of which appear in the course of a twelvemonth; and it will be illustrated by about 1000 figures of the most remarkable species. The first portion contains the Mammalia, and in point of execution leaves little to be desired, except its references to the works of such naturalists as have previously noticed the same species. The descriptions are drawn up with precision and judgment: without being diffuse, they are satisfactory, and evince great industry and observation. Yet perhaps it is to be regretted that the author has not given in Latin a brief recapitulation of the distinctive marks of each species, since in that case his work would have been of material service to foreigners as well as to his own countrymen. M. Dvigubsky is already known by his Primitiæ Faunæ Mosquensis, 1802: Prodromus Faunæ Rossicæ, 1804; and by two preceding publications on the indigenous animals of Russia; he therefore brings to the present undertaking the experience of years and the fruits of long application.

LIST OF THE PRINCIPAL NEW WORKS

PUBLISHED ON THE CONTINENT,

FROM OCTOBER, 1830, TO JANUARY, 1831, INCLUSIVE.

THEOLOGY.

1 Constant, Benj., de la Religion, considérée dans sa source, ses formes, et ses déve-
loppements. Tome IV. V. 8vo. 20s.
This work is now completed in 5 vols. price 2l. 8s.
2 De la Religion Saint-Simonienne. 8vo.
3 Monod (Pasteur de l'Eglise Reformée de Lyons), Sermons. 8vo.
4 Köthe, Dr. F. A. Concordia. Die Symbolischen Bücher der evangelisch-lutheri-
schen Kirche mit Einleitungen herausgegeben. gr. 8vo. Leipsig. 7s. 6d.
5 Konstitutionelle Kirchen-zeitung aus Bayern, Herausgegeben von A. C. Lerchen-
mütter. gr. 4to. Kempten. 15s.
6 Körner, J. Kaiser Julian der Abtrünnige oder die traurigen Folgen der Verunstal-
tung des reinen Christenthums. gr. 8vo. Schneeberg. 10s.
7 Döring, D. die deutschen Kanzelredner des XVIIIten und XIXten Jahrhunderts.
gr. 8vo. Neustadt. 11s. 6d.
8 Metger, C. H. das angeborne sinnliche Verderben des Menschen aus der Erfahrung
und Bibel. gr. 8vo. Leer. 10s.
9 Quix, Ch. Necrologium Ecclesiæ B. M. V. Aquensis. gr. 4to. Aachen. 3s.
10 Geist aus Luthers Schriften, herausgegeben von D. Zimmerman. III Bd. 3te
abthl. gr. 8vo. Darmstadt. 5s.
11 Palm, v. d. über die Mosaische Erzählung von der Schöpfung der Welt. gr. 8vo.
Wesel. 2s. 6d.
12 Ritter, D. Handbuch der Kirchengeschichte. 11ten Bdes. 2te abthl. gr. 8vo.
Bonn. 7s. 6d.
13 Röhr, D. Christologische Predigten. gr. 8vo. Weimar. 7s. 6d.
14 Fiedler, F. Fabula ecclesiastico-historica. Seriem XIX. sæculorum synchronistice
exhibens. gr. fol. Leipsig. 2s. 6d.
15 Die Fünf Bücher Mosis ; verständiget von S. P. Paulus. gr. 8vo. Cassel. 4s.
16 Paulini a S. Josepho, Cler. reg. Scholarum piarum præpositi gener. orationes
XXIII. habitæ in Archygymnassio Romanæ sapientiæ, ed. C. F. Chr. Wagner.
Vol. I. 8vo. maj. Cassel. 3s.
17 Daehne, D. de Præscientiæ Divinæ cum Libertate humana concordia. 8vo. maj.
Leipsig. 4s. 6d.
18 Rosenmüller, D. Handbuch der biblischen Alterthumskunde. 4r Bd. 1ste abthl.
gr. 8vo. Leipsig. 10s.
19 Spiess, J. C. ausgewählte Predigten. 3 Bde. gr. 8vo. Franckfurt. 15s.
20 Rosenmüller, Scholia in V. T. Part IX. vol. II. 8vo. maj. Leipsig. 9s.

GERMAN ALMANACKS FOR 1831.

21 Frauentaschenbuch. 10s.
22 Taschenbuch zum geselligen Vergnügen. 11s.

23 Urania. 10s.
24 Orphea. 10s.
25 Penelope. 9s.
26 Taschenbuch d. Liebe und Freundschaft. 8s.
27 Rosen. 12s.
28 Vergissmeinnicht. 12s.
29 Rheinisches Taschenbuch. 11s.
30 Veilchen. 7s. 6d.
31 Politisches Taschenbuch. 8s.
32 Almanach dramatischer Spiele. 6s. 6d.
33 Taschenbuch ohne Titel. 7s.
34 Historisches Taschenbuch. 10s.

LAW, JURISPRUDENCE, AND ADMINISTRATION.

35 Pinheiro Ferreira, Précis d'un Cours de Droit public interne et externe. 8vo.
36 Locré, Législation Civile, Criminelle et Commerciale de la France. Tomes XXII.
    XXIII. 8vo. 19s.
37 De Félice, Leçons de Droit de la Nature et des Gens. 2 vol. 8vo.
38 Recueil Général des Anciennes Lois Françaises, depuis l'an 420 jusqu'à la Révo-
    lution de 1789. Tome XXI. 8vo.
39 Procès des derniers Ministres de Charles X. 2 vol. 8vo. 16s. 6d.
40 Warnkönig, Prof. L. A. Doctrina juris philosophica aphorismis distincta in usum
    scholarum. 8vo. maj. Aachen. 7s.
41 Heise und Cropp, Juristische Abhandlungen, mit Entscheidung des Ober-appella-
    tionsgerichts der vier freien Städte Deutschlands. 2r Bd; gr. 8vo. Hamb. 15s.
42 Corpus juris civilis ins Deutsche übersetz von Dr. C. E. Otto. 4s hft. gr. 8vo.
    Leipzig. 2s. 6d.
43 Hartitzsch, D. das römische Privatrecht. gr. 8vo. Leipzig. 17s.
44 Gaji, Institutionum Comment. IV. a A. G. Heffter. 12mo. Bonn. 3s.
45 Mayer, D. das römische Recht nach seinen allgemeinen Grundsätzen. gr. 8vo.
    Stuttgardt. 12s. 6d.

MORALS, EDUCATION, AND POLITICAL ECONOMY.

46 Garnier, Précis d'un Cours de Psychologie. 8vo. 5s. 6d.
47 Doctrine de Saint-Simon. Ière Année. 8vo. 2de Edit. 1l. 10s
48 Krug, W. T. System der practischen Philosophie. 1r theil. Rechtslehre. 2te
    auflage. gr. 8vo. Königsberg. 9s.
49 Corpus Philosophorum optimæ notæ, qui ab restauratione litterarum ad Kantium
    usque floruerunt. Ed, A. G. Froerer. T. III. sect. 1. 8vo. maj. Stuttgardt. 7s.
50 Ohlert, D. der Idealrealismus als Metaphysik. 1r theil. gr. 8vo. Neustadt. 6s
51 Elvenich, D. die Moralphilosophie. 1r Bd. gr. 8vo. Bonn. 7s. 6d.

MATHEMATICS, PHYSICS AND CHEMISTRY.

52 Guillond, Traité de Chimie appliquée aux Arts et Métiers, et principalement à la
    fabrication des acides sulfuriques, &c. IIde partie. 12mo. 6s.
53 Pouillet, Elémens de Physique Expérimentale, et de Météorologie. Tome II.
    2e partie. 8vo.
54 Barailon, Méthodes nouvelles et faciles de calculer les Progressions génératrices,
    pour former les puissances et extraire leurs racines, de multiplier et de diviser.
    2de Edition, revue, &c. 8vo. 5s.
55 Montucla, Histoire des Recherches sur la Quadrature du Cercle, avec une addition
    concernant les problèmes de la duplication de la cube et de la trisection de
    l'angle. 8vo. 6s.
56 Rogg, S. Handbuch der Mathematischen Litteratur. Sect. I. 8vo. maj. Tubing. 16s.

NATURAL SCIENCES.

57 Cuvier et Valenciennes, Histoire Naturelle des Poissons. Tome VI. 8vo. 13s. 6d. — 4to. 18s.

58 Humboldt et Bonpland, Voyage. Sixième partie. Botanique. Révision des Graminées. Livraisons XXI. XXII. XXIII. folio. each 2l. 8s.

59 Geoffroy St. Hilaire et F. Cuvier, Histoire Naturelle des Mammifères, avec des figures originales coloriées, dessinées d'après les animaux vivans. Livr. XI. 4to. 9s.

60 Duperrey, Voyage autour du Monde. Première division. Zoologie, Livr. XIX. folio. 12s.

61 Lesson, Histoire Naturelle des Colibris. Livraison III. 8vo.

62 ————————————— suivi d'un Supplément à l'Histoire naturelle des Oiseaux Mouches. Livraison I. 8vo. 5s.

63 Almanach du Bon Jardinier pour 1831. 7s.

64 Dictionnaire Classique d'Histoire Naturelle. Tome XVI. 8vo. avec planches. 12s.

65 Guérin, Magasin d'Entomologie, ou Descriptions et Figures d'Insectes inédits ou non encore figurés; ouvrage destiné à établir une Correspondance entre les Entomologistes de tous les pays, &c. Liv. II. 2s. 6d.

66 Duhamel du Monceau, Traité des Arbres Fruitiers ; Nouvelle Edition, par Poiteau et Turpin. Livraisons LXV. LXVI. each 30s.

67 Redouté, Choix des plus belles Fleurs prises dans différentes familles du Règne végétal. Livraisons I. à XXIII. each 12s.

68 Wildenow, D. Grundriss der Kräuterkunde zu Vorlesungen entworfen. 3r praktischer theil. 8vo. Berlin. 12s. 6d.

69 Hessel, D. Krystallometrie der Krystallonomie und Krystallographie, mit 11 kupfern. gr. 8vo. Leipzig. 9s.

70 Presl, C. B. Symbolæ botanicæ. Fasc. I. folio maj. Prag. 1l. 1s.

71 Meigen, J. W. Systematische Beschreibung der bekannten europäischen zweiflügeligen Insekten. 6r theil, mit 12 steintafeln. gr. 8vo. Hamm. 17s. 6d.

72 Brown, R. Vermischte Botanische Schriften übersetzt von Dr. Nees von Esenbeck. IVr Bd. gr. 8vo. Nürnburg. 17s.

73 Frank, J. C. Rastadts Flora. 8vo. Heidelberg. 4s.

74 Wiedemann, D., aussereuropäische zweiflügelige Insekten. 2r theil. gr. 8vo. Hamm. 1l. 3s.

75 Zimmermann, D. Grundzüge der Phytologie. gr. 8vo. 17s.

76 Martius, Dr. von, Amœnitates botanicæ Monacenses. 3te liefer, mit 4 Kupfern. gr. 8vo. Frankfurt. 7s. 6d.

77 Germar, D. Grundriss der Krystalkunde. Mit 11 Kupfern. 8vo. Halle. 7s. 6d.

MEDICAL SCIENCES

78 Bourdon, Principes de Physiologie comparée. 8vo. 7s. 6d.

79 Menière, l'Hotel Dieu de Paris en Juillet et Aout 1830 : Histoire de ce qui s'est passé dans cette hôpital pendant et après les trois grandes journées. 8vo. 8s.

80 Denis, Recherches Expérimentales sur le Sang Humain. 8vo. 4s.

81 Cruveilhier, Anatomie Pathologique du Corps Humain. Liv. IX. folio. 9s.

82 Richard, Elémens d'Histoire Naturelle Médicale. 2 vols. 8vo. 18s.

83 Devreux, Mémoire sur les Tumeurs sanguines de la vulve et du vagin. 8vo. 3s. 6d.

84 Dictionnaire Historique de la Médecine Ancienne et Moderne, ou Précis de l'Histoire général technologique et littéraire de la Médecine, suivi de la Bibliographie médicale du 19e siècle, et d'un répertoire bibliographique par ordre de matières. Tome I. 2e partie. 8vo. 6s.

85 Béral, Nomenclature et Classification Pharmaceutiques. 4to. 12s.

86 Muro y Castella, Etude sur le Système organico-vital de l'Homme. 8vo. 4s. 6d.

87 Baudelocque, Traité des Hémorrhagies Utérines de l'Utérus, qui surviennent pendant la grossesse, dans le cours du travail et après l'accouchement. 8vo.

88 Tiedemann, Traité Complet de Physiologie de l'Homme. 2 vol. 8vo. 11s.
89 Orfila et Lesueur, Traité des Exhumations Juridiques et Considérations sur les changemens physiques que les Cadavres éprouvent en se pourrissant dans la terre, dans l'eau, dans les fosses d'aisance, et dans le fumier. 2 vol. 8vo. 10s. 6d.
90 Devergie, Clinique de la Maladie Syphilitique. Liv. XIV. 4to. 8s. —
91 Descourtilz, de l'Impuissance et de la Stérilité. 2 vol. 8vo. 12s.
92 Aulagnier, Dictionnaire des Substances Alimentaires indigènes et exotiques, et de leurs propriétés, &c. 2 vol. 8vo. 12s.
93 Foy, Cours de Pharmacologie. 2 vol. 8vo. 16s.
94 Meyer, Dr. F. J. F. Phytotomie. Mit 14 Kupfern. 8vo. *Berlin*. 15s.
95 Homöopathische und allopathische Leucht-und Brandkugeln. 1r Bd. 1s hft. gr. 8vo. *Leipzig*. 2s. 6d.
96 Hacker, Dr. Litteratur der syphilitischen Krankheiten vom Jahre 1794 bis mit 1829. gr. 8vo. *Leipzig*. 7s.
97 Rosas Dr. Handbuch der theoretischen und praktischen Augenheilkunde. 3 Bde. gr. 8vo. *Wien*. 2l. 2s.
98 Hüter, D. die dynamischen Geburtsstörungen. 2 Bde. gr. 8vo. *Berlin*. 16s.
99 Thomassen, D. Abhandlung über die Masern. gr. 8vo. *Osnabrück*. 5s.
100 Groos, Dr. die Lehre von der Mania sine delirio. 8vo. *Heidelberg*. 4s.
101 Handschuh, D. die Syphilitischen Krankheits-formen und ihre Heilung. gr. 8vo. *München*. 9s.
102 Riedel, D. Prags Irrenanstalt. gr. 8vo. *Prag*. 5s.
103 Tiedemann, F. Physiologie des Menschen. 1r Bd. gr. 8vo. *Darmstadt*. 17s. 6d.
104 Benedict, D. Bemerkungen über Hydrocele, Sarkocele, und Variocele. 8vo. *Leipzig*. 4s.
105 Brandes, Dr. die Mineralquellen zu Falinhausen. 8vo. *Lemgo*. 4s.
106 Böer, Dr. L. J. Libri de Arte Obstetricia. 8vo. maj. *Wien*. 13s.
107 Römer, D. A. Handbuch der Anatomie des Menschlichen Korpers. 2 Bde. gr. 8vo. *Wien*. 17s.
108 Bonnet, Dr. über die Natur und Heilung der Leber-Krankheiten. gr. 8vo. *Ilmenau*. 3s.

MILITARY:

109 Latour d'Auvergne, Mémoire sur l'Organisation Militaire. 8vo.
110 Manuel des Gardes Nationales de France, contenant l'Ecole de Bataillon, &c. 2 vol. 7s.
111 —— du Garde National à Cheval. 18mo. 3s. 6d.
112 Oostkamp, J. A. het Leven, de voornaamste Daden en Letgevallen van den Kommandeur Jan von Galen, Heer van Papendorp, met Platen. 8vo. *Leipzig*. 6s.
113 Nissen, N. Synchronistische Tafeln der Universal-Geschichte. imp. fo. 1l. 15s.
114 Blesson, L. grosse Befestigungskunst. 1ste abthlg. 8vo. *Berlin*. 17s. 6d.
115 Geschichte der Kriege in Europa seit 1792 bis Ludwig XVI. 4r theil. mit Plänen. gr. 8vo. *Leipzig*. 15s.

MISCELLANEOUS ARTS AND SCIENCES.

116 Prechtl, J. J. technologische Encyclopädie. 2r theil. gr. 8vo. *Stuttgardt*. 17s. 6d.
117 Unger, D. Uebungen aus der angewandten Mathematik. 1r Bd. mit 5 Kupfern. gr. 8vo. *Berlin*. 15s.
118 Schmöger, F. von, die ersten Elemente der Astronomie und Chronologie. gr. 8vo. *Regensburg*. 5s.

FINE ARTS.

119 Mionnet, Description des Médailles Antiques Grecques et Romaines, avec leur degré de rareté. Tome V. 8vo. 1l. 12s.
120 Vues prises dans les Pyrénées Françaises, dessinées par J. Jourdan, et accompagnéesd'un texte descriptif par E. Froissard. Liv. IV. V. folio. each 8s.

121 Hittorf et Zanth, Architecture Antique de la Sicile. Liv. VIII. folio.
122 Clarac, Mélanges des Antiquités Grecques et Romaines, ou Observations sur plusieurs bas-reliefs antiques du Musée Royal du Louvre, &c. 8vo.
123 Reveil, Musée de Peinture et de Sculpture. Livraisons 99 à 108.
124 Ecole Anglaise, Recueil de Tableaux, Statues et Bas-Reliefs des plus célèbres Artistes Anglais dépuis le temps d'Hogarth jusqu'à nos jours, gravé à l'eau-forte sur acier, accompagné de Notices descriptives, critiques et historiques en Français et en Anglais. Liv. I. à VIII. 8vo. each 1s. 6d.
125 Girault-Duvivier, Encyclopédie Elémentaire de l'Antiquité, ou Origine, Progrès Etat de Perfection des Arts et des Sciences chez les Anciens, d'après les meilleurs auteurs. 4 vol. 8vo. 1l. 12s.
126 Monumens Funéraires Choisis dans les Cimetières de Paris et les principales Villes de France : Liv. I. à IX. each 3s. 6d.
127 Cornelius, Peter von, Umrisse zu Dante's Paradies. Mit 9 Kupfern. gr. 4to. *Leipzig.* 9s.

HISTORY, BIOGRAPHY, VOYAGES, TRAVELS, &c.

128 Précis Historique, Généalogique et Littéraire de la Maison d'Orléans. 8vo. 6s. 6d.
129 Annuaire Historique Universel pour 1829. 8vo. 16s.
130 Duperrey, Voyage autour du Monde. IIIe Division. Historique. Livraison VI. 16s.
131 Schoell, Cours d'Histoire des Etats Européens depuis le bouleversement de l'Empire Romain d'Occident jusqu'en 1789. Tomes VII. à IX. 8vo. each 10s.
To be completed in 30 vols.
132 Polacki, Fragmens de l'Histoire de Pologne. Marina Muiszech. Liv. I. 8s.
133 Dictionnaire Complet, Géographique, Statistique et Commercial du Royaume de France et de ses Colonies, &c. Liv. VIII. IX. (NAB—SES). in 18mo.
134 La Garde Royale pendant les évènemens du 28 Juillet au 5 Aout. 1830. Par un Officier employé à l'Etat-Major. 2de édition. 8vo. 4s.
135 Bonnard, Costumes du XIIIe, XIVe, et XVe siècles, &c. Tome II. Liv. I. 4to. 6s. 6d.
136 Rifaud, Voyage en Egypte, en Nubie, et lieux circonvoisins, depuis 1805 jusqu'à 1827. Liv. I. à VIII. folio. each 10s. 6d.
To be completed in 3 vols. folio, each containing 100 plates, and 5 vols. 8vo. of text.
137 St. Hilaire, Voyage dans les Provinces de Rio de Janeiro et de Minas Geraes. 2 vol. 8vo. 20s.
138 De Viel Castel, Collection de Costumes, Armes et Meubles, pour servir à l'Histoire de France, depuis le commencement de la Monarchie jusqu'à nos jours. Liv. XXXI. 4to. 16s.
To be completed in 60 parts.
139 Histoire Générale des Voyages, ou Nouvelle Collection des Rélations de Voyage par mer et par terre, mise en ordre et complétée jusqu'à nos jours. Par C. A. Walckenaer. Tome XX, 8vo. 9s. 6d.
140 Les Incendies de la Normandie en 1830 ; Scènes historiques contemporaines. 8vo. 6s. 6d.
141 Schlegel, Fred. Tableau de l'Histoire Moderne, traduit de l'Allemand par M. J. Cherbuliez. 2 vols. 8vo. 20s.
142 Histoire Scientifique et Militaire de l'Expédition Française en Egypte. Tome III. (Expédition Militaire, Tome I.) 8vo.
The work will be completed in 12 vols. 8vo. or 60 livraisons, with an atlas in 4to. each livraison 6s. 6d.
143 Palmiere de Micciché, Pensées et Souvenirs Historiques et Contemporains. Tome IIe. 8vo.
144 Jean Temporal, de l'Afrique, contenant les Navigations des Capitains Portugais et autres faites au dit pays jusqu'aux Indes, tant Orientales qu'Occidentales, parties de Perse, Arabie heureuse, pierreuse et déserte ; ensemble la description de la Haute Ethiopie, pays du Grand-Seigneur Prête-Jean, et du noble fleuve du Nil, &c. Tome II. 8vo.

145 C. Cuvier, Introduction à l'Etude de l'Histoire Générale.' 8vo.
146 Carlyle, T. Leben Schillers, aus dem Englischen eingeleitet durch Göthe. gr. 8vo Frankfurt. 12s. 6d.
147 Stuart, M. romeinsche Geschiedenissen. Nieuwe Uitgave in twintig Deelen. Mit platen. Erstel Deel. 8vo. Leipzig, 10s.
148 Jahn, A. M. Reise von Mainz nach Egypten, Jerusalem, und Konstantinopol, in 1826—27. 5 hfte. gr. 8vo. Mains. 11s. 6d.
149 Lipowsky, F. J. Lebens-und Regierungsgeschichte des Churfürsten von Bayern, Karl Albert, nachmaligen Kaisers Karl VII. 8vo. Leipzig. 7s. 6d.
150 Lorentz, D. Handbuch der deutschen Geschichte. gr. 8vo. Halle. 6s.
151 Paganinis Leben und Charakter nach Schottky. Mit Bildniss. gr. 8vo. Hamburg. 2s. 6d.'
152 Mayerhoff, D. Johann Reuchlin und seine Zeit. Mit einer Vorrede des Prof. Neander. Mit Portrait. gr. 8vo. Berlin. 8s.
153 Münch, D. E. Geschichte des Hauses und Landes Fürstenberg. Mit Kupfern. 2r Bd. gr. 8vo. Aachen. 10s,
154 Rommel, D. von, Philipp der Grossmüthige, Landgraf von Hessen. 3 vol. gr. 8vo. Giessen. 1l. 10s.
155 Pahl, J. G. Geschichte von Wirtemberg. 6 vol. 8vo. Stuttgardt. 1l. 4s.
156 Schottky, J. N. Prag wie es war und wie es ist. gr. 8vo. Prag. 16s.
157 Wagner, G. W. Statistisch-topographisch-historische Beschreibung des Grossherzogthums Hessen. 3 Bde. gr. 8vo. Darmstadt. 10s.
158 Wit, J. Gen. v. Dörring, Fragmente aus meinem Leben III. Bdes. 2te abthlg. 8vo. Leipzig. 10s.'
159 Lamottefouqué, Baronin de, Blick auf Gesinnung und Streben in den Jahren 1774 bis 1778. 8vo. Stuttgart. 2s.
160 Adrian, Skizzen aus England. 1r thl. mit Kupfern. gr. 12mo. Frankf. 9s.
161 Geschichte der Staatsveranderung in Frankreich unter Ludwig XVI. 5r thl. gr. 8vo. Leipzig. 10s.
162 Schmidt, M. J. Geschichte der Deutschen. 26r und 27r thl. 8vo. Ulm. 16s.
163 Wiecke, K. W. Abriss der allgemeinen Geschichte 2té abthl. gr. 8vo. Glogau. 5s.
164 Plath, Dr. Geschichte des östlichen Asiens. 1r. thl. gr. 8vo. Göttingen. 18s.

CLASSICAL LITERATURE, PHILOLOGY, BIBLIOGRAPHY.

165 Querard, La France Littéraire, ou Dictionnaire Bibliographique, &c. Tome IV. 1ère partie (HA—KY). 8vo. 10s.
166 Bibliothèque Latine Française. Liv. XLVI. (Œuvres Complètes de Cicéron. Oraisons. Tome III.) 8vo. 9s. 6d.
———————— Terence, par Amar. Tome II. 8vo. 9s. 6d.
167 Bibliotheca Classica Latina ed Lemaire. L. A. Seneca, pars prima, et M. A. Lucani Pharsalia. Vol. I. 8vo.
168 Meincke, Dr. Aug. Quæstionum Scenicarum Specimen. III. 4to. Berlin. 4s. 6d.
169 Plutarchi Vitæ, c. G. H. Schæfer. Vol. VI. gr. 18mo. Leipzig. 6s.
170 Poetarum Latinorum, Hostii, Lævii, C. Licinii, Calvi, C. Helvii, Linnæ, C. Valgii, Rufi, Domitii, Marsi, aliorumque vitæ et carminum reliquiæ. Edidit M. A. Weichert. 8vo. maj. Leipzig. 10s.'
171 Lectiones variæ ex. M. T. Ciceronis editionibus Oxoniensi et Neapolitana descriptæ. Edit. Ernest. min. Supplm. Part. post. Vol. II. et III. gr. 8vo. Halle. 1l. 5s.
172 Lunemanns Wörterbuch zu Homers Ilias. 2te Auflage, besorgt von Dr. Ebert. gr. 8vo. Königsberg. 5s.
173 Vogel, A. Hercules secundum Græcorum poetas et historicos antiquiores descriptus et illustratus. gr. 4to. Halle. 2s. 6d.
174 Blume, Dr. Iter Italicum. 3r Band. 8vo. Halle. 6s.
175 Struve, Dr. Quæstionum de dialecto Herodoti Specimen. III. 4to. maj. Königsberg. 1s.
176 Truka, F. Praktisches Lehrbuch der cechischen vulgo bömischen Sprache. gr. 8vo. Brünn. 2s. 6d.

177 Wolfs, F. A. Vorlesungen über die vier ersten Gesänge von Homer's Ilias. 1r Bd. gr. 8vo. *Bern.* 5s.
178 Aetoli, A. Fragmenta collecta et illustrata ab A. Capellmann. 8vo. maj. *Bonn.* 2s. 6d.
179 Fuss, J. D. Carminum Latinorum. Pars nova. 8vo. maj. *Bonn.* 2s. 6d.
180 Gaal, G. von, Sprichwörterbuch in sechs Sprachen. 8vo. *Wien.* 7s. 6d.
181 Schwedisches Lesebuch, Herausgegeben von Freese und Lappe. Prosaischer theil. gr. 8vo. *Stralsund.* 7s.
182 Wagemann, D. des P. Ovidius fünf Trauerbücher travestirt, mit Allegaten des Latein. Textes. gr. 8vo. *Ludwigsburg.* 5s.
183 M. T. Ciceronis Oratio pro A. Cluentio. Ed. J. Classen. 8vo. maj. *Bonn.* 6s.
184 Justini, M. Martyris et Philosophi Apologiæ. Edid. J. W. J. Braunius. 8vo. maj. *Bonn.* 4s.
185 Lexicon Græco-Latinum manuale ex optimis libris concinnatum. Editio stereotypa. 16mo. *Leipzig.* 7s.
186 Seiler, A. Kurzgefasste Grammatik der Sorben-Wendischen Sprache. gr. 8vo. *Bautzen.* 4s.
187 Taciti, C. C. Dialogus de Oratoribus ed. Orell. 8vo. maj. *Zürich.* 5s.
188 Æschyli Persæ; Quæstion Æschylear. Specimen IV. Auct. Dr. Haupt. 8vo. maj. *Leipzig.* 7s.
189 Fritzsche, F. V. de Babyloniis Aristophanis Commentatio. 8vo. maj. *Leipz.* 2s.
190 Gurlitt, J. Archäologische Schriften, gesammelt von C. Müller. gr. 8vo. *Altona.* 10s.
191 Palairet, E. Thesaurus Ellipsium Latinarum, ed. M. Runkelius. 8vo. maj. *Leipzig.* 7s. 6d.
192 Taciti, C. C. Annales rec. G. H. Walther. IV. Vol. 8vo. maj. *Halle.* 1l. 5s.

MISCELLANEOUS LITERATURE.

193 Eberhard, A. G. Gesammelte Schriften. 20 Bde. 16mo. *Halle.* 1l. 5s.
194 Kurowsky-Eichen, F. v. Sämmtliche Werke. 1r Bd. 8vo. *Gotha.* 5s.
195 Kriegk, G. L. belehrende Darstellungen für das höhere Jugendalter. gr. 8vo. *Frankfurt.* 8s.
196 Paul, Jean, das Schönste und Gediegenste aus seinen Schriften, ausgewählt von D. Döring. 16mo. I.—VI. Bdchen. 18s.
197 Herder G. G. Sämmtliche Werke. 60 Bdchen. 16mo. *Stuttgart.* 3l. 10s.
198 Böhme, Jacob, Sämmtliche Werke, herausgegeben von K. W. Schiebler. 1r Bd. gr. 8vo. *Leipzig.* 4s.

POETRY, THE DRAMA, &c.

199 Almanach des Dames pour l'an 1831. 8s.
200 Boucher de Perthes, Chants Armoricains, ou Souvenirs de Basse-Bretagne. 18mo.
201 Thévenot, Hommages Poétiques et Poésies Diverses. 18mo. 5s. 6d.
202 Almanach des Muses pour l'année 1831. 4s. 6d.
203 Jacinthe Leclere, Chansons. 18mo. 4s.
204 Dupont, La Contre-Lettre, ou le Jesuite, drame en deux actes, 8vo. 2s. 6d.
205 Napoléon à Berlin, ou la Rediugote Grise, comédie historique. 8vo. 2s.
206 Dupaty et Regnier, Napoléon, ou Schoenbrunn et Ste. Hélène, drame historique. 8vo. 2s. 6d.
207 Anicet Bourgeois, Napoléon, pièce historique en trois parties. 8vo. 2s. 6d.
208 Mélesville, La Coalition, tableau populaire. 8vo. 2s.
209 Fontan, Jeanne la folle, ou la Bretagne au XIIIe Siècle ; drame historique en cinq actes, en vers. 8vo. 5s. 6d.
210 Martinez de la Rosa, Aben Hamet, ou la Révolte des Maures sous Philippe II. drame historique. 8vo. 6s. 6d.
211 Victor Ducange, Le Jésuite, drame en trois actes et en six tableaux. 8vo. 2s. 6d.
212 Oefele, von, Ludwig der Heilige in Ægypten. Schauspiel in 5 Aufzügen. 8vo. *Gera.* 3s.

213 Grabbe, die Hohenstaufen. Ein Cyclus von Tragödien. 2r Bd. 8vo. *Frank.* 7s.
214 Gräffe, K. H. die Reise zum Musikfeste, in neun Gesangen. 12mo. *Zurich.* 4s.
215 Toel, L. dichterische Versuche. 8vo. *Leer.* 8s.
216 Blankensee, G. Graf von, der Wanderer. Gedicht in zwey Gesängen. 8vo. *Breslau.* 2s. 6d.
217 Duller, E. die Wittelsbacher. Balladen. gr. 8vo. *München.* 5s.
218 Immermann, K. Fulifäntchen. Ein Heldengedicht in 3 Gesängen. 12mo. *Hamburg.* 4s.

NOVELS AND ROMANCES.

219 Stendhal, le Rouge et le Noir; Chronique du XIXe Siècle. 2 vol. 8vo. 20s.
220 Zschokke, les Matinées Suisses : seconde Série. Trad. de l'Allemand. 4 vols. 12mo. 16s.
221 Ricard, le Drapeau Tricolore. 4 vol. 12mo. 16s.
222 Adolphe Selmour, ou Cinq Ans de la Vie d'un Homme qui n'est pas Mort. Roman Historique. 3 vol. 12mo.
223 Bouilly, Contes Populaires. 2 vol. 12mo. 12s.
224 Pigault-Le-Brun, Contes à mon Petit-Fils. 2 vol. 12mo.
225 Louise Maignaud, les Etudiens : épisode de la Révolution de 1830. 4 vol. 12mo.
226 Harring Harro, Firn Malthes, des Wildschutzen Flucht. Scene in Bayrischen Hochlande. Eine novelle mit Liedern, 8vo. *Leipzig.* 4s. 6d.
227 Herbig, F. de Graven van Herst, eene vorspronkelike Nederlandsche Roman. Erste Deel. gr. 8vo. *Leipzig.* 13s.
228 Liebrocke, A. die Grafen von Löwenhaupt. Gemälde des XIII. Jahrhunderts. 2 thle. 8vo. *Leipzig.* 12mo. 9s.
229 Schopenhauer, G. Novellen. 2 thle. 12mo. *Frankfurt.* 14s.
230 Lessmann, D. Meister Marcola und die Nothlüge. 8vo. *Berlin.* 6s.
231 ———— das Spottgedicht. Ein Nachtstück. 8vo. *Berlin.* 6s.
232 Falco, B. die Rache des Amor. Eine Gallerie von Nachtstücken in Teniers Manier. 2 thle. 8vo. *Gera.* 13s.
233 Müchler, K. der Hausfreund. 8vo. *Berlin.* 5s.
234 ———— Kriminalgeschichten. 3r Bd. 8vo. *Berlin.* 5s.
235 ———— die Bigame. Eine Kriminalgeschichte. 8vo. *Berlin.* 5s.
235 Schmidt, H. der Dominikaner. 8vo. *Berlin.* 7s. 6d.

ORIENTAL LITERATURE.

237 Lois de Manon, publiées en Sanscrit, avec des Notes contenant un choix de Variantes et de Scholies, par A. L. Deslongchamps. 3e et dern. partie. 8vo.
238 Vendidad Sade. par E. Burnouf. Texte Zend. Liv. VI. folio. 16s.
239 Bohlen, das alte Indien : mit besonderer Rücksicht auf Ægypten. 2 thle. gr. 8vo. *Königsberg.* 1l. 2s.
240 Schlegel, A. W. von, Indische Bibliothek. 3ten Bdes. 1stes hft. gr. 8vo. *Bonn.* 4s. 6d.
241 Locmanni Fabulæ, ed. Dr. Roediger. 4to. *Halle.* 5s.

LONDON:

PRINTED BY C. ROWORTH, BELL YARD,
TEMPLE BAR

CONTENTS

OF

N°. XIV.

———◆———

THE

FOREIGN

QUARTERLY REVIEW.

ART. I.—1. *Traité de la Lumière.* Par J. F. W. Herschel, traduit de l'Anglais avec Notes par MM. P. F. Verhulst, Docteur en Sciences, et A. Quetelet, Directeur de l'Observatoire de Bruxelles. Tome premier. Paris. 1829. 8vo.
2. *Mémoires de l'Académie Royale des Sciences de l'Institut de France.*—*Mémoire sur la Diffraction de la Lumière*, Tom. V. *Mémoire sur la Double Refraction.* Tom. VII. Par M. A. Fresnel. Paris. 1826, 1827. 4to.

THE appearance of a French translation of Mr. Herschel's admirable Essay on Light brings it within the scope of a Review devoted to foreign literature and science; and we gladly avail ourselves of the circumstance to couple it with the two Memoirs whose titles we have transcribed as an introduction to the following remarks on one of the most interesting, most important, and, at present, most assiduously cultivated of all the branches of natural philosophy.

The *Essay on Light* was originally published in the Encyclopedia Metropolitana, and though the only treatise in our language which can be said to afford any thing like a systematic view of the present state of that interesting but difficult branch of physics, it does not seem hitherto to have attracted much attention; owing no doubt to its abstruse aspect, and the frequent recurrence of algebraic formulæ, so repulsive to all lovers of *science made easy.* By translating it into an idiom more generally understood, and placing it within the reach of the continental philosophers, from whom it must have been till now in a great measure excluded, not only by the language but also by the difficulty of access to that ponderous, expensive, and crude mass of literary and scientific matter, of which it forms one of the most valuable portions, MM. Verhulst and Quetelet have greatly extended its sphere of usefulness, and rendered at the same time an acceptable service to science. The two Memoirs of Fresnel give an account of the experiments, and explain the theoretical views, by which that ingenious, indefatigable, and much lamented philosopher, endeavoured to connect the various phenomena of optics with the hypothesis of an undulatory propagation of light through the medium of an elastic ether.

The science of light, like almost every other department of natural philosophy, is entirely of modern creation. Two, indeed, of its most remarkable properties, namely, its propagation in straight lines and the equality of the angles of incidence and re-flexion, were known even in the school of Plato, and are assumed as axioms in the treatise of *Optics* ascribed to Euclid. In the time of Ptolemy the subject of atmospherical refraction had become an object of attention to astronomers, though it would seem that Ptolemy himself had not been aware of the pheno-menon, or at least had not understood its importance, when he composed his Almagest, as no mention is made of it in that cele-brated work. But it may be affirmed that the knowledge of the *fact* of refraction constituted the whole of the ancient Dioptrics; for the law which it follows was not discovered till the time of Descartes. Alhazen, Vitello, and Roger Bacon, in the middle ages, successfully turned their attention to the subject, though it can hardly be said that their labours had any influence in accele-rating the discoveries of later times. Maurolycus, who lived in the sixteenth century, has been celebrated for explaining the sim-ple paradox proposed by Aristotle, viz. why the image of the sun formed by a beam of light passing through a very small hole of any figure whatever, triangular for example, always appears round? This philosopher had some vague notions respecting the true nature of vision and the functions of the different humours of the eye; he fell, however, into the error of supposing the images of objects not to be formed on the dark retina, but on the crystal-line humour; an erroneous opinion, which was also entertained by his still more celebrated contemporary, Baptista Porta. The true explanation of the manner in which the rays are refracted through all the humours of the eye, and form a distinct picture on the retina, belongs to Kepler, so famous for his discovery of the elliptic orbits and laws of motion of the planets. Snellius claims the honour of having been the first who discovered the true law of refraction, though the simple and elegant enunciation of the constant ratio of the sines is due to Descartes. Soon after that period the physical sciences began to make rapid advance-ment, and the optical properties of light to be studied with great care, in consequence of their application to the theory of the astronomical telescope.

But the most difficult, if not the most useful, questions con-nected with light, are those which relate to its physical nature, and the manner in which it is propagated through space. The first traces of speculation on this intricate subject are to be met with in the writings of Aristotle. This philosopher, laying it down as an axiom that the quantity of matter in a moving body is inversely proportional to the velocity, and that the velocity of light is infinite, conceived it to be immaterial, or denied it to be a substance. It is not, however, to the philosophers of ancient Greece that we need look for instruction in physics, respecting which their ignorance is not less conspicuous than their advancement in pure geometry and the sciences of abstract reasoning. Descartes was the first who speculated philosophically on the essence of light. According to Descartes the universe is filled with an extremely subtle fluid, composed of little globules *of the second element;* and he supposed light to result from a pressure on this fluid, produced by the agitation of the sun or other luminous body. Believing, with Aristotle, that its propagation is instantaneous, he was obliged to suppose the fluid to be entirely inflexible, in order that motion might be instantaneously communicated from one extremity of it to the other. In maintaining his opinion respecting the instantaneous transmission of light, it is curious to observe Descartes reasoning as follows :—" If," says he, " the motion of light is progressive, it will follow that the celestial bodies will not be seen in their true places, which is contrary to observation." That the stars are not seen in their true places, for the very reason which he assigns, is at present one of the best established facts in astronomy; and it is a striking instance of the acute and penetrating mind of Descartes, that he was for a long time the only one who perceived this mathematical consequence, which, had it been better examined, might have hastened, by fourscore years, the important discovery of the aberration.

Two theories, as most of our readers are aware, have long divided the opinion of philosophers respecting the nature and propagation of light. One of these consists in supposing it to be composed of particles of excessive minuteness, projected from the luminous body with a velocity equal to about 200,000 miles in a second of time. This hypothesis was adopted by Newton, and has been followed by the greater part of writers on optics. Its general principles are easily comprehended; and, having regard only to the more obvious properties of light, it affords an easy and intelligible explanation of the phenomena. With the aid of certain assumptions, which may be admitted without great difficulty, it also satisfactorily accounts for numerous classes of facts which have been discovered by the diligence of recent observers; and, which is of the utmost importance in order to establish any physical theory on permanent foundations, it readily admits of the application of mathematical reasoning, and can be pursued to its consequences by the same sort of analysis which embraces so many other phenomena resulting from the action of molecular forces. The other hypothesis, which is a modification of that of Descartes, is due to the celebrated Huyghens. It supposes light to be produced by the vibrations of an ethereal fluid, of great elasticity, which pervades all space and penetrates all substances, and to which the luminous body gives an impulse which is propagated with inconceivable rapidity, in spherical superficies, by a sort of tremor or undulation, as sound is conveyed through the atmosphere, or a wave along the surface of water. Both of these hypotheses are rendered probable by their giving a mechanical explanation of a vast number of observed facts; but they are both also exposed to difficulties of such a nature as to require the utmost ingenuity on the part of their respective supporters to combat successfully.

It is not our intention, in the following pages, to enter into a detailed examination of the evidences by which the two theories are supported; our object is only to explain the general train of reasoning by which they are respectively applied to the facts made known by observation; facts which are now become so numerous, that any theory which embraces them all must either be the true one, or at least have a close analogy to it.

Agreeably to the received doctrine of corpuscular action, the intensity of the force with which two molecules of matter attract or repel each other, depends on the mutual distance of these molecules, and the law according to which it varies may be such, that even within the narrow limits to which the sphere of action can be supposed to extend, there may be several changes from attraction to repulsion; that is to say, if at a certain distance two molecules attract one another, at a greater or less distance they may exercise a repulsive force, and thus the forces of attraction and repulsion alternately prevail according as the distances of the molecules are increased or diminished. Now in the corpuscular theory of light, the phenomena of reflexion and refraction are referred to the preponderance of the one or the other of these two forces. A molecule of light, approaching the surface of a smooth polished body, encounters a repulsive force, and is thrown off, making an angle with the surface equal to that by which it approached it, in the same way as an ivory ball rebounds when struck against an obstacle. Another molecule approaches the surface of a diaphanous body, where, owing to a difference in the nature or arrangement of the component particles from that which obtained in the former instance, it encounters an attractive force, which, acting in a direction perpendicular to the surface, changes the direction of the molecule, and accelerates its velocity.

On escaping from the medium, the same effects take place in an inverted order.

Admitting this reciprocal action of the molecules of light and other bodies to be the physical cause of reflexion and refraction, a difficulty presents itself in the outset, which has only been evaded by assumptions which the opponents of the corpuscular theory regard as violent and gratuitous. If a series of molecules, following one another in the same straight line, are animated with equal velocities, it is natural to suppose that, in impinging against the same surface, they must all be affected precisely in the same manner. For example, if a molecule of light is reflected from the surface of a body, we naturally conclude that every succeeding molecule, approaching the same point of the same surface, must be reflected in like manner; so that if reflexion takes place at all, it must be perfect. Experience, however, proves that this is by no means the case; for it is found that while some of the molecules are reflected from a given point, others of them, impinging against the same point, are refracted or absorbed; or it may happen that two succeeding molecules are refracted differently, as takes place with regard to certain species of crystals. The theoretical explanation of these phenomena by the Newtonian hypothesis, notwithstanding all the ingenuity and success with which it has been developed, is still unsatisfactory, and strikingly deficient in that simplicity which assures the mind that it has reached the last step in the process of generalization. Newton himself supposed the molecules to be subject to periodic changes with regard to their aptitude for attraction and repulsion; which changes he termed *accesses,* or *fits of easy reflexion and transmission;* terms sufficiently significative, though not very happily chosen. His followers have attempted to give a mechanical explanation of the *fits,* by ascribing to the luminous particles attractive and repulsive *poles,* analogous to those of the magnet, and supposing the disposition to be reflected or transmitted to depend on the pole which the molecule of light presents to the molecules of the body within whose sphere of action it comes. Thus, suppose two molecules of light to arrive successively at the same point of a surface, and that the first presents its attractive pole, the second the opposite : the first molecule, yielding to the attractive forces, is refracted, and said to arrive in an *access of easy refraction;* the second, obeying the influence of the repulsive forces, is reflected, and consequently said to arrive in an *access of easy reflexion.* According to this view of the subject, the luminous molecules are entirely independent of each other, and the term *pole* is only used to denote that their opposite sides have different physical properties. In addition to this peculiarity of constitution, they are also assumed to have a motion of rotation about their centres of gravity, which increases the mechanical resources of the theory, and gives the means of explaining the intricate phenomena of polarization.

When we speak of molecules endowed with attractive and repulsive forces, having poles, and balancing themselves about their centres of gravity, it is difficult to divest oneself. of the idea of sensible magnitude, or by the utmost strain of the imagination to conceive that particles, to which such properties belong, can be so amazingly small as those in question may be demonstrated to be. If, says Mr. Herschel, a molecule of light weighed a single grain, its effect would be equal to that of a cannon ball of 150 pounds, animated with a velocity of 1000 feet per second. How great then must be their tenuity if millions of molecules, collected by lenses or mirrors, have never been found to produce any sensible effect on the most delicate apparatus, imagined expressly for these experiments.

Until Newton had undertaken his memorable experiments, the cause of the different colours of objects had never received any satisfactory explanation; and such was the difficulty attached by the ancients to the subject, that Plato considered it as an usurpation of the rights of the Deity to attempt the investigation of this mystery of nature. The detection of the difference of refrangibility in the coloured rays of the solar spectrum, afforded a clue to the solution of the problem; and by a series of decisive experiments, Newton demonstrated (supposing the theory of emission true) that colour depends not on any modification of light acquired by reflection or refraction, but is inherent in the light itself; the solar beam being composed of rays of all the colours exhibited in the spectrum, which are differently affected in passing through refracting media. This hypothesis of different species of luminous molecules, is an unavoidable consequence of the theory; for if colour depended merely on a difference of the masses or initial velocities of the particles, it would result that the dispersion of the rays would always be proportional to the refraction, which is contrary to experience, as is well known. It is this circumstance, indeed, a difference in the dispersive and refractive powers of different substances, of which advantage is taken to destroy chromatism in the object glasses of refracting telescopes. The existence of rays of different colours is one of the ultimate facts to which the theory of emission leads, for of the circumstances which give one molecule the physical qualities necessary to produce the sensation of red, and another that of green, it is impossible to form any judgment.

We have already spoken of the amazing smallness of the luminous molecules, and of the enormous velocity (200,000 miles in a second) with which they are darted through space. There is another circumstance regarding them, which cannot fail to excite still greater astonishment, namely, the intensity of the forces that must be exerted to cause them to deviate from their natural rectilinear course. These are computed by Mr. Herschel as follows (we quote his own words):

" Whatever be the forces by which bodies reflect and refract light, one thing is certain, that they must be incomparably more energetic than the force of gravity. The attraction of the earth on a particle near its surface produces a deflexion of only about sixteen feet in a second, and, therefore, in a molecule moving with the velocity of light, would cause a curvature, or change of direction, absolutely insensible in that time. In fact, we must consider, first, that the time during which the whole action of the medium takes place, is only that within which light traverses the diameter of the sphere of sensible action of its molecules at the surface. To allow so much as the thousandth of an inch for this space is beyond all probability; and this interval is traversed by light in the $\frac{1}{12,672,000,000,000}$ part of a second. Now, if we suppose the deviation produced by refraction to be 30°, (a case which frequently happens,) and to be produced by a uniform force acting during a whole second; since this is equivalent to a linear deflection of 200,000 miles $\times$ sin 30°, or of 100,000 miles $= 33,000,000 \times 16$ feet, such a force must exceed gravity on the earth's surface 33,000,000 times. But, in fact, the whole effect being produced not in one second, but in the small fraction of it above mentioned, the intensity of the force operating it must be greater in the ratio of the square of one second to the square of that fraction; so that the least improbable supposition we can make gives a mean force equal to $4,969,126,272 \times 10^{44}$ times that of terrestrial gravity. But in addition to this estimate, already so enormous, we have to consider that gravity on the earth's surface is the resultant attraction of its whole mass, whereas the force deflecting light is that of only those molecules immediately adjoining to it, and within the sphere of the deflecting forces. Now a sphere of $\frac{1}{1000}$ of an inch diameter, and of the mean density of the earth, would exert at its surface a *gravitating* force of $\frac{1}{1000} \times \frac{1 \text{ inch}}{\text{diameter of the earth}}$ of ordinary gravity, so that the actual intensity of the force exerted by the molecules concerned cannot be less than $\frac{1000 \times \text{earth's diameter}}{1 \text{ inch}}$ $(=46,352,000,000)$ times the above enormous number, or upwards of 2×10^{44} when compared with the ordinary intensity of the gravitating power of matter."

Remote as such considerations are from the range of ordinary speculation, there is no way in which the subject can be viewed whereby the occurrence of numbers equally enormous can be avoided. Whether light be regarded as a substance *sui generis*, or as resulting from the agitation of an elastic medium, its prodigious velocity,—a fact resting on the most incontrovertible evidence—involves conclusions of a nature to astound even those who are the most habituated to the contemplation of the irresistible force of the agents which nature employs in accomplishing her purposes.

Of the numerous objections that may be urged against the Newtonian hypothesis, some of the principal have been stated with great force and eloquence by the celebrated Euler, in his *Opuscula Varii Argumenti,* and likewise in his *Letters.* One of these is, that the sun's mass and volume have undergone no sensible diminution since the epoch of the commencement of astronomical observations, notwithstanding the incessant discharge of luminous particles from every point of his surface. This objection is, however, easily met by a simple calculation. The sun's diameter is about 2000″, and at his distance, a second of a degree nearly corresponds to 460 miles. If then, we suppose the sun's diameter to undergo a diminution of two feet, which, considering his vast magnitude, and the great rarity of light, may be thought excessive, the diminution would only amount to about 800 feet in a year, and to 460 miles, or 1″ in 5000 years; so that after a lapse of thirty centuries, the diminution of the solar diameter would still be imperceptible, because in an observation of this sort so small a variation as 1″ could scarcely be appreciated by our best instruments.

Another objection to the Newtonian theory arises from the non-interference of the luminous particles in traversing space. Not only the sun, but every luminous body in the universe, is constantly sending forth rays in all directions; it may be supposed, therefore, that the molecules issuing from so many different points, must *necessarily* strike against each other, whereby their directions would be altered; yet no change in their direction, from a cause of this sort, has ever been observed, and a multitude of rays may be even made to pass through the same point, as the focus of a burning glass, without in the slightest degree interfering with each other. This objection is thus met by Mr. Herschel. "Experience," says he, "proves, that to keep up a continuous excitement in the eye, it is only necessary that the impression be renewed eight or ten times in a second. Now the velocity of light is nearly 200,000 miles in a second; supposing, therefore, that a hundred molecules reach the eye every second, each molecule may follow the preceding at a distance of 2000 miles." Hence it is easy to conceive that the chances of the collision of two molecules must be almost infinitely small.

A third objection is, that according to this theory it is necessary to conceive all transparent bodies to be perforated with holes, or pores, disposed in straight lines, and passing through every part of their surfaces in every direction : for no straight line can be imagined through which a ray of light will not pass. It follows, that diaphanous bodies, some of them apparently the most solid substances of nature, must be entirely destitute of matter, which is a palpable absurdity. It is evident that this objection supposes the constituent molecules of the body to be in absolute contact, and to have a sensible magnitude, but every thing which can be inferred from the discoveries of modern science respecting the constitution of bodies, goes to confirm the idea that there is no absolute contact. The elements of the densest bodies are kept asunder by heat; and, small as their mutual distances may be, sufficient space may be left to admit of the free passage of the still smaller molecules of light.

These (and many others of a similar nature might be mentioned) are some of the obvious difficulties that the theory of Newton has to encounter; there are others, however, of a more refined nature, arising from the peculiar modifications which light acquires in passing through particular substances, to which it is much more difficult to reply. But the objection which pressses with the greatest force arises from its want of explanatory power, and the consequent multitude of particular hypotheses that must be added to the general theory, in order to obtain a plausible explanation of numerous classes of new facts that are almost daily occurring to experimenters. In fact, the mechanical resources of the theory being limited to a difference of physical state in the opposite sides of the molecules, and their rotation about their centres of gravity, it possesses very little power of accommodating itself to new discoveries, and its opposers have some reason for objecting that every new phenomenon requires a new hypothesis.

The undulatory theory, as we have already remarked, is the fruit of the ingenious speculations of Huyghens; for although it had been maintained by Descartes, Hooke, and some others, that the sensation of light is produced by the vibrations of an extremely rare and subtle fluid, it is to the Dutch philosopher alone that the honour belongs of having not only reduced the hypothesis to a definite shape, and rendered it available to the purposes of mechanical explanation, but also of having shown that all the optical phenomena known at that time were deducible from it by rigorous mathematical reasoning. Owing to the success of Newton, in applying the corpuscular theory to his splendid discoveries, the speculations of Huyghens were long in a great measure neglected; indeed, the difficulty of pursuing investigations of so intricate a nature beyond the point to which they had been pushed by himself was so great, on account of the defective state of analysis, that few geometers were capable of successfully grappling with the subject. Our lamented countryman, the late Dr. Young, was the first from whom the theory received any valuable extension. By a train of mechanical reasoning, which in point of ingenuity has seldom been equalled, Dr. Young was conducted from the necessary *data* of the theory to some very remarkable numerical relations among some of the phenomena of optics apparently the most dissimilar, —to the general laws of diffraction which the most patient industry could never have detected by simple observation,—and to the true principles of the coloration of crystallized substances. So late as the year 1810, Malus made the important discovery, that light reflected under certain circumstances acquires the peculiar modification which results from double refraction, or becomes *polarized;* and he successfully explained the phenomena on the hypothesis of an undulatory propagation. But the Huyghenian theory has received, beyond all doubt, its greatest extension from the labours of Fresnel, a philosopher, whose original views and persevering industry had excited hopes for the further advancement of this branch of science, which have been unhappily frustrated by his premature death. In the two excellent papers, whose titles stand at the head of this article, he has made a triumphant application of the principles of the hypothesis to many of the most difficult and complex phenomena of optics, which formerly had not received, or had been thought incapable of, any theoretical explanation.

Among the difficulties which the undulatory theory has to encounter, one of the most formidable is common to it with all other questions which have reference to the propagation of motion through an elastic medium, of which it is impossible to define rigorously either the nature or its relation to ponderable matter. For want of a precise knowledge of the nature of the medium, the geometer can never be certain that the principles he has assumed embrace all the circumstances which affect the motion, so that he has not only to contend with the great and inherent difficulties which attend the application of the known methods of analysis to the vibration of elastic bodies, but is likewise reduced to the necessity of having recourse to experiment before he can have any assurance that his results contain an accurate expression of the phenomena. But though the inadequacy of our mathematical means may occasion embarrassment in the applications of the theory, it cannot in fairness be urged as an argument to diminish the probability of its truth. In the choice of a system, as is remarked by Fresnel, we ought to have regard only to the simplicity of the hypothesis; that of the calculations can be of no weight in the balance of probabilities, for nature, though she avoids the complication of means, does not embarrass herself with the difficulties of analysis.

One of the arguments most frequently urged in opposition to this theory is derived from the fact, that the nicest astronomical observations indicate no traces of the existence of a resisting medium in the regions of the planets. It is certain that the planets encounter no resistance in their orbits, their periodic times being exactly such as bodies placed at the same distance would require to circulate about the sun in a vacuum, according to the laws of gravity. The phenomenon of the aberration of light also proves that the medium is not, like the atmosphere, carried round with the earth in its orbit; for in that case the direction of the visual ray on reaching the eye must have suffered a variation corresponding to the orbital motion of the earth, and the small apparent change of position in the places of the stars, resulting from the earth's motion, combined with the rectilinear progression of light, would not have existed. It follows, therefore, that the earth and its atmosphere in traversing the medium through which light is conveyed, not only meet with no resistance themselves, but cause no disturbance whatever of its equilibrium. In this respect the luminous medium presents no analogy with ponderable matter; for whatever degree of rarity we assign to such matter, its resistance must still have a positive value, however small, the effects of which would be ultimately perceptible in their accumulation.

Granting, however, the existence of the elastic ether, it furnishes a mechanical reason for all the known phenomena of optics, and in many cases with as much facility and elegance as the rival theory of emission. In order to explain reflection and refraction, it is necessary to consider, that when a molecule of the luminous ether is made to vibrate, it communicates an impulsion to all those in its immediate vicinity, whence it may be regarded as a centre, from which a system of secondary waves emanates in all directions. In the case of reflection, the wave, before it reaches, and after it is thrown back from the reflecting surface, proceeds with the same velocity, because the elasticity of the medium in which it is propagated is the same, and the equality of the angles of incidence and reflection is easily demonstrated by tracing the path of the wave. With regard to refraction, it is assumed as one of the *postulates* or demands of the theory, "that in the interior of refracting medium the ether exists in a state of less elasticity, compared with its density, than in vacuo, (i. e. in space empty of all other matter); and that, the more refractive the medium, the less, relatively speaking, is the elasticity of the ether in its interior." Also, "that vibrations communicated to the ether in free space are propagated through refracting media by means of the ether in their interior, but with a velocity corresponding to an inferior degree of elasticity." These principles were assumed by Huyghens, and it is not difficult to conceive in what manner they may be applied to demonstrate the constant ratio of the angles of incidence and refraction. But something

more is wanting in order to complete the theoretical explanation of the various circumstances which attend the interruption
of the free propagation of the luminous waves; and no method
has as yet been found of calculating generally one of the most
important elements, namely, the intensity of the reflected and
refracted ray. Even the profound analysis of Poisson has failed
in accomplishing this object, although his researches have not
been altogether fruitless, inasmuch as they conducted him to a
plausible explanation of the relation that subsists between the
reflecting powers of a medium and its index of refraction, and the
diminution of the light reflected from the common surface of two
media in contact. The circumstance which chiefly perplexes
the subject is the necessity of having regard, not only to the
motion of the principal wave, but also to the motions of the
secondary waves, which proceed from every point of the reflecting
and refracting surface. It was in attempting to surmount this
difficulty that Dr. Young was conducted to the theory of the
interference of the luminous waves,—a theory which explains so
well a vast number of the most intricate phenomena of light, that
Mr. Herschel gives it the high praise of being, if not the actual
system of nature, at least one of the happiest hypotheses ever
invented by the human mind for grouping together large classes
of natural phenomena.

A general idea may be formed of the nature and objects of the
theory of interference by reasoning as follows: Conceive two
series of undulations, originally following different routes, to be
brought by the intervention of an obstacle, or other means, to flow
in the same direction, and to impinge on the same molecule of
the ethereal medium, the question is to determine the intensity
and direction of the resultant wave, or the motion of the molecule.
If the waves arrive simultaneously, or in the *same phase of vibration*, their joint effect on the molecule will evidently be equal to
the sum of their separate effects; but if a wave of the first system
succeeds one of the second, at a distance of time exactly equal to
the time of a semi-undulation, it is no less clear, that at the instant
when the molecule is about to recover its position of equilibrium
from which it was expelled by the first wave, it receives an impulse from the second wave in exactly the opposite direction, in
consequence of which it is prevented from recovering its original
position, and, the impulsive forces of the waves being supposed
equal, it must remain absolutely at rest. Here we have the singular phenomenon of two lights by their interference producing
darkness; a paradox which was first noticed by Grimaldi. These
two extreme cases were alone considered by Dr. Young; the
general problem of determining the result in the intermediate

cases, namely, when the two waves neither arrive simultaneously nor at intervals equal to a semi-undulation, was resolved by Fresnel, in his elaborate Memoir on Diffraction. In this memoir, Fresnel undertook a much more difficult investigation, namely, to determine the motion of the ethereal molecule when it is agitated, not only by two systems of waves, but by any number whatever; and in the course of his inquiries he was conducted to one of those fortunate results of analysis which sometimes unexpectedly occur to facilitate the computations of the geometer. The result in question was the very remarkable one, that the solution of the particular case, in which it is required to find the resultant of two waves separated from each other by a *fourth* of an undulation, comprehends that of the general problem; for whatever may be the number of the different systems of waves, and at whatever intervals they may succeed each other, it is always possible to substitute for each system its component, referred to two points, whose distance corresponds to a fourth of an undulation. Hence the total motion is reduced to that of two systems of waves succeeding each other at the aforesaid interval; and the intensity of the resultant is represented by the hypothenuse of a right-angled triangle, the two sides of which correspond to the respective intensities of the components of the two systems of waves. Fresnel subsequently proved, by a more direct process, that the wave resulting from the concourse of two others, whatever may be their relative directions, corresponds, both as to intensity and direction, with the resultant of two forces equal to the intensities of the primitive waves, and making with each other an angle which has the same proportion to the entire circumference as the interval which separates the waves of the two systems is to the length of an entire undulation.

Colour, which in the theory of emission is referred to certain differences in the physical nature and velocity of the luminous molecules, according to the undulatory system, depends on the velocity of the vibrations of the ethereal fluid, or the number of impulses it communicates to the nerves of the retina in a given time. But as this forms one of the most intricate parts of the theory, we will give the *postulate,* or hypothetical principle, on which the explanation rests, in the words of Mr. Herschel:—

" As in the doctrine of sound, the frequency of the aerial pulses, or the number of excursions to and fro from its point of rest, made by each molecule of the air, determines the pitch, or note; so, in the theory of light, the frequency of the pulses, or the number of impressions made on our nerves in a given time by the ethereal molecules next in contact with them, determines the colour of the light ; and that as the absolute extent of the motions to and fro of the particles of air determine the *loudness* of the sound; so the amplitude, or extent of the excursions of the ethereal molecules from their points of rest determines the *brightness* of the light.";

To this hypothetical assumption several objections immediately occur, and consequences have been deduced from it, which have been by some considered as fatal to the theory. For example, since the rapidity of the propagation is independent of the primitive impulse, and is determined solely by the degree of elasticity, which, in the case of the ethereal fluid, must be considered as uniform both externally and internally, with reference to a refracting substance, it follows, that all the rays, of whatever colour, ought to be propagated with equal velocity; hence, since refraction is caused by the difference of the velocity of propagation without and within the refracting substance, it follows, that the phenomenon of dispersion is impossible. Of this difficulty the theory hardly affords a satisfactory explanation. Fresnel has indeed attempted to remove it, but only by superadding another hypothesis, which may be admitted or rejected at pleasure, inasmuch as it does not appear to be susceptible of any experimental test. It is a result of analysis that the velocity of propagation in an elastic medium is the same, whatever may be the length of the undulation. But according to the undulatory theory of light, colour arises from a difference in the lengths of the undulations, or, what amounts to the same thing, in the number of vibrations of the ethereal molecules in a given time. Now Fresnel attempts to prove that the above result is only true when the radius of the sphere of the reciprocal action of the molecules is infinitely small in comparison of the length of an undulation, as is the case with the undulations of the atmosphere. When the radius of the sphere of action is comparable with the length of the wave, the smaller vibrations are propagated with a little less velocity, conformably to what the theory requires in order to account for the dispersion. Admitting, however, the existence of vibrations of different velocities, the way in which the eye is affected with the sensations of colours may be thus explained. The nerves of the retina, however delicate in structure, have still a great inertia in comparison of the molecules of the elastic ether. They can therefore only be put in motion by that ether by means of impulses received at regular intervals, corresponding to their proper degree of tension, in the same way as a heavy pendulum is made to vibrate by the slightest force, by the agitation of the air for. example, if the impulsive force is repeated at intervals exactly. equal to the time of one of its own oscillations. Now if we suppose the fibres to be so constituted that some of them vibrate more rapidly than others, those only which are in unison with the etherial vibrations will be agitated, and hence the sensation of the colour corresponding to that velocity of vibration. If there are no nervous fibres in unison with the ethereal vibrations, there will consequently be no sensation of light. Pursuing this train of speculation, Dr. Wollaston thought it probable that animals may exist, insects for example, incapable of perceiving the colours known to us, and all whose impressions of light are due to a class of vibrations beyond the limits of those which affect our organs.

If the corpuscular theory astonishes us by the extreme minuteness and enormous velocity of the molecules, the numerical results deduced from the principles of the other theory are not less overwhelming. The extreme smallness of the amplitude of the vibrations, and the almost inconceivable, but still measurable, rapidity with which they succeed each other, was calculated by Dr. Young, and is exhibited by Mr. Herschel in the following table :—

COLOURS.	LENGTHS of the Undulation in air, estimated in parts of an inch.	RATIO of these Lengths to one inch.	NUMBER of Undulations in a second.
Extreme Red . . .	0.000266	37640	458,000000,000000
Red	0.000256	39180	477,000000,000000
Intermediate . . .	0.000246	40720	495,000000,000000
Orange	0.000240	41610	506,000000,000000
Intermediate . . .	0.000235	42510	517,000000,000000
Yellow	0.000227	44000	535,000000,000000
Intermediate . . .	0.000219	45600	555,000000,000000
Green	0.000211	47460	577,000000,000000
Intermediate . . .	0.000203	49320	600,000000,000000
Blue	0.000196	51110	622,000000,000000
Intermediate . . .	0.000189	52910	644,000000,000000
Indigo	0.000185	54070	658,000000,000000
Intermediate . . .	0.000181	55240	672,000000,000000
Violet	0.000174	57490	699,000000,000000
Extreme Violet. .	0.000167	59750	727,000000,000000

Supposing the velocity of light to be 192,000 miles in a second.

From this table, as Mr. Herschel remarks, it appears that the susceptibility of the eye is confined within much narrower limits than that of the ear, the ratio of the extreme vibrations being nearly as 1.58 : 1, a value somewhat below that of a minor sixth, and consequently much less than an octave.

A considerable portion of the third book of Newton's Optics is devoted to the subject of the inflexion of light, which has always

formed one of the stumbling blocks of the corpuscular theory.
Many of the phenomena, indeed, seem incapable of explanation
on that theory, while they are all susceptible of being deduced
analytically from the principles of the undulatory system, and the
doctrine of interference. . Grimaldi had remarked, that when a
ray of light is admitted into a darkened room, through a very small
aperture, the shadows of bodies exposed to it are much larger
than they ought to he, if the rays passing very near the extremities
of these bodies proceed in straight lines ; and that the shadows
are bordered with fringes of different colours, always more distinct in proportion as the aperture through which the light is admitted is smaller. When the ray on which the experiment is
made consists of undecomposed or common light, the fringes are
only three in number; but with a ray of simple light, that is, a
ray which contains only one of the colours of the spectrum, they
are much more numerous, and vary in size according to the colour
of the light from which they are produced, the narrowest being
given by the violet ray, and the largest by the red. The Newtonian explanation of the phenomenon is, that when the rays pass
so near the interposed body as to come within the sphere of the
action of its molecules, an inflexion, that is, a partial reflexion or
refraction takes place, by which the light is decomposed, and the
coloured streaks appear both within and without the shadow.
But it is a remarkable circumstance that these fringes are entirely
independent of the density or form of the body exposed to the ray,
and are only affected by the dimensions of the space within which
they are intercepted, or that of the hole through which the ray is
introduced. It is therefore evident that the production of the
colour is in no way connected with the refringent power of the
body, nor with any attractive or repulsive forces which its molecules exercise on those of light; for such forces cannot be conceived to be altogether independent of its density, how small
soever the surface may be which is exposed to the action of the
light. Another circumstance connected with this subject appears
equally conclusive against the supposition of the action of molecular forces. When the opaque body is advanced nearer to the
luminous point, or hole through which the light is admitted, the
fringes which border the shadow, intercepted on the screen at the
same distance as before, become greatly enlarged while they preserve their proportional distances. Now if the light is bent from
its rectilinear path by a repulsive force exercised by the molecules
of the body by which it passes, the enlargement of the fringes is
a phenomenon which ought not to happen, for it is inconceivable
that such a force should be modified by the distance passed over
by the light from an arbitrary point which has absolutely no con-

nexion with the body in which it is supposed to reside. Dr. Young showed how this phenomenon could be accounted for on the undulatory hypothesis, by supposing the rays which pass near the body to interfere with those which strike against it and are reflected, and which, by that reflexion, have lost half an undulation. But the simplest and most satisfactory explanation was given by Fresnel, who showed the supposition of reflexion to be superfluous, and that it is only necessary to regard the opaque body as an obstacle to the propagation of the waves emanating from the luminous point. Having computed from theory the path of the wave, and the magnitude and distances of the fringes, Fresnel submitted his results to a severe experimental test, and found the most perfect conformity to subsist between theory and experiment. Thus a phenomenon which appeared inexplicable, or had at least been accounted for in a very unsatisfactory manner on the Newtonian hypothesis, received a complete explanation from the principles of the undulatory doctrine; and it is by no means the only instance in which the one theory has been found to apply readily to facts that seemed entirely irreconcilable to the other.

A multitude of curious consequences follow from the general principles of diffraction established by Fresnel, some of which have been developed with profound analytical skill by Poisson in the Memoirs of the Academy of Sciences. The subject has also been prosecuted to a great length in an experimental point of view, particularly by Fraunhofer, whose optical discoveries form the subject of an article in the second number of this journal. The most interesting of Fraunhofer's discoveries in respect of theory is that of the dark lines, or *deficient rays* as they are termed, of the spectrum, inasmuch as it affords the only means yet known of detecting any differences in the constitution of light emanating from different sources, for example from different stars. The detection of such differences, we are inclined to think, is in no way favourable to the undulatory hypothesis; for when light is regarded as the vibration of a medium, and consequently capable of being modified only by the elasticity of that medium, it cannot be supposed to differ in *kind*, however much it may differ in intensity, from whatever source the primitive impulse may be derived.

Another class of phenomena closely connected with the above, and of great interest in consequence of its relation to the permanent colours of bodies, is formed by the beautiful streaks or rings of coloured light exhibited by very thin substances, as plates of mica, soap-bubbles, or a film of air included between two plates of glass whose surfaces are slightly convex. The first

circumstance which strikes us as remarkable with regard to these
colours is, that whatever substance is employed for their production, they continue always exactly the same, and arranged in a
similar order, from the least thickness where they are most vivid,
to the greatest where they disappear. The only difference is in
the absolute extent of the space occupied by the colours of each
ring, which varies with the nature of the substance, and the more
or less rapid degradation of the colours. Mr. Herschel has devoted a long chapter to the examination of this subject, with a
view to the comparison of the explanatory powers of the two
theories. Although the undulatory hypothesis has been applied
to the different phenomena that have been observed, the explanations are not by any means free from obscurity and hypothetical
assumptions; nor are the objections brought against the Newtonian doctrine of a kind to carry with them conclusive evidence
against it. Yet there is one fact which deserves to be noticed,
and which Fresnel considers as a crucial instance to enable us to
decide between the rival doctrines. When two pieces of glass
not perfectly flat are laid on one another, the film of air included
between them gives out brilliant colours, which, when viewed
through a red glass, appear as a succession of bright and dark
streaks. Now these streaks are alike explicable on the principles
of both theories, with this distinction, however, that according to
the Newtonian theory the spaces between the bright streaks ought
to be *half bright ;* whereas, according to the theory of Huyghens,
they ought to be perfectly *black.* An appeal to experience ought
therefore to be decisive of the question; and Fresnel affirms
that the results of his experiments were perfectly conformable
with the consequences of the undulatory theory, and consequently
fatal to that of emission.

The last part of Mr. Herschel's treatise is devoted to the subject of double refraction, or that singular property which most
crystallized bodies possess of separating the rays of light which
enter their surfaces into two parcels, each of which pursues its
peculiar path in the interior of the crystal. This property was
first noticed by Bartholin. Newton does not appear to have bestowed great attention on it, at least he did not attempt to explain
it on the principles of his own theory, although the phenomena
accompanying it are undoubtedly the most interesting and important of all that come within the range of this department of physics.
He, however, made the remark that a ray of light, after having
undergone an extraordinary refraction, acquires *sides,* or distinct
relations to surrounding space—an idea which has since been
expanded into the theory of the *Polarization of Light,* which of
late years has occupied so much attention, and been the occasion
of so many interesting experiments. The Newtonian theory does

not readily lend itself to this class of phenomena; yet by means of certain arbitrary hypotheses, which have sometimes been too confidently put forward as laws of nature, the supporters of that theory have succeeded in framing analytical formulæ which embrace the greater part of the facts. Huyghens, who studied the phenomena with great care as they are exhibited by Iceland crystal or the crystallized carbonate of lime, was singularly fortunate in the explanation by which he connected them with his own system. In free space the luminous waves are propagated in spherical superficies, and the velocity of light is consequently the same in all directions; but in the interior of a doubly refracting crystal, Huyghens supposed the waves to assume a spheroidal form, in consequence of which the velocity of propagation is different in different directions; and by means of this simple modification of the general theory, he was enabled not only to represent the phenomena with accuracy, but also to compute with precision the deviation of the extraordinary ray. This hypothesis has been found to be in perfect agreement with numerous and comprehensive classes of phenomena since discovered, and has consequently received so great a degree of probability, that we shall offer no apology for entering more fully into its development.

In the undulatory system the theory of double refraction is founded on two postulates, one regarding the mode in which the luminous vibrations are propagated through the elastic medium, and the other the mode in which the elasticity is developed in the interior of the refracting crystal. The first of these assumes that the vibrations do not take place longitudinally, or in the direction of the visual ray, but in the direction perpendicular to it; in the same manner as when a blow is given to a cord tightly stretched, the motion is communicated rapidly in the direction of its length, while the vibrations are at right angles to it. In this respect the vibrations of the elastic ether differ from those of the atmosphere in the propagation of sound, for in this latter case the particles of the agitated air move backwards and forward in the direction in which the sound proceeds. The idea of transverse vibrations occurred to Dr. Young in attempting to connect with the theory of undulations some experiments of Dr. Brewster on bi-axial crystals, and was published by him before it had been suggested by any other writer. Fresnel, however, states, that he had previously arrived at the same conclusion from other facts. It seems at variance with the notions generally entertained respecting the communication of motion in elastic media; but the laws and mode of that communication are still among the most obscure parts of mechanical science, and the conclusion ought not to be rejected, if it is either indicated by the facts or forms an accurate

x 2

expression of the phenomena. Fresnel, indeed, attempts to prove
it to be a necessary consequence of the law of the interference of
waves, or rather that the law of interference depends solely on the
nature of the vibration; and grounds his demonstration on the
observed fact, that two pencils of light, polarized according to
rectangular planes, that is to say, of which the vibrations are all
at right angles to two rectangular planes, exercise no influence on
each other under the same circumstances in which the rays of
ordinary light exhibit the phenomena of interference; but when
the planes of polarization are not at right angles, but a little
inclined to each other, then the coloured light produced by the
interference of the waves begins to appear, and becomes more
distinct as the planes are more approximated to each other.
Now as the two pencils are never observed to interfere so long
as their planes of polarization are at right angles, but always to
produce when united the same intensity of light, whatever may
be the difference of the routes they have traversed, it follows
that the extraordinary rays are propagated by transverse vibrations;
and this fact being established, the principle of the conservation
of living forces makes it necessary that the ordinary rays be propagated in the same manner, consequently there are no vibrations
perpendicular to the surface of the wave, or, which amounts to
the same thing, parallel to the direction of the ray.

The second hypothesis on which the doctrine of double refraction is founded, is, that when a vibratory motion is given to the
molecules of the ethereal medium, the elasticity is unequally developed in the interior of the refracting crystal. In bodies not
crystallized, and in free space, the elasticity is developed equally
in all directions, and the length of the undulation being in the
inverse ratio of the square root of the elasticity, the surface of
the luminous wave is spherical, and light advances in all directions
with the same velocity; but in the case of an unequal development of elasticity the wave loses its spherical form, and assumes
that of a spheroid, or ellipsoid, according as the crystal has one
or two optical axes. This being admitted, the general laws of
double refraction are represented by a very simple construction.
Let us suppose a ray of light to enter a crystal in a given direction, and a point to be taken in this direction for the centre of an
ellipsoid: the ellipsoid will be determined when we know the
proportions of the lengths of the three axes, and their situation in
respect of the axes of the crystal. Now the relation of the axes
must be determined by experiment; they are respectively in the
inverse ratio of the square roots of the elasticity of the medium in
the same direction, and consequently the surface of the ellipsoid is
properly termed the surface of elasticity   With regard to the

situation of the axes of the ellipsoid, two of them are situated in the same plane with the axes of the crystal, and bisect the one the acute, and the other the obtuse angle which these axes make with each other; and the third is at right angles to the plane of the two first. Let us next conceive the ellipsoid thus determined to be cut by a plane passing through its centre and perpendicular to the luminous ray; the· section will be an ellipse, and its semi-transverse and semi-conjugate axes will represent respectively the velocities of the ordinary and extraordinary ray. The introduction of the ellipsoid is of great importance to the theory, inasmuch as it gives a geometrical surface easily calculated, at every point of which the luminous wave, setting out from the central point, arrives at the same instant.

Although the hypothesis of a medium in which the elasticity is greater in one direction than in another, is at variance with all our received notions of the properties of elastic fluids, yet analogies are not wanting to render it probable. It has been found by M. Savart, in his recent experiments relative to the propagation of sound, that the elastic force with which crystallized substances resist compression is greater in certain directions than in others ; and Professor Mitscherlich has also lately discovered that a similar property holds true with regard to their dilatation by heat. Though the mutual relations of these phenomena are not very well understood, they leave little reason to doubt that the ethereal fluid which conveys light is modified in the interior of certain substances by their internal structure.

We have already noticed the remark made by Newton, that the ray which undergoes the extraordinary refraction has its opposite sides affected by some virtue like magnetism, which gives them a distinct relation to opposite sides of space. When a ray of light, having acquired this modification, is made to fall on a plane reflecting surface under a certain angle of incidence, it escapes reflection altogether. Now, since in the case of ordinary light some portion is always reflected, whatever be the angle of incidence, it follows that all the molecules which compose the extraordinary ray must turn their similar poles, or homologous sides, towards the reflecting surface, or have their axes all arranged in the same direction. From this circumstance Malus gave the phenomenon the name of *polarization*, the effect being analogous to that which would be produced by a magnet on a series of magnetic needles, namely, that of arranging their axes all in parallel lines. Malus accidentally discovered that the same parallel arrangement of the molecules takes place when light is reflected from the surfaces of transparent bodies at certain angles which are different for different substances. In glass the polarization is complete when the ray makes with the surface an angle of

35° 25'. This discovery of Malus opened up a new field of interesting research, which has been industriously explored by
Brewster, Biot, Arago, Fresnel, and other experimenters, with
such success, that the results of their researches must henceforth
constitute the principal part of every systematic treatise of light.
The mechanical explanation of these phenomena, according to
the Newtonian theory, is suggested by the term employed to
designate them. The molecular forces of the crystal acting on
the luminous molecules, cause them to turn round their centres
of gravity till their axes assume certain determinate positions,
after which they remain at rest. This is the ordinary case; there
are some cases, however, in which the luminous molecules in
traversing the crystal assume no fixed position, but oscillate about
their centres of gravity in regular periods, the length of which
may be calculated. There are even cases in which they turn
with a motion of continuous rotation. It is in the explanation of
these peculiarities the system of emission has encountered great
and hitherto unconquered difficulties. Fresnel displayed consummate address in deducing the principal phenomena of polarization
from the principles of the undulatory hypothesis. According to
this philosopher polarized light is that of which the vibrations
remain constantly perpendicular to the same plane, which is *the
plane of polarization;* while the ordinary or direct light consists
in the reunion and rapid succession of an infinity of waves polarized in all directions. The act of polarization is thus made to
consist in the decomposition of all these little oscillations, whose
directions are variable, into two fixed directions at right angles to
each other, and in the separation of the two systems of waves,
either by the effect of reflection, or that of double refraction.*

Enough has perhaps now been said to enable us to form a
general notion of the mechanical reasoning by which the rival
theories account for the various phenomena of light. On a cursory view it must appear singular that two hypotheses, founded on
assumptions so essentially different, should concur in giving the
means of deducing analytically from their fundamental principles
so great a number of facts with equal precision and almost equal
facility; but it must be recollected that the laws which guide the
propagation of light are truths made known by observation, and
not dependent on any physical hypothesis. Let the connecting
cause of the phenomena be what it may, if the system we adopt
includes them all, it will always give us the means of deducing
the mathematical laws to which the phenomena are subject. In
order, therefore, to balance the probabilities of the two theories,
we have only to consider which affords the simplest means of

---

* Mémoire sur la Double Refraction.

grouping together and representing the phenomena; and, provided we reason accurately from the facts, the consequences we deduce must necessarily be elements of every possible system. So far as the corpuscular doctrine is available for the purposes of deductive explanation, it possesses all the characteristics of a good theory. It supposes the action of a force with which we are in some measure familiar. We are accustomed to contemplate the effects of attraction in the grand phenomena of astronomy; we perceive them at every instant in the downward tendency of all heavy bodies; and though they disappear among the small bodies of nature, they are re-produced in the phenomena of electricity, magnetism, capillary attraction, and various chemical actions, where they can be not only distinctly traced, but reduced to formulæ, and submitted to accurate calculation. The undulatory hypothesis is not seized by the mind with the same facility; yet it possesses some of the least equivocal characters of philosophical truth. Not only are new phenomena found to be in perfect accordance with its principles, but the consequences analytically deduced from those principles, when brought to the test of experiment, have been uniformly confirmed; and this not in a small number of particular cases, or where the consequences were so obvious as that they might have been foreseen, but in numerous instances, and where a train of reasoning has been employed so long and intricate that no sagacity could possibly have divined the result. Hence the hypothesis begins to be generally adopted by philosophers, or at least by those among them who are the most capable of appreciating the force of the reasoning on which it is founded. That it is entitled to be regarded as a physical truth it would be too bold to assert; that it even embraces *all* the phenomena cannot yet be affirmed; and subsequent observations alone can determine what we are to reject or admit concerning longitudinal, transversal, and circular; ordinary, and polarized vibrations. But it cannot be said that either theory has been demonstrated : and as the explanations and mathematical deductions founded on the one can be translated with more or less facility into the language of the other, it is not among the ordinary phenomena that we need seek for decisive grounds of preference. Till fortunate observations shall have produced some *crucial* instance, or the force of accumulating evidence have given a decided preponderancy, we must be content with knowing that light is propagated in straight lines, though in a manner unknown to us. Happily the useful properties of light are independent of any physical hypothesis respecting its propagation.

It may appear somewhat paradoxical that the hypothesis of the propagation of light by undulations should be much less accessible to mathematical analysis than that of the propagation of heat, with which it has in many respects so great an analogy, and both of-which, in all' probability, depend on the vibrations of the, same elastic ether.   The cause is this :—in the case of light, the primitive state of the luminous vibration, and all the modifications it suffers in consequence of encountering obstacles, must be taken into consideration; whereas heat is considered as resulting from the concourse of all the vibrations emanating from an infinity of different points, and therefore - the anomalies of its vibrations disappear in consequence of their fortuitous opposition, leaving nothing to be calculated but the general effect—the propagation of the wave.

From the brief account which our limits have permitted us to give of the progress of the science of light, it will easily be gathered that the undulatory theory is mainly indebted for its form and expansion to the labours of Young and Fresnel.   As giving a luminous exposition of the views and discoveries of these two philosophers, Mr. Herschel's Essay is a production of very great merit.   It would be unjust, however, to regard it as the mere statement of a theory already advanced to maturity.   Mr. Herschel has himself largely contributed both to the store of experimental facts, and the mathematical investigations by which they are connected with the theory, and shown to be necessary consequences of its principles.   The present work is stamped with the characters of originality and genius, and could have been executed only by one who was himself not only intimately acquainted with the phenomena he describes, and the delicate experiments by which they are exhibited, but also perfectly familiar with the resources of that sublime geometry which seizes a few general laws to deduce from them the principal phenomena of the universe.   In many places it bears the marks of haste, and wants the polish and condensation which belongs to a carefully revised production; but it has the merit of exhibiting a full and accurate view of one of the most interesting branches of physical science, and is therefore entitled to a high place among the best treatises of applied mathematics which have yet appeared in any language.

The translation is well and creditably executed, and in point of typographical accuracy considerably superior to the original. The formulæ and calculations are stated in the preface to have been for the greater part verified by M. Verhulst; and some corrections, supplied to the translators by Mr. Herschel himself, add to its value.   We ought to mention that the translation of the last part of the treatise, comprehending the subjects of polarization and double refraction, has not yet appeared. .

ART. II.—*Histoire de la Régénération de l' Égypte; Lettres écrites du Caire à M. le Comte Alexandre de Laborde, Membre de la Chambre des Députés.* Par Jules Planat, ancien officier de l'artillerie de la Garde Impériale, et chef d' état-major au service du Viceroi d'Egypte. 8vo. Paris. 1830.

THIS is the most recent and by far the most satisfactory account we have seen of the present condition of Egypt, under the administration of its celebrated ruler, Mehemed Ali. The author is, or rather *was*, an intelligent, laborious, and, above all, an honest-minded French officer of artillery, who, having been brought up in the school of La Fere, entered the Imperial Guard as an officer, made some campaigns, was present at the *funerals* of Waterloo, as the editor quaintly styles that memorable defeat, and subsequently left the service, like many more, from a feeling of disappointment and wounded national pride. He then turned his eyes to foreign countries where he might seek his fortune, and the then growing reputation of Mehemed Ali decided his choice. He went to Egypt, was recommended to the Pacha by the French consul, M. Drovetti, and taken into his service as Director of the Staff Corps, and Chief Instructor of the Military College which was then being formed. M. Planat remained in Egypt five years, till 1828, when he obtained leave to return to France for a short time, to see his friends and renovate his European ideas, with the view of returning to Egypt with new information which might be useful to his adopted country. A sudden illness, however, put an end to his career in the very prime of life; and his letters, written with all the frankness of friendly correspondence to Count de Laborde, have now been published in their original state. We like them all the better for this, notwithstanding a certain want of arrangement, owing to the writer having treated of subjects as they occurred to him at the moment, without any regard to priority of dates. The confusion arising from this deficiency we shall, however, endeavour to remove, so as to render the history of Mehemed Ali's administration intelligible to our readers. In the work, as it now stands, the account of the reforms effected in that country is intermixed with other matters, such as the wars against the Wahabees, the Nubians, and the Greeks, so as to perplex the attention of the reader.

The establishment of the Nizam jedid or regularly organized force, by Sultan Selim, which cost that monarch his life, had left a deep impression on the mind of many an intelligent Turk, and among others on that of Mehemed Ali, Pacha of Egypt. The recollection of the French and English armies, and their campaigns in that country, was still fresh in the memory of the people, and Mehemed understood the advantage to be derived from discipline and tactics against hordes of irregular Asiatics. Mehemed had been successful, more through artifice than force, in ridding himself of the Mamelukes; he was now the peaceful possessor of Egypt, but he knew that the Porte watched him with a jealous eye. The latter had, by a stroke of its wonted policy, commissioned him to carry on the war in the Hedjaz against the heretical Wahabees, who had profaned the sanctuaries of Mekka and Medina. Mehemed Ali accepted the commission, and retook the holy cities; but after this the war lingered on in the old Ottoman style, year after year, without any definitive success, until at last Tousoun Pacha, Mehemed's son, who commanded the army in Arabia, concluded a kind of truce with the Wahabee chieftain, Abdalla Saoud, during which both parties prepared themselves for a fresh struggle. It was about this time, July, 1815, that Mehemed Ali issued new regulations for the army, and enjoined the troops of Ismayl Pacha, his other son, to exercise after the European manner. The soldiers murmured, and called him Pacha of the Giaours, and the officers not being better disposed towards their new duties, a mutiny ensued. Mehemed, attended by Abdim Bey, took shelter in the citadel. Cairo was the scene of anarchy and plunder; and although the Viceroy succeeded in restoring order, it was with the understanding that the obnoxious regulations should be abandoned. Tousoun Pacha having just then returned to Egypt, where he died suddenly of the plague, Mehemed prepared a fresh expedition into Hedjaz, in September, 1816, which he entrusted to Ibrahim Pacha, whom M. Pianat styles his *adoptive* son. The Albanian troops, who had, as usual, stood prominent in the recent mutiny, formed part of the force sent to Arabia on this occasion. Ibrahim carried on the war with spirit, though with great loss, until 1818, when he penetrated to Derayeh, the strong hold of the Wahabees, and took prisoner Abdalla Saoud, who was sent to Constantinople, where he was barbarously put to death. Ibrahim afterwards returned to Egypt, leaving the remainder of his army to protect Mekka, Medina and Djedda.

Mehemed Ali now bethought himself of another expedition into Sennaar, where gold mines were reported to exist, and in which he might employ the greater part of his remaining irregular troops, who he saw would always be an obstacle to his favorite plan of the Nizam. The army for Sennaar left Cairo in June, 1820, under the command of Ismayl Pacha. It consisted of about 4000 men, Turks and Arabs. They overran Dongola, met with a spirited opposition from the Sheygya Arabs, and at last penetrated into the country of Sennaar. M. Caillaud accompanied this expedition, and his narrative has been given in

No. IV. of this Journal,* as well as an account of the disastrous events which followed, namely, the destruction of Ismayl Pacha and his suite, who were burnt to death by the Arabs of Shendy. At the news of this catastrophe the Defterdar Bey, who had arrived from Egypt with reinforcements, and was then occupied in the conquest of Kordofan, a dependency of the kingdom of Darfoor, hastened down to Sennaar to assume the command of the army, and after taking a dreadful revenge for the death of Ismayl, he established himself by terror in the new conquests, where he remained till the year 1824, when he was relieved by the regular troops which had been formed in Egypt in the meantime. After the departure of the last body of irregulars under the Defterdar, Mehemed Ali ordered the formation of a camp for the instruction of the officers whom he destined for the command of the new levies. He began by sending his own Mamelukes or body guards and attendants, and those of the principal officers of the state. He engaged as instructor Colonel Seve, formerly aide-de-camp to Marshal Ney, who had been recommended to him by M. Drovetti, the French Consul General. The camp was finally established at Assouan, on the furthest limits of Upper Egypt. That position was chosen in order to suit the constitutions of the blacks, who had been taken prisoners by the army of Sennaar, and who were now formed into regular battalions. To these were added, gradually, a number of fellahs or Egyptian Arabs, who either enlisted voluntarily, or were levied by the cachefs or chiefs of villages. A body of 4000 men was thus soon collected. Colonel Seve was assisted by several other French officers, who acted under his direction. The greatest difficulty was with the Turks or Mamelukes. Accustomed to a life of indolence and ease, these proud Osmanlees—seeing themselves obliged to give up their sumptuous dresses and their fine horses, to renounce the pleasures of Cairo, and to undergo hours of drilling on the sand in a sequestered corner on the borders of the desert—murmured loudly, swore at the Christians, and threw down their heavy muskets. Seve swore at them some big French oaths in return. The Turks soon learned to repeat his oaths, without understanding their meaning; they laughed, and by degrees cast off their sulkiness.

Seve went through his difficult task with great judgment and perseverance. He studied the different dispositions of his pupils; he talked to them in broken Turkish, laughed at their rich saddles and bridles, and told them how a handful of French infantry had defeated their numerous and brilliant Mameluke cavalry. · With the more refractory he was strict and severe, knowing he was supported by the authority of the Viceroy. Once, on the occasion of a platoon firing, a ball whistled past his ear. Without noticing this, " You are a set of awkward fellows," cried he— " prime and load again—present—fire! " No ball was heard to whistle this time. This trait of coolness and self-command won him those proud hearts. They became more familiar, courted his company, and by degrees forgot their prejudices. Several of his grown-up pupils became really attached to him.

A French medical officer, Mr. Dussap, set up a military hospital. Another Frenchman organized the arsenal at Cairo, established a foundry for cannon, an armoury and other accessaries. Saltpetre pits and gunpowder mills were also formed.

The camp of instruction was now removed northwards, nearer Cairo. This was effected gradually, out of consideration for the black recruits, who, coming from a latitude of 11 or 12°, would have felt the climate of Middle Egypt too cold for them. In 1823 the camp was established at Nekheli, near Syout. It was there that our author, lately arrived from France, saw Colonel Seve. He met there also the minister at war, Mohammed Bey, an intelligent old man. The latter questioned him about the news of Europe, and the occupation of Spain by the French army under the Duke of Angouleme. He seemed, however, to take but a very faint interest in all this. A Turk cannot understand the object of an invasion without the intention of permanent conquest. As for Seve, " he lived entirely after the oriental fashion; kept three women, natives of Abyssinia, by one of whom he had children; had fine horses, numerous domestics, and kept open table. He thus spent all the handsome salary the Viceroy allowed him."—p. 34.

Ibrahim Pacha, although nominally at the head of the army, was undergoing his exercise like the rest, acquiring the theory of field manœuvres, and giving to all the example of discipline and subordination. The character of this chief is described to be stern and impetuous, though easily appeased, brave and persevering, regardless of obstacles, and not without occasional sparks of generosity and high-mindedness. Short and thickset, his appearance has nothing agreeable; he looks a hardy and rude soldier.

At the end of 1823 the new Egyptian army already consisted of six regiments of five battalions, at 800 men for each battalion. The organization of the battalions was modelled after that of the French army. The regiments were numbered, and received their colours of white silk, with verses of the Koran in gold, and the cypher of Mehemed Ali. The soldiers wore jackets of red stuff, with trousers very full as far as the calf of the leg, then fitting close down to the ankle; a leather strap round the waist, and a cap instead of the turban. The arms and accoutrements were of French manufacture. About the same time the first field manœuvres took place in the presence of the Viceroy, of the French and English Consul-Generals, and of other strangers. Colonel Seve had laid down the plan and order of the manœuvres, and Ibrahim Pacha commanded the execution, which went off to the general satisfaction, and to the great exultation of the Viceroy, who received the compliments of his European guests.

The time had now arrived for trying this newly created army, which had cost so much pains, and see how it would behave in actual service. On the 5th January, 1824, the first regiment, 4000 strong, marched from the camp on the route to Sennaar, to relieve the irregulars of the Defterdar. These troops halted at Assouan, where their colonel, Osman Bey, joined them at the end of February. Just as the regiment was going to advance beyond the Cataracts, a formidable insurrection broke out in their rear. A sheik, who had the reputation of being a prophet, was at the head of the movement: 30,000 fellahs or peasants had assembled in the neighbourhood of Esnè, giving out that Mehemed Ali was dead, and from Esnè to Thebes the whole country was in revolt. Osman Bey, leaving the fifth battalion at Assouan, marched with the other four back to Esnè; but the spirit of revolt spread among his men, and 700 of them deserted. This was a most critical moment, on which the fate of the new institutions, nay, even of Egypt itself, depended. Osman Bey assembled his troops, made them take the oath of fidelity, and having secured his position at Esnè and relieved the irregular cavalry which had been surrounded by the insurgents, he sent messengers to the Viceroy to inform him of the state of affairs. Meantime a conspiracy had been hatched in the fifth battalion, left at Assouan, the object of which was to murder their officers and join the rebels. It was discovered in time; the soldiers were turned out without their arms, and, being questioned by the officers, denounced the leaders of the plot, who were immediately confined. The battalion then returned to its duty, and even attacked a convoy of boats manned by their own comrades, who were descending the Nile to join the rebels. This attack took place at the island of Philæ; the convoy was burnt, and most of the mutineers lost their lives. After this, the fifth battalion marched back to Esnè, to join the head-quarters of the regiment. Meantime the Viceroy had sent two more battalions from the camp, to attack the insurgents, while Osman Bey and the cavalry were fighting them on the other side. The peasants were cut to pieces by the regulars; 7000 of them remained on the field, many were taken prisoners, and the rest dispersed. The Viceroy had given orders to execute, without appeal, all soldiers found among the rebels: forty-five of them were shot on the banks of the Nile. Order being restored, the first regiment resumed its march in the month of June for Sennaar.

Osman Bey, following the course of the Nile, arrived at Dongola, and from thence, in September, at Cartoom, at the confluence of the White and Blue rivers, where he established his head-quarters and built barracks : by degrees the place became the centre of the commerce with Abyssinia and other parts of the interior. He sent two battalions into Kordofan as far as the frontiers of Darfoor. The Defterdar being thus relieved, he returned into Egypt with his irregulars, the greater part of whom being Albanians were sent off to the island of Candia.

Another regiment, the second, commanded by Mohamed Bey, was sent, about the same time, and on a similar errand, into Hedjaz. They embarked at Kosseir for Djedda. Achmet, Pacha of Djedda, under the authority of the Viceroy of Egypt, joined the expedition with some irregular cavalry, and provisions for forty days. The army marched in the latter end of 1824, and after halting a fortnight at Mekka, moved forward into the interior, first in an eastern direction, over the steep Jibel Cara to Raifa, which is represented as a fertile country, abounding in provisions. : The line of march then inclined to the south-east until they came in another fortnight to the village of Bakra, about 150 leagues from Djedda. From thence the army marched direct south, and on the 25th day's march from Mekka, they first spied out the Wahabees crowning the hills of Macheit. Their number might be from 10 to 12,000. The Egyptian army consisted of 5,000 regular infantry, some irregular cavalry, and several field-pieces. It seems that the Wahabees had heard of the arrival of the new troops from the Mekka travellers who traded with the interior, and had watched from their hiding-places some detachments of the advanced guard. Having been accustomed in their former wars with the Osmanlees to the sight of a superb cavalry, richly dressed and caparisoned, and shining with arms of every sort, they conceived but a poor idea of these humble infantry soldiers, marching quietly in files, dressed in coarse red stuff, and with *a long nail*, as they called it, at the end of their muskets. They rushed down, therefore, from their position, thinking of surrounding the Egyptians, who poured upon them a well-directed fire from both ranks. Surprised and daunted by the thick shower of balls which continued to fall upon them, the Wahabees ran back to their hills, pursued by the grenadiers and light companies, who hunted them through their fastnesses, and obliged them at last to abandon their position and retire precipitately into the interior towards Hedjilé, where it was impossible for the Egyptians, encumbered as they were with baggage, to attempt to follow them. This was the first action fought by the Egyptian

Nizam, or regulars. When the news reached Cairo, Mehemed Ali bounced from his divan with joy. The Colonel, Mohamed Bey, behaved gallantly on this occasion; he was, however, assisted by the French Captain Daumergue, one of the instructors, who had followed the expedition.

The Wahabees now learnt better to appreciate the new levies, and a war of outposts was carried on, in which prisoners being taken on both sides, the two armies became better acquainted with each other's strength. Another sharp engagement took place at Mehala, about two days journey west of Macheit, where a body of Wahabees entrenched in a village were driven out of it by the infantry, and might have been all taken had the cavalry charged in time. Mr. Vigoureux, another French instructor, repeatedly urged the commanding officer to execute a charge, but in vain. The Wahabees lost, however, about 1,500 men on the field, and the Egyptians also sustained a considerable loss. It is recorded in honour to the former, that their chief offered a double reward to those of his men who should bring in a prisoner alive, while Achmet, Pacha of Djedda, in the old Turkish spirit, gave merely a price for each head brought to the camp. At last the Egyptian army, having dispersed the Wahabees, returned towards the coast of the Red Sea, and encamped at Konfoudah, lat. 19°. Thence they marched again to the south along the sea-coast to Hachache, near Cape Djezan, whence they struck eastward into Yemen, and at last returned to Djedda, where they encamped, and from whence the regiment returned to Egypt, being relieved by the ninth regiment, in November, 1826, having lost in two years 1400 men upon a strength of 4,800, partly by the enemy and partly by disease. The regiment was well received by the Viceroy, who bestowed promotions on all the ranks. The men received a silver medal, and the privilege of wearing round their heads the small silk shawl striped green and yellow, worn by the Wahabees, with the ends hanging out from beneath their caps. This distinguishes the second regiment from the rest of the army. Mehemed Ali entrusted them also with the garrison of Cairo, " where," observes our author, " military posts are established, and guard-duty is performed the same as at Paris. The city is perfectly safe by night as well as day. Every serjeant is a sort of petty magistrate in police matters, and performs the duties of this new office with justice tempered with mildness."

We must now retrace our steps, in order to observe the progress of Mehemed Ali's Egyptian administration, which we have lost sight of awhile in order to follow his newly-created troops into distant regions. The Porte had been for some time urging the Viceroy to send his contingent to the war against the Greeks, and Mehemed Ali felt that he could no longer elude the orders of the Sultan consistently with his professions of allegiance. In the spring of 1824, he ordered, therefore, his four remaining regiments, 16,000 men in all, to prepare for embarkation, taking care, however, to direct the formation of three more regiments out of the depots of the former and the numerous recruits that flocked to the camp. About this time Colonel Seve formally embraced Islamism, and assumed the name and title of Solyman Bey, and the command of the 6th regiment, one of those destined for the Morea. As this occurrence made some sensation at the time in Christian Europe, it being the only recent instance of a Christian officer having publicly apostatised, we shall give the circumstances of the case from the narrative of our author, who was then on the spot.

Seve had completed his task : an army of 24,000 men was formed chiefly through his exertions. The Viceroy had assured him of his protection and of an independence for life, but rank in his army it was out of his power to give him ; he could not place a Christian officer in command over Osmanlees. He had given him at one time the temporary command of a battalion of blacks, but it was under the plea of instructing them, and even this had caused strong murmurs. In point of fact, Seve was only a *talemgi* (instructor) attached to the army; but in a civil capacity; but as he was a most valuable officer, he was given to understand that if he would but go through the formality of becoming a Mussulman, he should immediately be made a Bey, and have the actual command of a regiment of 4,000 men, with handsome appointments, and a new career would thus open before him. Seve was ambitious; he was thirty-six years of age; fancying he had nothing more to expect in Europe, he took the awful and irretrievable step: in June, 1824, he made profession of Islamism, and went through the necessary rites. We can hardly trust ourselves with any reflections on this painful subject. The attempt at an apology by M. Planat, dictated, we doubt not, by kind feelings towards a countryman and brother officer, is weak indeed; it reduces itself to this—that Seve was already a mere nominal Christian, one of that numerous class, particularly numerous in his age and country, who are quite indifferent about religious belief, and are satisfied with the easy admission of a Supreme Being, and, M. Planat adds, " of a future life." But, we would ask, what can be the object of a future life unless it he to award us punishment, or reward according to our deserts? Our indulgent casuist observes that " religion does not consist in the rites and ceremonies of an outward form of worship." But is there nothing else that distinguishes Christianity from Mahomedanism besides rites and outward forms? Are there no positive dogmas, no imperious duties which draw an impassable line between the Koran and the Gospel? " In the Koran," says M. Planat, " we find, *leaving apart the Prophet, however* (l), the same God, Creator, and Ruler of the Universe, just and merciful; therefore, M. Seve, in changing his religious practices, did not change his God." Alas! such is the logic, such are the arguments which, we say it not in scorn but in sorrow, too often pass current among our neighbours on the other side of the channel.

One of the most remarkable characters in Egypt, next to the Viceroy himself, is the Major General Osman Bey Noureddin. He was sent in early youth to Europe by Mehemed Ali, to finish his education; he spent several years in France and Italy, learned the languages of those countries, and made himself acquainted with European literature. On his return to Egypt, he translated into Turkish the French army regulations and manuals of exercise and manœuvres, which were adopted by the new troops. In 1821, he founded the elementary school of arts and sciences of Caser-el-ain, at Cairo, where about 600 boys, Turks and Arabs, under 18 years of age, are taught Turkish, Arabic, and Italian, drawing, arithmetic and geometry, and the infantry exercise. From this school the pupils proceed to the higher schools, or into the civil administrations.

In May, 1825, a military college was instituted for the instruction of officers in the scientific branches of their profession. A general staff corps was appointed at the same time, and Osman Bey was placed at the head of it with the rank of Major General. Our author, M. Planat, was engaged as director, or chief instructor, in the college, having other French and Italian professors under him. The students were taken from among the colonels, adjutants, and captains. The course of studies consisted of arithmetic, geometry, and drawing, the French language, the theory of infantry movements, and the study and practice of artillery, fortifications, topography, and ground surveying. The difficulties at first were considerable, the Turks being haughty and unmanageable; as the technical words were not to be found in the Turkish language, Osman Bey composed them with the assistance of the Arabic. As figure-drawing was repugnant to their religious ideas, Osman Bey used a stratagem; he left on the school-table a volume of Lavater's Physiognomy; the students looked at the plates and wondered, and began to ask questions like boys, such as why this head had only one eye? Then one of them was made to stand in the same position, &c. Thus, by degrees, they became interested, and one of them one day ventured to draw a head; his companions feared he had committed himself; but the Major General praised the attempt; the rest imitated the example, and a regular school of drawing was at last formed, though this branch of instruction was not officially included in the course.

The camp of instruction, with the college and staff, was now established near the village of Kangha, about four leagues north of Cairo, on the road to Syria, and on the verge of the desert. It is a plain of a firm sandy soil, above the level of the inundations of the Nile, and the climate is dry and healthy, though exposed to the *kamsin,* or hot south wind, which carries with it clouds of fine dust. A depôt (*nakhilè*) was also formed, as a sort of preparatory school for officers of infantry, in which 500 young men are organized into a battalion, and hence are promoted to commissions in the regular regiments as vacancies occur.

All these establishments and their accessaries have by degrees given rise to the village of Dgiaad Abad, which looks like a little European town in the rear of the camp. There are pretty houses with gardens, plantations of mulberry trees, wells supplied from the Nile by hydraulic machines, &c. At a distance of a mile and a half to the left of the camp, near the village of Abu-zabel, a large square building with an ample court in the middle was fixed upon as a military hospital. Dr. Clot, a French physician, was placed at the head of the medical department. He caused the old ruinous building to be pulled down and another built with the materials. Each side of the square contains eight dormitories, or wards, with forty beds each, and separated by wide corridors well aired. The building has no upper story, and the floor is raised four feet above the ground, which is very dry. In the middle of the spacious court are the dispensary, the baths, the kitchen, and a school of anatomy and dissecting room. This last was a great stumbling block to Mussulmans, and it required all the doctor's perseverance, in which he was powerfully seconded by Mehemed Ali, to carry the point. Religious prejudices were strong against the practice of dissection, and it has been thought prudent to keep it concealed from the people, every pupil binding himself by an oath not to divulge its secrets. One hundred young Arabs who had received some education (the Turks look down upon any pursuit which is not essentially military) were admitted as students, a uniform was given them, and after three years' practice they were eligible to the appointment of assistant surgeons in the army. The records of Arabian literature were ransacked to demonstrate that medicine was once in high favour among the believers; Abou Sana, whom we call commonly Avicenna, was extolled as the greatest light of the science, the study of anatomy was shown to be absolutely necessary in order to know the mechanism of the human frame, and at last prejudice was overcome. Lecturers on pathology, on chemistry, pharmacy, and botany were appointed, besides which the young men attended at the beds of the sick, and the surgical operations. This is perhaps the most useful establishment in all Egypt, and may be considered as a wonderful novelty in a Turkish country. The chief physician has about 1000 francs per month; the assistants and professors, all Europeans, have about 300. Another hospital has since been formed at Alexandria. A council of health is established at Cairo, composed of the Viceroy's protomedico, the chief physician of Abu-zabel, and two inspectors.

A commission of civil engineers for the superintendence of roads, bridges, and buildings, under the direction of M. Coste, has also been instituted, with fifty pupils, many of whom have since completed their instruction. Some of these have completed a *cadastre*, or new division, of Egypt, in sixteen departments, subdivided into districts and cantons, after the French model.

We must now pause, and give a general glance at all this creation effected by one man in the brief space of ten years. Those who have any idea of what Egypt was at the beginning of the present century,[*] a scene of anarchy, civil warfare and barbarism, a country distracted between a lawless militia and more lawless Osmanlee retainers of the Porte; those who know what the greater part of the vast Ottoman empire is even to this day, will best be able to appreciate the benefits of Mehemed Ali's administration. The regeneration of Egypt is far more complete than that which has been brought about by Sultan Mahmood in European Turkey, as the protected situation of the former country and the character of its population are more favourable to the attempt. But here some misgivings force themselves upon our minds. Will these institutions of Mehemed Ali take root in the soil, or will they end with the now nearly spun-out thread of his useful life? The interest we take in Egyptian affairs must depend mainly upon the solution of the above question, for if the whole structure is again to crumble into the dust in a few years, and the chaos of old Ottoman misrule to resume its sway, then the pageant is not worthy of arresting our attention. Is there any thing so radically vicious in Mahomedan society, as to prevent justice, order, humanity, and education from ever growing and thriving in it? Our author gives no opinion on the subject, but he points out an essential defect in the foundations of the new system. There are two castes, or rather races, in Egypt, the Osmanlees and the

---

[*] Ali Bey visited Egypt in 1807, and saw Mehemed Ali; and he gives a dismal account of the state of the country, the insubordination of the soldiery, and the weakness of the government.

Arabs, or Fellahs, cultivators of the soil; the former are the masters, they constitute the government, they furnish the officers, civil and military; the latter are subjects, little better than slaves. From both these the new system has dangers to apprehend.

" The Turks," says M. Planat, " have a certain outward show of politeness mixed with dignity, they are hospitable, tolerant and good-humoured, provided you do not talk to them about books and methods; grave and close in matters of business, but noisy in their amusements and extremely capricious; you must either do and talk as they do, or avoid them. Those who have arrived at middle age without having partaken of modern information, are very tenacious of their opinions; the least contradiction irritates them, their habit of commanding slaves cannot be rooted out of them; they are not however deficient in intelligence, but their indolence, and effeminate mode of living, have almost incapacitated them for mental exertion. The demonstrations they have now witnessed with their own eyes of the superior science of Europeans, have made them sensible of the emptiness of their former ignorant contempt of Christians; they feel that all their boasting, their fine horses and trappings, their shining Damascus blades, even their personal bravery, for brave they unquestionably are when roused, are insufficient to keep their ground among other nations. But it is a grievous mortification at forty years and upwards to have to begin a new life full of difficulty and labour, to submit like boys to a severe discipline, to give up cherished illusions, to renounce the incense of flattery, and cast off habits of long-assumed, and till now unquestioned superiority. What! submit to the same laws and regulations as their slaves! Such being the pupils we had to form, we were rejoiced when, after a few weeks of instruction, in which a certain management and tact were required, we found some of them enter, as it were, a new sphere of ideas, a new chord of their minds had been struck, they felt emulation, they began to court the instructors and the books they had before loathed. I have been surprised at times at the rapidity of the change, and at the zeal of application which succeeded their former apathy."—p. 70, &c.

On the other hand the mass of the subject people, with the exception of a few Copts in the cities, are of Arab descent, hardy, laborious, frugal and persevering, quick at learning, accustomed for ages to obey, and yet disliking the Turks, their masters; they have been easily induced to submit to the new discipline, and make excellent soldiers; they are brave, agile, careless of privations, marching barefooted if necessary, sleeping on the ground; they have easily divested themselves of old prejudices, which with them are not, as with the Turks, united with the enjoyments of command and of luxury. In their intercourse with the European officers, they exhibited none of the jealousy and pride of the Osmanlees. " The difference of religion," says M. Planat, " could hardly be said to draw a line between us and them. Why then," adds he, " not communicate the chief impulse of the reform to this nation ?" For a very simple reason, we would venture to answer, because Mehemed Ali, his friends and councillors, are Osmanlees, and as such do not wish to expose their empire to the chances of a revolution. For this reason no Arab officer is raised at present above the rank of a lieutenant. " Then," observes M. Planat, " the system of regeneration is established on a false base;"—not more so, we think, than *any other plan of regeneration begun by masters,* for the latter cannot be expected to cut their own throats in order to please theorists. Peter the Great did not begin by emancipating his serfs and those of his nobility; had he done so there would have been an end of Russian reform. Our author afterwards recollects himself, observing " that the intention of the Sovereign must be to effect regeneration by steps and gradations, whilst a fusion of the two races will probably take place in the mean time; these Turks," adds he, " seem to feel and understand, as if by instinct, that which in Europe is looked upon as a great secret of statesmanship."* Were Egypt to be effectually detached from the Ottoman empire, and the Osmanlees not recruited from the Levant, we think their race would become extinct, and the Arabs would effect their independence. We have heard it stated as a remarkable fact, that the marriages of the Turks in Egypt are mostly barren.

We find M. Planat returning frequently to the subject of the Arabs. He appears to have been less of a theorist than many of his countrymen, and rather a sensible practical man, such as the better order of Napoleon's officers certainly were. Moreover, he seems to have had no preposterous ambition, no transcendant opinion of his own merits, but to have been satisfied with the kindness and hospitality he had experienced in a strange land, sincerely attached to his superiors, and zealous for the improvement of that fine country which he had learned to consider as his own. That he was by no means deficient in warm feeling, we find a proof in the account he gives of the Egyptian mode of recruiting and its enormous abuses.

" At the epoch of the expedition to the Morea, the Viceroy ordered the formation of three more regiments to replace those that were sent away. Orders were given to the cachefs, or heads of villages, to furnish

---

* For an army of 50,000 men, which Mehemed Ali now has, about 3,000 officers were required. These were to be sought for among the Turks, the retainers of the pacha, beys, and other great people, their Mamelukes, body guards, pipe bearers, pages, writers, clerks, &c. This class being exhausted, any Osmanlee or Albanian petty officer of the old establishment, topgees or cannoneers, were taken, men accustomed to a life of alternate licentious indolence and violence and plunder. From such elements, it is easy to conceive that the formation of the officers gave much more trouble than that of the men. Even to the last, M. Planat observes, that the officers, although with many honourable exceptions, are still the weaker part of the Egyptian army.

recruits; 12,000 men were wanted, and the number sent to the camp of Kangha was 48,000! of which 36,000 were, after the inspection, sent back to their homes, having thus lost, many of them, forty days, and been dragged like felons, pinioned two by two, with ropes and heavy pieces of wood hanging from their necks. The roads were covered with these poor wretches, some with hardly a rag round their loins, extenuated with hunger and fatigue, driven by horsemen inured to this kind of service, and followed by the wives, children and old men, whose number arrived at the camp was above 20,000! In many cases the whole family came, and the house and field were abandoned."—p. 75, &c.

The management of the recruiting is left to the petty local authorities, Arabs themselves, who being uncontrouled, give full scope to their avarice, partialities and passions; numbers of families are thus ruined, while others have never furnished a recruit since the formation of the Nizam. The men rejected one year are often sent again the next, even when found defective or cripple; these poor *Fellahs* are so used to arbitrary oppression that they appear quite resigned to it, but many families leave the country in despair in order to avoid further vexations.

The intelligent Turks acknowledge the enormity of these abuses, but plead as their excuse, that the Arabs, with their proverbial cunning and trickery, would contrive to evade any plan of registry that might lead to a proper repartition of the conscription, and that every one of them endeavours to shift the burthen from his own shoulders to those of his neighbour. But as it appears that there is already a registry for the *miri*, or land-tax and house-tax, it would be an easy matter to ascertain at least the number of families. And if the sheiks do not act equitably, why not establish a municipal council in each village or district, composed of the *notables*, to whom all communal affairs should be referred? The most difficult task in forming a regular levy would be to ascertain the ages of individuals. There is, says M. Planat, hardly a Turk or Egyptian who knows the exact date of his birth or marriage; this uncertainty might be remedied in the next generation by issuing a regulation to the imams to keep henceforth a register of the circumcisions; and as to the present grown-up young men, they might be registered in classes of five years, from fifteen to twenty, and from twenty to twenty-five, out of which the number of recruits wanted might be drawn by lottery. After the latter period they ought to be exempted from serving, while at present there are men evidently past forty who have been enlisted. These regulations would produce another advantage, as young men, knowing their liability to the conscription, would not contract precocious marriages as they do at present, which tend to deteriorate the race. " If," our author concludes, "·you talk to a Turk of rank about these matters, he will readily admit the ⸱justice of your arguments, but if you press upon him the necessity of bestirring himself and making a beginning, you will find the usual resistance of apathy; *baccalum!* 'we will see!' is his motto."

There are, as we have already noticed, other materials besides the Fellahs, at the disposal of the Viceroy of Egypt for recruiting his army. These are the blacks from the interior, which his possessions of Sennaar and Kordofan enable him to draw to Egypt. This is a new and important feature of the Nizam. These blacks have been tried, have made distant campaigns, and are now mixed indiscriminately in the regiment with the Fellahs; though they are not so quick in learning their exercise as the Arabs, they are more intrepid, more faithful, and less disposed to desertion. They retain much of the pride of the savage, and his contempt for bodily pain and death. But the change of climate and of diet, and the fits of despondency to which they are subject, produce great mortality among them in the field. They answer better when assembled in stationary colonies, of which there is one at Heliopolis in Middle Egypt, which is in a thriving state.

M. Planat seems to have been persuaded that regeneration in the Ottoman empire must begin by the army, and be carried on through its instrumentality. However averse we may ⸱justly feel in Europe to a regeneration by the bayonet and effected by military instructors, we can be brought to believe that this is the only chance of regenerating Turkey, and indeed recent facts seem to prove it. The Koran, unlike the Gospel, was ushered in by the sword,—by the sword it has been supported and spread, and we fear that any reform in accordance with that code must, in some degree, partake of the same spirit. The formation of a regular and disciplined army, subject to the central government, furnishes the only possible means of checking the local tyranny of the pachas, beys and agas, of making these petty despots amenable to the general laws of the empire, of protecting the life and property of the subject, and, lastly, of instilling into the minds of all the first wholesome principle of universal ⸱justice, of certain duties and restrictions from which great and small must not swerve; no trifling point gained towards civilization. Till now, it is notorious that justice did not exist in Turkey, that every thing could be obtained, and every law evaded by force or money, and ·that the poor wretch who had neither could no more appeal to right against power than fight the Sultan himself. The very idea of such an appeal was regarded as absurd, and ridiculous; and the dreadful moral effects of this universal unbelief in ⸱justice are now conspicuous, the powerful believe in nothing, and the weak seek consolation in fatalism throughout the empire, as a last mental refuge from overwhelming oppression.

A curious episode, related by our author, comes here opportunely to exhibit in its true colours the old system of Ottoman government, which still prevails over a great part of the empire. In 1822, Abdalla, pacha of Acre, having bribed the emir of the Druses, a singular race of mountaineers, who inhabit the chain of Mount Lebanon, unrolled a forged firman, in which the Sultan was made to bestow on him the pachalick of Damascus, then held by Dervis Pacha. He then marched against Damascus, followed by his auxiliaries, but after ravaging the country, he was stopped by real firmans from the Porte, in which he was denounced as a rebel, and five pachas, including those of Damascus and Aleppo, were ordered to surround him and send his head to Stamboul. Abdalla, abandoned by the Druses, whose emir fled to Egypt, shut himself up in his fortress of Acre, and there braved the five pachas who had encamped under its wall with 9,000 irregulars. No one in their army understood the process of making approaches, the shot from their cannon passed over the ramparts without doing any damage to the garrison. Abdalla triumphed, and laughed at his enemies, the town was well supplied by sea, and this curious siege lasted ten months, to the great scandal of the whole empire. At last Mehemed Ali undertook the part of mediator, and obtained the pardon of Abdalla, on condition of his paying 60,000 purses to the Sultan; the emir Bechir returned to his mountain capital, Dair el Kamar, and the five pachas retreated home. This Abdalla was celebrated for his art in squeezing his subjects. One of his financial measures consisted in sending to those who were possessed of money goods from the government stores, such as corn, salt, and especially *soap,* to which he affixed an exorbitant price, which the forced purchaser was obliged to pay directly in cash. One of his threats when angry was to say to the object of his displeasure—" Take care I don't send you some of my soap!" Abdalla's soaps were the terror of Syria.—p. 52, &c.

We must now advert more particularly to an important epoch of Mehemed Ali's reign, namely, his expedition to the Morea, which has drawn upon him considerable obloquy. M. Planat gives a full account of the whole of these transactions. He entertains no doubt that Mehemed Ali, although at first not very eager to put himself forward, when once engaged in the war, acted sincerely in support of the empire, and of this we have felt throughout convinced. The cause of the Sultan, however objectionable it might appear in Europe, was that of the Osmanlees in general; and Mehemed Ali was too clear-sighted not to perceive that when an external attack was aimed at the head, all the limbs were interested in averting the blow: for the Turks already expected, and the event proved how truly, a war with Russia; and, indeed, at one time they imagined that a secret league of the Christian powers had been entered into for the destruction of the Crescent.

It was in July, 1824, that the Egyptian fleet, consisting of sixty-three ships of war, sailed, escorting 100 transports of all nations, with 16,000 regular infantry on board, four companies of sappers, field-pieces and heavy ordnance, and 700 cavalry, the whole under the command of Ibrahim Pacha. After being joined off Samos by the fleet of the Captain Pacha, they were attacked by the Greeks under Canaris, who set fire to a Turkish frigate. The Ottomans then bore away, and Ibrahim having collected his vessels together put back into Rhodes. Thence he sailed again, and anchored in Modon Bay in February, 1825. Immediately on his landing, Ibrahim marched with a body of chosen men to relieve Coron, which was besieged by the Greeks. The latter retired on his approach. He next turned himself against Navarino. On the 23d of March he sent 8000 men, with a battering train, to invest the place, and two days after he followed himself. The Greeks made several attempts to relieve it, but were always repelled with great loss. On the 7th of May, Ibrahim resolved to storm the fortress of Old Navarino, the taking of which would facilitate the reduction of the town of New Navarino. For this purpose it was necessary to dislodge the Greeks from an island or rock from which they annoyed the besiegers. Ibrahim sent orders to Modon, to Solyman Bey (Seve), to embark with two battalions of the sixth regiment, and attack the island by sea. The latter effected a landing, and carried the Greek redoubts at the point of the bayonet. About 100 Greeks escaped by swimming on board their ships. In this attack Solyman Bey received a sabre wound, and it was, we believe, on the same day that some Italian refugees, one of whom was the Piedmontese Count Santa Rosa, who had joined the Greeks, met a glorious death. In the night of the 12th of May, another attempt at relief was made by the Greeks from the interior, combined with a sortie from the garrison, both of which were repulsed by the Egyptians with great slaughter. The next day the garrison of Old Navarino surrendered on condition of having their lives spared, and being sent to some other part of the country, which they should name. The same conditions were granted three days after to the garrison of New Navarino; and Ibrahim, having given to his soldiers the spoils of the place, returned to Modon. He then went into the interior, defeated Pietro Bey of Maina, and other chiefs, and occupied Tripolitza. :He marched next upon Napoli di Romania, which he might, perhaps, have entered by escalade in the first moment of alarm of the Greeks. However, he satisfied himself with destroying Argos and the olive plantations in the plain, and returned to Tripolitza. He now sent parties of his men into the fields to reap the harvest which had been abandoned by the Greeks, and to secure and repair the corn mills. After many skirmishes the harvest was secured, and provisions for the army for eight months were brought into Tripolitza, besides a large booty and numbers of prisoners. Thus ended the campaign of 1825, which was most disastrous to the Greeks, who retained now in the Morea only Napoli and Monembasia, or Malvasia.

From the journal of this war, which M. Planat has derived from authentic sources, it appears clearly that the Greeks confined themselves to a partisan or guerilla warfare, and could not stand in the field against the Egyptians. The Arab soldiers fought bravely, and the whole management of the army appears to have been conducted with regularity and skill. Great devastations were committed by Ibrahim, especially in the fertile plain of Argos, although remonstrated against by one of the European officers who had accompanied his army. Yet fewer acts of personal cruelty were perpetrated than in the former wars carried on by the Ottomans, and the prisoners' lives were generally spared.

The campaign of the following year (1826) is memorable for the catastrophe of Missolonghi. Ibrahim, joined by the Seraskier Redschid Pacha, invested the place. The history of the siege is well known; the two outposts of Anatolico and Vassiladi were first taken by force, and the garrisons spared by Ibrahim and sent to Arta. Missolonghi was now closely pressed. The Greeks asked to be allowed to evacuate the place with arms and baggage, which was refused. They then, after having undermined part of the town, as a last resource of despair, determined to try and cut their way, sword in hand, through the besiegers' lines. They formed themselves into three columns; the first passed with only the loss of eleven men; the second lost thirty, but made its way through also; the third column, which was more encumbered with women and children, could not succeed, as the Egyptian troops were now pouring in to the defence of their lines. The unhappy Greeks were driven back into the town, which the besiegers entered along with them. A dreadful scene of slaughter now ensued. The Greeks fought from the windows and behind the walls for four hours. Several families having retired into the houses undermined, blew themselves up, with many of their enemies. The remainder were taken, and all those found with arms in their hands were put to death. Missolonghi was nothing but a vast heap of ruins and dead bodies of Christians and Mussulmans, all mixed together.

Before the siege of Missolonghi, Mehemed Ali had sent two more regiments, 8000 strong, to reinforce Ibrahim's army in the Morea. In the year following (1827) the Porte conferred on the Viceroy the command of the Ottoman fleet, coupled with the onerous charge of repairing and provisioning it. Mehemed Ali had in the mean time assiduously attended to the improvement of his own Egyptian navy, both in the *materiel* and in point of discipline. He had several frigates and corvettes built at Marseilles, Leghorn and Genoa. He also engaged several French naval officers in his service. A Board of Admiralty was established at Alexandria. The sailors are Arabs, and " they," says M. Planat, "rival *ours* in intelligence and skill. But the officers, like those in the army, are inferior to the men; whilst with the Greeks it is quite the reverse; they have good officers, but bad soldiers."—p. 211. The Major General Osman Bey, already mentioned, was also actively employed in organizing the navy. Indeed this Osman seems to be a universal man, and to have a hand in every thing. He translated the regulations of the French navy, from which he compiled a code for the Egyptian. He came, however, to an article in the former where, in case of some particular offences, disgrace and cashiering are the punishments awarded to the officer. " This will not answer here," shrewdly observed Osman; " our people have not such sensitiveness of honour; many would, perhaps, be glad to get out of the service at so cheap a rate. We must threaten them with degradation, and when that fails, with the bastinado." But then it must be observed, that the Egyptian officers, like the sailors, were in fact little better than slaves, pressed into the service, and governed chiefly by fear. The young men of the rising generation, being brought up under the present institutions, will probably be a different race of beings.

Mehemed Ali formed a naval school on board a corvette of one hundred young men. French naval officers acted as instructors, and afterwards as masters and masters' mates on board the fleet. The direction of this establishment was given to Hassan Bey Kouprousli, an old friend and companion of the Viceroy. The end of this man afforded a singular and rare instance of suicide in an Osmanlee. He had fallen under the Viceroy's disgrace on some charge of irregularity in his accounts, and been threatened in full divan to be brought before a court-martial. On his return on board his corvette, which was moored in the old harbour of Alexandria, he sent on shore under different pretences the pupils and their instructors; and to those who still loitered behind, he declared that unless they went away immediately they were dead men. Shortly after he fired his pistol into the powder store, and thus blew himself up. Eleven men, who had not understood or disregarded his orders, perished along with him!

The dock-yard of Alexandria was put in order. The confusion which previously existed in every department of the navy is incredible; the guns on board the ships were without proper carriages, some were found stowed in the holds; shot of all dimensions were heaped together; no inventory was kept of the ordnance or ammunition; the exhalations from the stagnant water, the filth of the decks, were enough to engender diseases. These things were altered; the old officers were exercised in the working of the ships, whilst the young ones were studying navigation; Arab boatmen were formed into battalions, and exercised as sailors, gunners and marines; and an Egyptian navy has at last been created, very different from the old Ottoman fleet. On the occasion of the sailing of a division with a convoy for the Morea, in the latter end of 1826, Osman Bey ordered a general salute of all the Egyptian ships, which was returned by the European men of war at anchor. He then assembled the captains and commanders, and led them to a large hall, where the Viceroy was seated, and from which there is a fine prospect of the old harbour. Osman Bey made them swear upon their honour to fulfil their duty, to seek for the enemy, and to fight him when met. He expatiated upon the national spirit which ought to animate them in the contest, and declared to them that, in future, promotions and distinctions would be bestowed upon merit alone; whilst those who should fail in their duties, disobey the new regulations, injure or disgrace their master's service, would be punished with the utmost rigour of the newly enacted laws. Osman spoke warmly and feelingly; his emotion communicated itself to his rude auditors, who perhaps for the first time felt the force of an appeal to their dignity as men. The Viceroy, Mehemed Ali, was seen to wipe his eyes several times.—p. 173.

On the 17th June, 1827, a Greek fleet of small vessels, with the frigate Hellas, having Lord Cochrane on board, appeared off Alexandria. In the night the Greeks directed three fire-ships against the Egyptian fleet, which was moored in the old harbour. The brig Tigranes alone caught fire, and was destroyed. Next day part of the Egyptian fleet, notwithstanding contrary winds, succeeded in putting to sea. The Viceroy, who happened to be at Alexandria, went about in his yacht giving orders, encouraging, and hastening the preparations. The batteries of the forts were put in readiness, a battalion of regulars was encamped at Figuiers point. The whole scene is represented by M. Planat as having been extremely animated. In the evening the whole fleet got under weigh, and the Viceroy's yacht in the midst of it. The Greeks meantime stood off. Mehemed Ali having given his final instructions to the admiral Mobarrem Bey, his son-in-law, to follow the Greeks, and bring them to action if possible, returned on shore. The fleet steered towards Rhodes, without, however, coming up with the enemy, and returned on the 29th to the harbour of Alexandria. Thus ended this alarm, which, however, as Osman Bey observed, had the good effect of keeping the Egyptians more on their guard since.

On the 5th of August, in consequence of orders from the Sultan, the combined Turkish and Egyptian fleet sailed for the Morea with the 10th regiment, to reinforce Ibrahim. The fleet consisted of two seventy-fours, several frigates and corvettes, besides smaller ships, in all seventy-five sail, and in the best condition. This was the fleet that was afterwards partly destroyed at Navarino. The brigs and schooners were furnished with twenty-four long oars, by means of which they could proceed at the rate of two miles an hour in case of calm, a contingency frequent in those seas. On the same day an event occurred, ominous to vulgar minds. Mohamed Bey, minister at war, a man devoted to the improvements of his country, and who might be considered Mehemed Ali's right arm, died of a violent disease. He had predicted his death the year before, and had a handsome monument raised for himself in the midst of plantations watered by fountains, by the side of the tomb of an old friend, whose death he constantly regretted. This was to the Viceroy a serious loss. Mohamed Bey was enthusiastically attached to his master, and often used to express his sincere admiration for a man who had done so much, although he had only learned to write at fifty years of age! He was proud to serve him, and only regretted that he should not be able to serve him long. In the most critical times he had by his decision and firmness saved his master's power, and we need not add his life, for in such cases the two words are synonimous in Turkey. He cleared Egypt of the remains of the Mamelukes; those who escaped were finally obliged to emigrate for ever beyond the cataracts. While Mehemed Ali was with the army in Arabia, in 1813, Latif Pacha came from Constantinople, secretly provided with a firman appointing him Pacha of Egypt, and succeeded in gaining the support of a strong party. Mohamed Bey, who was then minister of the interior in his master's absence, feigned to enter into Latif's views, and thus drew the latter to expose publicly his intentions, when Mohamed Bey, rallying his faithful ad-

herents, surprised him, and had him immediately executed. Although he was the second person in the state, he lived simply and
died poor.   He was known to have repeatedly, in times of need,
given up his salary to the treasury.   His house and furniture were
now sold to defray the remaining charges of his household. · Although stern in the performance of his duty, and harsh and pe-
remptory in his manner, he was never unjust, and he could also
be generous and indulgent.   Several instances, reflecting honour
on his character, are given by our author, who seems to have
been sincerely attached to the highly gifted old Mussulman. · Although perfectly undeceived with regard to the old prejudices and
ignorance of his countrymen, he was clear-sighted enough to
see where innovation ought to stop.   It having been represented
to him that young Osman Bey entirely neglected religious instruction and practice in the new schools, the old man severely
censured this omission, which he characterized as both improper
and imprudent.   He assembled one day the officers of the staff at
Dgiaad Abad, and the pupils of the military college, and said to
them :—" In future you shall not fail to perform your prayers ; I
have brought you two imams for the purpose, and Osman Bey
(who was then absent) shall attend too.   Woe to him who ab-
sents himself."   Next day the foundations of a mosque were laid
opposite to the school.—p. 149.

The treaty of London, of the 6th of July, was communicated
to the Viceroy after the departure of his fleet.   An English
officer, Col. Cradock, arrived towards the end of August on a
mission to Mehemed Ali.   To the proposal of withdrawing
Ibrahim from the Morea, the Viceroy mildly answered that he
was the subject of the Porte, and could not be a party to negotiations between the high powers,—that he certainly wished for
peace, but that must depend on the fiat of the Sultan, his master.
And he accompanied his answers with that courteousness of manner for which he is remarkable.   Being told that the Porte had
ordered Ibrahim to defend himself to the last extremity, he replied,
" Well ! I know my son, he will fight as long as he has a plank
of his fleet left."   However, he continued to assure the Franks
and the European travellers in his states, that whatever might be
the result of these affairs, he should continue to protect them with
all his power.   And he kept his word.

On the 28th of October an Egyptian corvette arrived at Alexandria, much damaged, and bearing the news of the defeat of
Navarino.   The report spread through the town ; the populace,
the Albanians, the Turkish gunners of Alexandria, and the families of the sailors on board the fleet, assembled round the
Viceroy's palace, crying loudly for revenge.   Mehemed Ali re-

tained all his presence of mind. The Albanians and the gunners were confined to their barracks, and their arms taken away; the families of the sailors were sent home, partly by persuasion, and partly by force. The guard of the district of the Franks was entrusted to the regular troops, and the storm was thus dissipated. We can feel, too, for Mehemed Ali on this occasion. That he was sorely grieved there can be no doubt; but he repressed his vexation, and said to his first drogman and confident, Boghos, " I expected as much, the Porte would have it so." The loss of the Egyptian fleet, however, though considerable in men, was not so great in ships as was at first imagined.

Satisfactory as the result of that combat was to the cause of Christianity and of humanity at large, it will not be uninteresting to our readers to hear the sentiments expressed in Egypt on the occasion :—

" The people here," says M. Planat, " begin to accuse the allies of a great abuse of power in the assumption of a dictatorship which rests upon no other foundation than that of force. There are men here among these Turks who know, though somewhat confusedly, that Europe is agitated from one end to the other by a struggle between power and liberty. They quote with a sort of sneer Spain and Poland, and ask why the great powers do not take under their protection the liberties of those countries as well as those of Greece? We are rather puzzled how to reply to their questions. The shameful piracies of the Greeks in the Archipelago, they think, ought to have been visited on the pirates themselves, and not on the Mussulmans, who are extensive consumers of European goods."—p. 100.

M. Planat speaks favourably and feelingly of the real champions of Greek independence, such as Canaris, Botzaris, and Miaulis, and of the few Europeans who truly and sincerely devoted themselves to the same cause; among others he mentions, with high praise, his own countrymen, Colonel Fabvier and St. Jean d'Angely. But he spares not " those noisy Philhellenes, those declaimers and poets who ranted in the newspapers about the descendants of Pericles and Leonidas, and filled the heads of people with the grossest delusions as to the real state of Greece." We believe that in our days sensible men are generally aware how cautiously vague reports and opinions concerning foreign and distant countries are to be received. Our author complains bitterly of the manner in which many European officers who had gone to assist the Greeks were treated by them; insulted, exposed to danger without being supported, receiving no pay and having exhausted their private means, they were glad to come away; several of these, whom he mentions, came to Egypt, where they were kindly received by the Viceroy. Many Greek families came also for safety, and found protection. All these, however, and other instances our author gives of Greek disorders, were the unavoidable effects of the miserable state to which Greece had been reduced, and of·the corruption, mistrust, and selfishness which had pervaded the mass of the Greek people during long ages of abject and barbarian oppression. It was only by putting an end to this brutalizing yoke, that any chance could be obtained of raising their national character. Unlike any other revolution, that of Greece risked nothing; it was no dubious experiment, for there was absolutely nothing more to lose, but every thing to gain ; and we consider it as a most providential dispensation that the independence of Greece was acknowledged before the breaking out of fresh troubles in the west of Europe, which else must have had the effect of weakening the interest, or at least cramping the exertions of the great powers in favour of that country.

All these new establishments, and the various foreign expeditions of Mehemed Ali, entailed an enormous expense on his treasury, which at one time was in a state of great disorder. We wish M. Planat had entered into some details about the Viceroy's financial means, which, besides the taxes, consist of mercantile profits, he being the first merchant in his states. He purchases at a fixed price the corn, cotton, and other harvest from the growers, and then sells it again, often at a great profit, to the traders and foreign merchants. The taxes are: the *miri* or land tax, the house tax, a capitation tax, and custom-house duties, which amount to only *three per cent.* on imported goods ! Every two or three years the Viceroy is obliged to send his own ministers to verify and audit the accounts of the different provinces, the collection of the taxes being left to the local authorities, who are often in arrear with the government, while they are guilty of exactions upon the inhabitants. All this is owing to the want of a regular system of internal administration, a thing unknown among Turks. For the same reason we know nothing of the budget, or of the amount of revenue: and we can only guess at some of the expenses, such as the army, because fixed salaries are now established, whilst before, the payment of the irregular troops was left entirely to the chiefs, who contrived to cheat both the government and the men. M. Planat's table of the pay of the officers and men of the Nizam will be found further on. Once, on his return from Alexandria to Cairo, Mehemed Ali was very wroth to find that his bills on the treasury, or exchequer bills, were negotiated at a great ·loss. The fault was laid on the Copt writers, who have all the accounts in their hands, as the Turks are no.clerks. It seems, however, that in 1826, Mehemed Ali had·projects laid before him of a regular plan of financial administration, especially for the collection and inspection of the revenue. He had also sent, about the same time, forty young men, some belonging to the first families in Egypt, to Paris, to form a sort of Egyptian College, and to learn mathematics, languages, medicine and other liberal professions, in order to choose from among them competent civil administrators. Some of these must, by this time, have completed their studies, and have returned home.

Our author reckons the population of Egypt at two millions and a half: we think it rather nearer three millions. In this calculation are not included the tribes of Bedowens, who are encamped in the neighbouring deserts, and who have now been brought to acknowledge the authority of the Viceroy, and furnish him with troops, especially irregular cavalry, to act as partizans and scouts. The Arab settled population consists of two classes, the Fellahs or labourers, and the descendants of Bedowen tribes, who have settled in the villages of the valley of the Nile, and who consider themselves of purer blood than the former. The other states subject to Mehemed Ali, are :—1. Dongola, Sennaar, and Kordofan, in short, the whole country beyond the Cataracts to the frontiers of Dar-foor and of Abyssinia. 2. The Hedjaz, including the Holy Cities, the Sherif of Mekka having no political power, and the Pacha of Djedda being subordinate to the viceroyalty of Egypt; and, 3, the island of Candia.* Of these the first might be made the most solid and important, as it is the most natural apanage of Egypt. A new military governor, Ruttem Bey, Colonel of the first regiment, was sent to Sennaar at the end of 1826, who took with him a French instructor and a surgeon. He received special instructions from the Major-General, Osman Bey, to establish hospitals the same as in Egypt, for the use of the natives as well as the military, to endeavour to conciliate the inhabitants to their new government, to encourage agriculture, to protect travellers and caravans from Abyssinia and other parts of the interior, and to form a corps of native infantry. Of the application and result of these wise measures we cannot speak from any subsequent reports, but we have no doubt things are better managed now than they were ten years since by the irregular troops under Ismayl Pacha, of whose mode of warfare M. Caillaud gave us such a revolting account.

The kingdom of Dar-foor is held by a Moorish dynasty of the

---

* The island of Candia is placed under Mehemed Ali's *military* superintendence; but the pachas of Candia and Retimo are still directly responsible to the sultan. The Sphactiotes, or Mountaineers, a wild race, professing the Greek religion, and never entirely subdued, continue at war with the Turks. A considerable portion of the population of the coasts profess Mahommedanism.

name of Kondgiaree, which is on hostile terms with the Egyptians, who have conquered from it the province of Kordofan. The chief force of the nation is their cavalry; the horsemen wear a coat of mail, and their appearance, says Mr. Planat, resembles that of the ancient Saracens. The inhabitants are of two races, as in Sennaar, the blacks, who are the subjects, and the Moors, of Arab descent, who are the rulers.

On the 1st January, 1828, the army of Mehemed Ali was comprised as follows:—

12 regiments, *alays*, of regular infantry, *peade*, of five *ortas* or battalions each, the battalion of 800 men	48,000
2 battalions supernumerary	1,600
1 battalion of cadets at the *nekhile* or depôt at Dgiaad Abad	500
3 battalions of artillery, *topgian*	1,800
Companies of waggon train	300
Ditto of gendarmes	150
12 companies of sappers, *baltadgis*, one with each regiment	700
2 ditto of artificers and pontonniers, *kouproudgis** . . .	160
The pupils and officers of the various military schools . .	1,000
Old Turkish artillery doing duty in the garrisons . . .	800
Albanian irregular infantry	6,000
Turkish cavalry, irregular	6,000
	66,960

Deducting however the losses recently sustained, especially by the army in the Morea, M. Planat reckons the whole at about 54,000 men, of whom 42,000 are regulars. Of this force, one regiment was in Sennaar and Kordofan, two were in Arabia, seven in the Morea, which soon after returned home, and the rest in Egypt. Part of the Albanian irregulars were in Candia. Thus the Egyptian armies were serving at the same time in Asia, in Africa, and in Europe. No reform had yet taken place in the cavalry, that body having been found more indocile than the infantry; attempts were made to embody them into squadrons, and accustom them to regular movements, but once in the field, as was the case in Arabia, they broke their ranks, and charged in their old tumultuous manner. Mehemed Ali had given orders, however, to have them all assembled at Djaffarich, in the Delta, and ranged into brigades of 1000 men, to be commanded by Beys. Previously they had been classed by cachefs or troops nominally of forty horsemen each, every chief being at the same time quarter master and paymaster, and subject to no inspection or review.

The general staff, *ridgial*, of the army consisted of Ibrahim Pacha, Generalissimo, the Minister at War, the Major General

---

* Companies of miners were being formed at the time.

Osman Bey, Selim Bey Colonel of the Staff, two chiefs of battalions, six adjutant-majors, six sub-adjutant majors, thirty-eight captains, ten lieutenants, and eight second lieutenants, these were assembled at the camp of Dgiaad Abad, where they attended the instructions at the college.

The monthly pay of the officers of regiments is as follows:—

	Egyptian piastres.	Francs.
1 colonel, *emir alay*	8000	2666
1 lieutenant-colonel, *kaimakan*	4000	
4 chiefs of battalion, *bin bachi*	2000 each.	
5 adjutant majors, *sag col agasi*, one of whom commands the fifth or depot battalion	1500 ditto.	
5 sub-adjutant majors	1000 ditto.	
1 first surgeon, *akim bachi*	1150	
5 assistant ditto, *akim*	1000 each.	
5 copts, writers, or accountants, *mallem*	} not stated.	
1 imam or priest		
1 captain, *jus bachi*, to each *boulouk* or company	500	
1 lieutenant, *mulasem evel*	350	
1 sub ditto, *mulasem*	250	

The serjeants, *chaous*, the corporals, and musicians, receive from one to two piastres per diem; and the privates half a piastre or not quite three and a half French sols, besides the rations, consisting of about two pounds (French weight) of bread, half a pound of meat, about one pound of rice, lentils and beans, and three pounds of wood for fuel, besides salt, oil, and soap. The officers have double and triple rations according to rank. We consider the soldiers' allowance as plentiful for that climate, and are not surprised that the poor Arab recruits, who were nearly starving in their wretched hovels at home, should consider their lot bettered by being in the service of the Viceroy, and thus made sure of a comfortable subsistence, which many of them share with their families, who follow them to the camp; and that although their pay is often a twelvemonth in arrear, they should seldom grumble provided their rations are issued to them regularly. We find, accordingly, that these men were faithful to their officers even when employed to repress insurrections among their own countrymen and fellow villagers.—pp. 123—190. With regard to the officers' pay, that of the colonel is truly splendid, too much so indeed in proportion to that of the company officers. A colonel with 33,000 francs, more than 1300*l.* sterling a year, in such a cheap country as Egypt, besides his rations, horses, servants, &c. is enabled to live like a prince: it must be observed, however, that he commands four thousand men, and answers in fact to one of our generals commanding brigades or divisions.

The clothing delivered to the troops consists of two jackets a

z 2

year, one of red coarse stuff for winter, and one of blue or white cotton cloth in summer, with facings of another colour, two pair of trousers, two ditto shoes, two shirts, and caps. The officers also receive two jackets a year, and a sabre on their being appointed. The officer's dress consists of a short jacket and trousers, both of crimson cloth, a *tarbouche* or cylindrical cap, a silk or cachemire sash, and red slippers. The higher ranks wear a profusion of gold lace, besides stars and crescents often enriched with diamonds.

We have entered into these details, because they serve to show the progress that discipline, comfort, and regularity have made in a few years, in a service which but the other day consisted of hordes of a barbarous and lawless militia. We may just notice one more institution of Mehemed Ali, which reflects honour on his wisdom and humanity, and that is a provision made for soldiers maimed or invalided in the service, another utter novelty among Ottomans.

Of the great mover of all this machinery, of Mehemed Ali himself, our author relates several personal anecdotes, all tending to impress our minds with the idea of a superior and even amiable character; we shall content ourselves with extracting some passages of the narrative of a visit he paid to the camp of Dgiaad Abad in December, 1826. The Viceroy arrived on the 24th at seven in the morning, and was received by the minister at war, the major general, and the staff, who had dismounted, and amidst the discharges of artillery, while the European band was playing the national Arab tune *Abou Lebdè.** He alighted at the house prepared for his reception, and there received the various bodies of officers. The ceremonial for every officer in his turn was to bend himself before the Viceroy, who was seated on his divan, and kiss the hem of his robe. Contrary to the invariable custom of the East, he would not allow any one to take off his shoes, so that " the vice-regal carpets were for the first time trodden by our shoes," says M. Planat, " to the great scandal of some old pipe bearers and other attendants of the strict Osmanlee school." A battalion of honour being appointed to do duty near his person, Mehemed Ali made them manœuvre before him, during which he conversed familiarly with the officers of the staff. Afterwards the pupils of the artillery school manned their guns and performed their evolutions. At half-past six the Viceroy's grandson Abbas Pacha, son of the late Tousoun, arrived. Mehe-

* With their usual tolerance, or rather haughty carelessness, the Turks allow their subjects to sing to their faces satirical songs against their despotism. The one above begins thus: " Sell thy cap to pay the taxes." During the late Greek war, it was not uncommon to hear the Greek patriotic hymn played by Greek musicians at Constantinople, before the coffee houses, and to a Turkish audience.

med Ali then dined in public under his tent, and afterwards retired
to his house. The following day was employed in visiting the
camp, the village, and the redoubts in front towards the Desert.
The weather being cold, the Viceroy made remarks on the effect
of too great a change of temperature on the constitutions of men,
of the difference between the winters in Arabia and those . of
Greece, and lastly on the disasters of the French in Russia, which
he explained to his officers.

On the 26th the great infantry manœuvres took place. The
Viceroy followed them on a sketch which was traced to him by a
staff officer. He had tendered his own pencil and the outside of
a despatch for this purpose, saying to the officer, " Just sketch
them down any way, *alla baballa.*" He was particularly pleased
with the formation of squares. At four in the afternoon he went
to the hospital of Abouzabel. Dr. Clot, the founder and head of
the establishment, took him to every part of it, and answered all
his numerous questions. He attended an examination of the Arab
pupils, who were purposely questioned on the subject of anatomy
and .dissections, to which they answered freely that the latter
were absolutely necessary to the medical student, and that the
great Abou Sana himself (*Avicenna*) had felt no scruple in this
respect. Mehemed Ali smiled, and at parting .with Dr. Clot
expressed his satisfaction and his gratitude for his zeal and care.

At seven he received the officers and students of the staff college, and questioned them one by one on their studies. He had
previously dismissed his attendants, and he looked, says M.
Planat, like a father in the midst of his children. He put on his
spectacles, examined the plans and topographical maps, and drawings of fortifications, which were very neatly executed. The
plan of the camp of Dgiaad Abad and its environs were shown
to him, a plate of which accompanies the present work. He
testified his agreeable surprise at seeing the progress his officers
had made. He read some translations into Turkish from the
French, particularly from La Fontaine's Fables, and laughed at
some passages in which the poet speaks freely of men in power.
He continued to occupy himself in this manner, with the only
interruption of smoking a pipe and eating two apples, till midnight, when he desired the officers to form a circle round his
divan; he was very friendly to all, especially to Osman Bey, and
exhorted the junior officers to redouble their zeal and courage,
as they had now overcome the first difficulties. " I am well
pleased with you, my children," said he, " if I had interest in heaven
I would perform miracles for you, but I am a mere man, and I
can only offer you promotion and salaries." Then, after a pause,
he added, with the expression of one who feels himself perfectly
content and at ease, " I find myself very well in this simple divan:

I should never wish to have one more sumptuous." " At half-past twelve we retired. Next day, the 27th, we accompanied him part of the way on his return to the capital."—pp. 174—181.

We shall not trouble our readers here with repeating after our author an account of the squabbles and pretensions of some of the French and Italian emigrants in Egypt, all of whom had ' not his good sense and modesty, nor the firmness and experience of Colonel Seve. General Boyer, who had come to Egypt at the latter end of 1824, to superintend the organization of the army, and had brought several other officers under him, and whose appointments were not less than 60,000 francs a year, could not agree, it seems, with the other officers who were there already, nor with the minister at war, and at last left the country in a huff, in August, 1826. When he went to take his leave of the Viceroy, his Highness, notwithstanding what had occurred, asked him politely to stay and dine with him, to which the general answered by excusing himself, saying, he had just breakfasted. Mehemed Ali, his old Osmanlee ideas perhaps recurring to him at the moment, thought the general suspected his intentions, and replied sharply, " Of what *I* eat, general, *you* may very well partake." The general then thought better of the matter, and sat down to table. The Viceroy, however, made him offers of service, told him that his custom house officers had orders not to visit his baggage, and wished him a good journey. Colonel Gaudin, who came to Egypt with Boyer, took his place as chief instructor, with a monthly salary of 1600 francs. An European instructor, or *talemgi*, was also appointed to every battalion; these instructors are divided into classes according to seniority, and receive from 140 to 383 francs a month, besides two uniforms a year, or 1000 piastres (333 francs) in lieu of them, rations, forage for a horse, and a yearly gratification; after making a campaign they have also an increase of pay.

General Livron was at the same time in the service of the Viceroy, who sent him to France as his agent to superintend the construction of ships, and the expedition of various articles he wanted. He had also several Neapolitan and Piedmontese officers in his service. A Colonel Rey, of the French artillery, came likewise, but got himself into trouble by shooting sparrows in the garden of the French consulate at Cairo, an offence which was considered so serious that a mixed Turkish and French court-martial was actually assembled to try the colonel, who was not yet in the Egyptian service. This ridiculous bubble, however, vanished in the air. This same Colonel Rey was stabbed in an affray at Cairo, but recovered. He finally left Egypt, we believe, much in the same way as General Boyer.

ART. III.—*Lieben, Lust, und Leben der Deutschen des sechszehn-ten Jahrhunderts in den begebenheiten des Schlesischen Ritters,* Hans von Schweinichen, *von ihm selbst ausgesetzt.* (The Loves, Pleasures, and Life of the Germans of the Sixteenth Century, in the Adventures of the Silesian Knight, Hans von Schweinichen, narrated by himself.) Breslau. 1823. 3 vols. 12mo.

WRITERS of memoirs are too apt to assume that their materials will be interesting to posterity in proportion as they are new or important to themselves.   Hence they fill their diaries with no-tices of public events, with detailed accounts of their own con-duct on occasions of ceremony, " the battles, sieges, fortunes that they have passed;" while they glide rapidly and silently over their domestic habits and feelings, employments and amusements. The effect of this mistake is chiefly felt, when, at the distance of cen-turies, habits and manners have undergone a complete revolution, and that which was familiar and common-place to the writer, gra-dually overspread with the dust and weather-stains of antiquity, has become to the reader a matter of doubt, curiosity and con-jecture.   When we look back to some name which has survived the influence of time, and endeavour from the bare and meagre memorials of his conduct on public occasions to realize to our-selves the portrait of the man as a whole, how much do we regret the absence of those little details and still-life accompaniments, without which the picture wears so shadowy and unreal an aspect; how anxious do we feel to be informed how this man of courts and battle-fields looked, when, throwing aside the holiday garb of his public appearance, he resumed the quiet undress of every-day existence—what were his loves and enjoyments, his amuse-ments, his friendships, his prejudices—whether he rose late or early, prosed much in conversation, drank " not wisely, but too well," and paid his debts regularly, or not at all. Nay, at the distance of a century or too, even his wardrobe becomes a matter in which we are interested, as tending to the completeness and coherency of the picture which is presented to the mind's eye; and we feel indebted to the antiquarian who takes the trouble, by recovering from the state-paper office his taylor's accounts (pro-bably unpaid), to inform us whether he wore a pea-green slashed doublet or. an orange tawney. The Spectator and Tatler, for in-stance, are already acquiring in this way an interest which at first they did not possess; as correct and lively sketches of these little peculiarities of dress, manners and customs, for which we should search in vain in more elaborate productions of the day, and which, though only removed from us by a century, have already begun to assume an antiquarian dignity in our eyes. Montaigne's gossip about his tastes and personal habits, impertinent as it may have appeared to his cotemporaries, is now to us among the most interesting portions of his desultory essays. What would we not give for a minute description of a day at Tusculum with Cicero, or a faithful record of one of Cæsar's youthful days of mingled business and revelry, philosophy and folly! How delightful would it be, if, instead of having to collect our ideas of the mysteries of the Roman toilette and domestic economy from such works as Bottiger's Sabina, and Meiners, we could, in some unexplored recess in Pompeii or Herculaneum, come suddenly upon a genuine number of the Diurnalia, or Augustan Gazette, with its medley of scandal, advertisements, fashionable departures from Rome for Baiæ or the Campagna, Patrician alliances in high life by special license of the Pontifex Maximus, gallantries of " an *august* personage," the new pantomime by Pylades or his rival Bathyllus,* or the last interesting gastronomical arrival of Rutupian oysters fresh from Britain!† Hence it is that Pliny's Letters, formal as they are, and the Noctes of Aulus Gellius, are interesting from the glimpses they afford into the private life of the time. Hence also such a work as Pepys's Memoirs, with all its details of eating and drinking, his deep meditations on new suits, even amidst the horrors of the plague of London, his minute descriptions of masquerades and junketing parties of all kinds, partly from its spirit of perfect *naiveté* and candour, partly from the graphic truth with which it delineates scenes of which we find elsewhere but scattered and imperfect notices, possesses for the present age an interest which few modern memoirs, though dealing with more stirring periods and events of greater public importance, can hope to obtain.

What Pepys's work is to the times of Charles II. these Memoirs of Hans von Schweinichen are to the private life of the Germans in the sixteenth century. His life falls within a period when the vast change in manners and the habits of society, produced by the discoveries in science and strange revolutions of empire and opinion which the first half of the sixteenth century witnessed, give a peculiar interest to these sketches of " The Loves, Pleasures and Life of the Germans," (as the editor styles this autobiography): while the open-heartedness of the narrator; his love of good eating, and still more of good drinking; and his admiration of fine dresses, in which he rivals Pepys himself; his frugality in his own case, with his liberality towards his prodigal and bankrupt master, impart an amusing personal and individual interest to these antiquarian or political details.

---

* Tacit. Annal. i. 54.			† Juvenal, iv. 141.

At the time when our knight commences his auto-biography, the internal feuds and dissensions of Germany had, under the rising ascendancy of the House of Austria, been in some measure composed; the usurpation of the nobles considerably checked; the rights of the citizen recognised; the police of the country protected by standing armies against the recurrence of anarchy or the dominion of " Faustrecht;" the peasant, though still a vassal, beginning to sleep within his cottage and beneath his vine-tree in peace, safe from the sudden invasion of the robber chiefs, who now no longer secure ,in their mountain fortresses, since the discovery of gunpowder, were gradually endeavouring to procure by industry and the cultivation of the soil the means of subsistence, which they had formerly drawn from robbery and violence.   Intelligence was rapidly diffusing itself with the increase of printing; the sciences, the productions, the wealth and literature of other countries were finding their way into this vast empire. In religion, the long-established dominion of Rome, consecrated as it seemed by immemorial possession and early prejudices, had been everywhere shaken to its foundations, and in many places trampled in the dust, by the energy of Luther.   The spell which had fettered inquiry in matters of faith was dissolved, and those principles which had at first been asserted in the discussion of religious questions were speedily transferred to secular affairs and the political relations of the ruler and the subject.   In politics, the dawn of popular institutions and unity among the German body becomes perceptible; in manners, an increase of extravagance and pomp, a gradual desertion of the baronial castle for the court, and a relaxation in the stiffness of ceremonial forms.   In morals, the good effects of the change of things was, perhaps, more problematical.   The admirers of the good old times might say with some truth, that with the rudeness of the feudal system and its fantastic usages, much which was really worthy and valuable in it had been swept away; that artifice had too often succeeded to open violence, and deceitful smoothness to rough sincerity of demeanour; calculation and manœuvring to straight-forward simplicity and self-devotion.   The Belial of feud and warfare had only been replaced by the Mammon of trade and avarice, and Germany, in her new state of existence, looked as if a turbulent army had suddenly marched off her soil, and left their deserted camp as a market-place for pedlars and suttlers to cheat and wrangle in.

Life, in short, had already begun to assume its prosaic aspect, and the reader who opens these memoirs of the sixteenth century in the hope of finding them gilded by any of the lingering glories of chivalry, will soon be disenchanted.   Even here, and at this early period, he will be able to trace the increasing preponderance of " the needful" over the beautiful: the dawn of a national debt, the maturity of pawn-broking and cent. per cent., and the rapid advance of those days when no mail is used but his Majesty's, and the wandering knight with his lance and palfrey gives way to the commercial traveller with his gig and pattern-card. Indeed, in one art, of which we moderns are a little too apt to claim the sole credit of invention—we mean the art of raising the wind, or living at the expense of our neighbours—we doubt very much whether any thing of importance could be added to the discoveries of Duke Henry of Liegnitz, the honoured master of our Silesian knight. " *Quærenda pecunia primum est*" was his motto, and that of all connected with him, to his dying day, and in this line, his fertility of invention, boundless assurance, and easy condescension towards his victims, render these memoirs a most interesting contribution to the philosophy of " Tick," and valuable as a practical guide to the art even in the nineteenth century. Not that our hero, however, amidst this system of swindling and money-making, is altogether deficient in some of the better features of the times of chivalry: he is no fire-eater, no doubt, and looks attentively at both sides of his coin before he parts with it; but something of the true heart and devotion of Götz and Sickingen, of Schartlin and Rothenhahn, he inherits and displays in the steadiness of his adherence to his ruined and even selfish master Duke Henry, and in that " constant service of the antique world" with which he devotes his purse and his personal labours to one who in many cases repays them with the characteristic ingratitude of the prodigal.

Hans's parents were Protestants, both of noble families in Silesia; and young Schweinichen, who was born in 1552, was educated till his ninth year at his paternal castle of Merkschutz, his time being divided between his studies at the village school, and the pastoral, though somewhat peculiar employment for the heir of two noble houses, with sixteen quarterings (which he takes care to set forth at length), of herding geese at home.* Sometimes this labour was varied by searching for eggs in the stables and among the corn, on which occasions his mother used to reward him, when successful, with a few copper coins. At the age of twelve he was transferred to Liegnitz, where the old duke, Frederick III. was at that time detained in custody on account of his debts, in a species of imprisonment within the rules of court. Succeeding an extravagant father, he had increased to an enormous extent the debts of the state, till at last he had been deposed by the authority of the emperor, and the dukedom tranferred to his

---

* Vol. i. p. 26.

son Henry, he being burdened, however, with the maintenance of his father and his family, and with the discharge, as far as practicable, of his debts.   Henry—" of thriftless father thriftless son" —instead of paying off any part of these, soon made matters, as we shall afterwards see, much worse.   It was while the old duke was residing *in custodia* at Liegnitz that young Schweinichen was introduced to him, and where he became the companion and fellow-student of the young Duke Henry.   Here he found the advantage of a small allowance of pocket-money which his father had made him.   Young as he was, he soon contrived to discover that his tutor at court was a great admirer of the fair sex, and by enabling him to gratify his tastes in this way by a few of the silver groschen he had been allowed for the purchase of books, he escaped with only two floggings during his incumbency.   At court he acted as page, and afterwards as cellar-master, a situation which seems to have been by no means a sinecure, for the duke generally refused to go to bed when tipsy, and Hans was obliged on such occasions to carry him thither, and sleep in the room with him.   From this situation, however, such as it was, he was removed for a time, in consequence of having been employed as the unconscious instrument in circulating a pasquil against the duke, and restored again to his old haunts, though not exactly his old Arcadian occupations and ornithological pursuits, at Merkschutz.

Two traits in his character here began to develope themselves, at first sight a little inconsistent, but which Hans throughout contrived to reconcile wonderfully with each other.   The first is a strong regard for what is commonly called the main-chance, which manifests itself in a most careful annual enumeration of the prices of corn and grain, and regular entries of every disbursement made by himself, from tavern-bills to knightly entertainments, travelling expenses, wedding and funeral charges—a practice which he continues to his death.   The other is a fancy for dress worthy of Pepys or Sir Piercie Shafton himself.   He dwells with the delight of a lover on a fustian suit and silk barret-cap, given him by his father when he went to school at Goldberg, and a long dangling white feather, which was the gift of his mother;[*] as also on another dress-suit with one leg yellow and the other black, in which he exhibited on a journey to Lublin, in which he accompanied the court.   Sometimes the two propensities to which we have alluded are mixed up together in rather a singular manner, and rounded off with a pious sentiment.   " This year," observes he, after his mother's death, which happened when he was six-

---

[*] Vol. i. p. 45.

teen, " my allowance from my father was eleven thalers sixteen silver groschen, and I was dressed in mourning. God give me good fortune and happiness in time to come. Amen. This year the grain was sold at the following prices," &c.

All these affectionate reminiscences of the departed glories of his wardrobe, and the frequent attendances at wedding feasts, for which he had exchanged his care of the geese, it may be imagined are symptomatic of an early disposition on the part of Hans to recommend himself to the fair sex, and accordingly he seems to have been a practised gallant and almost indispensable guest at all the dances and merry-makings in the neighbourhood of Gold-berg. One of his chief favourites was Catherine, the daughter of old Albert Bock, who used to drink to him in Latin, and Hans was very glad to find he was able to answer her in the same lan-guage, the only good result it would appear of his Goldberg education, or his studies under the amorous pedagogue of Liegnitz. In the course of a few years more we find him more seriously in-volved in a love passage with a lady of Swabia, whom he had encountered as usual at a wedding, but this connection was broken off by the unlucky accident of the lady proving a mother before she could become a wife. Next year, however, he dates as the commencement of his first serious attachment, of which he speaks with a degree of mystery. " This year," says he, " I experienced for the first time what love was, having fallen in love with a maiden so that I could not sleep. But I never had the boldness to disclose it, when and whereupon I conclude that first love is deepest. This year has flown by without my being aware of it."

It would, perhaps, have been well if Hans had not resorted to other modes of making time fly, but " sine Cerere et Baccho friget Venus." And his drinking powers, which afterwards com-manded the admiration of his cotemporaries, began about this time to be developed. The practice of drinking to excess, always the vice of the northern nations, had not, among other abuses, been much affected by the Reformation. On the contrary, sove-reigns prided themselves on maintaining at their court some fellow, often a fool, or dwarf, who would undertake to challenge and lay under the table in fair combat any stranger whom the court might think it hospitable to place in that horizontal position. Hans's coup d'essai in the art took place on one occasion when his father had invited some young men of the neighbourhood to accompany him to a wedding, and like that of the Cid it was a " coup de maitre."

" Among the party," says he, " was Caspar Ecke von Tscheswitz, a young hot blood; and with him I entered the lists at the wine. As I was unaccustomed to it, and drank freely, it was not long before I was under the table, and so drunk that I could neither walk, nor stand, nor speak, but was carried away like a dead man. I slept two nights and two days on end, till every one thought I would die. But, God be praised, matters turned out better. And since then I have learned not only how to drink, but have got a tolerable assurance that it would be no easy matter for any one to intoxicate me, and since then I have continued the practice stoutly; whether for my health and happiness, I shall mention in another place."

We cannot perceive from his Memoirs that either his health or his peace of mind suffered materially from this habit, though it occasionally placed him in situations which were comic enough. On one occasion at Gustrow, in Mecklenburg, where he had been carousing with his companions, the servant being rather dilatory in bringing a torch, the whole party appear to have fallen down stairs. Hans was no where to be found, but next morning he was discovered, like a second Regulus, in an empty wine cask, which lay conveniently at the bottom of the stairs to receive him, and in which he had passed the night in a state of insensibility. The only moral, however, which he seems to deduce from this catastrophe is, that master and servant ought not to get drunk at the same time, for he blames nobody but the servant, who was not sufficiently sober to light them down. Some years afterwards he performed a remarkable feat in this way at Fellensberg, when on a visit along with his master the duke to the court of Nassau, and where his character as a potent drinker soon came to be known, Hans having of course taken good care that it should not be hid under a bushel. On this occasion he twice drank off the welcome cup, containing three quarts of wine, and left a poor courtier, who had been rash enough to do him reason in a similar draught, utterly extinguished on the floor. And, indeed, until the gout and the infirmities of old age diminished his exhaustive powers, he seems to have been regarded on all hands as a most successful and formidable toper.

But there were better traits in the character of the young Hans than drinking and merry-making; namely, his dutiful affection to his father and mother, of whom he never speaks but with devoted attachment and real feeling. His mother died suddenly during his absence with his father in Poland.

" There came," says he, " intelligence to my father and myself, as we were on the way, that if my father wished to see his dear wife and I my dear mother again alive, we must make all speed, for there was no hope of her life. Which was a sad and evil message to my father, and to me particularly, for I knew I was her beloved Hans. And though we would gladly have hurried on, it could not be done on account of the robbers who were lying in wait for the duke's party, and would willingly have plundered the silver waggons; so with grief of heart were we compelled to remain with the rest till we reached Kalisch. From thence we travelled night and day, and reached home on the 13th of May, 1569, about five in the evening, after an absence of eleven weeks. But when we came into the court at Merkschutz, my father and I learned the melancholy news that my dear mother had died on the 2d of May, and had been buried in the church at Merkschutz the Sunday before we arrived, which was no joyful return to us. I would rather that the Poles had slain me outright than have experienced the sore heart's griefs on my home coming. Nor was it less heart-breaking to my dear father, but was the means of shortening his life. But when I began to reflect thereafter that I was a man and subject to grief, and that it was God's good will and providence that my dear mother should be taken from the world during my absence, I resigned her, and with grief and sorrow and childish tears put on my mourning; lamenting this year not merely with my outward garb, but with christian mourning of heart and countenance, staying as much at home as possible."

In 1573, being now twenty-one, he followed in the suite of the young dukes, Henry and Frederick, to Mecklenburgh; and, in 1574, we find him dividing his time pretty much between the court and his paternal mansion. Whether these visits to the court were owing to the good looks of the ladies or not he professes himself unable to say, but from the animated description which he gives of the garden of the court at Liegnitz at this time, there is little doubt they had a large share in the matter. He is almost betrayed into poetry when describing the goodness of the wines, the sweetness of the music, the gaiety of the dances, the beauty of the women, and the grace and condescension of the court.

" There was no sorrow or mourning. Nothing but delight and joy. If I had been to fall from Heaven on any spot on earth, it would have been among the ladies at Liegnitz I would have lighted ; for *there* were daily sports of riding, running at the ring, dancing, and other pastimes, very pleasing to the young folks, of whom I was one."

It must be admitted, however, that Hans's proceedings with regard to the fair sex were very peculiar, and the more so when we consider the extreme animation and interest with which he always approaches the subject. In most of his youthful attachments we find him proceeding with the greatest possible fire and vivacity for a time, but the moment he sees that matters are coming to a point, he cools, perceives that Heaven has determined otherwise, and with the most perfect sang froid lets the matter drop. This is very amusingly displayed in an affair about this time with the youthful daughter of Simon Promnitz. The first hint of the liaison occurs in an entry made by Hans in his journal, on occasion of his receiving an invitation from the young lady's mother to be present at her servant's wedding. " I saw plainly," says

Hans, " that the invitation was not on account of the maid but the mistress, her daughter Jungfer Hede." He went notwithstanding, and shortly after we find the business in full train.

" The young lady was only about fourteen years old, and had a fortune of 10,000 rix thalers, which the duke would willingly have assigned to me. I had no dislike to the maiden. She was fond of eating sugar, which I bought for her at different times, and once to the extent of two dollars at a time. I might have been easily induced to marry her, for my father would have liked the connection, and her guardians were in favour of it."

The Frau Kittlitzen no doubt endeavoured to injure her by some calumnious reports as to her personal habits, her inability to cook, and so forth, but these do not seem materially to have influenced him, for he had sense enough to see that these observations were dictated by mere envy, the lady Kittlitzen having a daughter of her own for whom she wished to secure him. Still he keeps dawdling on for about two years, merely remarking that both he and his intended were very young. It seemed, however, as if matters would now be brought to a point, for a certain Nickel Geisler, an old bachelor, whom he describes as looking more like a Jew than a nobleman, about this time came forward as a suitor to the young lady. His pretensions being sanctioned by her mother and guardians, she sent privately for Hans, and communicated to him her distress. One would have thought there would now have been an end of his irresolution, but Hans told her with much gravity, that he felt persuaded it was not the will of Heaven that he should marry for three years to come; that she might consult her own wishes, and either take the old Jew or leave him, but that if she intended to wait for him (Hans) she must do so for three years at least. " This answer," as might be expected, " pleased her not much." She turned from him weeping, and told him she would wait for him as long as he wished. To this appeal Hans made no reply.

Meantime Geisler laid his proposals before the duke, who thinking the match between Hans and the young lady a very eligible one, and willing to give him an opportunity of redeeming the time before it was too late, sent him a message by his chamberlain, that this was the day when the bridal wreath was to be given to the lady, and that both she and the duke wished that Hans should slip in and lay hold of the wreath before old Geisler. This advice again threw Hans into a state of perplexity.

" I was so agitated," says he, " that I broke out into a cold sweat. I could not answer, but remained for a time speechless, for I felt as if I should say no, but could determine upon nothing. Till at last, while I was endeavouring to decide, a voice seemed to whisper in my ear—Take not the wreath; take not the wreath. And so I started up, and said, that I thanked his highness for the favour, but my affairs suited not with marriage. When I had said this, I felt my heart suddenly quite light and joyful, from which I concluded that it was not the will of God, for otherwise there was no impediment on the face of the earth. The maiden was young and beautiful, gentle and rich, and would willingly have taken me; while I, on the other hand, was in the very flower of my age, and at that very time of life best suited for marriage, according to the proverb, four years before beard-cutting and four years after is the time to marry. But God is all-powerful, what he wills not comes not to pass. In this way the marriage was put off, which I have never had occasion to repent. And so ended my second courtship, from which I gather that it was not the will of God."

And so ended also his third, for in the course of a few pages more we find him uttering the same sentiment of resignation on the termination of another brief liaison with the daughter of the lady of. Kittlitzen.

Meantime his master, Duke Henry's pecuniary embarrasments had increased to such a height that he was obliged to commence a system of begging, swindling, and free quarters in all corners of Germany, which he pursued steadily from 1572 to 1576. In this wandering and disreputable life, Hans was his constant companion, and the person on whom the obnoxious duty of raising the supplies very often devolved. Henry kept moving with his whole suite from town to town, borrowing on all hands, from princes of the empire, nobles, ladies, abbots, nuns, peasants, Jews, dwarfs; from any one, in short, who, decoyed by his plausible manners, would either lend or make him a present of any sum however small. Twice in the course of these rambles he was arrested for debt, at Cologne and at Emmerich, till at last, after increasing his debts to an extent which made those of his father appear a mere cypher, and spending, among the rest, about half the patrimony of poor Hans, who continued to supply his extravagance to the last, he was deposed by the Emperor in 1576, and the dukedom given to his younger brother Frederick.

To Hans himself, still in the flower of youth, and with a natural love of rambling and adventure, this life of alternate beggary and splendour, to-day feasting with counts of the empire or enjoying the splendid hospitality of the Fuggers of Augsburg, (then among the most distinguished merchants in Europe,) to-morrow pawning jewels and even dresses to raise the necessary funds for travelling or subsistence; with its risks and dangers, its rapid changes of scene and society, was not without considerable attraction. In 1576 he attended Henry into Poland, to the throne of which the duke had at that time some pretensions; and the account which our biographer gives of their visit to Cracow, affords no bad spe-

cimen of the general character of their proceedings. Among
their other revels, Duke Henry was invited to the house of the
woivode, Peter Parovskyn, whose interest he was anxious to
secure, in order to further his views upon the throne. The banquet was a splendid one, and the health of the duke repeatedly
drunk as king of Poland, the guests attesting the sincerity of their
allegiance by breaking their glasses on their heads. Dancing
succeeded, and when the party broke up, so freely had the duke
indulged, that he was under the necessity of being supported on
his horse by two of his attendants as he rode home. When Hans,
who had charge of the duke's wardrobe, came to undress him as
usual, he perceived to his consternation that a jewel and chain of
the value of 17,000 rix-dollars, and a purse containing 100 florins,
were both gone. It was in vain to put any question to his grace,
he was in no condition to answer; while Hans himself, who had
ably seconded his master at the supper table, was just as little
prepared to follow out the examination. No remedy remained
but to go to bed and endeavour to sleep off his intoxication.
" Drunk, as I was, however," said he, " I slept but little."
When with the morning cool reflection came, all the information
the duke could give as to the missing articles was, that during the
dance he had given the chain to one person to hold, and the purse
to another; but to whom he had totally forgotten. Hans was in
despair, and went out to take counsel with his comrades. In
going out he met his father, who, to his great relief, told him that
as they were leaving the banquet the night before, a Pole had put
into his hands a purse containing 100 florins, which he supposed
must be the duke's, and so it proved to be. This raised Hans's
spirits, but still the more important article was missing. But in
about an hour came another Pole inquiring for the duke's chamberlain, and produced the chain and jewel perfectly safe. " Thus,"
says Hans, " our mourning was turned into joy." Hans rewarded
his honesty cheaply enough by taking him to his lodgings, drinking
with him, and finally presenting him with a donation of ten florins,
which he received with much gratitude. " I must say," he observes, " these were as honest Poles as one would wish to meet
with.—Thanks be to God who helped me out of this scrape!"

In Augsburg, to which the duke and his locust-like troop of
attendants next removed, he contrived to levy some of his heaviest
contributions. He gambled daily, a practice which then appears
to have been carried to great excess, and, being well versed in the
mysteries of the dice-box, generally won, frequently to the extent
of 200 or 300 florins daily. Hans himself following, *passibus
æquis,* also gained 300 florins on one occasion at a sitting. At
this time the riches of the citizens of Augsburg rivalled those of

the Venetian nobility during the best days of her commerce. The well-known merchant, Fugger of Augsburg, on whose purse Hans, on behalf of the duke, seems to have made a very determined attack, though without success, portioned his daughter with 200,000 rix dollars. He entertained the duke in the most sumptuous manner, but on pretext that he had made large advances for the King of Spain, declined his proposal for a loan of 4000 dollars. The only present which he was disposed to make him, namely, a ship of glass cunningly wrought by some Venetian artist, was broken by the awkwardness of Hans as he was placing it upon the table. Having failed with Fugger, he next tried his powers of persuasion on the town council, and wonderful to say, succeeded in obtaining from them a loan of 1000 dollars, on the duke's acknowledgment, for a year and without interest. The force of spunging could no further go. The whole of this sum was applied in satisfying the landlord's bill, who had already become clamorous for payment. This supply, however, enabled the duke for some time longer to protract his career of dissipation at Augsburg. Some particulars which Hans gives as to a ball at which he was present are curious. He had been invited to the marriage of a nobleman of the place, and the duke, who felt anxious to get admission into the party, prevailed upon Hans to take him with him as his servant. " I know not how it was, however," adds Hans, " but the servant managed to get so tipsy, I was obliged to lead him away." The duke having before night slept off his intoxication, sent a message boldly to the bridegroom, to say he would be happy to make one of his party in the evening, and the bridegroom, much flattered by the proposal, immediately sent a carriage to conduct his Highness to the banquet.

" In Augsburg it is the custom at dances that two persons, dressed in long red cloaks trimmed with white ermine, begin the dance, and no one is allowed to begin till they have set the example and performed the figure. When they turn, the others who dance must do the same, and when they embrace each other in the dance, the dancers do the same. And these persons are often bribed before-hand by the young men to embrace each other pretty frequently, that they may have an opportunity of doing the same with their partners. I have done so myself, and for half-a-dollar have procured many a pleasant hug in the course of the dance. My former servant was now again become my lord and master. When I saw him, I asked his grace how he had come thither? He answered, that he came there because he knew there were to be many fair dames there who had a mind to me, and that he was afraid of me, and wished to prevent my being entrapped! And truly I must confess, that in all my life-time I never looked on fairer ladies than these, for they were seventy in all; all dressed in white damask to please the bride, and covered all over with chains and jewels. And the hall large and handsome, sparkling with gold and silver, so that one might have taken it for the true paradise or the kingdom of heaven. I was very joyous, for as I said, the ladies were fair, and choice, courteous and kind in talk. In the evening I attended a rich maiden of the house of Herberg home to her father's house; it was said her father's fortune exceeded two tons of gold. I was received by him as if I had been a count, and nobly treated; stayed two hours and enjoyed myself. Then her father, as was the custom in the place, conveyed me home to my lodging in a coach, attended with torches. . . . . I often wished such a life might last for many years."

But these golden times in Augsburg could not last long. The worthy citizens began to get tired of the expensive amusement of entertaining this brainless prodigal duke; his supplies from the gaming table became less frequent; and with all Hans's exertions in the finance department, the funds began to fail. On one occasion Hans was obliged to sell a chain which his father had given him, for sixty-five dollars, which the duke with consummate effrontery pocketed, and even refused Hans the loan of six dollars of his own money, a piece of ingratitude which naturally vexed him much. Matters at last came to a crisis when they reached Cologne. Here the duke had contrived to run up a bill of about one thousand dollars, and the host, like his brother of Augsburg, became clamorous for payment. Two weeks did Hans continue to put him off on some pretext or other; but at last it became obvious that no alternative remained but payment or imprisonment. Hans's former success with the town council of Augsburg suggested to his master the plan of trying his eloquence upon the magistracy of Cologne, and accordingly he received full powers to treat with them for a loan of ten thousand dollars. Hans was received by them with all imaginable respect, and delivered in presence of the council a long oration, to which in all probability they listened with the more patience, that, like Yorick with the Franciscan, they had predetermined not to lend him a single sous. He was conducted back under a guard of honour, and informed that the council would send a written answer in a few days. Accordingly, in due time, appeared the envoys of the town council, who took their revenge upon Hans in a speech as long and as hypocritically respectful as his own, bestowing many compliments upon his eloquence, but concluding with the information that the council were under the necessity of absolutely refusing the loan, but had sent his grace a present of two hundred florins. This composition Henry had the meanness to accept.

In the midst of these delicate distresses arrived the astounding intelligence (15th April, 1576) that the dukedom had been taken from him and given to his brother Frederick, the fourth of that name. And now mine host, despairing of payment by means of negotiation, took the step of laying an arrest to the extent of his bill, which had mounted up to 2354 dollars, on the horses and furniture of the duke, all of which were immediately inventoried and taken possession of by the officers under form of law. It was in vain that Hans endeavoured to soften the obdurate creditor; it was in vain that the duke pleaded his privilege as an electoral prince of the empire. The electoral chamber of Cologne replied that their jurisdiction entitled them to arrest even the goods of the emperor himself; though, in consideration of the duke's rank, his person should remain untouched. Accordingly, the horses and carriages of the duke were sold to the extent of the debt; and so ended their compulsory sojourn in Cologne, the latter part of which had been rendered more disagreeable by the prevalence of a destructive pestilence. Hans's only precaution was a very simple one. He believed, he says, it was impossible he should die of the disease. He contented himself with taking a little vinegar and dry toast every morning,—which he followed up by liberal allowances of liquor in the evening.

At Emmerich, to which the duke removed in the course of his rambles, Hans records an odd adventure with a spirit or monster of some kind who haunted their lodgings, and who seems to have had many of the propensities and playful gambols of our own Robin Goodfellow :—

" Two nights before," says he, " a spirit or goblin had washed all the rooms, put the house to rights, and made the beds. On the third night the creature came to my bed ; it had a club, such as dwarfs generally bear, and it shook its wings over my head. When I awoke and saw it, I was terrified, and was about to call out, but his grace being asleep, I let it alone, and recommended myself to God. As there were lights in the chamber, I saw that the creature retired into a corner of the room and laughed. In the morning I told the duke, who would not believe me. The next night, being a little drunk, I was asleep ; so the creature came to Heilung, who lay beside me in bed. He cried out, ' O help me, holy Virgin !'—Though I heard him cry out very well, I let him alone and said nothing. Then the goblin came to my side, and laughed loudly and vanished, but so that I wist not where it disappeared.

" In the morning I told the maids in the house, and advised them to keep the ghost away, or else he would probably suffer for his visits. When they heard this they were glad that I had seen him; they told me I must be very lucky since he came to me first ; and that I must do nothing to him, for as long as he appeared I and my master should be fortunate. When I heard this I was well content.

" After this, when the cook one day left her cooking pots and things unwashed, in the morning they were all found cleaned and polished. They told me I should give him something to drink, the which I did, and usually laid out for him milk or beer, mixed with honey and sugar. He would come to it when he thought proper, nodding with his head to me as I lay in bed, and drink to me, which I have often seen. And as long as the goblin continued to appear, the duke and all of us enjoyed good luck and prosperity. Nor did I after the first time feel any terror, except once, which was the last time I saw him. His grace having risen early to write, told me to strike a light and waken the page who made his lemonade for him. The pages slept in the chamber above the duke's, to which the ascent was by a winding stair. When I had got about half up stairs, the monster met me so suddenly that I was dreadfully terrified and knew not what to do. He went by me so close that I touched him; then began to laugh, and said, 'Thou knowest not thy fortune, but thou wilt soon know how it shall fare with thee.' After this he was seen of none, and since his disappearance little luck fell to the share of my master and myself."

The following gentle passage of arms, which also took place at Emmerich, is more original than chivalrous :—

" The duke had a Captain Grotticken in his service, who talked as if he would eat up all mankind. One evening he had a quarrel with a Netherlander, and each challenged the other. I parted them that night, but next morning came the Netherlander to call out Grotticken. Grotticken, who had a wooden leg, unloosed it softly in bed, and kept the Netherlander engaged in conversation till he thought he had got him within his reach, and then rising up in bed, he smote the Netherlander with the wooden leg over the neck, and laid him flat on the ground. He got up, however, shortly, and made the best of his way out; and so ended the scuffle, for he did not challenge him again."

At Emmerich a second arrest of the duke's goods and chattels took place ; and now, unable any longer to keep off the evil day, the duke decamped one morning, leaving on the table a note for Hans, in which he concluded, " I will not pillow my head in idleness. Money, with God's help, I will have, that we may get out of this vile country, and away from this people. And so good morrow, dear Hans.—Henry."

" Thus said the duke—thus did the duke infer;" and Hans, adopting his example and advice, immediately set about raising five hundred dollars, on pledge, from a Jew named Humpel, a feat which he successfully accomplished. Another contribution of one hundred from an old maid, in whose house he had lived, enabled him finally to make an honourable retreat from Emmerich.

It is needless to pursue farther, with any minuteness, this life of swindling and extravagance, of profusion and beggary ; for enough has been already done to show sufficiently the nature of the school in which Hans passed his early life. It says a great deal for his natural good sense and good feeling, that when he abandons his wandering habits, returns to his paternal castle and

marries, he seems never to have relapsed into his former free and
easy habits, or to have thought for an instant of wandering beyond his confine. On his return, indeed, he had at first a good
deal on his hands. His father was dead, his fortune almost
ruined, his family depending on him for support, so that when he
revisited his home, in 1577, after an absence of two years and a
half, he says, that " much as he had wished for his return, he at
first longed as eagerly to be gone again." His time was now
passed between the court at Liegnitz, where he retained his situation of Hofmeister, and occasional visits to Schweinichen, where
matters were managed by his brother. In his concluding reflections on the year 1578, he observes, " I have been obliged this
year, as becomes a young man, to bestir myself in my employment, have had but few days of idleness, and truly eaten my bread
in the sweat of my brow. And though I have met with many
annoyances, and bitter winds have blown upon me, I have not
heeded them, but let them blow over. I have done my duty, and
not left undone what I knew to be right."

His steadiness was perhaps secured by another event which
now took place. With all his irresolution in matters matrimonial, the time was drawing near when the inconstant was to be
fixed. The young lady of Schellendorff had long been a favourite
with him, but in his usual vacillating way he had kept wavering
and manœuvring for years, without coming to the point, notwithstanding many invitations from the young lady's mother, who at
last began to think the case was hopeless. Hans, however, was
really in earnest this time. " I went," says he, " to Hernsdorf,
where I stayed two days and courted the young lady. I meant
very truly by her, and was right sorry to part. She told me not to
marry till I came again, and so I departed in God's name. The
young lady's mother had told her not to set her heart on me; that
I was a courtier and would deceive her, and that I would set off
and no one could tell when I might return again. But the young
lady would not be persuaded nor guided, but remained firm."
Her firmness, Hans tells us, was rewarded, for their marriage
shortly afterwards took place with great pomp, the whole court
assisting at the nuptials. A very accurate bill of fare is added
by Hans, as a sort of " piece justificative" relative to the magnificence and expense of the entertainment.

We must now make rather a sudden transition from this
scene of gaiety to one of gloom ; from the wedding tables to the
" funeral baked meats," which some years afterwards were destined to adorn the board at Schweinichen. When we next present our Swabian knight to our readers, the fire of youth is nearly
extinct, the last relics of its follies, saving an occasional potation,

are gone; he is become a farmer, and a peacemaker in his neighbourhood; one by one, old friends and relations have dropped
off, and he begins to feel somewhat solitary in his pilgrimage
through life; gout and other ailments, the legitimate offspring
of those carousals which had once crowned him with glory, are
beginning to break down his strong frame, when they are suddenly followed by a more serious and irreparable blow, in the
death of his wife. There is so much good feeling and natural
pathos in his account of her loss, which took place in 1601, that
we cannot better conclude than by some extracts from his journal
descriptive of that event. She had been ill for nearly a year
before, and although constantly attended by two physicians,
" which," as Hans observes, " cost me a deal of money in medicines," gradually grew worse.

" When she perceived that her time in this world could not be long,
she thought of me as her true husband; and, to prove the truth of her love
to me, directed her and my confidential friend, the Counsellor Antony
Scholtz, to make her testament, wherein she left to me all her effects,
except twenty Hungarian florins, which were to be sent after her death
to her sister, Frau Hese Manschwitz; which testament she then, as soon
as it was ready, with great eagerness and joy deposited in the Chancery.
Next day she, with much piety, received the sacrament in her own chamber. After these Christian duties were performed, she said to me, 'Now
I have finished what I have to do in this world. Let God call me when
he pleases, he will find me ready. His will is mine.' . . . As her swelling became greater, she said to me, ' Dear heart, you see my stay in this
world cannot be much longer, but bear it with patience. We have lived
long in love and truth with each other, have borne many cares and
much grief and want together, and still the greatest sorrow remains for
you, to bear my loss. As for me, my sorrows will be over. I have
borne many an annoyance quietly that I might not make you angry. So
when God shall take me from the world, do not repine nor grieve loudly,
that God in heaven may not be offended; but mourn and lament for me
like a Christian, not like a heathen, and think that we shall meet again
at the last day in greater joy than here. Lay me in the earth honourably,
but without pomp, and bury me within the church, that you also may be
beside me.' How deeply I felt in my heart all these heartbreaking words
all good men will readily believe; they penetrated through marrow and
bones, through heart and soul. All this I promised, with weeping eyes
and sad heart, to perform. . . . . As the disease continued to increase,
notwithstanding the assiduity of the physicians, and all my exertions,
my dear wife became weaker and weaker, and several times her speech
failed her. On the 14th she said to me, ' My dear heart, how sad is
parting! Now that the time is come in earnest, I pray of you again,
as I did before, that when God shall call you too away, you will cause
yourself to be laid beside me. And now God bless you, and keep you
well in body and soul, and guide you hereafter to eternal life, as I hope
in his grace it shall soon be with me. And observe, when night and

day divide, will be the hour of my departure to my heavenly father. If I am unable to speak, pray beside me, and make the 23d Psalm, " the Lord's my Shepherd," be sung to me. I would die with it in my ears. And now I pray you change my place, and lay my bed under the window,'—which was done. This last speech of my dear wife sank sorrowfully into my heart, and with heartbreaking grief did I thus receive her blessing. After this she spoke nothing but a few words, and about midnight fell into a state of complete weakness, from which, however, she was a little revived by applications of different kinds, and lay still the whole night. Next morning was Palm Sunday, and Herr Merten, the curate, came over to her, prayed beside her, and comforted her, and asked her if she was willing to die when her hour should come. Thereon she lifted up her hands and said yes. She spoke no more, but during the prayer she made signs that she prayed too; after this she said nothing to me or others, but lay still with her eyes closed, till one o'clock, when, without a struggle, she died, here in Liegnitz, in my house, in the upper chamber, and near the window looking into the street. The deep grief and desolation which this separation left in my heart, as if it would have burst with sorrow, I cannot express, but will leave it to every honest mind to imagine. After this breach in my house of mourning, I had the corpse dressed in her grave clothes, which she had caused my sister to make during her lifetime, covered with a dark cloak and decently veiled, and placed it on a table till the coffin should be prepared. It was afterwards placed in a well-pitched coffin, and lights burned for three days and nights round it, while I attired myself in mourning. A sorrowful Palm Sunday and a heart-breaking martyr's week has this been to me. I had lived twenty years and five weeks in peaceful and contented marriage with my dear wife, who now sleeps in God; while at home and in health, I can say we had never for a single night slept apart, nor gone to rest but in peace and kindness with each other, and thus these twenty years had seemed to me but a brief time. Much sorrow, much anxiety and suffering had we borne together; three children she had brought to me alive into the world, though God has taken them all again. And during these twenty years she has manifested to me all love and truth, and tended me in my many sicknesses with a care for which in this world I cannot recompense her, but God will reward her richly for it in another."

With this touching picture we shall take our leave of the honest-hearted old Swabian knight, who survived his wife fifteen years. In the Church of St. John, at Liegnitz, a square stone, on which is sculptured a rude effigy of the deceased in armour, with a sword in his hand, and over which his dusty banner still waves, commemorates his death on the 23d of August, 1616.

ART. IV.—*Considerations sur la Pêche de la Baleine.* Par A. de la Jonkaire. Paris. 1830. 8vo.

THIS is a respectable pamphlet, on a subject of considerable importance, and we gladly avail ourselves of its appearance, to lay before our readers some account of the progress and present state of the Whale Fishery. We shall, however, take a good deal wider range than is taken by the author of the pamphlet.

It is probably true, as has been sometimes contended, that the Norwegians occasionally captured the whale before any other European nation engaged in so perilous an enterprize. But the early efforts of the Norwegians were not conducted on any systematic plan, and should be regarded only in the same point of view as the fishing expeditions of the Esquimaux. The Biscayans were certainly the first people who prosecuted the Whale Fishery as a regular commercial pursuit. They carried it on with great vigour and success in the twelfth, thirteenth and fourteenth centuries. In 1261 a tithe was laid upon the tongues of whales imported into Bayonne, they being then a highly esteemed species of food. In 1338, Edward III. relinquished to Peter de Puyaune a duty of £6 sterling a whale, laid on those brought into the port of Biarritz, to indemnify him for the extraordinary expenses he had incurred in fitting out a fleet for the service of his Majesty. This fact proves beyond dispute that the fishery carried on from Biarritz at the period referred to must have been very considerable indeed; and it was also prosecuted to a great extent from Cibourre, Vieux Boucan, and subsequently from Rochelle and other places.*

The whales captured by the Biscayans were not so large as those that are taken in the Polar seas, and are supposed to have been attracted southward in pursuit of herrings. They were not very productive of oil, but their flesh was used as an article of food, and the whalebone was applied to a variety of useful purposes, and brought a very high price.

This branch of industry ceased long since, and from the same cause that has occasioned the cessation of the Whale Fishery in many other places—the want of fish. Whether it were that the whales, from a sense of the dangers to which they exposed themselves in coming southwards, no longer left the Icy Sea, or that the breed had been nearly destroyed, certain it is that they gradually became less numerous in the Bay of Biscay, and at length ceased almost entirely to frequent that sea. And the fishers being obliged to pursue their prey upon the banks of Newfoundland and the coasts of Iceland, the French fishery rapidly fell off.

---

* See *Mémoire sur l'Antiquité de la Pêche de la Baleine, par Noel*, 12mo. Paris, 1795.

. The voyages of the Dutch and English to the Northern Ocean, in order, if possible, to discover a passage through it to India, though they failed of their main object, laid open the haunts of the whale. The companions of Barentz, who discovered Spitzbergen in 1596, and of Hudson, who soon after explored the same seas, represented to their countrymen the amazing number of whales with which they were crowded. Vessels were in consequence fitted out for the Northern Whale Fishery by the English and Dutch, the harpooners and a part of the crew being Biscayans. They did not, however, confine their efforts to a fair competition with each other as fishers. The Muscovy Company obtained a royal charter, prohibiting the ships of all other nations from fishing in the seas round Spitzbergen, on pretext of its having been first discovered by Sir Hugh Willoughby. There can, however, be no doubt that Barentz, and not Sir Hugh, was its original discoverer; though, supposing that the fact had been otherwise, the attempt to exclude other nations from the surrounding seas, ou such a ground, was not one that could be tolerated. The Dutch, who were then prompt to embark in every commercial pursuit that gave any hopes of success, eagerly entered on this new career, and sent out ships fitted equally for the purposes of fishing, and of defence against the attacks of others. The Muscovy Company having attempted to vindicate its pretensions by force, several encounters took place between their ships and those of the Dutch. The conviction at length became general that there was room enough for all parties in the Northern seas; and in order to avoid the chance of coming into collision with each other, they parcelled Spitzbergen and the adjacent ocean into districts, which were respectively assigned to the English, Dutch, Hamburghers, French, Danes, &c.

The Dutch being thus left to prosecute the fishery without having their attention diverted by hostile attacks, speedily acquired a decided superiority over all their competitors.

When the Europeans first began to prosecute the fishery on the coast of Spitzbergen, whales were everywhere found in vast numbers. Ignorant of the strength and stratagems of the formidable foe by whom they were now assailed, instead of betraying any symptoms of fear, they surrounded the ships and crowded all the bays. Their capture was in consequence a comparatively easy task, and many were killed which it was afterwards necessary to abandon, from the ships being already full.

While the fish were thus easily obtained, it was the practice to boil the blubber on shore in the North, and to fetch home only the oil and whalebone. And, perhaps, nothing can give a more vivid idea of the extent and importance of the Dutch fishery in the middle of the seventeenth century, than the fact that they constructed a considerable village, the houses of which were all previously prepared in Holland, on the Isle of Amsterdam, on the northern shore of Spitzbergen, to which they gave the appropriate name of *Smeerenberg.** This was the grand rendezvous of the Dutch whale ships, and was amply provided with boilers, tanks, and every sort of apparatus required for preparing the oil and the bone. But this was not all. The whale fleets were attended by a number of provision ships, the cargoes of which were landed at Smeerenberg, which abounded during the busy season with well-furnished shops, good inns, &c.; so that many of the conveniences and enjoyments of Amsterdam were found within about eleven degrees of the Pole! It is particularly mentioned that the sailors and others were every morning supplied with what a Dutchman regards as a very great luxury—*hot rolls* for breakfast. Batavia and Smeerenberg were founded nearly at the same period, and it was for a considerable time doubted whether the latter was not the most important establishment.†

During the flourishing period of the Dutch fishery, the quantity of oil made in the North was so great that it could not be carried home by the whale ships; and every year vessels were sent out in ballast to assist in importing the produce of the fishery.

But the same cause that had destroyed the fishery of the Biscayans, ruined that which was carried on in the immediate neighbourhood of Spitzbergen. Whales became gradually less common, and more and more timid and difficult to catch. They retreated first to the open seas, and then to the great banks of ice on the eastern coast of Greenland. When the site of the fishery had been thus removed to a very great distance from Spitzbergen, the most economical plan was found to be to send the blubber direct to Holland. Smeerenberg was in consequence totally deserted, and its position is now with difficulty discoverable.

But though very extensive, the Dutch Whale Fishery was not, during the first thirty years of its existence, very profitable. This arose from the circumstance of the right to carry it on having been conceded, in 1614, to an exclusive company. The waste inseparable from such great associations, the wastefulness and unfaithfulness of their servants, who were much more intent upon advancing their own interests than those of the Company, increased the outlays so much, that the returns, great as they were, proved little more than adequate to defray them, and the fishery was confined within far narrower limits than it would otherwise

* From *smeeren*, to melt, and *berg*, a mountain.
† De Reste, Histoire des Pêches, &c. tom. i. p. 42.

have reached.   But after various prolongations of the charter of
the first Company, and the formation of some new ones, the trade
was finally thrown open in 1642.   The effects of this measure
were most salutary, and afford one of the most striking examples
to be met with of the advantages of free competition.   Within a
few years the fishery was vastly extended; and though it became
progressively more and more difficult from the growing scarcity of
fish, it proved, notwithstanding these disadvantages, more profitable to the private adventurers than it had ever been to the Company; and continued for above a century to be prosecuted with
equal energy and success.   The famous John de Witt has alluded
as follows to this change in the mode of conducting the trade:—

" In this respect," says he, " it is worthy of observation that the authorized Greenland Company made heretofore little profit by their fishery,
because of the great charge of setting out their ships; and that the train-
oil, blubber and whale-fins were not well made, handled, or cured; and
being brought hither and put into warehouses, were not sold soon enough,
nor to the Company's best advantage.   Whereas now that every one
equips their vessels at the cheapest rate, follow their fishing diligently,
and manage all carefully, the blubber, train-oil and whale-fins are employed for so many uses in several countries, that they can sell them
with that conveniency, that though *there are now fifteen ships for one that
formerly sailed out of Holland on that account*, and consequently each of
them could not take so many whales as heretofore; and notwithstanding
the new prohibition of France and other countries to import these commodities; and though there is greater plenty of them imported by our
fishers—yet those commodities are so much raised in the value above
what they were whilst there was a company, that the common inhabitants do exercise that fishery with profit, to the much greater benefit of
our country than when it was (under the management of a Company)
carried on but by a few."*

The private ships sent by the Dutch to the Whale Fishery
were fitted out on a principle that secured the utmost economy
and vigilance on the part of every one connected with them.   The
hull of the vessel was furnished by an individual who commonly
took upon himself the office of captain; a sail-maker supplied the
sails, a cooper the casks, &c.   The parties engaged as adventurers in the undertaking.   The cargo being brought to Holland
and disposed of, each person shared in the proceeds according to
his proportion of the outfit.   The crew was hired on the same
principle; so that every one had a motive to exert himself, to
see that all unnecessary expenses were avoided, and that those
that were necessary, were confined within the narrowest limits.
This practice has been imitated to some extent in this and some
other countries, but in none has it been carried so far as in

* True Interest of Holland, p. 63.   8vo. ed.   London, 1746.

Holland. It appears to us that it might be advantageously introduced into other adventures.

When in its most flourishing state, towards the year 1680, the Dutch Whale Fishery employed about 260 ships, and 14,000 sailors.

The English Whale Fishery, like that of Holland, was originally carried on by an exclusive association. The Muscovy Company was, indeed, speedily driven from the field; but it was immediately succeeded by others that did not prove more fortunate. In 1725 the South Sea Company embarked largely in the trade, and prosecuted it for eight years, at the end of which, having lost a large sum, they gave it up. But the legislature having resolved to support the trade, granted, in 1732, a bounty of twenty shillings a ton to every ship of more than 200 tons burden engaged in it; but this premium being insufficient, it was raised, in 1749, to forty shillings a ton, when a number of ships were fitted out, as much certainly in the intention of catching the bounty as of catching fish. Deceived by the prosperous appearance of the fishery, parliament imagined that it was firmly established, and in 1777 the bounty was reduced to thirty shillings. The effects of this reduction showed the factitious nature of the trade, the vessels engaged in it having fallen off in the course of the next five years from 105 to 39! To arrest this alarming decline the bounty was raised to its old level in 1781, and of course the trade was soon restored to its previous state of apparent prosperity. The hostilities occasioned by the American war reduced the Dutch fishery to less than half its previous amount, and gave a proportional extension to that of England. The bounty which had in consequence become very heavy, was reduced, in 1787, to thirty shillings a ton; in 1792 it was further reduced to twenty-five shillings; and in 1795 it was reduced to twenty shillings, at which sum it continued till 1824, when it ceased.

It appears from accounts given in Macpherson's Annals of Commerce,* that the total bounties paid for the encouragement of the Whale Fishery in the interval between 1750 and 1788, amounted to no less than £1,577,935. It will be seen from the official account, which follows, and which is now published for the first time, that there are no means of furnishing any accurate account of the sums paid as bounties from the year 1789 to 1813 inclusive; but it is notwithstanding abundantly certain that the total bounties paid during the period from 1789 to 1824 considerably exceeded a million. Here then we have a sum of upwards of TWO MILLIONS AND A HALF laid out since 1750 in pro-

* Vol. iii. p.511; vol. iv. p. 130.

moting·the Whale Fishery.　Now we believe that if we estimate
the entire average value of ·the *gross* produce of the Northern
Whale Fishery, (and it is to it only that the preceding statements
apply,) during the last three or four years, at £375,000 a year, we
shall be about the mark.　But had the £2,500,000 expended in
bolstering up this branch of industry been laid out as capital in
any ordinary employment, it would have produced £125,000 a
year of *net* profit; and deducting this sum from the above, there
remains only £250,000 to replace the capital wasted and ships
lost in carrying on the fishery, and to afford *a clear national
profit!* Whatever, therefore, may be the value of the Whale Fishery
as a nursery for seamen, it is absurd to regard it as contributing
anything to the public wealth.　The remark of Dr. Franklin, that
he that draws a fish out of the sea draws out a piece of silver, is
ever in the mouths of those who are clamouring for bounties and
protection against competition.　But we apprehend that even
Franklin himself, sagacious as he was, would have found it rather
difficult to show how the wealth of those is to be increased who
in fishing up one piece of silver are obliged to throw another of
equal value into the sea.　We subjoin

*An Account of the Number of Ships annually fitted out in Great
Britain for the Northern Whale Fishery, of the Tonnage and
Crews of such Ships, and of the Bounties paid on their account
from 1789 to 1824.*

Years.	Ships.	Tons.	Men.	Bounties paid.
1789	161	46,599		
1790	116	33,232	4,482	
1791	116	33,906	4,520	
1792	93	26,983	3,667	
1793	82	23,487	3,210	
1794	60	16,386	2,250	
1795	44	11,748	1,601	The documents from
1796	51	13,833	1,910	which the amount of
1797	60	16,371	2,265	bounties paid in these
1798	66	18,754	2,633	years could be shown,
1799	67	19,360	2,683	were destroyed in the
1800	61	17,729	2,459	fire at the late Cus-
1801	64	18,568	2,544	tom House.
1802	79	23,539	3,129	
1803	95	28,608	3,806	
1804	92	28,034	3,597	
1805	91	27,570	3,636	
1806	91	27,697	3,715	

1807 to 1813 } There are no documents in this Office by which the
account for these years can be rendered.

Years.	Ships.	Tons.	Men.	Bounties paid. £. s.
1814	112	36,576	4,708	43,799 11
1815	134	43,320	5,783	41,487 14
1816	130	41,767	5,542	42,746 13
1817	135	43,548	5,768	43,461 6
1818	140	45,040	5,903	45,806 1
1819	140	45,093	6,291	43,051 8
1820	142	45,092	6,137	44,749 18
1821	140	44,864	6,074	42,164 0
1822	124	38,182	5,234	32,347 4
1823	120	37,628	4,984	32,980 2
1824	112	35,194	4,867	29,131 15

JOHN COVEY,
Reg. Gen. of Shipping.

Office of Registrar General of Shipping,
Custom House, London, 16th Dec. 1830.

It is not even certain whether the expenditure of £2,500,000 upon bounties would really have had the effect of establishing the Whale Fishery upon a solid foundation, but for the occupation of Holland by the French, and the consequent hostilities in which she was involved with this country. These did more to promote and consolidate the British fishery than any thing else. The war entirely annihilated that of the Dutch. And our government having wisely offered to the fishers of Holland all the immunities enjoyed by the citizens of Great Britain in the event of their settling amongst us, many availed themselves of the invitation, bringing with them their capital, industry and skill. In consequence of this signal encouragement, the Whale Fishery of England was prosecuted with greater success than at any previous period. And at the termination of the late war in 1815, there were 134 valuable ships and about 5,800 seamen engaged in the northern fishery, and about 30 ships and 800 men in that to the south.

After peace was restored, the English capitalists and others became apprehensive lest the Dutch should engage anew with their ancient vigour and success in the Whale Fishery. But these apprehensions were without any real foundation. The Hollanders, during the twenty years they had been excluded from the sea, had lost all that practical acquaintance with the details of the fishery, for which they had long been so famous, and which is so essential to its success. The government attempted to rouse their dormant energies by the offer of considerable premiums and other advantages to those who embarked in the trade. Three companies were in consequence formed for carrying it on, one at Rotterdam, one at Harlingen, and one in South Holland. But their efforts have been very limited, and altogether unfortunate. In 1826 the company of South Holland was dissolved, while that

of Harlingen despatched four ships, and that of Rotterdam two.
In 1827, Rotterdam sent only one ship and Harlingen two; and
in 1828 one solitary ship sailed from Holland, a feeble and last
effort of the company of Harlingen!

Such has been the fate of the Dutch Whale Fishery. The
attempts to revive it failed, not because the ships sent out were
ill-calculated for the service, but because they were manned by
unskilful seamen. In the early ages of the fishery this difficulty
would have been got over, because owing to the fewness of competitors, and the scanty supply of oil and whale fins, even a small
cargo. brought a high price; but at present, when the fishery is
prosecuted on a very large scale and at a very low rate of profit
by the English, the Americans, the Hamburghers, &c. no new
competitor coming into the field could expect to maintain himself
unless he had nearly equal advantages. The Dutch have, therefore, done wisely in withdrawing from the trade. Any attempt
to establish it by the aid of bounties and other artificial encou-
ragements, would be one of which the ultimate success must be
very doubtful, and which could lead to no really useful result.
During the twenty years preceding the late French war, the fishery
of Holland was gradually declining, and had, in a great measure,
ceased to be profitable. It would be folly to endeavour to raise
anew and at a great expense, a branch of industry that had become
unproductive at a former period, when there is no ground for
supposing that it would be more productive at this moment.

We have already noticed several changes of the localities in
which the Whale Fishery has been carried on at different periods;
within these few years another has taken place even more important. The seas between Spitzbergen and Greenland are now
nearly abandoned by the whalers, who resort in preference to
Davis's Straits and Baffin's Bay, or to the sea which washes the
coast of West Greenland. The Dutch fishers first began to frequent Davis's Straits in 1719; and as the whales had not hitherto
been pursued into this vast recess, they were found in greater numbers than in the seas round Spitzbergen. From about this period
it was usually resorted to by about three-tenths of the Dutch
ships. It was not till a comparatively late period that Davis's
Straits began to be frequented by English whalers; and even so
late as 1820, when Captain Scoresby published his elaborate and
valuable work on the Whale Fishery, that carried on in the
Greenland seas was by far the most considerable. But within the
last few years the Greenland fishery has been almost entirely deserted. The various discoveries made by the expeditions recently
fitted out by government for exploring the seas and inlets to the
westward of Davis's Straits and Baffin's Bay, have made the
fishers acquainted with several new and advantageous situations

for the prosecution of their business. What further revolutions the fishery may be destined to undergo it is impossible to foresee, but there can be little doubt that the same results that have happened elsewhere will happen in Davis's Straits; and that it will be necessary to pursue the whale to new and perhaps still more inaccessible haunts.

The sea in Davis's Straits is less incommoded with field-ice than the Greenland and Spitzbergen seas, but it abounds with icebergs; and the fishery when carried on in Baffin's Bay and Lancaster Sound, is more dangerous, perhaps, than any that has hitherto been attempted.

The following Table gives a view of the produce of the Northern Whale Fishery during the three years ending with 1827.

Years.	Number of Ships Dispatched.	Number of Whales Captured.	Quantity of Oil.	Quantity of Whalebone.
			Tons.	*Tons.*
1825	110	501	6,597	360
1826	94	510	7,087	390
1827	88	1,155	13,179	732

It appears from this and the previous table, that the number of ships sent out has declined nearly a half since 1820. The bounty was repealed in 1824, and the ships fitted out have since fallen off in the ratio of 112 to 88 or 90. This is a sufficient proof of the insecure foundation on which the trade had previously rested.

The Whale Fishery has for a lengthened period partaken more of the nature of a gambling adventure than of a regular industrious pursuit. Sometimes the ships do not get half a cargo, and sometimes they come home *clean.* The risk of shipwreck is also very considerable. It appears from Mr. Scoresby's tables, (vol. ii. p. 131,) that of 586 ships sent to the north during the four years ending with 1817, *eight* were lost. This period was, however, uncommonly free from disaster. It would seem, too, that the risk of shipwreck is greater in Davis's Straits than in the seas to the east of Greenland. In 1819, of sixty-three ships sent to Davis's Straits, no fewer than ten were lost; in 1821, out of seventy-nine ships, eleven were lost; and in 1822, out of sixty ships, seven were lost. But the last season has in this respect been the most disastrous. Of eighty-seven ships that sailed for Davis's Straits, no less than eighteen, or twenty-two per cent. of the whole, have been totally lost; twenty-four returned *clean,* or without having caught a single fish; and of the remainder not one had a full cargo, only one or two being *half fished!* · If we estimate the value of the ships cast away, including the outfit, at £7,000 each, the loss from shipwreck only will be £126,000. It seems very doubtful whether, in the present critical state of the fishery, it will easily recover from so dreadful a blow.

A little work on " Discovery and Adventures in the Polar Seas and Regions," forming part of the " Edinburgh Cabinet Library," and compiled with great care and ability, was published in the course of the last year. We borrow from it the following instructive details with respect to the fishery in 1829, and the changes that have taken place during the last twenty years in the ports at which the fishery ships are fitted out.

RESULT OF THE FISHERY OF 1829.

Ports.	No. of Ships.	Tonnage.	Fish.	Oil.	Bone.	
				Tons.	Tons.	Cwt.
Aberdeen . . .	11	3,322	84	1,171	63	14
Berwick	1	309	11	147	8	16
Dundee	9	3,031	77	1,005	54	9
Hull	33	10,899	339	3,982	235	19
Kirkcaldy . . .	4	1,261	51	649	37	0
Leith	7	2,393	71	862	48	4
London	2	714	2	32	2	3
Montrose . . .	4	1,301	39	481	27	11
Newcastle . .	3	1,103	45	541	29	10
Peterhead . . .	12	3,429	118	1,445	78	16
Whitby	3	1,050	34	357	21	8
Totals . . .	89	28,812	871	10,672	607	10

Estimated Value.

10,672 tuns of Oil, at £25 . . . . £266,800
607½ tons of Whalebone, at £180 . . . 109,350
————
£376,150

' In the commercial tables presented to the House of Commons in 1830, the entire proceeds of last year are stated at £428,591 : 6*s.* 6*d.*; but this, of course, includes also the southern fishery. Of this amount there were exported to foreign countries, *oil* to the value of £73,749 : 10*s.* 6*d.* and *whalebone* amounting to £40,666 : 15*s.* 6*d.*; making in all £114,416 : 6*s.*

" There has also been a somewhat singular change in the ports from which the fishery is chiefly carried on. In London were undertaken all the discoveries which led to its establishment; and for some time a complete monopoly was enjoyed by the great companies formed in that city. Even between the years 1780 and 1790, the metropolis sent out four times the number of vessels that sailed from any other port. It was observed, however, that her fishery was, on the whole, less fortunate than that of the new rivals which had sprung up; and her merchants were so much discouraged, that, in Mr. Scoresby's time, they equipped only seventeen or eighteen vessels. They have since almost entirely abandoned the trade, employing last year and the present not more than two ships.

"Hull early became a rival to London, having sent out vessels at the very commencement of the fishery. Although checked at first by the monopoly of the great companies, as soon as the trade became free, she prosecuted it with distinguished success. In the end of the last century that town attained and has ever since preserved the character of the first whale-fishing port in Britain.

Whitby engaged in this pursuit in 1753, and carried it on for some time with more than common success; but her operations have since been much limited. Liverpool, after embarking in the undertaking with spirit, has now entirely relinquished it. Meantime the eastern ports of Scotland have steadily carried on, and even extended their transactions, while those of the country at large were diminishing. The increase has been most remarkable at Peterhead; and indeed this town, as compared especially with London, must derive a great advantage from avoiding, both in the outward and homeward voyages, 600 miles of somewhat difficult navigation.

"The following summary has been collected from Mr. Scoresby, as the average quantity of shipping fitted out in the different ports for nine years ending with 1818; and the comparison of it with the number sent out in 1830, will show the present state of the trade:—

		Average of 1810—18.		1830.	
ENGLAND—	Berwick	$1\frac{7}{9}$		1	
	Grimsby	$1\frac{4}{9}$		0	
	Hull	$53\frac{4}{9}$		33	
	Liverpool	$1\frac{8}{9}$		0	
	London	$17\frac{8}{9}$		2	
	Lynn	$1\frac{4}{9}$		0	
	Newcastle	$4\frac{7}{9}$		3	
	Whitby	$8\frac{8}{9}$		2	
			$91\frac{5}{9}$		41
SCOTLAND—	Aberdeen	$10\frac{8}{9}$		10	
	Banff	$\frac{8}{9}$		0	
	Burntisland	0		1	
	Dundee	$7\frac{5}{9}$		9	
	Greenock	$\frac{8}{9}$		1	
	Kirkcaldy	$\frac{7}{9}$		5	
	Kirkwall	$\frac{6}{9}$		0	
	Leith	$8\frac{7}{9}$		7	
	Montrose	$2\frac{7}{9}$		4	
	Peterhead	$6\frac{8}{9}$		13	
			$40\frac{1}{9}$		50
	Total		$131\frac{6}{9}$		91.

Of the ninety-one ships fitted out in 1830, four only were for Greenland.

We have already seen that, as a source of national wealth, the Whale Fishery is of exceedingly little importance. Neither does it seem to be of so much consequence as a nursery for seamen as is commonly supposed. The number of those employed in the northern fishery does not exceed 4,500; and it may be doubted whether the casualties to which they are exposed do not, in a public point of view, more than balance the increased skill and hardihood they acquire from being engaged in so perilous an occupation.

There seems no reason to apprehend any deficiency in the supply of oil from a falling-off in the fishery. We have seen, from the foregoing statements, that the fish oil imported in 1829, amounted to 10,672 tons. But at present about half this quantity of olive oil is annually imported; and as olive oil is loaded with a duty of £8 : 8s. a ton, it is obvious that if this duty were reduced, as it ought to be, to £3 or £4 a ton, the increased quantity imported would go far to balance any falling-off in the supply of train oil. When a coarser species is required, rape and linseed oil may be advantageously substituted for that of the whale; and that such would be the case no one can doubt, were the prohibitory duty of £39 : 18s. a ton, with which it is loaded, reduced to a reasonable amount, that is, to less than a *tenth* of its present magnitude. Tallow may also be applied to several purposes to the exclusion of train oil. Although, therefore, the Whale Fishery should decline, we need not fear that any material injury will thence arise to the industry of the country. And it would be most impolitic to attempt to bolster it up, either by resorting to the exploded system of bounties, or by laying heavy duties on the oils or tallow imported from other countries.

The South Sea Fishery was not prosecuted by the English till about the beginning of the American war. And as the Americans had already entered on it with vigour and success, four American harpooners were sent out in each vessel. In 1791, seventy-five whale ships were sent to the South Sea, but the number has not been so great since. In 1829 only thirty-one ships were sent out, of the burden of 10,997 tons, and carrying 937 men. The *Cachalot*, or spermaceti whale, is particularly abundant in the neighbourhood of the Spice Islands; and Mr. Crawfurd, in his valuable work on the Eastern Archipelago, (vol. iii. p. 447,) has entered into some details to show that the fishery carried on there is of greater importance than the spice trade. Unluckily, however, the statements on which Mr. Crawfurd has founded his comparisons are entirely erroneous, neither the ships nor the men employed amounting to more than a fifth or sixth part of what he has represented.

But errors of this sort abound in the works of those who had better means of coming at the truth. Mr. Barrow, in an article on the Fisheries, in the *Supplement to the Encyclopædia Britannica*, states the number of ships fitted out for the Northern Whale Fishery in 1814 at 143, and their crews at 7,150; and he further states the number of ships fitted out for the southern fishery in 1815 at 107, and their crews at 3,210. In point of fact, however, only 112 whale ships cleared out for the north in 1814, carrying 4,708 men, and in 1815 only twenty-two whale ships cleared out for the south, carrying 592 men! How Mr. Barrow, who has access to official documents, should have given the sanction of his authority to so erroneous an estimate, we know not. In the same article Mr. Barrow estimates the entire annual value of the British fisheries of all sorts at £8,300,000. But were this the place to enter upon the investigation, it would be very easy to show that in rating it at £3,500,000, we shall certainly be beyond the mark.

We annex a detailed account of the progress of the Southern Whale Fishery since 1814.

An Account of the Number of Ships annually fitted out in Great Britain, with their Tonnage and Crews, for the Southern Whale Fishery, and of the Bounties on their Account from 1814 to 1824, both inclusive.

Years.	Ships.	Tons.	Men.	Bounties paid, £.
1814	30	8,999	794	5,600
1815	22	6,985	592	8,000
1816	34	10,332	852	4,500
1817	42	14,785	1,201	10,000
1818	58	18,214	1,643	6,600
1819	47	14,668	1,345	9,100
1820	68	19,755	1,827	9,100
1821	55	14,398	1,396	8,300
1822	44	11,432	1,022	7,400
1823	59	17,669	1,536	6,800
1824	31	9,122	796	7,300

An Account, of the Number of Ships fitted out in the different Ports of Great Britain, (specifying the same) for the Southern Whale Fishery, their Tonnage, and the Number of Men on Board, during the Three Years ending 5th of January, 1830.

Ports.	Year ending 5th January, 1828.			Year ending 5th January, 1829.			Year ending 5th January, 1830.		
	Ships.	Tons.	Men.	Ships.	Tons.	Men.	Ships.	Tons.	Men.
London . .	31	10,158	874	21	7,000	604	31	10,997	937
Greenock .	2	216	28	nil.			nil.		

JOHN COVEY,
Reg. Gen. of Shipping.

Office of Registrar General of Shipping,
Custom-House, London, Dec. 16, 1830.

For a lengthened period the Americans have prosecuted the Whale Fishery with greater vigour and success than, perhaps, any other people. They commenced it in 1690, and for about fifty years found an ample supply of fish on their own shores. But the whale having abandoned them, the American navigators entered with extraordinary ardour into the fisheries carried on in the northern and southern oceans. From 1771 to 1775, Massachusetts employed annually 183 vessels, carrying 13,820 tons, in the former, and 121 vessels, carrying 14,026 tons in the latter. Mr. Burke, in his famous speech on American affairs in 1774, adverted to this wonderful display of daring enterprise as follows:

" As to the wealth," said he, " which the colonists have drawn from the sea by their fisheries, you had all that matter fully opened at your bar. You surely thought these acquisitions of value, for they seemed to excite your envy, and yet the spirit by which that enterprising employment has been exercised ought rather, in my opinion, to have raised esteem and admiration. And pray, Sir, what in the world is equal to it ? Pass by the other parts, and look at the manner in which the New England people carry on the Whale Fishery. While we follow them among the trembling mountains of ice, and behold them penetrating into the deepest frozen recesses of Hudson's and Davis's Straits : while we are looking for them beneath the Arctic Circle, we hear that they have pierced into the opposite region of polar cold ; that they are at the antipodes and engaged under the frozen serpent of the south. Falkland Island, which seemed too remote and too romantic an object for the grasp of national ambition, is but a stage and resting-place for their victorious industry. Nor is the equinoctial heat more discouraging to them than the accumulated winter of both poles. We learn that while some of them draw the line or strike the harpoon on the coast of Africa, others run the longitude and pursue their gigantic game along the coast of Brazil. No sea, but what is vexed with their fisheries. No climate, that is not witness of their toils. Neither the perseverance of Holland, nor the activity of France, nor the dexterous and firm sagacity of English enterprise ever carried this most perilous mode of hardy industry to the extent to which it has been pursued by this recent people; a people who are still in the gristle and not hardened into manhood."

The unfortunate war that broke out soon after this speech was delivered, checked for a while the progress of the fishery; but it was resumed with renewed vigour as soon as peace was restored. The American fishery has been principally carried on from Nantucket and New Bedford in Massachusetts; and for a considerable time past the ships have mostly resorted to the southern seas. " Although," says Mr. Pitkin,* " Great Britain has, at various times, given large bounties to her ships employed in this fishery, yet the whalemen of Nantucket and New Bedford, unprotected and unsupported by any thing but their own industry and enterprise, have generally been able to meet their competitors in a foreign market."

France, which preceded the other nations of Europe in the Whale Fishery, can hardly be said, for many years past, to have had any share in it. In 1784, Louis XVI. endeavoured to revive it. With this view he fitted out six ships at Dunkirk on his own account, which were furnished with harpooners and a number of experienced seamen brought at a great expense from Nantucket. The adventure was more successful than could have been reasonably expected, considering the auspices under which it was carried on. Several private individuals followed the example of his Majesty, and in 1790 France had about forty ships employed in the fishery. The revolutionary war destroyed every vestige of this rising trade. Since the peace the government has made great efforts for its renewal, but hitherto without success; and it is singular, that with the exception of an American house established at Dunkirk, hardly any one has thought of sending out a ship. But there is no reason to think that this will be any longer the case. The French government issued in December, 1829, an ordonnance which cannot fail to render fishing adventures lucrative, even though no fish should be taken. By this law a bounty of 90 francs a ton is given on every vessel fitted out for the Northern fishery; and not satisfied with this they give a double bounty, or premium of 180 francs (£7 : 2s.) a ton, to every ship fitted out for the fishery that goes beyond—the *sixtieth* degree of north latitude! Every one except those who framed this precious regulation, knows that it is idle to attempt fishing in

---

* Commerce of the United States, 2d ed. p. 46.

the Greenland seas under the 70th degree of latitude, and that even in Davis's Straits the whalers must go beyond the 62d degree. If, therefore, any vessel really thinks of fishing, were it only to give the crew a little exercise or amusement, she must go beyond the 60th degree, and become entitled to the high bounty. And in point of fact such is the *wisdom* of the French government, and such their zeal to promote this branch of industry, that a ship of 400 tons, fitted out on pretence of fishing, which should make a summer excursion to the seas round Iceland, would, although she never struck a harpoon, be entitled to a bounty of £2800! Instead, therefore, of there being only *seven* whale ships in France, as was the case in 1829, we shall be surprised if ministers have not to congratulate the chambers on this number being increased to 700 before the end of the present year. We are quite sure that were our government to offer such a bounty, we should not have 90, but 9000 ships engaged in the trade! Mr. Sadler and Lord Bexley cannot but be gratified at seeing that the mercantile system, though sapped on all sides, and tottering to its fall in England, should be so well bolstered up, and so vigorous in France.

M. de la Jonkaire, though, like all good Frenchmen, an admirer of bounties and prohibitions, suspects that the existing law, however excellent in spirit, requires *modification*, and that ships may be fitted out not so much to catch the whale as the bounty.

" Perhaps," says he, " we may even accuse the ordinance of December last of extravagant liberality; for, after all, bounties are only a tax levied on *all* the members of the community for the benefit of a *few; it is a* privilege which should only be granted on the score of great public utility, and the burden of it should always be lightened as much as possible. Now, it follows from the last ordinance that a vessel of 500 tons obtains a bounty of 90,000 francs (£3600), for a voyage of four or five months: this is not merely giving encouragement to the fishery, but actually paying all its expenses. Let us not deceive ourselves, the advantage which this branch of industry is likely to derive from it is only illusory; it is certain that speculators will send their vessels for the sole purpose of catching the bounty, and not of catching the whales; if they even return *clean*, the voyage will be a profitable one. There is no doubt whatever that this measure will send a number of vessels to sea, but it is not so certain that it will form whale-fishers. The fictitious impulse which it will give to this branch of commerce will soon be extinguished, without having been productive of any durable fruits."— p. 44.

Hamburgh, Altona, and other ports on the Elbe, carry on the Whale Fishery with considerable success. They usually send from fifty to sixty ships to the North. In 1818, Gluckstadt sent eighteen ships; while France, with her vast population and her system of bounties, only sent five!

ART. V.—HELIAND. *Poema Saxonicum Seculi Noni. Accur\
ratè expressum ad exemplar Monacense, insertis e Cottoniano \
Londinensi Supplementis, nec non adjecta lectionum varietate, \
nunc primum edidit* J. Andreas Schmeller, Bibliothecæ Regiæ \
Monacensis Custos etc. (Erste Lieferung: Text.) Monachii, \
Stutgartiæ et Tubingæ. Sumptibus J. G. Cottæ. 1830. \
Royal 4to.

THE Heliand* is a production of no ordinary interest, whether
we regard its subject, its style, its age, or its language. It may
be necessary for the information of such of our readers as
are not versed in poetic antiquarianism, to premise by way of
introduction, that the work before us is a poem of the ninth
century, and therefore venerable from its antiquity, besides
being interesting in a literary point of view, as are all the productions of such a remote period. It is written in a dialect
which very closely resembles the language of our Anglo-Saxon
ancestors, and is, therefore, of the utmost importance to the
student of that language, and through it, of the English, in all
its æras and stages of perfection. Our Saviour, as the name of
the poem testifies, is the principal character in it, and the subject
is a narrative of his life as detailed in the Four Gospels, the
events of which are thrown together into one continued narrative; it has a claim, therefore, upon the attention of the Biblical
critic, as illustrative of the interpretation then attached to portions of Holy Writ, the meaning of which, even at present,
gives rise to controversy. In addition to these recommendations,
we may add, that it possesses the advantages of a lofty style,
the sentiments are vigorous and natural, the circumstances which
the fancy of the poet has induced him to engraft upon the main
subject are interesting, as connected with the manners and feelings, and modes of thinking of the period in which he lived,
and they are valuable, as illustrative, in a certain degree, of the
state of society of the æra. The episodes, of which, unfortunately, there are too few, branch off in a natural manner from the
detail of the chief incidents, and in this respect, they present a
favourable contrast to the abruptness of their introduction, and
the tediousness of their details, in the poems of Cædmon and
Beowulf. Accompanied by so many recommendations in its
favour, we need not be surprised that a correct edition of it
should have long been desired by the literati of the continent:

---

* Heliand, the Saviour. The Saxon King, Alfred, shall here appear in the novel
character of an etymologist. He is so called says he because, *he sothlice hys folc* HAL
gedeth from hyra synnum; i. e. he truly maketh his people to be *healed* from their sins.
—*Alfred's Bede,* i. 21.

our wonder should rather be,—if such a subject had not long ceased to excite our wonder,—that its publication should have been so long neglected in this country.   This neglect affords a very remarkable, although unfortunately, by no means a solitary instance of the supine indifference with which we regard the philological treasures contained in our great public libraries.   The contrast which it exhibits between our inattention to similar monuments of antiquity, and the zeal and enthusiasm displayed by our German brethren, is as little flattering to our national vanity, as. it is creditable to our national literature.   Since the very commencement of the seventeenth century, a manuscript of the Heliand has existed in a well-known public library ; its value has been pointed out, and its importance dilated upon by each succeeding catalogue-maker; and yet no Englishman has been found willing or capable to undertake the task of being its editor. It is needless for us to inquire whence proceeds this apathy; it is sufficient to observe, that by the publication before us we are deprived of the only chance which remained of atoning for our long neglect; and our regret that the title-page bears the name of Munich instead of London, is only diminished by the satisfaction of finding that the task of editorship has fallen into such able hands.

Two manuscript copies of this poem are known to be in existence, both of them more or less imperfect ; so much so, that although one supplies *lacunæ* in the other, they would not, if united, furnish us with a complete whole.   The first, and the more generally known of these, is preserved in our own island ; and as we have already hinted, forms part of the Cottonian Library, the basis of the manuscript collection of the British Museum.*   This volume has long been esteemed one of the most important philological treasures of that splendid library. It is a small quarto, written upon vellum, in a hand in general very plain, (as may be seen in the specimen engraved by Hickes in the first plate of his Franco-Theotisc Grammar,) and is distinguished by the usual neatness which characterises the productions of the Saxon scribes.   Dr. James, who gives the earliest description of these MSS., informs us that this volume formed part of the collection of Canute, and the tradition clings to it still, for it is generally known by the name of King Canute's Bible. He has not, it is true, made us acquainted with his grounds for such an assertion, nor is there any external evidence or document in the volume itself which authorizes us to assent to it.   Something may be said for, as well as against, the admis-

---

* Marked Caligula, A. vii.

sion of this tradition. If we wish to dissent from it, we may state that the opinion we entertain of the dialect in which it is written, (of which more hereafter,) would incline us to accept this story with considerable hesitation; for the Scandinavian origin of Canute would render an infinitude of words and expressions used in this volume perfectly incomprehensible. But on the other hand, we should bear in mind that we are not told that it was written for Canute's use, or even that he read it, and therefore this argument should fall to the ground; and the perfect authenticity of the legendary tales told of another Saxon MS.* in the same collection, should guard us against too scrupulously rejecting this information which Dr. James gives us. Fancy may supply us with arguments,—if the term be not misapplied,—by allowing us to suppose that the tradition came with the volume into the hands of Sir Robert Cotton; or rather, that it might be embodied in a more tangible shape upon some fly-leaf which has fallen a victim to the hands of the binder. This reminds us that prefixed to the text are several illuminations,† which, whether they supply the place of the folio that contained the information we are in search of, or not, might be brought forward as an argument against the antiquity of our copy of the Heliand. These very splendid paintings represent some of the leading events in the New Testament history. From the style of art displayed in them, as well as from the costume of the figures introduced, the best judges have assigned no higher antiquity to them than the age of King Stephen. But we get rid of the difficulty thus caused by referring to Wanley, who, with every appearance of probability on his side, conjectures that they formed part of some Latin copy of the Gospels, and that the circumstance of their bearing upon the events described in the Heliand induced Sir R. Cotton to have them inserted in his codex, without sufficient regard to the preservation of unity of *costume.* Be that as it may, the writing of the poem itself indicates an antiquity prior by many centuries to the alleged date of the paintings. Wanley and Astle,—the highest possible authorities upon such questions,— enable us to fix the middle or latter end of the ninth century as the period in which this manuscript was transcribed.

For nearly two centuries this copy was the only one known,

---

* Nero, D. 4. See the curious History given of it in *Raine's History of North Durham,* folio, 1830, p. 67.

† The subjects are, the Annunciation, the Meeting of Mary and Elizabeth, the Nativity, the Appearance of the Heavenly Host to the Shepherds, the Infanticide, Symon meeting our Saviour in the Temple, the Adoration of the Magi, and the Baptism of our Lord by John.

and it was from it that the sole chance of an edition was to be
expected.   Fortunately for the interests of literature, however,
a second manuscript was discovered.   From certain hints long
ago thrown out, the Germans had a vague idea that the " Codex
Cottonianus" was not the only copy extant, and that a diligent
search amongst some of their monastic libraries might be rewarded by the discovery of another.   Duchesne (ii. 326) is supposed to have seen a manuscript of it, which supposition rests
upon the circumstance of his having quoted the preface of a
Gospel Harmony, written in Saxon.   Eckhard regrets that instead of publishing the preface, Duchesne did not publish the
text, or at least inform the world where this manuscript was to
be found.   It seems more than probable that he did not do so
because he had his information through the medium of the *Catalogus Testium Veritatis*, where a preface exactly similar occurs,
the most interesting passages of which we have extracted in the
note which will be found at page 387.   But there was undoubtedly correct information regarding the existence of such a manuscript, for Eckhard states that Pez communicated to him some
fragments which he had extracted from a manuscript at Würtz-
burg, and Zeigler, librarian there, confirmed his testimony by
stating that he had seen this manuscript.   Eckhard searched
there for it in vain, but after many years of disappointment, the
long-sought treasure was recovered in 1794.   The fortunate individual by whom this achievement was performed, was Gerard
Gley, who, although a Frenchman, was remarkably well versed
in German antiquities, as his volume upon the *Language and
Literature of the Franks* (published in 1814) evinces.   Whilst
ransacking the library of the Cathedral Church at Bamberg, he
chanced to meet with a manuscript, which, imperfect as it
was, he immediately recognised to be the Heliand.   Who does
not envy him his feelings at such a moment?   It was a discovery infinitely more important than any which rewarded the
enthusiasm of "honest Tom Hearne," whose morning and
evening prayers always contained the petition, that he might be
the favoured instrument of dragging to light some manuscript
which had never been printed ; a petition, which by the by, must
have frequently been granted in his searches through the Bodleian.   But to return to Gley.   He soon made public the information through the medium of the periodical publications of
Germany, and accompanied it with specimens of the text.   He
resolved to lose no time in printing the whole ; and for the purpose of doing so in a manner consistent with its merit, he associated himself with Reinwald, the well-known author of the
Glossary to Ulphilas.   However, for reasons we are unable to

state, this literary partnership did not publish. Reinwald's papers were in 1812, added to the Library of Munich; Gley's were carried by him into France, and subsequently deposited in the library of the Institute. Gley fixes the date of this poem to be A.D. 820. He is undoubtedly induced to do so from finding in the preface published by Duchesne, already quoted, that a Harmony of the Four Gospels was composed by the command of Louis le Debonnaire. We are unable, however, to ascertain whether the manuscript mentioned by him, from Flaccius Illyricus, is to be identified with the Heliand; if such be the case, there must be a third copy in existence, for we believe the Munich manuscript contains no such preface, and the Cotton one most assuredly does not. It must be admitted that, although there is no positive proof against such a supposition, the style and language are to a certain degree a confirmation of it, as they bear a strong resemblance to the oaths of the Carlovingian princes taken at Strasburg in 842, and at Coblenz in 860. Should this be the case, it must destroy the force of the encomia bestowed by Hickes upon its antiquity, in which it must yield to the fragment of Isidore of Seville, the Weisenbrun Hymn, the combat of Hiltibrand and Hathubrant, and the rule of St. Bennet.

Detached portions of the poem in the mean time, (all of which, with the exception of those published by Gley, are from the Cotton Codex,) had found their way into works of importance. Francis Junius is the first who is known to have paid anything like critical attention to the volume. The enthusiasm with which he entered upon the investigation of every subject connected with the ancient languages of the North, induced him to transcribe the whole, which he undoubtedly intended for the press. We cannot take upon ourselves to state what plan he had resolved to adopt in his edition; but as we find his transcript unaccompanied by grammar, glossary, translation, or note, this circumstance renders it probable that it was to be brought out in the same manner as the Saxon poem of Cædmon,* that is, without the slightest explanation of any kind. Upon the death of Junius in 1678, this copy, together with several other valuable manuscripts, passed to the Bodleian Library, where it probably has seldom since been disturbed.

Our countryman, Dr. Hickes, of whom we have every reason to be proud, was the next to draw the attention of the world to the Heliand. He first mentions it in his "*Institutiones Grammaticæ Anglo-Saxonicæ et Mæso-Gothicæ*," Oxon. 1689, and

---

* Two editions of this poem are at present announced as being intended for publication; one by Dr. Grundtvig of Copenhagen; the other under the joint care of Messrs. Thorpe and Taylor.

subsequently in his " *Thesaurus Linguarum Veterum Septentrio-nalium.*" In the latter work he is much.more .copious, for he prints as much as amounts to nearly fifteen pages of the present edition. With these extracts he gives us a Latin version, which justice obliges us to admit, however unwillingly,. is not always so correct as it might be, and as it should have been ; it is also dis-figured with many more errors than the disadvantage of translating from a single manuscript, with its perplexity of accompanying errata,. can excuse. The high opinion which he expresses of its merits, like every other opinion of his, is entitled to carry great weight with it ; and we shall have occasion farther on to direct the attention of the reader to it.while .making a few. observations upon the language of the poem. The subject of the Doctor's book rendering it more popular abroad than at home, the eulo-gium of the Heliand which it contained naturally brought it into merited notice upon the continent. Accordingly, about the year 1760, we .find Klopstock .anxious to procure a transcript from England, that he might publish it with a translation and notes; but for reasons unknown, the project was not carried into execution. Some fragments of it were printed at Copenhagen by Nyerup, which completes the list of those who have done. anything towards its illustration, until we arrive at the discovery of the second copy at Bamberg. In addition to these, we must add the name of J. Scherer, the late Librarian at Munich, who for many years meditated the honour of being its editor, and after having written copious prolegomena, and a large body of notes, (" *more suo, id est eruditè,*" as Ihre has said of his countryman Wachter,) was upon the eve of.sending his copy to the press,. when he was cut off by death. Our present worthy editor, upon succeeding last year to Scherer's situation, considered the duty of editing the Heliand as devolving upon him with the office. And we know no one who could have done it more ample justice. He has evinced his attachment to, and knowledge of, the early language and literature of his country by his edition of the Gospel of St. Matthew in the Mæso-Gothic of Ulphilas, and the Francic of Tatian ; nor must his equally learned and curious " *Bauerisch Worterbuch*" be forgotten. The manner in which he has exe-cuted his task in this first portion of his undertaking,.is by no means inferior to what we should expect from him ; and should the second, and more important part of the work, equal the anticipations which the correctness of the present authorizes us to entertain, we may safely say that it will entitle him to rank in the highest class of grammarians and philologists. The plan he has adopted in the text is judicious, for it presents us with exact. transcripts of both the copies ; although only one.is adopted in

the text, and printed entire, yet each is kept so distinct, that even
if we had the two originals before us, we could not, by their aid,
have a more correct idea of the discrepancies of the versions.
The Munich copy is printed *literatim;* the folios which are·want-
ing in it are supplied from a transcript of the Cotton MS.; the
words; syllables, or letters, which in the least point vary in the
two copies, are distinguished by that portion of the ' text being
printed in italics; and the corresponding portion of the Cotton
one is given at the bottom of the page. In those pages of ·the
text, which from the deficiency of the Munich MS., are printed
upon the sole authority of the Cotton one, the editor has pointed
out to us what he considers errors of the copyist, or irregular
and uncommon inflexions of words, by printing these anomalous
portions in italic letter. The editor informs us in his preface
that he has never been so fortunate as to have it in his power to
examine the Cotton manuscript, and that the readings which he
gives from it rest upon the authority of a transcript made by
Mr. Schlichtegroll, whom the literati of Germany sent hither for
that purpose; Having made a careful collation of those passages
in the work under consideration, which are printed from the
Cotton manuscript *alone,* we have been enabled to detect sundry
omissions and errors, of no very great moment it is true, but
which might easily have been avoided by ordinary care and circumspection. It was our intention to have presented our readers
with a list of these errata, an intention which we have abandoned
upon learning that the whole publication is to be· re-collated,
with the Cotton manuscript, by Mr. Reinwald, and that the collation is to appear in the Prolegomena which are to form a portion of the concluding number of the work. It is but justice to
Mr. Schmeller to state, that no discredit can possibly be attached
to him on this account, but on the contrary, in many of the instances in which he has offered a conjectural emendation of the
transcript of Schlichtegroll, he is supported by the manuscript
itself—a most satisfactory proof of his acquaintance with the
grammar and structure of the language. The second part of the
work is to contain a grammar, a glossary, some observations
upon the passages doubtful of meaning, accompanied with'proposed emendations, besides an inquiry into the relative merits of
the two copies, and the peculiarities which distinguish each. ' It
is obvious that in this lies the difficulty of the undertaking; and
as the editor will not avail himself of the prior labours of
Reinwald, and is prevented by some law process from using those
of Scherer, we cannot in reason complain if some months elapse
before the work be completed.

Those who are conversant with the poetic remains of any of·

the Gothic nations, at least of any antiquity, will easily imagine
that the versification of the Heliand is alliterative. But to many
of our readers, this explanatory term may require some little
explanation. Alliterative metre, then, is formed without the
slightest dependence upon the aid of terminal rhyme, and the
accuracy of the whole depends upon the existence of two or
more words in the first hemistich, and one in the second, all of
which shall commence with the same letter, provided that letter
be a consonant, but should the rythm hinge upon a vowel, each
of these was considered capable of forming the requisite alliteration for the other. This was the rule as it stood in its strictest
form; but considerable license was allowed, and indeed the poet
seems to have considered his object attained if the alliteration
was perceptible to the ear, although the words by which it was
formed were not placed in the situation above specified. This
measure was long a favourite with the poets of England and
Scotland,* and numerous specimens of it are to be found from
the time of Cædmon, the monk of the eighth century, to the
nameless Romancer who describes the battle of Flodden in the
sixteenth. We must admit that although very harmonious lines
frequently result from this measure, yet it is productive of many
disadvantages. The bard being bound down by its arbitrary
laws, which laid a chain upon almost each alternate word, was
induced to employ terms in secondary and oblique senses, and
hence we not unfrequently meet with expressions which we have
difficulty in reconciling with the sense of the passage in which
they occur, while their detached meaning is simple and obvious.

We now proceed to make a few passing remarks upon the
language in which the poem is written. Smith, the early cata-
logue-writer of the Cottonian Library, in describing the Heliand,
tells us that it is composed " *in Lingua Franco-Danica.*" Where
he obtained this piece of information we know not, nor will we
pause for the purpose of refuting such an absurdity. The
opinion of Hickes, however, is of more weight, both from his
experience in such matters, and because the decision he pronounced upon the question has remained undisputed until a
very recent period. He expresses himself so warmly upon the
value of the manuscript that we will not deprive our readers of
the pleasure of perusing a translation of the whole passage.

" Amongst the books, whether in print or in manuscript, which are
essential towards the attainment of a correct knowledge of the Franco-
Theotisc language, there is a volume in the Cottonian collection to
which I would direct your attention. It is a paraphrastic Gospel

---

* The allusions of Chaucer and Gascoigne are well known, and need not here be
repeated.

Harmony in rythm, and agrees in metre, style, and the general structure of its diction, very closely with the version of Genesis generally attributed to Cædmon. I am inclined to rank this volume amongst the Franco-Theotisc writings, and yet I am aware that arguments may be urged against the truth of this position. I was formerly induced to view it as the production of some Anglo-Saxon, who flourished between the conversion of his nation to the Christian faith, and the first irruption of the Danes : in other words, between the years 601, and 793. Between these two dates the Anglo-Saxons must, of necessity, have used the Franco-Theotisc language in the same pure and unalloyed state in which they introduced it into this island. Subsequently, however, I withdrew it from the Saxons, and attributed the merit of its performance to some Frank, whom we may suppose to have completed it under the reign of Charlemagne. But whether this manuscript be Anglo-Saxon, or Franco-Theotisc, I consider it of the utmost importance. It surpasses every other monument of the same age by the copiousness of its style, and the splendour of its diction ; its antiquity is demonstrated by the purity of its language ; and upon the whole, it may be placed in the next rank of excellence to the Gospels of Ulphilas, to which alone, in my opinion, it should yield in the estimation of every student of the ancient northern languages."

The doubts which very naturally arise in the mind of the reader, as to the final inference to be drawn from the hesitating and contradictory sentiments here expressed, are removed by finding that Hickes must have decided in favour of the Francic character of the Heliand, for in his Grammar of that language the authorities for several of his inflections of nouns and verbs, as well as many of the rules of syntax, are derived from its pages. In this point, as also in some others in the preceding quotation, with all due deference, we cannot agree with him. For instance, we consider his position as incapable of defence when he asserts that the language which the Saxons introduced into England must have been Francic, for there is evidence almost amounting to proof that it must have been Scandinavian. But to return ; we think that all who take the trouble of turning over the pages of his Francic Grammar, will find enough in it to convince them that the language there illustrated, and the language of the Heliand, have sufficient marks of contradistinction to prevent them from being identified. Not only do they differ in exterior appearance, but there are internal evidences which evince their distinction. The manner in which several of the nouns and verbs are inflected in the Cotton Codex differs so widely from the form used by the undoubted Francic authors Tatian and Otfriid, that a distinct paradigma is given us by Hickes. And as if this were not evidence sufficiently convincing, he tells us expressly that these inflections of the Heliand approach very nearly to the Saxon mode of declension, so nearly indeed, that he is compelled to style them the Saxon forms of the Franco-Theotisc. We venture, in the outset, to dissent from an arrangement which includes the language of the poem we are considering amongst those of the Francic writers. We allow that they have much in common, as much indeed as clearly testifies that they are descended from one common parent, and are sister dialects. But they have also many points of discrimination, and many discrepancies which cannot be reconciled with each other; and we observe many peculiarities which are far from common to both. This difference commences with the first rudiments of the grammar, and pervades it until we reach its most refined niceties; it is alike observable in the alphabet and in the syntax. Although our opinion is that the Heliand is certainly Saxon, we admit that there are in it many forms of inflection, as well as entire vocables which do not occur in the pages of any Saxon writer, and which indicate an origin decidedly Francic. We remark a deficiency, besides, of those words of Scandinavian descent, of which so many are to be found in some of our Saxon poetry, more especially Beowulf, whose Danish origin has been so satisfactorily demonstrated. In conformity with this, many words are illustrated in the Glossary of Schilter, for which we search in vain in the Dictionary of Lye. As these occur in the principal part of the line, forming its very stamina, and as the very existence of that vital and constituent element, the alliteration, hangs upon them, we cannot consider them mere dialectal variations, which may be accounted for by supposing them the arbitrary changes of the scrivener by whom the manuscript was copied, and that he adopted this mode of accommodating it to the language of his tribe and æra. Upon the whole, then, we have no hesitation in saying, that it is written in Saxon, with a very slight commixture of Francic, so slight indeed as almost to render the term Franco-Saxon a misnomer, but enough to prevent us from considering it as pure Anglo-Saxon, or the Danish or Norman forms of that language.* In other words, it is written in that language generally styled old Saxon, or pure Saxon—a language equally distinct from the Anglo-Saxon, the Dano-Saxon and the Francic. But the most satisfactory way for

---

* When we speak of the Danish dialect of the Saxon, we wish it to be understood that we do so merely because it is a theory supported by the authority of Hickes. We shall avail ourselves of a future opportunity of expressing our views upon this subject.

all parties, is that the reader should judge for himself, which we hasten to enable him to do by the subjoining specimen. The text of the Heliand here given in general follows the Munich copy, save in one or two instances, where that suggested by the Cotton one has been admitted as preferable. The lines are arranged according to the style of Saxon poetry, and that the alliteration may be the more easily perceived, those letters by which it is formed throughout, are distinguished by being printed in the italic character. We may here state that the adoption of this rythm is another argument against the Francic origin of this poem, for although the Anglo Saxon and Scandinavian poetry is universally formed in this measure, our memory does not supply us with any Francic or Almannic poem (with the exception of the Weissenbrun Hymn and the very curious fragment of Hilti-brand and Hathubrant) which we can quote as an instance of it of having been employed by those nations. The Latin trans-lation aims at nothing higher than a faithful interpretation of the text of the preceding column, and it is hoped that the desire to attain that object will form a sufficient excuse for its stiffness and constraint. We have a few words to say in offering our Saxon version to the reader. We have taken the trouble of forming it that he may compare it line by line, and word by word with the corresponding passage of the Heliand, and in doing so he will not fail to observe how closely the two columns agree, how seldom we are under the necessity of forming our portion by inserting a word in it which has not its prototype in the Heliand, and how frequently the Saxon is attained by simply altering a few vowels or liquids of the original, into others of a similar enunciation. We have not at-tained this end by the compromise of any characteristics which distinguish the language of our ancestors, nor do we wish to arrogate any merit to ourselves, when we assert that it is entirely in keeping with the genius of their poetry, and that the whole might rank with the paraphrase of Cædmon, or the fragment of Judith, so closely do they resemble each other in style and manner. The Latin translation will be found a sufficiently accurate key to this version, except in the very few instances pointed out in the notes. The subject we have chosen is the introduction to the Sermon on the Mount, and the first of the Beatitudes, founded upon these words : "And seeing the multi-tudes, he went up into a mountain : and when he was set, his disciples came unto him, and he opened his mouth, and taught them, saying, Blessed are the poor in spirit, for theirs is the Kingdom of Heaven." *Matt.* v. vi. 2, 3.

Heliand.	Latin Translation.	Saxon Version.
Than sat im the landes hirdi	Tunc sedebat se terræ custos,	Thænne sæt him se landes hi
Geginuuard 'for them gumun ;	Eregione(et)coram hominibus;	Ongeanweard fore tham gun
Godes egan barn :	Dei proprius filius :	Godes agan barn
Uuelda mid is *spracun*,	Voluit cum ejus sermonibus,	*W*olda mid his spræcum
*S*pabuuord manag,	Sapientia dicta multa,	*W*isa * word manag
*L*erean thea *l*iudi,	Docere hunc populum,	*L*æran thone *l*eode
Huo sie *l*of gode, ·	Quà illi laudem Deo	Hu tha *l*ofe gode ·
An thesum *uu*eroldrikea,	In hoc mundo .	On thissum *w*eorold rice
*Uu*irkean sculdin.	Agere debent.	*W*eorcian sceoldan.
Sat im tho endi suuigoda,	Sedebat se tunc, atq. tacebat	Sæt him tha, and swigode
Endi *s*ah sie an lango.	Procumbebatq. se per longum,	And *s*ah and-langne
Uuas im *h*old an is *h*ugi,	Fuit *ill*is amicus in ejus mente	.Wæs tham *h*old on his *h*yg
*H*elag drohtin !	Sanctus Dominus !	*H*alig drihten !
*M*ildi un is *m*ode ;	Benignus in anima ejus,	*M*ild in his *m*ode
Endi tho is *m*und antloc,	Et tunc os reseravit,	And tha his *m*uth onleac
*Uu*isde mid is *uu*ordun, .	Docebat cum ejus verbis	*W*isade mid his *w*ordum
*Uu*aldandes sunu !	Gubernantis filius !	*W*ealdandes sunu !
*M*anag *m*arlic thing	Multa præclara	*M*anag *m*ærlic thing
Endi them *m*annum	Et illis hominibus	And tham *m*annum
*S*agde *s*pahun uuordun,	Dixit sapientibus verbis	*S*ægde *s*wæsum † wordum
Them the he te theru *s*pracu	His quos ille huic sermoni	Thæm the he te thære *s*pr·
Crist alouualdo	Christus omnipotens	Crist alwealda !
Gecoran habda	Electus erat.	Gecoren hæfde
*H*uuilike *uu*arin allaro	Qui fuerunt, omnium	*H*wilce wæron allera
*I*rminmanno	Miserorum	*E*arm-manna
Gode uuerthoston,	Deo maxime dilecti	Gode weorthestan
Gumono cunnies	Hominûm gentis.	Gumena cynnes
*S*agde im tho te *s*ode	Narravit illis tunc pro certo,	He sæde him tha to sothe
Quad that thie *s*alige uuarin	Dixit, eos faustos esse,	Cwæth that hii sælige wæı
*M*an an thesoro *m*iddilgard	Homines in hanc orbe,	*M*anne on thissum *m*id gearde
Thie her an *i*ro *m*ode uuarin	Qui hic, in eorum mente erant	Tha her on heora *m*ode w
*A*rme thurb *o*dmodi	Pauperes humilitatis causâ.	*E*arme thruh *e*admode
Them is that euuiga *r*iki	Illis est ista æterna regio,	Thæm is *æ*lifes rice
Suuido *h*elaglic	Valde sanctum munus	Swithe *h*ælag lic
*A*n hebanuuange	In cœli campo	*A*n *h*eofon wange ·
Sinlib fargeben.—P. 38.	Perpetua vita data.	Sin lif forgifen.‡

But although we have expended much time in exhibiting th claims of the Heliand upon the attention of those who are curiou in the study of language, we would not, by any means, wish t confine its interest within a circle so circumscribed, or to pass i over as unworthy of the attention of the poet and the man o taste. The author of it has not confined himself in a servil manner to the History of the Four Evangelists; it is not a trans lation from them,—it is a poem founded upon the events the

* Wisa (wise) has here been introduced, because the Saxon language does not authoriz the use of any of the compounds of Spaha,' which is rather singular, as it is found i the other Scandinavian and Teutonic branches of the Gothic. See a beautiful etymo logy of it in Wachter, voce *Spæchen*. By the adoption of *wisa* the alliteration is preserved but transferred from the letter *s* to *w*.

† Swæs ; here again the presence of Spaha causes a difficulty, which we hav attempted to remove by substituting swæs, an adjective, which Lye renders *blandus*.

‡ We subjoin an English version for the purpose of rendering the sense of the tex

detail. Adopting their history as his groundwork, the poet incorporates with it scenes and events from his own imagination; and by blending these together, in a manner by no means deficient in skill of design or power of execution, he forms a whole, in which we find numerous passages breathing the spirit of true poesy. We shall endeavour to convey an idea of the manner in which the more highly coloured passages of the poem are depicted by the fancy of the bard, by offering to our readers a portion which we consider a fair specimen of his manner. We select for this purpose a description which includes nearly the whole interview between the Magi and Herod. However, we are aware that the simple energy of the original is but feebly conveyed in the version which we here attempt to give; and in addition to the proverbial imperfection of a translation, as the medium of conveying a correct idea of the merit of an original, a special apology is requisite for the first " Essay of an Apprentice in the divine art of Poetry."

There came from far
Three prophets, following the shining star,
A Heaven-directed band : wild ways they trod,
Their only guide the beacon light of God.
Their's was the wish that child of Heaven to see,
To be his slaves, to offer on bent knee
The tribute of their worship. Still the flame
Shone, till the kings to Herod's palace came.
Within that palace, feasting in high state,
Surrounded by his courtiers, Herod sate.
He had the art to wear no trace of sin,
Whilst all was utter worthlessness within.

---

more obvious, the object of the Latin one being rather to illustrate the grammatical construction of the original.

Then the ruler of the land seated himself,
The Son of God !
Opposite the people.
He wished with his discourse
To teach that people
Many wise sayings :
In what manner
They should praise God
In this world.
He sat and was silent,
And reclined himself.
He, the Holy Lord,
Was faithful to them in his soul,
And also affectionate in his mind.
Then the Son of the Almighty
Opened his mouth,
And taught in his words
Many excellent things.

And to these men
Whom he had selected
To this conference,
(Who were of all
The human race,
Of the progeny of men,
By God the most beloved,)
To these Christ Omnipotent
Said for a truth,
That those men
Were happy in this world,
Who here in their minds
Were humble in spirit.
To them is an eternal region,
A very holy gift given,
Even everlasting life
In the kingdom of heaven.

To smooth the brow with most dissembling art,
Whilst hate and vengeance rankled at his heart.

The monarch spake: " Declare to all around,
What cause thus leads you from your native ground ?
Into strange regions have ye wander'd, where
No breath reminds you of your native air :
Ye are far distant from your Eastern strand,
Ye are but exiles in a stranger's land.
And yet the red gold shines on every slave,
And ye have all that royalty can crave.
I mark your aspect, and your bearing proud,
Ye are no hirelings from the vulgar crowd.
Nature's nobility speaks from your face,
And marks you branches of a kingly race.
My eyes have ne'er beheld so fair a train,
Since first my sceptre ruled this wide domain."

Then spake the strangers from the Eastern land,—
" Easy the task to answer thy demand,
To show thee why we left our distant home,
And through far climes, what faith has bid us roam.
Holding communion with the God of love,
   Prophets once lived, to whom the task was given
To proffer us assistance from above,
   And cheer us on, with comfort drawn from Heaven.
Within our land there dwelt in other years
   One who was wise beyond the sons of earth ;
Though now his lot is where life hath no tears,
   Yet still his name is cherished, and gives birth
To lofty thoughts.   To him our God revealed
His counsels, through long ages kept concealed.
The time of his probation here was spent,
   And he was beckoned from this world away,
The spirit was recalled, which God had lent
   To teach his will unto the sons of clay.
But when the fated time at length drew near,
When he must quit each pleasure and each tear,
When death must part him from all household mirth,
And wrench each link that bound him to the earth,
And guide his soul to realms of purer light,
   He summon'd his companions round his bed,
Although the shadows darkened into night
   Which gathered o'er his eyes ; and thus he said
To those, the heirs of promises, whose power
Should long outlive the struggle of that hour :
" In future ages, to this world shall rise
" A mighty chief, the powerful and the wise ;
" From noble ancestry this conqueror springs,
" And in his veins shall flow the blood of kings.

" And God, his father, shall each prince command
" To bow, and yield their sceptres to his hand :
" And his the rule of Heaven and earth shall be
" Till time shall melt into eternity.
" In the same hour which gives this conqueror birth,
" A star shall shed its lustre on the earth,
" When ye shall see that star of heav'nly ray,
" Gird up your loins and hasten on the way.
" And it shall be your leader through each wild,
" Until ye reach the birth-place of that child."
—Long years have passed since these words were spoken,
  But still the might of God remains the same :
Aud we have seen on high the shining token,
  And owned the truth established by the flame,
Each morn the splendour of the heaven-born star
  Rose to our sight, to guide us on our way,
And led by it, we wandered from afar
  O'er heath and mountain, many a devious way.

This specimen enables us to form a fair estimate of the
manner of the poet. We are uncertain whether we should
mention, as a subject of approbation, or as a cause of regret, that
the wild and yet poetic legends of the middle ages find no place
in the pages of the Heliand. We search in vain for the marvellous history or even the names of the three Magi, [*] although its
frequent recurrence shows that it must have been one of the
most pervading fictions of the age. The specimen we have
printed exhibits, it is true, a departure from the simplicity of the
Gospel, but it is sober reason compared to the highly wrought
fictions of the Romance. The crucifixion is completed without
the aid of the blind knight Longeus, [†] and what is still more

---

[*] According to the Legend they were named Melchior, Balthazar and Gaspar.
They are very frequently mentioned in the theological writings of the middle ages, but
the most copious account is to be found in a small volume, *enprynted at Westmester by
Wynkyn the Worde.* As it is far from being common, the title is here given entire.
" Here begynneth the lyf of the Thre Kynges of Coleyn fro that tyme they sought our
Lord God Almyghty and came to Bedleem and worshypped hym and offred to hym
vnto the tyme of their deth (as it is drawen out of dyuers bokes and put in one) and
how they were translate fro place to place."

[†] We willingly quote some lines from the singular poem of the Visions of Pierce
Plowman, which the reader will observe is written in the same rythm with the Heliand.
  Ac ther cam forth a blynde knyght with kene spere yground
  Hihte *Longeus* as the lettere telleth. and longe badde lose hus sight
  By fore Pilate and oth[r] peuple, in the place he hovede
  Ac maugery hus meny teth. he was mad that tyme
  To jouste with J. H. C. this blynde Juwe *Longeus*
  For alle bii were unhardy. that hovede the oth[r] stoude
  To touche hym oth[r] to tryne hym. oth[t] to take hym doune and grave hym
  Bote this blynde bachelor. that bar hym thorw the herte
  The blood sprang down. by the sper and unsperrede the knyghtes eyen.
                      Edit. Whitaker, p. 343.

astonishing, there is no trace of the commonest, of all common legends, the Harrowing of Hell.* As if to make atonement for these, we find some passages where the poet is original, but they exhibit merely moralizations of certain events, or what used some years ago to be termed improvements. But while we disclaim all intention of lowering our bard, by placing him on a level with a methodist parson, we are compelled to admit that in this respect only, we are a little disappointed with him. The passages which are of the nature we state, are as follows: a moralization upon the parable of the Master of the Vineyard and his Labourers, extending through two pages; upon the healing of the two blind men near Jericho, the same length; a digression upon the crime and repentance of Peter, one page; and an episode† upon Satan attempting to procure the pardon and to save the life of our Saviour through the intervention of the wife of Pilate, whom he terrifies by dreams. Upon the whole, this poem adheres to the prototype in a manner which we should not have expected, and which is the more singular, since the nearly coeval productions of Cædmon and Judith are entitled to the merit of being ranked as original pieces of poetry, for although the plot of each is borrowed from Scripture, the incidents and dialogue spring from the fancy of the bard.

But if the Heliand be deficient in the legends which were engrafted by the superstition of those dark ages upon the true history, it is equally so in those perverted interpretations which the clergy of the time wrested out of seemingly obvious passages, by which they authorized their innovations. One specimen among many will suffice, as exemplifying the judicious manner in which these passages are rendered by our poet, who seems in this instance to have trusted to the voice of his own sound common sense. In speaking of the institution of the sacrament of the Lord's Supper, he calls it " *helag belidi.*" Now throughout the whole of this poem, the word " belidi" is used to express an image, an example, a type, sign, or representation, but most frequently a parable. This exhibits a most satisfactory proof that the ridiculous doctrine of the actual presence in the Eucharist was either not promulgated then, or that it was rejected with the contempt it deserved. Many other examples, equally convincing, might be selected, but that which we have cited

---

* The Harrowing of Hell is founded chiefly upon an incorrect interpretation of that article of the Crede, which states that our Saviour *descended into Hell.* The reader is referred to the exposition of this article by Pearson, to the Gospel of Nicodemus, the Visions above cited, page 353, et seq., and to a dissertation bearing this title in the Dramatic Mysteries of Hone.

† Cfr. Visions of Pierce Plowman, p. 357.

would be enough to have entitled our bard to an honourable station amongst the members which compose the " *Catalogus Testium Veritatis,*"* had this monument of the purity of his faith fallen under the inspection of its author.

We cannot bid this interesting production adieu without expressing our cordial thanks to its editor for the pleasure and information which he has afforded us, and 'of adding our voice to the approbation which all must bestow upon this new instance of his zeal, his industry, and his learning.

---

* In this curious and almost unknown work, the passages occur to which we have already alluded in the beginning of this article, which cannot find a more appropriate place than in the paper designed to illustrate a similar production. The poem here spoken of is at present unknown, and the description given of it (of which the following are the most interesting portions) is such as to make its discovery an object most ardently to be desired. We give the most interesting portions of the description. " Præcepit namque Ludovicus, piissimus Augustus, cuidam viro de gente Saxonum, qui apud suos non ignobilis vates habebatur, ut vetus ac novum Testamentum in Germanicam linguam poetice transferre studeret ; quatenus non solum literatis, verum etiam illiteratis, sacra divinorum præceptorum lectio panderetur. Qui jussis imperialibus libentur obtemperans, nimirum eo facilius, quo desuper admonitus est prius, ad tam difficile tamque arduum se statim contulit opus ; potius tamen confidens de adjutorio obtemperantiæ, quam de suæ ingenio parvitatis. Igitur a mundi creatione initium capiens, juxta historiæ veritatem, quæquæ excellentiora summatim decerpens, et interdum quædam ubi commodum duxit, mystico sensu depingens, ad finem totius veteris ac novi testamenti interpretando more poetico, satis faceta eloquentia perduxit. Quod opus tam lucide, tamque eleganter juxta idioma illius linguæ composuit, ut audientibus ac intelligentibus non minimam sui decoris dulcedinem præstet. Juxta morem vero illius poematis, omne opus per *vitteas* distinxit, quas nos lectiones, vel sententias possumus appellare.

. " Ferunt eundem vatem, dum adhuc artis hujus penitus esset ignarus, in somnis esse admonitum, ut sacræ legis præcepta ad cantilenam propriæ linguæ, congrua modulatione coaptaret. Quam admonitionem, nemo veram esse ambigit, qui hujus carminis notitiam, studiumque ejus compositoris atque desiderii anhelationem habebit. Tanta namque copia verborum, tantaque excellentia sensuum resplendet, ut cuncta Theudisca poemata suo vincat decore."—*Edit. fol.* 1562. p. 93.

Does not this story of the Heaven-taught poet, and the subject upon which he exercised his powers, remind us strongly of our own Cædmon ?

ART. VI.—1. *Histoire Financière de la France depuis l'origine de la Monarchie jusqu'à l'année* 1828, par M. Bresson. 2 tom. 8vo. Paris. 1829.

2. *Annuaire du Budget, ou Dictionnaire Annuel des depenses et des recettes de l'état,* par M. Roch. 2 vol. 8vo. Paris. 1830.

THESE àre curious volumes; not only as affording a view of the past and present systems of administering the revenue of a country so important in itself, and in its relations to the British empire, but as furnishing philosophy with materials for a natural History of Finance. The administration of national revenue could have no existence in the rudest state of despotic government, when all was managed by " the strong hand;" and contributions were levied from the people, by the same means as booty from the enemy. The most ancient of the French Taxes, the *Taille,* partakes exactly of this character, and may be traced to the practice of the feudal lords supplying their occasional wants by exactions from their vassals, equally arbitrary in amount and in apportionment. When the kings became lords paramount in fact, as well as in title, they levied this tax, in their own name, on all the vassals of their kingdom; but ventured not to extend its operation to those who had before levied it for themselves : hence the exemption of the nobles and ecclesiastics, which was perpetuated by the selfishness of their successors, and by the impotence, or pusillanimity, of the kings. In some provinces it was a tax only on real property according to its valuation in the public register : but, in general it was a personal tax, and proportioned to the supposed circumstances of each individual. The apportionment was regulated, for some centuries, by commissioners under the appointment of the treasury. This (as may well be supposed) was attended with such monstrous abuse, that in the time of Lewis XIII. that duty was exclusively referred to a royal commissioner in each district. This indeed increased the royal revenue near nine millions of livres; but the people wished the former system back again, and the power of the crown was enormously augmented. It is curious to observe how the original character of any institution seems to descend, like the idiosyncrasies of a family constitution, from generation to generation. This tax, so arbitrary in its origin, continued to be equally so in its progress, and this alone could be augmented at pleasure, without the formality of registering in the courts or parliaments, but merely by a decree of the council; and that often issued without even consulting the sovereign. It may readily, therefore, be conceived, how this became the *dernier resort* in all the emergencies of state, till it was at last swept away in the terrible expurgation of the revolutionary fire, which it had so much contributed to kindle. One other grand lesson is to be learned from the history of this tax;—it was, at first, occasional only, and especial circumstances were thought necessary to be alleged, in justification of its being levied; it became permanently established,—and when? on the first establishment, by Charles VII. of a standing army; thus exhibiting the connection between a permanently oppressive tax, and a permanent means of enforcing it.

As society becomes somewhat less rude, even despotism is obliged to veil its spoliations; and cunning, " the wisdom of the weak," begins to be substituted for open force. Hence the first recorded measure of the first recorded French minister of finance (Marigny A.D. 1301.) is the debasing of the coin. It is *not* surprising that this gross mode of swindling should have suggested itself to the financiers, and been blindly tolerated by the people, of a barbarous age; but it *is* extraordinary that the same clumsy trick was repeated, and tolerated through successive ages of increasing improvement in political institutions, and general knowledge; though doubtless in some degree, controlled in proportion to the progress of these. Thus, whilst in England the nominal pound of silver was gradually reduced to less than a third of a real pound, and the pound of gold was coined into nearly four times the same nominal value; in Scotland the nominal pound of silver was, by successive reductions, brought to the thirty-sixth part of a real pound, and the pound of gold was coined into twenty-eight times the same nominal value.

It is not, however, easy to conceive how even the tyranny of the beginning of the fourteenth century could succeed (as is said by Bresson, tom. i. p. 195.) in forcing individuals to carry in good money to be exchanged for bad at the Exchequer: for, in the elegant language of Swift,

" I think, after all, it would be very strange
" To give current money for base in exchange,
" Like a fine lady swapping her moles for the mange,
　　　　　" Which no body can deny."

Yet the more refined chicanery of Louis XIV's age seems to have surmounted even this difficulty—" Enfin on annonça, en 1653, une diminution d'un sixième sur les monnaies par gradation. Cette operation engagea les particuliers à preter leur argent soit au financier, soit au roi." That is, capitalists brought in their old coin and received security, it is to be supposed, for one sixth more; thereby adding to the interest, or rente, a bonus of 15⅔ per cent., at the expense of the nation, whose money was depreciated. Indeed the depreciation of money always involves, besides the national loss in the transaction, a further suffering from increased taxation—for the nominal price of labour and commodities rising in proportion as the currency is depreciated, government, continuing to have the same demand for labour and its products, must in order to command these, raise, by taxation, a larger portion of such currency. '

Obvious. as these truths are—much lauded as is the enlightenment of the nineteenth century, and conspicuous as Britain stands in that light, she, with her excessive issue of inconvertible paper-currency, has no right to ridicule the blind or abject submission of remoter times, and other countries :

> —— Quid rides ? mutato nomine de te
> Fabula narratur. .   .   .   .   .   .
> Cogeris et pictis tanquam gaudere tabellis, ·
> Nescis quod valeat nummus, quem prebeat usum.

From the disquisitions under the word *Gabelle* in Du Cange, ànd Mènage, a tax on salt would seem to have been early introduced, (certainly before the time of St. Louis,) but it was not made perpetual, and organized as a royal monopoly, till the reign of Philip de Valois. The word originally signified any tax; but from the odious character of the tax on salt, became appropriate to that; as the Devil for the chief of the evil ones. It seemed to comprehend all that was objectionable in any tax. It was a monopoly, a word of itself implying multiplicities of abuse; it was a *royal* monopoly, a mighty aggravation of ills—as including a large expenditure in management, that is a large payment by the people, in proportion to the net produce received into the exchequer; with an unlimited power of supplying deficiencies by extending the scale of extortion. For the manufacturers of salt could sell only to the king at the king's buying price, and the consumer could buy it only of the king at the king's selling price. Nor was the consumer allowed to judge of the quantity he should want; but was compelled to purchase in proportion to the number of his family; and that, which, with a poor prudent man, would have been a reason for economising, was insisted on by the king as the proper measure of expenditure. And if by this measure, a man found himself possessed of a redundant quantity of salt, and his next neighbour happened to find his allotted quantity unequal to his wants, he must, under grievous penalties, supply his deficieney, not from the redundancy of his neighbour, but from the royal stores. Nor was this all: different provinces were subjected to different rates of exaction. To judge of these rates, we must premise, that in those wholly exempt from the gabelle, salt varied in price from two to eight or nine livres the quintal. In some provinces, " les provinces de grandes gabelles," the average quantity required to be purchased per head was above nine pounds, and the price sixty-two livres per quintal. In some twenty-five pounds weight per head above eight years of age, and sixteen livres the quintal. Conceive next door neighbours unequally supplied, in proportion to their wants, throughout all the provinces subject to the tax ; and contiguous provinces, separated only by imaginary lines, supplied at such very different rates, prohibited under the severest penalties, from accommodating each other's wants, and subjected to the most hateful system of espial to prevent their doing so. And can we wonder that the people should, after centuries of endurance, have been at length, roused into contempt and hatred of a government, at once so gratuitously, and so cruelly oppressive? Again, it may be useful to observe, that this disgrace, even of a despotic government, and of barbarous ages, is, as far as part, at least, of the mischievous principle is concerned, not without parallel in the present age, and in this country. Till within a few years, this very article of salt was taxed, on one side of the Tweed, at fifteen shillings a bushel, and on the other, at only six shillings. And to this day, home-made spirits in Scotland and Ireland are subject only to a duty of three shillings per gallon, whilst in England the impost is eight shillings. It is unnecessary to dilate on the temptations, which such a state of things affords to smuggling; and it is hardly possible, by any dilatation, to convey an adequate idea of the evils introduced into the social system by the prevalence of smuggling. For not only is the principle of common honesty undermined, but a feeling of disloyalty to government, and of hostility to its agents is generated, not merely in the manufacturers, but in the necessarily much more numerous class, the consumers of illicit products. With respect to government, in case of any political crisis, such a feeling might have a very sinister influence : and, in regard to its agents, it tends to personal collisions, that terminate often in homicide, sometimes in murder, and always in fostering a spirit of tyrannical and mercenary oppression in the informers and enforcers of the law; and a habit of mean evasion and spiteful resentment in the infringers of it.

Taxes having such tendencies were in France by no means confined to one or two articles; but, under the name of *Droits de Traite,* or Transit Duty, attached to almost every article of import and export as regarded the kingdom in general, and as related to the interchange of commodities between province and province :—for, strange as it may seem, the different provinces, though immediately contiguous, and under the same royal canopy, were separated by artificial barriers, along which, war between the smugglers and excisemen was eternally waged. Some of this is ascribable to the circumstance of the kingdom having been formed by successive annexations of independent states, and the difficulty of uniting, under one system of government, people accustomed to look on each other with the hatred peculiar to borderers,—" Solito inter accolas odio,"—" uno amne discretis, connexum odium."—But Bresson refers the whole to the caprice of one individual, King John, who entailed a galling system, which, after four hundred years, it required the force of a revolution to break. Several of the provinces, it seems, had refused to contribute to his imposition on their woods and forests, (called, in the language of the French finance, " les aides,") and he punished them by ordaining, that these provinces, (many of them in the heart of the kingdom,) should be considered as alien to France, and that commodities passing into their territories should be subjected to the same duties as if exported to a foreign country. What blindness of anger was here! as if he could punish the provinces receiving the commodities, without including in the punishment the unoffending provinces, which produced them.

It is curious to observe, here, that taxes were then only levied on exports. Apparently, it was imagined that goods going out of the kingdom must impoverish it; and that exportation should be discouraged by a tax, from which imports, for a like reason, should be exempted: as if the exporters were such inveterate enemies to their country, that they would impoverish it, at the expense of beggaring themselves, by sending abroad products, for which they were to receive no equivalent. *Now*, the great burden of taxation is laid on imports,—upon just as absurd principles—as if a native would buy of the foreigner what he could produce cheaper at home,—or as if he could only pay the foreigner in gold; and as if, when he paid him in gold, he gave greater value than he would have done in any other commodity: for these are the assumptions, on which are founded all the jargon about the balance of trade, and the dangers of free trade. On this latter subject, however, there is some hazard of our being misunderstood; we speak here only of the abstract principle, which, however just, cannot, after having been abandoned for ages, be at once adopted without great loss to many, and great injustice to some. Restricted trade is like West Indian slavery,—no one can doubt its iniquity: but, having been so long established, other equitable claims are created, and due notice and long preparatory measures are required for its total abolition. Thus it was, that the fetters imposed by *Jean le Bon* on the intercourse of two-and-thirty of his provinces, continued to gall them for three hundred years, before any minister attempted even to procure their relaxation: and then the wisdom of Colbert could only effect a very partial relief to fifteen of them. The rest continued a century and a quarter longer, subject to the restraints we have named: and even those not regulated by any common rate of impost; but each under a tarif of its own, so as to embarrass the general commerce of the kingdom to a degree, which an Englishman of the present times can scarcely conceive, or, conceiving it, can scarcely believe that it could have been borne for a day.

Perhaps it was this obstructed communication, which made public roads of so much less consequence in France, and continued there a system, as inefficient for the purposes of construction and repair, as it was degrading and tyrannical to those whose forced labour was applied to these operations. This was the Corveé, of all the taxes the one which engaged the greatest numbers in support of the revolution that abolished it. It is thus well characterised by Bresson:*—"Impôt en nature, que l'on exigeait des paysans ; des hommes qui n'avaient que leur salaire pour vivre, condamnés a travailler sans salaire ; des familles, qui ne subsistoient que par le travail de leur chef, devoueés à la faim et à la misère ; ...... enfin la forme absolue des ordres, la dureté des commandemens ; la rigueur des amendes et des exactions, unissant la desolation à la misère, et l'humiliation au malheur : tel est le tableau des corveés :" but it is only the outline. What a terrible filling up of the picture might be made, if we consider that the engineer, engaged for making or repairing a road, had an unlimited power over the gratuitous labour of the district, to supply all his deficiencies in the materials employed, or in the mode of applying them, and the labour in which he might be so lavish. One fact alone may give an idea of the extent to which the persecution of the poor labourer might be carried. Under the pretext of forcing the peasant to more unremitted toil, the task assigned to him was to be performed at a distance of several leagues from his home.† But the grievance was not only in the peasant being required to construct the public work, from which he, of all men, derived the least benefit, but that he *alone* was required to perform it. The maxim of Roman Law was "ad instructiones, reparationesque itinerum et pontium nullum genus hominum, nulliusque dignitatis ac venerationis, meritis, cessare oportet."‡ And the same was the principle of the multitudinous old English statutes, and of the acts

---

* T. i. p. 23.   † Bresson, t. i. p. 24.

‡ Corp. Jur. Civ. 11. 74. 4.

which consolidated them,* compelling all classes to contribute to the formation and maintenance of public roads. Such, at least, was the theory of our law—from which, however, the practice differs in two circumstances remarkably elucidatory of national character. In the first place, though the law requires the co-operation of " all occupiers of lands and *tenements* within the parish,"—in practice, *they* only are called upon, who have the easy means of co-operation,—namely, the rural population:—and, secondly, even the rural population very seldom indeed call upon the labourer to fulfil his part.

The exemption, however, of French nobles from taxation was not, as generally supposed, quite universal. They were subject to the *taille* for lands in their own occupation, and to the capitation; at least to that part of it, which was general and personal, and from which " the Dauphin himself was not excepted." It was levied at a prescribed rate on each of the twenty classes, into which the population was divided; the other part was levied on the classes subject to the *taille,* at a per centage on that tax. This was not introduced till the desperate state of Louis le Grand's affairs drove him to the attempt; and the glare of his character, operating on national vanity, enabled him to establish it, at first as a temporary, and then, (according to the course of such things,) as a permanent impost.

Nobility in France having pecuniary privileges, it became an object of speculation and purchase, and the kings, from a very early period, entered into the disgraceful traffic; thus at once contaminating the fountain of honour, and admitting pollution to the stream. To such excess did this arrive, that it was calculated that there were not less, throughout the kingdom, than four thousand offices conferring hereditary nobility, and all vendible; besides innumerable inferior places, the possession of which exempted from the *taille,* and other burdensome or degrading taxes. Successive administrations increased the number of these, merely in order to have more for sale, till it became difficult to imagine a new name; for the name, and the money, were all that was wanted; and they were not fastidious in their choice. There were the king's wine-coopers, wig-makers, tasters of his salt-butter, and visitors of his fresh, triers of his cheese, searchers of hog's tongues, inspectors of calves, and controllers of pigs. Such dignities, however, might be enjoyed by commoners; for, says Bresson, " on conçoit que les offices d'essayeurs de fromage, et de langueyeurs de cochons n'anoblissaient pas." As they failed to ennoble, it might have been apprehended that ridicule

---

* 7 Geo. III. c. 42, & 8 Geo. III. c. 5.

would stop the sale; but, on the contrary, Louis le Grand, who among his many other meannesses, had been one of the greatest salesmen, was told by his minister, Pontchartrain, " toutes les fois que votre majesté crée un office, Dieu crée un sot pour l'acheter;" and this notwithstanding the infamous trick, often resorted to, of abolishing the offices, so sold, without indemnification to the purchasers, and bringing them, under another name, again into the market; where again, they found another buyer.

Such public profligacy, in the highest ranks, could not fail to demoralize the people, and when royalty and nobility suffered so severely from the tyranny and injustice of the people, they were only reaping the harvest, which themselves had sown.

It is instructive to observe how fiscal regulations sometimes tend to perpetuate abuses of another kind; and care, therefore, should be taken not to give governments an interest in upholding them. The wretched laws concerning apprenticeships, in early ages, were procured from the ignorance of legislators, by the monopolizing spirit of the individuals, or corporations, who had obtained, at a high price, their own privileges, and the protection of their lords; to whom, as legislators, they represented themselves as, unable to continue such payments, unless allowed to limit the number of their competitors, and to derive, from the prolonged services of their pupils, some indemnification for their future rivalry. Hence throughout Europe, a servitude of many years was imposed for the teaching of businesses, most of which might have been learned in a few months. The government of France insisted on sharing with the master in the plunder of his servant, and established a tax on the indentures of apprenticeship, and another on the admission of the apprentice to exercise his business as a master. The consequence of this was, the perpetuation and extension of the laws of apprenticeship. To be a draper required a youth to serve three years as an apprentice and two as a journeyman; to pay 300 livres on being bound, and 3,000 on setting up for himself. A cobler (savetier) served three years as apprentice, and four as journeyman, paying to the king 15 livres on his indenture, and on becoming a master in the business, 360 livres, " avec chefs-d'œuvre." If the king wore the chef d'œuvre of a cobler, he must have rivalled the economy, which we have somewhere seen recorded of Marie Antoinette, who, boasting to Turgot of her compliance with his sumptuary regulations, showed him her *souliers de vert uni;* and might almost have merited the courtly reply, *il sied bien que l'univers soit à vos pieds.*

The government, in fact, were convinced of the iniquity of all this by the arguments of Colbert, a century before; and what was the consequence? they granted, on receiving an ample bonus, the right of exercising a profession without any previous apprenticeship. Thus allowing a law, which they admitted to be unnecessary and unjust, to continue in force, that they might benefit by selling exemption from its operation.

There were several minor sources, both perpetual and occasional: such were the droit d'aubaine, that stigma on French hospitality, confiscating the property of strangers dying in their territory. The *dixmes et viugtiemes* were income taxes at 10 and 5 per cent. *Sols pour libre* was a per-centage occasionally added to all taxes. *Domaine d'occident* was a tax of 3 per cent. on all imports from America. *Joyeux événement* was an exaction by a new king for the pretended confirmation of the privileges and immunities of individuals and corporate bodies, (like the extortions practised by our second Charles, under the writs of *quo warranto*.) The vexations nature of this may be imagined from the fact; that Louis XV., when he assumed the government in 1723, let this tax to be farmed at 23 millions, and the farmers collected 41: the collection was fixed to begin in 1744, and only completed five months before his death; so that for thirty years the contractors had been squeezing and harassing the people on the score of the *joyeux événement*.

This kind of tax was never regularly authorised by enrolment in the registers of the parliament of Paris; nor do we find that the kings ever ventured to force its enrolment, by appearing in person to command it, a measure occasionally resorted to in the case of an unpopular impost. The king was then said to be *seant en son lit de justice;* of which name when the reason was asked by an Englishman, he was answered by a French wit (we think Marmontel) *c'est le lit où la justice dort.* The true origin, however, of this odd name, (which we believe is not generally known in England,) Bresson might have found in Le Duchat, who cites a remonstrance made by the parliament of Paris to Charles IX. in March, 1571: " Sire, votre cours de parlement à Paris . . . . est la cour des pairs de France ; la cour des droits de regale ; la cour du domaine de votre couronne; la justice eslite, autrement nommée lict de votre justice."*

Our object has hitherto been to give a general idea of the sources of French revenue under the old regime, and in so doing, somewhat has been incidentally shown of the mode of administration; but the general principle of this remains to be explained.

While the royal revenue consisted of the product of the royal

---

* L'Histoire Chronol. de la Chancell. de France.   Paris, fol. 1676, p. 154.

domains, the seneschal had the charge of it, in the early periods of taxation the grand chamberlain. But when the system of im- posts became. more complicated and extended, under Philip le Bel, it was found necessary to appoint a minister exclusively for finance. Under all these forms of administration the royal do- mains wasted away; .a fortunate circumstance for nations that possessed any institutions to resist extortions resorted to for sup- plying that waste; for, then, kings became dependent on their people, whose opinions and affections they were necessarily com- pelled to respect and conciliate.

Unhappily such was not the case in France; and the readiness with which arbitrary power could supply its own cravings ren- dered it facile to the rapacity of its minions: so that in 1783 this once rich monarchy was reduced, exclusive of its forests, to an income of 62,500*l.* sterling. The methods, at once mean and atrocious, by which such devastation had proceeded, may be judged by one transaction, so late as 1781. The domain of Fenestrange was alienated, professedly for 50,000*l.* sterling; but the purchaser had an order on the secret service fund for 50,000*l.* sterling, with which he paid for Fenestrange.

We have described the rude mode of taxation in the earlier ages, and the mode of administration partook of the same cha- racter. The first superintendant of finances was Marigni, in 1301. In 1315 he quarreled with a prince of the blood—they gave each other the lie, and drew their swords at the council table; and finally, Marigni was condemned unheard, one of the counts in the indictment being witchcraft. The next superintendant, La Guette, died of the rack; his successor, Remy, on the gallows. There is then a gap in the list for above 50 years: Bresson sup- poses from deficiency in the annals of those remote periods: .per- haps, as Milton says was the case for some years with the sceptre of Northumberland, the treasurer's key " was too hot for any one to venture to take it up." Ambition, however, like love, " will hope, where reason would despair," and Montaigu, in 1381, assumed the office, was executed, and succeeded by others, whose ministries and fates we have no room to notice.

At the accession of Francis I. in 1515, the revenues were 7,650,000 livres, which he .raised to 15,730,000, extorted from the people by the same arts of meanness and rapacity, which we have before detailed as the resources of the crown; and squan- dered in wars of personal ambition, or personal jealousy and envy of Charles V., or lavished on his mistresses, or permitted to be absorbed by the insatiable cupidity of his mother.

Now, for the first time, we hear of a *national*, or, more pro- perly speaking, a *regal* debt. It amounted to about a fourth of the revenue. Cossé, become minister of finance, had recourse, soldier-like, to the simplest and easiest, though not the least burdensome, mode of supplying the wants of the state. In fourteen years he raised seven-and-twenty loans, at 8⅓ per cent., on the security of the revenues of the city of Paris, adding 21,528,000 to the public debt. This, however, was, in itself, a proof of the improvement of public credit, and of an amended morality, or at least of a more enlightened selfishness, in the conduct of government, which could inspire such confidence. The *addition* to the *debt* exceeded by nearly one half the *whole* of the *revenues* fifty years before.* " D'O seems to have been the scape-goat of financiers. " Les historiens rapportent, que D'O avoit tous les vices, sans avoir aucune vertu." That such a man should be ten years the minister of the unprincipled Henry III. is not surprising; but that he should be continued under Henry IV., and suffered to live in oriental luxury and ostentation, whilst he ground the people, betrayed the best interests of his master, and reduced him literally to rags, and almost to famine, is a melancholy proof of the weakness of Henry's character, and how unavailing would have been his aspirations for the good of his people, but for the firmness, activity, and intelligence of Sully. Among the discoveries of Sully, on a rigid examination of the abuses which his predecessors had established into a system, was a bargain by D'O to have for himself a fifth share in the profits of the contract which he had made with the farmers of the salt duty. This may serve as a specimen of the man and the times.

At length Henry IV. entrusted the management of the finances to Sully, who justified the confidence by a zeal, activity, and integrity, difficult to be matched in ministerial history. Yet we cannot find that he is entitled to the praise of any profundity in the science of finance, at all superior to that of the age in which he lived. The wonderful additions which he made, at the same time, to the revenues of the monarch, and the comforts of the people, were accomplished solely by improvements in the mode of administration, not in the nature of the taxes imposed.

His notions concerning the evils of encouraging luxurious products were singularly narrow, even for that age; and were contravened by the king, who encouraged, by his assistance as well as countenance, the establishment of the most costly manufactures; " persuadé que sa richesse dependait de celle de ses sujets; que multiplier les genres d'occupation c'était s'assurer de leur bonheur, et de leur tranquillité même." This was statesman-like, arguing on the actual condition of society, and not attempting a

---

* Compare Bresson, tom. i. p. 146, and p. 154.

forced accommodation of that condition to abstract notions, compatible only with an imaginary state of things. Henry was here anticipating the useful part of the " Fable of the Bees," which, more than a century afterwards, excited such public indignation and alarm; because the Dutch philosopher was as prejudiced as the French minister, and was not contented with tolerating luxury and its attendant evils, as necessary to the present construction of society, but as necessary and good in themselves.

In the administration of the taxes, however, such as he found them, there was ample scope for the exercise of Sully's characteristic zeal, sagacity, firmness, and integrity. What the labour was may be partly conceived by the fact, that, at his accession to power, though 150 millions were taken from the purses of the people, only 30 reached the king's coffers. The English reader may form an idea of the enormity of this abuse, from comparing this rate of 400 per cent. in the expense of collection with that of 6 per cent. which is the cost of collection in the British empire.

The first great reform introduced by Sully was the having recourse to the old Roman method of letting, by public auction, the taxes that were to be farmed ;—at once securing the best terms for the public, and giving the fullest proof of ministerial integrity. When this mode had been so long practised, and recorded in the most familiar histories, it might be supposed that an opposite mode could only have been adopted by the effrontery of the most corrupt and despotic government, and only submitted to in the abjectness of an ignorant age. But the opposite mode was renewed, and continued to the end of the old regime in France; and fifty years have not elapsed since government-loans were made by private contract with the prime minister of England, and enormous profits accrued, under the name of a bonus, or share, to himself, his friends, or the enemies he wished to make friends. The merit of abolishing this nefarious, but long-established system, forms no small part of the praises due to the pecuniary disinterestedness of the younger Pitt.

Sully found the greatest confusion in the accounts of the subordinate financiers, or rather " une apparence de confusion, au milieu de laquelle les financiers voyaient très clair." To remedy this he sent forms of account, every item of which was required to be filled up, and accompanied with the necessary vouchers,so that no pretence was left for obscurity, or omission, or for the slurring of details under generalities. But he not only guarded against future imposition, but entered into a rigorous examination of erroneous or unliquidated accounts of former receivers-general, and other financial agents, whom he compelled to disgorge their spoils; particularly such as had procured themselves to be rated as creditors of the king, without having really made any advances of money. These were all fair game; but when he reduced, by a royal edict, the interest of debts, both public and private, contracted at 10 and 12 per cent. to 6¼, he was, in fact, making the king a fraudulent bankrupt, who, to keep himself in countenance, lent his authority to enable every other debtor to become the same.

This want of faith to the public creditor shows that he was blinded by the very common sophistry which persuades men that they are not personally to be accused of cheating, when they do not personally benefit by the cheat, though the injustice inflicted is the same, whoever reaps the profit; and if the inflictor would scrutinize his own mind, he would infallibly discover that he was bribed by some advantage to himself—as Sully was by the forwarding his favourite object of increasing the royal revenue, and his own reputation for doing so, without augmenting the national burdens.

Whenever Sully could act in person, his own incorruptibleness and decision of character effected great reforms; but when his power was delegated, the corruption of the age immediately came into operation, and added one proof to the millions which history affords, that when despotic power produces good, it is but " a happy accident," and that nothing but the visitation of an enlightened public can afford any permanent control on official men, especially when their individual responsibility is lost in the members of a joint administration. Hence, when Sully appointed a court to audit public accounts, and punish malversation in finance, " l'orage ne tombait que sur ceux qui n'avaient pas assez volé pour acheter des protections."*

The general result, however, of Sully's administration entitled him to the gratitude of his contemporaries, and the admiration of posterity. He reduced the *taille* five millions of livres; the transit, and other smaller imposts, one half; while he added four millions to the king's revenue, redeemed 135 millions of debt, and left 35 millions in the treasury, besides a value of 12 millions in arms and ammunition in the magazines, five millions expended on the fortifications of the frontier-towns, and above 26 millions on public works, and royal gratuities.—All this in a ministry of fifteen years, at the commencement of which the king and the people were in a like state of impoverishment.

The excellence of Sully's character, and the precarious prosperity of a despotic government, were painfully exhibited when

---

* Bresson, tom. i. p. 214.

the death of Henry IV. let loose the hungry and exasperated courtiers, whom the probity of the minister, supported by the authority of the king, had so long kept at bay. In four years, Mary de Medici, and her minion, Concini, had dissipated all the treasures of her husband, for whose loss she appeared to feel fully indemnified by exercising the power, as regent, of reversing his whole system of government, reducing the people to misery and poverty, and insulting them by revelling with her favourites in the most ostentatious luxury. Henry was murdered in 1610, and in 1614 the states-general were summoned to be consulted on the embarrassment of the finances, of which an entirely false statement was presented. Bresson, for once, speaks out, " on n'y trouva qu'un tissue de mensonges." Of the few recommendations, on which the different orders of the states could agree, (for their deliberations were " shivered into small frays and bickerings,") some were pretended to be adopted till the states had separated, and then all went on as before. The government debentures were at a great discount, ministers bought them on their private account in the market, and paid themselves in full at the treasury. Public institutions of every description were suffered to decline for want of funds, whilst the public burdens were augmented, and the most especially vexations of all taxes, the *sol par livre* on all transactions, was renewed.

A succession of ministers hurried the nation down the same road to ruin, till Effiat, under Richelieu, professedly recurred to the system of Sully; how successfully was evinced by his being able to borrow at 10 per cent., whilst, under the regency of Mary de Medici, the rate had been from 20 to 33 per cent. But in six years Effiat died; and his successors had recourse to the old system of extravagant expenditure, supported by pledging the sources of income, and forfeiting credit by failing to redeem the pledges, exasperating the public mind, and producing extensive individual distress by the suppression of all charges on the revenue of the city of Paris, and the abolition of nearly a hundred thousand offices and privileges of recent establishment. In the utter confusion resulting from such measures, the government contrived to flounder on for another thirty years. During this period the amount of taxation exceeded that at the death of Sully by fifty-three millions, of which thirteen millions only were available for the augmented expenditure of government. Richelieu, in his Political Testament, states the annual taxation, during his ministry, to have been seventy-nine millions, from which the net receipt was only thirty-three. The mode in which this was applied may be imagined from the single observation, which the details enable us to make, that while the whole ordinaries and extraordinaries of war do not equal nineteen millions, the royal domestic establishment, pensions, gratuities, and extraordinaries of the king's expenditure exceeded ten millions.

At the accession of Louis XIV. in 1643, the anticipations of the revenue included those of 1646, while salaries were extensively in arrear. No remedy was sought for such difficulties but by carrying to greater excess the system of fraud and extortion. It appears that the putting up to sale of the grand resource of an hereditary monarchy—the power of creating hereditary nobility—had been carried to such an extreme, as even to have exceeded the joint demands of vanity and cupidity, in the most opulent individuals, who were now, therefore, *compelled* to purchase patents of nobility; regardless of the opinion which Quintilian has so well expressed, " Omnium beneficiorum ista natura est, nt'non sit necessitas, sed potestas. Quicquid in honorem alicujus inventum est, desinet privilegium vocari posse, si cogas." This was a gross abuse and violent extension of a feudal custom, by which all persons, possessing lands of the value of a knight's fee, were compellable to assume knighthood, to pay the fees customary on initiation, and perform the services required of the order. On the institution of standing armies, these services were generally commuted for money; and, in order to obtain the fees and commutations, the sovereign was accustomed, on emergencies, to enforce this usually dormant power. In England it was frequently resorted to as late as Elizabeth's time, but more particularly in the weaker reigns of James and his successor; and its abolition was one of the last concessions which Charles made, just before the final rupture with his parliament. The forced purchases of nobility were at this period the more tyrannical, as, only five years before, all patents of nobility acquired in the preceding thirty years had been suppressed ; so that insecurity of enjoyment had been added to the other causes of indifference to these venal, and now imposed honours.

But the measure, which perhaps stamps more than any other the character of the age, is that which Mazarin gladly adopted on the suggestion of the parliament, to levy a tax on all connected with the public revenue, and to revoke all securities for money advanced to the king ; because—and the reason assigned marks a more total insensibility to the principles of equity than even the measures it justified—" almost all affected by the ordinance were men of mean birth, or of overgrown wealth."

Among the other expedients of the period was that invented by a Monsieur Tonti, and which gave name to our Tontines, now so well known as to require no explanation. Emery in his two administrations, together only three years, created 167 offices, and added 87 millions to the public debt; money was depreciated one-sixth; but in spite of all this, loans were contracted for at 20 and 25 per cent., as in the time of Mary de Medici, when she departed from Sully's system, instead of 10 per cent., at which Effiat between the two periods had borrowed by following that system. Not that there was any deficient ability in the ministry of the respective periods, but simply that there were no political institutions to controul the influence of individual characters,—that Sully and Effiat were honest, and that Richelieu and Mazarin were knaves. In Mazarin's account were 23 millions for *secret service:* well might Fouquet say, " Sire, il n'y a rien dans les coffres de votre majesté,—mais M. le Cardinal vous en prêtera."

The result of all this is a lesson which all subsequent statesmen may have read, but apparently without instruction ; the current expenses were 60 millions, the revenues 48 ; and " l'excès et la multiplicité des impôts detruisaient ces revenues."

Mazarin died, possessed of enormous wealth, estimated by some historians at 160 millions of livres; it is certain that he bequeathed twenty-eight to his favourite niece. He had told the king, " Je vous dois tout, sire, mais je crois m'acquitter, en quelque sorte, avec votre majesté, en vous donnant Colbert." This was high praise, and well merited. Colbert's ambition was not perhaps, m the extended sense of the word, more *disinterested* than Mazarin's; but it was not of the same vulgarly sordid cast. He coveted power as the means of proving how enlightened were his views of the evils of society, and of the modes of remedying them ; and we must charitably ascribe to the influence of his age and country, the unjustifiable proceedings, by which he obtained that power. The great evil which first attracted his attention was the number of offices of which the holders were not only exempt from taxation, but the capital which they had employed in purchasing the place was withdrawn or withholden from commerce; and that to so enormous an amount, that trade and manufactures were starved, and men's minds were alienated from the cultivation of them. Multitudes of these offices were suppressed without mercy: and as much of the public debt was known to have been incurred under the most fraudulent circumstances, many recent transactions were equitably annulled;· but revocations with long retrospect involved in wretchedness hundreds of innocent families, who either inherited claims which had never been disputed, or had paid a full equivalent for what they possessed, in the confidence of government continuing to pay what, by previous payments, they had admitted to be due. The interest of all state creditors was arbitrarily reduced : and this, coming upon capitals which had been similarly reduced by former ministers, brought them in many cases to half, and in some to less than half of their original value: and when these successive operations had proportionally diminished their value in the market, they were paid off at the rate of such diminution. Such was the commencement of the career of Colbert; and yet this is not reckoned among the six epochs, when Bresson admits, not that the government had committed an act of bankruptcy, but " manqué essentiellement à la foi publique."

It seems extraordinary that after the actual losses he had occasioned to the public creditors, the minister could still obtain money at ten per cent.; and his credit for personal disinterestedness, as far as money was concerned, and for general talent, enabled him also to succeed in establishing a bank of deposit, where sums might be lodged and withdrawn at pleasure, with an interest of five per cent. for the time they remained. This was found a most useful resource for the wars, in which Louis's ambition so often involved him; for in 1678, the amount of deposits was fourteen millions of livres. This might, in part, be attributed to the low state of trade and manufactures offering so little means of employment for capital. That state of things, however, Colbert exerted himself most powerfully to amend; and his efforts exhibit a singular compound of ignorance and intelligence. He encouraged and established, at great expense, various manufactures;— among others, workmen and machines for weaving stockings were procured from England: the glass manufactory from Venice, cloth, lace, and tapestry works were introduced from Flanders, &c. These grand designs set kindred minds to work; and Riquet suggested to Colbert the magnificent plan of uniting by a canal, the Mediterranean and Atlantic, which Bresson calls, and not improperly, " un des plus beaux ouvrages qui soient sortis de la main des hommes:" but he does not tell us that this splendid work has never paid the expense of its construction, the tolls never furnishing the interest of the capital employed. It was an undertaking worthy of a great minister, and a great nation: but it affords an impressive lesson as to the caution with which governments should follow rather than lead in mercantile improvement, and foster rather than give birth to any great enterprize dependent on trade, which, when wanting an assistant, is sure to call for him; and if he come uncalled, he is likely to remain unemployed.

The difficulties with which Colbert had to contend were immense. The ambition of his master, and his minister Louvois, required enormous sums for the armies; and a powerful navy, for the first time in France, was launched by the creative genius of the controller of the finances. The vanity of Louis, in peace, continued much of the profusion in war; and the minister was obliged to make a compromise with the monarch, supplying abundant funds for his ostentatious magnificence, and thus conciliating his protection in the execution of plans for national improvement and economy.

Honour, however, is due to Colbert, as the founder of the Academy of Sciences, and that of Painting and Sculpture. He established the Observatory, originated the Journal des Savans, and much extended the Royal Library. He reformed the constitution of the great companies trading to the East Indies and North America, and made large advances to enable them to extend their operations. Such monopolies and associations were no doubt necessary, to enable the nation to compete with similar united capitals in England and Holland; but it is grievous to think that so enlightened a mind should have carried the monopoly-system into all the details of internal trade and commerce, forcing every description of merchants and artizans to form themselves into companies, submit to regulations imposed upon them by a minister of state, necessarily ignorant of their best interests, and pay a fee too for this application of his wisdom.

The general result, however, of Colbert's administration of twenty-two years, proves him to have been indefatigable, incorruptible, of comprehensive views, and grand designs. During a period of unprecedented expenditure, he reduced the annual charge for the public debt from fifty-two millions to thirty-two; and the revenues, at the same time being raised from eighty-nine millions to one hundred and five, left a disposable revenue of seventy-three millions, instead of thirty-seven : and, what is perhaps most of all creditable to his character, he annually relieved the people from a portion of one of their most oppressive and vexations taxes. The *taille*, a few years before his accession to the ministry, amounted, during war, to fifty-three millions; at his death, also in the midst of war, it did not exceed thirty-five millions.

The highest testimony to the merit of Colbert is found in the changes which took place on his removal. The very year after his death, seventy-five millions were added to the public debt, and three millions to the odious *taille*. Every year added to financial distress and popular suffering. New loans were raised, new offices created, the salaries of old offices increased, tontines renewed ; and in 1695, a capitation (or property-tax, for it was levied at different rates on different classes) was resorted to, and perhaps was the least objectionable, as calculated to press most on the opulent classes. Letters of nobility were sold at the price of two thousand crowns, and there were five hundred purchasers. " Mais la resource fût passagère, and la honte durable." All nobles, ancient and modern, were compelled to register their arms, and pay a tax for the use of armorial bearings. In 1699, annuities were granted to the amount of four hundred thousand livres, which Bresson deprecates, as encouraging celibacy and selfishness. And so they do; but in certain states of society, the disposition to, and the facilities for gratifying these, *will* exist, and government may be allowed to participate in the profits of transactions which it cannot prevent. This apology cannot be made for lotteries, which were now renewed: for here government monopolizes the profits of a ruinous and demoralizing practice, which it might wholly suppress: and perhaps the bitterest satire on governments becoming lottery-keepers is to be found in their abolition, as an immoral institution, by a decree of the Convention, which, at the very time, (November, 1793,) was sanctioning all the atrocities of the revolutionary tribunal. The lottery of the minister Chamillard was of a strange kind, though Bresson does not notice the monstrosity, which seems to set all calculation at naught, and expect that no one would calculate, or that none but those of one age would buy; for the tickets were all of one price, and the prizes were annuities to the winners. Purchasers enow were found to make the profit considerable.

The rush to ruin was precipitous. The expense of the first year's war was one hundred and forty-six millions; of the eighth, two hundred and twenty-six. In 1702, exchequer bills were at par: in 1708, at thirty discount. The nation was sunk in wretchedness and exhaustion. Consumption was miserably reduced, and taxation proportionally unproductive.

Desmarets, a convicted felon, (for he had been dismissed, after Colbert's death, on account of embezzlement and swindling) was called to save the state, and acted perfectly in character. His first measure was to reject all claims created by anticipation on the revenues of the current year; he seized on the funds in the Bank of Deposit, for which he finally gave the depositors an equal sum in rentes, or what we should call stock, at one per cent., whilst he was borrowing at twelve. All holders of stock of former creation were paid only half their dividends; but recent lenders, to encourage more, were paid in full. He debased the coin,—he taxed as aliens those who had paid for their naturalization; families, who had removed from one province, were treated as aliens in another; and by rigid levyings of old taxes, and various devices for new, he contrived to extort still further contributions from the convulsive grasp of a sinking people.

M. Bresson's reflections on these transactions afford a melancholy example how much long familiarity with them has perverted moral judgment in France : " Quelque injustes qu'ils fussent, ils pourroient être legitimés par le besoin;" and because, " lors de son entrée en place il étoit generalement jugé impossible de soutenir la guerre une seule année, et elle fut soutenue sept années .... Demarets montre de quoi est capable un *bon* administrateur."

As a comment on this text, let us cite, in his own words, the statement in the very next page : " Les dettes exigibles de l'état montaient à 710,994,000 livres, et le manque de fonds etait de 788,757,364 livres." The revenues of the current and subsequent year were anticipated to an amount exceeding 240 millions. There was, indeed, an arrear of taxes due to government of above forty millions; but that was a debt of so desperate a nature, as to be considered not a portion of the wealth of the state, but a measure of the impoverishment of the people. Government debentures were at eighty per cent. discount.

Amidst such individual ruin and dishonour, and amidst such desolation of his people, Louis le Grand, " before whom the earth had trembled, fell sick, and perceived that he should die." What a lesson for ambition, had ambition ever learned to read !

One of the first measures of the succeeding regency was the institution of a commission of inquiry, whose retrospect extended to 1687. In that period were found 4410 persons, who had entered the department of finance without fortune, and who now possessed, according to their own statement, 800 millions, of which the commission left them in possession of 493. Multitudes were thus thrown into desperate circumstances, either from the sums they were justly compelled to refund, or from those unjustly withholden by the government, who practised, in the one case, the dishonesty which they punished in the other. This state of general demoralization and pecuniary distress prepared the way for the favourable reception of the wild speculations and golden promises of the notorious John Law, whose schemes had been rejected by most of the governments of Europe, and even by the reckless Desmarets himself, eight years before: for, however unprincipled, that minister was a calculating man of business and perspicacity, and at once detected the baselessness of the splendid visions, which fascinated the ill-regulated imagination of the Regent Orleans. Law was a Scotch adventurer, who had fled from the gallows in England, where he had been condemned for having " killed his man and triumphed o'er his maid." But a noble demeanour and conciliatory address procured him, with the French, a favourable audience, and he could develope his plans with eloquent enthusiasm. These plans, Bresson says, have been often described and little understood;

but, unfortunately, Englishmen can have no difficulty in comprehending both the elements of them—an unlimited issue of Bank paper without funds—and mercantile and mining speculations without foundation. The whole odium of this systematic delusion is usually thrown upon Law, because he was the active partner—but the king (that is, Orleans, in his name) was the first in the firm. The bank was established by royal patent, its paper received on a par with specie at the exchequer, and, finally, the king paid the company their shares, and declared the institution a royal bank. This, in the ignorance which then prevailed on the true principles of banking, gave it, for a time, a great additional credit. But royal authority and royal wants became the only rules in the management: excessive issues ensued, specie disappeared; and, however the infatuation of the French might dispose them to receive the bank paper as an equivalent, they were soon taught, by a proportionately excessive rise in the exchanges, how lowly, by all other nations, that paper was estimated. Foreign merchants, in order to procure specie for their creditors abroad, found themselves obliged to sacrifice a nominal amount of Bank paper larger than the amount of specie which they had to remit: this difference in the amounts was the measure of the discount to which the paper had fallen; the name of a discount, once heard in the money-market, excited alarm.

Law had been made controller of the finances, and gave notice that all public creditors, who would not consent to be reduced to two per cent., should be paid off, in Bank paper of course; and as most persons had chosen the latter alternative, the number of the holders of this trash was enormously increased. Government, as ignorant as it was unprincipled, endeavoured to uphold the credit of the paper by penal proclamations, which only confirmed the general fear. The market-price sank to one half. Government began to vacillate, at first sanctioning the depreciation, then ordering the value to be at par; this put an end to all confidence, and what had sold for twenty-thousand livres might be bought for 200. The general result was, that 511,900 persons, principally heads of families, were found to hold paper to the amount of 2,288 millions, of which the government would only make itself responsible for 1,700 millions.

The administration of Dodun, from 1722 to 1726, is remarkable for the establishment of a sinking fund; the plan was to levy an income-tax of two per cent., (which debtors, as in our amended income-tax, were allowed to deduct from their creditors,) for twelve years, on all proprietors, excepting the public creditor, which (unless meant as some indemnification for the frequent robberies committed on him,) was an erroneous exception; for a public creditor is as much bound as any other person to bear the national burdens in proportion to his property, the mode of acquiring it making no difference in the duty of paying for protection in the enjoyment of it. At the expiration of the twelve years, the fund accumulated from the tax was to form a sacred deposit, the interest of which was to be annually applied to the liquidation of the public debt. The tax was soon abandoned; and, as has been the fate of most sinking funds, the money was applied to other purposes; but six millions were afterwards annually taken from the consolidated fund, as we should call it, and applied to the reduction of debt.

In 1745, confidence seems to have been restored. Machault borrowed ten millions; and, setting aside a million a year for the discharge of principal and interest, the liquidation was accomplished in fifteen years. This resembles, and may have suggested our plan of raising one per cent. more than is actually wanted, on each occasion of a loan, applying that excess as a sinking fund for the reduction of the remainder. This minister might have saved the state, and superseded the revolution, if his enlightened views, approved by the good sense of Louis XV., had not been blasted by the superstition and pusillanimity of that monarch. He proposed to levy a twentieth on all rents, to be paid by all classes. The clergy alone resisted, and were compelled to submit, but availed themselves of their private access to the king, to alarm his conscience on the score of sacrilege, &c., and he granted them an immunity, on their promise of a large voluntary contribution. The other privileged orders were thus taught the benefits of resistance, and the chance for political salvation was lost.

In 1759, Silhouette quashed the contracts of the farmers-general, levied the taxes by his own agents, and raised seventy-two millions by offering a share of his profits to the contractors for the loan. The enormous profits made by farmers-general had been long notorious; yet the knowledge of that, and the advantage derived from their suspension, did not prevent their revival; and, in 1774, we have, from the treachery of a clerk, a copy of the bargain made with them, by which it appears, that this private contract was the secret channel through which the douceurs of the crown percolated to favourites and mistresses, and to the mistresses of favourites, and the favourites of mistresses without end, among whom were found, " indistinctement confondus les noms les plus augustes, et les plus inconnus."

Silhouette made another attempt at reform, borrowed from the practice of England, imposing the highest proportion of taxes on articles of luxury, so as to throw the burden more on the rich : and to the eternal disgrace of the boasted patriotism of the parliament of Paris, the edict was only put on their registers by royal authority, and, from their factious opposition, was soon obliged to be revoked.

By such weakness and corruption, affairs were brought to a crisis, from which it was thought some " bold bad man" alone could extricate the state. The Abbé Terray answered the description. For five years this man exercised every species of public extortion, and was guilty of the most cruel oppression, to feed his own cupidity.

Louis XV. died, and Terray was not long tolerated by his benevolent successor. Nor were the monarchs more contrasted than the ministers. Terray was succeeded by Turgot, the philosopher and philanthropist. In his celebrated letter to the king, on entering upon office, he laid down three fundamental principles for his administration of the finances. " 1. Point de banqueroute ; ni avouée, ni masquée par des reductions forcées. 2. Point d'augmentation d'impôts ; la raison en est dans la situation des peuples, et encore plus dans le cœur de votre majesté. 3. Point d'emprunt ; diminuant toujours le revenu libre, il nécessite, au bout de quelque tems, ou la banqueroute, ou l'augmentation d'impositions." These objects could only be effected by not allowing expenditure to exceed receipt ; and that necessitated a rigour, which rendered the minister odious to the courtiers, and perhaps not very acceptable, in the detail, to the young king, however he might generally approve the principles.

His first measure was to abolish the hateful *corvée* throughout the kingdom. He took off eight sous per livre from the transit duties, and a free trade, in grain, was allowed throughout the interior. There were three years arrears on all pensions, of which he paid, at once, two years, on all not exceeding 400 livres. Of this class the whole arrears were discharged before he quitted the ministry, and those due to other pensions, and to the public creditors in general, were in course for a like liquidation ; he simplified the forms for receipt of dividends, and paid off the principal of those whose dividends were too small to pay the expense of receiving them. He established a Discount Bank, which, by discounting bills of Exchange at four per cent., might bring down the general rate of interest to that rate. The success of his measures was found by the re-establishment of public credit. Government debentures were in some cases at par, and he was enabled to negotiate a loan in Holland for sixty millions of livres, at less than five per cent., a novelty in the history of French Finance; how much of this was due to the character of Turgot, was proved by his dismissal putting an end to the negotiation, and his successor not being able to raise a much smaller sum at less than six and a quarter per cent.

Clugni, in a five month's administration, re-established the corvée, the duties on becoming apprentices and masters in trades, the eight sous per livre. of transit duty, &c., in short, did all he could to undo the good which Turgot had effected.

. He was succeeded, in 1776, by one who had been a banker's clerk, and who, having private information of the peace about to be concluded at Paris in 1763, and speculating in the English funds, gave commencement to a fortune now estimated to be at least eight millions of livres. This was Necker. He had quitted the business of banking, and aspired to place, to which he endeavoured to recommend himself by publications exhibiting an acquaintance with the principles of commerce and public credit, and his efforts were aided by the assiduity of his wife (the Mademoiselle Curchod of Gibbon), in cultivating the acquaintance of men of rank and literary eminence.

" Probity and publicity" were the watch-words of Necker; and, whatever might be his other motives, he proved his respect for both, by his far-famed " Compte Rendu," in which were exposed, side by side, the vices of the old system, and his own comprehensive and beneficent plans. Nor was courage for the execution of them wanting, when, in one day, he suppressed above four hundred offices in the king's domestic establishment. The farming of taxes, the fruitful source, as we have before explained, of corruption, in which king and people were alike deceived, were almost entirely suppressed. The valuation of real property throughout the kingdom, begun in 1771, having been completed, the vingtièmes were assessed at a rate not to be altered for twenty years; and the *taille* and capitation tax, hitherto so arbitrary in the apportionment, were fixed, for each province, at an invariable sum. Instead of subjecting the provinces to the exactions of government agents, he granted them an assembly of proprietors, who apportioned the taxes, suggested to the king the most equitable mode of levying them, and of providing for the construction of roads, and other business of the district. This was an admirable preparation for a national representative assembly; had it been sooner introduced, and steadily persisted in, the nation would have been gradually accustomed to the blessings of such an institution, and to the discharge of its duties, and would not have come to the work of political regeneration, besotted with ignorance, and intoxicated with the draught of new power.

Before Necker's accession to office, there had been a series of bankruptcies (which had come to be considered one of the resources of government), and, after fifteen years of peace, an increasing deficit. After five years of war, his " Compte Rendu" showed a surplus of ten millions; he had borrowed 530 millions at a less interest than had ever been known in times of war,—the

discount on exchequer bills, which had been sixteen per cent.,
was reduced to eight, and all this was accomplished without any
addition to the burdens of the people.

His successors, as usual, reversed all the measures they found
recently established or in progress. In Nov. 1783, Calonne was
substituted, who may be considered as having put the last apple
into the pannier : the ass did not kick and die, but kicked and
killed. Calonne was appointed by an influence characteristic of
the old system. His patron was d'Harvelay, the court banker,
" qui voulait faire donner la place de Contrôleur-General à Calonne, qu'il aimait, moins cependant que ne l'aimait Madame
d'Harvelay." The minion was worthy of the patronage. His
measures were opposed by the parliament of Paris: he quarrelled
with them, and endeavoured to supersede their authority by calling an assembly of the Notables in February, 1787. To procure
their sanction to the extraordinary changes and additional impositions he proposed, all his art and all his eloquence were employed ;
but all could not conceal the astounding fact, that whilst in 1781
it had been declared, on royal authority, that there was then a surplus of revenue amounting to ten millions, it was now declared,
on the same authority, that there had been a continually growing
deficit from the year 1776, which Calonne confessed to having
increased by 35 millions, making the total deficit 115. The out-
cry was loud, and sounded over Europe. The king, sensible to
the disgraceful situation in which he was placed, forbade all publications on the subject. But Necker, indignant at his veracity
being impeached, and rejoicing in the opportunity of exhibiting
a comparison between the results of his own administration and
Calonne's, disregarded the prohibition, and had a vindicatory
tract printed, which was answered by a lettre-de-cachet, banishing
him twenty leagues from Paris : but that did not prevent Fleury,
the successor of Necker, from declaring, in a letter to Calonne,
that Necker was in the right. A copy of this letter was conveyed
to the king, who, on questioning Calonne on the subject, detected
him in a lie, and yet was weak enough to support Calonne, by
dismissing, on his demand, the minister who had furnished his
majesty with the means of his detection. He was thereby em-
boldened to demand also the dismissal of Breteuil; but as he
was a favourite of the queen, she took that occasion to represent the dangerous and disgraceful tendency of Calonne's measures, and he was dismissed at the very moment of his imagined
triumph.

Fourqueux was controller of the finances for one month, De
Brienne for three, and Lambert for a year. During these changes
nothing was effected for the redemption of the state. At length

Necker was recalled. No objection, as before, on the score of his religion, was now made to his entrance into the council, and he met there no opposition to his measures. However, he found affairs in so ruinous a condition that nothing could retrieve them but the authority of the states-general. In obtaining the royal assent for doubling the proportion of the third estate in that assembly, so that they constituted one half of the whole, he created the revolution. But he had reason, from experience, to apprehend, that if the third estate were to constitute, as heretofore, only a third of the assembly, the remaining two thirds, being of the privileged orders, would, as heretofore, resist all the attempts to abolish their exemptions; without which abolition no hope could be entertained of saving the state, or of relieving the wretchedness and oppression of the people.

The difficulties of the finances were stated by Necker to consist in a deficit exceeding 56 millions, with anticipations of revenue amounting to 260. Besides other debts, there were 76 millions of suspended payments, and 80 millions of arrears in the collection of taxes. The means for remedying these evils were detailed, and loans proposed. But, in the midst of these plans, the king, having determined no longer to continue the conciliatory conduct towards the assembly, which Necker had made a condition of his services, requested him to withdraw from the kingdom in as private a manner as possible. Necker justified the confidence of his master, whose new councillors had advised him to send the popular minister to the Bastile; he took, in the most secret manner, the shortest route into Germany, and wrote thence to assure Messrs. Hope, of Amsterdam, that he continued to them the private pledge of his own fortune, to the amount of two millions of livres, as a security for their supplying Paris with corn.

Whilst he was hastening to his quiet home on the banks of the Leman Lake, the Bastile was destroyed, and the throne of the multitude was erected on its ruins. At Bâle he met the king's letter of recall. His journey thence to Versailles was a triumphal progress; but, in the mean time, enthusiasm and ignorance had felt their power, and reason and experience were no longer listened to. Necker negotiated a loan for 30 millions at 5 per cent. The assembly refused their sanction to more than $4\frac{1}{2}$.: only $2\frac{1}{2}$ millions could be raised: and a subsequent attempt to borrow 80 millions—half to be paid in specie, and half in government debentures—was equally unsuccessful. The April deficit of 56 millions had increased in September to 61. This and all other financial embarrassments were fully represented by Necker, and, with the addition of his proposed remedial measures, submitted to the assembly; but the impatience of impassioned ignorance

suspended all plans, and the assembly, assuming the management
of the royal treasury, cut, as they thought, the Gordian knot, and
(in addition to 160 millions of the Discount Bank-paper ordered
to be received as specie,) they issued 400 millions of assignats,
for which the property of the crown and clergy were pledged,
and which were to be received in payment on the sale of such
property. In vain did Necker protest against such wild proceedings ; and Mirabeau's astute eloquence urged the assembly to
discharge the whole floating debt by an additional issue of 1,900
millions of assignats. The sum of his orations may be found in
one sentence : " partout ou se trouvera un porteur d'assignats,
vous conterez un defenseur necessaire de vos mesures, un crean-
cier interessé à vos succès ;" and this, whether the assignats continued to be held, or were exchanged for what was now called
national property. Necker, finding his services superseded, his
wisdom and experience set at naught, resigned his office, declining all remuneration, and leaving two millions of his property in
the national coffers.

After various wild enactments came the sweeping Law on
Finance, in 1798, which ordained the public debts of every description to be liquidated by a payment of two-thirds in notes
payable to bearer, but exchangeable only for national property,
and in the purchase-money of which also these notes could only
constitute a limited proportion. They fell, immediately on the
issues, to 80 per cent. discount, and were soon of no value whatever. The remaining third of the public creditor's claim was
entered in the " Great Book," and forming the basis of the
present debt of France under the name of Tiers Consolidé, records the bankruptcy of the nation, and the payment of a dividend
of 6s. 8d. in the pound.*

It was at this crisis of infamy and audacity that the government
proposed, and the legislature sanctioned, the most farcical gas-
conade that ever stamped the character of a people. A loan
was opened (to be repaid in ten years) at 5 per cent., with
the bonus of tickets in an annual lottery, of which the prizes
were to be furnished from a fourth of all contributions to be levied
by the French armies in England. This was acting the hunter-
salesman of the lion's skin on a grand scale. But the sale did
not take place—not a sous was bid.

When the consulship was established, (Nov. 1799,) there was
not specie enough in the treasury to expedite couriers to the

---

* So numerous had been the frauds on the public creditor, that, notwithstanding the
enormous debts incurred by successive administrations, the interest, after this last transaction, did not exceed thirty-eight millions of livres.

armies with intelligence of the change. Gaudin, (afterwards Duc de Gäete,) became Minister of Finance, and was the only unchanged minister from 1799 to 1814; so that a systematic arrangement may now be considered as commenced, which included, indeed, many evils inseparable from a despotic administration, but many regulations, also, worthy of imitation.

. The first measure was an increase of 4 per cent. on all taxes, but payable partly in specie, and partly in debentures of the late Directory, which had lost all value in the market. Notes were issued, which were to be valid payment for national property about to be sold. A deposit in specie was required as security from persons entering on office: and thus the new government was set in motion. A register of all real property was ordered, by which an invariable apportionment of taxation should be obtained, the proprietor be secured in the remainder of his property, without fear of the ignorance, caprice, or injustice of the collector; and the government could ascertain beforehand what sum might certainly be expected from the existing tax, or from any additional per-centage which it might be necessary to impose. This wise measure was entirely Bonaparte's. Gaudin organized the collection of the direct taxes in the way which is still pursued, and seems to have been taken from that adopted in England. A sinking-fund was established; and, however feeble its means, the recurrence to the principle, and the other measures we have specified, retrieved the public credit so far, as to raise considerably the price of stocks, which, under the Directory, had been so low as 10 per cent., and came at one period of the empire to be at 80. The Bank of France was formed, and the Sinking Fund subscribed, in crowns, for five thousand shares. Bills were drawn on the receivers of taxes, who paid the amount in specie, not into the Treasury, but into the Sinking Fund, to be exclusively applied to the redemption of these bills, which immediately obtained a credit equal to the best commercial paper. Bonaparte was justly proud of the amendment in the finances, and the revival of credit, and caused forty copies of the *Compte Rendu* for 1802 to be sent to England. It ought, however, to be considered, that he, as representing the French nation, was really in the situation of a bankrupt, who, having freed himself from claims on account of the past, starts unincumbered, and, with all the advantages of experience, requires only activity and circumspectness to secure success.

However false the principles of taxation under the empire, the administration seems to have been judicious. At the commencement of each year, Napoleon fixed the sum to be appropriated to each department, and limited the expenditure of each minister for the year: but this quota could only be drawn from the Treasury in such monthly sums as were determined by a special monthly decree of the Emperor; thus twelve times in the year modifying the general apportionment, in conformity with the particular circumstances of receipt and expenditure, or of unexpected emergency. This order extended to all the annexations of the empire, and in them the burden of public debts was completely removed by the sale of public property, principally that of useless ecclesiastical establishments—a benefit so sensibly felt after the storm of conquest had passed away, that even the Pope, on his restoration, had the good sense to confirm the alienations which had enabled him to enter on an unembarrassed revenue.

In 1812 all was order and prosperity in the finances. The expenditure was equalled by the receipts, and Napoleon had accumulated, from foreign institutions, &c., a reserve-treasure of 120 millions in gold.

In spite of the exhaustion of twenty-four years of revolution, despotic government, continual war and absurd legislation, the actual improvement of France was proved (says Bresson) by a comparison of the excess of exports over imports, which, in 1788, was only 75 millions; in 1812, 126 millions. But this, at all times a false criterion, is a most fallacious statement, inasmuch as the France of 1812 included rich and commercial countries with which the France of 1788 had no connection, Holland and Hamburgh, for example, whose balance of exports in 1788 might, perhaps, exceed the total balance of them and France together in 1812, though comprehending 130 departments, and 42 millions of people.

In the twelve years, however, there had been expended in canals, bridges, roads, fortifications, harbours, public buildings and public institutions, a thousand millions; of which it is remarkable that the completion of the four passes over the Alps, justly called *entreprises gigantesques,* is only estimated at thirty.

Amidst this enormous expenditure, it is, as Bresson observes, consoling to remark ten millions appropriated in " La Vendée, pour en cicatriser les plaies."

In 1813 the revenue was about 900 millions; the civil expenture 350; and to the remainder of 550 was required an addition of 300, to repair the disasters of the preceding year and meet the dangers of the present.

In 1814 the Baron Louis became the financial minister of the restored monarch, as he became since, and is now again, of Louis-Philippe; and he seems to have prepared the way for his own triumph by stating the arrears due in his predecessor's account at 1645 millions; whilst the Duc de Gäete maintained, and by the

Compte Rendu of 1817 was afterwards admitted to have proved, that it did not equal 504 millions. The calculated expenditure of 1814 was 827 millions, and the receipts were taken at 520. The claimants on account of arrears had their choice of exchequer bills, to be paid off in three years, with interest in the mean time at 8 per cent.; or inscriptions for stock in perpetuity, at 5 per cent. For payment of the exchequer bills were pledged the sale of royal woods, the surplus expected in the revenues of 1815, and the product of the sale of the property of communes, &c., and the common resort, the sinking fund. But all these proved insufficient, and the claimants became proprietors of stock to their respective amounts. Thirty millions of the king's personal debts were made a part of the national debt, twenty-five milhons were fixed for the civil list, and eight millions for the members of the royal family.

On Napoleon's eruption from Elba, he obtained, from the notorious contractor and speculator Ouvrard, fifty millions, at an interest of 10 per cent, and with a bonus of 3; and in order that this might not be known in the stock-market it was charged on the sinking fund.

The hundred days cost the nation 600 millions of livres—and what else?

In November, 1815, a treaty bound France to pay the allies, in five years, 700 millions in specie, by daily and equal instalments; and, annually for three years, 130 millions, for maintaining 150 thousand men of the army of occupation. All claims too, that could be substantiated by foreign communities, or individuals, the government became pledged to pay; and by a separate treaty, all British subjects who, being creditors of France, had, contrary to the treaty of 1786, had their effects confiscated by the French government, were to be indemnified.

The means devised for answering those prodigious demands were found quite inadequate; payment to the allies was suspended, and the possibility of provisioning their troops became very doubtful. French capitalists, alarmed by the late sudden vicissitudes, kept aloof; but the bold and clear-sighted Ouvrard suggested and negotiated a plan by which difficulties " were shook to air." It was proved to the allies, that an attempt to raise the funds due for the current half-year would, in the present state of public credit, still further reduce that credit, and render future payments still more impracticable. The only means, therefore, of accomplishing all purposes was by raising the credit of the French funds, and this was to be effected by the allies accepting stock at 5 per cent., yielding rentes to the amount of thirty millions, and commissioning the houses of the Hopes and the Barings

to sell the same on their account.   Concurrently with the adoption
of this plan by the allies, a diplomatic note announced that the
army of occupation was to be reduced one fifth.   Immediately,
government securities rose; foreigners and natives contended for
shares, and the Hopes and Barings, from assignees, became purchasers of the stock of the allies.   When the stock was inscribed
in the " Grand Livre," it was done at 53 fr. 85 c. (about 9¼ per
cent.); and Ouvrard tells us that in a short time it rose to 65 fr.   ·

This mode of satisfying foreign creditors was extended to the
claims of foreign states and individuals, which were compromised
for Inscriptions in the Great Book, yielding about sixteen millions of Rentes, of which England had three.   The loan was no
sooner opened than foreigners and natives rushed into competition, and even an armed force was required to keep order at the
place of subscription.   The rate of interest, instead of 9¼, as in
the preceding year, did not quite equal 7½ per cent.   This rapid
improvement in public credit under circumstances of such extraordinary disbursement, is ascribable primarily to the extension of
the market by bringing the allied sovereigns to become purchasers
of stock, and by the superabundance of capital in proportion to
employment for it, in all the trading nations of Europe.   To this
must be added the high honour and magnanimity displayed by
the French legislature in taking on itself the whole of the public
debts, without regard to the character of the government under
which they had been contracted.   Subsequent regulations, too,
contributed to the same effect.   In 1819 auxiliary *Grands Livres*
(called, quaintly enough, *Petits Grands Livres*) were opened in
the provinces, and by familiarising the people with the subject,
and facilitating the means of investing and drawing out their
money, added greatly to the demand for public securities, which
was still further increased by reducing, in 1822, the minimum of
an investment from fifty livres to ten, and giving various facilities
for transfer and receipt of dividends in these small accounts.   This
was in fact establishing savings banks on government security,
but with this disadvantage compared with ours—that the depositors might learn to be stock-jobbers, of which the moral mischief would be incalculable.

Another fiscal regulation, extended to the provinces, appears to
be of unmixed good: communes and towns which possessed a
public property were obliged to print, for the information of the
public, an annual statement of receipts and disbursements.   If
this were adopted with us, how many scandalous jobs (in which
sometimes the highest families participate) would be prevented!
how many charities, now diverted into private channels, would
diffuse blessings among multitudes!

. In 1821, so great was the improvement in public credit, that government could borrow at about 5¼ per cent. This was obtained by public competition in sealed proposals, and the contract given to the highest, which added to the national confidence in the integrity and strength of the government. In this year nineteen millions were abated in the tax on real property throughout the poorest provinces and those which had been most exposed to hostile invasion; and there was a reduction common to all amounting to seven millions more.

In 1822 a loan was voted in the Chamber of Deputies (with only nineteen dissentients) of 207 millions, for conducting the Spanish expedition.

In 1823 the Bank of France lent, at 4 per cent., 100 millions to government, who issued besides, 74 millions of exchequer bills.

In 1824 Spain acknowledged a debt of 58 millions to France, but Villele failed in attempting to reduce the 5 per cents (then at 102) to a 3 per cent. stock.

During all these financial and military operations above 100 millions had been furnished, by private persons, for making various canals, bridges, &c.; public corporations had been allowed to borrow money for various improvements; and the shares being made very small, brought the most moderate capitals into activity —a circumstance of great general importance, as well as of probable advantage, to any particular undertaking.

The wisdom and firmness of Louis XVIII. had left affairs in so flourishing a condition, that his successor ventured to propose an indemnity to emigrants and their families, whose property had been confiscated to an amount, as it was calculated, of more than 987 millions. The idea was as creditable to the monarch as the adoption of it was to the character of the nation. Indeed that adoption might have been anticipated, from the fact that the confiscated property of individuals, though protected by the same securities, had always borne a less price in the market than the properties of the state or of public bodies. To attempt to pay the principal of so large a sum, raised by loans, might have endangered public credit; and even an inscription of such a sum in the Great Book, and the consequent bringing of probably a large portion of stock suddenly into the market, might have deranged the system that was now going on so prosperously. It was, therefore, arranged that one-sixth of a thousand millions should be inscribed annually for five years, (beginning June, 1825,) bearing an interest of 3 per cent. As a counterbalance to this annual increase of the quantity of the debt, it was ordered that the sinking fund, whose annual purchases amounted to 77½ millions, should, during those five years, not accumulate such purchases, but that an equal sum of the national debt should be cancelled; and at the same time it was ordered that the sinking fund should not be applied to the purchase of any stock above par, which was enlarging the market for the newly created stock.

- In 1825 the measure was carried for the voluntary reduction of the 5 per cents.—an option being given (without the threat of being paid off) for the stock, as before, to be transferred to a 3 per cent. stock at 75, or to a 4½ per cent. stock at par, redeemable in ten years. The proprietors of more than 634 millions accepted these terms, (very few the latter alternative,) and the saving from this operation enabled government to remit above 6 millions of the tax on real property: but it is grievous to hear that the motive for these successive reductions had a political object, the disfranchisement of many whose right of voting at elections depended on the amount of their direct taxes.

Bresson is of opinion that the reduction ought to have been made on articles of consumption, and doubtless, if of luxurious consumption, it might be so; but in the extraordinary subdivision of landed property in France, a diminished land-tax would be a great relief to the productive classes. This relief, however, has been too much neglected in all French taxation. The old leaven of the exemption of the higher orders still operates, and though now no class, by name, be exonerated, the wealthy are in fact too lightly burthened: there is no tax, for example, on carriages and horses of pleasure, none on men-servants; whilst these articles pay a thirty-fifth part of our whole taxation.

The great deficiency of M. Bresson's work is the want of the details of the late national budgets, though he gives us all the *items* of the receipt and expenditure of the city of Paris, and the same for the household of Napoleon. These deficiencies, however, are well supplied by the other work which stands at the head of this article,—certainly one of the most instructive of the tribe of " Annuals,"—which gives us all the details of national receipt and expenditure, as stated or elicited in the Chamber of Deputies in their session of 1829. From this we shall be able to give our readers a pretty accurate idea of the state of the French finances, and their mode of taxation, as they stood just before the late revolution.

The state of the French finances then appeared a very flourishing one, because the government for several years had been able to command annual loans at a diminishing interest. But the necessity for such loans proves that the Sinking Fund, which Bresson, and Ouvrard in his Memoirs, both vaunt so much, as amounting to upwards of seventy-seven millions of livres per annum, was a mere fallacy.

In speaking of the public debt, the French express it, not like us, by the amount of capital, but by that of annual interest (Rentes), which is much more convenient and instructive, at least for all usual occasions. At the period of the Greek Calends—cum mula pepererit—and when the national debt is to be paid off, it may be requisite to talk of the principal.

In 1814, then, the interest of the debt was 63,300,000. (In 1818 the sinking fund was endowed, as they call it.) In 1820, when all demands of the allies were finally settled, the interest was 188,341,200. In 1828 it amounted to 200,350,947. In 1829, 202,973,883. Such was the state of the permanent or funded national debt of France on the 1st of January, 1829.*
But to this must be added a floating debt, of which the interest amounts to six millions, besides 3,200,000 paid to the Receivers General, as interest on anticipated revenue, which, though not called floating debt, is assuredly of the very same nature.

The other·items of expenditure make the total of the budget of
1829, as proposed by the Minister 979,935,329
Reduced by the Chamber to 972,739,879
Of these items we cite the civil list of twenty-five millions, only to notice that the identity of name has often led to very erroneous comparisons with our own, which provides for the payment of ambassadors, judges, and several other expenses not charged on the civil list of France.

Payment and indemnity to the Catholic Clergy . 26,796,500
Establishments for Ecclesiastical Education . . 2,600,000
Repairs of buildings, and other items, make the sum total of expense on account of what was lately called the established religion, and now only " the religion of the majority of Frenchmen," 35,921,300; and to the honour of French liberality, (and, be it added, of Catholic toleration,) there was an item in the budget, for " Christian congregations not Catholic," amounting to 720,000 livres, or about a fiftieth part of what was appropriated to the then religion of the state; and the sixth Article of the new Charter evinces the continuance of the same spirit.

The army (including the *materiel* of artillery, and engineers, and military schools) are estimated in round numbers at 186 millions; marine 58 millions; colonies, 7.

Under what may be called pensions, the charges appear heavy,

---

* Those who would wish to see the debt expressed in amount of capital, will find the necessary data in being informed that this interest is paid in the following proportions of Rentes:—

At 5 per cent 165,217,546
4½ do. 1,029,237
3 do. 36,727,100

Total of interest as above ....202,973,883.

but in the several changes of the government it has been necessary to conciliate many, who, as malcontents, might have disturbed the new establishments. Hence pensions to peers and senators, and their widows, 979,000; civil pensions, 1½ million; military, above 45½ millions; ecclesiastical, nearly 5½; miscellaneous, 1½ millions; and in the nature of pensions may be considered the charge of the Legion of Honour, 3,400,000. The payments as wages to the deputies are 600,000; to the peerage, 1,784,000. Before quitting the subject of expenditure we cannot but notice, as interesting to our gentlemen of the turf, that the late French government incurred considerable expense in improving their breed of horses, for there is a charge for the stud of brood mares and stallions of 1,840,000 livres.

Of receipts, the total calculated on by the budget was 979,252,224
Of expenses (as above) 972,739,879
_____
Leaving an expected surplus of 6,512,345
_____

In the items of receipts, the most important is that of the direct taxes, which bear exclusively on real property, and constitute about a third of the whole revenues, (in round numbers about 327½ millions.) This, as it affects lands, must tend, by throwing poor soils out of cultivation, to raise the price of corn, and other raw produce; and as real property is excessively subdivided in France, must operate as a heavy burthen on the industrious classes. In England the land-tax (including the poor cess, which indeed constitutes about four-fifths of the whole) is only about one-ninth of our revenue; and even this, as our landed property is much less subdivided, falls principally on the opulent classes. Their tax on salt, so much a necessary of life, is about an eighteenth (44¼ millions) of the whole revenue, while with us it has been wholly abolished. The expense (128 millions) of collecting the revenue in France is at the rate of about 13 per cent.; whilst with us it does not average above one half that rate.

These comparative statements, joined to the observations which we made, as suggested by the historical details, may enable the English reader to form a general idea of the system of French finance up to the period of the late extraordinary and unexpected Revolution. Here a new æra commences; some symptoms have already been exhibited of a disposition to set at naught the lessons of dear-bought experience which France has already been taught, as the preceding outline of her financial history clearly shows. Let us hope that these symptoms are only transitory, and that we shall soon see her again tranquilly pursuing the same prudent course from which she was only forced by the madness and folly of the late government.

ART. VII.—*Briefe über einen Theil von Croatien und Italien,
an Caroline Pichler, von* Therese von Artner. (Letters on
part of Croatia and Italy, addressed to Caroline Pichler, by
Theresa von Artner.) Pesth. 1830. 8vo.

THE present age, with all its gallantry, does not, we believe,
allow the productions of female tourists to hold a very exalted
rank in the circle of literature, and this verdict, pronounced in
the teeth of prejudice, we dare not take upon ourselves to protest
against. Indeed it must be confessed that those of our own fair
countrywomen who have of late entered the arena have in no
wise contributed to alter this opinion; from the chaotic mass of
maudlin sentiment, vulgar common-place, and useless directions,
contained in Mrs. Starke's Manual, down to that *ne plus ultra*
of coxcombry, " *Rome in the Nineteenth Century,*" there is nothing
that is worth the trouble of a first, or will bear a second perusal,
except the lively narrative of Lady Morgan, who, in her wildest
flights of absurdity, is always interesting from her liveliness; her
information not being like that of most others in the inverse proportion to her vanity. The work before us, though hardly to
be classed with those of the above description, neither arrogates,
nor is entitled to much praise for depth of information or elegance; it consists of letters addressed by an Austrian lady to the
celebrated novelist, Caroline Pichler, with whose name, if not
with her works, most of our readers are, we apprehend, well acquainted. The first of these is occupied in the description of
one of the most interesting districts of Europe, but that unfortunate
" Dux femina facti," which we believe never prospered since
Dido's time, seems to hang like an incubus over the otherwise
entertaining narrative; as we ever and anon find ourselves betrayed
into episodes about the spring of life, roses of love, &c. invented,
we suppose, in compliment to the antiquated gallantry of some
old battered general in the military provinces of Croatia. Really,
ladies, when they do travel, should adopt the buckskin *propria
quæ maribus*, like the old empress mother of Russia.

Leaving the town of Agram, in June, 1825, our tourist travelled by Petrinia to Sziszeg, passing through a district called Turo-
polye, consisting of twenty-four departments, the inhabitants of
which boast of a nobility, the date of whose patents must throw
the pretensions of the greatest part of our own aristocracy into
the shade; Bela IV., King of Hungary, in reward for their services
against the Mongols and Bulgarians, granted them the dignity of
nobility, and at the same time the more important privilege of
freedom from taxation, about the year 1260. It must, as our

author observes, be curious enough to see these primitive dignitaries, each possessing about the same quantity of land as an Irish peasant, inhabiting a cottage, rudely constructed of wood, without a chimney, but proud nevertheless of their distinction, and parading on Sundays with a blue mantle, the sole insignia of their rank.

. The first town of note visited by Therese von Artner is Sziszeg, (anciently Siscia,*) a colony founded by the Romans, probably in the reign of Augustus, which still retains many curious relics of its former grandeur. Its situation, at the confluence of the Kulpa and Save, is most favourable for commerce, and would, if the intermediate districts ever became civilized, render it a great entrepôt for the produce of Carniola, Carinthia, and Croatia, on its way to the Black Sea. In ancient times a canal ran through the heart of the town, opening on each side into a river, and underneath the canal ran a tunnel arched with tiles, of sufficient size to allow a horseman to pass through: so well had this been constructed that a very little trouble would again render it serviceable. The end indeed was only lately closed up by a merchant, into whose cellar it disgorged itself, on account of the frequent flooding it occasioned, and who being, we suppose, an honest man, did not choose, even with so excellent an excuse, to allow his customers' wine to be partially diluted. Another ruin of the same kind exists not far from the town, at a castle called Rastovich, (from which an aqueduct brought water to their colony,) extending to a distance of several miles to another fortress called Moszlovina. Who can deny after this the practicability of Mr. Brunel's undertaking? Innumerable sarcophagi have been discovered in excavating under some of the vineyards; they were generally found enclosed in a small vault; and, what is rather unusual, frequently contained the remains of two, sometimes of three, bodies. The interior of these sarcophagi was also not uncommonly streaked with marks of fire, and contained fragments of charcoal, which, together with the circumstance of finding the lacrymatories and other relics melted, leads our authoress to suppose that part of the corpse was frequently burnt within the coffin.

We are next introduced into one of the military departments which form the territorial line of division between Austria and Turkey. In consequence of the lawless and marauding habits of the natives on each side of the border, every establishment is made to assume as martial an air as possible,—the earth is sown with dragons' teeth ready to start up into an armed force at

---

* Not Siscium, as our authoress cites it, vid. *Plin. H. N.* iii. 28.—" Colapis in Saum influens juxta Sisciam.

a few hours notice,—every elevated spot of ground is crowned with a watch tower; and between the incursions of freebooters and the plague, the country is kept in a continual state of excitement. The institution of this military system, which so well accords with the disposition of the inhabitants, is owing to Maria Theresa, and her successors have done all in their power to follow up the spirit of her plans. The domestic arrangements betray the same precaution against an external attack; each house is inhabited by three, frequently by more families, the oldest of which receive particular attention from the rest, being lodged in the large hall, which serves as an eating room for the whole; the rest being in the true patriarchal style obliged to sleep in small chambers or cabins which encircle the court.* Each inmate has, however, a voice in the common council. In order to provide more effectually for the security of individuals, and at the same time to insure a ready obedience to any military summons, government do not allow any insulated houses to be erected. Hence a military district (*Regiments-bezirk*) generally consists of a string of villages, the size of which is not considerable enough to weaken any local attachments, (that which our tourist passed through on her road to Glina consisted of nine hundred and thirty-six houses,) while at the same time domestic duties and military services bring a large body in daily intercourse with each other, accustom them to act in concert, and as all political differences are out of the question, create an union of opinion and feeling which, far more than any positive institutions, render them attached to the country, and its eager defenders against foreign aggression. And yet these people, though apparently not yet emerged from the barbarous condition of the feudal times, are by no means dead to literary pursuits; to every regiment (i. e. every village) is attached a library, which, besides military and scientific works, always contains at least those of Schiller, Wieland, and Goethe; translations of Walter Scott's novels are likewise frequently met with, and always popular.

The dress of the men (that of the ladies we shall not venture upon, but send a translation, if required, to the Morning Post) is as simple as can be well imagined, consisting of a pair of white linen pantaloons, a shirt held together by a leathern belt; to this some add a cloth jacket, with or without sleeves, and this part of the dress alone admits of any ornament. The head is covered

---

* We cannot help noticing the similarity of customs in the Homeric times on the reception of a guest.—Odyss. Δ. 296.

αργειη δ'Ελενη δμωησ' εκελευσεν
δεμνι' υπ αιθουση (open portico) θεμεναι.
Ατρειδης δε καθευδε μυχω δομου υψηλοιο.—Id. 304.

with a red cap or a hat. The constant appendages to this attire
are a knapsack, gun, pistols and knife. The gallant old general,
under whose superintendence our authoress was favoured with
such opportunities of observing the manners and customs of this
interesting people, to put a finishing stroke to his politeness,
treated her with a national dance, termed *colo.* The myrmidons,
(*Serressaner,* a select body intrusted with the duties of watching
over internal quiet and external invasion,) being summoned, stood
in a circle to the number of thirty, and amongst them were some
females of a pretty advanced age. They danced in pairs, one
seizing the other round the belt, so that the arms were crossed
behind, and in this position they began to move three steps forward and one back. The slowness and irregularity with which
this was at first executed gave it more the resemblance of the
reelings of a half tipsey crowd than a dance. By means, however, of an air, which the performers never ceased humming, the
steps became more regular, and the quickness of the motions
gradually increased. The spirits of the performers, enlivened by
the indulgence in their national amusement, were at length wound
up to a high pitch of excitement: and the finale, like that of our
Vauxhall fireworks, closing with a general explosion, must have
been no slight trial to the nerves of our travelling heroine. It
appears that a formidable dancer, one of the most ruffian-looking
of the whole party, in a red jacket and cap, and bristling with all
the apparatus of war, drew, with a look of wild delight, a pistol
from his belt, and fired it into the air; his example being followed
immediately by the rest of the troop. A lively feeling of injury,
promptness to anger, and a sense of honour which never forgives
an insult, form, as might be expected, the characteristic features
of a race nursed like this in a constant state of moral excitement;
as our friend Bailie Nicol Jarvie has it, " they are clean anither
set frae the like o' huz," the children sport with dirk and pistol
instead of coral and rattle, and are thus enabled to ape their more
formidable sires with considerable success. One example of this
we find in the work before us. Some children, employed in
watching cattle, agreed to while away the time in playing at odd
and even; the loser to be punished by a slight beating with a
knotted handkerchief. The girls of the party suffered the penalty
in good humour, but when they attempted in return to pay off one
of their companions, a boy ten years old, the urchin drew his
pistol and shot one of them. On being brought before the court,
and questioned concerning the deed, he exhibited the most perfect
indifference. On being asked whether he was aware that he
would be hung, " You may do so," he replied, " for I am in your
power," superior force affording in his mind the only indisputable

claim to authority. The murderer's youth saved him from the gallows, no doubt to become a worthy aspirant to the noble qualities of Rob Roy's progeny, and a successful proficient in the admirable feats of " bringing down a black-cock on the wing wi' a single bullet, and driving a dirk through a twa-inch board."

The spirit of chivalry, whose departure from the more civilized parts of Europe has so often been pathetically lamented, found a resting place in these remote regions; it is not long since no youth could pay his addresses honourably to any of his countrywomen until he had made a marauding incursion across the border,

> " And struck three strokes with Croat brand,
> And marched three miles on southron land."

Though, lest the parent's strict notions of ceremony on this or any other point should interfere with the happiness of the young couple, a kind of Gretna Green had been established over the border; where the first priest whom the fugitive pair happened to meet was fee'd to betrothe them, instead of having his turkeys stolen by the candidate for connubial bliss.

Our traveller next proceeds from Carlstadt to Fiume by the Louisen-Strasse, a magnificent road undertaken by some patriotic nobles of Austria under the patronage of the emperor; the whole length of this pass, by which a communication is opened to Hungary with the sea, is ninety miles, its breadth about twenty-six feet; the engineer was the Baron von Vukassovich, who did not live to see it completed, being killed at the battle of Wagram. Before his death, however, he had the satisfaction of seeing it carried over the mountain ridge which separates Croatia from the Adriatic. Here it was necessary to force a passage through the mass of rock which crowns the summit, and of which a single column has been left standing in commemoration of the difficulties encountered; on this the bold projector proposed merely to inscribe the words—PER GLI INCREDULI—a modest rebuke to those who once derided his Herculean labours. The pass itself is called Porta Hungarica.* From this height the traveller looks down upon the town of Fiume, which lies at his feet; the vegetation as he descends becomes more and more luxuriant; the sea, which is bounded by Istria and the Island of Cherso, assumes the appearance of a vast and tranquil

---

* We are sorry to find that the traffic upon this road has not been sufficient to repay a moderate interest upon the sums expended in its formation. The tolls levied have indeed been much lowered, but now that the freedom of navigation in the Black Sea and the passage of the Dardanelles have been secured, the corn of Hungary and the adjoining countries, which might otherwise pass through Fiume or Trieste, finds a vent through the port of Odessa.

lake. Mrs. von Artner, overcome by her feelings, went into hysterics at the sight of a pine tree, on which she makes some touching reflections: this indeed appears an orthodox piece of ceremony among female voyagers, for the lady, whose travels we mentioned before, hurried out of her coach at the first glimpse of the dome of St. Peter's, and plumped down on her knees, amid ejaculations and tears, to the amazement of the startled vetturino who, poor man, justly doubted of the sanity of his cargo.

From Fiume the road led to Trieste, the flourishing condition of which town much delighted our tourist. It is indeed astonishing to observe how rapidly the trade of the place has increased since it was declared a free port: the warehouses were full of goods of every description from every nation.

" With patriotic joy," she continues, " I remarked that in consequence of the recent encouragement which has been given to our manufactures, the English muslins and linens no longer exhibit a superiority over our own, but fall far short of them in colour, taste and cheapness. One of my companions, who had not seen Trieste for forty years, wondered also at the increase of artisans; some time since it was impossible to furnish a house in the town, whilst operatives of every description are now found there in abundance."

We need hardly add, that the increase of commerce has been accompanied by a corresponding improvement in the style of buildings, both public and private, and a taste for cleanliness, comfort, and magnificence has, in consequence, been universally diffused. The voyage from Trieste to Venice is described in a manner so truly German, that we are sure an extract from the conclusion will not be unpleasant to our readers.—p. 128.

" Having left Trieste in the evening," (says our authoress,) " exhaustion would not permit me to pass the night on deck, which the pleasing temperature of the air would have otherwise warranted me in doing. I was obliged to retire for some hours to the ladies' cabin. At the grey of the morning I again ascended the deck, and though the scene I had left was no longer present, yet its place was supplied by one full as beautiful. The whole creation swam in the mildest colours. The rapidity of the steam-boat had again brought us near the coast, heaven and earth melted in a kiss. The sea was of a silver blue, and to the eye seemed only an enormous fish, covered with delicate scales; the pure blue of the atmosphere was varied with the ruddy dawn and the grey mist, whose tints gradually melted into each other, while the white sails of numerous vessels glided on every side, amid streaks of rose colour and silver. All was brightness and melting serenity; no where was a shadow to be seen, except when the compressed steam burst from the safety valve, and a coal-black, gigantic serpent of smoke, issued forth into the pure atmosphere, like sin entering into paradise."

The account of Venice contains nothing which can arrest our

attention: a minute description of its churches, palaces, and other works of art being now quite familiar to all who feel any interest in such subjects. We may pardon the feelings of an Austrian when defending the conduct of her government towards this fallen city; she says, and we think with some degree of justice, that nothing can be more unfair than to draw a parallel between the present condition of Venice and its former splendour, and to lay the difference to the account of the Austrian administration. For centuries the republic had been on the decline. The discovery of the passage round the Cape was a death-blow to her mercantile activity, and the league of Cambray put a limit to her conquests. When Bonaparte took possession of Venice, in what state did he find her once formidable navy? Only twenty ships were in the docks; of these, two had been begun since 1732, two since 1743, and two since 1752, nor was there any probability of their being completed. Yes—let his be the blame who first violated the neutrality of states too weak to defend themselves, who took armed possession of them without even the plea of their occupation by the enemy being dangerous to his own country, and who surrendered them to that enemy and a foreign yoke, in order to purchase an involuntary acquiescence in his own unprincipled conquests. At this day the Venetians may complain of the apathy of their masters, but not of actual oppression; the yoke may not be easy, but the burthen is light. We grant, indeed, that as long as the Austrian rule endures, Venice will never rise from her state of degradation; her very look is that of a body from which the spirit has fled: the first calm moments of death may, indeed, cheat us into a belief that the spirit is still there; yet the delusion is but transitory, decay will soon stretch his " effacing finger" over the beautiful surface, and the mouldering form will soon convince us of the reality of dissolution.

Our authoress had the good fortune to be present at Vicenza during the celebration of the festival of *La Rua* or *La Ruota,* which is founded upon a legend resembling that of Castor and Pollux at the battle at the Lake Regillus.—p. 208.

" The festival of La Ruota is celebrated on the day of Corpus Christi, which happened to be that of my arrival at Vicenza. Its origin is dated from a victory of the Vicentines over the Paduans, who had long held the former under subjection. The exact account cannot be traced to any historical foundations, though two legends exist on the subject. According to the first, two knights of the town, by name Sforza Pisano and Verlatta, placed themselves at the head of their fellow-citizens against their oppressors, and took a most conspicuous part in the battle, which ended in so complete a route of their opponents, that the general lost a wheel of his chariot, which the Vicentines brought home in triumph, and which gave occasion to this festival. According to the second tradition, the two heroes are said to have penetrated as far as Padua, to have there thrown the tyrant from the window of his own palace, and on their triumphant return, to have been met by processions of their grateful countrymen, each of the various corporations bearing the emblems of its trade, amongst which that of the notaries was particularly distinguished by a wheel, which has in consequence been preserved at the annual commemoration of the victory."

In a rather interesting chapter upon the education and manners of women, p. 239, et seq. we find a very just censure passed upon the practice of encouraging them to look upon marriage as a freedom from all restraint, and a mere passport for indulging in all those vices to which the females of that genial clime are so prone. Mothers are taught to look upon their children in the light of necessary evils; the custom of having them nursed in the country up to a certain age deadens, if it does not destroy, all the affections which nature has so wisely implanted; they return as strangers, in whom the parents take no delight, and if ever deemed worthy a passing thought, are only brought to remembrance as materially interfering with the mother's vicious pursuits. The loose conduct of the female sex leads of course to a corresponding depravation of the male; as long as the candle lasts, there will be found moths to hover round its rays: who can wonder at the supineness of the Italians in political affairs, when all domestic duties are thus unnaturally neglected? To make a good citizen, a man must be virtuous in his private relations; there may be, nay, we every day see exceptions, but in the mass the bonds of public and private morality are, we believe, inseparably connected.

The system of municipal government carried on under the auspices of Austria does not appear to us well calculated either to ensure an easy collection of the revenue, or to provide against abuses in the distribution of the public burthens. Our authoress's account is rather confused, but as far as we can collect, the arrangement is as follows. The towns are governed by a council, at the head of which is a podesta. The *Borghi* and *Communi* (perhaps small towns and villages) select from the mass of their proprietors a deputation, which must be approved of by the governor, (we suppose the military commandant.) These consult respecting the management of all public improvements, the repairing of roads, and the distribution of the funds arising from public institutions within their boundaries, as well as of so much of the public revenue as may be *allotted* to them. The decisions of this assembly are then submitted to a provincial assembly, which consists of nobles, commoners and deputies from the towns. Should these assent, ·it is then laid before a central-council, (*congregation* is the word used, but our translation is, we think, nearly correct,) of which there are two, one at Venice, the other at Milan : each formed of two individuals, a noble proprietor and an inhabitant of one of the towns. Having passed through these ordeals, the assent of the emperor is the only remaining sanction requisite to enable the bill to pass into a law. But should either the provincial assembly, or central council, refuse to pass a mea-sure submitted for their approval, *an appeal lies from the commu-nities* (*Gemeinden,* perhaps the first assembly is meant) *to court.* The business of the central councils consists in the imposition and collection of taxes, the examination of public accounts, the· division of military services, the allotting of sums for the repairs of embankments, roads, and the expenditure of the tolls collected on them. An account of their proceedings must be delivered in to the emperor, whose commands they likewise receive directly. All these officers give their services gratuitously, except the *podestas* of Venice and Milan, each of whom receives a salary of two thousand florins. The above must be a very meagre outline of the form of government ; the duties of the respective bodies are, it will be perceived, by no means accurately defined, but the whole seems admirably adapted to fulfil the purpose for which we take it for granted the system was put together ; i. e. to create perpetual jealousies and disputes between the different depart-ments, and thus to lay the whole at the mercy of the Austrian despot.

If the administrative bodies were independent, it might per-haps be wise to consider the dignity and influence of office as a sufficient remuneration for its irksome duties; but what honour can there be in serving as deputy's deputy for a foreign master, and how will such influence be exerted except in receiving bribes for the partial execution of a disagreeable duty? Our good lady reasons somewhat curiously in assuring us of the equal distribu-tion of the imposts, and fairness in their application; the former is proved by recourse never having been had to military force in their collection. This merely proves that they are not heavy, not that they are equally imposed ; and, indeed, this is perhaps allow-ing too much to the argument. Taxes in France, from which the nobility were exempt, were long paid patiently by the lower orders; a day of reckoning, indeed, came at last, as we trust it will in Italy; but how much mistaken would he have been who had argued from the apparent contentment of the people, that they were well and impartially governed. Again, an appeal is made to the goodness of the roads, in order to bear out the asser-tion that the money raised is fairly applied ; this is indeed suffi-

cient evidence that the whole is not squandered; but until we
know the sums collected and works performed, we shall be inclined to suspend our judgment upon this point.

In a further part of the work, p. 325, it is indeed hinted, that
the authoress knew more than she could disclose; the truth is
imparted to us, but not the whole truth. That the people may be
happy under such a government is possible—that they will remain
for ever contented with what a party in England would term
their *virtual representation,* is ridiculous to suppose; they have
not even the consolation of the slaves of an African despot :—
" Happy are ye," said an Emperor of Morocco to his subjects,
" happy people, who have only to obey laws made by your representative through the prophet, and I am he!' "

ART. VIII.—*Histoire de la Vie et des Ouvrages des plus célèbres
Architectes du XIe Siècle jusqu'à la fin du XVIIIe.* Par
M. Quatremère de Quincy. Deux volumes, gr.-in-8vo., avec
47 Planches. Paris, 1830.

WERE it not that the name of Radical Reformers would mix us
up with the Cobbetts and Hunts, and other worthies of that
stamp, in whose celebrity we are by no means ambitious of par-
ticipating, we too should proclaim ourselves such; since we
must confess—indeed it would be useless for us to attempt to
conceal it—that we are, in our way, staunch advocates for liberty'
and reform. Like most other reformers, however, and champions of liberty, we are not over and above tolerant towards our
opponents, as the reader will doubtless be convinced by the
time he shall have perused this article. That our paper will
scandalize and horrify many of the " *legitimates,*" be they either
ultra-Palladianists or ultra-Grecianists, is also tolerably certain;
and yet even they ought to feel obliged to us, inasmuch as we
hereby afford them a very fair opportunity of coming forward to
re-state, more satisfactorily than they have hitherto done, all that
can be advanced in support of their own exclusive systems.

The only apprehension which we entertain, is, that our readers
in general may not care one straw either for ourselves or our
adversaries, but very unceremoniously skip over altogether an
article with so very unpromising a title, or with one that promises nothing but a repetition of ten-times repeated dulness. It
must be confessed that our subject is by no means a popular
one,—that it cannot be rendered so lively as a chapter on political economy, so intelligible to the uninitiated as a pamphlet
on the Bullion question, so immediately interesting to elderly

gentlemen and young ladies as a profound dissertation on geology. The fact is, architecture has no *lay* votaries; with here and there a solitary exception, it is studied by none but those who design to follow it as a profession, for while every *ology* and *onomy* (hardly excepting ideology and gastronomy, those two opposite poles of human learning,) are comprised in the circle of modern education, this pursuit alone is excluded from the catalogue, as being altogether too mechanical in its nature and principles to have anything in common with the other liberal arts. Hence it happens, that even persons of general information in other respects are not ashamed to avow their complete ignorance of even the elements of architecture; or, what is far worse, they often betray the most ludicrous ignorance, while, on the strength, perhaps, of knowing a few technical terms, they affect to understand something of it. For whether people know either one order from another or not, or one single rule of the art, they can all criticise *buildings*, deciding most authoritatively on the merits or defects of any piece of architecture, nay, at a single glance too, and without being able to assign the least valid reason for either censure or approbation:—*stat pro ratione voluntas.* This, it will be said, is the mere *tirade* of exaggeration: persons of common-sense do not commit themselves in that egregious manner. We know not whether many sensible persons are guilty of such *bêtises;* we should say not, since few who deserve that appellation would venture to speak decisively on what they never studied: but we can prove that many who pretend to direct the opinion of others in architectural matters, frequently display a profundity of ignorance that is truly astonishing; and that too, not merely in private conversation, but they absolutely record their blunders in print. For instances of this nature we have not to search far: tourists, topographers, and newspaper critics, would supply a tolerably bulky collection of them; nor would such a tome fail alternately to excite our commiseration and risibility, keeping us in a state of perpetual oscillation between groans and laughter. One tourist, who does not seem a positive ignoramus in other respects, informs us that the palace built by Charles V. at Grenada, strikingly resembles that designed by Inigo Jones, and intended to be erected at Whitehall; another compares the magnificent temple at Balbec, a pile adorned in a style of the most exuberant profuseness, with the little rustic-looking church on the west side of Covent Garden market. Then again, we were, not many years ago, informed by the newspapers that the front of one of the new club-houses in St. James's Street was copied from that of Whitehall Chapel, and that the gateway at the corner of Grosvenor Place was in imitation -of the arch of Constantine, which might with equal, truth have been asserted of its opposite neighbour leading into Hyde Park. Although we do not expect to meet with any profound architectural criticism in the columns of a newspaper, yet even there we should not discover equal ignorance on any other subject; but when we find similar, nay still more egregious blunders in publications which, it is to be presumed, have at least more labour and care bestowed on them, than can be afforded for the hasty paragraphs of a newspaper, we are indeed surprised, and feel that nothing except the complete ignorance of the public on such matters could protect such works from universal ridicule.

‘ We offer no apology for these apparently desultory remarks, which may at first sight seem to have very little to do with the general scope and purport of our article; because, we think that the above instances, and they are but very few compared with what we could have produced, go a considerable way towards proving, not only that the generality of otherwise educated persons know nothing whatever of architecture, but also that they presume every one else to be equally unacquainted with it. Neither is the draftsman, the nature of whose task would, we might imagine, almost preclude the possibility of any strikingly gross inaccuracy as to positive matter of fact, however incapable he may be of expressing the more delicate touches of character, always free from the charge of strangely misrepresenting what his pencil undertakes to describe. We do not here allude to those mediocre and frequently paltry performances which are little better than caricatures of the buildings professed to be pourtrayed, but to works of some character, in which we have reason to expect something like a scientific knowledge of the art, whose productions form the subjects of the draftsman's or painter's delineations. We could point out some curious instances of this species of graphic lying, to say nothing of minor offences against veracity, occasioned either by sheer carelessness, or by the utter indifference to truth on the part of the artist; who is satisfied himself, and thinks all the rest of the world ought to be satisfied too, if he only produces a showy effect of light and shade. In a publication, not exactly a hundred years old, much extolled by the critics as a prodigy of excellence for the beauty of its plates, we have observed many very singular blunders; in some places the letter-press descriptions give the lie direct to the engravings; or it may be that the latter give the lie to the text. With regard, too, to the manner in which the descriptions to architectural views are generally drawn up, nothing can be more paltry and inane than they are for the most part. The writer, perhaps, informs us how many columns and windows there are in the front of a building, which, by the by, is hardly necessary when the view is before our eyes; and if he does this without committing any palpable mistake, we may think both him and ourselves exceedingly lucky, since it is not every one who can accomplish that. One of these erudite gentlemen, * in a late number of a popular work of this kind, called a gateway at the palace of Fontainebleau a portico, misled in all probability by the French word *portail*, which he anglicized by a term conveying a totally different meaning. It is true, that the literary, or more properly the letter-press portion of such works is beneath all criticism,—frequently little better than mere pilferings from ordinary guide books, and utterly destitute of any original information, much more of anything like critical remark; still, as works of this class are mere articles of luxury, as they are not for the circulating-library but for the drawing-room table, the slovenly carelessness they for the most part evince, shows how little the purchasers of them are shocked at inconsistencies and nonsense that would disgrace a twopenny publication, and that pass current with impunity, only because reviewers and readers are, on these subjects, even more ignorant, if possible, than the writers of such stuff.

And this brings us to one very important consideration, namely, by what especial fatality has it happened, that architecture, which even our commonest school books assert to be one of the fine arts, and which, if we might trust to the magnificent language held by some of its professors, is the queen and sovereign of them all, embracing in her boundless domain the whole extent of human knowledge, combining mathematics with æsthetics, and all the mystic harmonies both of numbers and forms;—how happens it that architecture has never become a branch of ornamental education, but is, on the contrary, looked upon as little better than a mere mechanical trade? If we are not greatly mistaken, this neglect may be traced in some degree to two very opposite causes; the study is at once too easy and too difficult. Paradoxical enough! the reader will exclaim; nevertheless we cannot help thinking that such is really the case. When we say

---

* The phraseology these writers make use of, is oftentimes, at the best, singularly awkward and erroneous: thus we meet, again and again, with such expressions as, 'columns supporting a portico;' which is not much unlike saying that the walls of a room support the room itself; 'columns with Corinthian capitals and entablatures,' a kind of paraphrastic circumlocution, that is recommended by no particular propriety or elegance. And why 'entablatures,' as if there was a plurality of that part of the order, and one entablature was piled above the other; or each column had its own distinct piece of entablature, severed from the rest. Another will tell us of a portico 'receding back at the top, without a pediment;' which is not palpable nonsense only because it is utterly unintelligible.

easy, we mean apparently so : and certainly any person who is
not quite an idiot, may, in the course of a few hours, learn the
names of the different orders, and to distinguish one from the
other, and .may pick up some half-dozen technical terms : behold him then established ,as a critic for life, and all further
study would be absolutely superfluous to one who does not intend to follow the art professionally.   Besides, are not the orders
every thing—the all-and-all in architecture?   It would be quite
idle, therefore, for a gentleman critic to pretend to know any
thing farther : and even the less he knows of these, the less
danger there will be of his being mistaken for a builder.   No
wonder, then, when such is the case, when the whole science is
thought to consist in knowing a few cabalistic words, such as
Doric, Ionic, &c., if those thus initiated utter. egregious twaddle
in a tone of authority, adopt the most imbecile prejudices, and
circulate the shallowest criticisms.   On the other hand, those
who would really be at some pains to acquire such a competent
knowledge of architecture as would be sufficient to enable them
to appreciate all its.beauties, and to judge of its productions as
they do of those of its sister arts, are apt to be discouraged from
proceeding by the dry technical details, and the still more intolerable pedantry, which more or less pervade every treatise on the
subject.

There is, in fact, hardly a single elementary work on architecture, that is not either by far too superficial to be instructive,
or too replete with mere technicalities to adapt itself to the
wants of the general reader, who is at once embarrassed by
meeting with such numerous *minutiæ*, for which he has no occasion, and disappointed at finding so little of that which he really
requires, and which would invest the subject with permanent
interest, with spirit and vitality.   Each writer goes over too
nearly the very same ground, and contemplates his matter from
precisely the same point of view as most others have done before
him.   Instead of attempting to render architecture a popular
pursuit, all those who have treated of it seem to have been
rather ambitious of involving it in a certain mysticism, and to have
laboured to confound what is merely conventional with what is
really essential.   Instead of any thing like generalization of
principles, or originality of views, we meet with insulated rules,
and the dull quackery of monotonous routine ; while puerile
trifling, or anile superstition, is suffered in many cases to exclude
even a glimpse of common sense.   In almost every other branch
of knowledge, the student is able to provide himself with theoretical and critical, as well as practical works ; but here he ought to
be endued with more than ordinary ardour and perseverance, if he

would collect for himself the insulated scraps of criticism, and the few really useful original remarks that, " few and far between," are scattered over a wide expanse of almost unvaried sameness. After examining an entire architectural library for this purpose, he will probably find his toil rewarded by the acquisition of what would hardly suffice to fill a moderate-sized volume. Lest this sentence should be deemed too sweeping; if necessary, we should apprize our readers that we do not include in the class of works to which we are now alluding, those which treat more expressly of the archæology and history of architecture, for many of them have really enriched that department of literature, both in our own and other languages. Yet, however meritorious and interesting works of this latter character may be, the very qualities that give them their value prevent their becoming popular; besides which, the ample and expensive form in which they are generally published, necessarily limits them to few purchasers. It is in works that ought to be text books on the art, and which, if properly executed, would become so, that we desiderate more intelligent and critical views, with such a tolerably fair degree of industry in addition as would prevent the appearance of that liberal transcription from preceding authors, which even candour must allow to be very much like bookmaking and plagiarism. We are aware that in elementary treatises on the same pursuit, be it what it may, much must be substantially the same; yet we have a right to expect that each succeeding one shall exhibit either some originality of remark, a more lucid exposition of the subject, or a refutation of long-established errors; or that at any rate it shall recommend itself by greater popularity of style. To this last-mentioned quality there are few books on architecture that have much pretension: of those that are really useful, the majority can be considered as little more than works of reference, not as readable books, which may be perused with satisfaction even when their contents are known; nor does this arise from positive necessity, owing to the technicality of the subject. That which constitutes the mere *accidence* of the art does not, indeed, admit of much variety of phraseology, or of any particular allurements of style; yet even here, dryness may, to a certain extent, be avoided, while all beyond this is susceptible of as much interest as any other topic of critical disquisition. The jejuneness, therefore, which so frequently disappoints, and the crudity that so generally disgusts us, are not to be imputed to the barrenness and intractability of the subject, but to the indolence, if not the incompetence of the writer. In proof that dullness and dryness are not inseparably allied to similar topics, we would or could point out one or two papers that appeared a few years since in a

periodical entitled " Annals of the Fine Arts;" to the literary·
part of some of Mr. Papworth's publications, and some chapters
of a work with the rather affected title of the " Union of Painting,
Sculpture, and Architecture." It must be acknowledged that,
with the exception of what is exclusively technical or practical,
our architectural literature is in this country exceedingly scanty.
No one can accuse the members of this profession of expatiating
on the merits of their own productions, for those who have published their designs have generally done so without comment, or
rather without any other explanation than mere references to their
plates, even when in justice to themselves, if not for the satisfaction of their readers, they ought to have explained what cannot
otherwise be understood, and to have pointed out how far they
were controuled by unfavourable circumstances. This is the more
to be regretted, because we feel that it is the want of sufficiently
explanatory and well-written descriptive letter-press that hinders
such works from being interesting to many who would else derive
both instruction and gratification from them. Even such works as
the *Vitruvius Britannicus* and its successors contain the *minimum*
of information beyond what is to be obtained from the plates
themselves, thereby leaving those who consult them in the most
perplexing ignorance as to numerous particulars, which it is impossible for them to know without every part of such structure being either minutely delineated, or what is omitted in the drawings
being supplied in the text. The deficiency here complained of is
not peculiar to English works of this class, although it is certainly
more uniformly to be observed in them; for some foreign ones
are tolerably satisfactory in what relates to their historical and
descriptive matter; in proof of which we may refer to the letter-
press accompanying Schinkel's collection of designs, which, never-,
theless, cannot be accused of being unnecessarily prolix. To say.
the truth, the Germans have displayed far more zeal and industry
than ourselves, not only in mere matter-of-fact elucidations, but
in whatever appertains to architectural criticism and bibliography;
nor do we here allude to their Hirts, and Stieglitzes, and Mollers,
but to the numerous articles on such subjects to be met with in their
journals, many of which are written not only with intelligence, but
a truly *con amore* spirit; while in this country,—so complete is the
indifference manifested towards such pursuits, that hardly a single
literary journal thought it worth while to notice the appearance of
such a work as Murphy's Arabian Antiquities of Spain. Neither
is it architectural books alone which experience this neglect: it is
the same as regards buildings, for where are we to look for any
thing like an intelligent and candid appreciation of their merits?
A random paragraph in a newspaper, not always free from the

suspicion of puffing, may occasionally inform us that such or such a building has been lately erected ; but rarely, indeed, do we meet with any thing more, except in the shape of that small wit which assails the spire in Langham Place, and the egg-shell on the new palace. Our critics—if that appellation be not a positive misnomer—display far more talent in seeing obvious defects, than in detecting beauties, to the perception of which, indeed, their petty parrot-like study will not assist them : hence, we presume, it has happened that one of the most original and tasteful of all the recent edifices in the metropolis, so truly antique in its spirit and Greek in its feeling, although at the same time so dissimilar from any other piece of architecture, has escaped being *honored* by their notice. Although, too, almost every one concurs in censuring the building at the end of St. James's Park, no one has thought proper to assign any more satisfactory reason for his disapprobation than what is implied in vague and sweeping epithets : according to such enlightened judges, it is bad, *because* it is bad : yet we are of opinion that no extraordinary sagacity is required to point out *how* it happens, that a building with so much ornamental detail, and with so much embellishment that is beautiful in itself, produces altogether so poor an effect.

We have, perhaps, taken more pains than was necessary, to show the general apathy and want of information that prevail with regard to architecture, and which cannot but be regretted, both because an abundant source of great intellectual enjoyment is thereby cut off, and because men of talent in the profession are deprived of the encouragement they would feel, were they certain that the public could competently appreciate merit in this particular art. Another, and certainly no small advantage that would accrue to architects themselves, from the art itself being in some degree understood by persons in general, is, that they would not be so frequently exposed as they now are to impertinent and ignorant interference, since those by whom they were employed would be better aware of the numerous difficulties that fetter the practitioner, and would, at the same time, be better disposed to listen to, and comprehend his explanations. We do not assert too much when we say that, considered merely as a study, without any ulterior object, architecture is capable of affording quite as much, and as intense and constant enjoyment, as music, painting, or any other intellectual pursuit. For confirmation of this, we may confidently appeal to the testimony of those who have taken it up in that view : they are indeed but a very small minority,— prodigiously outnumbered by the dilettanti and cognoscenti in the other fine arts, yet animated with as decided enthusiasm. If such be really the case—if, setting aside all collateral interests

and questions of utility, this study contains so much. to repay
those who must look for their remuneration to the study itself,
it is indeed astonishing that, in this age of multifarious education,
architecture should not have been enlisted into the corps of sciences and accomplishments taught at our academies of every
grade; but, on the contrary, discarded by universal consent, as if
too insipid or mechanical to merit attention. ." Are you serious,
or bantering?—would you really have young persons, then, do
nothing but draw columns, and learn to discourse of the orders, of
plans and elevations, and go and stare at buildings?—and all for
what?—merely that they may in time talk of such things as cleverly as an ordinary mason." In this manner would objections
be shaped on the very first proposal of the plan we recommend,
and to many they would appear unanswerable; for nothing is
more common than for persons to suffer themselves to be ridi-
culed out of doing a thing, by the sophistry of an argument *ex
abusu,* or rather by the downright caricature of reasoning. There
is nothing that may not thus be represented in the most absurd
and ludicrous light; yet in spite of this very convenient species
of humour, which is so frequently resorted to by those who can
annoy, although they are unable to combat, the world believes that
music is something more than merely fingering keys and scraping
strings, and that it would not be a very candid explanation to say
that reading is only staring at printed paper. With such rea-
soners the mental gratification is nothing : unless the object of
pursuit be something tangible, they affirm that it is a mere chi-
mæra of the fancy,—inane and worthless.

We, however, are of opinion that the study of architecture has
far more to recommend it as a branch of education for young
persons of *both* sexes, than some of those things which it is now
considered indispensably necessary for them to learn; and as the
recommendations it possesses of this nature have never been done
justice to, we shall perhaps be excused, if we briefly advert to
a few of them. The connection of architecture with the other
fine arts, and the convenience of knowing at least so much of it
as will enable us to judge how far the accessories in a picture are
correct, where buildings are introduced, are too obvious to be
insisted upon; neither is it necessary to expatiate on the superior
advantages possessed by the traveller who has qualified himself by
a competent study of the subject, for enjoying the local beauties
of the cities he visits. It might be conceived that the additional
interest which an acquaintance with the various styles of architecture imparts to historical studies, and the kind of *memoria technica*
furnished by the various reminiscences connected with celebrated
buildings, would alone form a sufficient reason for directing the

attention of the youthful pupil to such studies. But there is another very important consideration in its favour,—one that ought immediately to satisfy the *cui-bono* sceptics who may not see the value we impute to it as a mere accomplishment: which is, that nothing tends more to refine the taste, and to divest it of all taint of vulgarity, than early familiarizing both the eye and the mind with those exquisite forms of beauty transmitted to us in the remains of ancient art ;—that nothing is better calculated to elevate our ideas, than frequent contemplation of structures distinguished either by the sublimity of their dimensions, or the harmony of their proportions. So far then, what is urged in favour of dancing as a bodily accomplishment may, *cæteris paribus*, be urged in behalf of architecture, namely, that the study of it forms habits of gracefulness: in either case it is the general, not the particular and insulated advantages that constitute the chief value of the acquirement. It is not in order that they may be able to draw columns, for that is merely the means not the end of the pursuit, that we would suggest the propriety of ladies applying themselves to what has hitherto never been included within the circle of female acquirements; but that they may thereby cultivate their taste, and ground it upon something less baseless and shifting than mere feminine likings and dislikings. And when we consider how wide is the province—how influential the authority which the sex are apt to claim in such matters—how much, in all that regards ornamental furniture and interior embellishments, depends on the refined or trivial taste of our fairer halves; it must be acknowledged that to initiate them into such studies would not be an act of perfect disinterestedness. Independently of its subsequent advantages, the elementary practice of architectural drawing would be highly beneficial to the youthful pupil, inasmuch as it affords an immediate application of the simpler principles of geometry ; as it forms the hand to correctness—the eye to a scrupulous examination of forms ; and consequently implants habits of careful deliberation and attention, as well as the seeds of taste. Perhaps it will be thought that the accuracy and exactness required for delineating architectural detail would be not altogether compatible with that freedom of hand, which is desirable in other styles of drawing ; yet we can assure both young ladies and their mammas that there is very little danger of their becoming very rigid precisians as regards outline,* or rather that a little more exactness in this respect

---

* By *outline*, we do not mean a harsh and cutting contour,—for the latter is but too generally evident in the performances of juvenile and female draftsmen :—we plead guilty to the bull that has just escaped us. It will probably be objected that architectural drawing is both too laborious and too mechanical ever to become a fa

would be a decided improvement. After all, however, it is not imperatively necessary, that students of this class should actually delineate with their own hands the objects they have to study—for we would not absolutely terrify our fair readers with the idea of using compasses and ruler: it will be sufficient to draw the requisite examples *mentally*, following every line, until the figure be perfectly understood, and every part of it impressed upon the memory.

We shall hardly be suspected of wishing to throw any dash of the ridiculous on what we seriously recommend,—although many will not fail to laugh at such a notable scheme as that of converting architecture into an amusement for ladies,—and we will, therefore, venture to predict that they would discover it a somewhat more intellectual pastime than oriental tinting, and find that it would occasionally supply topics of conversation possessing a happy medium between the levities of chemical gases and the grave matters of millinery and lace. It would seem, nevertheless, as if women had by common consent agreed never to stray into this province of art, as if it were totally barren of all allurement—without aught to engage the imagination, or to exercise the judgment. The world has seen female mathematicians, one even holding a professorship in a learned university; it has seen female sculptors; and it has certainly *heard* of one female pope; but, as far as we have been able to ascertain, there is no recorded instance of one female architect. Now this may seem a most unfortunate admission on our part, inasmuch as the fact seems to prove that the pursuit must be in itself entirely unsuited to the sex. This circumstance is, indeed, rather an awkward one, when we first consider it; yet the argument that might otherwise very speciously be drawn from it falls to the ground, when we produce a parallel and still more extraordinary instance from an art which is certainly not considered interdicted to the exercise of female talent. Where, we ask, is the woman who has distinguished herself as a musical composer? What are we to think?—has the sex never furnished any competitors for that wreath; or has their insignificance prevented their failures being recorded? The question is rather a delicate one, for whatever might be the answer, it would hardly be compli-

---

vourite pursuit with those with whom drawing is only a recreation; and also that mere elevations and details are too formal a species of delineation. To which we reply, the force of these objections must depend entirely upon individual feeling: if the student should have little perseverance, or feel more disgust at the process, than satisfaction at the result of it, he can hardly hope to succeed; neither can he have any great relish for architectural beauty, who cannot feel its abstract merits in geometrical delineation. We may, here, further remark, that it is not a little singular that with us, ' formal' should convey an unfavourable meaning, while the '*formosus*' of the Romans implied the highest degree of beauty.

mentary; neither will it be deemed a proof of much policy and address on our part to have touched upon what may be likely to offend those whom we are trying to persuade, and should, therefore, endeavour to conciliate. Be that as it may, the inference we would have our readers draw from that very circumstance is tolerably obvious. Nor do we see why women should voluntarily forego all the gratification to be derived from an elegant pursuit, merely because it is one which the other sex have practically appropriated to themselves as a profession.* We have already dwelt too long on this division of our subject; otherwise we could adduce many reasons that recommend architecture, considered merely as an accomplishment and an amusement, to the youthful and female portion of society. As it is, we will content ourselves with mentioning one,—namely, that of all the fine arts, it is the only one incapable of receiving or transmitting the least moral taint. Poetry, music, painting, sculpture, do not always prove favourable to mental purity: even when their compositions have nothing that can shock either the most modest ear or eye, the impressions they make upon the mind are frequently such as are hardly reconcilable with delicacy, although it would be too harsh to say that they are incompatible with virtue: and hence it may sometimes happen, that an illiberal construction will be put upon the admiration excited solely by the excellence of art. There are likewise some branches of physical science, which, for very obvious reasons, female pupils can hardly be allowed to approach; but architecture is not obnoxious to the slightest inculpation on the ground of indelicacy: the other fine arts may—this *must* be pure. With great propriety, therefore, might it be termed the Virgin Art: inexpressibly lovely as are the forms it has at its command, the emotions they excite can hardly be called sensual, at least not in the usual acceptation of the word. It may, however, probably be said, that this merit, upon which we seem to lay so much stress, amounts after all to merely a negative one, and that in proportion to its inability to do any harm must be its incapacity for effecting any good. Yet surely a study which, if properly pursued, tends to exercise both the judgment and the taste, and supplies so much and such varied intellectual pleasure, unalloyed by any baser admixture, does not require to be vindicated

---

* By way of making some amends for the not very gallant tone of the above observations, and that we may pay a compliment where it is so well merited, we cannot resist citing here the example of a lady of rank, whose devoted application to, and proficiency in the study of architecture, form an exception to our rule. Under the tasteful direction of Lady Stafford, who has had a greater share in the designs than, perhaps, we are warranted in alluding to, Costessey Hall has become one of the richest and purest specimens of domestic Gothic in the kingdom, and from its architectural variety and splendour deserves to be entitled the Windsor of Norfolk.

merely because it does not effect what is beyond its province. If our avocations of this kind interfere with no moral duties, the most rigid code of morals demands no more. On reconsidering what we have thus stated in behalf of architecture, our arguments appear to us so much like mere truisms, that we should be tempted to strike them out, were it not that the subject has never been looked at in this point of view, which is not much to be wondered at, seeing that the study of the art has hitherto been treated of merely by practical men, who have regarded their readers as persons of the same class. Non-professional people would be considered by them in the light of interlopers. We ourselves, too, run some risk, not only of being looked upon by the Vitruvian fraternity as poachers trespassing on their manors, but as seeking to derogate from the honour of their art, by recommending it as pretty pastime for boys and girls, and by proposing to render its mysteries " intelligible to the meanest capacities." Although, however, we should hail any attempt to render the study of architecture more popular and generally accessible, we cannot point out any work adapted for such a purpose; the books that might effect so desirable an object still remain to be written, for notwithstanding the eager search continually making after novelty in literary subjects, that of which we are now speaking, which offers so wide a scope for originality of thinking, remains untouched. Of course we mean something not only in a more expanded form than Catechisms, Rudiments, and other manuals of that description, but altogether different from them,—something that would substitute a living principle of intelligence and taste, for a bundle of dry sticky rules,—that should be the production of the mind, not the mere operation of the pen.

Yet it is not books alone that are required: excellent as these might be, unless there were also motives to open and study them, their influence would be very confined, and operate but slowly. Before we can hope that architecture will attract many followers, as a liberal pursuit, the public must have proof that it really is one,—that, setting aside every consideration of utility, it is in this respect valuable for itself alone. The architect's ideas, even though they should exist merely on paper, belong as truly to art as those of the painter: the manual skill demanded in the one case is indeed infinitely less than in the other; but the mental power exhibited may be equally great. This however, it seems, people have yet to learn, for, except by professional men, such productions are considered absolutely valueless, and utterly inadmissible on the walls of a drawing-room. While the most mechanical productions, in the most doggrel style, frequently pass muster as pictures, and can find admirers to dote on the imbecility they

display, the sublimest conceptions, the most original and beautiful compositions in architecture would be rejected as totally
unfit for any other place than either the architect's own studio, or
that miserable refuge for the destitute, the library of the Royal
Academy.* It is hardly to be expected that those whose opinions
on matters of taste are only the echo of others' dicta, should affect
to value what they see generally slighted, and considered of so
little importance as to be treated as a mere humble dependent.
We are not very solicitous to claim acquaintance with one who
is uniformly banished to a side-table in the dining-, or to the
farthest corner in the drawing-room, but rather avoid him as if
his insignificance were contagious. The countenance which architecture receives from the Somerset House conclave is not much
unlike that bestowed on such unhappy nobodies whose presence
is tolerated, that their inferiority may be the more apparent; and
we have little doubt but that the vilest dauber of faces conceives
himself an infinitely greater artist than a Gandy or a Parke. In
the opinion of the academicians, any hole will do for architectural
drawings, and any method of hanging them, so that the walls be
but covered from top to bottom: it being of no moment with respect to such subjects whether three-fourths of them can be seen or
not; besides, those which are in the latter predicament are, at least,
beyond the reach of criticism. We are by no means apt to attach
much importance to affairs of mere etiquette, yet we cannot help
thinking that it would be better were architecture treated not quite
so unceremoniously, inasmuch as it would then have a chance of
meeting with some attention from the public. For our part, we
do not conceive it to be altogether politic, as far as the interests
of architecture are concerned, that architectural designs and models should be exhibited along with paintings; for in the kind of
partnership that subsists between the two arts, the one we are
here speaking of is invariably the junior partner; *proximus, longo
tamen intervallo.* Nay, it is not even the firm of " Painting and
Architecture:" for *that* would have some little show of respect,
—but merely " Painting and Co." We would advise her, there-

---

* While writing this, we learn with extreme regret and surprise, that Mr. J. Gandy's
drawings have just been disposed of by the hammer. Among them was his magnificent
series of designs for a palace, which were knocked down to Mr. Decimus Burton for a
few pounds! and many others of equal merit were purchased by the Wyatts and Wy-
attvilles for less, as a morning paper remarks, than they would have charged for the
plan of a pig-stye. Can any thing more strongly proclaim the ignorance and apathy
prevailing with regard to drawings of this class, than that works which, considered as
productions of art, were worthy of being placed in the cabinets of men of taste, should
sell as mere lumber? In the estimation of the public, a man who maps out race-horses,
and takes the portraits of donkeys, is an artist; but the poetical visions of a Gandy
will hardly earn for him the reputation of being a tolerable mechanic.

fore, to announce a dissolution of partnership in the gazette, and to open shop on her own account. In the " provinces," where you purchase your snuff and your coffee at the same counter, art must always be a general dealer; but surely it is hardly necessary that such should be the case in the metropolis of the British empire.

To speak less figuratively, it would, in our opinion, prove highly conducive to the interests of the art, and tend very much to engage public attention in its favour, were a separate Academy of Architecture established, which should have not only an annual exhibition of its own, but likewise a permanent gallery of prize designs and models, which latter ought to be put upon the same footing as the National Collection of Pictures, and opened gratuitously to visitors and students throughout the whole year. A series of models of the most celebrated buildings, both of ancient and modern times, properly classified and arranged in different rooms according either to their localities, styles, or dates, could not fail to be attractive. Even those for whom mere architectural drawings have at present no interest, would be gratified by such representations, and would acquire a relish for those of a different kind; while the scholar, the antiquary, the traveller—in short, every person with any tincture of liberal studies, would eagerly profit by the sources of instruction thus opened to them. Models are not only far more intelligible to persons in general than geometrical drawings, but likewise more satisfactory than perspective views, inasmuch as they exhibit the subject completely, from any distance and from any point. That the formation of such a museum would be an undertaking of some magnitude in point of expense, and a labour of many years, we are perfectly aware: but there can be no doubt that it would prove extensively beneficial, and be worthy of a civilized age and nation.*

What we have just said must be considered as little more than a brief and immature hint; and we have here introduced it rather for the purpose of showing what is *not* done, than with the slightest hope that any institution of the kind will ever be formed.

---

* Were one apartment, for instance, devoted to Grecian architecture, the subjects might be so arranged as to exhibit the progressive improvement or decline in each order. Of each of the principal edifices there ought to be two models; one exhibiting the building in its actual state, the other a restoration of it; on the walls of the room there might also be drawings and views of the same structures, or of such parts of them as could not be so well understood from the models themselves. Some exceedingly beautiful models of the Parthenon and other Athenian edifices were lately to be seen at Messrs. Browne and Co.'s gallery, University-street, which ought to be visited by every person of taste for the numerous specimens it contains of ornamental architecture and sculpture, and other works of *virtù*. We may here also mention Mr. Day's ingenious and tasteful models, executed both from his own designs, and those of living architects.

That which beyond every thing else would contribute to the advancement of the art is public encouragement, of which the portion that falls to its share is trifling indeed, although many will think that of this it is now certainly obtaining its full share. And so, in truth, it does, as far as mere building is concerned; and as far as encouragement means nothing more than pounds, shillings, and pence. Were architecture no more than shoe-making or coat-making, this would be all very well; the patronage it receives, sufficiently ample. The *trade* flourishes, but the *art*—how are we to finish the sentence? By " encouragement" we understand something more than employment, conceiving it to mean an intelligent appreciation, and liberal patronage of the powers of architecture as a fine art. If the majority of the public be altogether ignorant of its nature in this respect; if they are satisfied with the vulgar tawdriness of most of the terraces in the Regent's Park; if they affect to admire the 'style' of Belgrave-square, and fancy its dowdiness to be beauty, the old cast-off frippery it exhibits, grandeur,—it is almost idle to talk of encouragement. Quantity, not quality, is their criterion of merit: show them but huge buildings with plenty of columns,—and no matter how common-place, stale, or absolutely bungling and incoherent the things thus nicknamed designs,—their suffrages are won. Oftentimes has it been our lot to hear the vilest of all vile things in architecture extolled as fine; rarely indeed have we met with any one who admired the few really exquisite beauties to be met with in one or two pieces of architecture. Although no one has yet discovered the art of obtaining the flavour of a single slice of pine-apple from a cartload of turnips, our very goodnatured and indulgent public have ascertained that a score of tawdry little houses put together have quite the air of a palace; yet show them a shop-front designed with the most elegant gusto, and displaying more originality than is to be seen in half-a-dozen palaces, and they will be unable to perceive any particular merit in it.*

It must be admitted that the encouragement which architecture at present receives from us, is somewhat like that which a singer would feel in exerting his powers before a room of deaf spectators: there are some perhaps to whom the knowledge of the company's infirmity might give confidence and satisfaction; and there are

---

* There is a gem of this description in Bond-street, which is really a study for the beautiful invention and finished elegance it exhibits. It is, of course, far beneath the dignity of our critical wiseacres to take any notice of such things, but it is singular that it should have escaped the notice of a professional man, and that Mr. Elmes should not have introduced it into " Jones's Views of London," seeing that, for want of better materials, he was obliged to eke out that work by such subjects as the Licensed Victuallers' School at Kennington.

also many, doubtless, styling themselves architects, who may be of opinion that the public are quite as well informed as is desirable.   At times, indeed, we do hear something like dissatisfaction and wonder expressed with regard to several of the new churches. In the former feeling we ourselves participate; not altogether in the latter, because it is tolerably evident that those who had the management of such jobs, either knew nothing of, or cared absolutely nothing for the architectural part of the concern.   No regard is paid in such cases to public opinion, and for very obvious, if not altogether satisfactory reasons;—namely, because there is no public opinion—no public interest about such matters: unable to judge for themselves, people believe whatever they are told, or at least fancy whatever they please.   It is unquestionably but a matter of taste after all; yet in most other things which are equally so, although the million do not quite relish *caviare,* they are not to be humbugged in so flagrant a manner. It is in vain for Mr. Colburn to assert in every newspaper in England, that some of his writers are quite equal to Sir Walter Scott: the world will not believe him, and works of intense interest and intense scandal drop, somehow or other, after a single brief season, into the tomb of all the Capulets.   Neither would it be possible for any theatrical manager—were he brainless enough to make the experiment, to palm off a cracked-voiced singer as the rival of a Billington or a Catalani.   In architecture, on the contrary, the public are for the most part so grossly ignorant that they do not even suspect they have anything whatever to learn; or they have perhaps picked up a few obsolete and worn-out scraps of criticism, which, like some kind of lies, are repeated from mouth to mouth until at last they are believed.   They read in some grandame's school-book that Inigo Jones was a great architect; and,—Heaven help us!—that he first introduced the Grecian style into this country.   Well, but admitting that Inigo might pass as a prodigy in his day, when the great Nash had not risen on the horizon of art, the only wonder now is, that he should have been admired so long, and indeed at all; for those who have examined his designs published by Kent must admit that there is very little to commend even in the best of them, while some of them are so hideous and barbarous, as to defy the power of imagination to conceive anything more truly detestable.   Yet this is the man whose name perpetually dins our ears whenever architecture is mentioned.   To what then, it will be asked, does Jones owe his reputation?—not to his own strength, but to the weakness of his contemporaries; to the accident of position.   He imported the Palladian style; and his name consequently forms an epoch from which a new æra assumes its date.   He was, in truth, little more than an indiscriminate imitator of the Venetian school, copying its defects and absurdities, its puerilities and vices, as well as its real merits. We admit that his errors and deficiencies are to be ascribed in a great degree to the age in which he lived; yet although this may excuse his defects, it does not remove them.

For at least a dozen times have we been on the point of apologizing to our readers for our apparently strange digressions. Some of them, too, may opine that we shall have concluded our article before we even touch upon the work that serves as the text to it. We are, however, now approaching that point, since, luckily, the mention of Inigo Jones has reminded us that two volumes of architectural biography by M. Quatremère de Quincy, are at this moment lying before us. It was with no small anticipations that we first opened them, for not only did the name of the author lead to expect something very superior to a mere dictionary-like compilation; but we trusted that we should meet with some important additions to this class of biography: we wish we could add that these expectations have been realized. According to the plan he laid down, M. de Quincy has noticed only the ‘ most celebrated’ architects ; so that of course we did not look for any new names in the earlier part of the work, since none had escaped previous notice in similar publications, but we did trust that we should discover among the later articles, some which, if the names themselves were not unknown to us, would yet supply many particulars of which we were ignorant. With the single exception, however, of the notice of Gondouin, there is nothing with which we were before unacquainted. To say the truth, notwithstanding the explana on he has given in his preface, we do not quite understand M. deiQuincy's ideas of celebrity, for if he has passed over many names as not coming up to that standard, he has introduced several which, in our opinion, are far beneath it. The author is so far consistent that he makes reputation rather than merit guide him in his selection ; and in conformity with this, has given a notice of Borromini, to which we do not object, inasmuch as he is certainly celebrated, and the record of his extravagances may operate as a useful warning to others. But it puzzles us to see Van Campen's name on the list of celebrated architects,—a name we hardly ever hear of, or see mentioned, although he had the merit of building one of the greatest masses of insignificance in all Europe, the Stadthouse at Amsterdam. He is, indeed, noticed by Milizia, but then his work is more comprehensive, and does not affect to confine itself to artists of first-rate distinction ; and we may remark that, with the exception of being somewhat more minute in the description of Van Campen's *chef-d'œuvre,* the French writer follows Milizia's account step by step. From this and one or two other circumstances, we suspect that his own convenience had its full weight in determining the biographer's opinion as to the necessary degree of celebrity; otherwise he would hardly have omitted many artists of quite as much pretension as several whom he has inserted in his collection, but of whom it was not so easy to meet with notices already prepared to his hand.

On the score of omission, M. Quatremère de Quincy is candid enough in his preface to admit that his work is very open to criticism in this respect; excuses of this kind, however, cost little, nor would there have been any occasion for such deprecation of criticism had he been conscious that he had passed over nothing which his readers had a right to expect as essential to his object. Instead of this we do not find a single Swedish, German, Spanish, or Portuguese architect mentioned in the whole work, and but very few English ones. In the appendix at the end of the second volume, are brief notices of about forty architects of less eminence than the preceding ones, and among them of our countryman Gibbs; no mention, however, is made of Vanbrugh, who, we should imagine, ought hardly to have been passed over in silence, if only on account of his singularities. Neither does M. de Quincy condescend to enrol among his 'plus célèbres architectes,' Adam, Stuart, Chambers, Wyatt; nor Ventura Rodriguez; nor Von Knobelsdorff, and Langhans; nor Quarenghi; none of whom are so obscure or so unworthy as not to merit a niche in this pantheon of genius, beside such men as Van Campen, Le Mercier, Mansart, Gabriel, and Antoine. Neither was Calderari, the countryman of Palladio, undeserving of being associated with him here. Still we must admit that M. de Quincy is tolerably impartial, since he has also omitted Dewailly, Ledoux, Leroi, and some French architects of no mean note. Some of the preceding cannot, it is true, be held up as exactly praiseworthy, much less as entirely faultless models: Robert Adam, for example, oftener calls forth our censure than our admiration; with a redundance of frivolous embellishment, most of his designs exhibit a penurious nakedness that forms a more singular than agreeable contrast; yet an able critic would experience no difficulty in eliciting much valuable instruction from his very defects; neither was he altogether without his merits, for even his least perfect works generally contain some good and original ideas, while in all that relates to interior distribution, and to piquant variety in the form and distribution of apartments, he was, for the most part eminently happy. If on no other account, he was certainly entitled to notice as having formed a kind of revolution in our architectural taste; and for venturing to deviate from the frigid, monotonous formality of his predecessors. With regard to Stuart, it cannot be said that he executed any great number of buildings, nor, with the exception of the chapel at Greenwich Hospital, of such importance as to claim for him extraordinary distinction as a practical architect; nevertheless, his name ought to occupy a prominent situation in the architectural history of the eighteenth century, since it is to his labours that we are indebted for emancipation from the vicious taste that had so long pervaded Europe. Like another Luther, he effected a reformation that has subverted the authority of Rome, and opened our eyes to its enormous abominations. Did we not fear that our comparison might appear rather too bold, not to say profane, we could pursue the parallel much farther, and point out some striking resemblances between the infallibility of the Vatican, and the infallibility of the college of Italian architects. Leroi is, we presume, excluded for nearly the same reasons as Stuart; but it is not so easy to divine wherefore the architect of Somerset house was not judged worthy of a place in M. de Quincy's " Elysium," especially as the materials for a biographical memoir of him might have been obtained without any difficulty. Among those whom we are surprised at not finding recorded in this work, we have mentioned James Wyatt, not because we ourselves entertain any very high opinion of him, but because he undoubtedly enjoyed quite as much celebrity or vogue as any of his contemporaries, certainly far more than he would have obtained had he been born half a century later. Hardly ever has an equal degree of reputation been acquired by similar mediocrity of talent; for his merits were little more than negative; and he was rather a clever builder of houses, than an artist. His style was feeble, and void of dignity,—insignificant and mannered; and is of that convenient ready-made sort which suits just every thing and nothing. It is by no means astonishing, therefore, that he was able to execute so much, but there can be little doubt that he would have achieved more for his reputation had he done less. It has been the fashion to talk of the simplicity and elegance of his designs, two qualities that have never struck us in any of the buildings of his that we have seen; for we are rather inclined to impute to them sterility of invention, meanness in the profiles, and a degree of nakedness that causes them to look unfinished. The taste of that man was surely not very refined, who conceived little upright ovals, like the old-fashioned looking-glass frames, to be graceful ornaments for the front of a house; or who over mere holes in the walls, for windows, sometimes introduced a series of panels, each containing, by way of embellishment, a rag of drapery, looking particularly like a dish-clout hung up to take the air, in that conspicuous situation. With such feelings, we are not at all indignant with M. de Quincy, although neither the Grecian beauties of the Oxford-street portico, nor the Gothic magnificence of the front of the House of Lords could induce him to apotheosize the architect whom our Horace Walpole, of virtú and critical memory, was pleased to commend. As for Ventura Rodriguez, and the others we have mentioned, whose names he has not inserted even in his appendix, we can only suppose that they altogether escaped M. de Quincy's erudite and laborious researches. The tenour of our preceding remarks renders it unnecessary for us to say that this work puts us in possession of hardly any new information whatever; and although it is a more readable book than Milizia's lives, it is by no means so useful as one of reference, particularly in Mrs. E. Cresy's translation, which contains several additional lives. We ought to observe, however, that M. de Quincy's volumes possess one great recommendation, namely, the plates, which are very well engraved, in outline, and give a specimen of each architect's style, commencing with the cathedral of Pisa, built by Buschetto, 1063, and terminating with Soufflot's church of St. Geneviève; and as what is considered the chef-d'œuvre of each master has been selected for this species of illustration, we may conclude that it so far faintly adumbrates the architectural glories of the last eight centuries. The elevations in general are upon far too small a scale to show more than the leading features of the design, and to serve as graphic illustrations to the text; but they are quite sufficient to convince any unprejudiced person that these masterpieces have nothing in common with Grecian architecture. Nevertheless, such as the Italian style is, people fancied that they perceived in it all the beauties of the antique, although one would think that the Pantheon at Rome was alone sufficient to convince them of their mistake. Grecian architecture was absolutely unknown except by name, consequently they are not to be censured for not appreciating what they had no conception of; but it is strange that they should have affected to despise the Gothic style as barbarous and disfigured by abundance of minute ornament and petty members,—for its irregularity and grotesque fancies, when their own style exhibited the same, with this especial difference, that the very qualities that were congenial to the one were at variance with the professed principles of the other. Where two or more orders are placed one over the other, as in many Italian façades, and they consist only of pilasters, or half-columns, the resemblance which the forms themselves bear to those of classical architecture merely serves to render the very contrary method of applying them more obvious : the likeness is of that kind which provokes a disadvantageous comparison, just as some single feature in the face of a plain woman sometimes calls to our recollection a beautiful countenance. What is termed Gothic architecture is, on the contrary, so totally dissimilar from the antique,—whether Grecian or Egyptian,— that we can no more compare them together than we can a horse and an eagle. We cannot, therefore, be shocked at the difference between the two, when similarity is quite out of the question. Instead of considering and admiring the Gothic and Lombard styles for their own peculiar beauties and modes of expression, the *cinquecento* critics very philosophically tried it by rules with which they have no more to do than an English jury with the laws of Confucius. They looked at such buildings with Vitruvius in their hands, and made the notable discovery that their proportions were faulty, or rather that there were no proportions at all : that is, they chuckled at their own sagacity because they could demonstrate that the eagle was not a quadruped! *ergo*, &c. forgetting all the while their own unbecoming procerity of ears, or in other words that their own ' regular' style was of rather an ignoble, mulish description, and that the alliance they claimed with the ancients might as well have been kept a secret. It is really diverting to hear with what gravity some of the orthodox critics descant on eurythmia, symmetry and proportions, in speaking of a species of architecture wherein it rarely happens that anything of the kind is to be observed; and to mark the ridiculous importance attached to the observance of a few specific rules, while the principles that first dictated them are altogether lost sight of. Such narrow-minded, grovelling, pettifogging criticism, which is punctiliously observant of the letter of architectural law, in trifles, at the same time that it disregards its spirit, pervades nearly all that has ever been written on the subject; the consequence of which is, that the opinions once so firmly established are now nearly valueless, and will soon be quite obsolete.

We ourselves will not act so unjustly towards Italian architecture, as its exclusive admirers have done towards every other style, for we admit that it has produced many noble and beautiful structures, although they are but few compared with the greater number. But the system itself is decidedly inferior to that of the Greeks, of which it is merely a dialect, not like the Gothic, a distinct language. It is, moreover, a dialect far less harmonious, polished, copious, and expressive than the parent language, and far better suited to the prose of common life, than to the poetry of art. One of the absurd and vulgar prejudices which well-bred people ought to be ashamed of, as fit only for ladies' maids and other slipslop gentry, is, that " Italian architecture" necessarily implies something very beautiful and elegant, whereas it as frequently means the very reverse. We have few buildings that in unmeaning jumble, barbarousness, and cumbrous frippery, rival Gibbs's Church, in the Strand, his first production after his return from the "classic soil of Italy," but which he might have designed with equal taste, had he confined his studies to a pastry-cook's shop. While it lasted, this blind and bigotted admiration of Italian architecture not only did much positive harm, but prevented much good, by rendering people totally insensible to the exquisite beauties of the styles which it superseded, both here and on the continent. It is perhaps our misfortune that we have no faith in cabalistic words and charms : the terms Doric, Ionic, or Corinthian, have no meaning for us, until we know how those orders are applied, since it not unfrequently happens that the order itself has far less to do with the general character of the edifice, than any thing else; and even in the best works of the Italian school there is generally something evincing a terrible obliquity of taste, and neutralizing what might otherwise be beauties. Palladio himself will furnish us with not a few examples of the most intolerable deformities, such as diminutive straggling columns, lofty pedestals, broken entablatures and pediments, hideous attics and balustrades, huge scrolls and other nondescript crankum ornaments. We are certainly not compelled to imitate his blunders and vices, together with his merits, yet even at the best, the style which derives its name from him, cannot, if it retain any thing of its original character, enter into any competition with Grecian architecture. So far then, we differ *toto cœlo* from a late writer (Gwilt) who carries his predilection for the Palladian school so far, as to doubt whether our national taste be at all improved since the time of Burlington and Kent, adducing in support of his opinion Lord Leicester's celebrated villa, designed by the latter. That Holkham House is one of the finest pieces of architecture of its class and period, that its interior displays a felicitous combination of beauties, and a remarkably pure and elegant taste, none will more readily admit than ourselves ; at the same time we cannot but feel that it would have been far more beautiful, more imposing in effect, more varied in its details, and also more picturesque, had its author been acquainted with Grecian architecture. To say the truth, Mr. Gwilt's opinion appears to us so extraordinary, that we could almost suppose him to have seen but very few of our lately erected buildings, which are not only very superior to any thing of a former period in all that relates to detail, but also for a decided improvement in design. Perhaps he will hardly allow that the study of Grecian form has had any beneficial influence on our taste in ornamental furniture; and if so, our astonishment ceases.   Mr. Gwilt, however, is not the only one who entertains similar views, for a writer in the *Gentleman's Magazine,* (for aught we can tell Mr. G. himself,) most lack-a-daisically bewails the degeneracy of the architecture of the present day.   " Pejor fit ætas," says this critic, " we boldly affirm that there is neither grandeur of effect, nor chastity of design in very numerous modern structures." With the qualification contained in the latter part of the sentence, the assertion must be allowed to be tolerably correct, since it is undeniable that there are many recent buildings to which the censure applies.   The question is, whether there have not, of late years, been erected a proportionably greater number of important buildings than at any former period of the two last centuries,* and distinguished by a nobler style of composition, and by greater purity and elegance of taste.   To this the answer cannot but be in the affirmative, unless we admit that the façade of the London University, with its rich decastyle portico; the New Corn Exchange, the most original and happy modern application of a genuine Greek style; the New Post Office,† the Church of St. Pancras, the Athenæum Club House, and the splendid group of ornamental buildings at Hyde Park Corner, besides many others erected both in the metropolis and various provincial towns, ought to yield the palm to such pieces of architecture as the churches and Companies' Halls in the city, or to such a specimen of decoration as Temple Bar, or such a sample of magnificence as the Adelphi or to such frigid mediocrity as Marlborough and Chesterfield Houses.   Should more satisfactory proof of the superiority of the present generation of architects over their predecessors be demanded, we would refer to the British Museum, as furnishing the

---

* Of forty-eight porticoes in London, forty-one have been erected since 1809, or within twenty years, an increase that evinces pretty strongly the greater attention now bestowed on ornamental architecture.

† Although we mention this building as exhibiting an improved style of design, it is rather to be commended for its simplicity and good taste, and for the noble appearance which it derives from its extent, than for any particularly fine quality it exhibits as a work of art.   The portico certainly deserves great praise; yet we think that Mr. Smirke has not availed himself as he might easily have done of the opportunities afforded by the nature of the structure.   Had he, instead of continuing the wall between the two antæ within the portico, made here an opening into the hall, with no other separation than two columns, in a line with the two centre ones in front, not only would the effect of such a vista have been exceedingly picturesque, and the perspective richly varied, but this circumstance alone would have given the whole building a very marked and appropriate character, different from that of any other public edifice.   Nor would this have been attended with the slightest inconvenience of any kind, either as regards the security of the building by night, or the necessary degree of shelter from the weather. Mr. Smirke is an exact copyist, and a sensible architect; but he is not a man of genius, and possesses but very little invention.

most ready means of comparing almost simultaneously the opposite tastes of the 17th and 19th centuries;—a stronger antithesis, a more violent contrast cannot be pointed out.

We by no means intend either to say that there were no structures of any merit erected during the last century, or to deny that several of those lately erected are very abortive efforts ; but even some of these latter would have been considered very creditable in point of design, had they been erected fifty or sixty years ago, and many that now scarcely excite attention would then have been esteemed of some importance.   While, however, we readily acknowledge that the present taste in architecture, both here and on the continent, is greatly superior to what it was in the days of the Palladios and Mansarts, we also feel that very much remains to be accomplished before architecture shall be emancipated from the errors and trammels of a mechanical system, and acquire that independence which is the birthright of every one of the fine arts. We have discarded most of the vicious tricks and unseemly grimaces, that were formerly reckoned very becoming and graceful, and are now acknowledged to be absurd; we have likewise naturalized among us many of the pure and refined beauties of Grecian architecture ; yet although this is laudable in itself, and was quite as much as could be expected, it will not suffice for the future.   We must either advance or retrograde : art cannot be kept stationary to one point, fixed for ever in the same attitude, without becoming spiritless, languid and insipid.   Of this there is ample evidence in the history, both of art and literature : after such a degree of excellence has been attained that further effort seems useless, and all that apparently remains to be done, is to adhere as closely as possible to the models thus furnished, then comes the drowsy age of indolent imitation and mechanical routine, getting every day more and more dull, till some new impulse be given to it, and intellect starts afresh.   Now that we have copied long enough to have got beyond mere school-boy exercises, it behoves us to aim at something higher than the mere *manner* of the antique,—to study its spirit,—since such study alone will enable us to produce anything superior to mere fac-similes, and elevate us from being the imitators, to being the rivals of the artists of Greece.

According to the present system, even our most unexceptionable specimens of architecture are little more than *centos*, composed of features, every one of which is borrowed from some ancient example, and thus put together with more or less skill ; a mode of designing that appears to be quite the reverse of that practised at the best period of the art, when every part of an edifice seems to have been designed expressly for that individual occasion, or so modified as to render it conformable to the character of the whole fabric. Hence that variety, and great latitude in design, which we observe in all the choicest examples of Grecian architecture, so that it is impossible to meet with any two precisely similar. Rarely indeed do the moderns attempt any novelty of this kind,—for mere fancies and caprices do not constitute invention: it requires consummate taste and skill in a painter to give a figure a new and happy attitude; but the veriest dauber can draw a man standing on his head. Before an artist can hope to become original through study, he must know what originality means, and must possess that innate delicacy of taste which will enable him to distinguish at once new modes of beauty from untried shapes of absurdity. But even while architects profess to copy the antique, they have altogether neglected some of its greatest merits: how they can look at such works as Stuart's Athens, and not be struck by one of the most palpable and effective beauties of Grecian architecture; or, if they perceive it, how it has happened that they have never hitherto adopted what would impart such spirit and variety to their compositions, is to us truly astonishing. In the former case what are we to think of their observation,—in the latter of their taste? What we allude to is, moreover, one of those remarkably simple things that without any precedent for it, would occur instinctively to any one who ever bestowed any thought upon a design. In all probability therefore, its extreme simplicity and propriety caused it to be quite overlooked by the followers of that school, which has distinguished itself by endeavouring to reconcile the most frigid and irrational pedantry with the most intolerable licentiousness.

The nineteenth century, however, has commenced auspiciously, and has already produced many fine monuments of architecture, far surpassing in grandeur of manner, in originality of design, in variety of composition, and in elegance of taste, the *classical* structures of modern Italy, and the vaunted *chefs-d'œuvre* of the age of Louis XIV. We have already mentioned some buildings as favourable specimens of the ability of our own living architects, nor will the student find beyond the Alps more congenial and correct models on which to form his taste. With far greater advantage, both to himself and his profession, might he now direct his steps towards Germany, where he will behold many recently erected structures of surpassing beauty. Several of the new buildings with which Schinkel has embellished Berlin are conceived in a spirit worthy of Greece itself; and must satisfy every one that that architect well merits the appellation of *Formendichter*, applied to him by his countryman Seidel, so poetical and picturesque is his composition, so tasteful his style, so happy his

invention. The new Theatre, the new Museum, and the Wacht-
gebäude, in that city, sufficiently attest his genius and his taste;
nor ought we to forget the truly princely mansion erected by him
at Krzescowice, for Count Potocki, compared with which most
of the bewondered palazzi and villas of Italy appear both mean
and barbarous. Leo Klenze, another of the living architects of
Germany, has also proved himself worthy of the name of artist,*
and has manifested in his designs the vigour of native talent combined with a masterly emulation of the antique. It is to him that
Munich is indebted for its Glyptotheca, which not only enshrines
some of the most valuable treasures of art in the world, but is a
beautiful work of art itself. Thus in Germany, which until lately
had hardly any modern structures that could be viewed with a
feeling short of disgust, and whose palaces were caricatures of
the worst French and Italian styles, a new æra of the art has commenced: that Gallomania which so long infected both their literature and their architecture, rendering them the imbecile imitators of a people by whom they were despised, is now, happily,
banished altogether; and Germany may be said to have emancipated itself from a double thraldom, intellectual as well as political. The little kingdom of Bavaria alone has already done
more for the advancement of the fine arts, than most of the weal-
thiest nations of Europe. Munich, its capital, possesses, in addition to the treasures of its Glyptotheca and Pinacotheca, numerous other attractions for every class of artists, and all persons
of taste : among others the noble frescoes that adorn the arcades
in the garden of the palace, where the pencils of Cornelius and
his associates have produced a series of truly magnificent historical compositions, while our English artists content themselves
with manufacturing pretty little namby-pamby subjects for al-
bums and annuals. Vienna, Dresden, Stuttgard, Leipzig, Weimar, Cassel, Darmstadt, and Carlsruhe, have likewise all of
them been considerably embellished of late years : in the last-
mentioned city, and in other parts of Baden, numerous public
and private buildings were erected by Weinbrenner, who died
March 1st, 1825; and whose autobiography was published not
long ago.

Denmark has never been distinguished for its taste in architecture, nor has that degree of improvement taken place for
which there was such ample room, and for which also, from time

---

* Both Schinkel and Klenze are men of varied and extensive attainments, and profi-
cients in many other branches of art besides that which they follow professionally. The
former has even displayed considerable talent as a landscape painter; and the latter
is an able scholar in architectural archæology. Schinkel was born at Neuruppin,
March 13th, 1781 ; Klenze in 1784.

to time, very favourable opportunities have presented themselves. If we may judge from the designs published by M. Hansen, a celebrated architect at Copenhagen, of the buildings executed by him, our opinion is anything but favourable. M. Hansen is undoubtedly original in 'his way,' for he displays many ideas that are more singular than beautiful; but his style is a strange medley of incoherent parts. The façade of the new Radhuus or Town Hall, at Copenhagen, has some good points, and but for the perverse taste it so studiously exhibits, and the hideousness of some of the details, might be pronounced a composition of considerable merit. We cannot now enter into such an analysis of the design as would justify our criticism, yet we may remark one curious instance of his infelicity, which is, that in the hexastyle Ionic portico, he has left the shafts of the columns plain, while he has fluted the faces of the antæ, or rather the pilasters; nor is it merely by solecisms of this kind that he offends.

Russia, so long an unknown region to the historians of the fine arts, will henceforth demand a chapter in the annals of architecture. At present, however, that country contains few structures that will satisfy a fastidious taste. The edifices in her two capitals are rather distinguished by a certain dreary vastness, than by grandeur of manner, and the finer qualities of art. Travellers descant on rows of palaces and palace-like edifices, adorned with "Grecian" columns and colonnades: whereas the truth is, the majority of these buildings are more like barracks, the chief attempt at design consisting only in such *parasitical* embellishment—if embellishment it may be termed—as meagre columns and pilasters stuck between the naked holes left for the windows. Hence there is an air of meanness and poverty arising from the incoherent contrast, which is totally at variance with art, whose object is to please. Greece has certainly not furnished the taste here displayed: in fact most of the architects employed have been either foreigners, or natives who have formed their style in Italy and France. Among the former was the ' celebrated' Quarenghi (born at Bergamo, 1744, died Feb. 1817,) whose name we have already mentioned. Greatly as he has been cried up, he gave no proofs of any superior talent: without anything particularly faulty or offensive, except as regards their vulgar, careless detail, his buildings exhibit little to call forth admiration; and his manner may be characterised as consisting in a certain second-hand gentility. Both his designs and those of Rusca are very monotonous, and their architecture a kind of reformed Palladian, or Italian, divested indeed of some of its excrescences, but colder and more insipid; for the vices that have been weeded out have not been succeeded by beauties transplanted from elsewhere. Of such reformers it may truly be said, *solitudinem faciunt, pacem appellant.* Far more ability and taste have been evinced by Stazov, Melkinov, Mikhailov, and some of the living native architects of Russia. The new Theatre at Moscow, designed by the last-mentioned of these, is a particularly noble pile of building, with a magnificent octastyle portico of the Ionic order, the columns of which are somewhat more than forty feet in height.

Our limits prevent us from extending, as we easily might do, this rapid and cursory glance at the architecture of those parts of the continent which have hitherto been quite over-looked by all writers on the subject. We must therefore content ourselves with having endeavoured to call the attention of professional men and others to the numerous fine buildings that are to be met with in places not yet mapped down in the connoisseur's chart. We are of opinion, too, that some of our topographical and architectural draftsmen might safely venture to speculate upon a professional tour to countries less familiar to us than France or Italy.

. Although we have said little on M. Quatremére de Quincy's work, we have sufficiently expressed our opinion of it. We cannot conscientiously recommend it as a performance evincing any particular research, or any very original and enlightened criticism. Almost all that it contains has been long ago given to the public: nevertheless it will be useful to those who possess no similar work of reference, and as it certainly possesses a very attractive exterior, and a considerable number of illustrations, it may thereby excite curiosity towards the subject, where it did not previously exist. The history of architecture, however, particularly of modern architecture, including all the *Post-Roman* styles, or those which had their origin subsequently to the overthrow of the empire, remains to be written; all that has hitherto been done being little more than imperfect outlines of such a history, or detached essays. There are likewise a multitude of topics connected with architecture as a fine art, none of which have yet been treated of at all; for writers on architecture, like architects themselves, have been content to tread in the beaten track of routine, without diverging to the right or the left. But if we have much to learn, we have also no little to unlearn,—not a few prejudices to abandon, and many irrational and superstitious opinions to discard. Whoever intends to overthrow the hydra absurdities that beset the entrance to the fane of art, ought to approach them resolutely, and combat them manfully: he must feel no compunctions, no qualms of heart, no misgivings, no apprehensions. Hardly may we hope that any one will devote his time and energies to what appears such a Quixotic enterprise; yet of one thing we may be certain, that until either the rights of art shall have been successfully vindicated, or time shall have silently worked a complete reform, so long must architecture. continue degraded and unhonoured. Nor do we absolutely despair of such reform taking place; nay, we may even venture to say that there is a prospect now dawning upon us, which, unless it should prove a mere mirage, announces that some of the finest productions of modern architecture, and some of the highest names in the art, are destined to be recorded in the annals of the nineteenth century.

ART. IX.—1. *Josephi Mariae Suaresii, Episcopi Vasionensis, Notitia Basilicorum.* Recensuit et observationibus auxit D. Christianus Fridericus Pohlius, Civitatis Lipsiensis Senator et Syndicus. Lipsiæ, 1804, 8vo.

2. *Manuale Basilicorum, exhibens Collationem Juris Justinianei cum Jure Graeco Postjustinianeo, Indicem Auctorum recentiorum qui Libros Juris Romani e Graecis Subsidiis vel emendaverunt vel interpretati sunt, ac Titulos Basilicorum cum Jure Justinianeo et reliquis Monumentis Juris Graeci Postjustinianei comparatos.* Digessit D. Christ. Gottl. Haubold, Eques Ordinis Sax. Virtutis Civicae, et Juris Professor Publ. Ord. in Academia Lipsiensi. Lipsiæ, 1819, 4to.

3. *De Basilicorum Origine, Fontibus, Scholiis, atque nova Editione adornanda.* Scripsit D. Carol. Guilielm. Ernest. Heimbach. Lipsiæ, 1825, 8vo.

IN this country the history of the civil law is so imperfectly understood, that there are probably many eminent lawyers who, in the whole course of their study and practice, never heard of such a book as the *Basilica*. A certain friend of ours in Lincoln's Inn, whom we rank among the most learned of the English lawyers, has a copy of this voluminous repertory of ancient jurisprudence, which long adorned the library of a celebrated bibliomanist, under the title of SANCTI BASILII OPERA, or the Works of St. Basil. Provided it was a fine copy with an ample margin, the contents of the book might be of little or no consequence to the possessor. This disinterested collector of books was not perhaps trained to the legal profession; but what shall be said of Mr. Pinkerton, who was educated as a lawyer, who advanced such high claims to general erudition, and who treated other men's errors with such merciless severity? "There is," as he is pleased to remark, "an originality in the Greek writers which forms and nurtures genius; the Latin only foster imitation. A divine or a physician ought to be grounded

H H 2

attention of modern lawyers was first directed by Angelo 'Poli-ziano, a man of singular talents'and attainments, who died in the year 1494. The earliest editions, containing the Greek text without a Latin version, were published by Viglius Zuichemus, a native of Friesland, who, after having been a professor of law in the universities of Padua and Ingolstadt, entered into holy orders, and became provost of the cathedral of Ghent.* His two editions, which both appeared in 1534, were followed by many others; and among these we must distinguish two different editions by Fabrot,† a very celebrated expounder of the Greek texts of the Roman law; but the fame of all former editors was totally eclipsed by Willem Otto Reitz, who published a splendid and most complete edition of Theophilus about the middle of last century.‡ This learned and judicious man, whose name we shall more than once have occasion to mention, was born in the year 1702, was appointed rector of the Gymnasium of Middelburg in Zeeland in 1741, and died in 1769. In the title-pages of different publications, he is described as *Jurisconsultus:* he had taken the degree of doctor of laws, but although eminently skilled in jurisprudence, his ordinary occupation was that of a classical instructor; and in the Dutch seminaries of learning, such attainments have very frequently been united in the same individuals. He belonged to a family which produced several scholars, and one of his brothers was the editor of Lucian, and the author of a work which is well known to philologers.§ Reitz's edition of Theophilus is so elaborate and satisfactory, that, in the opinion of Haubold, it is unequalled by any similar publication, except Ritter's edition of the Theodosian Code.‖

The *Corpus Juris Civilis,* as every student of the civil law is sufficiently aware, includes various constitutions written in the Greek language. The amended edition of the Code, *Codex repetitæ prælectionis,* was published in the year 534; but the emperor Justinian survived till the year 565, and during that long interval he promulgated many new laws. His Novels, or new Constitutions, which form the present collection, are one hundred and sixty-eight in number, and the greatest part of them appear to have been originally written in Greek; some were however written in Latin, and others were at the same time exhibited in both languages. These are followed by thirteen Greek edicts of

* Foppens Bibliotheca Belgica, tom. ii. p. 1153.

† Paris. 1638, 4to. Paris. 1657, 4to. Of the latter edition some copies have a new title, with the date of 1679.

‡ Hagæ Comitis, 1751, 2 tom. 4to.

§ Joan. Freder. Reitzius de Ambiguis, Mediis et Contrariis; sive de Significatione Verborum ac Phrasium ambigua. Traj. ad Rhen. 1752, 8vo.

‖ Hauboldi Institutiones Juris Romani Litterariæ, p. 205. Lipsiæ, 1809, 8vo.

Justinian, which properly conclude the body of the civil law; although the common editions comprehend various Novels of Leo, together with other ancient documents, all of which are only to be regarded as appendages. But as no branch of our present subject is so generally understood, we shall content ourselves with remarking, that the history of the Novels of Justinian has been very elaborately detailed by Biener,* and the history of the Novels of Leo by Beck and Zepernick.†

Of the Pandects of Justinian, different Greek versions have been mentioned by different writers. One version has been ascribed to Thalelæus, who was an antecessor in the time of that emperor; but Pohl and Heimbach have shewn, that there are no sufficient grounds for believing that he undertook such a task. Another translation is mentioned by Matthæus Blastares as having been executed by Stephanus, an advocate of Constantinople, who had been conjoined with Tribonian in the commission for compiling the Pandects. The same individual appears to have illustrated the other parts of Justinian's compilation; and some fragments of the works of Thalelæus and Stephanus have been published by Ruhnkenius. The Code was likewise translated into Greek: the translator is supposed to be the person who, in the scholia of the Basilica, is repeatedly described as Κωδικευτης. To many of the judges, as well as the suitors, in the Eastern empire, Latin must evidently have been an unknown tongue. When the seat of empire was transferred from Rome to Byzantium, the first emperors were anxious to transfer the use of the Roman language, and for a considerable period this continued to be at least the language of the court. Teachers of Roman eloquence were established in the second metropolis, and they doubtless found many pupils among the youth who aimed at a fashionable education, or were ambitious of preferment; but it was not to be expected that the great body of the people should be induced to unlearn one language, and to acquire another.

During the interval which elapsed between the reign of Justinian and that of Basilius, there were many Greek writers on the Roman Law; and not a few names have been recovered from the wreck of time by Lambecius, Suarés, Asseman,‡ and other

---

* Geschichte der Novellen Justinian's, von Dr. Friedrich August Biener, ordentl. Prof. d. Rechte zu Berlin. Berlin, 1824, 8vo.

† D. Caspar. Achatii Beck de Novellis Leonis Augusti et Philosophi, earumque Usu et Auctoritate liber singularis. Præmissa est Dissertatio de provida Dei Cura in dispensandis Jurisprudentiæ Fatis. Adjectis animadversionibus et mantissa commentationum ad argumentum spectantium, edidit D. Carolus Frider. Zepernick. Halæ, 1779, 8vo.

‡ Assemani Bibliotheca Juris Orientalis Canonici et Civilis. Romæ, 1762-6, 5 tom. 4to.

learned enquirers, and many accurate notices have now been added by Heimbach. Basilius, who has obtained a conspicuous place among the legislators of the empire, derived his lineage from Armenia, but was himself born in Macedonia, and is commonly known by the name of Basilius the Macedonian. He rose from an origin sufficiently humble, and after having been a groom, he became sovereign of the East. In the year 866, Michael the Third associated him in the government, under the title of Cæsar. His benefactor was a weak and dissolute prince; and when Basilius endeavoured to give a better direction to his conduct, he was exposed to suspicions and snares, against which he opposed the dagger of the assassin, and thus became sole emperor in the course of the ensuing year. Among candidates for empire, it is utterly vain to look for the most rigid principles of piety or virtue: Basilius however appears to have been a person of no ordinary character; of his taste for literature he has left a specimen in his Exhortations to his son Leo;* but his chief distinction arose from his attempt to form a complete body of law for the government of his dominions. The Eastern empire, in which the Greek language was vernacular, was governed by a collection of laws chiefly written in Latin ; and the different versions which had been executed, were without the sanction of public authority. It was therefore his object to select such enactments as were still in force, and, having digested them into the form of a regular code, to invest them with the imperial sanction. This great undertaking he did not live to complete. He died in the year 886, and was succeeded by his son Leo, who, in consequence of his studious propensity, obtained the surname of the Philosopher. His treatise on tactics was published by Meursius, and some of his other works are preserved in manuscript.† The body of Greek laws was completed under his direction: the date of its promulgation has not been ascertained; but as the student is referred to it in Leo's Ecloga, which was written in the year 910, the Basilica must have been in circulation before that period. Leo the Philosopher ended his reign and his life in the year 911, and was succeeded by his son Constantinus Porphyrogennetus, when only seven years of age. This learned prince likewise belongs to the catalogue of royal authors,‡ and from him the Basilica appear to have received their final revision. The revised edition is described by Theodorus Balsamon, in his commentary on the Nomocanon of Photius, as τὴν τελευταίαν

---

* Basilii Romanorum Imp. Exhortationum capita lxvi. ad Leonem filium, cognomento Philosophum. Lutetiæ, apud Federicum Morellum, 1584, 4to.
† Fabricii Bibliotheca Græca, tom. vi. p. 367, edit. Harles.
‡ Fabricii Bibliotheca Græca, tom. vii. p. 681.

ἀνακάθαρσιν;* and, according to the opinion of Heimbach, it was not divulged before the year 945. Whether the work has descended to our times as it was completed by Leo, or as it was afterwards reformed by Constantinus, has been disputed among the historians of the Roman jurisprudence. Brunquell avers that we now possess the Basilica in their revised form;† but Hoffmann considers this opinion as extremely doubtful,‡ and his suggestions seem to be confirmed by the subsequent investigations of Heimbach.§

This great digest of the law received the title of the Basilica, τῶν Βασιλικῶν, derived, according to some writers, from the name of the emperor Basilius, or, according to others, from the circumstance of its containing βασιλικὰς διατάξεις, or imperial constitutions. In the West it never obtained the force of law; and its utility therefore consists in the illustration which it furnishes to the Justinian body of law, from which it is chiefly compiled. Its utility in this respect has long been understood and acknowledged. The advantages to be derived from a careful examination of the Basilica, were first exhibited in the writings, and more particularly in the *Observationes*, of Cujacius, who left no source of information unexplored; and they have been formally enumerated by more recent writers.‖ A portion of the work was first committed to the press by Gentianus Hervetus, who published at Paris in the year 1557 a Latin version of the forty-fifth, forty-sixth, forty-seventh, and forty-eighth books, and of certain fragments of the twenty-eighth and twenty-ninth books. Of the sixtieth book, which is of great length, Cujacius published a Latin version at Lyons in the year 1566, and this version was reprinted at Hanau in 1596.¶ The different portions which had thus been edited, were combined together by Dionysius Gothofredus, and printed at Hanau in 1598, and again in 1606.** Cujacius had been occupied in preparing some other portions for the press; and after his death, which took place in 1590, Charles Labbé published his version of the thirty-eighth and thirty-ninth books, together with the Greek scholia. The book was printed

* Voelli Bibliotheca Juris Canonici veteris, tom. ii. p. 814.
† Brunquelli Hist. Juris Romani, p. 309.
‡ Hoffmanni Hist. Juris Romani, tom. i. p. 654.
§ Heimbach de Basilicorum Origine, p. 16.
‖ Eckhardi Hermeneutica Juris, p. 587, edit. Walchii. Lipsiæ, 1802, 8vo.
¶ In the *Themis, ou Bibliothèque du Jurisconsulte*, tom. vii. p. 165, tom. ix. p. 321, the reader will find an elaborate dissertation by Professor Biener of Berlin, " Sur l' usage que Cujas a fait des Basiliques, et sur les manuscrits de ce recueil qui existent dans les bibliotheques de Paris;" and in tom. x. p. 161, he will find " Observations sur la Dissertation de M. Biener relative à l' usage que Cujas a fait des Basiliques," by Professor Berriat St. Prix of Paris.
** See however Hugo's *Civilistisches Magazin*, Bd. ii. S. 414. Here the reader will find a valuable contribution to the history of the Basilica.

at Paris in the year 1609. But the most meritorious labourer in this department of literature and jurisprudence was Charles Annibal Fabrot, whose services entitle him to a more particular commemoration. He was born at Aix in Provence in the year 1580, and after having made great progress in his classical studies, he addicted himself to the study of law, and took his doctor's degree in the year 1606. He afterwards became an advocate in the parliament of Aix, and his merit procured him the friendship of several individuals of influence. In 1609 he was appointed a professor of law in the university of Aix, where he became second professor in 1632, and first professor, or dean of the faculty of law, in 1638. It was at this latter period that he published his valuable edition of Theophilus. This work he dedicated to the chancellor Seguier, who induced him to fix his residence in Paris, and, on the condition of his undertaking the formidable task of preparing an edition of the Basilica, procured him an annual pension of 2000 livres. Fabrot, who appears to have been a man of great application, published the Basilica in Greek and Latin, after an interval of nine years, having in the mean time been engaged in several other works.* He has retained Cujacius's version of the three books already specified, and has himself translated the remaining books. He has added the Greek scholia, which are likewise translated into Latin. Of the sixty books which composed this great work, he supposes that he has exhibited forty-one in an entire form, though Meerman, Reitz, and other writers are of opinion that this number admits of some abatement; and those portions which are manifestly defective, he has endeavoured to supply from the *Synopsis Basilicorum*, from Harmenopulus, and from other sources. His edition is almost entirely without annotations, and is otherwise deficient in what may be considered as necessary illustration. A dedication to his patron Seguier, consisting of twelve pages, is followed by a preface, extending only to the fourth page, and this again is succeeded by Suarés's *Notitia Basilicorum;* but with respect to the history of the ample compilation itself, or of any other portion of the Greek jurisprudence, he furnishes his readers with no further information. His work appears to have been urged with a degree of rapidity approaching to precipitation; for, as he informs us in the preface, he sometimes laboured to supply two different presses. He is the author or editor of many other works: his labours contributed to illustrate the history as well as the laws of the Greek empire; he was the editor of several of the

---

* Των Βασιλικων Βιβλια Η'. Βασιλικων libri lx. in vii. tomos divisi. Carolus Annibal Fabrotus, Antecessorum Aquisextiensium Decanus, Latine vertit, et Græce edidit ex Bibliotheca Regis Christianissimi. Parisiis, 1647, 7 tom, fol.

Byzantine historians, and the author of various publications on the civil and the canon law. He was involved in the controversy which Salmasius maintained with equal learning and pertinacity, on the doctrines of the Roman law respecting usury.* One of his last labours was his edition of the works of Cujacius, which he published in the year 1668, in ten volumes folio: he thus performed a very important service to the more learned students of jurisprudence; but his intense application to this undertaking produced a malady which terminated his life on the 16th of January 1659. He died at Paris, leaving a son named Guillaume Fabrot, who was a counsellor in the "Cour des Monnoyes."†

After an interval of more than a century from the date of Fabrot's edition, four entire books of the Basilica, namely, the forty-ninth, fiftieth, fifty-first, and fifty-second, were published by Reitz, of whose meritorious labours we have already had occasion to speak. They were first inserted in the fifth volume of Meerman's *Thesaurus Juris Civilis et Canonici*, and thirteen years afterwards they appeared in a separate form.‡ The editor has added a Latin version, together with notes. The separate volume contains Ruhnkenius's edition of the commentaries of Thalelaeus, Theodorus, Stephanus, Cyrillus, Gobidas, and other Greek lawyers, on the titles of the Pandects and Code, " *de Postulando* sive *de Advocatis*, nec non *de Procuratoribus et Defensoribus.*" These commentaries were first inserted in the third and fifth volumes of Meerman's extensive collection. Ruknkenius, who was so great a master of Grecian literature, and who had studied the civil law in the excellent school of Ritter, has translated them into Latin, and has illustrated them with annotations. At the suggestion of Hemsterhusius, he had resumed his juridical studies with the view of preparing himself for a law professorship;§ but after having exhibited this very adequate specimen of his proficiency, he returned to those elegant pursuits of classical philology which have rendered his name so justly celebrated.

---

* Epistola Car. Ann. Fabroti, Antecessoris Aquisextinsis, de Mutuo: cum Responsione Cl. Salmasii ad Ægidium Menagium. Lugd. Bat. 1645, 8vo.

† Terrasson, Hist. de la Jurisprudence Romaine, p. 480. Niceron, Memoires pour servir à l'Histoire des Hommes illustres dans la Republique des Lettres, tom. xxix. p. 355.

‡ Operis Basilici Fabrotiani Supplementum, continens libros quatuor Basilicorum, IL. L. LI. & LII. nunc primum ex Codice manuscripto Regiæ Bibliothecæ Parisiensis integre editos: Latine vertit, variautes Lectiones collegit, Notasque criticas ac juridicas, tam aliorum quam suas, addidit Gul. Otto Reitz, JCtus. Accedunt Thalelæi, Theodori, Stephani, Cyrilli, aliorumque JCtorum Græcorum Commentarii in Tit. D. & Cod. *de Postulando* sive *de Advocatis*, nec non *de Procuratoribus et Defensoribus*: novissime ex Codice MS. Bibliothecæ Lugduno-Batavæ edidit, Latine vertit, et castigavit David Ruknkenius. Lugduni Batavorum, 1765, fol.

§ Wyttenbachii Vita Davidis Ruknkenii: Opuscula, tom. i. p. 564. Lugd. Bat. 1821, 2 tom. 8vo.

·· In his sketch of the·history of the Basilica, we must not overlook the ancient *Glossæ,* which are not without their value.   They
were first published by Labbé, who ranks among the more learned
cultivators of Greek·jurisprudence, and were afterwards illustrated
by Schulting and by Röver.*

Basilius and his family·followed the example of Justinian, by
preparing different elementary works for the benefit of those en-
tering.upon the study of the law.   One of these, which in an
imperfect form occurs in the collection of Leunclavius,† appears
to have been promulgated in the name of this emperor, and of
his two sons Constantinus ·and Leo, each of whom had been
invested with the title of Augustus.   This work has frequently
been confounded with another 'Εκλογὴ τῶν Νόμων, prepared under
the auspices of Leo and his son Constantinus Porphyrogennetus.
The latter production remains in manuscript, but an edition of it
was meditated by the learned Mascou, and a few pages have
been published as a specimen.‡   It is however necessary to
remark, that the history of these two works is involved in no
small degree of obscurity.   Different manuscripts exhibit different titles; the preface belonging to the one compendium is
sometimes transferred to the other; and Constantinus, the son of
·Leo, is occasionally confounded with his own uncle of the same
name.§

. Long before the publication of the Basilica themselves, the
Synopsis Basilicorum had been committed to the press by Joannes
Leunclavius, or Loewenklau, a learned Westphalian, distinguished
as a·scholar and a civilian.   He was the editor and translator of
many Greek works, and the merit of his versions has been admitted by Huet, the most erudite bishop of Avranches.‖   One historian of the Roman law has, without any apparent ground, ascribed
this abridgement to Romanus Junior Lacapenus:¶ the name of the

---

* Caroli Labbæi Observationes et Emendationes in Synopsin Basilicωn, &c. cum
veteribus Glossis Verborum Juris, quæ passim in Basilicis reperiuntur. Paris. 1606,
8vo.—These *Glossæ* were afterwards printed with " Cyrilli, Philoxeni, aliorumque
veterum Glossaria Latino-Græca et Græco-Latina, a Carolo Labbæo collecta, et in
duplicem alphabeticum ordinem redacta." Lutet. Paris. 1679, fol. They are to be
found, with the emendations of Joseph Scaliger and other learned men, and the notes
of Schulting, in Otto's *Thesaurus Juris Romani,* tom. iii. col. 1697. Röver's "Specimen
Observationum et Emendationum ad Glossas veteres Verborum Juris," is subjoined to
his edition of the "Fragmentum veteris Jurisconsulti de Juris Speciebus et de Manu-
missionibus, quod servavit Dositheus Magister." Lugd. Bat. 1739, 8vo.

† Leunclavii Jus Græco-Romanum, tom. ii. p. 79.
‡ Püttmanni Memoria Gottfridi Mascovii, p. 119. Lipsiæ, 1771, 8vo.
§ Wæchtleri Opuscula juridico-philologica, p. 588. Lugd. Bat. 1733, 8vo.—" Inde
factum est," says Pohl, p. 6, " ut in universa juris Byzantini postjustinianei historia
nihil fere difficilius sit, quam harum Eclogarum aetatem et auctores definire." See likewise Heimbach, p. 93.

‖ Huetius de Interpretatione, p. 171.   Paris. 1661, 4to.
¶ Struvii Hist. Juris Romani, p. 340.

author remains altogether unknown. It was published from a manuscript which Sambucus had found at Tarento, a place within the limits of the district formerly called Magna Græcia, where the Greek language long continued to be vernacular. In the manuscript, the different subjects are digested according to the order of the alphabet; but the editor has arranged them in the order of the sixty original books. The text is accompanied with a Latin version, and a series of annotations occurs at the end of the volume.* With respect to the translation, a charge of plagiarism was brought against him by Freigius, a professor of law in the university of Altdorf.† A manuscript translation, executed by this professor, appears to have been communicated to him; but his knowledge of the Greek language and of the Roman law, and his skill as a translator, were such as to leave him little or no inducement to avail himself of this clandestine aid. The Synopsis was afterwards illustrated by Labbé, who published an ample collection of observations and emendations. Another *Synopsis Basilicorum*, which has never been printed, is preserved in different libraries. It is of smaller extent, and is commonly described by the Greeks as μιχρὸν κατὰ στοιχεῖον. Michael Attaliata is the author of a third Synopsis, which has been inserted in the collection of Leunclavius,‡ under the title of Ποίημα νομιχὸν, ἤτοι Πραγματιχή. From an epigram prefixed, it appears to have been composed in the third year of the emperor Michael Ducas, that is, in the year 1073. The author, who describes himself as a proconsul and judge, has not digested his little work in alphabetical order.

About the same period, a Σύνοψις τῶν Νόμων, or Synopsis of the Laws, was composed by the younger Michael Psellus, who had been preceptor to Michael Ducas. It is addressed to this emperor, and is written in verse. As it only consists of 1406 verses, it necessarily contains a very scanty outline of legal science: its value is not highly estimated by Augustinus,§ and other competent judges; but as a literary curiosity it is not entirely without

---

* LX. Librorum Βασιλικων, id est, Universi Juris Romani, auctoritate Principum Rom. Græcam in linguam traducti, Ecloga sive Synopsis, hactenus desiderata, nunc edita per Joan. Leunclaium, ex Joan. Sambuci, V. C. Bibliotheca. Item Novellarum antehac non publicatarum Liber. Adjunctæ et Adnotationes interpretis, quibus multæ leges multaque loca juris civilis restituuntur et emendantur. Basileæ, 1575, fol.

† Wæchtleri Opuscula, p. 589.

‡ Juris Græco-Romani, tam Canonici quam Civilis, tomi duo; Johannis Leunclavii Amelburnii, V. Cl. studio ex variis Europæ Asiæque bibliothecis eruti, Latineque redditi: nunc primum editi cura Marquardi Freheri, J. C. cum ejusdem Auctario, Chronologia Juris ab excessu Justiniani ad amissam Constantinopolin, et Præfatione, &c.— Francofurti, 1596, fol.

§ Augustini Emendationes et Opiniones, lib. iv. cap. iii. p. 175, edit. Lugd. 1559. 8vo.

its attractions. The lines of which it is composed are πολιτικοὶ στίχοι, or popular verses;* a mode of writing which, in many instances, had begun to supersede the more classical structure of Greek as well as Latin poetry. Accent or emphasis being substituted for quantity, lines were formed of a number of syllables corresponding with some particular species of verse; and some original defects in this mode of composition, might possibly be supplied by a peculiar adaptation of the voice. The modern Greeks, who speak a language which can scarcely be considered as different from that of their classical ancestors, retain or have adopted a pronunciation which appears to set at open defiance all the known and acknowledged rules of prosody: while they profess to regulate the voice by accent, they make long syllables short, and short syllables long; so that in their manner of reading an ancient poet, it is utterly impossible for our ears to recognize the melody of verse. They indeed tell us, what may be sufficiently true, that our ears are too obtuse to discover the delicacy with which they combine accent with quantity; but, at all events, it is very hard to imagine that their general system of pronunciation has been legitimately transmitted from the times of Homer, Pindar, and Sophocles. Psellus employs a verse of fifteen syllables, which seems intended to represent the iambic tetrameter catalectic. In the subsequent passage, he gives a general account of the *Corpus Juris Civilis:*

Πρῶτον δ'ἑρμηνευτέον σοι, πόσα τοῦ νόμου μέρη.
Τὸ μὲν γὰρ τούτων Κώδικος οὕτως ὠνομασμένον,
Πτυχίον δωδεκάβιβλον, ὅ φασὶ διατάξεις·
Ἔχει δὲ τοῦτο δόγματα, Δέσποτα, βασιλέων,
Ἀντιγραφάς τε νομικὰς, καὶ δικῶν ἀποφάσεις·
Τὸ δὲ καλοῦσι Δίγεστα, Ῥωμαικὴ δ' ἡ κλῆσις.
Ὑπάρχει δὲ τὸ Δίγεστα, Ἑλληνικῶς Πανδέκτης,
Ὅτι καὶ νόμων πέφυκε παντοδαπῶν δοχεῖον,
Καὶ πλεῖστοι συνεγράψαντο τοὺς νόμους τοῦ Πανδέκτου.
Τῶν δὲ Διγέστων, Δέσποτα, παντοδαπὰ τὰ μέρη·
Τὰ μὲν γὰρ πρῶτα λέγουσι περὶ συναλλαγμάτων,
Τετράβιβλος δ' ἡ σύνταξις, κλῆσις τῶν Πρώτων, πρώτη·
Τὸ μετὰ ταῦτα πέφυκεν ἑπτάβιβλον πτυχίον,
Ῥωμαικῶς λεγόμενον οὕτω, δὲ ἰουδίκης,
Ἤτοι περὶ τῶν κρίσεων, κ. τ. λ.†

---

* Ilgen ad Carmina Homerica, p. 656. Gaisford ad Hephæstionem, p. 247. Maltby, Lexicon Græco-Prosodiacum, p. lxiv.

† Michaelis Pselli Synopsis Legum, versibus iambis et politicis, cum Latina interpretatione et notis Francisci Bosqueti, selectisque observationibus Cornelii Siebenii, emendatius edidit Ludovicus Henricus Teucherus, p. 10. Lipsiæ, 1789, 8vo.—This work of Psellus may likewise be found in Meerman's *Thesaurus Juris Civilis et Canonici*, tom. i. p. 37.

We shall only transcribe other two verses, in which this juridical versifier states the maxim, that ignorance of fact, το φάκτου, but not of law, admits of a legal excuse:

Τοῦ νόμου μὲν ἡ ἄγνοια συγγνώμην οὐ λαμβάνει,
Τοῦ φάκτου συγγινώσκεται τοῖς νόμοις προσηκόντως.*

One of the latest Greek civilians of much note was Constantinus Harmenopūlus, a judge of Thessalonica, whom Suarés,† Jac. Gothofredus,‡ and other learned writers have erroneously placed in the twelfth century. He was born about the year 1320, and he appears to have died about the year 1380.§ He was a native of Constantinople, and having been trained in the best learning of that age, he gradually arrived at different stages of preferment, and was eminent for his knowledge of the canon as well as of the civil law.‖ In 1345 he composed his Πρόχειρον Νόμων, or Manual of the Laws, a work of considerable extent, and of considerable value.¶ Harmenopulus was better acquainted with the principles than with the history of the Roman law; and it may perhaps be sufficient to mention his strange averment that Justinian promulgated three different codes, namely, the Gregorian, Hermogenian, and Theodosian. He is said to have been initiated in Latin literature by Aspasius, a Calabrian monk, whom his father had attracted from Italy by the promise of an ample salary; but we must apparently suppose him to have derived his knowledge of the Roman law from Greek compilations. He makes a nearer approach to truth when he speaks of Gaius as the first of lawyers. His work has however been found of importance in elucidating various points of law; and many learned men have bestowed no inconsiderable labour in illustrating it as one of the last reliques of ancient jurisprudence. The Greek text was first published by T. A. Suallemberg,** and after a short interval a Latin version was added by Bern. a Rey.†† Another version was executed by Jo. Mercerus.‡‡ He was succeeded by Dionysius Gothofredus, who published at Geneva an edition including paratitla, various readings, and a *Nomenclator Græcarum Dictionum Juris, ad Harmenopulum.*§§ This editor has professedly adopted the translation of Mercerus; but, as Reitz has remarked, most of the notes are derived from the same source, and without any form of acknowledgment. An edition

---

* P. 118. This rule is taken from the Basilica, lib. ii. tit. iv. § 9.
† Suaresii Notitia Basilicorum, p. 16. ‡ Gothofredi Hist. Juris Civilis, p. 19.
§ Fabricii Bibliotheca Græca, tom. xi. p. 260. edit. Harles.
‖ Mastricht Hist. Juris Ecclesiastici, p. 318.
¶ Bachii Hist. Jurisprudentiæ Romanæ, p. 686. ** Parisiis, 1540, 4to.
†† Coloniæ, 1547, 8vo. ‡‡ Lugduni, 1556, 4to.
§§ Apud Guillelmum Læmarium, 1587, 4to.

of Harmenópulus was for some time meditated by Ruhnkenius;* but he finally abandoned the design, and it was afterwards adopted by Reitz, whose learned labours have so greatly contri- buted to facilitate the study of this branch of literature and juris- prudence. He lived to prepare his edition for the press, but died before its publication; and the late Baron Meerman inserted it in the supplement to his father's Thesaurus.† The text, ad- justed by a collation of various manuscripts, is printed without accents: it is accompanied with a new version, with notes of the editor himself, and of several other civilians; and besides other appendages, he has subjoined the Nomenclator of Gotho- fredus, corrected and enlarged.

Besides the works which have already been enumerated, seve- ral others of the same denomination have been printed,‡ and many more are still preserved in manuscript, particularly in the Vatican, and in the Imperial Library at Vienna. What we have hitherto stated may perhaps be sufficient to excite, though not to gratify, the curiosity of those who are capable of being interested in such disquisitions; and if any gentle reader is disposed to pro- secute his enquiries to a greater extent, we beg leave to refer him to the respective publications of Suarés, Haubold, and Heimbach.

Joseph Marie Suarés, author of the *Notitia Basilicorum,* was a native of Avignon, where his father was "Auditeur de la Rotte;" and having embraced the ecclesiastical profession, he became Bishop of Vaison in the year 1633. This high prefer- ment he resigned in favour of his brother in 1666: he afterwards retired to Rome, and was appointed Vicar of St. Peter's, and Keeper of the Vatican Library; and in this city he terminated his earthly career on the 8th of December 1677.§ He was evi- dently a man of learning, and was the author of various works. His account of the Basilica was written at Rome in 1637, and there it is said to have been printed during the same year; but we strongly suspect it to have been printed for the first time in Fabrot's edition of the Basilica. The editor states that it had been transmitted to him by Cardinal Francesco Barberini; a favour which would not have been very material if the tract had

---

* Bergmanni Præf. in Ruhnkenii Opuscula, p. xii. Lugd. Bat. 1823, 2 tom. 8vo.

† Hagæ Comitum, 1780, fol.

‡ Here we must not entirely overlook a publication which bears the following title: Τοῦ Ἀνατολικοῦ Νομίμου Βιβλία γʹ. Juris Orientalis libri iii. ab Enimundo Bonefidio, J. C. digesti ac notis illustrati, et nunc primum in lucem editi. Cum Latina interpre- tatione. *Excudebat Henr. Stephanus,* 1573, 8vo. The first book contains imperial constitutions; the second, pontifical sanctions of the archbishops and patriarchs of Constantinople; and the third, rescripts of other ecclesiastical dignitaries.

§ Niceron, Memoires des Hommes illustres, tom. xxii. p. 297.

been published ten years before; nor have we been able to find
this Roman edition in any library, or its title in any catalogue.
This tract of Suarés was reprinted by Simon van Leeuwen, at the
beginning of his edition of the *Corpus Juris Civilis,* and was
inserted in the twelfth volume of the learned and indefatigable
Fabricius's *Bibliotheca Græca,* where it is accompanied with
valuable annotations.   Still however the work was not to be
found in a very accessible form; and Dr. Pohl, syndic of Leipzig,
has performed an important service by publishing a separate
edition.   The notes of Fabricius are retained, and those which
he himself has added are numerous and able.   The text of
Suarés, who has been succeeded by many other enquirers into
the same branch of knowledge, is somewhat meagre; but in this
improved form his work ought to find a place in the library of
every scholar who professes to study the history of the Roman
law.   The historical notices are not confined to the Basilica, but
may be said to embrace the entire compass of the Greek jurisprudence of the empire.

From the publication of this early French bishop we pass to that
of a late German professor.   Haubold's *Manuale Basilicorum* is
a work of a different nature, but is likewise a valuable acquisition
to the more learned student.   Its plan is sufficiently described in
the lengthened title, which we have inserted at the head of this
article.   The collation which the reader must expect is not that
of passages actually quoted, and confronted with each other; it
consists in enumerating the succession of books and titles, and in
adding perpetual references to the parallel passages.   We also
find a very laborious series of references to the works of modern
civilians, who have illustrated the Justinian law from the Greek
jurisprudence; and he has prefixed an " Index chronologicus
Interpretum recentiorum e quorum observationibus Manuale
Basilicorum est digestum," in which he enumerates 188 books
or tracts.   Of his laborious undertaking, a considerable share of
the credit is due to a lawyer named Lehmann, who conducted
his researches under Haubold's direction.   This mode of employing a literary assistant is not uncommon in the German universities, which generally contain many young men of learning
and industry, willing to labour for a moderate remuneration.

" Quare haud moratus sum manum ipse operi admovere; cui tamen
rite perficiendo, perquam exigui otii mihi, homini aliis aut potius diversis
laboribus addicto, reliqui memor, tempestive circumspexi socium, qualem
in parte priori, hoc est, in ipsa juris Justinianei cum Basilicis collatione,
adornanda laetor me nactum esse virum ultra sortem, qua utitur, littera-
tum, Joannem Theophilum Lehmannum, Delitiensem, in urbe patria
forensibus negotiis nunc mancipatum, olim, quum adhuc Lipsiae degeret,

mibi familiarem, quem honoris causa nomino. Is, meis auspiciis, non
solum jus Justinianeum cum Basilicis diligentissime contulit, aptato ad
hunc finem exemplo editionis Fabrotianae praesertim in scholiis, quorum
cuique locum contextus, ad quem pertinet, calamo adsignavit; verum
etiam e supellectile librorum, quam possideo, optimos quosque inter-
pretes, qui jus Justinianeum e Graecis subsidiis vel illustraverunt, vel
restituerunt et emendaverunt, adnotavit."—*Praef.* p. v.

Christian Gottlieb Haubold, whose personal history may perhaps be unknown to most of our readers, was born at Dresden on
the 4th of November 1766. His father became professor of
natural philosophy in the University of Leipzig, and died soon
afterwards, leaving him in the sixth year of his age; but although
he was thus deprived of a parent, his guardians gave him an
excellent education. He entered the university in the year 1781,
and pursued a liberal course of study, but was not slow in
selecting jurisprudence as his proper department. His mother
had married as her second husband a printer named Saalbach,
who treated him with the kindness of a father, and who had
induced him to give an occasional attendance in the office, with
the view of preparing himself for continuing the business: he
was however too eagerly bent upon other pursuits, and during
his academical course he attended the lectures of no fewer than
ten different professors of law. In 1784 he took the degree of
master of arts, and in the following year that of bachelor of laws;
in September 1786, he qualified himself as *Magister legens,* and
during the ensuing semester he read his first course of lectures,
on the history of the Roman jurisprudence. Having taken his
doctor's degree in 1788, he was next year appointed extraordinary
professor of juridical antiquities, in 1796 ordinary professor of
the law of Saxony, and he successively attained to all the usual
honours belonging to the law-faculty.* He continued to read
lectures on the Roman and the Saxon law, and he devoted a very
uncommon degree of attention to their history and literature.
The various works which he published, chiefly relate to the
Roman law, and are almost all written in the Latin language;
they are the result of indefatigable research, and are uniformly
distinguished by extent of learning and solidity of judgment. In
all that relates to what the Germans describe as the literature of
the law, he was without a rival, and his works are of the greatest
value in directing the researches of the curious enquirer. Hugo,
Haubold, and Savigny have, each in his own department, given
a signal impulse to the juridical studies of the age; and before
we desist from our critical labours, we are not without some

---

* Autobiographieen Leipziger Gelehrten, herausgegeben von M. Heinrich Gottlieb
Kreussler, S. 39. Leipzig [1810] 4to.

faint hope of making their respective merits better known to English readers. This most learned and estimable professor died at Leipzig in the year 1824, at the premature age of fifty-eight, leaving a family to bewail his loss. His very able successor Dr. Wenck, well known even in this country as the author of *Magister Vacarius*, has already followed him to the grave.

Dr. Heimbach, a pupil of the same excellent school of jurisprudence, and now professor of law in the University of Jena, announces his having undertaken the laborious task of publishing a new edition of the Basilica; and we trust that some few of our readers, who may have accompanied us in our excursion over this unfrequented tract, are prepared to wish him eminent success.* The volume which he has now published as a prospectus, contains a learned and copious explanation of his plan, and is itself a valuable contribution to the history of the Greek jurisprudence. He has carefully traced the history of the Basilica, and of the sources from which they are derived; and has added notices, not only of the editions, but likewise of the various manuscripts preserved in various libraries. Nor has he neglected to give an account of the Greek scholia. His notices of Greek works on the civil law he prosecutes to a period much more recent than that of the promulgation of the Basilica. In reprinting this great work, he proposes to adjust the readings by a careful collation of manuscripts, and by consulting all the Greek and Latin

---

* In the course of last year Dr. Heimbach circulated proposals for publishing the work by subscription. His paper contains an address from the bookseller as well as from the editor; and as the latter explains the conditions of the subscription, we shall transcribe it at length. It is dated at Leipzig on the 13th of June 1830, and bears the signature of *Joannes Ambrosius Barth.*

"Quod per aliquot annos amicus Heimbachius mecum agitavit consilium, ejus recte nunc exsequendi adjutorem me habebit promtissimum, quippe qui certo confidam, edendo opere supra nominato jurisprudentiæ elegantioris omnium terrarum cultoribus, quid quod ipsis dicasteriorum adsessoribus? haud parum utilitatis allatum, nec vulgare bibliothecis ornamentum paratum iri. Quare quicquid in me est faciam, ut argumento longe gravissimo externa forma non indigna reperiatur, neque tamen liber nimio pretio constet. Hinc iis, qui subscriptis nominibus adjutores se profitebuntur, spondeo, omne opus, circiter CCCL. nitidæ chartæ plagulis complectendum, viginti Joachimicis esse venditurum, qui quidem nummi vix tertiam ejus pecuniæ partem efficiunt, qua Fabrotiana editio, si quando ejus adquirendæ rara alicui oblata fuit opportunitas, libenter redimi solet. Subscribendorum vero nominum cujusvis urbis bibliopolæ copiam præbebunt, ex quibus, qui duodecim nomina colligerunt, tredecim collegisse a me censebuntur. Universus liber in singulos viginti plagularum fasciculos dispertitus deinceps prodibit, quorum quisque iis, qui nomina professi sunt, soluto Joachimico cum octo grossis a me tradetur.

"Si qui viri docti communicandis benevole notis, libris, subsidiis editori humanissimo gratum facere forte constituerint, hos enixe rogatos volo, ut epistolarum, librorum, vel quicquid habuerint, ad illum transmittendorum negotium mihi injungunt.—Nihil magis in votis habeo, quam ut editori egregio ad opus arduum brevi perficiendum tempus et vigor, mihi autem in eo ornando doctorum hominum plausus et adjumentum rite adsint et subveniant."

texts which promise to afford any illustration : he undertakes to digest and correct the scholia, to add a Latin version of the scholia as well as of the Basilica themselves, and to accompany the whole with a commentary, and with several useful indexes. Of his duty as the editor of such a production, he seems to have formed a correct estimate; and it must be admitted that he has provided for himself a task of no ordinary magnitude. With our best wishes for the success of so laudable and so arduous an undertaking, we will venture to express a hope that, as Dr. Heimbach appears to be still young and ardent, he will endeavour to attain a more terse and classical Latinity, which could not fail to add another recommendation to his juridical disquisitions. We too frequently meet with Latin words rather than Latin idioms ; and although it cannot be said that the text of the Basilica abounds with classical Greek, we are nevertheless anxious to see it illustrated with some degree of taste and elegance.

Art. X.—1. *Paganini's Leben und Treiben als Künstler und als Mensch; mit unpartheiischer Berücksichtigung der Meinungen seiner Anhänger und Gegner; dargestellt* von Julius Max Schottky, Professor. (Paganini's Life and Labours as an Artist and as a Man; with an impartial Examination of the opinions of his adherents and his adversaries. By Professor Schottky.) Prag. 1830. 8vo.

2. *Paganini's Leben und Charakter, nach* Schottky, *dargestellt* von Ludolph Vineta. (Paganini's Life and Character, after Schottky, by Ludolph Vineta.) 8vo. Hamburgh. 1830.

Judging from the reception which some of our lighter articles have met with, we should be disposed to conclude that the majority of our readers have no objection to a little music between the acts, and we have therefore the less hesitation in selecting the present subject; but in case there may be some of a different opinion, who think that they perceive a too frequent recurrence to these topics in our pages, we should like to premise a few words in explanation.

In the first place, it will be recollected that ours is a *Foreign* Review, and that in Germany, Italy, France, and throughout the continent, music is a subject of surpassing interest,—that it is better understood and cultivated to a greater extent than in this country, and that the number of works which are constantly emanating from the press in regard to it is very considerable. As faithful chroniclers therefore of the literature of the age, we cannot, with any degree of propriety, pass over in silence a department of the fine arts so popular, upon which so much is said and written from one end of Europe to the other, and which is so frequently consecrated by genius of the first order. Music as a science, including composition, necessarily falls under the consideration of a Journal devoted to scientific and literary objects. To excel in it, besides a species of natural talent rarely to be met with in perfection, demands intellectual endowments of a high character, and we have already felt much satisfaction in bringing to light some of the relics of Mozart and Weber. The mere practice of the art, we admit, requires less mental culture, and is for the most part pursued by persons whose habits are less refined, whose intellectual stamp is of an inferior grade, and who, generally speaking, move in a lower sphere. We say in the general case; for, as occurs with respect to the Drama, there are sometimes to be seen a few splendid exceptions, which, when they exist, are always so much more to the honour of the individuals who stand so pre-eminent above their fellows. Indeed it may be observed, that the composer and the musical performer bear about the same relation to each other as the dramatist and the actor, and in the same way as we might feel inclined to trace the life and character of a Garrick, a Kemble, or a Talma, we are now induced to furnish a few, and but a few, particulars in the history of the illustrious Paganini. And as we apprehend that there are none, even of our unmusical friends, who have not heard of this renowned personage and his feats as an artist, one of the wonders of his age and of the world, and as a man possessing a character abounding in curious and characteristic traits, the source of a great deal of table-talk, and a great variety of absurd and groundless rumour and speculation, we shall consider no farther apology necessary for introducing to their notice this very extraordinary person.

Nicolo Paganini was born at Genoa in February, 1784; we are not informed as to his father's profession, if indeed he had any, all that we are told is, that his chief pursuit was to improve his circumstances, which were not the best in the world, by speculating in the lottery, so that when his little son, Nicolo, began at an unusually early age to give strong indications of musical talent, it seemed to him as if the wheel of fortune had at last been propitious, and he accordingly lost no time in setting to work to make the most of his prize. Having some skill on the violin himself, he resolved to teach him that instrument, and as soon as he could hold it, put one into his hands, and made him sit beside him from morning to night and practise it. The incessant drudgery which he compelled him to undergo, and the occasional starvation to which he subjected him, seriously impaired his health, and, as Paganini himself asserts, laid the foundation of that valetudinarian state which has ever since been his portion, and which his pale sickly countenance and his sunk and exhausted frame so strongly attest. As his enthusiasm was such as to re- quire no artificial stimulus, this severe system could only have been a piece of cool and wanton barbarity. He already began to show much promise of excellence, when a circumstance occurred which not only served to confirm these early prognostications, but to rouse him to exert all his energies. This was no other than a dream of his mother Theresa. An angel appeared to her, she besought him to make her Nicolo a great violin player, he gave her a token of consent, and the effect which this dream had upon all concerned we sober-minded people can have no idea of. Young Paganini redoubled his perseverance. In his eighth year, under the superintendence of his father, he had written a sonata, which, however, along with many other juvenile productions, he lately destroyed, and as he played about three times a week in the churches and at private musical parties upon a fiddle nearly as large as himself, he soon began to make himself known among his townsmen. At this time he received much benefit from one Francesco Gnecco, who died in 1811, and whom he always speaks highly of.

In his ninth year, being applied to by a travelling singer to join him in a concert, he made his first public appearance in the great theatre at Genoa, and played the French air " La Carmag- nole," with his own variations, with great applause.

His father now resolved to place him under the tuition of the well-known composer, Rolla, and for that purpose took him along with him to Parma. The particulars of their interview afford a striking proof of the proficiency which he had by this time ac- quired. As Rolla happened to be ill and lying in bed, the party were shown into the anti-chamber, when, observing upon the table one of the composer's newest concertos, the father beckoned to his son to take up his violin and play it, which he did at sight, in such a way that the sick man immediately started up, demanded who it was, and could scarcely be prevailed upon to believe that the sounds had proceeded from a little boy and his intended pupil, but as soon as he had satisfied himself that that was really the case, he declined to receive him—" For God's sake (said he) go to Paer, your time would be lost with me, I can do nothing for you."

To Paer accordingly they went, who received him kindly and referred him to his own teacher, the old and experienced " Maestro di Capella" Giretti, from Naples, who gave him instructions for six months, three times a-week in counterpoint. During this period he wrote twenty-four Fugues for four hands, with pen, ink, and paper alone, and without an instrument, which his master did not allow him, and, assisted by his own inclination, made rapid progress. The great Paer also took much interest in him, giving him compositions to work out, which he himself revised, an interest for which Paganini ever afterwards showed himself deeply grateful.

The time was now come when Nicolo was destined, like other youthful prodigies, to be hawked about the country, to fill the pockets of his mercenary father, who managed to speculate upon him with considerable success in Milan, Bologna, Florence, Pisa, Leghorn, and most of the upper and central towns of Italy, where his concerts were always well attended. Young Paganini liked these excursions well enough, but being now about fifteen years of age, he began to be of opinion that they would be still more agreeable if he could only contrive to get rid of the old gentleman, whose spare diet and severe discipline had now become more irksome to him than ever. To accomplish this desirable object an opportunity soon offered. It was the custom of Lucca, at the feast of Saint Martin, to hold a great musical festival, to which strangers were invited from all quarters, and numerous travellers resorted of their own accord, and as the occasion drew near, Nicolo begged hard to be allowed to go there in company with his elder brother, and after much entreaty succeeded in obtaining permission. He made his appearance as a solo player, and succeeded so well, that he resolved now to commence vagabondising on his own account, a sort of life to which he soon became so partial, that, notwithstanding many handsome offers which he occasionally received to establish himself in several places as a concerto player or director of the orchestra, he never could be persuaded to settle any where. At a later period, however, he lived for some time at the court of Lucca, but soon found it more pleasant and profitable to resume his itinerant habits. He visited all parts of Italy, but usually made Genoa his head-quarters, where, however, he preferred to play the part of the dilletante to that of the virtuoso, and performed in private circles without giving public concerts.

It was not long before he had amassed about 20,000 francs, part of which he proposed to devote to the maintenance of his parents. His father, however, was not to be put off with a few thousands, but insisted upon the whole. Paganini then offered him the interest of the capital, but Signor Antonio very cooly threatened him with instant death unless he agreed to consign the whole of the principal in his behalf; and in order to avert serious consequences and to procure peace, he gave up the greater part of it.

Those who know any thing of the gay, romantic sort of life

which artists in Italy, particularly those connected with the all-
engrossing object of music, usually lead, the diversified society in
which they mingle, and the incident and adventure which they
meet with, will not wonder that Paganini should have felt inclined
to pass his days there, among his own countrymen, who felt and
appreciated his talent, received him upon all occasions with the
most enthusiastic applause, showered down upon him all the gold
they could afford, besides flowers, garlands, and sonnets,

> " Of such sweet breath composed,
> As made the things more rich."

He loved the manners and customs of his country, its beautiful
scenery, its climate, but their kindred souls were still more congenial to his heart. He was their idol; wherever he went his fame
had preceded his approach, and the multitudes poured in to hear
him in streams as if he had been a worker of miracles. Having
music at their command at all hours of the day, there is no country
where concerts are worse attended than in Italy, and yet those
which he gave never failed. People seemed never to be satiated
with the delight of hearing him, and at Milan he gave, with the
most brilliant success, no fewer than nineteen concerts rapidly
succeeding each other. The only place in the whole of his pere-
grinations where he was unsuccessful was at Palermo in Sicily.
At Rome, Naples, and Florence he was eminently triumphant,
and at the former of these places his Holiness the Pope was
pleased to confer upon him the order of the *Speron d'Oro.*
. Much to his credit, Paganini bore his honours with singular
modesty. They never inflated him with exaggerated notions of
his own powers, and, above all, they never dazzled his vision so as
to blind him to the merit of his professional brethren. To Spohr,
the German violinist, so celebrated for the excellence of his *Cantabile,* and whom he met at Naples, he gave full credit for being
the greatest and most perfect *singer* upon his instrument. Conscious of his own immeasurable superiority in the aggregate of
the qualities for which all the greatest masters have been distinguished, he could well afford to admit the claim of a brother artist
in one branch of the art. But when any of them appeared in the
shape of rivals, no man ever felt more intense pleasure in beating
down all opposition. Whatever it was that his antagonist plumed
himself on, to that Paganini directed his efforts, and never rested
until he had come off victorious. Indeed if Spohr, instead of
acting as he did, had perilled his boasted Cantabile in action, we
very much doubt whether he would not have seen cause to have
repented of his temerity. He would in all probability have
shared the same fate with Lafont, the Parisian violinist, who

having, when at Milan, courted a public *assault* with the Genoese, (to borrow a fencing phrase,) received so many palpable hits that he was glad to retrace his steps homewards, and leave the latter in undivided possession of his own territories. The challenge here proceeded from Lafont, at whose earnest request Paganini agreed to join him in a concert. At the rehearsal the wary Italian manœuvred in such a way that his adversary must have been quite unprepared for the discomfiture which awaited him, and very probably might have been misled to anticipate an opposite result. The hour of the concert arrived, and the public were breathless with anxiety to witness the contest of the rival masters. Lafont played first. His fine tone and his graceful and elegant performance, as might be supposed, drew down much applause. Next came Paganini; but now it was not merely the purity of the intonation, the beauty of the style, the neatness and distinctness of the execution. A more powerful enchanter waved the magic wand, and it seemed to those present as if the soul of melody itself stood before them, confessed in all her charms, her grace and tenderness, her grandeur and sublimity. Besides the superiority of his adagio playing, Paganini was determined in feats of execution completely to outstrip his antagonist. The same passages accordingly which the latter had performed in single stops, he executed in double; rapid successions which the one had achieved in double ordinary sounds, the other produced in the most perfect manner in double harmonic sounds: where the one had accompanied his melody with chords, the other superadded to the chords the most rapid and distinct pizzicatos with the left hand: where Lafont had astonished his audience with his octaves and tenths, Paganini amazed them still more by stretching with the same ease and certainty fourteenths and sixteenths. Having now routed the foe at all points, he had amply made good his title to be proclaimed the victor.*

It was early in 1828 when Paganini arrived at Vienna, where

---

* The substantial accuracy of the above statement can be attested by many who were present upon the occasion. A Frenchman, however, will never admit that he is beaten, and in the same spirit that many of *la grande nation* still claim the honour of having triumphed at Waterloo, M. Lafont, in an egotistical letter addressed to one of the French journals, while he pretends to be doing ample justice to Paganini, broadly asserts his own supremacy, and that of the French school generally, and like Marshal Boufflers of old, who, when his army was cut to pieces, protested that he had not lost an inch of ground, most positively denies that he left Italy in consequence of the alleged defeat. But whatever may have taken place at Milan, recent events seem to have superseded the necessity of farther inquiry. Paris itself has at last surrendered to the victorious Paganini, and as Mr. Cianchattini, in his letter in the *Harmonicon* in answer to M. Lafont, predicted, his appearance has produced an effect upon the *artistes* of that capital as electrical as if Hercules himself had descended in the midst of the gladiators of ancient Rome.

he gave a great many concerts with a success equal if not superior to any which had hitherto attended his exertions. His performance excited the admiration and astonishment of all the most distinguished professors and connoisseurs of this critical city. With any of the former all idea of competition was hopeless; and their greatest violinist, Mayseder, as soon as he had heard him, with an ingenuousness which did him honour, as we ourselves have reason to know, wrote to a friend in London, that he might now lock up his violin whenever he liked.

In estimating the labour which it must have cost a performer like Paganini to have arrived at such transcendent excellence, people are often apt to err in their calculations as to the actual extent of time and practice which has been devoted to its acquisition. That the perfect knowledge of the *mechanique* of the instrument which his performance exhibits, and his almost incredible skill and dexterity in its management, must necessarily have been the result of severe discipline, is beyond all question; but more, much more, in every case of this kind, is to be ascribed to the system upon which that discipline has proceeded, and to the genius and enthusiasm of the artist. The miraculous powers of Paganini in the opinion of his auditors were not to be accounted for in the ordinary way. To them, it was plain that they must have sprung from a life of a much more settled and secluded cast than that of an itinerant Italian musical professor. It was equally clear, from his wild, haggard and mysterious looks, that he was no ordinary personage, and had seen no common vicissitudes. The vaults of a dungeon accordingly were the local habitation which public rumour, in its love of the marvellous, seemed unanimously to assign to him, as the only place where " the mighty magic" of his bow could possibly have been acquired. Then, as to the delinquency which led to his incarceration, there were various accounts. Some imputed it to his having been a captain of banditti; others, only a carbonaro; some to his having killed a man in a duel: but the more current and generally received story was, that he had stabbed or poisoned his wife, or, as some said, his mistress; although, as fame had ascribed to him no fewer than four mistresses, it was never very clearly made out which of his seraglio it was who had fallen the victim of his vengeance. The story not improbably might have arisen from his having been confounded with a contemporary violin-player of the name of Duranowski, a Pole, to whom in person he bore some resemblance, and who, for some offence or other having been imprisoned at Milan, during the leisure which his captivity afforded, had contrived greatly to improve himself in his art; and when once it was embodied into shape, the fiction naturally enough might have obtained the more credence, from the fact that two of his most distinguished predecessors, Tartini and Lolly, had attained to the great mastery which they possessed over their instrument during a period of solitude—the one within the walls of a cloister—the other in the privacy and retirement of a remote country village. At all events, the rumours were universally circulated and believed, and the innocent and much-injured Paganini had for many years unconsciously stood forth in the eyes of the world as a violator of the laws, and even a convicted murderer—not improbably, to a certain extent, reaping the golden fruits of that " bad eminence;" for public performers, as we too often see, who have once lost their " good name," so far from finding themselves, in the words of Iago, " poor indeed," generally discover that they have only become objects of greater interest and attraction. How long he had lived in the enjoyment of this supposed infamy, and all the benefits accruing from it, we really cannot pretend to say; but he seems never to have been made fully aware of the formidable position in which he stood until he had reached Vienna, when the Theatrical Gazette, in reviewing his first concert, dropped some pretty broad hints as to the rumoured misdeeds of his earlier life. Whereupon he resolved at once publicly to proclaim his innocence, and to put down the calumny; for which purpose, on the 10th of April, 1828, there was inserted in the leading Vienna journals, a manifesto, in Italian as well as German, subscribed by him, declaring that all these widely circulated rumours were false; that at no time, and under no government whatever, had he ever offended against the laws, or been put under coercion; and that he had always demeaned himself as became a peaceable and inoffensive member of society; for the truth of which he referred to the magistracies of the different states under whose protection he had till then lived in the public exercise of his profession.

The truth of this appeal (which it is obvious no delinquent would have dared to make) was never called in question, no one ever ventured to take up the gauntlet which Paganini had thrown down, and his character as a man thenceforward stood free from suspicion.*

* We mean by this that he has stood free from suspicion in the eyes of all who knew any thing about the matter, or gave themselves the trouble to inquire into it; with the rest of the world the maxim is reversed, and *calumny* not *truth* is most apt to prevail. When people hear a good story, if they do not know the individual to whom it relates, it is of no consequence to them whether it is true or false. We are sure, however, that no respectable publisher would ever knowingly give his sanction to such false and injurious statements as those we have alluded to in regard to Paganini, and we think that the editor of the *Nouvelle Biographie des Contemporains* owes the Chevalier some apology for having revived those absurd aspersions in the following circumstantial manner:—
" On assure qu'emporté par une passion violente et un caractere sombre, il assassina, dans

That such fictions should have got wind, is not at all to be wondered at; for, besides the circumstances which we have above noticed, the romantic gaiety of his disposition, and his love of gallantry in his younger days, were constantly prompting him to seek adventures and amusement by assuming different disguises and characters. Indeed the pleasure which he felt in making his audience stare and gape with astonishment was not always confined to the concert-room; it would seem that he would sometimes draw a long bow of another description, and enliven the conversation by retailing humorous anecdotes of his own invention. His masquerading propensities frequently found vent in travelling, and among strangers where he was not known; and we are told that, upon one occasion, finding himself seated *vis-a-vis* in a diligence with a very rich but not very bright fellow-passenger, he contrived to dispel the tedium of the journey by passing himself off for a certain well-known brigand, whose name at that time spread consternation and alarm throughout all Romagna—an announcement which, as it was any thing but belied by his personal appearance, produced an effect upon his companion of which, perhaps, we may form some idea by figuring to ourselves a condemned criminal on his way to execution.

His whimsicalities, his love of fun, and many other points of his character, are sometimes curiously exemplified in his fantasias. He imitates in perfection the whistling and chirrupping of birds, the tinkling and tolling of bells, and almost every variety of tone which admits of being produced; and in his performance of *Le Streghe* (The Witches), a favourite interlude of his, where the tremulous voices of the old women are given with a truly singular and laughable effect, his *vis comica* finds peculiar scope.

His command of the back-string of the instrument has always been an especial theme of wonder and admiration, and, in the opinion of some, could only be accounted for by resorting to the theory of the dungeon, and the supposition that his other strings being worn out, and not having it in his power to supply their places, he had been forced from necessity to take refuge in the string in question; a notion very like that of a person who would assert, that for an opera dancer to learn to stand on one leg the true way would be—to have only one leg to stand upon. We shall give Paganini's explanation of this mystery in his own words.

---

sa jeunesse, sa femme ou sa maitresse; quoi qu'il en soit, emprisonné à Gènes, il y resta pendant sept ans. Ce fut là, que pour adoucir les ennuis de sa captivité, il s'exerça à jouer du violon, et qu'il parvint à une dégré si etonnant de perfection, que le Roi de Sardaigne, d'après l'avoir entendu, le rendit à la liberté." Details like these, when untrue, are unworthy of any work of higher character than the *Infernal Magazine* or the *Horrific Register.*

" At Lucca, I had always to direct the opera when the reigning family visited the theatre; I played three times a week at the court, and every fortnight superintended the arrangement of a grand concert for the court parties, which, however, the reigning princess, Elisa Bacciochi Princess of Lucca and Piombino, Napoleon's favourite sister, was not always present at, or did not hear to the close, as the harmonic tones of my violin were apt to grate her nerves, but there never failed to be present another much esteemed lady who, while I had long admired her, bore (at least so I imagined) a reciprocal feeling towards me. Our passion gradually increased, and as it was necessary to keep it concealed, the footing on which we stood with each other became in consequence the more interesting. One day I promised to surprise her with a musical *jeu d'esprit,* which should have a reference to our mutual attachment. I accordingly announced for performance a comic novelty, to which I gave the name of " Love Scene." All were curiously impatient to know what this should turn out to be, when at last I appeared with my violin, from which I had taken off the two middle strings, leaving only the E and the G string. By the first of these I proposed to represent the lady, by the other the gentleman, and I proceeded to play a sort of dialogue, in which I attempted to delineate the capricious quarrels and reconciliations of lovers; at one time scolding each other, at another sighing and making tender advances, renewing their professions of love and esteem, and finally winding up the scene in the utmost good humour and delight. Having at last brought them into a state of the most perfect harmony, the united pair lead off a *pas de deux,* concluding with a brilliant finale. This musical scena went off with much eclat. The lady, who understood the whole perfectly, rewarded me with her gracious looks, the Princess was all kindness, overwhelmed me with applause, and, after complimenting me upon what I had been able to effect upon the two strings, expressed a wish to hear what I could execute upon one string. I immediately assented, the idea caught my fancy; and as the emperor's birthday took place a few weeks afterwards, I composed my Sonata ' Napoleon' for the G string, and performed it upon that day before the court with so much approbation that a cantata of Cimarosa, following immediately after it upon the same evening, was completely extinguished, and produced no effect whatever. This is the first and true cause of my partiality for the G string, and as they were always desiring to hear more of it, one day taught another, until at last my proficiency in this department was completely established."

We know no one who has been more cruelly misrepresented than the subject of this notice. In reality a person of the gentlest and most inoffensive habits, he is any thing rather than the desperate ruffian he has been described. In his demeanour he is modest and unassuming, in his disposition liberal and generous to a fault. Like most artists, ardent and enthusiastic in his temperament, and in his actions very much a creature of impulse; he is full of all that unaffected simplicity which we almost invariably find associated with true genius. He has an only son, by a Signora

Antonia Bianchi, a singer from Palermo, with whom he lived for several years until the summer of 1828, when he was under the necessity of separating from her in consequence of the extreme violence of her temper, and in this little boy all his affections are concentrated. He is a very precocious child, and already indicates strong signs of musical talent. Being of a delicate frame of health, Paganini never can bear to trust him out of his sight. "If I were to lose him," says he, " I would be lost myself; it is quite impossible that I can ever separate myself from him; when I awake in the night, he is my first thought." Accordingly, ever since he parted from his mother, he has himself enacted the part of the child's nurse; and that our readers may form some idea of the manner in which he acquits himself in this new capacity, and of the character of the young Paganini, we shall here insert a description with which we are furnished by a friend of his who happened to call upon him at his lodgings at Prague, in 1828, in order to take him out to dinner. We may mention that the youth goes by the classical cognomen of Achilles, Lyrus, Alexander.

· "Every thing was lying in its usual disorder; here one violin, there another, one snuff-box on the bed, another under one of the boy's playthings. Music, money, caps, letters, watches, and boots were scattered about in the utmost confusion. The chairs, tables, and even the bed had all been removed from their proper places. In the midst of the chaos sat Paganini, his black silk nightcap covering his still blacker hair, a yellow handkerchief carelessly tied round his neck, and a chocolate coloured jacket hanging loose upon his shoulders. On his knees he held Achillino, his little son of four years of age, at that time in very bad humour, because he had to allow his hands to be washed.

· "His affectionate forbearance is truly extraordinary. Let the boy be ever so troublesome, he never gets angry, but merely turns round and observes to those present, 'the poor child is wearied, I do not know what I shall do, I am already quite worn out with playing with him. I have been fighting with him all the morning, I have carried him about, made him chocolate, I do not know what more to do.' It was enough to make one die of laughing, to see Paganini in his slippers fighting with his little son, who reached to about his knee; sometimes the little Achillino would get into a rage, draw his sabre upon his father, who would retreat into the corner of the room and call out ' enough, enough ! I am wounded already,' but the little fellow would never leave off until he had had his gigantic adversary tottering and prostrate on the bed.

"Paganini had now finished the dressing of his Achillino, but was himself still in sad dishabille. And now arose the great difficulty, how to accomplish his own toilette ; where to find his neckcloth, his boots, his coat. All were hid, and by whom? By Achillino. The urchin laughed when he saw his father pacing with long strides through the apartment, his searching looks glancing in all directions. And upon his asking him where he had put his things, the little wag pretended astonishment, and held his tongue, shrugged up his shoulders, shook his head, and signified by his gesture that he knew nothing about them. After a long search the boots were found, they were hid under the trunk ; the handkerchief lay in one of the boots ; the coat in the box ; and the waistcoat in the drawer of the table. Every time that Paganini had found one of his things, he drew it out in triumph, took a great pinch of snuff, and went with new zeal to search for the remaining articles, always followed by the little fellow, who enjoyed it vastly when he saw his papa searching in places where he knew nothing was hid. At last we went out, and Paganini shut the door of the apartment, leaving behind him, lying about on the tables and in the cupboards, rings, watches, gold, and, what I most wondered at, his most precious violins. Any idea of the insecurity of his property never entered his head ; and fortunately for him, in the lodgings which he occupied the people were honest."

We must not omit the remainder of the scene,

" The day being cold, Paganini had put on a monstrous cloak. And as he was afraid that Achillino might catch cold, he took him up in his arms and carefully lapped him over and over with it. The little one, who wanted to breathe more freely, soon poked his head out,—it was like a fine spring day in the arms of winter."

In the discharge of his filial duties, Paganini has always shown himself to be quite as exemplary as in that of his parental. The wealth which he has amassed has been partly applied to provide for the comforts of his aged mother, and not unfrequently dispensed in acts of bounty towards his more necessitous relations and friends. Having now traversed Germany, Paris and London will complete his professional tour, after which he intends to revisit his native city and to see his mother once more. In this anticipation, during his stay at Vienna in 1828, she wrote to him as follows :

" I assure you that I pray to God every day to keep me in good health, as well as yourself, that our wishes may be accomplished. The dream has been realized ; what heaven predicted has come to pass. Your name flies from mouth to mouth, and art, through God's grace, has procured for you a comfortable livelihood. Beloved and esteemed by your countrymen, and in the arms of your friends, enjoy at last that quiet which your health requires. Your portrait, which you sent me in the letter, gave me great pleasure, and I have already read all the particulars in the newspapers. You can easily believe that such news afford extraordinary pleasure to a mother. Take care and do your utmost that your name may be immortal ; guard against the effects of the bad climate of those great cities, and remember that you have a mother who loves you from her heart."

Upon his return to Italy, however, it is not his intention to settle in Genoa, where, as Mr. Ludolph Vineta emphatically observes, " both he and Columbus were born." He proposes to spend the remainder of his days in Tuscany, the spot to which Catalani and other great artists have retired—the Val d'Arno—the climate of which he prefers to all others.

" There," says he, " prevails the eternal spring of Eden," (rather a flattering description of a Florentine winter). " There, under that sweet azure sky, and among that highly cultivated and polite people, will I await my last hour, and cheerfully will I die, having first inhaled the air of Dante and of Petrarch."

Unwilling to impair. the force of these exalted and classical sentiments by any comments of ours, we now respectfully take leave of the Chevalier Paganini, and in doing so we again recur to the *emphatic* words of Mr. Vineta.

· " Adieu Paganini, confide in Apollo, he will give ear unto thy prayer, and the last sigh of thy breast will die away as calmly and as easily in the Italian sky as the softest flageolet-tone of thy heaven-inspired immortal Cremona. Adieu Paganini ! !' "

ART. XI.—1. *Histoire de Pologne avant et sous le Roi Jean Sobieski.* Par N. A. De Salvandy. 3 tom. 8vo. Paris. 1829.

2. *Lettres du Roi de Pologne, Jean Sobieski, à la Reine Marie Casimire, pendant la Campagne de Vienne, traduites par M. Le Comte Plater, et publiées par* N. A. De Salvandy. 8vo. Paris. 1826.

POLAND has ever been esteemed the most singular country in Europe; singular from its history, its institutions, its usages, and above all from its retaining beyond any other nation the impress of its primitive state. It has resolved the problem whether the spirit of ancient institutions may not be adopted—however violently, because unnaturally adopted—by a modern and greatly changed system of society; it has exhibited the strange phenomenon of a considerable degree of civilization engrafted on a barbaric stock. It is the singularity of this phenomenon which in a great degree constitutes the interest of the subject, and makes Polish history at all times an object of attention to the curious reader. While other nations have advanced in the career of social improvement, or at least assimilated their respective usages to the change of circumstances, that country has for the most part pertinaciously adhered to those of remote antiquity. The modifications which Christianity and a state of society, in many respects different, have introduced into the moral picture, have, so far from destroying the peculiarity, only deepened the shades, and rendered the effect more striking. Poland, in short, might have been regarded as a gigantic landmark between barbarism and civilization,—a monument of other times ineffectually assailed by the great spirit which every where else has annihilated almost every vestige of what once existed, and shaken the old world to its very foundations.

If any one, at all conversant with the subject, were asked what periods of Polish history are the most interesting and striking, he would unhesitatingly name three,—that of Sobieski; that of Stanislas Leczsinski; and that which elapsed from the first partition in 1772 to the accession of the Emperor Nicholas. With the *second* of these periods the reader has a sufficient acquaintance, for general purposes at least, from Voltaire's beautiful romance of Charles XII. A portion of the *last* we have already developed. The present notice will therefore be restricted to the *first*, which we consider, and we are sure the reader will participate in the opinion, as among the most interesting in the whole range of modern history.

In many points of view John Sobieski is one of the greatest characters in royal biography, the greatest beyond all comparison in the regal annals of his country. A renowned sovereign, a devoted patriot, a man of genius, an accomplished scholar; he likewise joined all the spirit of ancient chivalry to all the fervour of Christian piety. Placed in order of time between Gustavus Wasa and Peter the Great, he equalled the former, if not in the romantic incidents of his life, certainly in strength of principle, in grandeur of conception, in vigour of purpose, and surpassed him perhaps in desperate valour; while both as a man and a hero he left the latter much behind him, though he had probably less of that comprehensive, prophetic grasp which characterized the mind of the Tsar. But more than either is he entitled to the grateful reverence of posterity; he was the saviour of Christendom, the bulwark of European liberty no less than of the faith of the Gospel. But for him, that might not have been a vain threat which destined the altar of St. Peter's to become the manger of the Moslem's horse.

This illustrious monarch was first introduced to the English reader by our countryman, Dr. Connor, who had the honour to be his physician, and whose work, however deficient in *literary* merit, and what is worse, however circumscribed in plan or inaccurate in details, is not without attraction. Subsequently his name had a place in our universal histories. But in those wretched compilations, without exception wretched and unworthy of our age and nation, or in the contemporary accounts of the Siege of Vienna, the reader would vainly look for any thing like a satisfactory portrait of this hero. As to M. de Salvandy's work, it is like most other human things,—a mixture of good and bad, but one in which the latter sadly predominates.   On the one hand it is more copious than any which have preceded it, and, to do it justice, *somewhat* more replete with facts. On the other it exhibits the worst vices of the French school : it is declamatory; vague, pompous; it shows a continual hankering after *effect*, and a constant effort to cover the author's sterility with the flowers of verbiage : then the everlasting allusions to a period of which every Englishman is sick, and to a name which every Englishman despises, those of Louis XIV., and the conceited vanity of assigning every possible event in every possible quarter, from the revolutions of an empire to the quarrels of the meanest domestics, to the ubiquitous influence of the *grand monarque,* comprize no inconsiderable portion of the work. After perusing it with the utmost attention, we have asked ourselves the question,—" What do these volumes really contain ?" Occasionally, however, we shall revert to them, but more still to the recently published correspondence of Sobieski, which unaccountably appears to have attracted little attention in this country.

The extraction of Sobieski was truly illustrious.   On the paternal side he belonged to one of the forty puissant branches sprung from the famous palatin Janik, who in the reign of Lesko the Black, acquired by his warlike exploits a name almost on a level with that of the Grecian Hercules.   His grandfather Mark, and his father James, Sobieski, the former palatin of Lublin, the latter castellan of Cracow,* were distinguished for bravery among a nation of heroes, no less than for their honours and possessions. His mother was the grand-daughter of the great Zalkiewski, who fell at Kabilta by the hand of the infidel.   With this illustrious man, Poland had drooped : her existence as a nation was threatened on the one hand by the Swedish Gustavus Adolphus, on the other by the Tartars.   But

" In the midst of these disasters," says Salvandy, on the faith of a

---

* A *palatin* governed a palatinate, or province, and was invested with extensive powers both civil and military.   A *castellan* was in some sort the deputy of the palatin, but was also powerful from his office, and the head of the nobility in his jurisdiction: he held his court as well as the palatin, commanded in the field, and administered the laws in time of peace.   As all offices were immovable, even by the king, they who filled them were not merely independent, but absolute in their respective districts. The curse of Poland was this want of subordination and of responsibility. We must not forget to observe that though the palatines were superior in dignity and power to the castellans, there was an exception for the castellan of Cracow, who ranked above all the palatins, though next to the Cardinal Primate of the kingdom.

Besides these officers, there was another class, the *starosts,* whose jurisdiction was military, but many of whom had likewise civil courts, and an authority equivalent to that of our barons under the Norman sway.   The starostas were benefices, the revenues of which the king could enjoy six months, on every vacancy, but which at the end of that period he was compelled to give away to some one of his followers.

MS. written by the hand of Sobieski himself, " in a distant fortress there passed an event destined hereafter to repair them. One summer day of this year (1629) a frightful storm visited the canton of Olesko, a little place in Black Russia, at the foot of the Carpathian mountains, on the confines of Lithuania and Poland, and in the centre of the most elevated plateau of these countries where two rivers have their source,— the Bug, which after joining the Vistula in the north, flows into the Baltic; and the Bog, which traverses the Ukraine and Tartary, and joins 'the Borysthenes, not far from the Euxine. The fortress, a feudal manor, occupies a magnificent situation on the summit of a *mohila*, or immense artificial hill, which once served either as altar or tomb to the Sclavi. The tempest shook to its base this steep mobila, this fortress hung in the clouds. In this place, which might command a view of all Poland, which is linked with the recollections of her ancient history, a child was born during the raging of the elements: the grand-daughter of Zalkiewski was its mother. While the awful peals of thunder rendered some of her attendant domestics deaf for life, the courageous Theophila supported the throes of nature undismayed."—tom. i. p. 154.

It is singular enough that this fearful collision of the elements accompanied John Sobieski's exit from, no less than his entrance on, the stormy stage of life.

The education of the future hero, like that of his elder brother Mark, whom a premature fate awaited, corresponded with his high fortunes. In his father's princely inheritance of Zalkiew, for princely we may well call a place which reckoned fifty villages, and a territory equal in extent to an English county among its dependencies, the owner of which too could muster some thousands of armed domestics, he was taught not only the theory of war, but languages, history, politics, philosophy, every thing in fact likely to be useful to one whom his birth and connections destined to the first offices in the state. This ready genius required little aid from instructors, and his active frame was rendered hardy and robust by martial exercises. In a word, whether listening to the counsels of a father, whom a cultivated understanding and great experience in the world rendered the best of teachers, or bearding the wild boar in the recesses of his patrimonial forests, he afforded sure presages of his future eminence. But the most agreeable of his occupations was in anticipating the vengeance which he vowed one day to take on the Osmanlis, the eternal enemies of his country, his religion and his race; vengeance to which, like the Carthaginian of old, he was sworn from his childhood. No wonder; for in the short space of half a century four males of his house had fallen under their sabres, and fate was soon to add a fifth. We shall see how a fire thus fed by the strongest incentives, by patriotism, religion, and a sense of personal wrongs, blazed furiously forth against the Moslems.

John· had scarcely attained his sixteenth year when he and Mark were sent on their travels. In France he became the friend no less than the pupil of the great Condé; in Italy he applied himself to the fine arts, to public law, and to the policy of princes; at Constantinople he leisurely surveyed the proportions of the gigantic· antagonist against which both as a Christian knight and a noble Pole he had been taught to nourish unextinguishable hatred. He was preparing to pass among the Tartars, when an alarming insurrection of the serfs, and an invasion of Tartars, summoned him to the defence of his order and country.

In no country in Europe was the slavery of the lower class, the cultivators of the ground, of all in fact who were not born of gentle blood, so utterly abject or galling as in Poland. The degradation of their condition originated in the worst age of Sclavonic history, when every fierce Pagan considered he had a right to do what he pleased with " the capture of his bow and spear." Where no warrior would descend to cultivate the ground, this ignoble duty was devolved on the vanquished: wars were undertaken for no other purpose than the procuring of hands for agricultural labours. As not only the strong man who became the prize of battle, but the women and children of whole districts were forcibly· carried away, these sons of bondage were rapidly multiplied, and each landed proprietor was enabled to leave his posterity an hereditary succession of serfs. The base condition of this class was thenceforward as inevitable as the degradation of certain Hindoo castes. The arbitrary nature of the rights thus originally acquired by lawless force, lost nothing by transmission through successive barbarians. For many ages any man might kill his *own* slave with perfect impunity; and if he killed another's, he had only to make about the same compensation as for the destruction of an ox. It was not until the time of Casimir the Great, whose efforts to improve the condition of the serfs, to raise them from a level with the brutes which perish to the dignity of men, demand the esteem of posterity, that a fine of a few crowns was attached to the wilful murder of a slave. *More* than this the enlightened monarch would have attempted, had he possessed the power; kings have seldom been the oppressors of the·poor, however they may have delighted in impoverishing the rich or humbling the great; but he had to deal with an aristocracy which held king and serf in subjection, and fiercely opposed every encroachment on what they called their privileges, that is, every thing tending to define their uncontrolled authority. Even this penalty was easily evaded in a country where each man, entrusted with the administration of the laws, palatine, castellan, or starost, or the hired judges and bailiffs of those officers, was interested in upholding these privileges. The tyranny to which the serf was subject, and which had no check beyond the feeble one of humanity; the rapacity which wrung from him not only what his lord might have some justice in claiming, but often what was necessary for the support of life; the severe chastisements which followed disobedience to commands frequently impossible to be fulfilled; the insults to which his wife or daughter was continually exposed from any Polish *noble*, however poor or mean in station (and where one hundred thousand were privileged to commit such insults, God knows they were common enough) were for a long time borne in hopeless sorrow. But human endurance has its limits: even the embruted soul of the serf was not without the feelings of nature, nor consequently insensible to the voice of indignation. Imperfect as was the system of Christianity in which he was reared, it yet sufficed to convince him that he was of the same nature as his haughty lord, and heir of the same hopes of immortality. He complained; his complaints were answered with stripes, fetters, or death. Sometimes partial insurrections followed, but as they were not conducted on any combined plan, they were speedily extinguished in blood. If he was in consequence taught to smother his vengeance, it only raged with the greater fury within: it wanted but a vent to burst forth and wrap in one blaze the persons no less than the possessions of the tyrants.

Such a vent was at length found. There was a Cossack chief, Bagdan Kurielniski, a native of the Ukraine, (then subject to Poland,) who had grown grey in the service of the republic, but was now become its most dreaded enemy. By a tyrannical intendant his property had been wrested from him, himself bound in fetters, his wife violated and murdered, and one of his sons stabbed on her corse. The Cossack's soul was on fire; he loudly proclaimed his wrongs; 300,000 of his countrymen and of the Tartars, whose Khan had espoused his cause, rose to avenge them. At the head of this imposing force, he cut in pieces the armies sent against him by the diet. As he advanced into Polish Russia, he was joined by the serfs who had previously massacred their lords, and by some hundreds, if not thousands of Arian and Calvinistic nobles, whom the intolerance of the diet had doomed to death. Like the Cossacks, the great bulk of the serfs, inhabiting the eastern dependencies of Poland and the Grand Duchy of Lithuania, were of the Greek church; so that religious animosity was added to the thirst for revenge. The fury of the assailants particularly fell on two classes of persons—Jesuits and Jews—the former as the merciless fomenters of persecution, the latter as the agents of the great, and the grinders of the poor.

Their delight was to compel all the monks and nuns they could seize not only to marry with each other, but under the up-raised poignard to consummate the rite. Thus rolled on this frightful inundation, destroying noble and priest in its progress, but breaking the chains of the peasant: it was at length arrested under the walls of Zamozsk, within which the remnant of Polish chivalry had met to make a stand.

The two Sobieskis hastened from the Ottoman capital to oppose this strange confederation of Arian and Calvinist, Greek and Moslem. Little did the sultan dream of the prize which escaped him.

Having supported the election of the Cardinal John Casimir, successor of Vladislas Wasa, to the throne of the republic, and having by a duel with a Paz created to himself everlasting hostility from that powerful Lithuanian family, John Sobieski eagerly commenced his military career—a career destined to prove unrivalled for splendour. In the outset the subordinate post which he necessarily filled, joined to the imbecility of the king and generals, obscured the lustre of his exploits. After a chequered campaign, but one in which his valour was uniform, an ignominious peace—and that too in spite of his remonstrances—was made with Bagdan: it was soon treacherously broken by the Poles, and heaven, as if to punish the guilt, brought or permitted many reverses on them. Of these none was more deeply felt by John than the loss of his brother Mark, who fell at Batowitz into the merciless hands of the Tartars. Other foes arose: on the one side the Swedish Charles Gustavus, on the other the Muscovite Tsar Alexis, ravaged the country with impunity. The Polish armies were annihilated; John Casimir driven from the throne; and for a time the nation ceased to exist. But some true hearts there were—and among these none was truer or braver than Sobieski's—who never despaired of the country: noble and peasant at length combined; the dissensions of her foes favoured the combination, and John Casimir was restored. Yet he had no great reason to rejoice at his return: if the foreign enemy remitted his blows, there remained one more to be feared, domestic rebellion, which was fomented by Austria. Nor did this subside until the hostile parties were obliged to desist from sheer exhaustion; until no man had strength enough left to raise a hand against his brother.

During these contentions, which, though they continued many years, are too obscure to be noticed here, Sobieski was gradually rising to the higher commands. When in 1660 the eastern provinces of the republic were again ravaged by the troops of Alexis, he was one of the chiefs in the Polish armies. His successes over the Muscovite general, Sheremetoff, and above all the brilliant victory he gained over the same enemy at Slobadyssa, where 70,000 of the Tsar's forces were killed or taken, drew on him the attention of Europe, and elevated him to a rank with the great captains of the age. His exploits during the six following years against the Muscovites and Tartars—exploits which it is impossible to enumerate in this place—procured him from his grateful sovereign first the elevated post of Grand Marshal, next that of Grand Hetman of the crown. In the former capacity he presided over the palace, the administration, the correspondence with foreign powers, &c.; he was the only subject, nay more, the only *man* in the realm, who by virtue of his office could inflict the punishment of death without appeal; nor without his sanction could that punishment be carried into effect by any other tribunal in any part of Poland. In the latter capacity he was invested with the supreme disposal of the military force of the state; he had the sole care of levying, organizing, and putting in motion the various armies, and these armies he commanded in the field. In short, he exercised powers which in other countries are essential to royalty, and was in his own the depositary of an authority superior to the king's. These two dignities were like all others immoveable: the king could confer but not revoke them: they were obviously too great to be lodged in the hands of the same individual. What enhanced the pride of their possession in the view of Sobieski was the fact that they had never before been united in the same person.

The joy of the Poles was great to see their favourite captain thus placed at the head of all the civil and military dignities *of the crown*—that is, *of Poland.* (*Lithuania,* though united with the republic since the accession of the Grand Duke Jagellon (1386) to the throne of the republic, had its great marshal, hetman, and chancellor, like Poland, whose authority was perfectly independent of their brother dignitaries of the crown.) He had long possessed the love of the army, which had once actually forced John Casimir to promote him; he had in an equal degree the confidence of the kingdom; both were justified in believing that he alone could save the country. Some such bulwark was soon necessary: in 1667 one hundred thousand Cossacks and Tartars invaded the kingdom. To meet these formidable numbers there were only 10,000 soldiers, ill equipped, ill paid, and for that reason not over zealous in her cause. "But," said the vice-chancellor of the crown, who spoke the sentiments of the whole nation, "if we have no troops, we have Sobieski, who is an army himself; if the public treasury be empty, his own revenues supply what is wanting; he burdens his patrimony with debts, that he may support the

men he has raised." This was literally true : at his own expense
the patriotic hetman raised the army to 20,000, and fearlessly
marched to meet the enemy. Having intrenched himself at Pod-
haie, he sustained during sixteen successive days, with unshaken
intrepidity, the impetuous onset of the assailants, on whom he
inflicted a heavy loss. He did more : on the morning of the
seventeenth, with his greatly diminished band—diminished as
much by desertion as by death—he issued from his fortifications,
audaciously assumed the offensive, and in a few hours utterly
routed Cossack and Tartar, with the Sultan Galga at their head,
and compelled them to sue for peace. Success so splendid had
been expected by no man. All Poland flocked to the churches to
thank God for having given her a hero in the time of her need.
All Europe was not less astonished, for all had predicted the
speedy extinction of the republic. And extinguished it would
have been but for one man, who thus added another century to
its duration.

: The services of the grand hetman during the reign of the feeble
and worthless Michael Wiezsnowiezki, who succeeded on the resignation of John Casimir, were not less signal or important. In
1671 he opened what at its close Christendom might well term *the
miraculous campaign:* With a mere handful of followers—indeed
he had never more—he not only triumphed over Cossack and
Tartar, but humbled the pride of the Turk, who, now that Candia
had fallen, had seriously set about the execution of his long-cherished schemes of conquest. Mahomet IV. was constrained to
flee, but he fled only to return with a new army. Sobieski, who
had but 6000 men; and who could not procure reinforcements by
the time they were wanted, retreated in his turn, but only to strike
more effectually when opportunity served. Sometimes he stationed his horsemen between the infidels and their country, cutting
in pieces detached parties, and giving freedom to the captives
whom they were carrying away. But the most daring of his
exploits was at Budchaz, where the sultan lay encamped with the
flower of the Osmanlis. After a march quite secret and incre-
dibly swift, he suddenly fell on them ; made a great carnage ;
reached even the imperial tents, and forced Mahomet to flee.
On this occasion the king—who, however, hated him because he
was popular and powerful—wrote to congratulate him, saying,
" Envy itself is compelled to acknowledge that, after God, your
ability alone, though at the head of so inconsiderable a force,
has saved Poland." The vice-chancellor wrote : " Glory to the
Most High, who, by means of your powerful hand, has again
raised a country which had despaired of itself, and made no effort
for its own preservation. We cannot thank you as we should,

but with heart and tongue we bless you : we do more than admire
—we revere the heroic deeds by which you have surpassed even
the wishes of your country." But the conqueror himself derived
little satisfaction from his splendid successes. The king, terrified
even in victory, consented in a *secret* treaty not only to the dis-
memberment of the kingdom, but to the humiliation of an annual
tribute as the price of peace.

If the kingdom had not disputes abroad, she was sure to make
them at home. After the conclusion of this ignominious peace,
she was torn in pieces by some half-dozen different factions, all
of them aspiring to the government of the state. The *poor* nobles
wanted an agrarian law—the rich confederated against them ; the
serfs clamoured for freedom—both poor and rich joined against
them ; the factions of Austria and France laboured with no other
end—monstrous as that end may seem—than to destroy Polish
independence ; and a party more powerful than all was resolved
to depose the king, not because his measures had proved disastrous
to the state, but because he was the creature of Austria, (he had
been caught by the common bait, the hand of an archduchess,) a
power detested by the great body of the Poles. As Sobieski
supported the authority of Michael, though his enemy, and refused
obedience to a factious diet, he did not escape vexation. His
soldiers were ordered to disobey him, and he himself to lay down
his authority, and appear before their high mightinesses. Indignant at this treatment of one who had so often saved the country,
the army instantly confederated—that is, assumed an independent
authority in opposition to the diet; they swore to defend Poland,
their own rights, and their glorious leader, against internal no less
than external enemies. Again, no inconsiderable number clamoured for the spoliation of the church, insisting, like the revolutionists of all times, on the competency of the state to seize her
temporalities : the result was a counter-confederation among the
clergy. In short, the anarchy of the kingdom was such as had
never been seen before—such as made its best friends despair of
its existence a single month. While the army passed into winter-
quarters (1672), the grand hetman in disgust retired to his estates.
Believing that all was over with Poland, Louis XIV. offered him
an asylum in France, with a dukedom and a marshal's truncheon ;
but the patriot would not abandon the abode of his fathers : he
hoped even against hope.

The hero had not long enjoyed the tranquillity of retirement
before he was required to appear at Warsaw to defend his character against a hired, perjured ruffian, who had denounced him
as a traitor to the Royal Confederation, as a self-elected body
were pleased to term themselves. He did appear, accompanied

by nearly all the more illustrious Poles, and a few regiments of horse. (Such, indeed, was the usual escort of this princely noble.) His presence struck faction dumb. As grand marshal of the crown, he insisted on the assembly being changed into a legal diet; as grand hetman, on the rupture of the ignominious peace with the Turk. Both demands were immediately granted; the very assembly which had appeared ready to proscribe him, were lavish in their praises of the hero " into whom the souls of all preceding heroes had passed,"—of him, " to whom nature had never before produced an equal, and never would in ages to come." In fact, it was discovered by his enemies—such were all who aimed at the subversion of the republic—that the hearts and voices of the nation were with him. They condemned the delator to death, but as the punishment could not be inflicted without the grand marshal's sanction, the fellow was permitted to live.

If Sobieski had procured the rupture of this disgraceful treaty, he could not so easily procure troops to meet the incensed Turks. After many grievous delays, however, and more grievous disappointments, not a few of which were caused by the intrigues of the Paz, who headed the troops of the Grand Duchy, and over whom, he, as hetman of the crown, had no authority, he organized an army, and prevailed on Michael to command it. According to custom, when the king was present, the bonzuk, or lance of the grand hetman, was lowered before the royal tent. One morning the army were overjoyed to find their hetman's bonzuk erect—a proof that the dastardly Michael had abandoned the field. The other moved on. The (so deemed) impregnable fortress of Kotzim, before which three hundred thousand of the Osmanlis had formerly failed, was stormed and taken by one-tenth that number of Poles, though it was garrisoned by a powerful Turkish army. The consequences of this glorious triumph were great; Moldavia and Wallachia placed themselves under the protection of the conqueror; the Turks retreated with precipation beyond the Danube; and Europe thanked God for " the most signal success which for three centuries Christendom had gained over the infidel." But the greatest remains to be told: he was preparing to follow up his career of victory, when news arrived of Michael's death, (the royal glutton died through eating voraciously of one thousand apples presented to him a few days before by the municipality of Dantzic,) and of the preparations for the election of a new king:—that dignity was reserved for the conqueror of Kotzim.

Among the usages which the Poles had continued to observe from their first establishment as a people, none was so striking as their universally assembling on every vacancy to elect a ruler.

That on the decease of one chief all the members of each barbarous tribe should meet to choose another was natural enough; but that a system adapted only to societies in the first stages of their existence—to the Sclavonic tribes, or the Indians of the New World—should be perpetuated when the science of government so much improved—when the advantages of the representative mode were so much better understood, is one of the most singular characteristics of this singular people. On ordinary occasions, indeed, each palatinate sent its deputies to the general diet; but the nobles, as if fearful that the power thus delegated would be abused, often followed the deputies and awed them by their presence. And even this modified system of representation was very slowly and partially adopted. Russia, for example, never returned deputies, but as many horsemen as pleased attended this diet, even on ordinary occasions. On *important* emergencies, such as the one under notice, every Polish gentleman vindicated his privilege to assist in the elections, and one hundred thousand horsemen appeared at Warsaw, armed as if for battle, and ready, if necessary, to support their respective candidates by the sword. The poor menial who while at home shrunk under the whip of his master, now felt all the importance of his privileges as a *noble*, —felt that even *he* was considerable enough to be bribed. Yet, after all, the real power of election was for the most part lodged with the great landed proprietors on whom the rest were dependent, and the object of whose suffrages the rest were constrained to support. To see one of these territorial lords ride to the field of election, escorted by some thousands of his dependent lances, was as magnificent but it was not less melancholy: how soon might these gallant warriors fall by the hands of each other!

Most readers are aware that on the present occasion the leading candidates were Charles of Lorraine, who was supported by Austria, and Philip of Neuburg, the creature of Louis XIV. All Europe indeed pointed out the saviour of Poland as the fittest to wear the crown; but then the choice of the one candidate would ensure the alliance of the emperor, the other of the French king—an advantage which no *Piast*, or native prince could bring. At length (April 20, 1674) the diet opened, all the chivalry of Poland, and the Grand Duchy being ranged under the ensigns of their respective palatinates, their eyes intently fixed on the proceedings of the deputies, who were seated in the open air, and whom they had constituted their representatives until the preliminaries were settled,—not for the giving of their suffrages. Many of the assembled chiefs eyed one another with no friendly glance, and at each scowl the sabres of their respective followers half-leaped from the scabbard. The French candidate's proposals were but coldly received. The Paz, who with the Lithuanians supported Charles, being elated at this first appearance of success, proposed the exclusion of a *Piast* as preliminary to the examination of the claims of any other candidate. (The blow was aimed at Sobieski, who was not yet returned from the army.) The proposal was received with indignation by many of the Poles, but generally approved by the Lithuanians. As usual, a dispute arose between these hostile people when the conqueror of Kotzim was announced. The shouts which rent the air at his approach, the suspension of all business in the diet while all Warsaw thronged around him, eager to see and bless him, were omens of his near elevation. Yet it was probably unknown to himself; for he proposed a *third* candidate, the Prince of Condé. Instantly a great multitude shouted " *a Condé!*" but the Lithuanians, and all whom the perfidy of Louis had disgusted, cried " *a Lorraine!*" The assembled pospolite ranged themselves into two lines, to fight for one or the other of these candidates, when by the address of the Bishop of Cracow, who exercised the functions of the inter-rex, bloodshed was avoided: having chaunted a psalm in concert with the attendant clergy, he ordered each palatinate to advance according to custom, and register the votes of its nobles. Instantly the two formidable lines were broken, and the assembled nation was preparing to approach, palatinate after palatinate, for that purpose, when the president of Russia, (the reader will not confound the Polish provinces under that name with the empire of the Tsars, of which the proper name was Muscovy,) Stanislas Jablonowski, harangued the people in favour of a *fourth* candidate. Having in an eloquent speech stated his objection to Lorraine and Condé (Philip was set aside almost by common consent)—objections which were really unanswerable—he cried, " Let a Pole reign over Poland!" " *A Piast! a Piast!*" and " *God for Poland!*" was the response of the fickle multitude. The president continued :—

" We have among us a man who has ten times saved the republic by his head and arm; who is hailed, both by the whole world and by ourselves, as the first and greatest of the Poles. By placing him at our head, we shall best consecrate his own glory; happy shall we be in being able to honour by an additional title the remaining days of one who has devoted every day to the interests of the republic; happier still in securing our own safety by rescuing genius and patriotism from the shackles cast over them, and investing both with new energy and power." " We know that such a king will maintain our nation in the rank it occupies, because he has hitherto maintained it in its present elevation—an elevation too to which he himself has raised it." "Poles!" concluded the animated speaker,—" if we here deliberate in peace on the election of a king; if the most illustrious potentates solicit our suffrages; if our power be increased, and our liberties left to us—whose is the glory? Call to mind the wonders of Slobadyssa, Podbaic, Kaluz, Kotzim—imperishable names!—and choose for your monarch JOHN SOBIESKI!"

The effect was electrical: all the Polish and Lithuanian palatinates shouted " Long live King John III.!" The soldiery drew their swords, swearing to exterminate all who did not join the cry. The Paz raised what opposition they could; but finding the popular current too strong to be stemmed, they sailed with it. Sobieski was proclaimed. Like his predecessors he signed the *pacta conventa*—a compact, however, of which the conditions were drawn up by the nobles, and favourable only to their order. Like them, too, he showed his bounty to the state and army: he performed as much as any of his rivals had proposed. He redeemed the crown jewels which had been pledged with the Jews; he built two fortresses to protect the frontier; he founded a gymnasium for the education of the Polish nobles; he raised and supported several regiments during the subsequent wars with Turkey; and presented the whole army with several months pay. Whether he accepted the crown with much avidity is doubtful. Some writers say that he intrigued for it with great art, and that the address of Stanislas was concerted with him. There is no evidence in support of such an assertion, but much to oppose it. Thus much, however, is certain, that his ambitious wife left no means untried—flattery, bribes, promises—to strengthen his party.

The new king was almost immediately called on to justify the confidence reposed in him by a gallant nation. While obtaining his accustomed successes over the Tartars, he was suddenly assailed by Mahomet at the head of an amazing, and what is more, a disciplined host. He had but 8,000 men left, and the arrival of supplies was of all things the most contingent. He threw himself into Lemberg, where he was speedily invested. All Poland believed him lost, yet he sent for his queen and children, resolved, that if conquered, their bones and his should there find a tomb. Taking advantage of a heavy fall of snow which a high wind blew in the face of the foe, he one day issued from the fortress, led on his heroic band, shouting his favourite war-cry of *Christ for ever!* and after a sharp conflict again routed the infidels, who fled with precipitation before this second Cœur de Lion. Well might all Christendom cry *a miracle!* for such wonders had never been wrought since the heroic days of Crecy and Poitiers. It was hoped that such disastrous defeats would deter the Moslems from opposing a captain who appeared as if raised up by Providence to be their scourge, if not their destruction; but this time their pride was exasperated; they levied another and more formidable army, (three hundred thousand strong,) which they confided to the Pacha of Damascus, the most resolute, if not the ablest of their generals. His surname of *Shaitan,* or *the Devil,* was sufficiently expressive of his renown. The Polish king's forces might reach ten thousand, yet fearful as were the odds, he scorned to retreat. Having entrenched himself between two small villages on the banks of the Dniester, he supported, during twenty successive days, the most desperate efforts of the enemy; whose formidable artillery—the same that had reduced Candia—showered continued destruction into his camp. Never before had his situation been so critical. The bombardment was terrific, and was not remitted day or night; the ranks of the Poles were thinned by it, no less than by the frequent sallies which the king led to the very centre of the dense ranks of the Moslem. Shaitan was utterly confounded at such supernatural resistance; it gave way to admiration of this great hero. He proposed terms of peace, which the Polish and Lithuanian nobles were eager to accept, but which Sobieski heard with rage. " Tell your master," replied the latter, " that if such proposals are renewed to me, I will hang up the messengers!" In an hour the firing recommenced :—

····" This time the bombardment was dreadful : the batteries had been brought nearer, and elevated on high redoubts which overlooked the whole camp. The besiegers relaxed not night or day: the Poles had no place of refuge but the ditches at the foot of their intrenchments, (every where besides was marked by death and conflagration :) during three weeks they had heard nothing of Poland, and in this long silence every hope of succour had fled. To these evils famine was now added : a little wood which had supplied the horses with grass and the men with acorns, was exhausted; soon the ammunition began to fail, and what was worse than all, the most courageous to droop. From the distance of a musket shot to the boundaries of the horizon, the camp of the infidel was seen to extend on all sides like a huge wall. The Christian camp was a prison which held out no other prospect than a sepulchre; it was thinned by desertion; and those who remained murmured : ' Why not accept a peace which, in fact, king Michael had accepted on an occasion of much less peril? was not necessity a law which the whole world might sanction without dishonour ?'

" Michael Paz having opposed, in a council of war, all the propositions of the king to assure the safety of the army, came up to him at the head of a mutinous band, expatiated on their desperate condition, and acquainted him with their resolution to desert *en masse.* ' Desert who will,' answered the king, ' *I* shall remain; the infidels must pass over my corpse before they reach the heart of the republic.' After a pause he added, ' I might have conquered, now I can but die. I know who has filled the soldiers with the spirit of discouragement and rebellion ; it is to be expected that they who'arrive the last on 'the field should be the first to speak of flight.' He mounted a horse, and rode along the line. ' My friends,' cried he, ' I have drawn you from worse scrapes than this. Does any one think my head is weakened with wearing a crown?' At his voice the army begins to breathe; his tranquil assurance gave hope even to the most dejected."—*Salvendy,* tom. xi. p. 367.

: As the balls and shells fell thick among this heroic band, Sobieski ordered them to be returned by his own guns and mortars. And returned they were, with interest. The alacrity of the soldiers in gathering up every ball and shell as they fell, in thrusting them into the ever-active engines, aud dashing them in the faces of those who had sent them, would have roused the patriotism of the most insensible, and inspired even cowards with bravery. The Turks were thunder-struck at seeing so brisk a fire all at once resumed; they doubted not that the Tartars, their allies, who occupied the left bank of the Dniester, had suffered supplies to be poured into the camp. Forty-eight hours of inaction followed. What could this mean? Doubtless the Polish monarch was planning something decisive. So thought the Moslem, and the anticipation kept them on the alert throughout two nights. On the morning of October 14th, 1676, their astonishment knew no bounds when they saw the Pole calmly issue from his entrenchments, with his few followers drawn up for battle, apparently as confident of the result as if legions had compassed him. They could not believe *a mere man* would attempt such a thing: from that moment their superstition invested him with supernatural powers. The Tartars exclaimed that there was no use contending with " the wizard-king." The Pacha Devil was indeed superior to the weakness; but another reason made him loth to prolong the contest: he knew that Radziwil was approaching at the head of the pospolite. The moment, therefore, he saw John give the signal for battle, he offered an honourable peace, which was immediately accepted.—Is this history or romance?

But John would have made no peace with the infidel had he obtained the support he solicited from the Christian powers of Europe. He had long formed a plan which, to use his own words, " would have returned the barbarians conquest for conquest; would have driven them into the solitudes that had vomited them forth on Europe; nay, would have done more than exiled the monster to its native deserts, would even have exterminated it, and restored the Byzantine empire." To carry into effect this magnificent design, he required no more than the co-operation of two of the powers most exposed to the inroads of the Ottomans. In vain did Innocent XI. invite Europe to unite with " a prince

who · for 'thirty years had been the bulwark of the Christian republic—the brazen wall against which all the efforts of the barbarians had failed;" a prince " whose holy trophies adorned the
vaulted roofs of the Vatican;" "the lieutenant of the God of
Hosts, whose arm was predestined not only to bear the sceptre,
but to break the heathen yoke under which nations groaned."

During the following few years, while the Polish hero was
supposed to be slumbering under the laurel wreath, his very
existence was embittered by constant and unavoidable anguish.
On one side, the intrigues of his wife, a Frenchwoman by birth,
and like all Frenchwomen too desirous of power to hesitate at
the means by which it might be obtained; on the other, the
turbulent conduct of some nobles, who by their fatal *vetos* audaciously dissolved every diet disposed to redress the crying grievances
of the nation, and thereby reduced the authority of this patriotic
king to a vain name, occasioned him vexations enough. Uxorious
beyond all example in one of his character; blind to the imperfections—we might say the vices—of a woman, whose unprincipled
ambition plunged the whole machine of government into confusion; he offered but a feeble opposition to her wily intrigues, she
contrived to wield what little power the constitution allowed him.
Then his disputes with the senators who were secretly in the interest of either France or Austria, and who disputed still more
fiercely with each other, sometimes so far as to forget his presence, and to draw the sword on each other on the very steps of
the throne—made his indeed a crown of thorns!

But of this more hereafter. We must now proceed to the most
glorious epoch in this hero's life.

In 1683, the Turks, after seven years' preparation, put into
motion the most formidable army which Europe had seen for some
time. Whither was its destination? Not Poland, because throughout their vast empire there was not a soul which quailed not at
the · bare mention of " the wizard king;" and because an envoy
from Mahomet had arrived to assure that King of the Sultan's
friendship. The infamous Louis well knew—he who had stirred
up the Sultan to an exterminating war on the Empire. Nay more,
to prevent Sobieski from affording any assistance to Leopold, he
by his gold fomented a conspiracy among the leading Poles, the
object of which was to dethrone if not assassinate that hero, whose
single arm he dreaded more than the resistance of all Austria.
Fortunately the victim detected the hellish plot by intercepting a
letter from the French ambassador to Louis. He hastened to the
diet, and read the correspondence, which implicated not a few who
were present; yet with the magnanimity of his character, he expressed his conviction that the whole was a gross fabrication.

" But," added the politic king, who had resolved to espouse the cause of Leopold, or rather that of Christendom, " convince the world also that it *is* an imposture ; declare war against the infidel !" The diet listened with indignant wonder, and the declaration was voted almost unanimously, by none more zealously than those whose names were thus alarmingly compromised.

In the mean time the Turkish vizir and generalissimo, Kara Mustapha, swept the Hungarian plains with amazing rapidity. The politicians who, like Leopold, expected that he would confine his operations to that kingdom, were in utter consternation when they found that instead of wasting his time in the siege of petty fortresses, he poured his vast hordes over the Austrian dominions, and approached the capital. The dastardly Leopold fled with a train of arch-duchesses, leaving the Duke of Lorraine (the same who had contested the Polish crown with Sobieski) to defend his states, and Stahremberg his capital. On the 15th of July that capital was first invested. Europe was in consternation ; Rome trembled for herself, and well she might, for the instructions of the vizir involved her utter destruction. The Pope continually despatched couriers to press the march of Sobieski. The Emperor, the Duke of Lorraine, and all the German princes solicited him by daily messengers to do once for Europe what for thirty years he had done for his own country—to save it from the Moslem yoke. He was not inattentive to the call, but he encountered even more than the usual difficulty in levying and equipping his troops. With the subsidies he received from the Pope and his own revenues he at length assembled at Cracow an army of 16,000 strong. Yet not the vizir, nor Leopold, nor Europe, were sure that *he* would march. His dissatisfaction with the Emperor, who had ever been his bitter enemy ; and the dislike which as a Pole he must naturally feel towards Austria, were considered more than sufficient to keep him far from the field. But the Christian triumphed over the Pole ; he warred in good earnest for the defence of the faith ; nor, as a hero, could he be supposed insensible to the immortal glory of being the deliverer of Europe. But the siege was prosecuted with vigour, and deputies from Silesia, Moravia, and Austria again arrived at Cracow to implore the speedy aid of his own arm, which they esteemed of more value than hosts. The minister of the Emperor and the papal nuncio fell at his feet, embracing his knees like the humblest suppliant. Leopold offered to guarantee the crown to his son James, to bestow on that prince the hand of an arch-duchess, and to cede to him and his heirs the kingdom of Hungary, if he would recover it from the infidel, and save Vienna. (How these promises were fulfilled we shall soon perceive.) He marched, and Europe breathed.

The campaign of Vienna has been too often celebrated by historians and poets to be related here. We can allude only to such particulars respecting it as are less known, or we should rather say, scarcely known at all; and these must relate exclusively to Sobieski. They are derived from the recently published letters of the hero. These letters are interesting, not merely as containing an accurate account of the campaign, but as exhibiting the inmost thoughts of a great king, clothed in the utmost simplicity of language, yet possessing considerable merit as compositions. By most of our readers the extracts we proceed to make from them will be deemed by far the most interesting portion of this article. They are indeed admirable for the chivalric tone, the deep piety, the originality, the patriotism, and the playful fancy of the writer.

· At Heilbrunn the King was met by the Duke of Lorraine, whom he thus describes :—

" He has the height of Prince Radziwil, the features of Chetmaki, and is about the same age; his nose is very aquiline, just like a parrot's beak. He is deeply marked with the small-pox, and his face has more down on it than the thistle; ·his uniform is grey, without ornament, except some lace buttons; his hat has no plume; his boots are yellow, or rather were three months ago; his war horse is tolerable, but the bridle, saddle, and indeed the whole harness are very mean, and much the worse for wear. Yet, for all this, he has not a vulgar appearance; he looks the gentleman, or even the man of distinction."—" He wears a mean light-coloured wig; in short, he cares very little about his appearance; but I shall agree with him very well, he is deserving of a higher destiny."

The two captains having concerted their plan of operations, John encamped on the Danube, where he was joined by the imperial forces, and by the flower of the German chivalry. He was saluted by them with unbounded acclamations; the sovereign princes of the empire, who would have scorned to obey an equal, were eager to receive the orders of so renowned a warrior. His exultation was extreme to find himself at the head of 70,000 men, having never before commanded half so many; with these he thought himself a match not only for the 300,000 Turks and Tartars, but for the whole infidel world. The appearance of the troops too pleased him. " We may apply to these Germans," he writes, " what we say of horses—they do not know their own strength." Both they and his own forces had need of strength and agility besides. After the harassing passage of the Danube, the Calemberg, a chain of steep, abrupt, rugged mountains, abounding with gorges and precipices, and narrow pathways obstructed with rocks and trees, had to be surmounted. The ascent occupied three days; what with the labour accompanying it, and the scarcity of provisions, he declared that he and his followers were so wasted that any one of them bid fair to outstrip the deer. But he had other toils, which few besides himself could have sustained.

" Continual harangues, my interviews with the Duke of Lorraine and other chiefs, innumerable orders to be given, prevent me not only from writing, but from taking food and rest. These duties become the more frequent, now that Vienna is at the last extremity, and that a distance of four miles only separates us from the enemy. Add the ceremonial of the interviews, the difficulties arising from etiquette about one thing and another—as who shall march first or last; who shall have the right, who the left; then come councils without end, delays, indecisions; and all this not only wastes time, but breeds misunderstanding. Besides, numbers of princes arrive day and night from all parts of Europe; then there are the counts and knights of so many different nations—all these *will* see me, and take up my time."

He omits to mention another task which was more imperative than all the rest; he was forced to write innumerable letters—by night too, for he had no leisure by day—to his tyrannical queen, who so far from consulting his repose, insisted on being acquainted with every thing that happened from his own pen, and daily tormented him, not only with new demands, but with reproaches when, as was often the case, they were too exorbitant to be fulfilled. Yet how tenderly does he expostulate with her:—

" I must complain of you, to yourself, my dear and incomparable Mariette. How comes it that you have no better opinion of me after all the proofs of tenderness I have given you? Are you serious in saying that I do not read your letters? Can you believe it when in fact, amidst all my cares and anxieties, I read every one of them three times at least—the first, when they arrive; the second, when I retire to rest or am disengaged; the third, when I sit down to answer them! All this enumeration of the years of our union, the number of our children, &c. should have had no place either in your letter or your head. If I do not always write so much at length as you wish, is it not possible, my dear, to account for my haste without the help of injurious surmises? The champions of Europe and Asia are but a few miles distant from each other. I have every thing to inspect, even to the slightest details."

Nay he forgets his own unequalled toils and cares in his anxiety for this most unreasonable of women. In the very same letter (written long before the dawn of September 5,) he says—

" I beseech you my love, for my sake do not rise so early—what constitution could bear it? Could any one's especially who retires to rest so late as you? You will afflict me greatly if you do not listen to my request; you will deprive me of tranquillity; you will impair my health, and what is much worse, you will injure your own—you who are my only consolation in this world. As to our mutual affection, let us try in which of the two it will soonest cool. If my age is not one of ardour, my heart and soul are young as ever. Did we not agree, my love, that *your* turn would come next—that you would have to become the wooer? Have you kept your promise, my darling? Do not saddle me with your own faults; on the contrary, prove to me by words, by letter, and above all, truly prove to me that you will cherish a constant attachment for your faithful and devoted Celadon, who is now compelled to finish his letter in rapturously saluting his amiable and well-beloved Mariette."

Who would suppose such a letter written by a husband of fifty to a wife of fifty?

On the morning of September 11, the allied army reached the summit of the Calemberg, from which the Austrian capital and the wide-spread gilded tents of the Moslems formed a magnificent prospect—the latter as terrific as magnificent. Great was the astonishment of Kara Mustapha to behold heights which he had confidently deemed inaccessible, glittering with Polish lances. He did not then know that " the wizard King" was there, but the unwelcome intelligence was soon conveyed to him. Like a prudent man, however, he concealed the fact, and like a brave one he made his dispositions for battle. Sobieski did the same; but he was at first incommoded with a fierce wind which blew directly in the face of his followers. " Our horsemen," said he, " can scarcely keep the saddle; one might fancy the aërial powers let loose against us; this may well be, for the vizir is reputed a great magician." The wind, however, fell, as if the elements were willing to suspend their own conflict to behold the fiercer one of man.

September the 12th is a day which ought to be annually commemorated by Christian Europe. Having heard mass and communicated—a pious practice which he never neglected when any great struggle was impending—the King descended the mountain to encounter the dense hosts of the Moslems on the plains below. The shouts of the Christian army bore to the infidels the dreaded name of *Sobieski!* The latter were driven to their entrenchments after some time. On contemplating these works, he deemed them too strong and too formidably defended to be forced. Five o'clock P.M. had sounded, and he had given up for the day all hope of the grand struggle, when the provoking composure of Kara Mustapha, whom he espied in a splendid tent tranquilly taking coffee with his two sons, roused him to such a pitch that he instantly gave orders for a general assault. It was made simultaneously on the wings and centre. *He* made towards the pacha's tent, bearing down all opposition, and repeating with a loud voice, *Non nobis, non nobis, Domine Exercituum, sed nomini tuo da gloriam!* He was soon recognised by Tartar and Cossack, who had so often beheld him blazing in the van of the Polish chivalry; they drew back, while his name rapidly passed from one extremity to the other of the Ottoman lines, to the dismay of those who had refused to believe him present. " Allah!" said the Tartar khan, " but the wizard is with them sure enough!" At that moment the hussars, raising their national cry of " *God for Poland!*" cleared a ditch which would long have arrested the infantry, and dashed into the deep ranks of the enemy. They were a gallant band; their appearance almost justified the saying of one of their kings —" that if the sky itself were to fall, they would bear it up on the point of their lances." The shock was rude, and for some minutes dreadful; but the valour of the Poles, still more the reputation of the leader, and more than all, the finger of God, routed these immense hosts; they gave way on every side, the khan was borne along with the stream to the tent of the now despairing vizir. " Canst not *thou* help me?" said Kara Mustapha to the brave Tartar, " then I am lost indeed!" " The Polish king is there!" replied the other; " I know him well! Did I not tell thee that all we had to do was to get away as quick as possible?" Still the vizir attempted to make a stand; in vain,—as well might he have essayed to stem the ocean tide. With tears in his eyes he embraced his sons, and followed the universal example—of flight. Europe was saved! Let some extracts from the conqueror's letter on the occasion describe the rest:—

" *From the Vizir's Tent, Midnight, Sept.* 13.

" Only joy of my soul, charming and well-beloved Mariette!*

" God be for ever praised! He has given our nation the victory—a triumph such as past ages have never beheld. All the artillery, the whole camp of the Mussulmans, with infinite riches, are become our p   . The approaches towards the city, the fields around us, are covered with the dead infidels, and the survivors flee in consternation. Every moment our men bring in camels, mules, and sheep which belonged to the enemy, besides a multitude of prisoners. We have also a great number of deserters, mostly renegades, well equipped and mounted. The victory has been so sudden and extraordinary, that both in the city and our camp, the alarm did not all at once subside, every instant the enemy's return was dreaded. In powder and ammunition he has left us the value of a million florins.

" This very night I have witnessed a spectacle which I had long desired to see. Our baggage train set fire to the powder in several places; the explosion resembled the judgment day, but no one was hurt. On this occasion I remarked how clouds are formed in the atmosphere. But, after all, it is a bad job; there is above half a million lost.

---

* The uniform commencement of *all* the king's letters to the queen, with one single exception.

" The vizir in his flight has abandoned every thing, all but his horse and the dress he wore. I am his heir; the greater portion of his riches is become mine.

" As I advanced with the first line, driving the vizir before me, I met one of his domestics, who conducted me to his private tents; they occupy a space equal in extent to Warsaw or Leopol. I have obtained all the decorations and ensigns usually borne before him. As to the great standard of Mahomet which his sovereign had confided to him, I have sent it to the Holy Father by Talenti. We have also rich tents, superb equipages, and a thousand fanciful things equally fine and valuable. I have not yet seen every thing, but what I have seen is beyond comparison superior to what we found at Kotzim. Here are four or.five quivers, mounted with rubies and sapphires, which alone are worth many thousands of ducats. So, my life, you cannot say to me what Tartar women say to their husbands who return without booty—" Thou art no warrior, for thou hast brought me nothing; none but the foremost in battle ever gain any thing."

After speaking of other trophies, for the detail of which we cannot afford room, he continues—

" To-day I have visited the capital; it could not have held out more than five days longer. The imperial palace is full of holes made by the balls; these immense bastions, full of crevices and half-fallen in, look frightful.

" All the troops (imperial) have done their duty well; they ascribe the victory to God and us. The moment the enemy gave way (and the chief struggle was where I stationed myself, opposite the vizir,) all the cavalry of their army rode up to me at the right wing, the centre and left having little to do; among these were the Elector of Bavaria, the Prince of Waldeck, &c. They embraced me, kissed my cheek; the generals saluted my hands and feet; soldiers and officers, on foot and horseback, exclaimed, *Ah! unser brave König!* (Ah, our brave King!) All obeyed me even better than my own soldiers. . . . . The name of *saviour*, as well as embraces, has been given me. I have been in two churches where the people kissed my hands, feet, clothes; others, at a greater distance cried out—' Let us kiss your victorious hands!'

" To-day we follow up the pursuit into Hungary; the electors say they will accompany me."

Some . other circumstances omitted by the royal scribe accompanied his entry into Vienna. Amidst the acclamations of the countless thousands who thus hailed their saviour, not a few contrasted him with the despicable poltroon who had abandoned them, and could not avoid exclaiming, " Why is not this *our* king!" They followed him into the church of the Augustines, where, as the clergy were not immediately in attendance, he himself chaunted the *Te Deum.* Shortly afterwards the same service was performed in the cathedral; the King was present, his face prostrate on the steps of the altar. Then it was that a priest, adapting the words of the Gospel to the hero, read aloud, " There was a man sent from God whose name was JOHN!" The effect was electrical on the assembled audience; there was sublimity in the application.

It is impossible to describe the transports of the Christian world when the result of the campaign was known. Protestants as well as Roman Catholics caught the enthusiasm; every pulpit, " at Mentz as at Venice, in England as in Spain," resounded with the praises of the illustrious victor. At Rome the rejoicings continued a whole month. Innocent XI. bathed in tears of gratitude and joy, remained for hours prostrate before a crucifix. The standard of the prophet was triumphantly borne from church to church, from convent to convent, as the most undoubted signal of the favour of God towards his people, and the success of his lieutenant.

But what was the reward the deliverer of the empire received at the hands of Leopold?

The reader's heart would be sickened quite as much as his indignation raised, were he to peruse the accounts given by the writers of the period, of the base ingratitude of the Austrian towards one who, at a great personal sacrifice, had preserved the crown on his head. He did not fulfil any one of his pledges; there was no arch-duchess for prince James; no longer any intention of guaranteeing the Polish throne to him, or of ceding Hungary. But this is not the worst; when compelled, for decency's sake, to make his acknowledgements to his preserver in person, he insulted rather than thanked him. Worse than all, he even refused to supply the Polish army with provisions or beasts of burden, though the King was going to fight *his* battles in Hungary. The same baseness was continued to the very close of the campaign. But ingratitude, quite as much as hypocrisy, has ever characterized the house of Austria; and of that detestable house the most detested member is Leopold.

We cannot follow this greatest of heroes through his Hungarian campaign. We can only observe that the country was conquered for the Emperor; that though Sobieski sustained a momentary check from a new army of the infidels at Strigonia, October 7th, yet at the same place, five days afterwards, he gained over them a victory, which he truly called " greater than even that of Vienna." " Thanks be to God!" ejaculated he piously, " Hungary is free at last from the infidel yoke after two centuries of bondage!" The impatience of his nobles to return to their fire-sides constrained him, very much to his mortification, to return with them.

What must strike the reader most deeply in contemplating the results of this astonishing campaign, is the fact that from its close

Turkey ceased seriously to disquiet the central powers of Europe: She no longer dreamed of extending her conquests: her only care thenceforward was to act on the defensive,—to preserve, if possible, the integrity of her actual dominions. To this great prince had providence reserved the glorious task of placing bounds to the previously incessant progress of Islamism in Europe. When the torrent threatened to overwhelm the Christian nations;—when from Portugal to Muscovy all was breathless apprehension;—when the Pope himself, like his predecessors of old, trembled lest the Eternal City should become the prey of an enemy more ferocious than Goth or Hun;—Sobieski fearlessly stepped forth, and amidst the blessings of countless millions, erected the bulwark of Christian freedom. From that moment the torrent began quietly to sink into its native channel. Not that the Osmanlis made no effort to recover some of the Hungarian fortresses they had lost; not that the Polish king no more took the field against them—for twice or thrice in the decline of his life he again marched at the head of his lances; but they never again met him with confidence in their own strength, nor consequently without defeat. Generally they did not wait for his onset, but fled long before he could reach them. .

Allusion has before been made to the troubled spirit of the Polish king—troubled by the turbulence and treason of his nobles. The fatal *veto* continued to be his bane;—nay, as if the glory he had acquired was too great to be enjoyed unmixed by any human being, his cares were increased tenfold after the campaign of Vienna. In the wretched constitution of the Poles, it was not enough that when two parties disagreed on any great measure the less successful should confederate—that is, erect the standard of civil war: *any individual gentleman*, however poor, had the power of annulling by his simple veto any decree he pleased, even when approved by every other member of the diet—unanimity, without a single dissentient voice, being as necessary to the passing of such a decree, as to finding a verdict by our jury. In neither case does the absurdity require exposure. There was, to be sure, a remedy for the evil, and a precious one it was. If the dissentient member were poor, he might be bribed to withdraw his opposition; and if this generally successful argument were equally ineffectual, he might be removed by assassination. Not unfrequently, when the courageous dissident lanced his veto, and made haste to quit the indignant assembly, he was cut down before he could mount his horse. But a more common case was, that he who thus daringly put a negative on the proceedings of a whole diet had protectors powerful enough to screen him from the consequences, or at least rich enough to secure him a competency in some neighbouring country, until the desire of vengeance was allayed by time.

The mortifications sustained by the king on thus seeing his most patriotic measures for the good of Poland neutralized, were not the worst evil; his very person, no less than his dignity, was subject to continual insults. One called him a tyrant, even on his throne; another told him he had reigned long enough; a Paz invited him to descend and fight a duel. True it is that the sober portion of the members, who were by far the most numerous, espoused the cause of their outraged ruler, and compelled the audacious traitors to apologise; but could that poor satisfaction heal the wounds of offended majesty, or make him hopeful of a republic whose bosom was lacerated by such disgraceful scenes? In vain did he beseech, expostulate, remonstrate, threaten; in vain did he exhibit the true picture of the ruin such dissensions must bring on the country. What can be more dignified or affecting than his address, delivered with much difficulty, at the close of a stormy diet, (1688,) in reply to the accusations of *despot, destroyer of liberty, traitor,* &c. which a few of the more violent members abundantly applied to him? how prophetic its tone!

" He was well acquainted with the human heart who said, that minor sorrows will speak out, while great ones are mute. The whole world will marvel in contemplating us and our councils. Even nature herself must be seized with astonishment: that all-bountiful parent has endowed every living thing with the instinct of self-preservation, and given to the vilest creatures arms for their own defence; but *we* are the only beings on earth which turn these arms against ourselves. This instinct is wrested from us—not by any superior power, or inevitable destiny—but by a voluntary delirium, by our passions, by our eagerness to destroy one another. What one day will be the melancholy surprise of posterity to see that, while elevated to such a height of glory, while the Polish name filled the whole earth, we have suffered our country to fall into the gulf of ruin?—to fall, alas! for ever! For myself, I may from time to time have gained her battles, but I am powerless to save her. I can do no more than leave the future of my beloved land—not to destiny, for I am a Christian—but to God, the High and Mighty.

" True, it has been said—and the saying has been addressed to myself—that there was a remedy for the evils of the republic; that the king should not be the destroyer, but the restorer of the public liberty. Has he then destroyed it? Senators, that holy liberty in which I was born and nurtured is guaranteed by my oaths, and I am not a man to commit perjury. To maintain it has been the labour of my whole life; from my infancy the blood of all my race has inspired me with devotion to it. Let him who doubts the fact, go visit the tombs of my ancestors; let him follow the path by which they have welcomed me on to immortality. Their blood will tell him the way to the country of the Tartars, and the Wallachian deserts. From the bowels of the earth, from beneath the cold marble, he will hear a voice crying—' Learn of me how noble and sweet it is to die for one's country!' I might also invoke the memory of my father, who was four times elected to preside in this sanctuary of our laws, and who deserved the glorious name he obtained— that of the bulwark of liberty. Believe me all this tribunitian eloquence would be better employed against those who, by their disorders, call down on our native land the terrible denunciation of the prophet, which, alas! even now I hear sounded above our heads—' *Yet forty days and Nineveh shall be no more!*'

" Your illustrious highnesses know that I am no believer in auguries; I do not seek after oracles; I place no reliance on dreams. It is not from auguries, but from faith, I learn that the decrees of Providence cannot fail of accomplishment. The power and justice of Him by whom the universe is governed, regulate the destiny of states : where even during the lifetime of the prince *any* crime is attempted with impunity— where altar is raised against altar, and strange gods followed under the very eye of the true one—*there* the vengeance of the Highest has already begun its work."

The monarch ended his speech, (it will be found too rhetorical, but the fault is certainly not his, but the historian Zaluski's,) by asserting his unfeigned respect for Polish liberty, and his firm resolution to maintain it unimpaired. His words deeply affected the senators, but the impression was short-lived; ere long he was doomed to undergo the same mortifications from the same quarters. He found royalty in such a country too heavy a load for an old man to bear; he ordered his chancellor to prepare the act of abdication. Instantly the voice of faction was hushed; all Poland, not excepting his very enemies, prayed him to remain at his post. All feared that if *he* retired from public life, there would indeed be an end to the existence of the republic. After a short struggle between his inclination and his sober judgment, he submitted to the unanimous wish of the people; for with him patriotism was second only to religion.

The lot of Sobieski in this life was doomed to be as unhappy as it was splendid. These everlasting contentions of his nobles he might have borne—with pain indeed, but at the same time with resignation—had he been blessed with domestic felicity. But his family occasioned him even greater pangs than his diet. His queen intrigued more criminally than ever; his second son, Alexander, at her instigation, laboured to alienate the hearts of the Poles from his elder brother, Prince James, that on the death of the king the crown might fall to him; then the hatred between the elder son and the mother, and between the daughter-in-law and the mother-in-law : the everlasting quarrels that ensued from these fruitful sources, to the scandal of the court and nation, made the old man's life as painful as his crown. Sick of the court, he fled into the forests, or wandered from one castle to another, or pitched his tent wherever a beautiful valley, picturesque landscapes, the mountain torrent, or any natural object attracted his attention. Sick too of the world, he sought for consolation in religion and philosophy. With his intimate friends he discoursed on the nature of the soul, the justice of heaven, the wonders of another life more mysterious even than this—of a life dreaded yet affording hope eternal, and too easily obtained by the cares and sorrows of a day. There might be something of pedantry in his manner, but he was sincerely attached to letters. He not only cultivated them with assiduity himself, but recommended the study of them to others, and patronized all who excelled in them. Under his reign, distracted as it was, more books issued from the Polish press than during the two centuries preceding. He was no mean poet, and his example produced a host, if not of *good* poets, of versifiers; and the diffusion among a fierce ignorant people even of a *taste* for literature was something. The sciences also, astronomy especially, were cultivated with ardour.

At length the end of this great man approached. The immediate cause of his death is wrapt in mystery. He had been recommended to take a strong dose of mercury (his infirmities for some time had been neither few nor light): was it too strong for his constitution to support? So at least thought some—so even he appeared to suspect. If a deed of darkness was actually committed, the veil which covers it will not be raised in this life; the perpetrators and their motives are known only to the Omniscient. At the queen's entreaty, the prelate Zaluski visited him on his deathbed, to recommend him to make his will. " Bishop," he replied, " I am surprised that a man of your sense should argue thus. Can you expect any good thing from the times we live in? Look at the inundation of vice, the contagion of folly, and tell me whether you seriously believe our last wishes will be regarded. Unhappy monarch! while living, our commands are disobeyed;—dead, will they be listened to more readily?"

" On Corpus Christi day," says Zaluski—a day which singularly enough was the one also of his birth and election—" he accepted the sacrifice of dying, more willingly than twenty-three years preceding he had accepted that of reigning." " On that solemn day, without a murmur, he laid down his life and crown in exchange for another life, and, as I most firmly believe, for another crown."

It is some consolation to find that his last illness brought the Poles to a sense of the blessing they were about to lose. All Warsaw flocked to the church to celebrate the double anniversary of his birth and accession—little dreaming, however, that his last hour was come—and to pray God for his restoration to health. When informed of the circumstance, he was affected, but he had no wish that their prayer should be granted. The moment he expired, the sun had disappeared below the horizon, and a tempest arose, so sudden, so extraordinary, so fearful, that an eye witness could not find words to describe it.

" With this Atlas," adds the good rhetorical bishop, " in my eyes at least—may I prove a false prophet !—the republic itself has fallen. Thus we seem not so much to have lost him, as to have descended with him to the tomb. He wore the crown so as to confer more lustre on the regal dignity than he received from it. It might be truly said that our country and our glory lie in the same sepulchre with him. At least I have but too much reason to fear our power has passed away for ever. The grief at this mournful intelligence is universal. The inhabitants weep as they accost one another in the street; those who are less affected are not less frightened at the fate reserved for us. What grief was ever more natural ? He was perhaps the first king under whose reign not one drop of blood was shed in reparation of his own wrongs. He had but one fault—he was not immortal. Born for the universe, he lived only for his country. Many ages will elapse before such a present will be vouchsafed to the world :—an excellent and great man, a marvellous assemblage of the best qualities which we should not believe nature could produce in the same person unless she had once astonished the world with the prodigy !"

The bishop was but too true a prophet. John III. was the last independent prince of the country; with him ended Polish greatness. A prey, first to the Swede, then to the Russian, her first magistrate was in fact but the first of slaves. Frederic Augustus, Augustus III., and Stanislas Poniatowski reigned only at the nod of the Autocrat.

Great as were alike the talents and virtues of Sobieski, impartial biography cannot conceal his defects. No man better understood the interests of Poland, and to do him merely justice, no man ever held them dearer; but in his internal administration we find a degree of feebleness, of weakness even, not to be expected in one of his vigorous understanding. Was it that he saw the hopelessness of attempting the regeneration of Poland? This seems the more probable from the failure of his efforts to give due influence to the crown by rendering it hereditary. Yet there is little doubt that had he acted with as much decision in the cabinet as in the field, he might have achieved something, perhaps much; and thereby have done his people more real service than by all his victories. But *non omnia possumus omnes;* the glory of a hero, a patriot, and a philosopher, is enough for one man.

The weakness of the king in private life was still more lamentable. Who but must smile with as much contempt perhaps as pity to see him bend so humbly before the imperious Maria Casimira? who but must wonder at his pitiful blindness as to the real character of that unprincipled woman? We say *unprincipled,* and we could adduce proofs enough that the epithet is but justly applied; let one suffice. When married to Sobieski, her second husband, she had been a widow three weeks. There, as in the case of Denmark's queen, the funeral baked meats might well have been served at the marriage table. What but infatuation—and infatuation too admitting of no excuse—must have prevented him from perceiving that a woman so ready to forget, and outrage the memory of a man so strongly devoted to her as Radziwil had been, was not worthy of a second love—that instead of being the solace, she would be the curse of his existence. What wonder that she should make that existence so wretched—that she should betray the second husband as she had insulted the first—that she should pour the venom of her own breast into the bosoms of her children, and sow the seeds of the shameful dissensions which happened between Alexander and James before the hero had lain dead twenty-four hours? May not the unhappiness of the king be traced to this first and most fatal error? " If eternal justice rule this ball," is there not retribution in this? We dare not pronounce, but we are sure that history and biography are equally pictures of the moral justice of heaven.

ART. XII.—1. *La Grande Semaine des Polonais, ou Histoire des Memorables Journées de la Revolution de Varsovie;* traduit du Polonais, par un Polonais. Paris. 1831. 8vo.

2. *The Polish Cause. Speech of the Marquis Wielopolski at the Public Dinner given at the Crown and Anchor on the 9th of March,* 1831. Translated from the French MS. 8vo. London.

3. *La Question Polonaise, par Lucien de St. Firmin, étudiant en Droit.* Paris. 1831. 8vo.

WE have seen in the preceding article the almost prophetic denunciations which the misgovernment of ancient Poland and the disunion of her nobles elicited centuries ago from some of the best patriots of that country, from Casimir, Sobieski, Zaluski, and others. These were too truly verified in the course of the eighteenth century. The Swede, and the Saxon, the Russian, the Austrian, and the Prussian, nay even the Ottoman, were alternately courted and called in by the various factions to interfere in the intestine controversies of the country, and to bestow on Poland successive kings, supported by foreign swords. And when the *protection* thus invoked was felt as a yoke, and the nation winced under it, another power was appealed to, and another equally *disinterested* protection readily obtained.   But never would the proud magnates agree to look among themselves and in their own incoherent institutions for the causes and the remedy of so many evils.   Had Poland earnestly taken this wiser course; she might have filled in Europe the station which Russia has since attained, but she let the opportunity escape her, and we see the consequences.   At last the partitions came; and it was not till long after the first of those flagitious transactions, when Poland was reduced to one-half of its former extent, that an attempt was made to alter the defective laws of the country, by the constitution of May, 1791.   That constitution, however, came too late; it only served to shed a lustre over the funerals of Poland; a lustre which was heightened by the resistance of the gallant Kosciuszko and his companions in arms.   Poland ceased to exist as a nation.   The romantic exertions of the emigrant Poles, their devotion to France, their hopes of Bonaparte's interference in favour of Poland, their repeated disappointments, somewhat soothed at last by the establishment of the Duchy of Warsaw at the peace of Tilsit in 1807, the conquest of that duchy by the Russian armies in 1813 after Napoleon's retreat; and, lastly, the erection of this same portion of ancient Poland into a kingdom by the Emperor Alexander in 1815; all these vicissitudes have been narrated and commented upon in a former article of this review.   We then observed that the great obstacle to the tranquillity of Poland and the satisfaction of the Poles consisted in the placing of the crown of a small constitutional kingdom on the brow of the absolute Sovereign of an immense adjacent empire, between which and Poland feelings of national enmity, kept alive by frequent and cruel warfare, had existed for ages.   An Emperor of Russia, even with the best intentions towards the Poles, would necessarily be influenced by the interests, the prejudices, and the pride of his natural subjects, and the same hand which governs with absolute sway forty millions of men, could hardly direct the constitutional movement of a small neighbouring state with the delicacy its complicated machinery requires.   As it was, the contact of the two governments forced to move on together, might be compared to the jogging of the *pot de terre* by the side of the *pot de fer* in the French fabulist. The instance of Hungary being attached to the crown of Austria has been alleged, but we consider the two cases as by no means similar.   The constitution of Hungary is feudal, the peasants are serfs; Hungary forms an ancient and powerful part of the hereditary dominions of the Emperor,—there is no recent bitter hostility between it and the other parts, there is no preponderating mass in the assemblage of states which constitute the Austrian empire, which swallows up the interests of the others; the German interest is felt, it is true, as the interest of the Court, but it is not supported by the blind instrumentality of forty millions of subjects. The greater part of the Austrian dominions is inhabited by various Sclavonian races, as jealous of their customs and local and municipal precedents as the Hungarians themselves. The crown of Austria cannot therefore be considered as autocratical in the same sense as that of Russia. The chivalry of Hungary have long mustered under the imperial standards, and the recollections of many a hard-fought field serve to keep alive their hereditary loyalty. But the Polish armies have never yet met the Russians on the field of battle but as foes, and fifteen years peace could hardly prove sufficient to obliterate the mementos of five centuries.

Oginski states that the Emperor Alexander told him in confidence, that he had met with " many obstacles at Vienna" to the re-establishment of the kingdom of Poland. These obstacles sprang mainly from a natural jealousy of the additional power which would thus accrue to the Russian crown, rather more we suspect, at least on the part of the Austrian and Prussian cabinets, than from zeal for Polish independence, and we are confirmed in this idea by seeing it stated that a counter-project was proposed and discussed in the Congress of a *fourth partition* of Poland, that is to say of the Duchy of Warsaw, between the three powers. This would have been a final blow to all the hopes of the Polish patriots. Alexander resisted the proposal firmly, and was probably supported by France and England in his view of the subject, as being an expedient preferable to the total annihilation of Poland. That there was policy in this determination of Alexander, that he had in view the addition of power to his crown, by being made to rule over the two great Sclavonian nations, there can be no doubt, but it is also certain that at that period he was kindly and liberally inclined towards the Poles, and we have good authority for stating that he never looked so much at his ease and in such a flow of spirits as when mixing in Polish society at Warsaw. Persons who had an opportunity of observing him both there and at St. Petersburgh, were struck with the change in his countenance when he returned to his own Russian capital, where he appeared thoughtful, reserved, and almost gloomy. Alexander had also given some hopes of incorporating Lithuania with the new kingdom, hopes which perhaps he could not have realized without wounding the pride and incurring the animadversion of his Russian nobles; but the disappointment was bitterly felt by the Poles. Secret societies were formed at Warsaw and in other parts of Poland, having for their object the future emancipation of all the

ancient provinces of the kingdom.   A spirit of mistrust and hostility was thus fostered in the breasts of the Polish people towards
their Russian neighbours and fellow subjects, and all prospects of
cordiality between the two nations were at an end.   At last the
Russian conspiracy of 1825 broke out, and although it was not
proved that the Polish secret societies had been engaged in it, yet
it is now admitted that they had knowledge of it, and that several
of their members had interviews at Kiiow with Pestel, Mouravieff
and others of the Russian conspirators.*   The Poles say that
being made acquainted with the views of the latter, which went
the length of establishing (absurd it must sound to all men in their,
senses) *a republic in Russia!* they, the Poles, conceived a just
contempt for the plot and the plotters, and determined, to have no
further connection with them.†   They did not, however, reveal
the Russian conspiracy against the, imperial government, and for
this, one of them, Krzyzanowski, was afterwards sentenced to undergo a correctional punishment.

But the circumstance which aggravated the soreness felt by the
Poles of Warsaw, and which may be considered as having led
ultimately to the late revolution, was the appointment of Constantine as commander-in-chief of the Polish army.   This was a
great error in Alexander, who must have been perfectly well acquainted with his brother's temper and disposition.   In fact, the
principal gravamen of the Polish charges falls upon that arbitrary
personage, who seems to have been a most unfit man to rule over
a spirited and proud people; we say *rule*, because although Constantine was nominally nothing more than generalissimo of the
Polish army, yet he had, especially since the death of the Emperor's Lieutenant Zayonczek, in 1826, monopolized by degrees
the authority of a Viceroy, interfering capriciously in civil and
criminal matters.

We shall now give our readers a concise statement of the Polish
grievances by referring, seriatim, to the various articles of the
Constitution of 1815 which have been infringed at different times.

It was provided by Art., 10, that the Russian troops which
might have occasion to pass through the territory of the kingdom,
were to be entirely at the charge of the Russian treasury.   Russian
regiments, however, have been stationed at Warsaw and in its

---

* See an article on Poland in the *Revue Encyclopédique* of November last.
† It is a remarkable fact, that the Poles had on former occasions calculated on the
co-operation of Russian malcontents from the country beyond the Borysthenes, for
which see Dombrowski's Letters in Vol. I. of the " History of the Polish legions in
Italy," of which a notice will be found among the Critical Sketches in the present
number.   And in 1794, during Kosciuszko's struggle, Russian malcontents from the
same quarter had communicated with the Poles by means of secret emissaries.

vicinity for years past, and have been lodged and supplied with necessaries at the expense of the inhabitants.

Art. 16 guarantees the liberty of the press, the latter being subjcet to the laws for the repression of its abuse. During the last twelve years a strict censorship has been established.

Articles 18 to 21 confirm the old principle—*neminem captivari permittemus nisi jure victum;* individuals could not be arrested, except in the cases and under the forms provided for by the law, the motives of their arrest to be signified in writing to the prisoner, who was to be brought within three days before the proper authority, and if found innocent, to be immediately discharged; bail was also admitted for offences not capital. These provisions, however, have been repeatedly violated; persons have been detained in prison without being brought to trial, others have been brought before military courts, under the pretence that they had been at one time military men, which is the case of most people of the better classes in the country. In cases where the proper court acquitted a prisoner, the latter has been sent before another tribunal, and another, until a sentence has been obtained according to the wishes of the executive. It is true that the independence and inviolability of the judges were guaranteed, but in some instances these magistrates have been removed from one court, where they were found acting in opposition to government, to some other district, where they became comparatively inefficient.

Art. 21 secures to every Pole the liberty of travelling and of removing his property at pleasure, but of late years passports were only obtained with the greatest difficulty, and in many instances altogether refused. Travellers arriving at Warsaw were taken direct to the Grand Duke's residence of Belvidere, there to wait for an audience from Constantine and to answer his interrogatories.

Articles 39, 91—93, left at the disposal of the King the revenues of the state, raised conformably to the budget, which was to be voted by the Diet every four years. But the details of the expenditure have never been submitted to the Diet, and although the minister of finances regulated his department with proper economy, yet he was obliged to submit to superior orders, and part of the revenues passed into improper hands. From papers found in the police office, it results that a sum of 6000 florins or about £150 sterl. per diem was paid to informers, who had become the pest of society at Warsaw. Loans were also granted by the treasury to unprincipled speculators, who never repaid either capital or interest. It would appear as if the Emperor himself was not aware of this misapplication of the public monies.

Art. 47—48, prescribes the responsibility of ministers and superior officers of the state. But this principle became null in praetice, and when the last Diet had the boldness to impeach some of the ministers, it was dissolved, and no further notice taken of the accusation.

Art. 87 says, the Diet ought to be assembled once every two years, and yet from 1820 to 1825, none was convoked. Since Nicholas's accession only one Diet has been assembled.

Art. 95 declares that the debates shall be public. However, an ordonnance, dated February, 1825, abolished their publicity. This was the only illegal act which Alexander signed himself.

Art. 110 and 111 limit the nomination of senators or members of the upper house to the class of persons paying 2,000 florins or 1,200 francs direct taxes. In a country like Poland, this condition was essential to the dignity and independence of the senate, and to the support of the conservative or aristocratic principle; and yet by a singular inconsistency it was violated the year before last, and civil officers were named senators, who had no income but the emoluments of their office.

Art. 135—137, prescribed the formation of a municipal council in every palatinate or province of the kingdom, for the purpose of electing the civil officers, controlling the local expenditure, making the electoral lists, &c. This was a provision truly constitutional, and highly creditable to the framers of the charter. Without municipal rights there can be no political liberty. Of late years, however, this provision was also infringed on in the instance of the palatinate of Kalisz, one of the eight into which the kingdom is divided. It happened that the members of this province were the strongest oppositionists in the Diet, and the palatinate of Kalisz was on this account deprived of its general council!

A council of legislation, composed of members of the Diet and of the senate, had been appointed to revise or remodel the civil and criminal laws of the country. The council was slow in its labours, entrusted the details to men destitute of legislative information, who merely looked upon their employment as a sinecure, and after occasioning an expenditure of large sums of money, produced at last a bad imitation of the French civil code, which satisfied nobody. The project of a law of divorce was particularly objected to, and was rejected in the last Diet by a majority of 69 votes.

Art. 153 provides for the formation of a militia for the internal security of the country. This force, however, was never organized.

Such are the complaints of violation of the charter, as stated by the Poles themselves. Even making allowance for some exaggeration, it is evident that there were sufficient grounds for dissatisfaction. The constitution of 1815, though perhaps not *the best possible,* would, had it been faithfully observed, have satis fied most reasonable men. It is true that a strong party still existed, who, looking back to the former independence and integrity of the kingdom, would never have rested without making attempts to re-unite the vast provinces which have for half a century been annexed to the Russian, Austrian, and Prussian dominions. Improbable as these expectations may appear, they were entertained by sanguine men, and secret societies, as we have already observed, were formed to further their views. This of itself would have been sufficient to obstruct the progress of conciliation, and the establishment of cordial relations between Russia and Poland. But the conduct of the Russian delegates at Warsaw, and especially of Constantine, increased these difficulties tenfold.

The latter alienated the army by his capricious severity, and by his gross and insulting conduct, which, it is stated, was carried so far as actually to strike officers of rank in presence of their men, a thing unheard of in any other military nation in Europe. It was among the young officers that the late revolt broke out, and even now that the cause has become national among all the educated classes, yet its warmest and most determined champions are undoubtedly to be found in the ranks of that army, embittered by traditional recollections and exasperated by recent illtreatment.

In speaking of the manner in which the revolution of Warsaw broke out, we cannot but deplore the acts of violence and vengeance that accompanied it. The movement was no doubt precipitated by impetuous students and subaltern officers, without the concurrence of the higher and more influential classes; this is admitted by the Marquis Wielopolski himself in his speech. " In every nation," says he, " there are the young who are hurried too rapidly away, the mature who pursue the proper pace, and the old and debilitated who march too slowly." Therefore it is essential that " the mature" should direct important national movements, and this has proved, as we earnestly hope it will continue to prove, the salvation of France during the last crisis. The taking away the lives of Russian officers of rank whom the insurgents met singly in the streets of Warsaw, is also a matter of deep regret. Several of these individuals had rendered themselves obnoxious to the Poles, it is true, but others were merely doing duty with the garrison, and their only crime was that of being Russian officers.* Two Polish generals were also murdered, whose senti-

* The following are the names of the officers killed in the night of the 29th of November :—Generals Gendre, Hauke, Trembicki, Siemiontkowski, Blumer, Potocki,

ments are acknowledged to have been patriotic, one of whom, Stanislas Potocki, being unaware of the extent or object of the insurrection, was endeavouring, as in duty bound, to quell the tumult, and the other, General Nowicki, whose name in his reply to the challenge being mistaken for that of the Russian General Lewicki, was killed by one of his own friends. Several Polish regiments fought against their brethren on the first day, although they subsequently joined the popular cause, after Constantine's retreat. The conduct of the last-mentioned personage during the insurrection, appears to have been marked by a singular want of resolution and of presence of mind, which, notwithstanding his personal bravery in the field proved on former occasions, must be fatal to his character as a commanding officer. It is positively asserted that with his Russian troops and the Polish regiments that remained faithful to him, he might have quelled the insurrection before it had assumed a national character. However this may be, he remained inactive for four days outside of Warsaw, and it was only on the 3d of December that the Polish troops, tired out with his vacillations, left him to return to that capital.

In the subsequent conduct of the Polish councils, until the beginning of hostilities, we think we have perceived, as elsewhere, two principles at work, one prudent, cautious, and moderate, and the other, rash, reckless, and intemperate. These two principles may be styled the Oromasdes and the Arimanes of modern liberty. Unfortunately the latter spirit is too apt to gain the preponderance in revolutions. The spirit of the clubs, and the meddling of students in grave deliberative questions, must always prove mischievous to the cause of rational freedom. Among military men, also, in several countries of the Continent, there are but too many whose notions of patriotism and liberty are strangely associated with visions of conquest and of military sway and license, which anomalies they reconcile together in their heads by a series of sophisms such as these, namely: that the forms of liberty must become the same for all nations; that they are to be of the last approved French manufacture; and that the French liberals being entrusted with the high mission of planting liberty all over the world, their armed propagandists have therefore a right to interfere wherever dissatisfaction is stirring, and even to stir it where it lies dormant. Sentiments like these have been publicly proclaimed, to the astonishment of the sober part of the community, by men of no obscure names, by enthusiasts young and old. A more absurd or mischievous creed cannot possibly be imagined.

and Nowicki; Colonels Sass and Mieciszewski, and the Vice-President Lubwidski. Generals Dyakow and Fench were wounded.—See " La Grande Semaine des Polonais," p. 22.

If acted upon, it would lead to a succession of revolutions, dismemberments of countries, and wars, until all the world, all Europe at least, became constituted under one form of government,* which would in all probability be a new military despotism like that of Napoleon, who in some way or other is still evidently the patron saint of most of these pseudo-liberals. It has been gravely asserted that the liberties of France are not safe so long as there exists one absolute monarchy in Europe; nay, so long as there is an hereditary aristocracy of wealth and influence in any one country.* Now this is really going too far. We do not think we have much chance of seeing, in our days, republican institutions prevailing in Russia, Austria or Bohemia, Hungary or Croatia, or in Turkey; and therefore the consequence would be, that we must reconcile ourselves to pass the remainder of our lives amidst an incessant war of principles.

In order to show that we do not exaggerate the views of the ultra-liberal or *movement* party, we will quote, out of a thousand, one passage of the pamphlet which stands third at the head of this article, written by a *law student* at Paris :—

" As long as the other nations that sympathise with regenerated France shall not have overthrown the despotism which weighs upon them, France will be in a critical state of transition, in which she ought not to remain. It is therefore a matter of necessity *that she should assist every where the rising of the masses* that wish to follow her example ; *she must proclaim a war of principles on which her own existence depends.* In order to live free and happy, she ought to associate all other nations to a partnership of her new institutions ; she must raise them to her own level, she must impress on them her own movement, in a word, *she must carry every where thought and civilization at the point of the bayonet.*"— *La Question Polonaise*, p. 9.

We should be ashamed to confound the cause of Polish independence with the monstrous system of political ethics above exposed. Since the sword has been drawn from the scabbard on the banks of the Vistula, we have admired the gallantry and determination of that brave nation, and sincerely trust that their resistance may be the means of finally obtaining for them the objects of their long-cherished hopes, the establishment of their national independence on a solid basis, and a free constitution. By their own heroic efforts, single and unsupported, they have already achieved so much as to inspire us with confidence that they will finally accomplish these great objects, even if left to themselves. These efforts, however, have given them so much the greater claim to the active and immediate, but friendly mediation of

---

* See passim the speeches of MM. Lafayette, Mauguinn, Lamarque, and Co., and the columns of the *National, Constitutionnel,* and *Courrier Français*.

Great Britain and France in their favour.   Let us hope that the ancient sympathies of the distinguished statesman who now directs the British councils, have been awakened in favour of oppressed Poland, and enlisted his powerful advocacy in her cause.*

We shall now conclude this short article on the Polish question by giving some statistical notes on the present social and econo- mical condition of Poland, which we extract from an elaborate statement by Dr. B. Zaydler, a Polish writer, which appeared in a recent Italian journal.

" The kingdom of Poland is divided into *eight* palatinates; *viz.* Ma- sovia, Cracow, Sandomir, Kalisz, Lublin, Plotsk, and Augustowa.   The population, according to the last census in 1829, was (exclusive of the army) 4,088,290, which may be thus classed :—

" *By their several races:*		*By their religion:*	
The real Poles	3,000,000	Roman Catholics	3,400,000
Rusini, or Rusniacks, from the eastern parts of ancient Po-		Greek Church	100,000
		Lutherans	150,000
land	100,000	Calvinists	5,000
Lithuanians	200,000	Jews	400,000
Germans	300,000	Other Sects	5,000
Jews	400,000		
	———		———
	4,000,000		4,060,000

" The population of the towns is to that of the country as one to five.

Employed in agriculture, there are householders	.	1,871,259
Their families and servants		2,221,188
Manufacturers		140,377
Their families		358,035
Tradesmen		49,888
Their families . . . . :		131,331
Landed proprietors		4,205
Copyholders		1,886
Freeholders in towns		41,654
Persons employed under government		8,414
Patients in the 592 public hospitals		5,376
Prisoners in the 76 prisons		7,926

" The proportion between the nobles and the plebeians is as one to thirteen.

" According to a verification made by the senate in 1824, there were in the kingdom 12 princes, 74 counts, and 20 barons, besides the inferior or untitled nobility.

---

* The limits to which this article is necessarily confined, prevent us from entering into a variety of other considerations which the subject naturally suggests.   We feel the less regret, however, in abstaining from further discussion at present, in conse- quence of finding, since this article was written, that the whole question has been taken up, and treated *au fond*, with a leaning in favour of the Poles certainly, which is very natural, but at the same time with great calmness and temperance, in a pamphlet en- titled " Thoughts'on the Present Aspect of Foreign Affairs," published by Ridgway.

" The city of Warsaw reckoned, in 1815, only 80,000 inhabitants; it now amounts to 140,000, besides the garrison. The provincial towns are Lublin, having 13,400 ; Kalisch, 12,100 ; Plotsk, 9,200, &c. The population of the kingdom has been increasing since 1815, at the rate of 100,000 individuals every year.

" It appears from Dr. Rodecki's statistical tables published at Warsaw, in 1830,—that there are Jews in almost every town of the kingdom of Poland ; that in 14 of these, their number is equal to that of the Christians, while in 114 it is greater : in three, the inhabitants are either all Jews, or almost entirely so. In Warsaw alone they muster 30,000. Their number is fast increasing. They monopolize almost all trade, to the exclusion of the Christian population. The government has endeavoured to check this evil, but with little success ; and with this view Professor Chiarini has been employed in translating the Thalmud, and in laying down a plan of reform for that singular people.*

" ' The Catholic religion being that of the great majority of the kingdom, is under the *special protection of the government,* without infringing, however, on the public freedom of other forms of worship, and on the equality of individuals of every communion in the enjoyment of civil rights. The Catholic hierarch consists of the Archbishop of Warsaw, primate of the kingdom, and eight bishops, one for each palatinate. There are 1,638 parish churches, 117 auxiliary ones, 6 colleges, 11 seminaries, 151 male convents, and 29 female. In 1819, Pope Pius VII. suppressed by a bull 31 male convents and 13 female. The number of the clergy of the Latin Catholic Church is 2,740. The Greek Catholics have a bishop at Chelm, 287 parish churches, one seminary, and five male convents. Their priests amount to 354. There are, besides, six churches of the Russo-Greek communion under the jurisdiction of the Bishop of Minsk, 29 Lutheran and 9 Calvinist churches, having their respective consistories, 2 of the sect of Philippines, 274 synagogues, and 2 Mahomedan mosques with their imams !

The University of Warsaw was founded in 1816 in lieu of that of Cracow, and it consists of five faculties, having 48 professors, and about 750 students. There are besides at Warsaw four lyceums, besides other schools, Sunday schools for mechanics, and girls' schools. In the provinces are 11 palatine schools and 14 district ones. In all the kingdom there are 1756 professors or teachers, nearly 30,000 students, and about 11,000 female pupils.

" In all chief towns of palatinates there are civil and criminal courts, besides commissions of peace in every district. The two courts of appeal and the supreme court assemble at Warsaw. The senate takes cognizance of offences against the state ; there are also a court of commerce and a territorial court.

" The army consisted, in 1830, of eight regiments of infantry of the line, besides the guards, four regiments of light infantry, eight regiments of cavalry, besides the yagers of the guard, two brigades of foot artillery, and two ditto of horse, a corps of engineers, &c., in all 36,000 men.

---

* See No. XII. of this Review.

The arsenal and foundery are at Warsaw.   There are two fortresses in
the kingdom, Zamosk and Modlin.   Every individual from 20 to 30
years of age is subject to military service, except in cases of exemption
provided by the law.   The two new military schools, formed in 1825,
near Warsaw, have educated already 7,000 pupils.

" The budget of 1827 consisted as follows : —

	Receipt.	*Florins.**
Direct taxes		17,646,652
Indirect ditto		40,685,630
Income of national lands and forests		7,048,265
Income from tolls and rates on bridges, roads, &c.		3,769,955
Receipt from mines, mint, prisoners' labour, &c.		2,837,600
Total		71,988,102

	Expenses.	*Florins.*
Civil list reduced in 1822, from 2,324,705 to		1,508,150
Vice-roy, senate, council of state		924,609
Ministry of public instruction and religious worship		3,831,821
Ditto of justice		2,528,301
Ditto of interior or home department		3,178,909
Ditto of war		30,927,795
Ditto of finances		5,155,936
Secretaryship of state		223,000
Superior central authorities		944,965
Commissions of administration in the Palatinates		3,666,526
Pensions, repair of roads, public buildings		11,422,007
Extraordinaries		1,866,410
Charges on separate administrations		2,837,600
Total		69,016,030

" There are in the kingdom, especially about Kielce, mines of iron,
zinc, coals, and also copper and lead.

" Of the 451 towns in the kingdom 353 consist more than half of
wooden houses; 83 are entirely of wood; 6 have half their houses
made of brick; and 9 consist of more brick than wooden houses.
Warsaw contains 1,540 brick and 1,421 wooden houses.

" Besides the towns, of which 214 are national property and 237
belong to private families, there are in the kingdom 22,365 villages,
5,373 of which are national, and 16,992 private property.

" The communications have been extensively improved since 1815.
Two fine substantial roads cross the whole kingdom, one from Kalisz
to Brzesk Litewski, another from Cracow to the Niemen, both passing
through Warsaw.   Diligences have been established; inns and post
houses erected; 523 bridges have been constructed or repaired.   Em-

---

* The Polish *florin* is about sixpence sterling. , It is divided into 30 *groschet*.

bankments, in great part of stone, have been raised to restrain the waters of the Vistula. The other rivers have been cleansed, and a canal has been cut to join the Narva to the Niemen.

" The city of Warsaw has wonderfully improved since the peace. New streets, squares, palaces, gardens, private and public buildings have been constructed either by government or by individuals assisted, in many instances, by the public treasury. The streets are well lighted, several of them have been Macadamized. The management of prisons has been ameliorated, the convicts are employed in the public works, mendicity has been suppressed. A society of beneficence has been formed at Warsaw, as well as a society of the friends of science. A new exchange, a new theatre, the new church of St. Alexander, new barracks, and a monument to Copernicus, by Thorwaldsen, have been raised.

" The exports of the kingdom consist chiefly in corn and cattle, besides honey, wax, timber, wool, hides, and tallow. The imports are wines, tobacco, colonial produce, and articles of luxury and fashion.

" The manufactures of woollen cloth, linen, carpets, and leather, have thriven since the peace. While in 1815 there were hardly one hundred looms for coarse woollen cloths, there are now above six thousand, which now supply the whole kingdom, including the army. More than ten thousand families of foreign workmen, chiefly German and Swiss, have expatriated to Poland, where they have built new towns and peopled districts formerly deserted. There are numerous distilleries of spirits, and the brewing trade is also very extensive; they brew porter and ale equal to those of England. By the former laws of Poland commerce was depressed, and no noble, however poor, could, without degradation, resort to it, whilst he often served in a menial capacity a richer nobleman.

" The balance of trade between the kingdom of Poland and the neighbouring states in 1827, stood as follows :—

	Florins.
Imports from Russia	11,079,683
Exports to ditto	14,548,522
Imports from Prussia	20,318,433
Exports to ditto	15,544,730
Imports from Austria	8,527,480
Exports to ditto	91,967
Imports from the republic of Cracow	748,857
Exports to ditto	2,880,265

" Agriculture, which is still the principal occupation of the population, suffers under a depression of prices, In 1827, they reaped 4,439,399 *korzecs** of rye, 3,183,023 of oats, 1,506,062 of barley, and 751,076 of

* A *korzec* is nearly two hundred weight. It is divided into 32 *garniecs*, of four *kwartz* each.

wheat, besides 4,288,185 *korzecs* of potatoes, and hay, flax, hemp, and honey. The cattle are improving both in quantity and quality.

" In 1827 there were in the kingdom 694,728 cows ; 475,946 oxen; 259,990 calves, 703,207 pigs, about two million and a half sheep, 192,841 horses, 8,771 stallions, 167,901 mares. About one half of the extent of the territory of the kingdom may be reckoned to be cultivated, one-fourth of the remainder is occupied by forests, and the rest by marshes and uncultivated lands.

" Since the establishment of the Grand Duchy of Warsaw, the peasantry of that part of Poland have been emancipated ; they live on the estates of the great landlords, each family having a cabin and thirteen acres of ground, on condition of working for the owner three days in the week. They may remove themselves, by giving up their tenement. Several proprietors have adopted the system of free labour and wages."

CRITICAL SKETCHES.

Art. XIII.—*La Vita di Cola di Rienzo, con osservazioni, &c. di* Zefirino Re *Cesenate.* (The Life of Cola di Rienzo, with Observations, &c. by Zefirino Re, of Cesena.) 2 vols. 8vo. Forlì. 1828.

THIS is not an entirely new work, but a reprint, according to the excellent fashion of the present day, of an old book, increased in value by investigations, criticisms, illustrations, &c. &c., the produce of modern study. The original Life is a very pleasing and natural piece of contemporary biography, and as such, would still be highly interesting, even had it no other merit. The present editor indeed sees cause, and we think upon sufficient grounds, to dispute the authorship of *Tommaso Portifiocca, Scriba-Senato Romano,* (or Clerk to the Roman Senate,) to whom it has been usually ascribed, but he deems its contemporaneity to be fully established by the " I saw" and " I heard," which the biographer frequently uses in relating the particulars of his history. And we moreover fully agree with Signor Zefirino Re, that—

" The truth which shines in pure resplendence throughout his narrative breathes of that golden age, and of the modest simplicity with which the two Villanis wrote their celebrated histories, as well as of the vivacity with which the bold Dino lashed the vices of his fellow-citizens."

Perhaps this may be somewhat overrating the *Vita di Cola di Rienzo,* considered merely in a literary point of view. But we, nevertheless, think the whole reading public is much indebted to our editor for this revival of a nearly unknown work, narrating an episode in the history of the Middle Ages but little better known, and from the very anomaly of its character peculiarly interesting to the philosophical historian, whilst it affords to the politician, especially to the young, and, therefore, hot-headed, politician, a lesson from past times not inapplicable to the actual state of the world.

Cola di Rienzo may, not improbably, be best known to some of our readers by the successful tragedy of our talented countrywoman, Miss Mitford ; and what is more remarkable, we believe his chief claim upon the sympathy and the curiosity of his own countrymen arises from the circumstance of his bold enterprize and the fair promise of its dawn having inspired the genius of Petrarch with the finest of his *Canzone;* we mean that beginning—

" Spirto gentil, che quelle membra reggi."

Aristocratic contemners of the low-born Roman Tribune have indeed asserted, contrary, we think, to all internal evidence, that the *Canzone* in question was addressed to one of the Colonna family, and a full quarter of Signor Zefirino Re's present publication consists of a commentary upon the said *Canzone,* destined to reinstate Cola in the glory of really being the object of Petrarch's poetical enthusiasm ; a question which the English reader may deem more important to the history of the poet than to that of the demagogue. It is the extraordinary phenomenon of Cola di Rienzo's rise, and temporary rule amidst the intense feudalism of the 14th century, that renders his life worthy the attention of every reflecting mind. And to all such, more especially to all who love to speculate upon the varieties of human nature, upon the changes induced by circumstances upon human characters, we would recommend the unknown contemporary biographer's work. · It is· written, we think, with great impartiality, notwithstanding the writer's manifest admiration of his hero, especially of his eloquence, concerning which he repeatedly exclaims, when recording its employment or its influence, *Deh! come bene parlava!* Oh! how.well he spoke! ·

Cola di Rienzo was of low origin, being the son of a publican and a washerwoman. His name, aristocratical as it sounds, is composed of two familiar abbreviations, Cola of his own name Nicholas, and Rienzo, or Rienzi, (for it is written either way,) of his father's, Lorenzo. It is as if in speaking of Jack Cade, we substituted the Christian name of his father for the surname, and supposing that worthy person to have been denominated Jem, called him Jem's Jack : so that Miss Mitford, who probably meant to dignify her protagonista by giving him only the last part of his appellation, deeming it, perhaps, surname or the name of a birth-place, has merely changed the Jack for the Jem. We own the Italian Jem is the more sonorous of the two. Cola, as his biographer invariably calls him, enjoyed the advantage of an education far superior to his birth or his parents' means, for which he was probably indebted to a class of men as much over-reprobated in these philosophical· times, as they were over-venerated of yore, we mean the monks, who frequently bestowed much gratuitous pains upon the instruction of youths displaying talents worthy of cultivation.

·. Cola's imagination seems to have been heated by ideas and images of the ancient power and liberty of his native Rome, and its vague fires were directed against the feudal oppressors of the Eternal City, by the murder of his brother, for which he could obtain no satisfaction, no justice. He now addressed himself to inflaming his fellow-citizens by oratorical declamations upon the liberty of their forefathers and their own thraldom; and succeeded so well, that in May, 1347, he effected his own election to the classical office of Tribune. With this plebeian title he obtained an absolute authority, which he at first administered with the inflexible integrity and the simplicity of a Cato. He compelled the haughty barons to forego their acts of arbitrary and licentious violence, and submit to the controul of the law ; and during this period of pure greatness and glory, the Tribune was acknowledged as a potentate by all the states of Italy, as well as by some others. But when did man exercise despotic power without himself experiencing its baneful effects? Vanity was the first fruit of its noxious influence on Cola. He claimed the right of deciding the great cause then pending between Joanna Queen of Naples, accused of having sanctioned the murder of her husband, and Lewis King of Hungary, that husband's brother ; and he proceeded to summon emperors and electors, popes and cardinals, before his judgment-seat. It is needless to say, that this last step provoked most formidable enmity. Yet even that enmity he might by possibility have defied or defeated ; but so rapid was the deteriorating action of despotism upon our Tribune's character, that within eight months from his elevation, his luxury, insolence, cruelty, and tyranny had exasperated the whole population of Rome to such a degree, that in December, the legate, sent by Pope Clement VI. to act against this usurper of his temporal authority, found it no arduous task to excite the citizens to insurrection against their lately idolized Tribune.

Cola with some difficulty escaped from the popular rage, and fled from Rome. He spent about three years in concealment; then, apparently recovering his original boldness and enterprize, he visited the court of the Emperor Charles IV. and ere long established himself in his imperial majesty's good graces. He next repaired to Avignon, then the papal residence, where he was thrown into prison, and for a while closely confined. But upon trial he was cleared of all the crimes, especially the heresy, laid to his charge; and so complete was his acquittal, that the new pope, Innocent VI., named him Senator of Rome, and sent him back thither, with the legate, Cardinal Albornoz, to suppress the disorders that had arisen since the Tribune's flight.

During the six years and a half which had elapsed since that event, Rome had been harassed with factions, desolated and oppressed by the great barons, and tyrannized over by another Tribune, who had all his predecessor's faults without any of his great qualities. A strong party in the city declared for Cola, and on the 1st of August, 1354, he re-entered Rome, under his new title of Senator, resuming his former sovereignty. But in his exile the ex-tribune had learnt to seek consolation in wine, and habitual inebriety now added a character of irrational caprice to his previous cruelty and tyranny. He forfeited the good will of his subjects yet more speedily than before, and by the 8th of October, his conduct had provoked a tremendous popular tumult. The first alarm seems to have restored him to his original self; and as a short specimen of the quaint old work before us, we translate part of the account of Cola's conduct upon this occasion.

" When the Tribune saw the tumult increase, and himself deserted, he hesitated greatly, and asked his three companions what could be done; and wishing to remedy the mischief, he took courage, and said, ' It shall not go thus, on my faith!' Then he armed himself in complete armour, in knightly guise, and took the banner of the republic, and presented himself alone in the balcony of the upper saloon. He extended his hand, making signs for silence, and that he was about to speak. Without doubt, had they listened to him, he would have broken and changed their opinions, and the attempt would have been defeated. But the Romans would not listen; they acted like hogs; they threw stones, shot arrows, ran with fire to burn the doors. So many were the darts and arrows, that he could not hold out in the balcony; one dart struck his hand! Then taking the banner, he spread out the silk, and with both hands shewed the golden letters and the arms of the Roman citizens..... But these tender modes were of no avail; the senseless people did worse and worse, and shouted, ' Death to the traitor!'

We must tell the result somewhat more briefly than our good Italian biographer. Cola now thought only of saving his life. For this purpose he exchanged his armour for the clothes of one of the meanest of his domestics, and taking a quantity of bedding upon his head, endeavoured to mingle with the rabble, (who were breaking into the blazing palace) as one of themselves carrying off plunder; but he was recognised by some magnificent ornament which he had neglected to take off, and falling into the hands of the infuriated multitude, was put to death with every circumstance of indignity. Such was the end of a demagogue of high talent, liberal education, and originally, it would seem, of excellent intentions.

ART. XIV.—1. *Henri III. et sa Cour, Drame Historique, en Cinq Actes, et en prose.* Par Alexandre Dumas. Paris, 1829. 8vo.

2. *Jeanne la Folle, ou la Bretagne au* 13*me Siècle, Drame Historique, en Cinq Actes, et en vers.* Par L. M. Fontan. Paris, 1830. 8vo.

THE revolution which has deposed the classical school of the Corneilles and Racines, and given the romanticists absolute possession of the French stage, preceded by very many months, we believe, the memorable week of July, which transferred the crown of Charles X. to Louis Philip.   Nevertheless, we conceive the two revolutions to be intimately connected, and strong political excitement to be the chief cause of the prevalent French passion for historical dramas; the only kind of play now capable, as we are assured, of drawing full houses to either that once most classical of theatres, the *François*, or the minor Parisian play-houses.   We are not sure that we do not greet the dramatic revolution with more unmixed satisfaction than the political; for although we have no doubt but what its first fruit must be an inundation of bad dramas, we still think that it opens a prospect of future tragedies, in which the best parts of the adverse schools may be blended together, producing a result infinitely superior to any thing the French stage has yet known.   And the worst evils that threaten to attend the progress to a " consummation so devoutly to he wished," are dullness and absurdity.   Of the probable progress and termination of the political revolution, we are not here called upon to hazard any conjectures.

It would be most agreeable to us could we await the perfect amalgamation we have ventured to prognosticate, ere we felt called upon to notice the dramatic vicissitudes now in course.   But we conceive that all changes occurring in foreign literature imperatively demand our attention; and we have therefore selected the two historical dramas now before us, as illustrations of the transition in question.   We shall begin with that which enjoys the honours of the *Théâtre François,* which has transformed the best comic actress now extant, Mlle. Mars, into a first-rate tragedian, which is the rage in Paris, and which actually does produce upon the stage a very powerful effect.   We wish we could bestow equal commendation upon it as a literary production.

M. Dumas altogether rejects the trammels of verse, or even of a prose style at all elevated above the ordinary tone of conversation. Neither does he trouble himself to devise any very masterly or artificial conduct of his story, or development of his characters.   These last unfold themselves with a prompt frankness which the censorious might term bald; and which we can understand only by supposing that the author never meant his work to be read, and relied upon the actor's talents to relieve or disguise his own idleness or unskilfulness.   We shall extract part of a scene between Catherine of Medicis and her hireling astrologer, as at once opening the business of the play, and affording an average sample of M. Dumas' dialogue, as well as an instance of the sort of baldness of which we have spoken.   The Queen-mother says :—

" The Duke of Guise and St. Megrin are my enemies. But it is this young gentleman of Bordeaux who especially disturbs me. Better educated, less frivolous than Joyeuse or d'Epernon, St. Megrin has acquired an ascendancy over Henry that frightens me. Father, he would make him a king.

"*Ruggieri.* And the Duke of Guise?—

Cath. Would make him a monk. Neither would suit me. I must have him something more than a child, and something less than a man. What! shall I have depraved my son's heart by voluptuous indulgences, and smothered his intellect under superstitious puerilities, only that another than myself may seize upon his mind and govern him at pleasure? No. If I have given him a fictitious character, it was that that character might subject him to me, that I might continue regent, though France had a king. Thus far I have succeeded. But these two men!—

"*Rug.* Well, cannot your valet de chambre, René, prepare them perfumed balls, such as you sent the Queen of Navarre a couple of hours before her death?

"*Cath.* No; they are essential to me: they maintain that irresolution in the king's soul which constitutes my strength. I seek only to fling other passions athwart their politics, to distract their attention for an instant; then I make my way between them to the king, whom I shall thus have insulated with his weakness, and I regain my power."

This may suffice to show the open-hearted, straight-forward manner in which M. Dumas' personages disclose their own turpitude. The story corresponds with this mode of painting characters. The plot for interrupting the political purposes of Guise and St. Megrin, in which the queen desires the conjurer's aid, is to make Guise jealous of his wife and St. Megrin, who are already desperately in love with each other, although the strict virtue of the duchess has prevented even a declaration. Catherine succeeds in every purpose of mischief, but none of benefit. The duke scarcely makes a five minutes pause in his cabals with the *Ligueurs*, whilst he just compels his wife to make an assignation with her lover. And how, gentle reader, think you he compels her? Heroically she prepares to drink the poison he offers her, but when he pinches her arm black and blue with his gauntleted hand, she yields, observing that a woman can die but not bear pain. We pity women sincerely if they cannot; and moreover we hope this new school will not bring the rack, wheel, and other forms of torture, upon the stage as sources of the pathetic. St. Megrin falls into the snare and is assassinated; the duchess faints or dies, we know not which; and the curtain drops upon the duke's intimation that he will now see about dethroning the king. The best scenes are those in which the duchess betrays her love.

We proceed to M. Fontan's Drama, which we must confess is infinitely more to our taste, although we believe it is far less popular than *Henri Trois et sa Cour.* Our preference is, perhaps, partly influenced by *Jeanne la Folle's* being in verse, as we must further confess our reluctance ever to see gorgeous tragedy despoiled of her natural garb of dignity; but we also think that this piece displays much more boldness and originality of genius than the other, and thence holds out far greater promise of improvement; for we by no means consider M. Fontan as being either beyond the need of improvement, or as having reached the height to which he is capable of soaring. We must begin our *critique* of his historical drama with cavilling at his title: He calls it *Britanny in the* 13*th century:* yet the main part of the story turns upon the apprehended subjugation of Britanny to William the Norman, King of England. Whether this be William the Conqueror, or William Rufus, is not explained; but as the latter prince died in 1100, we are at a loss to imagine what danger could threaten Britanny from either in the 13th century. The play consists of the plots of a wicked and deformed younger brother, Conon, to rob his amiable elder brother, Arthur, of the affections of their father, Duke Hoel, of his birthright, and of his plighted bride, Alicia, the daughter of William the Norman. At length Conon involves Arthur in suspicious appearances of parricidal and fratricidal intentions, and obtains a sentence of death against him, the execution of which is only prevented by the intervention of Jeanne. This personage, who gives her name to the play, passes with all her acquaintance for a witch, and is so designated in the *Dramatis Personæ;* though, as far as we can judge, she is simply mad: her only supernatural feat being the knocking a stout young man (the bearer of Arthur's death-warrant), on the head with a bludgeon, an operation which the audience does not indeed see, the curtain falling as she lifts her club, but which she accurately describes in the next act. In the fifth act Conon requires his old doting father to surrender his duchy to him during his life-time, and, upon his positive refusal, murders him. We shall translate part of the subsequent scene. Conon stands confounded at his own crime, when Jeanne rushes in, and exclaims :—

" Aha ! The deed is done. There's blood for blood.
                    [*Throwing down Arthur's death-warrant.*
" *Conon.* 'Tis well.   And Arthur?
" *Jeanne.* Rescued.
" *Conon.* Rescued !
" *Jeanne.* Duke !
He's now the Duke—Hear'st not the glad acclaims?
" *Voices without.* Arthur for ever !
" *Jeanne.* Hear'st thou ?
" *Voices without.* Arthur! Arthur!
" *Jeanne.* He comes!—Young Arthur, our Liege Lord; our Duke !
" *Conon.* Woman, thou hast betrayed me !
" *Jeanne.* Aye, indeed !
                    *   *   *   *
The self-same death we here must die together,
United by our murders. 'Twas to die
I came ; I, murdress of my foster-son.
                    *   *   *   *
Did the old man, beneath thy ruthless axe,
Like him implore for mercy?   Was't one blow?
Did one suffice?   [*Flames are seen through the windows.*
" *Conon.* What sudden light?   Away !
" *Jeanne.* We go not hence !   I tell thee—no escape !
See how the fire its hundred arms of flame
Extends, devouringly t' encircle us.
" *Conon.* At least I'll dearly sell my life.   [*Drawing his sword.*
" *Jeanne.* Already
That idle hope is lost.   Oh, my precautions
Are taken !—Every path for thee is closed.
Submit !—No human aid can snatch thee hence.
                    *   *   *   *

My Lords of Brittany, pray take the field
For crook-backed Conon l · Shed for him your blood !
Expel the English foes. A throne, a palace !
Quick for our crook-backed duke a stately palace !
Then form his court.   Bow, haughty vassals, bow
Your heads before his high deformity !
Long reign the noble duke !—Conon, look up !
  [*The flames increase, and part of the Palace falls.*
.See ! There's an opening !—Now escape !—escape !
  [*He stabs himself, whilst the Sorceress laughs, and the whole Palace falls in.*"

We must add one concluding remark upon what appears to us M. Fontan's system of rhyme.   Every French scholar knows that French poetry does not, like English, prohibit the use of identical syllables as rhymes ; that is to say that *impel* might, according to French rules, rhyme to *repel*.   But never did we see rhymes of this kind swarm as they do in this author's pages, and we cannot but conceive that he must consider *these* as the only perfect rhymes, and those which we deem more correct as only to be tolerated when no better can be had. In a page taken at random we find the rhymes as follows :—Faiblesse, blesse ; vaillant, assaillant ; lutte, chute ; pas, pas ; fuite, suite ; toujours, jours ; insolente, lente ; ici, ceci.   Six identical to two rhyming syllables.   The effect is, to our ear, peculiarly disagreeable.

ART. XV.—*Details and Observations on the Cholera, which has prevailed in the Government of Orenburg, from Autumn, 1829, to Autumn, 1830.* Published by the Supreme Medical Board of Russia (in the Russian language.)

A TRANSLATION of these reports into German, with a commentary, has been prepared by Professor Lichtenstein, of St. Petersburg, and has probably by this time issued from the press.   The importance of the subject induces us to give our readers the conclusions at which the Russian Medical Board has arrived.

Many persons might have remained ignorant of the character of the Cholera Morbus, so long as it was confined to India and Persia, but its approach towards the centre of modern civilization renders it a subject of mingled curiosity and apprehension.

For the information of those who are not aware of the magnitude of this evil, we shall first offer a description of the character of this disease derived from the account of the epidemic in India in 1817.   This epidemic arose at Jessore, 100 miles from Calcutta, and continued for many months, constantly spreading its ravages till it reached in one direction to Bombay, and in the other extended along the whole coast of Coromandel; reached Ceylon, and stretched across the Straits of Sunda to China: it was also subsequently carried to the Mauritius.   The cholera will sometimes travel against the wind and the monsoon itself, and is not arrested by coldness of temperature.   The proportion of persons it attacked in the epidemic just mentioned, in Bombay for instance, was

15,945, out of a population of 200,000 or 220,000 inhabitants, and it is asserted that all the persons who did not receive advice, 1,294 in number, perished, independently of those who died in spite of medical attendance. This disease produces in many cases immediate death, all sensorial power being extinguished in an instant, "just as the electricity from a Leyden jar is discharged, on the contact with the brass rod." Where the disease is mortal, but dissolution does not take place so rapidly, the symptoms. are " violent vomiting with painful cramps, damp clammy sweats, cold and bloodless extremities, burning heat at the stomach, a sudden death-like countenance." The skin under the nails becomes incurvated, the palms of the hands and soles of the feet become shrivelled, and at last all pulsation totally ceases. In many of these cases the patients are in dreadful agony, and require sometimes six people to hold them in their beds.

From India the Cholera has extended to Persia, and is now no longer an Asiatic disease, having, after entering Russia, made an alarming progress towards us: it is now in Gallicia. Regarding it as a contagious disorder, the British government has prudently adopted measures to prevent its importation. Having given a description of Cholera, as it appeared in India, we now lay before our readers the information published by Professor Lichtenstein, of St. Petersburg. The most prominent features are:—

The disease first showed itself in Orenburg the 26th August, 1829, and later in the village of Massina, February 6, 1830. The number of sufferers amounted to 3590, of whom 2725 recovered, 865 perished. Considering the apprehensions excited as to the results, the treatment adopted must be esteemed very effectual. From the combination of individual observations and experience, the medical board has arrived at the following conclusions; which, with reference to the strongly disputed point, as to the contagiousness of the distemper, as well as a general insight into its nature, and the remedies applied, will be found of the highest importance.

, 1. That the disease, prevailing at Orenburg within the specified period, was actually the Cholera.

2. The important question, whether the disease originated in Orenburg itself, or was introduced from its boundaries on the Kirgish side, in spite of the most rigid investigation on the part of the local medical boards, is yet undecided.

· 3. The other question, however, which does not yield to it in importance, viz., whether the disease be contagious, is now more satisfactorily settled than the first. From the first observations on it, independent of the description of the Staff Physician of Sokolon (all of which appear at length in the work,) we might be induced to think that the Cholera did not communicate itself to the patient by immediate contact. However, in the progress of the malady, the local boards, as well as the physicians, have been fully convinced that the cholera does in fact disseminate itself from one man to another, and by this means travels from place to place.

4. From all observations collected, we must come to the conclusion that the contagiousness of the Cholera, though in some instances incontestible, is nevertheless not so apparent as that of the plague and yellow fever. The infectious power is not so visible in its operation on all who come in collision with those afflicted with it. This is most conspicuous in the primary stage of the disorder.

5. All this tends to confirm the decision of the medical board, (also included in this summary,) which was contained in their treatise issued on this subject. In this it is declared that the Cholera, in common with many other epidemical disorders, becomes in process of time contagious, and may then extend itself by communication.

6. The police, and quarantine regulations adopted in the Orenburg government, were doubtless of great benefit. Nevertheless it occurred, as related by the Staff Physician, that the inhabitants, after the inforcement of a fourteen days quarantine, were visited by this disease. Allowing that this happened without any recent intercourse with persons and places affected, we must concede that the term of fourteen days was scarcely adequate for the full development of the latent malady in the subject. It has resulted from observation that the contagiousness really exists.

7. Confiding in these remarks, and not in any theories that may have obtained on the subject, we must allow that the progress of the disease at Orenburg was of the most rapid nature. In the course of twelve to eighteen hours from its commencement, the disease has been known to terminate fatally.

8. The Cholera, partaking of the character of the plague, can recur, and affect the same persons again.

9. Change of weather and climate has apparently no influence on the progress of the Cholera. The cold, in contradiction to the early observations, has not the least power over it. It was in December and January that it attained its utmost malignity, and extended itself in some places at a temperature of 27° to 30° Reaumur.

10. The Faculty of Orenburg adopted no other police or precautionary measures against the Cholera than those prescribed in the directions of the medical board. They consist in an entire separation of the patient from the sound members of the community, and in a faithful application of all external influences, which may benefit the patient.

11. The protecting power of camphor has, it appears, on this occasion proved ineffectual. In none of the observations collected is it mentioned.

12. In the treatment of the Cholera, the necessity of the immediate application of medical means has been abundantly established. The lapse of a few hours, without recourse to the assistance of art, will render the disease very dangerous, often incurable. The "*médecine expectative*" cannot be made available here. The strongest remedies must be applied without the least temporization or intermission.

13. From amongst the multitude of remedies we may select the chief, viz., bleeding, calomel, opium, warm covering and friction.

14. Oil of cajeput, volatile alkali, and muriatic acid, fail of their expected operation here.

15. The mortality of this epidemic was not so extensive as it is described to be in its ravages in the south of Asia. A census of the mortality was taken in the Orenburg government, where the people were in the habit of concealing the disease in its incipient state, and where little attention is paid to cleanliness and salubrity of dwellings. If we compare the details in the lists of the dead, we shall find some districts which have suffered more severely than others.

ART. XVI.—*Taréas de un Solitario, o nueva Coleccion de Novelas.* (Tasks of a Solitary, or a New Collection of Tales.) Madrid, 1829. 12mo.

THE Western Peninsula of Europe appears to have been almost the birth-place of chivalrous romance, as well as of the beautifully simple ballad, historical or legendary, to which, in Spanish, the name of *romance* is especially given; probably from its having been one of the earliest forms of composition in the language of the country, when termed indifferently the vulgar tongue, and the *langue Romane* or *Romans.* Yet such works of fiction, moral, pathetic, or impassioned, as under the name of novel or romance, now delight most parts of Europe, are in Spain* almost unknown. What Spanish literature does afford of the kind is little, and that little dull, cold, extravagant, and uninteresting. Under existing circumstances of this nature, we gladly hail a volume, even of the size and description of the one before us, although in any other language with which we are acquainted it could not have commanded an instant's notice. We have perused it with some satisfaction, and trust that its reception will be such as may encourage its author to cultivate and exert talents evidently equal to better things.

This tiny volume contains an allegorical dream and five short stories, concerning which the author says, " If I have sometimes imitated, I have at other times invented, and never have I translated."

From this declaration we draw the conclusion, that the tale of *El Cuadro Misterioso,* or the Mysterious Picture, being altogether new to us, is original. Of the other four, two are founded upon Shakspeare's Twelfth Night, and Much Ado about Nothing; a third is borrowed from Washington Irving's sleeping hero; and the fourth from an old Italian story, we forget whether of Bandello, or some other *Novelliero.* All are, however, as the author avers, imitated, not copied or translated ; some are transferred to Spanish ground, and all are varied and adapted to his own taste. This is sometimes done happily, as when in his *Agravio Satisfecho,* or the Expiated Insult, taken from Much Ado about Nothing, he substitutes thé great captain of Spanish history, Gonsalvo de Cordova, for Dogbery, as the detector of the plot against the reputation of Hero; but we cannot say that we think all our Solitary's alterations, improvements, or that he, as yet, discovers any peculiar skill in the management or construction of a story. Our impression is, nevertheless, strong that, if he would take the pains, he could write an effective tale. His language is excellent ; and, in fact, it has never before been our good fortune to read any thing in Spanish that so clearly and powerfully bore the impress of the spirit of these cultivated and stirring times, as our anonymous author's Tasks, which, by the way, might, we conceive, more appropriately bear the title of Lord Byron's earliest publication, Hours of Idleness.

The introductory Vision is by far the cleverest thing in this tiny

* Don Quixote is a satire, or a satirical romance ; a title which will include most good Spanish tales. Cervantes's own serious romance, *Persiles y Sigiemunda,* is unreadable.

volume, and from it we shall take our specimen. The author supposes that during a visit to the *Biblioteca Real,* or Royal Library, in the new edifice built for its reception, while profoundly meditating upon the contempt professed for Spanish literature by those nations whose writers have most freely plundered its treasures, he lays his head upon a ponderous folio, (not one of those whence the spoilers had drawn their booty we presume,) and falls asleep. He now dreams that he sees numbers of ragged, meagre, miserable looking beings enter the library and seize upon the books, which at their touch are converted into splendid garments. We translate part of the description of subsequent proceedings, both because we think it lively and fanciful, and because we suspect that few of our readers may be aware how much the best French authors are indebted to the contemned literature of Spain.

"Amongst the crowd were a few less shabby in dress and mien than the rest. In one of these, distinguished by his courtly air, polished manners, and harmonious language, I immediately recognized M. Le Sage. This personage accosted Don Vicente Espinel with a fine speech or two, and politely disencumbered him of his cloak. Next admiring his doublet and ruff, he very quietly appropriated those articles likewise; and finally, unable to withstand the attractions of the hat, he set that, with all its graceful feathers, upon his own head. Then, leaving poor Espinel in complete *dishabille,* he himself appeared so bravely and gallantly equipped, that he looked like a real Spaniard.

"At this moment I observed a very solemn gentleman, who, with a theatrical step and great assumption of importance, walked up to Guillen de Castro, and, as though doing him a prodigious favour, snatched the *Cid's Tizona** from his side, buckled on the golden spurs presented to the hero by Doña Urraca, and suffered neither helmet, shield or gauntlet to escape him. When thus armed a knight, he retired with so martial an air, that I deemed it had been the very Ruy Diaz de Bivar himself. How was I scandalized when in the spoiler I discovered the celebrated Corneille!

"Shortly afterwards appeared an *exquisite,* trimmed and perfumed, with the airs of nobility, and some order at his breast. The signs could not deceive, and I knew that this was Florian. He, without wasting time in compliments, laid hands upon P. Gines de Hita, taking from him Boabdil's scymetar, Zoraida's caftan, and Muley's turban. All which prizes he so skilfully arranged upon his own person, that he seemed a legitimate Abencerrage.

"Who could have believed it! Not even the fair sex was safe from the rapacity of these intruders! There wanted not manufacturers of comedies who despoiled Doña Maria de Zayas of her cap and silk skirt, and left her blushing and out of countenance at the affront offered to her."

It can hardly be necessary to explain, that of the authors here named, the Spanish have supplied the French with more than the ground-work of those pieces upon which rests the reputation of the latter. We now take our leave of the Solitary, but we hope not for long; and as we have heard that foreign authors do sometimes take a hint from our critiques, we sincerely wish that these remarks may meet our Spanish novelist's eye, and animate him to that labour and those exertions which alone, we firmly believe, are requisite to insure his achieving something very superior to the present little volume.

---

* The name of one of the *Cid's* swords.

ART. XVII.—*Histoire des Legions Polonaises en Italie, sous le Commandement du General Dombrowski.* Par L. Chodzko. 2 vols. 8vo. Paris. 1829.

GENERAL DOMBROWSKI was one of the principal officers who had fought under Kosciuszko, in the last war of Polish independence, against the Russians and Prussians in 1794. He left his country, after the taking of Warsaw, and repaired first to Berlin and afterwards to Paris, where a number of Poles had assembled and held their meetings at the Hotel Diesbach, endeavouring to induce the Directory to some resolution, or at least demonstration, in favour of the reintegration of Poland.* The French government, however, having made peace with Prussia, could not openly give umbrage to the latter power, and replied to the Polish refugees by evasive words. Dombrowski having no confidence in these intrigues, bethought himself of another project. In October, 1796, he laid before the Directory a plan for raising a Polish legion in which the refugees might enlist, and which would be swelled by deserters from the Austrian service. By this means the *nucleus* of a Polish army would be formed to act under the orders of France until an opportunity should be given it to re-conquer Poland. The plan was considered advantageous to the French government, but the French constitution forbade the enlistment of foreign troops in the service of the Republic. To evade this difficulty, the Directory said " they would endeavour to prevail on their good allies, the Cisalpine Republic, which Bonaparte had just formed at Milan, to take the Polish Legion into their pay," thus saddling the Italians with the expense of a corps, which was to serve, however, under the orders of the French generals, and assist in their campaigns. Dombrowski repaired to Milan, and the general-in-chief of the army of Italy, Bonaparte, referred him to the Lombard Congress. A convention was signed in January, 1797, by which the Polish corps was taken into the pay of Lombardy. They were to be commanded in their own language, to have their own national uniform, but to wear the French cockade. Two battalions were formed at first, but the number was soon increased to four, amounting to more than three thousand men.

The first services of these Polish auxiliaries were required against the Republic of Venice, the fall of which reflected but little credit on the French cause. Colonel Liberadzki was killed in entering Verona, where an insurrection had broken out. The Poles fought bravely on every occasion, and they, as well as our author, a Pole himself, never seem to have doubted for a moment the justice of any aggression in which the French were engaged. Themselves the victims of oppression in their own country, they became the unreflecting instruments of a parallel injustice in other lands. Thus moral evil perpetuates itself.

The Polish Legion, after the fall of Venice and the peace of Campoformio, was stationed at Rimini, on the frontiers of the remaining Papal territory, then at peace with the French and Cisalpine republics. On the 22d of December, 1797, a revolt broke out in the neighbouring town of Pesaro: a troop of armed patriots, as they were then called, attacked

* See the article on Oginski's Memoir on Poland, No. VI. of this Review.

the garrison, took possession of the military posts, and arrested the commandant and the Roman governor, Monsignor Saluzzo. The latter sent a message to General Dombrowski, as the officer *of a friendly power*, requesting his intervention. Dombrowski answered, " that being in the service of *a neutral power*, he could not order his troops to advance beyond the frontiers of the Roman territory, but that if the governor thought his life in danger, he would, on his personal responsibility, give him the assistance humanity required;" and he sent the second battalion of his Legion, together with a thousand Cisalpine infantry and cavalry, under General Lecchi. The sequel is curious and characteristic of those transactions: we quote M. Chodzko's words.

" The *papal troops* (not the insurgents) were driven from all their posts; the governor (who had required the general's friendly assistance) and some hundreds of men were made prisoners of war; and two pieces of cannon, a vast quantity of ammunition and stores fell into the hands of the Italian and Polish troops. A provisional municipality was installed, a civic guard formed, &c. The papal troops seeing this, retreated to Fano and Urbino; but General Lecchi *pursued them* even there, and found the population (so says our author) tired of the pontifical yoke, and preferring the new government of the conqueror and the strict discipline of the republican troops to the vexations of the papal soldiers. Deputations from the Adriatic provinces came to General Dombrowski, requesting to be occupied by the victorious army. Their wishes *were speedily granted.*"—vol. ii. pp. 47—48.

It may be remarked that this violation of the Roman territory took place before the tumult at Rome on the 27th of December, in which the French general, Duphot, was killed, and which served afterwards as a pretext for the invasion of the whole Roman territory by the French in February, 1798. It is but justice also to observe that Bonaparte had no share in these transactions, he being then in Egypt.

The Poles marched to Rome with the French army under Berthier. There the pageant of a republic was got up on the Capitol, and Roman consuls appointed. But the country-people were not so easily persuaded: two formidable revolts broke out, one at Frosinone and Ferentino, the other near Terracina. The Poles were sent, with some French troops, to put down the insurrection. Frosinone was burnt, Terracina was pillaged, the insurgents were slaughtered without mercy: "The bayonet of the republicans cleared the earth of them." Such are Mr. Chodzko's words, and he calls the Italian country-people who fought for their homes and their country against the intrusion of insolent foreigners—he calls them in every instance *rebels!* The Roman, Neapolitan, Tuscan peasantry, *rebels against the French!* Suwarrow, if we recollect right, in 1794, called the Poles rebels against Russia. We cannot follow our author in the narrative of similar horrors during the whole of that and next year, 1799. From Rome the Poles and French went on to Naples. Similar insurrections or *rebellions* broke out, and similar means were adopted to quell them. Sessa, Traetto, Castelforte, were taken by storm, the people slaughtered without mercy, the towns burnt, the walls razed. The same scenes took place on the return of the army to the North, in passing through Tuscany, where another insurrection had broken out at Arezzo and Cortona. The Poles being generally in the advance, were mostly sent against the insurgents. · Brave to rashness, stern and uncompromising, they appeared among the terrified Italians as the ministers of republican wrath, and left behind them a fearful remembrance. When in cantonments, however, they preserved a strict discipline, and being Catholics they attended to their religious duties, different in this from their allies, the French.

: In, June, 1799, we find the Polish Legion engaged at the terrible battle of La Trebbia, against their old enemy Suwarrow, who had, as if by magic, been transported from the banks of the Vistula to those of the Po. The Poles, animated by national hatred, fought like lions during those three days : they lost *one half of their numbers.* The French were obliged to retire towards Genoa. The Polish Legion was again engaged at the murderous battle of Novi, on the 15th of August, 1799. At the end of that disastrous campaign the Legion, reduced to 800 men, was stationed at Marseilles, where it recruited to fill up its thinned ranks.

The following year (1800) Bonaparte resumed the command, and victory smiled once more on the French. The Polish troops were not present at Marengo, but they fought against the Austrians at Peschiera and Legnago. After the conclusion of the armistice which led to the peace of Lunéville in 1801, the two Polish Legions, that of the Danube and that of Italy, were assembled in the latter country, forming altogether a body of nearly 15,000 men. The greater part of them was afterwards embarked at Leghorn and Genoa under the command of Jablonowski, and sent to St. Domingo, where they almost all perished in that disastrous expedition! Of those who remained in Italy, some entered the service of the Italian Republic, and some that of Naples, after the second invasion of that kingdom by the French. " Such, after five years hard fighting in the service of France, were the fate and the reward of the Polish Legions."—vol. ii. p. 323.

Dombrowski remained in Italy. He had never during his foreign campaigns lost sight of the prospects of his native country. He was continually making plans, more sanguine than practicable, for bringing about the re-establishment of Poland; but his schemes, on being submitted to cool-headed statesmen, appeared shorn of all their brilliant colouring, and were rejected. The first project of Dombrowski was laid before the cabinet of Berlin in March, 1796. In it he proposed to begin the revolution in Austrian Poland; that Prussia should march her troops into those provinces under the pretence of maintaining order, drive the Russians beyond the Dniester, and lastly establish a Prussian prince on the constitutional throne of Poland.

Dombrowski's second plan was still more hazardous and romantic. He proposed, in 1797, to march with his Legion from the Venetian states into Austrian Croatia, deceive the Austrian troops by a feint, then throw himself into the Turkish territory, and after crossing Servia, enter Bukowina and Gallitzia, there to stir up insurrection. The French government, it was observed, would not be compromised by this movement, *in which it could always deny having taken any part.*"—vol. ii. p. 327, *et seqq.* The Directory approved of the plan, and sent it to Bonaparte, but that general had just signed the preliminaries of Leoben with

Austria! It was now necessary to be circumspect towards the latter power, and Dombrowski proposed to make common cause with Austria against Russia and Prussia, and to place the Archduke Charles on the throne of Poland. This plan was sent, in 1798, to General Bernadotte, the French ambassador at Vienna.

In July, 1800, another project was laid by Dombrowski before Bonaparte. It was to march rapidly with the Polish Legions from the Rhine to Egra in Bohemia, and thence through Moravia into Gallitzia, surprising the Austrians, and hoisting the standard of Polish independence. At the general peace a compensation might be given to Prussia in Germany, and to Russia in Turkey, for the loss of their respective shares in Poland.—p. 281.

But enough of these dreams. Dombrowski lived long enough to think them so himself. That brave veteran, after repairing to Napoleon's camp in 1806, and contributing to the formation of the Dutchy of Warsaw, retired to Posen, where he enjoyed a short period of repose. He was again in the field in the famous campaign of 1812; and in that of the following year, after the death of Poniatowski, he led the remains of the Polish army across the Rhine. After the peace the Emperor Alexander named him Senator Palatine of the new kingdom of Poland, with the decoration of the White Eagle. Dombrowski was now past sixty, and his health was seriously impaired by constant fatigue and the wounds he had received. He retired to his estate of Winagora, in Prussian Poland, where he died, in the midst of his family, in June, 1818, one year after Kosciuszko's death. He desired to be buried in the uniform he had worn during his Italian campaigns.

"A short time before his death, General Dombrowski, conversing with an officer formerly under his orders, expressed his bitter regret at seeing that all the efforts, the sacrifices made, the bravery displayed by the Poles in the service of the various chiefs who had led them to combat, had been of no avail to their own country. ' What have we to hope,' exclaimed he, ' or rather, what have we not to fear? I see no ties between the scattered parts of Poland, and no security against the chances of future events. Had Napoleon, after escaping from Elba, carried his eagles again to the banks of the Vistula, what would have been the consequence unto Poland? More bloodshed, more combats, more victims; but as for independence or liberty—never! Whosoever he be for whom the Poles have broken their spears, what advantage did they derive either from victory or defeat? Feeble because disunited, what conditions can they expect from the winner in the great game? None but what his own policy may suggest him to prescribe. . . . . What matters the yoke under which we are now bent? Whoever be the prince, whatever the government, let the Poles be united in sympathy, in their wishes, in their opinions—let them be united even in serving the sovereign who rules them at present. One day, perhaps, one day, if fortune, who has given him the empire, were to avert her face from him, Poland might then recover its independence, and acknowledge no other king but the one it should freely choose.'"

The lesson we derive from the whole of this melancholy narrative, and which becomes doubly important at the present moment, is, that *no people ought to trust to foreigners for the regeneration of their country.*

DENMARK.

PROFESSOR Thiele, Secretary to the Academy of Arts in Copenhagen, will shortly commence the publication, in Danish, of a series of *Thorwaldsen's Works;* editions in French and English will also appear. The first volume will contain the history of this great artist up to 1814, with seventy-three etchings of his various productions to that time. The second volume will continue the history to 1828. The engravings have been partly made in Rome by Bisser and Lindau, under the inspection of Thorwaldsen, and partly by the first artists of Copenhagen.

FRANCE.

The *Society for the Diffusion of Useful Knowledge* in this country lately addressed a series of questions to a kindred society* in Paris, with the view of obtaining some precise and accurate information as to the general system of education pursued in France. The replies, which were drawn up by a late head of the University, M. Vatismenil, fill an octavo pamphlet of forty-six pages. Our limits do not allow us to give an analysis of its contents, but the public will no doubt soon be made acquainted with them through the medium of the Society's newly established *Journal of Education.* It may, however, be our duty, in a future number, to take up the subject of education on the continent at length, and we shall then have great pleasure in communicating the substance of M. Vatismenil's extensive inquiries, and in doing justice to his able and enlightened views. As connected with this subject our readers will forgive us for introducing here the following tribute, from the *Journal des Debats,* to the eminent and distinguished person who was the primary agent in directing these inquiries to be made.

" There is a man now living in England, whose name is associated with all the blessings of modern civilization. A profound politician, and an impassioned orator; faithful to the public weal, and the friend of virtue —he is equally active in the abolition of the slave trade—in the establishment of the University of London—and in the emancipation of the catholics; and is undoubtedly the greatest and most extensive propagator of elementary education in the civilized world.

" Placed, by the power of his genius, at the head of the opposition, he has enjoyed the singular good fortune, after many years' struggle, to see the triumph of all his views; and the crowns that now adorn his brow have been won from the hands of his very enemies in politics. This man—who was formerly seen leaving the office of a lawyer—is raised on a sudden to the summit of power. He is seated, by our revolution,† on the wool-sack—the proudest throne of

---

* *Société du Bulletin Universel, pour la Propagation des Connaissances Scientifiques et Industrielles.*

† Our readers will smile at this sally of the lively Frenchman. We acknowledge the great impulse given to the cause of reform in this country by the late revolution, but the natural course of events in England, independent of all foreign influence, would have raised Lord Brougham to his present elevation in a very few years.

liberty; and exercises there that royal popularity, the generous influence of which is felt throughout the whole extent of the civilized world."

The first number of a monthly publication devoted to charitable institutions has just appeared at Paris. Prefixed is a preliminary report, drawn up by Baron De Gerando, on the plan of the society.

Biagioli, the author of the well-known Italian Grammar and other works, died at Paris in December last. His Commentary on Dante is among the best that have appeared on that difficult poet, and shows Mr. Biagioli to have been every way qualified to diffuse a taste for the vast conceptions of the Italian Homer. M. Biagioli has left several works in MS. particularly a new Dictionary in Italian and French, and French and Italian, which has been long announced.

At the sitting of the Academy of Sciences on the 13th of December, Baron Cuvier made a verbal report as to some collections of natural history recently brought from India by M. Dussumier. This gentleman has for the last ten years devoted a large portion of his time and a part of his fortune in collecting subjects of natural history. This is the sixth voyage he has made to India and China, and the sixth time that he has loaded the Museum with his presents; but the present exceeds in magnificence all the previous gifts. It presents a large addition of mammalia, quadrupeds, birds, reptiles, fishes, mollusca, and testacea. M. Dussumier is anxious to set out upon another voyage to Canton and Manilla, and M. Cuvier, in the name of the Academy, recommended him to the favourable notice of the government.

It appears from a list of the dramatic pieces played at Paris during the two last years (from the 1st of January, 1829, to the 31st of December, 1830,) that no less than 3558 have been performed.

M. Magendie has been nominated to the chair of Medicine of the Society of Medicine.
M. Navier has been appointed Professor of Analysis of the Polytechnic School; and M. Pouillet, Professor of Physics at the same School.

M. de Parchappe, an old pupil of the Polytechnic School and officer of artillery, who quitted France on the restoration of the Bourbons, has just returned from a long and extensive journey in South America. M. de Parchappe was the friend and companion of the unfortunate Bompland and of the intrepid traveller D'Orbigny. He devoted his particular attention to the geography of the countries through which he travelled, and has brought home valuable materials for a knowledge of the republic of Buenos A res, and the manners and customs of its inhabitants. The author himself traced the courses of the Parana and the Uragai, two considerable rivers hitherto very little known, as well as most of the rivers of that vast territory as far as Patagonia. His travels are now preparing for publication.

GERMANY.

A cheap edition of the *Augusteum,* or Dresden's Museum of Ancient Monuments, is about to appear.

A handsome edition of the *Corpus Juris Canonici,* in one vol. 4to., with notes and parallel passages, will speedily appear.

Counsellor Feder, of Darmstadt, is employed on a new edition of Statius, for which purpose he has made a large collection of MSS., some of which have been procured from Spain.

Dr. Walz, of Tubingen, who has been ransacking the libraries of France and Italy for the last three years, has announced an edition of the *Rhetores Græci*, in seven vols.

Professor Creuzer has lent the whole MS. of his edition of Plotinus to this country for impression.

Dr. Hermann, of Heidelberg, will shortly publish an extensive *Introduction to the Study of Greek Antiquities.*

Professor Moser, of Ulm, has collected a large and hitherto inedited mass of materials for the illustration of a new edition of Cicero's *Disputationes Tusculanæ.*

Died in November last, at Pesth, in his 49th year, the celebrated Hungarian poet *Charles Kisfaludy*. He was the first projector of the Hungarian Almanack of the Muses, the Aurora, and particularly distinguished himself in dramatic literature. He has already had honourable mention made of him in this Journal, see No. V. p. 60.

We have seen a prospectus of a new Italian and German, and German and Italian Dictionary, by Dr. Valentini of Rome, who has been many years established in Berlin as a Professor of his native language. Judging from the prospectus and specimen of the work which accompanies it, the new Dictionary promises to excel all that have hitherto appeared in copiousness and lexicographical arrangement.

A Biography of Ancient and Modern Jews is about to appear, in *Hebrew*, by E. Carmoly. Chronological tables will be prefixed for the purpose of facilitating the *historical* arrangement of the subject, which will appear in alphabetical order.

The publication of Messrs. Ehrenberg and Hemprich's Natural History Collections, made during their travels though Libya, Egypt, Nubia and Abyssinia, from 1820 to 1825, is now proceeding at Berlin. Of the *zoological* division, the first part of the *Mammalia*, the first of the *Birds*, and the first of the *Insects* have just appeared.

Dr. Eschscholtz, the naturalist, who accompanied Captain Kotzebue in his Second Voyage round the World, is publishing a Zoological Atlas, containing figures and descriptions of the new animals discovered during that voyage.

A German translation of the Spanish Epic, the *Araucana*, of Ercilla, (an article on which poem appeared in this Review some numbers back,) has just been published by a Mr. Winterling.

Herr Kaufmann, of Berlin, who is already favourably known by some considerable versions from Shakspeare, is now engaged in a translation of BURNS. He proceeds under the eye of the Berlin *Society for Foreign Literature*, of which he is a member. Goethe, in a letter to one of his friends, thus speaks of him and his undertaking: *ein talent-voller junger Mann, und glücklicher Uebersetzer beschäftigt sich mit* BURNS, *ich bin sehr darauf gelegen.*

The literary deluge, which commenced in Germany in 1814, still continues to increase. For the 2000 works, which were then about the annual compliment, we have now nearly 6000. The catalogue of the last Leipzig fair (Michaelmas, 1830) contains 3444 articles, of which 2764 are actually published, and if these are added to the 3162, announced in the Easter catalogue, the number of books published during 1830 will amount to 5962. The number published in 1829 was 5314; in 1828, 5654; in 1827, 5108; previously to which the number had never exceeded 5000. Magazines and popular encyclopædias have increased in the same proportion, and the public has showed as great a desire to read as the learned have to write. Private libraries are diminishing, while public ones are daily increasing.

A collection of the works of the most eminent philosophers who have flourished from the revival of letters to the time of Kant, is now in the course of publication at Stuttgardt. It will include Bacon, Descartes, Spinoza, Locke and Hume, and select portions of the works of Leibnitz.

The publication of Ersch and Gruber's *Encyclopædia of Arts and Sciences,* which had been suspended for a considerable time, is now resumed. The 21st part of the first section, the 7th part of the second, and the 1st part of the third have recently made their appearance.

The first volume of the *Life and Literary Correspondence of Fichte,* published by his son, has just appeared at Sulzbach.

The seventh volume of Mr. Von Hammer's History of the Ottoman Empire, including from 1699 to 1739, is just ready. The work is now announced to extend to two more volumes.

The *sixth* volume of Professor Wilken's *History of the Crusades* is just published at Berlin. It embraces the crusades of the first half of the thirteenth century.

HOLLAND.

An original novel or romance in the Dutch language is so great a rarity that *De Schildknaap* would deserve to be mentioned, even did it possess less merit than it actually does. This production belongs to the class of what are termed historical romances, and which are now so much in vogue in every country in Europe, where there is any demand for works of fiction. The tale— for as it consists of only a single volume, so ought it perhaps to be designated—has juster pretensions to the epithet " historical" than many others which assume it, the fictitious portion of the narrative being kept rather subordinate to the events and materials taken from history, than merely embellished by a few historical reminiscences, and incidental traits of costume. It is by no means, however, a dry chronicle of the period it illustrates, retaining the formality of history, without its dignity and authenticity: on the contrary, the author has neglected no opportunity of bringing forward whatever relates to the national manners and character of the Hollanders at the period he has selected for his purpose, namely, the middle of the thirteenth century. His details of this nature are touched with spirit, and exhibit great truth of local colouring; a merit that must give his work a value even in the eyes of those, be they his own countrymen or foreigners, who may not consider the story itself a performance of superior interest. The outline of this latter is simple, not to say meagre, enough: Sicco, the hero of the tale, is an orphan, educated at the court of Floris IV., who afterwards becomes the Squire (*Schildknaap*) and companion of William II., Count of Holland, accompanying him in his various military exploits; until disappointed in his attachment to the beautiful Christina von Wassenaar, he sets out on a pilgrimage to Jerusalem. After his return he joins the prince in Germany, whence he returns with him and his consort to Holland. Among the ladies in the suite of the latter is Agnes von Wallern, who wins the squire's affections, and returns his love; in consequence of which he becomes anxious to clear up the mystery hanging over his birth, and at length discovers that he is the son of Eppo Kamminga, Lord of Ameland. The union of the lovers does not however put an end to the narrative, which the author brings down to the period of William's untimely death in an insurrection of the West Friezlanders (1255) when; his horse sinking into the ice, the defenceless prince was ruffianously dispatched by them. After this melancholy event, Sicco and Agnes retire to their castle at Ameland, where they pass the remainder of their days in tranquillity. Few and unvaried as these leading incidents of the story are, and they certainly do not exhibit any great invention or contrivance, the work itself displays great ability, and may be recommended as affording an interesting and instructive picture of Holland in the thirteenth century.

Among the numerous imitations to which Jouy's Hermite de la Chaussée d'Antin has given birth, we may reckon Cramer's *Pelgrim der Nederlanden;* which, although it is far inferior to that prototype, displays some curious and rather striking, if not masterly sketches of national manners. Consistently with his character, the pilgrim does not confine his observations to the Dutch capital and its inhabitants, but makes various excursions to other places, and avails himself of the opportunity thus afforded to touch upon antiquarian and historical topics; and as very few tourists of our own have communicated much on the subject of Holland, these six little volumes will be found to supply the English traveller with some useful topographical information. As is the case with almost every other work of the kind, the scenes from real life are too overcharged in the colouring; the follies and extravagancies scattered throughout the whole mass of society, are concentrated in a focus till their force becomes unnatural and intense. Satirists are not much unlike those who should pick up all the weeds and stones out of a field, as a sample of the productions of the soil: they collect together all the vices and absurdities they meet with, and then say " this is society, this is the age." Such, however, is not society: were it such, it would be unendurable. We do not mean to say that the " Pelgrim" sins in this manner at all more than, if quite so much as, the generality of writers of the same class: yet there are one or two *traits* in his work that startled us not a little, and which certainly do not say much in favour of the morals of the Dutch. In his description of the fair at Amsterdam, he mentions, as a fact, what to us appears incredible, namely, that there was a public exhibition of the amours of a lion and lioness, of which notice was given in placards, and at which many *ladies* (*vele dames*) were present! After this we may believe almost any thing related of a people who can tolerate such disgusting indecency. Some of the most interesting and really valuable papers in this work are two or three biographical sketches, viz., Herreyns the painter, who died August 10th, 1827, and who is here said to have been one of the finest colourists after Rubens, Vandyke, and Jordaens; Andries Snoek, the celebrated tragedian, whom even Talma confessed to be unrivalled, and the no less celebrated Madame Wattier Ziesenis, the Siddons of the Dutch stage. This accomplished tragic actress was born at Rotterdam, April 13th, 1762, and died at Brussels, April 23d, 1827.

ITALY.

Mr. Marino Salomon, of Cephalonia, has published in Italian, at Bologna, an " exposition of the political causes which thwart the progress of agriculture in the Ionian islands, with notes on the past and present state of public administration." In the latter part the author has exposed the vices' and abuses of the old Venetian administration of those islands, the *provveditori*, or delegates sent by the senate, being generally needy nobles who went there to recruit their purses by all means in their power, extortion, fines, sale of offices, &c. The consequence was that industry was cramped, commerce fettered by monopolies, agricultural produce low; *currants* f. i. were one fourth or one fifth of their present value. The roads over the islands were detestable, no inns, no establishments for charity or education. One hundred sequins were sufficient to purchase a doctor's degree, and there is an anecdote of a nobleman who obtained a degree for his valet, and boasted he could have one for his horse. After this, the present administration must appear a blessing, and although the author does by no means flatter it, it is evident that under the English protection the Ionian islands have been far happier than ever they were before.

. A new scientific journal has been announced for publication at Padua under the title of *Annali delle Scienze del Regno Lombardo Veneto*. The principal professors of the university are among the contributors, among others Dal Negro and Da Rio. The first number was to appear in March, 1831. This publication is intended to fill up the void left by the cessation of the " Journal of Sciences of Pavia" in 1828. The *Annali di Storia naturale* continue to appear at Bologna.

A new edition of Gioia's celebrated work, *Filosofia della Statistica*, is being published at Milan in five volumes, octavo, with valuable additions by Professor Romagnosi.

We find that the system of mutual instruction is spreading fast in the schools of Tuscany, Parma and even Sicily. It is not admitted in Piedmont nor in the Roman states. In Austrian Lombardy it existed till 1822, when it was stopped, and we believe has not been since resumed.

Dr. Palloni, one of the most distinguished medical professors of Italy, died last year at Leghorn. His principal claims to the gratitude of his countrymen are: his having introduced vaccination into Tuscany in spite of the prejudices against it: his having by his wise regulations stopped the progress of the yellow fever which broke out at Leghorn in the autumn of 1804, and threatened all Tuscany and Italy. He was in consequence appointed Physician to the Board of Health of that port. In 1817 he also by his cares arrested the progress of the petechial fever, which was making great ravages at Leghorn. Respected by all the governments which followed one another in Tuscany, he was decorated with various orders, was member of the principal Italian academies, as well as of those of Berlin, Copenhagen and Wilna. The following are among the treatises he has published " Whether the yellow fever be contagious or not? Opinions on the fever which prevailed at Leghorn in 1804. Observations on the petechial typhus and on contagion in general. On the change in the climate of southern Europe. On the actual state of medicine, Leghorn, 1826. Account of a case of somnambulism, with reflections on this phenomenon."

POLAND.

On the 11th of May last a superb colossal bronze statue, which had been erected by the Poles to the memory of Copernicus at Warsaw, was first unveiled to the public. The Philomathic Society, after attending divine service in the Church of the Holy Cross, adjourned to the open place, when the venerable Julian Ursyn Niemcewitz from the raised platform of the monument addressed the assembled multitude with singular eloquence and power, and his words falling from the lips of a man óf more than eighty, moved whole masses of the listeners, now to enthusiastic plaudits, and anon to tears. He said that three centuries had passed since Copernicus had been gathered to the bosom of that earth whose motion round the central sun he had revealed. That the forgetfulness of the great services of the great was usually succeeded by the outburstings of grateful remembrance, and that posterity often dragged forth to immortal memory the names which had been resting in temporary oblivion. He spoke of this as the fate of Copernicus, and he honoured with deserved plaudits Staszyc who had defrayed half the expenses of the statue. He mentioned Thorwaldsen, who had modelled it. "Now," said he, "after ten years lingerings, shall every Polish heart vibrate with the satisfaction that beams from every Polish eye: and the sun on which Copernicus turned in perpetual gazing shall for the first time visit his image with its glorious beams." At this moment the tapestry fell which covered the statue, and he continued— "Henceforward ever present wilt thou be. Highest, happiest of the eternal! The honour of thy country—the glory of thy race. Let thy influence, watching over the temple of the national muses,* guard it from all degradation and aid the propagation of all knowledge and all truth. And how infinitely happy am I in the privilege of having lived to extreme old age, to perform this honourable office—*nunc dimitte, Domine, servum tuum.*" Every head was uncovered—every face turned towards the statue—and the heavens which for three days had been cloudy and dark, broke out into sudden brightness and sunshine. There was a burst among the people as if a miracle had really been wrought in celebration of the great festival, and a band of musicians and singers suddenly broke forth from the cupola of the Philomathic Society's edifice, with a hymn, of which what follows is a close translation.

> "O sun of glory! Let that glory shed
> Its most concentred radiance on his head—
> On him the orbits of the stars who drew,
> And nature's mystic lore and language knew:
> Illustrious man! Sarmatia's grateful tongue
> Has to the echoing world thy honours sung:
> Though Lechian voices loudest speak—yet all
> In blending accents hail thy festival!"

And after a short pause of breathless silence:

> "Son of the earth! to whom the power was given
> To measure the mysterious march of heaven,
> Be welcome now to fame's necropolis
> And take thy seat in glory and in bliss."

It seemed as if Urania, aided by the music of the spheres, had herself been calling him to her own celestial regions. Never was witnessed so superb an apotheosis.

The inscription on the pedestal, which is of grey Polish marble, is eminently simple and striking.

> "Nicolao Copernico
> Grata Patria."

It is repeated in Polish on another side. On the third are the seven planets of the old planisphere.

---

* Hall of the Philomathic Society, just opposite.

RUSSIA.

The Eleventh Volume of the Memoirs of the Academy of St. Petersburgh contains some posthumous Dissertations of Euler, who, before his death, had expressed a wish that the Memoirs might contain some of his papers for a series of forty years after his death. In 1823, the term being expired, there were still, found remaining in the archives of the Academy *fourteen* Dissertations of the celebrated mathematician, which are now published in this eleventh volume together with four Dissertations of Schubert and thirteen of Fuss.

ORIENTAL LITERATURE AND SCIENCE.

A long memoir was recently read, before the Academy of Inscriptions and Belles Lettres, by M. Abel Remusat, on a Journey in the interior of Asia, commenced in the year 399 of our era, and terminated twelve years after, by several Samanians or Chinese Buddhists. The original MS. is in the King's library, and Deguignes, who was acquainted with its existence, had intended to translate it, but gave up the design from the difficulty he found in ascertaining the names of the places mentioned by the travellers, the greater part of them having disappeared in the interval of fourteen centuries. To overcome this very difficulty was, however, the motive with M. Remusat for undertaking this memoir. By combining the materials furnished by other Chinese travellers, and the scanty assistance derived from the ancient books of India, he has succeeded in tracing, without any interruption, the whole series of places visited by the travellers. From this memoir, then, it appears, that Chi-fa-hian and his companions, after having quitted the city of Si-'an-fou, in Chen-si, passed through various states, came to the country of the Wigurs, then to Khotan, and afterwards to Cashmir; that after crossing the Himalaya Mountains and passing the Indus, in the environs of Attock or Peishawer, they found, on the left bank of that river, a population wholly Hindoo in language, customs and religion; having princes professing the Buddhist worship, and the proper names of the countries being in the Sanscrit language. We are led to hope that the whole of this curious memoir will speedily be published, together with a complete translation from the Chinese of the journey itself, from the interest attached to it as regards the ancient geography of India, and a knowledge of the Buddhist traditions. The notes which M. Remusat has added to his translation, bring us acquainted with other travels of a similar description, and contain copious researches into the state of Hindostan in the fourth and fifth centuries.

In an article *on the Christian Missions in China*, published in Number IX. of this Journal, we gave an account of the different religious systems of that empire. To such as took an interest in the subject, the information will be acceptable, that M. Panthier, a young French orientalist, has just published at Paris a very interesting memoir on the doctrine of Tao, translated from the Chinese, with a commentary, extracted from the Tao-Te-King of Lao-Tseu, and several Sanscrit works, proving the perfect conformity of certain philosophical opinions of China with those of India, which M. Panthier conceives to have been the cradle of those opinions. M. Panthier has given the original Sanscrit text of two *Oupanichads*, extracted from the *Vedas*, with a French and a Persian translation. It is pleasing to remark the appearance of this publication, as a symptom of the subsidence of that political effervescence which was excited by the memorable days of July, and of the desire of men of letters and science to return to their more tranquil and delightful pursuits.

LIST OF THE PRINCIPAL NEW WORKS

PUBLISHED ON THE CONTINENT,

FROM JANUARY TO MARCH, 1831, INCLUSIVE.

THEOLOGY AND ECCLESIASTICAL HISTORY.

242 Manifeste des Catholiques Français sur le devoir de soumission aux puissances, ou Traité des devoirs Catholiques dans les Revolutions. 8vo.

243 Discours sur l'Incredulité et sur la certitude de la Révélation Chrétienne. Par l'Evêque de Strasburg. 8vo. 7s.

244 Réligion Saint Simonienne, Association Universelle ou Organisation Definitive de l'Humanité, pour l'amélioration progressive, sous le rapport moral, intellectuel et physique du sort de la classe la plus nombreuse et la plus pauvre. In plano de deux feuilles.

245 Ostervald Argumens et Réflexions sur les Livres et les Chapitres du Nouveau Testament ; nouvelle edition revue et corrigée. 12mo. 2s. 6d.

246 Wahl, Dr. Clavis Novi Testamenti philologica. Editio minor. 4to. maj. *Leipzig.* 18s.

247 Hemsen, Dr. der Apostel Paulus, sein Leben, Wirken und seine Schriften. 4 bücher. gr. 8vo. *Göttingen.* 13s.

248 Lindberg, M. Libri Ecclesiæ Danicæ symbolici. 8vo. *Copenhagen.* 3s.

249 Niemeyer, Dr. Charakteristik der Bibel. 5 thle. gr. 8vo. *Halle.* 1l. 17s. 6d.

250 Rosenmüller, Dr. Scholia in V. T. in compendium redacta. Vol. III. 8vo. *Leipzig.* 18s.

251 Sailer, J. M. Sämmtliche Werke. 1—5r thl. gr. 8vo. *Sulzbach.* 1l.

252 Schenke, Prof. Ethica Christiana. 3 tom. Editio quinta. 8vo. maj. *Wien.* 17s.

253 Graser, Dr. Divinität. 3te. auflage. 2 thle. gr. 8vo. *Bayreuth,* 1l.

254 Paulus, Dr. exegetisches Handbuch über die 3 ersten Evangelien. I. 1—2. gr. 8vo. *Heidelberg.* 1l.

255 Waibel, A. A. Dogmatik der Religion Jesu. I—IV. Abhandlung. gr. 8vo. *Augsburg.* 4s. 6d.

256 Günther, F. H. G. De Mortis Jesu Christi fine salutari ; Commentatio præmio regio ornata, 4o. maj. *Göttengen.* 3s.

257 Leo, M. Geschichte der Christlichen Religion und Kirche. 2 thle. 8vo. *Leipzig.* 7s. 6d.

258 Ludewig, A. Historisch-Kritische Untersuchungen über die verschiedenen Meinungen von der Abkunft unsers Herrn und Heilandes. 8vo. *Wolfenbüttel.* 2s. 6d.

259 Olshausen, Dr. Biblischer Commentar über sammtliche schriften des Neuen Testaments. 1r bd. gr. 8vo. *Königsberg.* 15s.

260 Planck, Dr. Geschichte der protestantischen Theologie. gr. 8vo. *Göttingen,* 7s. 6d.

261 Bibliotheca Sacra patrum ecclesiæ Græcorum. Pars III. 12mo. *Leipzig.* 4s. 6d.

262 Theile, Dr. tabulæ rerum dogmaticarum compendiariæ, Pars 1or. 4to. maj. *Leipzig.* 3s.

263 Francolm, Dr. Die Mosaische Sittenlehre. 8vo. *Breslau.* 8s.

264 Hald, Historia Ecclesiastica Synoptice enarrata. Pars 1a. 4to. maj. *Copenhagen.* 4s.

265 Haurenski, C. Alethophilus, oder der neue Glaube in der Christenheit. gr. 8vo. *Neustadt.* 12s.

266 Kapp, Dr. Grundsätze zur Bearbeitung Evangelischer Agenden. gr. 8vo. *Erlangen.* 6s.
267 Les Voyages de Jesus Christ, ou Description Geographique des principaux lieux et Monumens de la Livre Sainte avec une Carte et le plan de Jerusalem. 8vo. 8s.
268 Meditations Religieuses, en forme de discours, pour toutes les epoques, circonstances, et situations de la vie domestique et civile ; traduites de l'Allemand, Tome II. 2de partie. 8vo. 6s. 6d.

LAW, JURISPRUDENCE, AND ADMINISTRATION.

269 Recueil Général des Anciennes Lois Françaises, depuis l'an 420 jusqu'à la Revolution de 1789, par MM. Isambert, Decrusy et Taillandier. Tomes XX. XXI. XXII. Juin, 1687—10 Mai, 1774. 8vo.
270 Jouve, Essai sur la peine de mort, ou de la peine de mort considérée dans ses rapports avec le droit et l'interèt de la Société. 8vo.
271 Des Principes Politiques qui doivent servir de base à la legislation electorale. 8vo.
272 Lois Municipales, Rurales, Administratives et de Police, etc. Tome I. 8vo.
273 Ortolan et Ledeau, Le Ministère Public en France ; traité et code de son organisation, de sa competence et de ses fonctions dans l'ordre politique, judiciaire et administratif, avec le texte des lois, decrés, ordonnances, avis du conseil d'etat et instructions ministérielles. 2 vol. 8vo. 16s.
274 Kraut, Dr., de Codicibus Luneburgensibus. 4to. *Göttingen.* 2s.
275 Reimarus, Dr., Bemerkungen und Hypothesen über die Inscriptionenreihen der Pandectenfragmente. gr. 8vo. *Göttingen.* 3s.
276 Falck, Dr., Juristische Encyclopädie. 3te Ausgabe. 8vo. *Kiel.* 9s.
277 Corpus juris civilis, das, ins Deutsche, übersetzt von Dr. Otto, Schilling et Sintenis. 1r Bd. 1—6 Hft. gr. 8vo. *Leipzig.* 13s.
278 Droste-Hülshoff, Dr., Lehrbuch des Naturrechts, oder der Rechtsphilosophie. 2te Auflage. gr. 8vo. *Bonn.* 7s. 6d.
279 Pütter, Dr., die Lehre vom Eigenthum nach deutschen Rechten, aus den Quellen dargestellt. gr. 8vo. *Berlin.* 7s.
280 Zeller, P., Systematisches Lehrbuch der Polizeiwissenschaft, nach Preussischen Gesetzen. 1—8 Thl. gr. 8vo. *Quedlinburg.* euch 7s.
281 Duncker, J. F. L., Das Recht aus dem Gesetz des Lebens. 8vo. *Berlin.* 10s.
282 Baiernbriefe oder Geist der 4 ersten Ständeversammlungen des Königreiches Baiern. 1r Bd. 8vo. *Stuttgardt.* 16s.
283 Hin forna Lögbök Islendinga sem nefnist Gragas. Codex juris Islandorum antiquissimus, qui nominatur Gragas. Pars I. II. Cum 1 Tab. 4to. maj. *Copenhagen.* 2l. 2s.

MORALS, EDUCATION, AND POLITICAL ECONOMY.

284 Gordon, Alex. Exposé Historique et Philosophique placé en regard de la doctrine Saint Simonienne. 8vo. 2s.
285 Duchesne, Essai sur les Finances. 8vo. 9s. 6d.
286 Bulletin de la Société des Etablissemens Charitables. Tome I. No. 1. 8vo. 2s. 6d.
287 De l'Education et de l'Instruction, à Madame * * * * à Bourdeaux. 18mo. 1s.
288 Gesner, J. G. die Deutsche Landwirthschaft, nach ihrem jetzigen Stande dargestellt. 1r theil. gr. 8vo. *Stuttgardt.* 4s. 6d.
289 Hegel, Dr. Encyclopädie der philosophischen Wissenschaften im Grundrisse. 3te ausgabe. 8vo. *Heidelberg.* 17s. 6d.
290 Heinroth, Dr. Geschichte und Kritik des Mysticismus. gr. 8vo. *Leipzig.* 12s. 6d.
291 Horst, Dr. Deuteroskopie. 2 bdchen. gr. 8vo. *Frankfurt.* 12s.
292 Krause, G. F. Versuch eines Systems der National und Staatsökonomie von Deutschland. 2 theil. gr. 8vo. *Leipzig.* 18s.
293 Meyer, J. F. von, Blätter für höhere Wahrheit. 10te sammlung. 8vo. *Berlin.* 8s.
294 Krug, Prof. Universal philosophische Vorlesungen. gr. 8vo. *Neustadt.* 14s.

MATHEMATICS, PHYSICS AND CHEMISTRY.

295 Toucas, H., L'Arithmétique rendue facile au moyen de l'Algebre mixte. 8vo.
296 Berzelius, Traité de Chimie, traduit par A. J. L. Jourdan sur les MSS. inédits de l'auteur et sur la dernière edition Allemande. *Chimie Minerale.* Tome III. 8vo. 7s.
297 Mémoires de l'Academie Royale des Sciences de l'Institut de France. Tome X. 4to. 21s.
298 Desroches, Traité Elémentaire de Chimie et de Physique. 8vo. 8s.
299 Memorie della Reale Academia delle Scienze di Torino. Tomo XXXIV. 4to. 1l. 10s.
300 Gauss, C. F., Principia generalia theoriæ figuræ fluidorum in statu æquilibrii. 4to. *Göttingen.* 3s.
301 Brandes, H. G., de Cometarum caudis disquisitio mathematica. Pars 1a, cum II Tabulis. 4to. *Leipzig.* 2s.
302 Naumann, Dr., Lehrbuch der reinen und angewandten Krystallographie in 2 Bdcn. Mit Kupfern. gr. 8vo. *Leipzig.* 1l. 15s.
303 Pohl, G. F., der Elektromagnetismus, theoretisch-practisch dargestellt. 1ste Abthlg. Mit Kupfern. gr. 8vo. *Berlin.* 10s.
304 Elementar-Lehrbuch der dynamischen Wissenschaften. 1r Bd. Statik. Mit Kupfern. gr. 8vo. *Berlin.* 17s.

NATURAL SCIENCES.

305 Jaume St. Hilaire, la Flore et la Pomone Françaises. Livraisons LIII.—LX. 8vo. each 3s.
306 Iconographie du Regne Animal, de M. le Baron Cuvier, etc. par Guérin. Livraisons X. XI. 8vo. each 6s.
307 ——————————————————————————— colorié, 15s.
308 Lesson, Histoire Naturelle des Colibris; Suivi d'un Supplément à l'Histoire Naturelle des Oiseaux-mouches. Livraisons V. VI. 8vo. each 5s.
309 Magasin de Conchyliologie, ou Descriptions et figures de Mollusques vivans et fossiles, inédits ou non encore figurés, par F. E. Guérin. Livraisons III. IV. 8vo. each 2s. 6d.
310 Magazin d'Entomologie, ou Descriptions et Figures d'Insectes inédits ou non encore figurés. Livraisons III. IV. 8vo. each 2s. 6d.
311 Temminck, Nouveau Recueil de Planches Coloriées d'Oiseaux. Livraison 87. 4to. 10s. 6d.; folio, 15s.
312 Barjanel, Traité Complet de la Culture de l'Olivier, redigé d'après les observations et expériences de M. l'Abbé F. Jamet. 8vo.
313 Lesson, Centurie Zoologique, ou Choix d'Animaux Rares, nouveaux ou imparfaitement connus; enrichi de planches inédites. 3r Livraison. 8vo.
314 Bartling, Dr. Ordines naturales plantarum eorumque characteres et affinitates adjecta generum enumeratione. 8vo. *Gottingen.* 12s.
315 Linnæi, C. Genera Plantarum. Editio nona c. C. Sprengel. Tome I. 8vo. maj. *Gottingen,* 11s. 6d.
316 Wagler, Dr. Natürliches System der Amphibien. Mit Kupfern. folio. *Stuttgardt.* 1l. 4s.
317 Wiedemann, Dr. Achias Dipterorum, genus a Fabricio conditum. Cum tab. lithogr. II. 8vo. *Keil.* 2s. 6d.
318 Abbildungen aller bis jetzt bekannten europäischen zweiflügeligen Insekten. 1s hft. Mit 10 steintafeln. gr. 8vo. *Hamm.* 3s. ditto coloured, 9s.
319 Martius, Dr. Amœnitates botanicæ Monacenses. Fasc. I.—IV. gr. 4to. *Frankfurt.* each 4s.
320 Dann, Dr. Commentatio de paracusi sive de auditus hallucinationibus. 4to. maj. *Berlin.* 7s.
321 Dierbach, Dr. Abhandlung über die Arzneikräfte der Planzen. gr. 8vo. *Lemgo.* 7s.
322 Girardin, Considerations générales sur les Volcans, etc. 8vo. 5s.
323 Cuvier, Cours de l'Histoire des Sciences Naturelles et de la Philosophie de l'Histoire Naturelle. 2me partie. Livraison XIII. 8vo.

324 Duperrey, Voyage autour du Monde, executé par ordre du Roi. Botanographie. Phanerogamie, par M. Ad. Brogniart. VIIIme livraison. 4to.

325 Boisduval et Lecoute, Histoire générale et Iconographie des Lepidoptères et des Chenilles de l'Amérique Septentrionale. Livr. I.—VII. 8vo. each 6s.

326 Alexis Noel, Collection Entomologique, ou Histoire Naturelle des Insectes peints d'après nature. Livraisons I.—VI. 8vo. each 4s.

327 Dictionnaire Classique d'Histoire Naturelle. Tome XVI. (T—Z). 8vo. 8s. pl. noirs, 4s. pl. color. 15s.

328 Redouté Choix des plus belles Fleurs, prises dans differentes familles du Règne Végétal. Livraison XXIV. 4to. 12s.

329 Jaume St. Hilaire, Les Dahlia, ou histoire, description, et culture des plus belles espèces et variétés de Dahlia; ouvrage orné de figures peintes d'après nature. Par Mlle. Guillon. 1re livr. folio. 10s.

MEDICAL SCIENCES.

330 Heiberg, Dr., Commentatio de Coremorphosi. 8vo. *Christiania.* 7s. 6d.

331 Hueck, Dr., das Sehen seinem äussern Processe nach entwickelt. gr. 8vo. *Gött.* 4s. 6d.

332 Langenbeck, Dr., Novum Theatrum Anatomicum Göttingen. Cum V Tab. 4to. maj. *Göttingen.* 3s.

333 ————— Nosologie und Therapie der Chirurgischen Krankheiten. 4r Bd. gr. 8vo. *Göttingen.* 15s.

334 Hasper, Dr., über die Natur und Behandlung der Krankheiten der Tropenländer. 2 Thle. gr. 8vo. *Leipzig.* 1l. 5s.

335 Pallatides, Dr., de Vita Somatica. 8vo. maj. *Wien.* 3s.

336 Das Hamburgische allgemeine Krankenhaus. Mit Kpfrn. gr. 4to. *Hamburg.* 15s.

337 Simon, Dr., der Vampirismus im XIX Jahrhundert. 8vo. *Hamburg.* 4s. 6d.

338 Blasius, Dr., Handbuch der Akiurgie. 2 Thle. 8vo. *Halle.* 15s.

339 Hahnemann, S., Reine Arzneimittellehre. 1r Thl. 3te Auflage. gr. 8vo. *Leipz.* 10s.

340 Hiort, J. J., de functione retinae, particula prima Commentatio. Vols. I. II. Cum 1 Tab. 8vo. *Christiania.* 8s.

341 Barrey, Histoire Impartiale de la Vaccine, ou Appreciation du bien qu'on lui. attribue et du mal qu'on lui impute; Mémoire qui a obtenu le prix, etc. 8vo.

342 Lepelletier, Physiologie Médicale et Philosophique. Tome I. 8vo. 7s.

343 Cloquet, Jules, Pathologie Chirurgicale, Plan et Methode qu'il convient de suivre dans l'enseignement de cette Science. 4to.

344 Gendrin, Mémoire Medico-Legal sur la mort violente du Duc de Bourbon, Prince. de Conde, etc. 8vo. 3s.

345 Piorry, du Procédé Opératoire à suivre dans l'exploration des organes par la Percussion Médiate, et Collection de Mémoires sur la Physiologie, la Pathologie et. le Diagnostie. 8vo. 6s.

346 Keraudren, Mémoire sur le Cholera-Morbus de l'Inde. 8vo. 1s. 6d.

347 Lallemand, Recherches Anatomico-Pathologiques sur l'Encephale et ses dependences. 6e Lettre. 8vo. 3s.

348 Mérat, Dictionnaire Universel de Matière Medicale et de Thérapeutique Générale. Tome III. (E—K.) 8vo. 7s.

349 Cloquet Anatomie. Liv. LI. LII. fol. 18s. (This work is now completed.)

350 Simon, Dr., Versuch einer kritischen Geschichte der verschieden artigen besonders unreinen Behaftungen der Geschlechtstheile. 2 Thle. gr. 8vo. *Hamburg.* 1l. 1s.

351 Clarus, Dr., Tabellarische Uebersicht der zum wissenschaftlichen Studium der Heilkunde nöthigen Vorlesungen. gr. 8vo. *Leipzig.* 3s.

352 Hohl, A. F., de Aneurysmatis, cum Tabula, 8vo. maj. *Halle.* 2s. 6d.

353 Schnurrer, Dr., die Cholera-Morbus, ihre Verbreitung, ihre Zufälle, etc. 8vo. *Stuttgardt.* 4s.

354 Elsner, Prof., über die Cholera. Ein Versuch dieselbe zu deuten. 8vo. *Königs-. berg.* 2s.

MILITARY.

355 Decker, Traité de l'Art de combattre de l'artillerie à cheval ; traduit de l'Allemand, avec des notes relatives à l'armée Française, par Ravichio de Peretsdorff, 8vo. 8s.
356 Gaspard de Pons, le Comte, de la necessité d'accélérer l'avancement dans notre armée. 8vo.
357 Jomini, Baron de, Tableau analitique des principales combinaisons de la guerre. gr. 8vo. *St. Petersbourg.* 7s.

MISCELLANEOUS ARTS AND SCIENCES.

358 Abbildungen von Schlosserwaaren im neuesten Wiener, Pariser und Londoner Geschmack. Ein Handbuch für Baukünstler, etc. von Th. Hölzel. Livraisons I.—XXII. qu. 4to. *Prag.* 8s.
359 Fiedler, C. W., Lehrbegriff der grundsätzlichen Färber-und Zeügdrukerkunst. 2 Thle. 8vo. *Göttingen.* 10s.
360 Köhler, H. G., über die zweckmässigste Einrichtung der Gewerbschulen und der Polytechnischen Institute. gr. 8vo. *Gottingen.* 2s.
361 Woelfer, M., die Treppen-Baukunst in ihrem ganzen Umfange. Mit 20 Kupfern. 8vo. *Berlin.* 15s.
362 Bunsen, R. G., Enumeratio ac Descriptio Hygrometrorum quæ inde a Saussurii temporibus proposita sunt. Commentatio præmio regio ornata. 4to. maj. Mit Kupfern. *Gottingen.* 5s.
363 Encyclopèdisches Wörterbuch der Wissenschaften, Künste und Gewerbe, herausgeg. von Pierer. 1—15 Bd. gr. 8vo. *Altenburg.* each 10s.
364 Boner, C., Vollständiger Unterricht über die Anlage der Bohr-oder der Artesischen Brunnen. 2te Auflage nebst Kupfern. gr. 8vo. *Münster.* 4s.
365 Leblanc, Choix de Modèles appliquées à l'enseignment du dessin des machines, avec un texte descriptif. 2ème partie. 4to. avec Atlas. 12s. (To be completed in three parts, each 12s.)
366 Lettres à Clemence sur la Musique, par Madame E. L. 18mo. 5s. 6d.
367 Annuaire, pour l'an 1831, présenté au Roi par le Bureau des Longitudes. 18mo. 1s.
368 Connaissance des Tems, ou des Mouvemens Celestes pour l'an 1833. 8vo. 8s.
369 Dictionnaire Technologique, ou Nouveau Dictionnaire Universel des Arts et Métiers et de l'Economie Industrielle et Commerciale. Tomes XVII. XVIII. et pl. 31, 32. 20s.
370 Robertson, Mémoires Récréatifs et Anecdotiques du physicien aéronaute. Tome I. 8vo. 10s.
371 Brunel Varennes, Metroscopographie, ou Nouveau Système de Perspective, également applicable à toutes les parties de l'Art du dessin pittoresque, et a toutes les opérations geodésiques ou topographiques. 4to. 15s.
372 Gaetzschmann, M. F., Anleitung zur Grubenmauerung. Mit 35 Platten. fol. *Schneeberg.* 1l. 5s.

FINE ARTS.

373 Beschreibung der Stadt Rom, von E. Platner, C. Bunsen, E. Gerhard, und W. Rösteli. Mit Beiträgen von B. G. Niebuhr. 1r bd. gr. 8vo. *Stuttgardt.* 1l. 2s.
374 Brönsted, Lettre sur quelques médailles cufiques dans le Cabinet du Roi de Danemark, avec XII planches. gr. 4to. *Copenhagen.* 1l. 5s.
375 Vue des Ruines de Pompei d'après l'ouvrage publié à Londres en 1829, par Sir W. Gall et J. P. Gandy. Livraisons XX. XXI. 4to. each 8s.
376 Ecole Anglaise. Recueil de Tableaux, etc. accompagnés de notices, descriptions, critiques, et historiques en Français et en Anglais. Livraisons IX. à XII. 12mo. each 1s. 6d.
377 Reveil, Musée, de Peinture, et de Sculpture. Livraisons CIX. à CXVIII. each 1s. 6d.
378 Museum Etrusque de Lucien Bonaparte, Prince de Canino, (fouilles de 1828, 9). Vases peints, avec inscriptions. 4to. 30s.

379 Sestini Descrizione di molte medaglie antiche Greche esistente in piu Musei, comprese in 41 tavole incise in rame e distribuite secondo il sistema geografico numismatico. 2 vols. 4to. 2l. 2s.

380 ——— Descrizione delle Medaglie antiche Greche del Museo Hedervariane dal Chersoneso Taurico fino a tutto la Tessaglia e Isole appartementi alla medesima e alla Macedonia. 4 parts, 4to. 2l. 12s. 6d.

381 Trente Vues de la Grèce, représentant des contrées et des Monumens que l'on trouve encore aujourdhui. Cahiers I. II. 8vo. each 6s.

HISTORY, BIOGRAPHY, VOYAGES, TRAVELS, &c.

382 Aletheia, Zeitschrift für Geschichte, Staats-und Kirchenrecht von Dr. Münch, Jahrgg. 1830. 12 Hfte. gr. 8vo. *Haag.* 2l.

383 Genealogisch-historisch-statistischer Almanach, 8r Jahrg, für 1831. 16mo. *Weimar.* 8s.

384 Dahlmann, Quellenkunde der deutschen Geschichte, nach der Folge der Begebenheiten für eigne Vorträge der deutschen Geschichte geordnet. gr. 8vo. *Göttingen.* 2s. 6d.

385 Esmark, J., Reise von Christiania nach Drontheim durch Oesterdalen und zurück über Dovre nebst einem Abstecher nach Junteland. 8vo. *Leipzig.* 7s.

386 Fichte, J. G., Leben und literarischer Briefwechsel herausgegeben von seinem Sohne J..H. Fichte. 1r Theil. 8vo. *Sulzbach.* 8s.

387 Martens, G., Supplement au recueil des principaux traités d'Alliance, de paix, etc. Tome XI. 2e partie. gr. 8vo. *Göttingen.* 12s. 6d.

388 Plass, H. G., Vor-und Urgeschichte der Hellenen. 1r Bd. gr. 8vo. *Leipzig.* 12s. 6d.

389 Richter's, J. P. Fr., Leben nebst Charakteristik von H. Döring. 16mo. *Erfurt.* 3s.

390 Rotteck, E. von, Allgemeine Geschichte. 9 vol. 7te Auflage. gr. 8vo. *Freiburg.* 3l. 12s.

391 Kaiser, A., Russland wie es ist. 4 Thle. 8vo. *Leipzig.* 16s.

392 Schollеr, K. Fr., Italienische Reise. 2 Bde. gr. 8vo. *Leipzig.* 17s.

393 Schirach, C. von, Geschichte unserer zeit. In jährlichen Uebersichten der wichtigsten Ereignisse. 1r Jahrgang, das Jahr 1829. gr. 8vo. *Hamburg.* 10s.

394 Silbert, J. P., Lichtpunkte aus der hellen Kammer eines historischen Denkers. 2 Bde. 16mo. *Wien.* 5s.

395 Raumer, Fr. von, Briefe aus Paris und Frankreich im Jahre 1830. 2 Thle. gr. 12mo. *Leipzig.* 15s.

396 Schaab, Dr., die Geschichte der Erfindung der Buchdrucker-Kunst. 2 Bde. Mit Kupfern. 8vo. *Mainz.* 12s.

397 Schiller's Leben, verfasst aus Erinnerungen der Familie. 2 Thle. 8vo. *Tübingen.* 15s.

398 Rotteck, Dr., Allgemeine Geschichte. 6 Bde. 7te Auflage. gr. 8vo. *Freiburg.* 1l. 16s.

399 De Lamotte-Langon. Cinq Mois de l'Histoire de Paris en Mille Huit Cent trente. 8vo. 10s.

400 Belanger, Voyage aux Indes Orientales par le Nord de l'Europe, les provinces du Caucas, la Georgie, l'Arménie et la Perse, suivi de détails topographiques, statistiques et autres sur le Pegou, etc., pendant les années, 1825, 6, 7, 8, 9. Zoologie. Liv. I. II. 4to. each 14s.

401 Zielinski, Histoire de Pologne. 2 vol. 8vo. 20s.

402 La Grande Semaine des Polonais, ou Histoire des Memorables journées de la Revolution de Varsovie, par un Polonais. 8vo. 2s.

403 Dix Jours de 1830: Souvenirs de la dernière Revolution, par A. S., Officier d'Infanterie de l'Ex-Garde Royale. 8vo. 4s.

404 Faune, Souvenirs du Midi ou l'Espagne telle qu'elle est sous ses pouvoirs religieux et monarchiques. 8vo. 8s.

405 Annuaire Historique Universel pour 1829. 8vo. 16s.

406 Duperry, Voyage autour du Monde. IIIe Division. Historique. Livraisons V. VI. VII. folio. each 16s.

407 Barbichon, Dictionnaire Complet de tous les lieux de France et de ses Colonies. Ouvrage entièrement neuf. 2 vols. 8vo. 16s.
408 Laborde, Itinéraire Descriptif del Espagne. 3me edition. Tome VI. avec Atlas, in 4to. The work is now completed, price 4l.
409 Lévi, Nouveaux Elemens d'Histoire Générale Redigés sur un plan Méthodique et entièrements neuf, etc. in 8vo.
410 Balbi et De la Roquette, Essai Historique Geographiques et Statistiques sur le Royaume des Pays Bas. In plano. 8s.
411 Voyage de la Pérouse, redigé d'après ses MSS. originaux, suivi d'un Appendice renfermant tout ce-que l'on a découvert depuis le naufrage jusqu'à nos jours, et enrichi de notes; par M. de Lesseps, Consul Général de France à Lisbonne, et seul débris vivant de l'Expedition dont il était interprète. 8vo. 9s.
412 Rifaud, Voyage en Egypte, en Nubie et lieux circonvoisins depuis 1805 jusqu'en 1827. Livraisons VIII. IX.
    To be completed in 5 vols. 8vo. of text, and 3 vols. folio of plates.
413 Dictionnaire Geographique Universel. Tome VIII. 1e partie. 8vo. 9s. 6d.
414 Memoires de Constant, premier valet de Chambre de l'Empereur, sur la Vie privée de Napoléon, sa Famille et sa Cour. Tomes V. VI. 8vo. 20s.
415 Biographie Ardennoise, ou Histoire des Ardennois qui se sont fait remarquer par leurs ecrits, leurs actions, leurs vertus et leurs erreurs. 2 vols. 8vo. 20s.
416 Schoell, Cours d'Histoire des Etats Européens depuis le bouleversement de l'Empire Romain d'Occident jusqu'en 1789. Tome X. 8vo. 10s.
417 Chroniques Pittoresques, et Critiques de l'Oeil de Boeuf des petits Appartemens de la Cour et des Salons de Paris sous Louis XIV. la Régence. Louis XV. et Louis XVI. Tome V. 8vo. 10s.
418 Humboldt et Bonpland, Voyage. Rélation Historique. Liv. VI. 2e partie. 4to. avec Atlas. 3l.

POETRY, THE DRAMA, &c.

419 Auffenberg, von, der Renegat von Granada. Dramatisches Nachtgemälde, in 5 abtheilungen. 8vo. *Franckfurt.* 9s.
420 Herrmann, G. Moritz, Kurfürst von Sachsen. Vaterländ. Schauspiel, in 5 aufzügen. 8vo. *Leipzig.* 4s.
421 Welker, P. H. Thüringer Lieder, mit 4 abbildungen. gr. 12mo. *Gotha.* 7s.
422 Zedlitz, Baron von, Todtenkränze. Canzone. 2te auflage. 8vo. *Wien.* 7s.
423 Atterbom, Dr. die Insel der Glückseligkeit, Schauspiel, in 5 Abenteuern. gr. 8vo. *Leipzig.* 7s. 6d.
424 Les Trois Catherines, Scènes Historiques du Règne de Henri VIII., en trois époques. Par Deport et Monnais. 8vo. 4s.
425 Robespierre, ou le 9 Thermidor. Drame en trois actes et neuf tableaux. Par Bourgeois et Francis. 8vo.
426 Yseult Raimbauld, Drame Historique en quatre actes. Par M. Paul Foucher, 8vo. 4s.
427 Theveneau, Napoléon, ou trois epoques de la France; poëme en trois chants. 8vo.
428 Scribe, Théatre. Tome IX. 8vo. 9s. 6d.
429 ——— et Bayand, les trois Maitresses ou une Cour d'Allemagne; comédie. 8vo. 3s. 6d.

NOVELS AND ROMANCES.

430 Pigault Le Brun. Contes à mon petit-fils. 2 vol. in 12mo. 8s.
431 Victor Hugo, Notre-Dame de Paris. 2 vols. 8vo. 20s.
432 Vermond. Chroniques Populaires de Berry, recueillies et publiées pour l'instruction des autres Provinces. 2 vols. 12mo. 12s.
433 Bouilly, Contes Populaires. 2 vols. 12mo. 12s.
434 Zschokke, Les Matinées Suisses, traduites de l'Allemand. 2de série. 4 vols. 12mo. 16s.
435 Signob, La Lingère, Roman Populaire. 5 vols. 12mo. 21s.
436 Vallée, La Figurante, Roman de Mœurs. 4 vols. 12mo. 16s.
437 Lamothe-Langon, Le Duc et le Page. Roman de Mœurs. 4 vols. 12mo. 16s.
438 Janin, J. J. die Beichte. 8vo. *Leipzig.* 4s. 6d.

439 Laun, Fr. der Verliebte Onkel und seine Nichten. 2bde. 8vo. *Leipzig.* 5s.
440 Kellstab, L. die Aventure. Eine Novelle. 8vo. *Berlin.* 7s. 6d.
441 Spindler, H. der Geheimnissvolle, oder die beiden Verbrechen. Russische Novelle. 8vo. *Leipzig.* 4s.
442 Numsen, Dr. die Bonvivants, Charakterbilder. 1r bd. 12mo. *Leipzig.* 6s.
443 Storch, L. die Fanatiker, Historischer Roman aus der 2ten Hälfte der 16ten Jahrhunderts. 2thle, 8vo. *Leipzig.* 10s.
444 Lohmann, Fr. neueste gesammelte Erzählungen. I.—VI. *Leipzig.* 12mo. each 8s.
445 Sayowskin, M. die Russen im Jahre 1612. Ein historischer Roman. 2thle 8vo. *Königsberg.* 10s.
446 Satori, J. Blanca von Castilien, oder das Opfer der Politik. Eine historische Erzählung. 2 bde. 8vo. *Leipzig.* 7s. 6d.
447 Konradin von Schwaben, der letzte Hohenstaufen. 2thle. 8vo. *Leipzig.* 7s. 6d.
448 Huber, Th. Erzählungen. 6 thle. 8vo. *Leipzig.* 1l. 2s. 6d.
449 Spazier, N. O. die Uzkokin. 8vo. *Leipzig.* 6s.
450 Storch, L. Kunz von Kauffung. 3 thle. 8vo. *Leipzig.* 12s. 6d.

CLASSICAL LITERATURE, PHILOLOGY, BIBLIOGRAPHY.

451 Virgilius, variet lect. et perp. adnot. illustrat. a C. G. Heyne. Editio IV. e. Wagner. vol. I. p. 1, 2. Editio splendidior. 8vo. maj. *Leipzig.* 2l. 10s.
452 Ditto, common paper, 17s.
453 Horatii, G. Fl. in Vitam Suetonio conscript. notas varior colleg. suasque et comment. perpet. adjec. Dr. Richter. 4to. *Zwickau.* 7s.
454 Justini Historiæ Philippicæ. Secund. vetustissim. Cod. edid. Dr. Duebner. 12mo. maj. *Leipzig.* 8s.
455 Nitzsch, Prof. de Historia Homeri maximeque descriptorum carminum ætate meletemata. Fasc. I. 4to. *Hannover.* 7s.
456 Hirschfeld, G. Schemoth Hannir daphim, oder Synonymik zur Beförderung der Hebräischen Sprache. 2te Ausgabe. 8vo. *Berlin.* 4s.
457 Terentii, P. Afri., Comoediae Sex, cum interpr. Donati, ed A. H. Westerhovius et Stallbaum. 6 vol. 8vo. *Leipzig.* 24s.
458 Becker, Dr. Demosthenes als Staatsbürger, Redner, und Schriftsteller. 1e Abthlg. Litteratur des Demosthenes. gr. 8vo. *Quedlinburg.* 6s.
459 Jacobi, Dr. Handwörterbuch der griechischen und römischen Mythologie. 2e Abthlg. gr. 8vo. *Coburg.* 8s.
460 Anecdota Græca, e Codd. Regiis descripsit, annotatione illustravit J. F. Boissonade. vol. III. 8vo.
461 Recherches Historiques et Critiques sur l'etablissement de l'Art Typographique en Espagne et en Portugal, avec une notice des villes ou cet art a été exercé pendant le XVe Siecle dans ces deux Royaumes, etc. 8vo. 2s. 6d.
462 Glay, Catalogue Descriptif et Raisonné des MSS. de la Bibliotheque de Cambrai. 8vo.
463 Vie d'Agricola par Tacite, traduite par Lucien Bonaparte. 8vo. 3s. 6d.
464 Lindberg, J. C. Lettre à Bröndsted sur quelques Medailles Cufiques dans le Cabinet du Roi de Danemark, recemment trouves dans l'ile de Falster, et sur quelques MSS. Cufiques. 4to. avec 12 planches. 1l. 5s.
465 Reuvens, Lettres à M. Letronne, sur les Papyrus Bilingues et Grecs, et sur quelques autres monumens Greco-Egyptiens du Musée d'Antiquités de l'Université de Leiden. 4to. avec Atlas in folio. 2l.
466 ————————————————————— vellum paper, 4l.
467 Poetæ Scenici Græcorum, rec. et annot. instrux. H. Bolite. vol. I.—X. 8vo. maj. *Leipzig.* each 6s.
468 Schmidt, M. Leitfaden zur gründlichen Erlernung der russischen Sprache, in 2 Thlen. gr. 8vo. *Leipzig.* 7s.
469 Thucydidis de bello Peloponnesiaco. Libri VIII. Recog. F. F. Haacke. Editio minor. 8vo. maj. *Leipzig.* 8s.
470 Aristotelia von Dr. A. Stahr. 1r thl. das Leben und die verlornen Briefe des Aristoteles. gr. 8vo. *Halle.* 4s. 6d.

471 Ciceronis de Oratore, libri III. Edid. Henrichsen. 8vo. maj. *Copenhagen.* 12s. 6d.
472 Ernesti, J. A. Clavis Ciceroniana. Editio sexta. 8vo. *Halle.* 10s,
473 Hartung, Prof. über die Casus, ihre Bildung und Bedeutung. gr. 8vo. *Erlangen.* 6s.
474 Grimm, G. de Hildebrando antiquissimi carminis Teutonici fragmentum. folio. *Gottingen.* 4s. 6d.
475 Neues allgemeines Handwörterbuch der Deutschen Sprache. 2 Bde. 8vo. *Göppingen.* 12s.
476 Kärcher, K. Kurzgefasstes Handbuch des wissenswürdigsten aus der Mythologie und Archäologie des Klassischen Alterthums. Mit 62 Tafeln. 8vo. *Karlsruhe.* 1l. 2s. 6d.
477 Kulemkamp, B. Versuch eines äst hetischen Kommentars zum allgemeinen Deutschen Conversations-Lexikon. 1e & 2e Abthlg. gr. 8vo. *Gotha.* each 3s. 6d.
478 Lambini, Dr. Monstroliensis in universitate litterarum Parisiensi olim regii profess. Tullianæ emendationes. 8vo. maj. *Coblenz.* 17s.
479 Leutsch, Dr. Thebaidis cyclicæ reliquiæ. 8vo. maj. *Göttingen.* 2s. 6d.
480 Isaei Orationes XI. cum aliquot deperditarum fragmentis Recogn. G. F. Schömann. 8vo. maj. *Griefswalde.* 15s.
481 Legis, Dr. Alkuna, Nordische und Nord-Slawische Mythologie. Mit 13 Kupfern. gr. 8vo. *Leipzig.* 10s.
482 Rask, Prof., a Grammar of the Anglo-Saxon Tongue. 8vo. *Copenhagen.* 15s. 6d.

MISCELLANEOUS LITERATURE.

483 Isographie des Hommes Célèbres, ou Collection de fac-simile de Lettres Autographes et de Signatures. Livraison complémentaire, in 4to.
484 Zschokke, H. Ausgewählte Dichtungen, Erzählungen und Novellen Taschen-Ausgabe, in 10 banden. 2te auflage. 16mo. *Aarau,* 2l. 8s.
485 Jean Paul, das Schönste und Gediegenste aus seinen verschiedenen Schriften, 10 bdchen. 8vo. *Leipzig.* 2l.
486 Weber, Dr. Vorlesungen zur Æsthetik, vornehmlich in Bezug auf Göthe und Schiller. 8vo. *Hannover.* 8s.
487 Campe, J. H. Sämmtliche Kinder-und Jugendschriften. 4te ausgabe. 37 bde. 8vo. *Braunschwig.* 3l. 15s.
488 Tromlitz, A. von, Sämmtliche Schriften. Taschenausgabe. 18 bde. 16mo. *Dresden.* 2l. 5s.
489 Hauff, W. Sämmtliche Schriften. 36 vols. 16mo. *Stuttgardt.* 1l. 16s.
490 Hoffmann, C. T. W. erzählende Schriften. 18 vols. 12mo. *Stuttgardt.* 18s.

ORIENTAL LITERATURE.

491 Nalus Maha-Bhárati episodum c. F. Bopp. Second. Edit. emend. fasc. 1us. 4to. *Berlin.* 8s.
492 Bohlen, Dr. Das Alte Indien, mit besonderer Rücksicht auf Ægypten. 2 thle. gr. 8vo. *Königsberg.* 1l. 2s.
493 Cirbied, Grammaire de Denis, de Thrace, tirée de deux MSS. Arméniens de la Bibliotheque du Roi; publiée en Grec, en Arménien et en Français, etc. 8vo.
494 Anthologie Erotique d'Amarou. Texte Sanscrite, traduction, notes et glosses; par A. L. Apudy. 8vo. 9s.
495 Vendidad Sade, par Burnouf. Texte Zend. liv. 6. 16s.
496 Kabuktian Sahari Harian; dan Tombohiang Jang Dijadkan deri Parochianus Romanus. Exercises et Prières en Malai. 12mo.

INDEX

SEVENTH VOLUME

FOREIGN QUARTERLY REVIEW.

—

A.

London: C. Roworth and Sons; Bell-yard, Temple-bar.